FINANCIAL
ACCOUNTING
THEORY
AND ANALYSIS

TEXT AND CASES

Tenth Edition

Richard G. Schroeder
University of North Carolina at Charlotte

Myrtle W. Clark
University of Kentucky

Jack M. Cathey
University of North Carolina at Charlotte

WILEY

JOHN WILEY & SONS, INC.

Vice President and Publisher   *George Hoffman*
Acquisitions Editor   *Michael McDonald*
Project Editor   *Brian Kamins*
Marketing Manager   *Amy Scholz*
Executive Media Editor   *Allison Morris*
Media Editor   *Greg Chaput*
Production Manager   *Janis Soo*
Assistant Production Editor   *Elaine S. Chew*
Marketing Assistant   *Laura Finley*
Editorial Assistant   *Jacqueline Kepping*
Cover Designer   *Seng Ping Ngieng*
Cover Image   *© Robin MacDougall, Getty Images, Inc.*

This book was set in 9/11 Meridien by Aptara, Inc. and printed and bound by Courier Westford, Inc. The cover was printed by Courier Westford, Inc.

This book is printed on acid free paper.

Evaluation copies are provided to qualified academics and professionals for review purposes only, for use in their courses during the next academic year. These copies are licensed and may not be sold or transferred to a third party. Upon completion of the review period, please return the evaluation copy to Wiley. Return instructions and a free of charge return shipping label are available at **www.wiley.com/go/returnlabel**. Outside of the United States, please contact your local representative.

Library of Congress Cataloging-in-Publication Data
Schroeder, Richard G.
    Financial accounting theory and analysis : text and cases / Richard G. Schroeder, Myrtle W. Clark, Jack M. Cathey. –10th ed.
                p. cm.
    Includes index.
        ISBN 978-0-470-64628-1 (hardback)
    1. Accounting. 2. Accounting—Problems, exercises, etc. I. Clark, Myrtle. II. Cathey, Jack M. III. Title.
    HF5625.A2394 2011
    657—dc22

                                                            2010028571

Printed in the United States of America
10 9 8 7 6 5 4 3 2 1

Preface

Accounting education has experienced many dramatic changes over the life of this accounting theory text. The publication of the tenth edition represents over thirty years in its evolution. At its inception, much of what was then considered theory was in reality rule memorization. In recent years, the globalization of the economy has impacted the skills necessary to be a successful accountant and caused accounting educators to develop new methods of communicating accounting education. Emphasis is now being given to the incorporation of ethics into the curriculum, the analysis of a company's quality of earnings and sustainable income, the use of the World Wide Web as a source of information, an increased emphasis on the international dimensions of accounting, the development of critical thinking skills, the development of communication skills, and the use of group projects to develop cooperative skills.

This edition of the text is a further extension of the refocusing of the material to suit the needs of accounting professionals into the twenty-first century. Among the changes in this edition that were designed to accomplish this objective are:

- Expanded use of the Web by including cases and updates on the textbook companion site at *http://www.wiley.com/college/schroeder.*
- Added a tutorial on the FASB ASC in the solutions manual.
- Added a test bank to the solutions manual containing over 250 multiple choice and over 200 essay questions.
- Updated the disclosure examples throughout the chapters and updated the financial analysis sections of each chapter using Hershey and Tootsie Roll as the example companies.
- Added 5–10 FASB ASC cases in each chapter.
- Added new "Room for Debate" cases in several chapters.
- Updated the discussion of the sources of GAAP to incorporate the FASB ASC in Chapter 1.
- Added a discussion of the FASB's Accounting Standards Codification in Chapter 1.
- Updated the discussion of the FASB-IASB "Norwich Agreement" and their joint conceptual framework and financial statement presentation projects in Chapter 2.
- Updated the discussion of the IASB-FASB "Roadmap to Convergence" project that is attempting to arrive at a common set of high-quality global accounting standards and the removal of the need for the reconciliation

requirement for non-U.S. companies that use IFRSs and are registered in the United States in Chapter 3.

- Updated the discussion of the impact of international versus U.S. GAAP accounting standards in Chapter 3 to incorporate SEC's decision to partially eliminate the Form 20-F reconciliation requirement for foreign companies.
- Added a discussion of the IFRS on the use of GAAP for small and medium-sized entities in Chapter 3.
- Added a discussion of the FASB-IASB discussion paper on revenue recognition in Chapter 5.
- Updated the discussion of the proposed new format for the statement of comprehensive income in Chapter 6.
- Added a discussion FASB-IASB financial statement presentation project in Chapter 6.
- Added a summary of FSP FAS 157-4 to the discussion of fair value measurements in Chapter 7.
- Added a discussion of the proposed format of the statement of financial position in Chapter 7.
- Added a discussion of the proposed format of the statement of cash flows in Chapter 7.
- Added a discussion of the reissued IAS No. 39, "Financial Instruments: Recognition and Measurement," in Chapter 10.
- Added a discussion of IFRS No. 7, "Financial Instruments: Disclosures," in Chapter 10.
- Added a discussion of IASB's exposure draft on income taxes in Chapter 12.
- Added a discussion of the FASB-IASB joint project on accounting for leases in Chapter 13.
- Added a discussion of the proposed amendment to *IAS No. 19*, "Retirement Benefit Costs" in Chapter 14.
- Added a discussion of the "acquisitions method" in Chapter 16.
- Added a discussion of accounting for "noncontrolling interests" in Chapter 16.
- Added a discussion of the revised *IFRS No 3*. "Business Combinations," in Chapter 16.
- Added a discussion of *IFRS No 8*. "Operating Segments," in Chapter 16.
- Added a discussion of the SEC's interpretive guidelines regarding the disclosure of items in the MD&A section of the 10-K report in Chapter 17.
- Added a discussion of the "Final Report of the Advisory Committee on Improvements to Financial Reporting to the United States" in Chapter 17.

The publication of this text would not be possible without the assistance of many individuals. We are extremely indebted to our colleagues; Gurav Kumar, Benjamin, and Stephen Zeff whose comments and criticisms contributed to the 10th edition. Additionally, we thank our research assistant, Meloyde Gordon for her help.

We extend our thanks to the editorial staff at John Wiley & Sons, including Michael McDonald, Acquisitions Editor, Brian Kamins, Project Editor, and Jacqueline Kepping, Editorial Assistant. Our thanks also goes to the production staff on the book, Elaine Chew, Assistant Production Editor of John Wiley & Sons, as well as our copyeditor, Chris Thillen.

Contents

CHAPTER 1

The Development of

Accounting Theory

In its simplest form, theory may be just a belief; but for a theory to be useful, it must have wide acceptance. Webster defines *theory* as:

> Systematically organized knowledge, applicable in a relatively wide variety of circumstances; a system of assumptions, accepted principles and rules of procedure to analyze, predict or otherwise explain the nature of behavior of a specified set of phenomena.[1]

The objective of theory is to explain and predict. Consequently, a basic goal of the theory of a particular discipline is to have a well-defined body of knowledge that has been systematically accumulated, organized, and verified well enough to provide a frame of reference for future actions.

Theories may be described as normative or positive. *Normative theories* explain what should be, whereas *positive theories* explain what is. Ideally, there should be no such distinction, because a well-developed and complete theory encompasses both what should be and what is.

The goal of accounting theory is to provide a set of principles and relationships that explains observed practices and predicts unobserved practices. That is, accounting theory should be able to explain why companies elect certain accounting methods over others and should enable users to predict the attributes of firms that elect various accounting methods. And as in other disciplines, accounting theory should also be verifiable through accounting research.

The development of a general theory of accounting is important because of the role accounting plays in our economic society. We live in a capitalistic society,

1. *Webster's 11th New Collegiate Dictionary* (Boston: Houghton Mifflin, 1999).

which is characterized by a self-regulated market that operates through the forces of supply and demand. Goods and services are available for purchase in markets, and individuals are free to enter or exit the market to pursue their economic goals. All societies are constrained by scarce resources that limit the attainment of all individual or group economic goals. In our society, the role of accounting is to report how organizations use scarce resources and to report on the status of resources and claims to resources.

As discussed in Chapter 4 there are various "theories of accounting," including the fundamental analysis model, the efficient markets hypothesis, the capital asset pricing model, the human information processing model, positive accounting theory, and the critical perspective model. These often competing theories exist because accounting theory has not yet developed into the state described by Webster's definition. Accounting research is needed to attain a more general theory of accounting, and in this regard the various theories of accounting that have been posited must be subjected to verification. A critical question concerns the usefulness of accounting data to users. That is, does the use of a theory help individual decision makers make more correct decisions? Various suggestions on the empirical testing of accounting theories have been offered.[2] As theories are tested and either confirmed or discarded, we will move closer to a general theory of accounting.

The goal of this text is to provide a user perspective on accounting theory. To this end, we first review the development of accounting theory to illustrate how investor needs have been perceived over time. Next we review the current status of accounting theory with an emphasis on how investors and potential investors use accounting and other financial information. Finally, we summarize current disclosure requirements for various financial statement items and provide examples to show how companies comply with these disclosure requirements.

The Early History of Accounting

Accounting records dating back several thousand years have been found in various parts of the world. These records indicate that at all levels of development, people desire information about their efforts and accomplishments. For example, the Zenon papyri, which were discovered in 1915, contain information about the construction projects, agricultural activities, and business operations of the private estate of Apollonius for a period of about thirty years during the third century B.C.

According to Hain, "The Zenon papyri give evidence of a surprisingly elaborate accounting system which had been used in Greece since the fifth century B.C. and which, in the wake of Greek trade or conquest, gradually spread throughout the Eastern Mediterranean and Middle East."[3] Zenon's accounting system contained provisions for responsibility accounting, a written record of all transactions, a personal account for wages paid to employees, inventory records, and a record of asset acquisitions and disposals. In addition, there is evidence that all the accounts were audited.[4]

2. See, for example, Robert Sterling, "On Theory Structure and Verification," *The Accounting Review* (July 1970), 444–57.

3. H. P. Hain, "Accounting Control in the Zenon Papyri," *The Accounting Review* (October 1966), 699.

4. Ibid., 700–701.

Later, the Romans kept elaborate records, but since they expressed numbers through letters of the alphabet, they were not able to develop any structured system of accounting. It was not until the Renaissance—approximately 1300–1500, when the Italians were vigorously pursuing trade and commerce—that the need to keep accurate records arose. Italian merchants borrowed the Arabic numeral system and the basis of arithmetic, and an evolving trend toward the double-entry bookkeeping system we now use developed.

In 1494 an Italian monk, Fra Luca Pacioli, wrote a book on arithmetic that included a description of double-entry bookkeeping. Pacioli's work, *Summa de Arithmetica Geometria Proportioniet Proportionalita,* did not fully describe double-entry bookkeeping; rather, it formalized the practices and ideas that had been evolving over the years. Double-entry bookkeeping enabled business organizations to keep complete records of transactions and ultimately resulted in the ability to prepare financial statements.

Statements of profit and loss and statements of balances emerged in about 1600.[5] Initially, the primary motive for separate financial statements was to obtain information regarding capital. Consequently, balance sheet data were stressed and refined in various ways, while expense and income data were viewed as incidental.[6]

As ongoing business organizations replaced isolated ventures, it became necessary to develop accounting records and reports that reflected a continuing investment of capital employed in various ways and to periodically summarize the results of activities. By the nineteenth century, bookkeeping expanded into accounting, and the concept that the owner's original contribution, plus or minus profits or losses, indicated net worth emerged. However, profit was considered an increase in assets from any source, as the concepts of cost and income were yet to be developed.

Another factor that influenced the development of accounting during the nineteenth century was the evolution in England of joint ventures into business corporations. Under the corporate form of business, owners (stockholders) may not be management. Thus many individuals, external to the business itself, needed information about the corporation's activities. Moreover, owners and prospective owners wanted to evaluate whether stockholder investments have yielded a return. As a consequence, the emerging existence of corporations created a need for periodic reporting as well as a need to distinguish between capital and income.

The statutory establishment of corporations in England in 1845 stimulated the development of accounting standards, and laws were subsequently designed to safeguard shareholders against improper actions by corporate officers. Dividends were required to be paid from profits, and accounts were required to be kept and audited by persons other than the directors. The industrial revolution and the succession of the Companies Acts in England also increased the need for professional standards and accountants.

In the later part of the nineteenth century, the industrial revolution arrived in the United States, bringing the need for more formal accounting procedures and standards. Railroads became a major economic influence. These companies created the need for supporting industries, which in turn led to increases in the

---

5. A. C. Littleton, *Accounting Evolution to 1900* (New York: AICPA, 1933).

6. John L. Carey, *The Rise of the Accounting Profession* (New York: AICPA, 1969), 5.

market for corporate securities and an increased need for trained accountants as the separation of the management and ownership functions became more distinct.

Initially anyone could claim to be an accountant, for there were no organized professions or standards of qualifications, and accountants were trained through an apprenticeship system. Later, private commercial colleges began to emerge as the training grounds for accountants. These institutions emphasized the quality of value, but discussions of the nature of value in accounting education did not surface until much later. At the end of the nineteenth century, widespread speculation in the securities markets, watered stocks, and large monopolies that controlled segments of the U.S. economy resulted in the establishment of the progressive movement. In 1898 the Industrial Commission was formed to investigate questions relating to immigration, labor, agriculture, manufacturing, and business. Although no accountants were either on the commission or used by the commission, a preliminary report issued in 1900 suggested that an independent public accounting profession should be established to curtail observed corporate abuses.

Although most accountants did not necessarily subscribe to the desirability of the progressive reforms, the progressive movement conferred specific social obligations on accountants.[7] As a result, accountants generally came to accept three general levels of progressiveness: (1) a fundamental faith in democracy, a concern for morality and justice, and a broad acceptance of the efficiency of education as a major tool in social amelioration; (2) an increased awareness of the social obligation of all segments of society and introduction of the idea of the public accountability of business and political leaders; and (3) an acceptance of pragmatism as the most relevant operative philosophy of the day.[8]

The major concern of accounting during the early 1900s was the development of a theory that could cope with corporate abuses that were occurring at that time, and capital maintenance emerged as a concept. This concept evolved from maintaining invested capital intact to maintaining the physical productive capacity of the firm to maintaining real capital. In essence, this last view of capital maintenance was an extension of the economic concept of income (see Chapter 5) that there could be no increase in wealth unless the stockholder or the firm were better off at the end of the period than at the beginning.

During the period 1900–1915, the concept of income determination was not well developed. There was, however, a debate over which financial statement should be viewed as more important, the balance sheet or the income statement. Implicit in this debate was the view that either the balance sheet or the income statement must be considered fundamental and the other as residual and that relevant value could not be disclosed in both statements.

The 1904 International Congress of Accountants marked the initial development of the organized accounting profession in the United States, although there had been earlier attempts to organize and several states had state societies. At this meeting, the American Association of Public Accountants was formed as

---

7. Gary John Previts and Barbara Dubis Merino, *A History of Accounting in America* (New York: Ronald Press, 1979), 136.

8. Richard Hofstadter, *Social Darwinism in American Thought* (Philadelphia: University of Pennsylvania Press, 1944).

the professional organization of accountants in the United States. In 1916, after a decade of bitter inter-factional disputes, this group was reorganized into the American Institute of Accountants (AIA).

In the early 1900s, many universities began offering accounting courses. At this time no standard accounting curriculum existed.[9] In an attempt to alleviate this problem, in 1916 the American Association of the University Instructors in Accounting (AAUIA) was also formed. Since curriculum development was the major focus at this time, it was not until much later that the AAUIA attempted to become involved in the development of accounting theory.

World War I changed the public's attitude toward the business sector. Many people believed that the successful completion of the war could at least partially be attributed to the ingenuity of American business. As a consequence, the public perceived that business had reformed and that external regulation was no longer necessary. The accountant's role changed from protector of third parties to protector of business interests.

Critics of accounting practice during the 1920s suggested that accountants abdicated the stewardship role, placed too much emphasis on the needs of management, and permitted too much flexibility in financial reporting. During this time financial statements were viewed as the representations of management, and accountants did not have the ability to require businesses to use accounting principles they did not wish to employ. The result of this attitude is well known. In 1929 the stock market crashed and the Great Depression ensued. Although accountants were not initially blamed for these events, the possibility of governmental intervention in the corporate sector loomed.

Accounting in the United States since 1930

One of the first attempts to improve accounting began shortly after the inception of the Great Depression with a series of meetings between representatives of the New York Stock Exchange (NYSE) and the American Institute of Accountants. The purpose of these meetings was to discuss problems pertaining to the interests of investors, the NYSE, and accountants in the preparation of external financial statements.

Similarly, in 1935 the American Association of University Instructors in Accounting changed its name to the American Accounting Association (AAA) and announced its intention to expand its activities in the research and development of accounting principles and standards. The first result of these expanded activities was the publication, in 1936, of a brief report cautiously titled "A Tentative Statement of Accounting Principles Underlying Corporate Financial Statements." The four-and-one-half-page document summarized the significant concepts underlying financial statements at that time.

The cooperative efforts between the members of the NYSE and the AIA were well received. However, the post-Depression atmosphere in the United States was characterized by regulation. There was even legislation introduced that would have required auditors to be licensed by the federal government after passing a civil service examination.

9. For example, students now taking such accounting courses as intermediate, cost, or auditing are exposed to essentially the same material in all academic institutions, and textbooks offering the standard material for these classes are available from several publishers.

Two of the most important pieces of legislation passed at this time were the Securities Act of 1933 and the Securities Exchange Act of 1934, which established the Securities and Exchange Commission (SEC). The SEC was created to administer various securities acts. Under powers provided by Congress, the SEC was given the authority to prescribe accounting principles and reporting practices. Nevertheless, because the SEC has acted as an overseer and allowed the private sector to develop accounting principles, this authority has seldom been used. However, the SEC has exerted pressure on the accounting profession and has been especially interested in narrowing areas of difference in accounting practice. (The role of the SEC is discussed in more detail in Chapter 17.)

From 1936 to 1938 the SEC was engaged in an internal debate over whether it should develop accounting standards. Even though William O. Douglas (then the SEC chairman, and later a Supreme Court justice) disagreed, in 1938 the SEC decided in *Accounting Series Release (ASR No. 4)* to allow accounting principles to be set in the private sector. ASR No. 4 indicated that reports filed with the SEC must be prepared in accordance with accounting principles that have "substantial authoritative support."

The profession was convinced that it did not have the time needed to develop a theoretical framework of accounting. As a result, the AIA agreed to publish a study by Sanders, Hatfield, and Moore titled *A Statement of Accounting Principles*. The publication of this work was quite controversial in that it was simply a survey of existing practice that was seen as telling practicing accountants "do what you think is best." Some accountants also used the study as an authoritative source that justified current practice.

In 1936 the AIA merged with the American Society of Certified Public Accountants, forming a larger organization later named the American Institute of Certified Public Accountants (AICPA). This organization has had increasing influence on the development of accounting theory. For example, over the years, the AICPA established several committees and boards to deal with the need to further develop accounting principles. The first was the Committee on Accounting Procedure. It was followed by the Accounting Principles Board, which was replaced by the Financial Accounting Standards Board. Each of these bodies has issued pronouncements on accounting issues, which have become the primary source of generally accepted accounting principles that guide accounting practice today.

Committee on Accounting Procedure

Professional accountants became more actively involved in the development of accounting principles following the meetings between members of the NYSE and the AICPA and the controversy surrounding the publication of the Sanders, Hatfield, and Moore study. In 1936 the AICPA's Committee on Accounting Procedure (CAP) was formed. This committee had the authority to issue pronouncements on matters of accounting practice and procedure in order to establish generally accepted practices.

The CAP was relatively inactive during its first two years but became more active in response to the SEC's release of ASR No. 4 and voiced concerns that the SEC would become more active if the committee did not respond more quickly. One of the first responses was to expand CAP membership from seven to twenty-one members.

A major concern arose over the use of the historical cost model of accounting. The then-accepted definition of assets as unamortized cost was seen by some critics as allowing management too much flexibility in deciding when to charge costs to expense. This practice was seen as allowing earnings management (see Chapter 5) to occur.

Another area of controversy was the impact of inflation on reported profits. During the 1940s several companies lobbied for the use of replacement cost depreciation. These efforts were rejected by both the CAP and the SEC, which maintained that income should be determined on the basis of historical cost. This debate continued over a decade, ending when Congress passed legislation in 1954 amending the IRS Tax Code to allow accelerated depreciation.

The works of the CAP were originally published in the form of *Accounting Research Bulletins* (*ARBs*); however, these pronouncements did not dictate mandatory practice and received authority only from their general acceptance. The *ARBs* were consolidated in 1953 into *Accounting Terminology Bulletin No. 1*, "Review and Resume," and *ARB No. 43*. *ARBs No. 44* through *No. 51* were published from 1953 until 1959. The recommendations of these bulletins that have not been superseded are contained in the FASB Accounting Standards Codification (FASB ASC; discussed below) and referenced throughout this text where the specific topics covered by the *ARBs* are discussed. Those not superseded can be accessed through the cross-reference option on the FASB ASC website (http://asc.fasb.org).

Accounting Principles Board

By 1959 the methods of formulating accounting principles were being questioned as not arising from research or based on theory. The CAP was also criticized for acting in a piecemeal fashion and issuing standards that, in many cases, were inconsistent. Additionally, all of its members were part-time and as a result their independence was questioned. Finally, the fact that all of the CAP members were required to be AICPA members prevented many financial executives, investors, and academics from serving on the committee. As a result, accountants and financial statement users were calling for wider representation in the development of accounting principles. The AICPA responded to the alleged shortcomings of the CAP by forming the Accounting Principles Board (APB). The objectives of this body were to advance the written expression of generally accepted accounting principles (GAAP), to narrow areas of difference in appropriate practice, and to in the method of establishing accounting principles was quickly squelched when the first APB chairman, Weldon Powell, voiced his belief that accounting research was more applied and pure and that the usefulness of the end product was a major concern.

The APB was composed of from seventeen to twenty-one members, who were selected primarily from the accounting profession but also included individuals from industry, government, and academia. Initially, the pronouncements of the APB, termed "opinions," were not mandatory practice; however, the issuance of *APB Opinion No. 2* (see FASB ASC 740-10-25 and 45) and a subsequent partial retraction contained in *APB Opinion No. 4* (see FASB ASC 740-10-50) highlighted the need for standard-setting groups to have more authority.

This controversy was over the proper method to use in accounting for the investment tax credit. In the early 1960s the country was suffering from the effects of a recession. After President John F. Kennedy took office, his advisors suggested an innovative fiscal economic policy that involved a direct income tax credit (as opposed to a tax deduction) based on a percentage of the cost of a qualified investment. Congress passed legislation creating the investment tax credit in 1961.

The APB was then faced with deciding how companies should record and report the effects of the investment tax credit. It considered two alternative approaches:

1. The *flow-through* method, which treated the tax credit as a decrease in income tax expense in the year it occurred.

2. The *deferred* method, which treated the tax credit as a reduction in the cost of the asset and therefore was reflected over the life of the asset through reduced depreciation charges.

The APB decided that the tax credit should be accounted for by the deferred method and issued *APB Opinion No. 2*. This pronouncement stated that the tax reduction amounted to a cost reduction, the effects of which should be amortized over the useful life of the asset acquired. The reaction to this decision was quite negative on several fronts. Members of the Kennedy administration considered the flow-through method more consistent with the goals of the legislation, and three of the then-Big Eight accounting firms advised their clients not to follow the recommendations of *APB Opinion No. 2*. In 1963, the SEC issued Accounting Series Release No. 96, allowing firms to use either the flow-through or deferred method in their SEC filings.

The fact that the SEC had the authority to issue accounting pronouncements, and the lack of general acceptance of *APB Opinion No. 2*, resulted in the APB's partially retreating from its previous position. Though reaffirming the previous decision as being the proper and most appropriate treatment, *APB Opinion No. 4* approved the use of either of the two methods.

The lack of support for some of the APB's pronouncements and concern over the formulation and acceptance of GAAP caused the Council of the AICPA to adopt Rule 203 of the Code of Professional Ethics.[10] This rule requires departures from accounting principles published in *APB Opinions* or *Accounting Research Bulletins* (or subsequently *FASB Statements* and now the FASB ASC) to be disclosed in footnotes to financial statements or in independent auditors' reports when the effects of such departures are material. This action has had the effect of requiring companies and public accountants who deviate from authoritative pronouncements to justify such departures.

In addition to the difficulties associated with passage of *APB Opinions No. 2* and *No. 4*, the APB encountered other problems. The members of the APB were, in effect, volunteers. These individuals had full-time responsibilities to their employers; therefore, the performance of their duties on the APB became secondary. By the late 1960s, criticism of the development of accounting principles again arose. This criticism centered on the following factors:

1. *The independence of the members of the APB.* The individuals serving on the board had full-time responsibilities elsewhere that might influence their views of certain issues.

---

10. The AICPA's Professional Code of Ethics is discussed in more detail in Chapter 17.

2. *The structure of the board.* The largest eight public accounting firms (at that time) were automatically awarded one member, and there were usually five or six other public accountants on the APB.

3. *Response time.* The emerging accounting problems were not being investigated and solved quickly enough by the part-time members.

The Financial Accounting Standards Board

Due to the growing criticism of the APB, in 1971 the board of directors of the AICPA appointed two committees. The Wheat Committee, chaired by Francis Wheat, was to study how financial accounting principles should be established. The Trueblood Committee, chaired by Robert Trueblood, was asked to determine the objectives of financial statements.

The Wheat Committee issued its report in 1972 recommending that the APB be abolished and the Financial Accounting Standards Board (FASB) be created. In contrast to the APB, whose members were all from the AICPA, this new board was to comprise representatives from various organizations. The members of the FASB were also to be full-time paid employees, unlike the APB members, who served part-time and were not paid.

The Trueblood Committee, formally known as the Study Group on Objectives of Financial Statements, issued its report in 1973 after substantial debate—and with considerably more tentativeness in its recommendations about objectives than the Wheat Committee had with respect to the establishment of principles. The study group requested that its report be regarded as an initial step in developing objectives and that significant efforts should be made to continue progress on refining and improving accounting standards and practices. The specific content of the Trueblood Report is discussed in Chapter 2.

The AICPA quickly adopted the Wheat Committee recommendations, and the FASB became the official body charged with issuing accounting standards. The structure of the FASB is as follows. A board of trustees nominated by organizations whose members have special knowledge and interest in financial reporting is selected. The organizations originally chosen to select the trustees were the American Accounting Association; the AICPA; the Financial Executives Institute; the National Association of Accountants (The NAA's name was later changed to Institute of Management Accountants in 1991), and the Financial Analysts Federation. In 1997 the board of trustees added four members from public interest organizations. The board that governs the FASB is the Financial Accounting Foundation (FAF). The FAF appoints the Financial Accounting Standards Advisory Council (FASAC), which advises the FASB on major policy issues, the selection of task forces, and the agenda of topics. The number of members on the FASAC varies from year to year. The bylaws call for at least twenty members to be appointed. However, the actual number of members has grown to about thirty in recent years to obtain representation from a wider group of interested parties.

The FAF is also responsible for appointing the members of the FASB and raising the funds to operate the FASB. Until 2001 most of the funds raised by the FAF came from the AICPA and the largest public accounting firms. However, the Sarbanes-Oxley Act of 2002 required the FASB to be financed by fees assessed against publicly traded companies, instead of by donations from the interested parties in the private sector. The purpose of this action was to increase the independence of the FASB from the constituents it serves. The FAF currently collects

FIGURE 1.1   *Structure of the FASB*

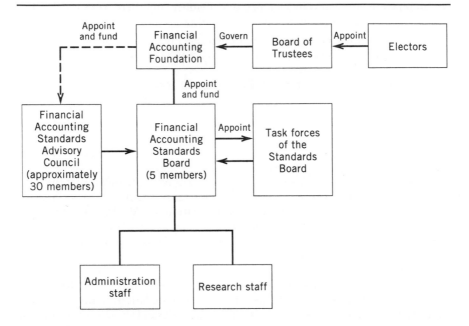

more than $23 million a year to support the activities of the FASB. Figure 1.1 illustrates the current structure of the FASB.

Both the FAF and the FASB have a broader representation of the total profession than did the APB; however, most of the members are usually CPAs from public practice. The structure of the FAF has recently come under scrutiny by the SEC. In 1996, Arthur Levitt, chairman of the SEC, voiced concern that the FAF's public interest objectives were at risk. He suggested that the FAF be reorganized so that most of its members would be individuals with strong public service backgrounds who are better able to represent the public free of any conflict of interest. He went on to suggest that the SEC should approve the appointments to the FAF.[11] To date there has been no change in the method of appointing FAF members, and changes in the structure of either the FAF or the FASB are likely to be evolutionary.

Section 108 of Sarbanes-Oxley established criteria that must be met in order for the work product of an accounting standard-setting body to be recognized as "generally accepted." The SEC responded by issuing a policy statement stating that the FASB and its parent organization, the FAF, satisfy the criteria in Section 108 of the Sarbanes-Oxley Act and, accordingly, the FASB's financial accounting and reporting standards are recognized as "generally accepted" for purposes of the federal securities laws.[12] Consequently, the FASB is the organization having

11. R. Abelson, "Accounting Group to Meet with SEC in Rules Debate," *New York Times*, 5 May 1996, D5.

12. Securities and Exchange Commission, "Commission Statement of Policy Reaffirming note two different fonts the Status of the FASB as a Designated Private-Sector Standard Setter," Washington, D.C., April 23, 2003.

the authority to issue standards for financial accounting. Thus, throughout this book, pronouncements of the FASB and those of its predecessor organizations not superseded or amended are presented as GAAP.

The Mission of the FASB

The FASB's mission is to establish and improve standards of financial accounting and reporting for the guidance and education of the public, including issuers, auditors, and users of financial information.

In attempting to accomplish this mission, the FASB seeks to:

1. Improve the usefulness of financial reporting by focusing on the primary characteristics of relevance and reliability and on the qualities of comparability and consistency (discussed in Chapter 2)

2. Keep standards current to reflect changes in methods of doing business and changes in the economic environment

3. Consider promptly any significant areas of deficiency in financial reporting that might be improved through the standard-setting process

4. Promote the international comparability of accounting standards concurrent with improving the quality of financial reporting

5. Improve the common understanding of the nature and purposes of information contained in financial reports

Types of Pronouncements

Originally, the FASB issued two types of pronouncements, *Statements of Financial Accounting Standards (SFASs)* and *Interpretations*. Subsequently, the FASB established two new series of releases: (1) *Statements of Financial Accounting Concepts (SFACs)* and (2) *Technical Bulletins*. *SFASs* conveyed required accounting methods and procedures for specific accounting issues and officially created GAAP. *Interpretations* were modifications or extensions of issues pronouncements. *SFACs* are intended to establish the objectives and concepts that the FASB will use in developing standards of financial accounting and reporting. To date, the FASB has issued seven *SFACs*, which are discussed in depth in Chapters 2, 6, and 7. *SFACs* differed from *Statements of Financial Accounting Standards* in that they did not establish GAAP. Similarly, they are not intended to invoke Rule 203 of the Rules of Conduct of the Code of Professional Ethics. It is anticipated that the major beneficiary of these *SFACs* will be the FASB itself. However, knowledge of the objectives and concepts the board uses should enable financial statement users to better understand the content and limitations of financial accounting information. *Technical Bulletins* were strictly interpretive in nature and did not establish new standards or amend existing standards. They were intended to provide guidance on financial accounting and reporting problems on a timely basis.

On July 1, 2009, the FASB ASC became the single source of generally accepted accounting principles. The FASB ASC became effective for interim and annual periods ending after September 15, 2009. On that date, all pronouncements issued by previous standard setters were superseded. The FASB had three primary goals in developing the Codification:

1. Simplify user access by codifying all authoritative U.S. GAAPs in one spot.

2. Ensure that the codified content accurately represented authoritative U.S. GAAPs as of July 1, 2009.

3. Create a codification research system that is up to date for the released results of standard-setting activity.

The Codification is expected to:

1. Reduce the amount of time and effort required to solve an accounting research issue
2. Mitigate the risk of noncompliance through improved usability of the literature
3. Provide accurate information with real-time updates as Accounting Standards Updates are released
4. Assist the FASB with the research and convergence efforts

The FASB ASC is composed of the following literature issued by various standard setters:

1. Financial Accounting Standards Board (FASB)
   a. Statements (FAS)
   b. Interpretations (FIN)
   c. Technical Bulletins (FTB)
   d. Staff Positions (FSP)
   e. Staff Implementation Guides (Q&A)
   f. Statement No. 138 Examples
2. Emerging Issues Task Force (EITF)
   a. Abstracts
   b. Topic D
3. Derivative Implementation Group (DIG) Issues
4. Accounting Principles Board (APB) Opinions
5. Accounting Research Bulletins (ARB)
6. Accounting Interpretations (AIN)
7. American Institute of Certified Public Accountants (AICPA)
   a. Statements of Position (SOP)
   b. Audit and Accounting Guides (AAG)—only incremental accounting guidance
   c. Practice Bulletins (PB), including the Notices to Practitioners elevated to Practice Bulletin status by Practice Bulletin 1
   d. Technical Inquiry Service (TIS)—only for Software Revenue Recognition

Additionally, in an effort to increase the utility of the FASB ASC for public companies, relevant portions of authoritative content issued by the SEC and selected SEC staff interpretations and administrative guidance have been included for reference in the Codification, such as the following:

1. Regulation S-X (SX)
2. Financial Reporting Releases (FRR)/Accounting Series Releases (ASR)

3. Interpretive Releases (IR)
4. SEC Staff guidance in:

    a. Staff Accounting Bulletins (SAB)

    b. EITF Topic D and SEC Staff Observer comments

Effective July 1, 2009, the FASB will no longer issue Statements of Financial Accounting Standards. Changes to authoritative U.S. GAAP, the *FASB ASC,* will be publicized through an Accounting Standards Update (ASU). Each ASU will:

1. Summarize the key provisions of the project that led to the ASU,
2. Detail the specific amendments to the FASB Codification, and
3. Explain the basis for the Board's decisions.

Emerging Issues

One of the first criticisms of the FASB was for failing to provide timely guidance on emerging implementation and practice problems. During 1984 the FASB responded to this criticism by (1) establishing a task force, the Emerging Issues Task Force (EITF), to assist in identifying issues and problems that might require action; and (2) expanding the scope of the *FASB Technical Bulletins* in an effort to offer quicker guidance on a wider variety of issues.

The EITF was formed in response to two conflicting issues. On the one hand, accountants are faced with a variety of issues that are not fully addressed in accounting pronouncements, such as interest rate swaps or new financial instruments. These and other new issues need immediate resolution. On the other hand, many accountants maintain that the ever-increasing body of professional pronouncements has created a standards overload problem (discussed in more detail below). The FASB established the EITF in an attempt to simultaneously address both issues. The goal of the EITF is to provide timely guidance on new issues while limiting the number of issues whose resolutions require formal pronouncements by the FASB.

All members of the task force occupy positions that make them aware of emerging issues. Current members include the directors of accounting and auditing from the largest CPA firms, representatives from smaller CPA firms, and the FASB's director of research, who serves as chairman. It is also expected that the chief accountant of the SEC will attend task force meetings and participate in the deliberations.

The EITF discusses current accounting issues that are not specifically addressed by current authoritative pronouncements and advises the FASB staff on whether an issue requires FASB action. Emerging issues arise because of new types of transactions, variations in accounting for existing types of transactions, new types of securities, and new products and services. They frequently involve a company's desire to achieve "off–balance sheet" financing or "off–income statement" accounting.

Issues may come to the EITF from a variety of sources. Many are raised by members of the task force themselves; others come from questions asked by auditors. Occasionally, an issue may arise because of a question from the SEC or another federal agency. An issue summary is prepared, providing the basis for each issue brought before the EITF. Issue summaries generally include a discussion of the issue, alternate approaches to the resolution of the issue, available references pertaining to the issue, and examples of the transaction in question. An issue summary is not an authoritative pronouncement—it merely represents the views of the EITF members at that time.

The task force attempts to arrive at a consensus on each issue. A consensus is defined as thirteen of the fifteen voting members. A consensus results in the establishment of GAAP and constitutes an accounting standards update to the FASB ASC.

Standards Overload

Over the years, the FASB, the SEC, and the AICPA have been criticized for imposing too many accounting standards on the business community. This *standards overload* problem has been particularly burdensome for small businesses that do not have the economic resources to research and apply all the pronouncements issued by these authoritative bodies. Those who contend that there is a standards overload problem base their arguments on two allegations: (1) not all GAAP requirements are relevant to small business financial reporting needs; and (2) even when GAAP requirements are relevant, they frequently violate the pervasive cost-benefit constraint (discussed in Chapter 2).

Critics of the standard-setting process for small businesses also assert that GAAP were developed primarily to serve the needs of the securities market. Many small businesses do not raise capital in these markets; therefore, it is contended that GAAP were not developed with small business needs in mind.

Some consequences of the standards overload problem to small business are as follows:

1. If a small business omits a GAAP requirement from audited financial statements, a qualified or adverse opinion may be rendered.

2. The cost of complying with GAAP requirements may cause a small business to forgo the development of other, more relevant information.

3. Small CPA firms that audit smaller companies must keep up to date on all the same requirements as large international firms, but they cannot afford the specialists that are available on a centralized basis in the large firms.

Many accountants have argued for differential disclosure standards as a solution to the standards overload problem. That is, standards might be divided into two groups. One group would apply to businesses regardless of size. The second group would apply only to large businesses, small businesses, or particular industries. For example, the disclosure of significant accounting policies would pertain to all businesses, whereas a differential disclosure such as earnings per share would apply only to large businesses.

The FASB and various other organizations have studied but have not reached a consensus. A special committee of the AICPA favored differential reporting standards.[13] The FASB had historically taken the position that financial statement users might be confused when two different methods are used to describe or disclose the same economic event, but in 2009 the International Accounting Standards Board (IASB) issued a pronouncement that omits or simplifies the applicability of its standards and disclosure requirements for small and medium-sized companies (see Chapter 3). The attempt to harmonize U.S. and international GAAP may result in the adoption of a similar FASB standard; however, bankers

---

13. Special Committee on Accounting Standards Overload, *Report on the Special Committee on Accounting Standards Overload* (New York: AICPA, 1983).

(a major source of capital for small businesses) and financial analysts have fairly consistently criticized differential reporting requirements as a solution to the standards overload problem.[14]

Standard Setting as a Political Process

A highly influential academic accountant stated that accounting standards are as much a product of political action as they are of careful logic or empirical findings.[15] This phenomenon exists because a variety of parties are interested in and affected by the development of accounting standards. Various users of accounting information have found that the best way to influence the formulation of accounting standards is to attempt to influence the standard setters.

The CAP, APB, and FASB have all come under a great deal of pressure to develop or amend standards so as to benefit a particular user group. For example, the APB had originally intended to develop a comprehensive theory of accounting before attempting to solve any current problems; however, this approach was abandoned when it was determined that such an effort might take up to five years and that the SEC would not wait that long before taking action. The Business Roundtable engaged in what initially was a successful effort (later reversed) to increase the required consensus for passage of a *SFAS* from a simple majority to five of the seven members of the FASB. Congressional action was threatened over the FASB's proposed elimination of the pooling of interest method of accounting for business combinations (see Chapter 16).

Two of the most notable examples of the politicizing of accounting standards involved the issues of employee stock options and fair value accounting. By the early 1990s, the awarding of employee stock options to company executives had become widespread. This was especially true in the new technology companies, where stock options were a major component of employee compensation. As a result, the FASB developed a preliminary standard that would have required companies to expense the fair value of the stock options granted to executives and other employees. The proposed standard was met with widespread opposition. Companies in the high-technology industry expressed the most vocal objections. Many of these companies had been reporting no earnings, and they feared that a required expensing of stock options would greatly increase their losses or lessen whatever earnings they might ever report. When it became evident that the FASB was determined to proceed with the standard, they appealed to members of Congress. Subsequently, proposed legislation was introduced in both the House and the Senate that ordered the SEC not to enforce the FASB's proposed standard on expensing stock options. As the FASB continued on toward issuing a standard, the Senate responded by passing a resolution that urged the FASB not to move ahead with its standard. One senator even introduced legislation that would have required the SEC to hold a public hearing and cast a vote on each future standard issued by the FASB, a procedure that probably would have led to the demise of the FASB. At that point, SEC Chairman Arthur Levitt, who had been on record as strongly favoring the FASB's proposed standard, counseled the FASB not to issue a standard that required the expensing of the fair value of stock options in the

14. Barbara J. Shildneck and Lee Berton "The FASB's Second Decade," *Journal of Accountancy* (November 1983), 94–102.

15. Charles T. Horngren, "The Marketing of Accounting Standards," *Journal of Accountancy* (October 1973), 61–66.

income statement; otherwise, its future existence might be at risk.[16] A watered-down version of the stock option standard was passed in 1995; however, a standard based on the original FASB proposal was later adopted. See Chapter 15 for a further discussion of accounting for stock options.

The fair value controversy was just as contentious. In September, 2006 the FASB published *Statement of Financial Accounting Standards No. 157*, "Fair Value Measurements," now contained at FASB ASC 820-10, which outlined the method to be used when determining fair values such as is required by FASB ASC 320-10 for marketable securities. Later in 2008, a market crisis occurred that resulted in a credit crunch for banks. Critics maintained that the requirement to use fair value to measure investments caused or exacerbated the market crisis by forcing a downward spiral of valuations based on distressed institutions. The SEC responded with a study that recommended retaining the fair value requirements.[17] This did not silence the critics, and the *Wall Street Journal* reported that its analysis of public filings revealed that thirty-one financial firms and trade groups had formed a coalition in early 2009 and spent $27.6 million to lobby legislators about the fair value requirement.[18] Subsequently, public hearings were held in Congress that resulted in several heated exchanges—including one congressman telling FASB Chairman Robert Herz, "Don't make us tell you what to do, just do it," and another stating, "If you don't act, we will."[19] The outcome was that the FASB issued a modification FAS 157-4, *Determining Fair Value When the Volume and Level of Activity for the Asset or Liability Have Significantly Decreased and Identifying Transactions That Are Not Orderly* (see FASB ASC 820-10-65), that was generally thought to lessen the impact of the fair value requirements. However, a subsequent study of the impact of FAS ASC 820-10-65 on seventy-three of the largest banks in the United States found that a large majority of the banks reported that the adoption of the new requirements did not have a material impact.[20]

Economic Consequences

The increased pressure on the standard-setting process is not surprising, considering that many accounting standards have significant economic consequences. *Economic consequences* refers to the impact of accounting reports on various segments of our economic society. This concept holds that the accounting practices

16. The events surrounding this controversy are documented in Steven A. Zeff, "The Evolution of U.S. GAAP: The Political Forces Behind Professional Standards (Part II)," CPA Journal Online, February 2005, http://www.nysscpa.org/cpajournal/2005/205/index.htm.

17. *Report and Recommendations Pursuant to Section 133 of the Emergency Economic Stabilization Act of 2008: Study on Mark-To-Market Accounting* (Washington, DC: Securities and Exchange Commission, 2008).

18. Susan Pulliam and Tom McGinty, "Congress Helped Banks Defang Key Rule," *Wall Street Journal*, 3 June 2009, http://online.wsj.com/article/SB124396078596677535.html.

19. Financial Executives Institute, "Levitt, Beresford on Congress, FASB and Fair Value; Breeden Calls for Merger of SEC, CFTC and PCAOB FEI Financial Reporting Blog" (March 26, 2009), http://financialexecutives.blogspot.com/2009/03/levitt-beresford-on-congress-fasb-and.html.

20. Jack M. Cathey and Richard G. Schroeder, "The Impact of FSP FAS 157-4 on Commercial Banks," Unpublished Working Paper, 2009.

a company adopts affect its security price and value. Consequently, the choice of accounting methods influences decision making rather than just reflecting the results of these decisions.

Consider the release of the FASB's pronouncement on other postretirement benefits (OPRBs) *FASB Statement No. 106*, "Other Post Retirement Benefits" (see FASB ASC 715-10-30, 60, and 80). The accounting guidelines for OPRBs required companies to change from a pay-as-you-go basis to an accrual basis for health care and other benefits that companies provide to retirees and their dependents. The accrual basis requires companies to measure the obligation to provide future services and accrue these costs during the years employees provide service. This change in accounting caused a large increase in recorded expenses for many companies. Consequently, a number of companies simply ceased providing such benefits to their employees, at a large social cost.

The impact on our economic society of accounting for OPRBs illustrates the need for the FASB to fully consider both the necessity to further develop sound reporting practices and the possible economic consequences of new codification content. Accounting standard setting does not exist in a vacuum. It cannot be completely insulated from political pressures, nor can it avoid carefully evaluating the possible ramifications of standard setting.

Evolution of the Phrase "Generally Accepted Accounting Principles"

One result of the meetings between the AICPA and members of the NYSE following the onset of the Great Depression was a revision in the wording of the certificate issued by CPAs. The opinion paragraph formerly stated that the financial statements had been examined and were accurate. The terminology was changed to say that the statements are "fairly presented in accordance with generally accepted accounting principles." This expression is now interpreted as encompassing the conventions, rules, and procedures that are necessary to explain accepted accounting practice at a given time. Therefore financial statements are fair only to the extent that the principles are fair and the statements comply with the principles.

The expression "generally accepted accounting principles" (GAAP) has thus come to play a significant role in the accounting profession. The precise meaning of the phrase, however, evolved rather slowly. In 1938 the AICPA published a monograph titled *Examinations of Financial Statements*, which first introduced the expression. Later, in 1939, an AICPA committee recommended including the wording, "present fairly . . . in conformity with generally accepted accounting principles" in the standard form of the auditor's report.[21]

The meaning of GAAP was not specifically defined at that time, and no single source exists for all established accounting principles. However, later Rule 203 of the AICPA Code of Professional Ethics required compliance with accounting principles promulgated by the body designated by the Council of the Institute to establish such principles, except in unusual circumstances. Currently, that body is the FASB.

The guidance for determining authoritative literature was originally outlined in *Statement of Auditing Standards (SAS) No. 5*. Later, *SAS No. 5* was amended by *SAS*

---

21. Zeff, "The Evolution of U.S. GAAP."

No. 43. This amendment classified the order of priority that an auditor should follow in determining whether an accounting principle is generally accepted. Also, it added certain types of pronouncements that did not exist when *SAS No. 5* was issued to the sources of established accounting principles. *SAS No. 43* was further amended by *SAS No. 69*, whose stated purpose was to explain the meaning of the phrase "present fairly . . . in conformance with generally accepted accounting principles" in the independent auditor's report.[22] *SAS No. 69* noted that determining the general acceptance of a particular accounting principle is difficult because no single reference source exists for all such principles. In July 2003, the SEC issued the *Study Pursuant to Section 108(d) of the Sarbanes-Oxley Act of 2002 on the Adoption by the United States Financial Reporting System of a Principles-Based Accounting System* (the Study). Consistent with the recommendations presented in the Study, the FASB undertook a number of initiatives aimed at improving the quality of standards and the standard-setting process, including improving the conceptual framework, codifying existing accounting literature, transitioning to a single standard-setter regime, and converging FASB and IASB standards.

In 2008, the FASB issued *SFAS No. 162, The Hierarchy of Generally Accepted Accounting Principles.*[23] *SFAS No. 162* categorized the sources of accounting principles that are generally accepted into descending order of authority. Previously, the GAAP hierarchy had drawn criticism because it was directed toward the auditor rather than the enterprise, it was too complex, and it ranked FASB Concepts Statements, which are subject to the same level of due process as FASB Statements, below industry practices that are widely recognized as generally accepted but are not subject to due process.[24]

According to *SFAS No. 162*, the sources of generally accepted accounting principles were:

1. AICPA Accounting Research Bulletins and Accounting Principles Board Opinions that are not superseded by action of the FASB, FASB Statements of Financial Accounting Standards and Interpretations, FASB Statement 133 Implementation Issues, and FASB Staff Positions.

2. FASB Technical Bulletins and, if cleared by the FASB, AICPA Industry Audit and Accounting Guides and Statements of Position.

3. AICPA Accounting Standards Executive Committee Practice Bulletins that have been cleared by the FASB and consensus positions of the FASB Emerging Issues Task Force (EITF).

4. Implementation guides published by the FASB staff, AICPA accounting interpretations, and practices that are widely recognized and prevalent either generally or in the industry.

---

22. *Statement on Auditing Standards No. 69*, "The Meaning of Present Fairly in Conformity with Generally Accepted Accounting Principles in the Independent Auditor's Report" (New York, 1993), para. 1.

23. *Statement of Financial Accounting Standards No. 162: The Hierarchy of Generally Accepted Accounting Principles* (Norwalk, CT: FASB, 2008).

24. *Study Pursuant to Section 108(d) of the Sarbanes-Oxley Act of 2002 on the Adoption by the United States Financial Reporting System of a Principles-Based Accounting System* (Washington, DC: SEC, July 2003).

Finally in 2009, the FASB issued *SFAS No. 168, The FASB Accounting Standards Codification and the Hierarchy of Generally Accepted Accounting Principles—a replacement of FASB Statement No. 162. SFAS No. 168* identified the FASB ASC (discussed below) as the official source of U.S. GAAP.

In this chapter and throughout much of the book, special attention is given to the pronouncements referred to in Rule 203 of the AICPA Code of Professional Ethics. The reason for this special attention is apparent. Practicing CPAs have an ethical obligation to consider such pronouncements as the primary source of GAAP in their exercise of judgment as to the fairness of financial statements. Opposing views as well as alternative treatments are considered in the text narrative; however, the reader should keep in mind that the development of GAAP has been narrowly defined by the AICPA.

Despite the continuing effort to narrow the scope of GAAP, critics maintain that management is allowed too much leeway in the selection of the accounting procedures used in corporate financial reports. These criticisms revolve around two issues that are elaborated on later in the text: (1) Executive compensation is frequently tied to reported earnings, so management is inclined to adopt accounting principles that increase current revenues and decrease current expenses; and (2) the value of a firm in the marketplace is determined by its stock price. This value is highly influenced by financial analysts' quarterly earnings estimates. Managers are fearful that failing to meet these earnings estimates will trigger a sell-off of the company's stock and a resultant decline in the market value of the firm.

Previously, SEC Chairman Levitt noted these issues and indicated his belief that financial reports were descending "into the gray area between illegitimacy and outright fraud." As a consequence, the SEC has set up an earnings management task force to uncover accounting distortions. Some companies have already voluntarily agreed to restructure their financial statements as a result of this new effort by the SEC. For example, SunTrust Bank, Inc., of Atlanta, though not accused of any wrongdoing, agreed to a three-year restructuring of earnings for the period ended December 31, 1996.[25]

The FASB's Accounting Standards Codification

Over the past fifty years, financial accounting professionals have had to manage hundreds of accounting standards promulgated by several different accounting standard setters. Many of these accounting professionals became convinced that accounting standards had evolved to the point that they could not keep up. The large number of standards is not a new issue, but the issue was becoming more unmanageable with each passing year. The members of FASAC recognized the problem and in 2001 suggested that the FASB address the issue of efficient access to U.S. GAAP by initiating a simplification and codification project. During 2002 and 2003, the FASB began various projects to address these issues, and in early 2004, the FASB accelerated its efforts on the codification and retrieval project. In September 2004, the FAF trustees approved funding for the FASB's codification and retrieval project. In June 2009, the FASB announced that the Codification would be the single source of authoritative nongovernmental U.S. GAAP effective for all interim and annual periods ending after September 15, 2009.

---

25. E. McDonald, "SEC's Levitt Pushes Harder for Changes in Fiscal Reporting and Some Cry Foul," *Wall Street Journal*, 17 November 1998, A2.

The concept is relatively simple and involved the following steps:

1. Restructure all U.S. GAAP literature by topic into a single authoritative codification.
2. Modify the standard-setting process to focus on updating the codification.

The major reason for embarking on the codification process was that researching multiple authoritative sources complicated the research process. For example, using the previously existing structure, an individual needed to review existing FASB, EITF, AICPA, and SEC literature to resolve even a relatively simple issue. As a result, it was easy to inadvertently overlook relevant guidance. Codifying all existing U.S. GAAP literature into one authoritative source eliminates the previous need to research multiple sources. In addition, creating one source will allow the FASB to more easily isolate differences in its ongoing effort to converge with international accounting standards. The codification represents the sole authoritative source of U.S. GAAP. Creating the codification is only the first step, and it is only part of the overall solution. Going forward, the standard-setting process will be changed to focus on the codification text. By implementing such an approach, constituents immediately will know the revised codification language as soon as the standard setter issues the standard. This approach eliminates delays and ensures an integrated codification. The FASB has also developed a searchable retrieval system to provide greater functionality and timeliness to constituents.

The FASB ASC contains all current authoritative accounting literature. However, if the guidance for a particular transaction or event is not specified within it, the first source to consider is accounting principles for similar transactions or events within a source of authoritative GAAP. If no similar transactions are discovered, nonauthoritative guidance from other sources may be considered. Accounting and financial reporting practices not included in the Codification are nonauthoritative. Sources of nonauthoritative accounting guidance and literature include, for example, the following:

i. Practices that are widely recognized and prevalent either generally or in the industry
ii. FASB Concepts Statements
iii. American Institute of Certified Public Accountants (AICPA) Issues Papers
iv. International Financial Reporting Standards of the International Accounting Standards Board Pronouncements of professional associations or regulatory agencies
v. Technical Information Service Inquiries and Replies included in AICPA Technical Practice Aids
vi. Accounting textbooks, handbooks, and articles

The FASB ASC stipulates that the appropriateness of other sources of accounting guidance depends on its relevance to particular circumstances, the specificity of the guidance, the general recognition of the issuer or author as an authority, and the extent of its use in practice (FASB ASC 105-10-05-3).

This text takes a historical approach to the development of accounting theory that traces the evolution of accounting standards. As such, we refer to all authoritative pronouncements by their original titles with a parenthetical reference to either the fact that they have been superseded or where they are now contained in the FASB ASC. We have included several cases in the assignment material for each chapter that utilize the FASB ASC.

The Role of Ethics in Accounting

Ethics are concerned with the types of behavior society considers right and wrong. Accounting ethics incorporate social standards of behavior as well as behavioral standards that relate specifically to the profession. The environment of public accounting has become ethically complex. The accountants' Code of Professional Ethics developed by the AICPA has evolved over time, and as business transactions have become more and more complex, ethical issues have also become more complex.

The public accountant has a Ralph Nader–type overseer role in our society. This role was described by former Chief Justice of the United States Warren Burger:

> Corporate financial statements are one of the primary sources of information available to guide the decisions of the investing public. In an effort to control the accuracy of their financial data available to investors in the securities markets, various provisions of the federal securities laws require publicly held corporations to file their financial statements with the Securities and Exchange Commission. Commission regulations stipulate that these financial reports must be audited by an independent certified public accountant . . . .[26]

By certifying the public reports that collectively depict a corporation's financial status, the independent accountant assumes a public responsibility transcending any employment relationship with the client. The independent public accountant performing this special function owes ultimate allegiance to the corporation's creditors and stockholders as well as the investing public. This "public watchdog" function demands that the accountant maintain total independence from the client at all times and requires complete fidelity to the public trust.

The SEC requires the filing of audited financial statements in order to obviate the fear of loss from reliance on inaccurate information, thereby encouraging public investment in the nation's industries. It is, therefore, not enough that financial statements be accurate; the public must perceive them as being accurate. Public faith in the reliability of a corporation's financial statements depends upon the public perception of an outside auditor as an independent professional.

Justice Burger outlined the very important role accountants play in our society. This role requires highly ethical conduct at all times. The role of ethics in accounting is discussed in detail in Chapter 17.

Accounting in Crisis—The Events of the Early 2000s

On January 1, 2001, Enron's stock was selling for over $90 per share. From that time until the early summer of 2001, nineteen investment research firms reviewed

---

26. *U.S. vs. Arthur Young and Co. et al.*, U.S. Supreme Court No. 8206871 U.S.L.W. 4355 (U.S. Mar. 21, 1984), 1.

its performance and twelve had given it a "strong buy" recommendation, while five others had recommended it as "buy."[27] Additionally, the company's 2000 annual report indicated that its auditor had not found any significant accounting problems. However, on August 14, 2001, it was announced that the company's president, Jeffery Skilling, had resigned after only six months on the job for "purely personal reasons."

Enron used what were termed *special-purpose entities* (SPEs) now termed variable interest entities (VIEs) to access capital and hedge risk.[28] By using SPEs such as limited partnerships with outside parties, a company may be permitted to increase its financial leverage and return on assets without reporting debt on its balance sheet.[29] The arrangement works as follows: An entity contributes fixed assets and related debt to an SPE in exchange for an ownership interest. The SPE then borrows large sums of money from a financial institution to purchase assets or conduct other business without the debt or assets showing up on the originating company's financial statements. The originating company can also sell leveraged assets to the SPE and record a profit. At the time these transactions took place, the FASB required that only 3 percent of a SPE be owned by an outside investor. If this guideline is met, the SPE didn't need to be consolidated and the SPE's debt was not disclosed on the originating company's financial statements.

Enron used SPEs to new degrees of complexity and sophistication, capitalizing them with not only a variety of fixed assets and liabilities but also extremely complex derivative financial instruments, its own restricted stock, rights to acquire its stock, and related liabilities. Additionally, as Enron's financial dealings became more complicated, the company apparently also transferred troubled assets that were falling in value, such as certain overseas energy facilities, its broadband operation, or stock in companies that had been spun off to the SPEs. As a consequence, the losses on these assets were kept off Enron's books.

To compensate partnership investors for assuming downside risk, Enron promised to issue additional shares of its stock. As the value of the assets in these partnerships fell, Enron began to incur larger and larger obligations to issue its own stock farther down the road. The problem was later compounded as the value of Enron's stock declined.

On October 16, 2001, the company reported a third-quarter loss and its stock dropped to about $33 a share. On October 28, as some of the problems with the SPEs were made public, a special committee of the board of directors of Enron was established under the chairmanship of William C. Powers, dean of the University of Texas Law School. The Powers Committee Report concluded that some Enron employees were directly involved in the SPEs and were enriched by tens of millions of dollars they never should have received. The committee also found that many of the transactions were designed to achieve favorable financial statement results and were not based on legitimate economic objectives or to transfer risk.

27. Analysts' recommendations take different forms but can be generally categorized as (1) strong buy, (2) buy, (3) hold, (4) underperform, and (5) sell. This issue will be covered in more depth in Chapter 17.

28. Special-purpose entities are discussed in greater depth in Chapter 16.

29. Financial leverage involves the use of debt financing as described in Chapter 11. Return on assets is calculated as net income/total assets and is discussed in more detail in Chapter 7.

In the meantime, the company's stock went into a free fall. On October 22, 2001, the SEC requested information about the company's off–balance sheet entities, and its stock price fell to just above $20. On November 12, the company announced restated earnings for the period 1997–2000 that resulted in $600 million in losses, and its stock price fell to about $8 per share. Later, on December 2, the company filed for bankruptcy and its stock became virtually worthless. How did this happen? What can be done to prevent similar episodes in the future?

The Enron case was just one in a series of accounting and auditing failures that include HealthSouth, WorldCom, and Tyco. These failures were triggered by a series of events that critics have attributed to the change from a manufacturing to a service economy in the United States and the resulting large increase in consulting services by public accounting firms.

Historically, accounting has been considered a highly trustworthy profession. Public accounting firms trained new accountants in the audit function with oversight from senior partners who believed that their firm's integrity rode on every engagement. That is, new auditors were assigned client responsibility after minimal formal audit training. Most of the training of new accountants took place on-site, and the effectiveness of the new auditor depended on the effectiveness of the instructor.

CPA firms have always called their customers "clients" and have worked hard to cultivate them. Partners routinely entertained clients at sporting events, country clubs, and restaurants, and many CPA firm employees later moved on to work in their clients' firms. Any conflicts in these relationships were at least partially offset by the CPA firm's commitment to professional ethics.

These relationships changed as information technology advisory services grew in the late 1970s and early 1980s. Also in the mid-1980s, the AICPA lifted its ban on advertising. As a result, revenue generation became more critical to partners' compensation. Thereafter, the profit structure of CPA firms changed dramatically; and in 1999, revenues for management consulting accounted for more than 50 percent of the then–Big Five's revenue.

As a result, the audit function evolved into a loss leader that public accounting firms offered in conjunction with vastly more lucrative consulting engagements. But as pubic accounting firms competed more aggressively on price for audit engagements, they were forced by cost considerations to reduce the number of procedures performed for each client engagement. This resulted in increased tests of controls and statistical models, and fewer of the basic, time-consuming tests of transactions that increase the likelihood of detecting fraud. In addition, junior auditors were frequently assigned the crucial oversight roles usually filled by senior partners, who were otherwise engaged in marketing activities to prospective clients. This reduced the effectiveness of the instructor–new accountant training process.

Two major changes in the accounting profession have taken place in the wake of the accounting scandals:

1. Arthur Andersen, formerly one of the Big Five audit firms, has gone out of business.

2. In July 2002, President George W. Bush signed into law the Sarbanes-Oxley Bill, which imposes a number of corporate governance rules on publicly traded companies.[30]

---

30. The act is discussed in depth in Chapter 17.

Enron was the fourth major audit failure affecting Arthur Andersen (AA) since 1999. In May 2001, Andersen paid $110 million to settle Sunbeam's shareholders' lawsuit. In June 2001, Andersen agreed to pay a $7 million fine to the SEC in the Waste Management case. Andersen had already agreed to pay part of a $220 million suit to settle a class action case related to Waste Management, which had overstated income by approximately $1 billion. On May 7, 2002, Andersen agreed to pay $217 million to settle civil litigation over its audits of the Baptist Foundation of Arizona.

The demise of AA was felt by its employees and across the economy. The company was the fifth-largest auditing firm in the world, employing 85,000 people in eighty-four countries. In 2001, AA reported U.S. revenues of $9.3 billion. But during this same year, the company began to unfold. AA was fined or paid more than $100 million to settle lawsuits for audit problems concerning two clients, Waste Management and Sunbeam. After Enron's October 2002 third-quarter earnings announcement, AA's independence from Enron began to be questioned because the firm had provided significant nonaudit services to Enron in addition to its fees associated with the Enron audit. Andersen received $47.5 million in fees from Enron. Of this amount, $34.2 million, or 72 percent, was audit related and tax work. Total fees for other services totaled $13.3 million. Also, Enron had outsourced some internal audit functions to Andersen, a practice that is now specifically prohibited by Sarbanes-Oxley.

On January 10, 2002, AA notified the SEC and the Department of Justice that its personnel involved with the Enron engagement had disposed of a significant number of documents and correspondence related to the Enron engagement. Five days later, AA dismissed the lead partner and placed three other partners involved with the engagement on leave. AA also placed a new management team in charge of the Houston office. These moves were in an apparent attempt to distance the firm's home office from the problems concerning Enron.

On February 2, 2002, the Powers report was released. It suggested that the home office of AA was well aware of accounting problems at Enron. As the report stated, the evidence suggested that AA did not function as an effective check on the disclosures reported by Enron. Also, the report noted that AA expressed no concerns to Enron's board of directors about accounting problems at Enron.

In response, on February 3, 2002, AA announced that former Federal Reserve Board Chairman Paul Volcker had agreed to chair an independent oversight board (IOB). The objective of the IOB was to review all policies and procedures of the firm and to ensure the quality and credibility of the firm's auditing process. The IOB had authority to mandate any changes in policies and procedures needed to ensure quality.

In March 2002, the Justice Department openly questioned AA's involvement with Enron and the eventual document shredding. Following a week of negotiations between AA and the U.S. Justice Department concerning a possible criminal indictment for obstructing justice, a criminal indictment against AA was unsealed on March 15. On May 2, a federal jury trial began in Houston. Finally, on June 15, AA was convicted of a single count of obstructing justice. AA was barred from conducting and reporting on the audits of SEC-registered companies after August 2002 and subsequently went out of business.

The Sarbanes-Oxley Public Company Accounting Reform and Investor Protection Act of 2002 (SOX) was passed by Congress to address corporate accountability in response to the financial scandals that had begun to undermine citizens' confidence in U.S. business. Specific provisions of the legislation are discussed in depth in Chapter 17. In summary, SOX established the Public Company Accounting Oversight Board (PCAOB). The PCAOB has the responsibility of setting auditing standards, reviewing the practices and procedures u sed by public accounting firms in conduction audits, and ensuring compliance with the provision of the legislation.

SOX also places new legal constraints on corporate executives by requiring corporate presidents and chief financial officers to certify the accuracy of a company's financial statements. Specifically, they are required to indicate that they have reviewed both quarterly and annual filings that based on their knowledge, the reports do not contain any untrue statements or material misstatements of facts; and that based on their knowledge, the financial information in the reports is fairly presented. Additionally, SOX puts the accounting profession under tightened federal oversight and establishes a regulatory board—with broad power to punish corruption—to monitor the firms and establishes stiff criminal penalties, including long jail terms, for accounting fraud.

Finally, SOX changes the way the FASB is funded. Previously, about a third of FASB's annual budget came from voluntary contributions from public accounting firms, the AICPA, and about one thousand individual corporations. Under SOX, those voluntary contributions are replaced by mandatory fees from all publicly owned corporations based on their individual market capitalization. But the fees are to be collected by the PCAOB. The SEC oversees the PCAOB. As a result, some fear that SOX has inadvertently made FASB more vulnerable to political pressure. Some have called SOX one of the most significant legislative reform packages since the New Deal of Franklin D. Roosevelt;[31] others have likened it to medical history, when a correct diagnosis was followed by an inappropriate or even harmful therapy such as the nineteenth-century practice of "bleeding" patients who were suffering from fever. This therapy turned out to be the opposite of what is necessary and beneficial because it weakened patients precisely when they needed strength to combat the cause of the fever.[32] The critics of SOX see a flaw in the system in that the auditor is retained and paid by the client, thereby making the auditor beholden to the client and its management. As a consequence the auditor, though he or she may not realize it, ends up seeing things through the eyes of management. While it is too early to determine which view will turn out to be correct, SOX will undoubtedly significantly affect the accounting profession.

International Accounting Standards

A truly global economy emerged during the 1990s, as many U.S. companies generated significant amounts of revenue and profits in foreign markets. Multinational companies are faced with decisions on the allocation of resources to their most efficient uses. These allocations cannot be accomplished without accurate and reliable financial information. Companies seeking capital or investment

31. R. R. Miller and P. H. Pashkoff, "Regulations under the Sarbanes-Oxley Act," *Journal of Accountancy* (October 2002), 33–36.

32. J. Ronen, J. Cherny, and T. W. Morris, "A Prognosis for Restructuring the Market for Audit Services," *CPA Journal* 73, no. 5 (May 2003), 6–8.

opportunities across national boundaries face cost and time issues. Capital-seeking firms must reconcile their financial statements to the accounting rules of the nation in which they are seeking capital, and investors must identify foreign reporting differences. The increasingly global economy requires that this process be simplified. Thus there is a push to harmonize international accounting standards.

The IASB is an independent private sector body that was formed in 1973 to achieve this purpose. Its objectives are

1. To formulate and publish in the public interest accounting standards to be observed in the presentation of financial statements and to promote their worldwide acceptance and observance

2. To work generally for the improvement and harmonization of regulations, accounting standards, and procedures relating to the presentation of financial statements[33]

These objectives have resulted in attempts to coordinate and harmonize the activities of the many countries and agencies engaged in setting accounting standards. The IASB standards also provide a useful starting point for developing countries wishing to establish accounting standards.[34]

The IASB has also developed a conceptual framework titled the *Framework for the Preparation and Presentation of Financial Statements*.[35] The conclusions articulated in this release are similar to those contained in the FASB's Conceptual Framework Project. That is, the objective of financial statements is to provide useful information to a wide range of users for decision-making purposes. The information provided should contain the qualitative characteristics of relevance, reliability, comparability, and understandability.

At the time this book was published, the IASB had issued forty-one Statements of Accounting Standards (IASs) and ten Statements of Financial Reporting Standards (IFRSs). However, since it has no enforcement authority, the IASB must rely on the "best endeavors" of its members. Neither the FASB nor the SEC is a member of the IASB, so its standards have no authority in the United States at the present time. However, the SEC recently ruled that foreign companies that adopt IASB standards are eligible to list their securities for sale on U.S. stock exchanges (see Chapter 3 for a further discussion of this issue). As noted in Chapters 2 and 3, there is also a movement to have IASB standards become GAAP for U.S. companies. The emergence of multinational corporations has resulted in a need for the increased harmonization of worldwide accounting standards. The role of the IASB is discussed in more detail in Chapter 3, and the IASB standards are reviewed throughout this text in chapters dealing with the issues addressed by each IAS or IFRS.

33. International Accounting Standards Committee, *International Accounting Standards 1996* (London: IASC, 1996), 7.

34. The FASB and IASB are now coordinating their efforts to develop a new conceptual framework and a combined set of accounting standards, as discussed in Chapters 2, 3, and 5.

35. *Framework for the Preparation and Presentation of Financial Statements* (London, England: IASC, 1989).

Cases

• Case 1-1 Sources of GAAP

The FASB ASC is now the sole authoritative source for all U.S. GAAP.

a. What are the major goals of the FASB ASC?
b. How is the FASB ASC expected to improve the practice of accounting?
c. What literature is now contained in the FASB ASC?
d. What should an accountant do if the guidance for a particular transaction or event is not specified within the FASB ASC?

• Case 1-2 Accounting Ethics

When the FASB issues new standards, the implementation date is frequently 12 months from date of issuance, and early implementation is encouraged. Becky Hoger, controller, discusses with her financial vice president the need for early implementation of a standard that would result in a fairer presentation of the company's financial condition and earnings. When the financial vice president determines that early implementation of the standard will adversely affect the reported net income for the year, he discourages Hoger from implementing the standard until it is required.

Required:

a. What, if any, ethical issue is involved in this case?
b. Is the financial vice president acting improperly or immorally?
c. What does Hoger have to gain by advocacy of early implementation?
d. Who might be affected by the decision against early implementation? (CMA adapted)

• Case 1-3 Politicalization of Accounting Standards

Some accountants have said that politicalization in the development and acceptance of generally accepted accounting principles (i.e., standard setting) is taking place. Some use the term *politicalization* in a narrow sense to mean the influence by governmental agencies, particularly the SEC, on the development of generally accepted accounting principles. Others use it more broadly to mean the compromising that takes place in bodies responsible for developing these principles because of the influence and pressure of interested groups (SEC, American Accounting Association, businesses through their various organizations, Institute of Management Accountants, financial analysts, bankers, lawyers, etc.).

Required:

a. The Committee on Accounting Procedure of the AICPA was established in the mid- to late 1930s and functioned until 1959, at which time the Accounting Principles Board came into existence. In 1973, the Financial Accounting Standards Board was formed, and the APB went out of existence. Do the reasons these groups were formed, their methods of operation while in existence, and the reasons for the demise of the first two indicate an increasing politicalization (as the term is used in the broad sense) of accounting standard setting? Explain your answer by indicating how the CAP, APB, and FASB operated or operate. Cite specific developments that tend to support your answer.

b. What arguments can be raised to support the politicalization of accounting standard setting?

c. What arguments can be raised against the politicalization of accounting standard setting? (CMA adapted)

• Case 1-4 Generally Accepted Accounting Principles

At the completion of the Darby Department Store audit, the president asks about the meaning of the phrase "in conformity with generally accepted accounting principles," which appears in your audit report on the management's financial statements. He observes that the meaning of the phrase must include more than what he thinks of as "principles."

Required:

a. Explain the meaning of the term *accounting principles* as used in the audit report. (Do not in this part discuss the significance of "generally accepted.")

b. The president wants to know how you determine whether or not an accounting principle is generally accepted. Discuss the sources of evidence for determining whether an accounting principle has substantial authoritative support.

c. The president believes that diversity in accounting practice will always exist among independent entities despite continual improvements in comparability. Discuss the arguments that support his belief.

• Case 1-5 The Evolution of the Accounting Profession

The nineteenth century witnessed the evolution of joint ventures into business corporations.

Required:
Discuss how the emergence and growth of the corporate form of business affected perceptions regarding the role of the accounting profession in financial reporting in England and the United States.

• Case 1-6 Accounting in Crisis

During the early 2000s, the role of accounting and the auditing profession changed and several accounting scandals were uncovered.

Required:

a. What conditions caused accounting and the auditing profession role to change during this time?

b. What major changes occurred as a result of the accounting scandals at that time?

• Case 1-7 The FASB

The FASB is the official body charged with issuing accounting standards.

Required:

a. Discuss the structure of the FASB.

b. How are the Financial Accounting Foundation members nominated?

c. *SFAC No. 2* describes a number of key characteristics or qualities for accounting information. Briefly discuss the importance of any three of these qualities for financial reporting purposes. (CMA adapted)

FASB ASC Research

For each of the following research cases, search the FASB ASC database for information to address the issues. Cut and paste the FASB ASC paragraphs that support your responses. Then summarize briefly what your responses are, citing the paragraphs used to support your responses.

• FASB ASC 1-1 Variable Interest Entities

In this chapter, we discuss how Enron and other companies use Variable Interest Entities (VIEs) to keep the effects of transactions and events off corporate balance sheets.

1. How does the FASB define a VIE? In other words, how does an entity qualify to be a VIE?

2. Is a company that meets the definition of a VIE required to consolidate the VIE?

• FASB ASC 1-2 Status of *Accounting Research Bulletins*

Portions of *ARB No. 43* are still considered GAAP. Three of the most important issues covered in *ARB No. 43* are revenue recognition, treasury stock, and comparative financial statements. Find the appropriate sections of the FASB ASC, originally contained in *ARB No. 43*, that address these issues. Cite the sources and copy the relevant information.

• FASB ASC 1-3 Accounting for the Investment Tax Credit

The accounting alternative treatments for the investment tax credit originally outlined in APB Opinions 2 and 4 are still considered GAAP. Find and cite the FASB ASC paragraphs and copy the relevant information.

• FASB ASC 1-4 Securities and Exchange Commission Comments

SEC observers frequently provide comments at EITF meetings. Find, cite, and copy the observer comments on:

1. Revenue recognition—customer payments and incentives

2. Debt with conversions and other options

3. Software cost of sales and services

- FASB ASC 1-5 Generally Accepted Accounting Procedure Guidelines

Find the guidelines for determining GAAP in the FASB ASC.

Room for Debate

- Debate 1-1 Which Body Should Set Accounting Standards in the United States?

Team Debate

Team 1: Argue that the SEC should set accounting standards in the United States.

Team 2: Argue that the FASB should set accounting standards in the United States.

- Debate 1-2 Should the Scope of Accounting Standards Be Narrowed Further?

Team Debate

Team 1: Pretend you are management. Argue against the narrowing of accounting choices.

Team 2: Pretend you are a prospective investor. Argue for the narrowing of accounting choices.

CHAPTER 2

The Pursuit of the

Conceptual Framework

The Conceptual Framework Project (CFP) represents an attempt by the FASB to develop concepts useful in guiding the Board in establishing standards and in providing a frame of reference for resolving accounting issues. Chapter 1 summarized the development of accounting from its early stages until the present. This review revealed that accounting practices were initially developed in response to changing economic conditions, and no attempts were made to establish a "theory of accounting" prior to the twentieth century. Subsequently, individual writers and later authoritative bodies undertook efforts to explain the goals of accounting. Most of the initial approaches were more descriptive of existing practice than normative in nature. Later efforts have attempted to develop and build on a normative theory of accounting.

The Early Theorists

Although debates about issues such as the existence of a science of accounting and the need to develop a theoretical framework began to appear in the early 1900s,[1] the first attempts to develop accounting theory in the United States have been attributed to William A. Paton and John B. Canning.[2] Paton's work, based on his doctoral dissertation, was among the first to express the view that all changes in

---

1. See, for example, A. Smith, "The Abuse of Audits in Selling Securities," *AAPA Year Book* (1912), 169–180; and H. R. Hatfield, *Modern Accounting: Its Principles and Some of Its Problems* (New York: Appleton, 1909).

2. S. A. Zeff, "The Evolution of the Conceptual Framework for Business in the United States," *Accounting Historians Journal* 26, no. 2 (December 1999): 89–131.

the value of assets and liabilities should be reflected in the financial statements, and that such changes should be measured on a current value basis.[3] He also maintained that all returns to investors (both dividends and interest) were distributions of income, and consequently he espoused the entity concept rather than the prevailing proprietary concept.[4] An additional contribution of this work was an outline of what Paton believed to be the basic assumptions or postulates underlying the accounting process. Paton's basic assumptions and postulates can be viewed as the first step in the development of the conceptual framework of accounting. Canning's work suggested a framework for asset valuations and measurement based on future expectations as well as a model to match revenues and expenses.[5] At this time, the balance sheet was viewed as the principal financial statement, and the concept of capital maintenance was just emerging.

During this early period, significant contributions to the development of a conceptual framework of accounting were also made by DR Scott.[6] Scott was viewed as an outsider; however, his writings have proven to be quite insightful. Scott was originally trained as an economist and was heavily influenced by the views of his colleague, the economist and philosopher Thorstein Veblen. He adopted Veblen's view that many academics were overly occupied with refining the details of existing theories when there was a need for the reexamination of fundamental assumptions. Both Scott and Veblen viewed the industrial revolution as changing the fundamental fabric of our society. An example of the manner in which Veblen influenced Scott is contained in Lawrence and Stewart:[7]

> Veblen believed men acquired habits of thought unconsciously and the thoughts men get are shaped by their daily activities. Any change in daily activities, such as that occasioned by the Industrial Revolution, would be expected to lead to a major shift in previous habits of thought. Scott saw the scientific method as the new habit of thought coming to dominance.

Scott believed the industrial revolution caused managers to look for new methods of maintaining organizational control. As a result, scientific methods such as accounting and statistics became organizational control tools.

Scott contributed to the development of accounting theory by recognizing the need for a normative theory of accounting. This view, described in several publications from 1931 to 1941, evolved into a description of his conceptual framework in "The Basis for Accounting Principles."[8]

---

3. W. A. Paton, *Accounting Theory—With Special Reference to Corporate Enterprises* (New York: Roland Press, 1922).

4. The proprietary theory holds that a firm's assets belong to its owners, whereas under the entity theory the firm and its owners are viewed as separate. See Chapter 4 for a discussion of this issue.

5. J. B. Canning, *The Economics of Accountancy* (New York: Roland Press, 1929).

6. Scott had no first name. He was named DR and used the two initials without spacing or punctuation in his publications.

7. C. Lawrence and J. P. Stewart, "DR Scott's Conceptual Framework," *Accounting Historians Journal* 20, no. 2 (December 1993): 104.

8. DR Scott, "The Basis for Accounting Principles," *The Accounting Review* (December 1941): 341–49.

In his first important work, *The Cultural Significance of Accounts*, Scott argued that accounting theory was not a progression toward a static ideal but rather a process of continually adapting to an evolving environment.[9] The notion of adaptation later became one of Scott's principles in his conceptual framework. He approached accounting from a sociological perspective. The basic premise presented in *Cultural Significance* was that the economic basis of any culture is shaped by the institutional superstructure of the society in question. This view later evolved into his orientation postulate.

Scott's next important work was a response to the American Accounting Association's "A Tentative Statement of Principles Underlying Corporate Financial Statements" (discussed later in the chapter). Scott criticized the AAA monograph as having a too-narrow view of accounting in that it addressed only accounting's transaction function.[10] Rather, he saw accounting as encompassing other important functions, such as managerial control and the protection of the interests of equity holders. He also viewed accounting as having both an internal control function and an external function to act for the protection of various economic interests such as stockholders, bond holders, and the government.

Although Scott's first two works contain what were to become elements of his conceptual framework, the first step in its articulation is contained in "Responsibilities of Accountants in a Changing Environment."[11] In this work he again alluded to the influence of the industrial revolution on a changing economy and saw it as requiring improved financial reporting to meet the needs of all investors. Scott supported Paton's earlier acceptance of the entity theory and went on to emphasize that accounting must meet the needs of external users. This view is an example of why Scott was considered an outsider, because the prevailing view was that accounting should be designed to benefit the firm's management or proprietor (the proprietary theory).

In 1941 Scott unveiled his conceptual framework in "The Basis for Accounting Principles."[12] He maintained that it could serve as a vehicle for the development of internally consistent accounting principles. Scott's framework includes the following hierarchy of postulates and principles to be used in the development of accounting rules and techniques.

- *Orientation Postulate.* Accounting is based on a broad consideration of the current social, political, and economic environment.

- *The Pervasive Principle of Justice.* The second level in Scott's conceptual framework was justice, which was seen as developing accounting rules that offer equitable treatment to all users of financial statements.

- *The Principles of Truth and Fairness.* Scott's third level contained the principles of truth and fairness. Truth was seen as an accurate portrayal of the information presented. Fairness was viewed as containing the attributes of objectivity, freedom from bias, and impartiality.

9. DR Scott, *The Cultural Significance of Accounts* (Houston: Scholars Book Co., 1931).

10. DR Scott, "The Tentative Statement of Principles," *The Accounting Review* (September 1937): 296–303.

11. DR Scott, "Responsibilities of Accountants in a Changing Environment," *The Accounting Review* (December 1939): 396–401.

12. Scott, "The Basis for Accounting Principles."

- *The Principles of Adaptability and Consistency.* The fourth level of the hierarchy contained two subordinate principles, adaptability and consistency. Adaptability was viewed as necessary because society and economic conditions change; consequently, accounting must also change. However, Scott indicated a need to balance adaptability with consistency by stating that accounting rules should not be changed to serve the temporary purposes of management.

Even a cursory review of Scott's framework reveals how far ahead of his time he was. His ideas were later incorporated by Moonitz in "Accounting Research Study No. 1" and by the AAA in *A Statement of Basic Accounting Theory* (both discussed below). It was not until much later that the deductive approach to accounting theory that Scott had advocated since the early 1930s began to be employed by authoritative standard-setting bodies.

Early Authoritative and Semi-Authoritatve Organizational Attempts to Develop the Conceptual Framework of Accounting

In the mid-1930s professional organizations became interested in formulating a theory of accounting. In 1936 the American Accounting Association released a statement titled "A Tentative Statement of Accounting Principles Affecting Annual Corporate Reports."[13] The statement's goal was to provide guidance to the recently established SEC; however, it was widely criticized by academics as relying too heavily on the historic cost model and the convention of conservatism.[14] To its credit, the AAA statement highlighted the distinction between the current operating performance and all-inclusive concepts of income, which continue to be discussed today as the issue of sustainable income.[15]

In 1938, the American Institute of Accountants (AIA)[16] also published a monograph, *A Statement of Accounting Principles*, written by Thomas H. Sanders, Henry Rand Hatfield, and Underhill Moore, that ostensibly described accounting theory.[17] The goal of this publication was to provide guidance to the SEC on the best accounting practices. However, the study did not accomplish its objective because it was viewed as a defense of accepted practices rather than an attempt to develop a theory of accounting.[18] In 1940, the AAA published a benchmark

---

13. American Accounting Association, "A Tentative Set of Accounting Principles Affecting Corporate Annual Reports" (Evanston, IL: AAA, 1936).

14. See, for example, Scott, "The Tentative Statement of Principles"; and G. Husband, "Accounting Postulate: An Analysis of the Tentative Statement of Accounting Principles," *Accounting Review* (December 1937): 386–410.

15. See Chapter 5 for a discussion of this issue.

16. The AIA was later renamed the American Institute of Certified Public Accountants (AICPA).

17. T. H. Sanders, H. R. Hatfield, and U. Moore, *A Statement of Accounting Principles* (New York: AICPA, 1938).

18. See, for example, W. A. Paton, "Comments on 'A Statement of Accounting Principles,'" *Journal of Accountancy* (March 1938): 196–207; and A. Barr, "Comments on 'A Statement of Accounting Principles,'" *Journal of Accountancy* (April 1938): 318–23.

study by Paton and A. C. Littleton, *An Introduction to Corporate Accounting Standards*.[19] While this study continued to embrace the use of historical cost, its major contribution was the further articulation of the entity theory. It also described the matching concept, whereby management's accomplishments (revenue) and efforts (expenses) could be evaluated by investors. This monograph was later cited as developing a theory that has been used in many subsequent authoritative pronouncements.[20]

Standard-setting bodies were initially reluctant to deal with the issue of accounting theory. At its inception, the Committee on Accounting Procedure (CAP) had considered developing a comprehensive set of accounting principles but dropped the idea because of the belief that the SEC might not be patient enough to allow the CAP enough time to develop the project and, as a consequence, might decide to develop its own accounting standards. Subsequently, the CAP had both internal disagreements and disagreements with the SEC over a number of issues. These disagreements were at least partially caused by the CAP's case-by-case issuance of accounting standards that in many instances were inconsistent due to the lack of an overall theory of accounting. By 1958, the CAP's problems caused the president of the AICPA, Alvin R. Jennings, to voice the belief that additional research was needed to examine accounting assumptions and develop authoritative pronouncements.[21] Jennings established the Special Committee on Research Programs to review and make recommendations on the AICPA's role in establishing accounting principles.

The committee's report proposed the establishment of the Accounting Principles Board (APB) to replace the CAP.[22] It also proposed the establishment of a research division to assist the APB. The committee report identified four broad levels that the development of financial accounting should address: postulates, principles, rules for the application of principles to specific situations, and research.[23]

The committee's definition of these levels avowed that "postulates are few in number and are the basic assumptions on which principles rest. They necessarily are derived from the economic and political environment of the business community."[24] The committee report stated that a fairly broad set of coordinated accounting principles should be formulated on the basis of the postulates. The committee's first charge to the APB's research division was to commission studies on the postulates and principles that would serve as the foundation for future authoritative pronouncements. This can be viewed as the first real attempt to establish a conceptual framework of accounting by an authoritative body.

19. W. A. Paton and A. C. Littleton, *An Introduction to Corporate Accounting Standards* (Sarasota, FL: American Accounting Association, 1940).

20. R. K. Storey, "Conditions Necessary for Developing a Conceptual Framework," *Journal of Accountancy* (June 1981): 84–96.

21. A. R. Jennings, "Recent Day Challenges to Financial Reports," *Journal of Accountancy* (January 1958): 28–34.

22. American Institute of Certified Public Accountants, *Report of the Special Committee on Research* (New York: AICPA, 1959).

23. Ibid., 63.

24. Ibid.

The AICPA accepted the committee's recommendations and in 1959, the APB replaced the CAP. An accounting professor, Maurice Moonitz, was chosen as the APB's director of research. He took on the responsibility of developing the accounting postulates and appointed another accounting professor, Robert T. Sprouse, to collaborate with him on the principles research study. The outcome was a disaster.

The postulates study, titled *The Basic Postulates of Accounting,* "Accounting Research Study No. 1," was published in 1961.[25] It consisted of a hierarchy of postulates encompassing the environment, accounting, and the imperatives as follows:

Group A: Economic and Political Environmental Postulates

This group is based on the economic and political environment in which accounting exists. They represent descriptions of those aspects of the environment that Sprouse and Moonitz presumed to be relevant for accounting.[26]

A-1. Quantification
Quantitative data are helpful in making rational economic decisions. Stated differently, quantitative data aid the decision maker in making choices among alternatives so that the actions are correctly related to consequences.

A-2. Exchange
Most of the goods and services that are produced are distributed through exchange and are not directly consumed by the producers.

A-3. Entities
Economic activity is carried on through specific units of entities. Any report on the activity must identify clearly the particular unit or entity involved.

A-4. Time period (including specification of the time period)
Economic activity transpires during specifiable time periods. Any report on that activity must specify the period involved.

A-5. Unit of measure (including identification of the measuring unit)
Money is the common denominator in terms of which goods and services, including labor, natural resources, and capital, are measured. Any report must clearly indicate which monetary unit is being used.

Group B: Accounting Postulates

The second group of postulates focuses on the field of accounting. They are designed to act as a foundation and assist in constructing accounting principles.

B-1. Financial statements (related to A-1)
The results of the accounting process are expressed in a set of fundamentally related financial statements that articulate with each other and rest on the same underlying data.

---

25. M. Moonitz, *The Basic Postulates of Accounting,* "Accounting Research Study No. 1" (New York: AICPA, 1961).

26. Notice the similarity to Scott's orientation postulate.

B-2. Market prices (related to A-2)

Accounting data are based on prices generated by past, present, or future exchanges that have actually taken place or are expected to.

B-3. Entities (related to A-3)

The results of the accounting process are expressed in terms of specific units or entities.

B-4. Tentativeness (related to A-4)

The results of operations for relatively short periods are tentative whenever allocations between past, present, and future periods are required.

Group C: Imperative Postulates

The third group differs fundamentally from the first two groups. They are not primarily descriptive statements; instead, they represent a set of normative statements of what should be rather than statements of what is.

C-1. Continuity (including the correlative concept of limited life)

In the absence of evidence to the contrary, the entity should be viewed as remaining in operation indefinitely. In the presence of evidence that the entity has a limited life, it should not be viewed as remaining in operation indefinitely.

C-2. Objectivity

Changes in assets and liabilities and the related effect (if any) on revenues, expenses, retained earnings, and the like should not be given formal recognition in the accounts earlier than the point of time at which they can be measured objectively.

C-3. Consistency

The procedures used in accounting for a given entity should be appropriate for the measurement of its position and its activities and should be followed consistently from period to period.

C-4. Stable unit

Accounting reports should be based on a stable measuring unit.

C-5. Disclosure

Accounting reports should disclose that which is necessary to make them not misleading.

The general reaction to the release of ASR No. 1 was that the results were self-evident and consequently didn't serve any useful purpose.[27] It was also not possible to determine whether the postulates could be transferred into a useful set of principles because the principles study was not published until the next year.

The principles study, Accounting Research Study No. 3, *A Tentative Set of Broad Accounting Principles for Business Enterprises* (published in 1962), argued for

---

27. W. Vatter, "Postulates and Principles," *Journal of Accounting Research* (Autumn 1963): 163–76.

the use of current values in accounting measurements.[28] The authors advocated different methods of determining current value for various balance sheet items such as replacement cost for inventories and plant and equipment, and the use of discounted present values for receivables and payables. Although the use of discounted present values for accounting measurements is widely accepted today and guidelines for its use are outlined in *Statement of Financial Accounting Concepts No. 7* (discussed later in the chapter), this concept was foreign to most accountants in the early 1960s. These views were also in conflict with the SEC's long-term advocacy of historical cost accounting. The result was that the APB dismissed the two studies as too radically different from GAAP for acceptance at that time.[29]

As a result, the APB was again faced with the same problems that daunted its predecessor, the CAP, when it dealt with issues case by case without an underlying foundation on which to base decisions. In an attempt to solve this problem, the APB commissioned another study by a retired practitioner, Paul Grady. The result, *Inventory of Generally Accepted Accounting Principles for Business Enterprises*, was in essence a summary of the then-accepted current GAAP.[30] Therefore, the APB still had little in the way of a foundation on which to base its decisions on current issues.

Later in the mid-1960s, the APB engaged in another attempt to develop a theory of accounting. A committee was formed and given the charge to enumerate and describe the basic concepts to which accounting principles should be oriented, and to state the accounting principles to which practices and procedures should conform. The original intention of this project was to develop a comprehensive theory of accounting. The published statement, *Basic Concepts and Accounting Principles Underlying Financial Statements of Business Enterprises*,[31] started off well by advocating the user approach suggested by the AAA's "A Statement of Basic Accounting Theory" (discussed later in the chapter) and defined accounting as a service activity whose function is to provide quantitative information; primarily financial in nature, about economic entities that is intended to be useful in making economic decisions.[32]

APB Statement No. 4 also addressed a new issue, the sophistication of users. It concluded that "users of financial statements should be knowledgeable and understand the characteristics and limitations of financial statements."[33] Unfortunately, the definition provided for the elements of the financial statements was again based on current accepted practice in that assets and liabilities were defined as being "recognized and measured in conformity with generally accepted accounting principles,"[34] but GAAP was defined as being the consensus at a particular time.

---

28. R. T. Sprouse and M. Moonitz, *A Tentative Set of Broad Accounting Principles for Business Enterprises*, "Accounting Research Study No. 3" (New York: AICPA, 1962).

29. "News Report," *Journal of Accountancy* (April 1962): 9–10.

30. P. Grady, *Inventory of Generally Accepted Accounting Principles for Business Enterprises*, "Accounting Research Study No. 7" (New York: AICPA, 1965).

31. *Accounting Principles Board Statement No. 4*, "Basic Concepts and Accounting Principles Underlying Financial Statements for Business Enterprises" (New York: APB, 1965).

32. Ibid., para. 9.

33. Ibid., para. 131.

34. Ibid.

As a result, the committee worked for five years before once again coming up with what was basically a description of existing practices. Additionally, the APB's report was published as a statement rather than as an opinion; consequently, its recommendations did not encompass GAAP and could be ignored without violating Rule 203 of the AICPA Code of Ethics, which requires compliance with accounting principles promulgated by an authoritative body.

The members of the CAP and APB were mainly accounting practitioners who apparently had little interest in developing a normative theory of accounting. In an attempt to fill this void, the AAA published *A Statement of Basic Accounting Theory* (*ASOBAT*) in 1966.[35] This monograph defined accounting as "the process of identifying, measuring and communicating economic information to permit informed judgments and decision by users of the information."[36]

Two new ideas arose out of *ASOBAT*'s definition of accounting. The members of the committee were mainly academics, so they looked upon accounting as an information system. Therefore they saw communication as an integral part of the accounting process. Additionally, the inclusion of the term *economic income* broadened the scope of the type of information to be provided to assist in the allocation of scarce resources. The committee also embraced the entity concept by indicating that the purpose of accounting was to allow users to make decisions. In essence they were defining accounting as a behavioral science whose main function was to assist in decision making. As a consequence, the committee adopted a decision-usefulness approach and identified four standards to be used in evaluating accounting information: relevance, verifiability, freedom from bias, and quantifiability. *ASOBAT* maintained that if these four standards could not be attained, the information was not relevant and should not be communicated. *ASOBAT* noted the inherent conflicts between relevance and verifiability in making one final recommendation. The monograph called for the reporting of both historical cost and current cost measures in financial statements. The current cost measures to be used included both replacement cost and price-level adjustments.

The publication of *ASOBAT* resulted in diverse opinions. Robert Morrison, the committee's only practitioner, voted for the monograph's release but requested that his concerns be published as a commentary at the end of the document. Morrison indicated that *ASOBAT* did not fulfill the committee's charge because it offered little in the way of basic accounting theory as the foundation for accounting principles. He also disagreed with the reporting of current cost information on the basis that it lacks verifiability.[37] On the other hand, another committee member, George Sorter, objected to the user needs approach because it assumed that user needs are known and well specified enough to allow information to be supplied to meet those needs.[38] Finally, one of the leading accounting theorists of the time, Robert Sterling, stated that *ASOBAT* contained very little that was new. He also found it to be inconsistent

35. American Accounting Association, *A Statement of Basic Accounting Theory* (Evanston, IL: AAA, 1966).

36. Ibid., 1.

37. Ibid., 97.

38. G. Sorter, "An Events Approach to Basic Accounting Theory," *The Accounting Review* (January 1969): 12–19.

and not completely logical. For example, he questioned the committee's ratio-nale for current costs as being that historical cost was deficient. He asked; "if historical cost is so inadequate, why report it at all?"[39]

The criticism of the APB resulted in yet another attempt to develop a conceptual framework of accounting. In a manner similar to *ASOBAT*, the Trueblood Committee's report on the objectives of financial statements (see Chapter 1) embraced the decision-usefulness criteria as the primary basis for the preparation and presentation of financial information. This committee was charged by the AICPA with proposing fundamental objectives of financial statements to guide the improvement of financial reporting. It was to find the answers to four questions:

1. Who needs financial statements?
2. What information do they need?
3. How much of the needed information can be provided by accountants?
4. What framework is needed to provide the needed information?

The Trueblood Committee adopted a normative approach as well as a user orientation in maintaining that "financial statements should serve primarily those users who have limited authority, ability or resources to obtain information and who rely on financial statements as their principal source of information about an enterprise's economic activities." The committee report specified the following four information needs of users:

1. Making decisions concerning the use of limited resources
2. Effectively directing and controlling organizations
3. Maintaining and reporting on the custodianship of resources
4. Facilitating social functions and controls[40]

Like its predecessors, the Trueblood Committee had difficulty agreeing on the answers to the questions proposed by the AICPA. As a result, it indicated that its final report be regarded as a first step in the process. The report listed the follow-ing objectives for financial reporting:

1. The basic objective of financial statements is to provide information useful for making economic decisions.
2. An objective of financial statements is to serve primarily those users who have limited authority, ability, or resources to obtain information and who rely on financial statements as their principal source of information about an enterprise's economic activities.
3. An objective of financial statements is to provide information useful to investors and creditors for predicting, comparing, and evaluating potential cash flows in terms of amount, timing, and related uncertainty.

39. R. Sterling, "*ASOBAT*: A Review Article," *Journal of Accounting Research* (Spring 1967): 95–112.

40. American Institute of Certified Public Accountants, *Objectives of Financial Statements* (New York: AICPA, 1973). The fourth purpose can be seen as derived from the work of Scott.

4. An objective of financial statements is to provide users with information for predicting, comparing, and evaluating enterprise earning power.

5. An objective of financial statements is to supply information useful in judging management's ability to use enterprise resources effectively in achieving its primary enterprise goal.

6. An objective of financial statements is to provide factual and interpretative information about transactions and other events that is useful for predicting, comparing, and evaluating enterprise earning power. Basic underlying assumptions with respect to matters subject to interpretation, evaluation, prediction, or estimation should be disclosed.

7. An objective is to provide a statement of financial position useful for predicting, comparing, and evaluating enterprise earning power.

8. An objective is to provide a statement of periodic earnings useful for predicting, comparing, and evaluating enterprise earning power.

9. Another objective is to provide a statement of financial activities useful for predicting, comparing, and evaluating enterprise earning power. This statement should report mainly on factual aspects of enterprise transactions having or expecting to have significant cash consequences. This statement should report data that require minimal judgment and interpretation by the preparer.

10. An objective of financial statements is to provide information useful for the predicting process. Financial forecasts should be provided when they will enhance the reliability of the users' predictions.

11. An objective of financial statements for governmental and not-for-profit organizations is to provide information useful for evaluating the effectiveness of the management of resources in achieving the organization's goals. Performance measures should be quantified in terms of identified goals.

12. An objective of financial statements is to report on the enterprise's activities affecting society that can be determined and described or measured and that are important to the role of the enterprise in its social environment. This objective was an attempt to draw attention to those enterprise activities that require sacrifices from members of society who do not benefit from those activities.

In addition, the Trueblood Committee report addressed the issues of the fallibility of single numbers in the financial statements and current costs. With respect to the former, the committee suggested that single number measurements that do not indicate possible ranges and dispersions in describing events are subject to uncertainty. With respect to current costs, the committee maintained that the stated objectives of financial reporting could not be achieved by using a single valuation basis such as historical cost. It concluded that different valuation bases should be used for different assets. The objectives enumerated by the Trueblood Committee became the basis for the first release in the FASB's conceptual framework project, *Statement of Financial Accounting Concepts No. 1*.

Statement on Accounting Theory and Theory Acceptance

The unsettled standard-setting process in the early 1970s caused the AAA to again consider accounting theory. In 1973, the AAA Committee on Concepts and Standards for External Financial Reports was charged with updating *ASOBAT* in light of the many changes in accounting that had taken place since it was originally issued. The committee deliberated over a four-year period. Since appointments to the committee were for two years, the committee membership changed during the second two-year period; however, six original members remained on the committee. Its report, *Statement on Accounting Theory and Theory Acceptance* (*SATTA*), turned out not to be an update of *ASOBAT*, but rather a review of the status of accounting theory and its acceptance.[41]

The committee's rationale for this approach was stated as follows:

> Fundamental changes have occurred since the publication of *ASOBAT* The basic disciplines traditionally utilized by accounting theory have been altered considerably, and accounting researchers have enthusiastically employed their new tools, perspectives and analytical techniques to explore a wide range of accounting issues from new directions.[42]

The committee's conclusion was that a single, universally accepted basic accounting theory did not exist. The committee's basis for this conclusion is examined in the following paragraphs.

SATTA first embarked on a review of accounting theories and found that a number of theories explained narrow areas of accounting. The committee noted that while there was general agreement that the purpose of financial accounting is to provide economic data about accounting entities, divergent theories had emerged because of the way different theorists specified users of accounting data and the environment. For example, *users* might be defined either as the owners of the accounting entity or more broadly to include creditors, employees, regulatory agencies, and the general public. Similarly, the environment might be specified as a single source of information or as one of several sources of financial information. The various approaches to accounting theory were condensed into (1) classical, (2) decision usefulness, and (3) information economics.

The Classical Approach

These studies covered the period from 1922 to 1962, with the exception of one monograph from 1975. *SATTA* maintained that all of these works were deductive in nature and criticized them as generally disconnected in that they did not cite or build on previous work. It was noted that many of the authors of these works were trained in economics because at the time, most universities did not offer Ph.D. degrees in business, and those that did required much work in economic theory. As a consequence, many authors included in this category were influenced by the neoclassical economic theory of the firm, which ignores historical costs and generally advocates the use of current values. *SATTA* subclassified the

---

41. American Accounting Association, Committee on Concepts and Standards for External Financial Reports, *Statement on Accounting Theory and Theory Acceptance:* AAA (Sarasota, FL: AAA, 1977).

42. Ibid., ix.

studies in this group into the deductive (true income) school and the inductive school. The deductive school theorists held that income measuring a single valuation base would meet the needs of all users. Studies included under this category were those by Paton, Moonitz and Sprouse, and Moonitz. Inductive school studies were viewed by *SATTA* as attempting to rationalize or justify existing accounting practice. The studies under this category included those by Hatfield and Littleton.[43]

The Decision-Usefulness Approach

The decision-usefulness studies, which include the AAA's "Tentative Statement," the Sanders, Hatfield, and Moore monograph, *ASOBAT*, and the Trueblood Report, focus on the recognition that usefulness is a basic objective of accounting. This approach stresses the use of decision models. Once a particular decision model is chosen, information relevant to the model is specified and accounting alternatives are compared to the data necessary for implementing the model. For example, the Trueblood Report stated that the basic objective of financial accounting is to provide information useful for making economic decisions.

A second focus of studies included under this category revolves around studies that examined the reactions by decision makers to reporting alternatives. Examples include the behavioral accounting studies discussed in Chapter 4 and a classic study by Ball and Brown investigating the information content of accounting numbers.[44]

Information Economics

Studies taking this approach use economic theory to specify the information necessary to make economic decisions. They treat information as a community that has costs and prices and examine whether regulation of external financial reporting is desirable. *SATTA* apparently included this category as an emerging method of developing accounting theory; however, information economics has not gained the prominence *SATTA* anticipated.

Criticisms of the Approaches to Theory

SATTA next embarked on a discussion of why none of the approaches to theory had gained general acceptance. *SATTA* raised six issues.

1. *The problem with relating theory to practice.* The real world is much more complex than the world specified in most accounting theories. For example, most theory descriptions begin with unrealistic assumptions such as holding several variables constant.

2. *Allocation problem.* Allocation is an arbitrary process. For example, the definition of depreciation as a *rational* and *systematic* method of allocation has led to a variety of interpretations of these terms.

3. *The difficulty with normative standards.* Normative standards are desired states; however, different users of accounting information have different desired states. As a result, no set of standards can satisfy all users.

---

43. It is interesting to note that DR Scott was not even mentioned in *SATTA*.

44. R. Ball and P. Brown, "An Empirical Evaluation of Accounting Income Numbers," *Journal of Accounting Research* (Autumn 1968).

4. *The difficulties in interpreting security price behavior research.* Market studies (such as the efficient market studies discussed in Chapter 4) attempt to determine how users employ accounting numbers. These studies have attempted to control for all variables except the one of interest, but there have been disagreements over whether their research designs have actually accomplished this goal.

5. *The problem of cost-benefit considerations accounting theories.* A basic assumption of accounting is that the benefits derived from adopting a particular accounting alternative exceed its costs. However, most existing theories do not indicate how to measure benefits and costs.

6. *Limitations of data expansion.* At the time *SATTA* was published, a view was emerging that more information is preferable to less. Subsequent research has indicated that users have a limited ability to process accounting information. (The issue of information processing is discussed in Chapter 4.)

The next section of *SATTA* noted that although the evolutionary view of accounting had considerable appeal, the evidence suggests that the existing accounting literature was inconsistent with that view. It suggested that the process of theorizing in accounting was more revolutionary than evolutionary and turned to a perspective developed by Kuhn.[45] He suggests scientific progress proceeds in the following order:

1. Acceptance of a paradigm.[46]
2. Working with that paradigm by doing normal science.
3. Becoming dissatisfied with that paradigm.
4. Searching for a new paradigm.
5. Accepting a new paradigm.

SATTA suggested that accounting theory at that time was in step 3 of this process because a number of theorists had become dissatisfied with the matching approach to specifying the content of financial reports.

Evaluation of SATTA

If the newly formed FASB was looking for a sense of direction from *SATTA*, they were undoubtedly disappointed. *SATTA*'s contention that no universally accepted theory of accounting was then in existence in essence left it up to the FASB to develop one. The FASB responded with its Conceptual Framework (discussed in the next section). *SATTA*'s focus on the philosophy of science perspective is not without its detractors. Peasnell (1978) concluded that *SATTA*'s theory approaches do not constitute paradigms,[47] because a paradigm is much more than a set of

---

45. T. Kuhn, *The Structure of Scientific Revolutions,* 2nd ed. (Chicago: University of Chicago Press, 1970).

46. *SATTA* defined a paradigm as "a kind of world view and focus for research." (*SATTA*, p. 42).

47. K. Peasnell, "Statement on Accounting theory and Theory Acceptance: A Review Article," *Accounting and Business Research* (Summer 1978): 217–28.

hypotheses. He also doubted the appropriateness of applying Kuhn's theory to accounting:

> Accounting is not a science, it is a service activity. Accounting, therefore, should be equated not with the sciences, but with fields like medicine, technology and law, of which the principal *raison d'etre* is an external social need.[48]

Peasnell also criticized *SATTA*'s distinction between the classical and decision usefulness approaches as "artificial."[49] Finally, he suggested that the inability of *SATTA* to reach a consensus was influenced by the committee that wrote *SATTA* because it was composed of several members who had strong advocacy positions on various approaches to theory development.

The FASB's Conceptual Framework Project

A motivating factor in the development of the Conceptual Framework Project (CFP) was the FASB's observation about the difficulties its predecessor, the APB, had experienced. As discussed above, the APB commissioned two studies on postulates and broad principles of accounting that were rejected as too radically different. Later, another committee was commissioned that resulted in *APB Statement No. 4*, which also was not fully accepted because it was viewed as a list of current practices rather than as a guide.[50]

The CFP first attempted to develop principles or broad qualitative standards to permit the making of systematic rational choices among alternative methods of financial reporting. Subsequently, the project focused on how these overall objectives could be achieved. As a result, the CFP is a body of interrelated objectives and fundamentals. The objectives identify the goals and purposes of financial accounting, whereas the fundamentals are the underlying concepts that help achieve those objectives. These concepts are designed to provide guidance in three areas:

1. Selecting the transactions, events, and circumstances to be accounted for
2. Determining how the selected transactions, events, and transactions should be measured
3. Determining how to summarize and report the results of events, transactions, and circumstances

The FASB intends the CFP to be viewed not as a package of solutions to problems but rather as a common basis for identifying and discussing issues, for asking relevant questions, and for suggesting avenues for research.

The CFP has resulted in the issuance of seven *Statements of Financial Accounting Concepts (SFAC): No. 1:* "Objectives of Financial Reporting by Business Enterprises"; *No. 2:* "Qualitative Characteristics of Accounting Information"; *No. 3:* "Elements of Financial Statements of Business Enterprises"; *No. 4:* "Objectives of Financial

48. Ibid., 220.

49. Ibid., 222.

50. For a discussion of the rationale for the CFP, see J. M. Foster and L. T. Johnson, *Why Does the FASB Have a Conceptual Framework?* (Norwalk, CT: FASB, 2001).

Reporting by Nonbusiness Organizations" (because the focus of this text is financial accounting, *SFAC No. 4* will not be discussed here); *No. 5:* "Recognition and Measurement in Financial Statements of Business Enterprises"; *No. 6:* "Elements of Financial Statements" (*SFAC No. 6* replaced *SFAC No. 3*); and *No. 7:* "Using Cash Flow Information and Present Value in Accounting Measurements."

SFAC Nos. 1 and *2* can be described as the goals to guide practice. They also indicate how these goals are useful in making qualitative decisions about what to report. Specifically, *SFAC No. 1* defines the primary objective of financial reporting as usefulness. *SFAC No. 2* describes how financial statements can be useful in qualitative terms. *SFAC No. 5* explains that *SFAC Nos. 1* and *2* provide guidelines for accountants to be able to recognize and measure accounting information. In addition, *SFAC No. 5* describes measurability and states that for an item to be reported, not only must it be measurable, but it also must meet the definition of an element provided in *SFAC No. 6*. *SFAC No. 7* provides a framework for using future cash flows and present value as the basis for accounting measurements. Each of these statements is discussed in more detail later in the chapter.

The CFP does not directly affect practice, and the *SFACs* are not intended to invoke application of Rules 203 or 204 of the Code of Professional Ethics, which specify how deviations from GAAP are to be disclosed.[51] *SFACs* affect practice only by means of their influence on the development of new accounting standards.

The FASB itself is the most direct beneficiary of the CFP. *SFACs* provide the Board with a foundation for setting standards and tools to use in resolving accounting and reporting questions. They also provide a framework that can be used to consider the merits of alternatives and promote greater efficiency in internal and external communications. The FASB staff is guided by pertinent concepts in the *SFACs* that might provide guidance in developing its analysis of issues for consideration by the Board. Discussion of the CFP concepts used was included in the basis for conclusions section of every new *SFAS* prior to the adoption of the Accounting Standards Codification in 2009. Although the CFP doesn't provide all of the answers, it narrows the alternatives and eliminates those that are inconsistent with it. It also is used to guide the development of neutral standards, which aids in the allocation of scarce resources and the efficient function of capital markets.

An additional benefit of the CFP is the reduction of the influence of personal bias on standard setting. Without the guidance provided by the conceptual framework, standard setting would be based on the individual personal frameworks of the members of the Board. This could result in inconsistent standards over time as the members and their individual frameworks change. Without a frame of reference, a rational debate cannot occur, and the appropriate treatment is in the eye of the beholder. The CFP also helps users of financial information better understand that information and its limitations because it provides a frame of reference for preparers, auditors, students, and faculty.

The FASB has indicated that no new statements of concepts are anticipated. However, the Board and the International Accounting Standards Board (IASB) are currently examining whether differences in their existing conceptual frameworks are impediments to convergence of accounting standards internationally

---

51. See Chapter 17 for a discussion of this issue.

(discussed later in the chapter). That is, much of their respective conceptual frameworks were developed over two decades ago, and the passage of time has led to increased complexity that was not anticipated; consequently, some modifications may be necessary. The specific content of *SFAC Nos. 1, 2, 5, 6*, and *7* as currently constituted is summarized in the following paragraphs.

Statement of Financial Accounting Concepts No. 1: "Objectives of Financial Reporting by Business Enterprises"

The foundation for *SFAC No. 1* was the Trueblood Committee's work on the objectives of financial statements; consequently, it is an attempt to establish normative accounting theory. As *SFAC No. 1* points out, external financial reporting by business enterprises is not an end in itself. Rather, it is a source of useful information furnished by management to financial statement users who can obtain the information in no other way. *SFAC No. 1* indicated that the overall objective of financial reporting is to give users a basis for choosing among alternative uses of scarce resources. While this objective may seem self-explanatory, it is important because it established that user needs are more important than auditor needs in the development of accounting standards. Consequently, effective financial reporting must meet several broad objectives. It must enable current and potential investors, creditors, and other users to execute these actions:

1. Make investment and credit decisions.
2. Assess cash-flow prospects.
3. Report enterprise resources, claims to those resources, and changes in them.
4. Report economic resources, obligations, and owners' equity.
5. Report enterprise performance and earnings.
6. Evaluate liquidity, solvency, and flow of funds.
7. Evaluate management stewardship and performance.
8. Explain and interpret financial information.

Following on the basic overall objective, *SFAC No. 1* stated that the FASB intends that these broad objectives will act as guidelines for evaluating the usefulness of new and existing GAAP to users making investment and credit decisions. This goal will help facilitate the efficient use of scarce resources and the operation of capital markets.

Statement of Financial Accounting Concepts No. 2: "Qualitative Characteristics of Accounting Information"

The second statement of concepts bridges the gap between *SFAC No. 1* and subsequent statements that describe the elements of financial statements and provide guidelines for their recognition, measurement, and disclosure. Specifically, *SFAC No. 2* addresses the question: What characteristics of accounting information make it useful? Later *SFACs* are concerned with how the purposes of financial accounting are to be attained.

SFAC No. 2 notes that accounting choices are made on at least two levels. First, the FASB or other agencies such as the SEC have the power to require businesses to report in some particular way or to prohibit a method that might be considered undesirable. Second, the reporting enterprise makes accounting choices between acceptable alternatives. *SFAC No. 2* attempts to identify and define the qualities that make accounting information useful by developing a number of generalizations or guidelines for making accounting choices on both levels.

More specifically with respect to second-level choices, the statement indicates that the primary criterion of choice between two alternative accounting methods involves asking which method produces the better—that is, the more useful—information. If the answer to that question is clear, it then becomes necessary to ask whether the value of the better information significantly exceeds that of the inferior information to justify any extra cost (cost-benefit analysis). If a satisfactory answer is given, the choice between alternatives should be clear. The qualities that distinguish better (or more useful) information from inferior (less useful) are primarily the qualities of relevance and reliability (discussed later).

Figure 2.1 illustrates the hierarchy of accounting qualities, discussed by *SFAC No. 2* in reviewing the characteristics of accounting information.

FIGURE 2.1   *A Hierarchy of Accounting Qualities*

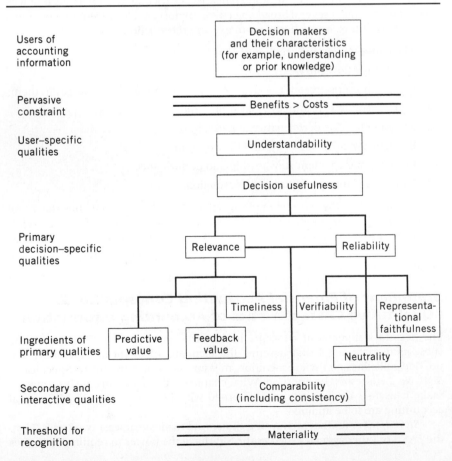

From Figure 2.1 we can see that the characteristics of information that make it a desirable commodity are viewed as a hierarchy of qualities, in which usefulness for decision making is the most important quality. However, the hierarchy does not distinguish between the primary qualities and other qualities, nor does it assign priority among qualities. In the following paragraphs, we discuss each of the hierarchical levels in detail.

Decision Makers and Their Characteristics

Each decision maker judges what accounting information is useful, and that judgment is influenced by such factors as the decision to be made, the methods of decision making to be used, the information already possessed or obtained from other sources, and the decision maker's capacity to process the information. These characteristics indicate that generally, managers and owners of small or closely held enterprises may find some external financial reporting information less useful than will stockholders of large, publicly held enterprises.[52]

Cost-Benefit Constraint

In general, unless the benefits to be derived from a commodity or service exceed the costs associated with providing it, the commodity or service will not be sought after. However, financial information differs from other commodities in that the costs of providing financial information initially fall on preparers (the enterprise), whereas the benefits accrue to both preparers and users. Ultimately, a standard-setting body such as the FASB must do its best to meet the needs of society as a whole when it promulgates a standard that sacrifices one of those qualities for the other, and it must constantly be aware of the relationship of costs and benefits.

Understandability

Understandability of information is governed by a combination of user characteristics and characteristics inherent in the information. This characteristic serves as a link between decision makers and accounting information. To meet the *SFAC No. 1* criterion of usefulness, the decision maker must explicitly understand the information. Understandability can be classified as relating to particular decision makers (Does the decision maker speak that language?) or relating to classes of decision makers (Is the disclosure intelligible to the audience for which it is intended?).

Decision Usefulness

SFAC No. 1 indicated that financial information is intended to be useful to decision makers. *SFAC No. 1* also established that relevance and reliability are the two primary qualities that make accounting information useful for decision making. Subject to constraints imposed by cost and materiality (discussed below), increased relevance and increased reliability are the characteristics that make information a more desirable commodity—that is, one useful in making decisions. If either of those qualities is completely missing, the information will not be useful. Although ideally the choice of an accounting alternative should produce information that

---

52. The FASB's Exposure Draft, "Financial Statements and Other Means of Financial Reporting," expands on this conclusion. This release examines the issues of what information should be provided, who should provide it, and where it should be presented. In addition, it examines the question, should GAAP be the same for all companies regardless of size? The FASB has not issued a final statement that addresses this question.

is both more reliable and more relevant, it may be necessary to sacrifice some of one quality for a gain in another.

Relevance

Relevant accounting information can make a difference in a decision by helping users to form predictions about the outcomes of past, present, and future events or to confirm or correct prior expectations. Relevant information has predictive value, feedback value, and timeliness.

Predictive Value and Feedback Value

Information can make a difference to decisions by improving decision makers' capacities to predict or by confirming or correcting their earlier expectations. Usually, information does both at once because knowledge about the outcome of actions already taken will generally improve decision makers' abilities to predict the results of similar future actions.

Timeliness

Having information available to decision makers before it loses its capacity to influence decisions is an ancillary aspect of relevance. If information is not available when it is needed or if it becomes available so long after the reported events that it has no value for future action, it lacks relevance and is of little or no use. While timeliness alone cannot make information relevant, a lack of timeliness can rob information of relevance it might otherwise have had.

Reliability

The reliability of a measure rests on how faithfully it represents what it purports to represent, coupled with an assurance for the user that it has that representational quality. To be useful, information must be both reliable and relevant. Degrees of reliability must be recognized. It is rarely a question of black or white, but rather of more or less reliability. Reliability rests on the extent to which an accounting description or measurement is verifiable and representationally faithful. Neutrality of information also interacts with those two components of reliability to affect the usefulness of the information.

Verifiability and Representational Faithfulness

Verifiability may be demonstrated by securing a high degree of consensus among independent measurers using the same measurement methods. Representational faithfulness, on the other hand, refers to the correspondence or agreement between the accounting numbers and the resources or events those numbers purport to represent. A high degree of correspondence, however, does not guarantee that an accounting measurement will be relevant to the user' s needs if the resources or events represented by the measurement are inappropriate to the purpose at hand. Social scientists have defined this concept as *validity*.

Neutrality

In formulating or implementing standards, the primary concern should be the relevance and reliability of the information that results, not the effect that the new rule may have on a particular interest. A neutral choice between accounting alternatives is free from bias toward a predetermined result. The objectives of financial reporting serve many different information users, who have diverse interests; thus, no single, predetermined result is likely to suit all interests.

Comparability and Consistency

The usefulness of information about a particular enterprise increases greatly if it can be compared with similar information about other enterprises and with similar information about the same enterprise for some other period or point in time. Comparability between enterprises and consistency in the application of methods over time increase the informational value of comparisons of relative economic opportunities or performance. The significance of information, especially quantitative information, depends to a great extent on the user's ability to relate it to some benchmark.

Materiality Constraint

Materiality is a pervasive concept that relates to the CFP qualitative characteristics, especially relevance and reliability. Both materiality and relevance are defined in terms of what influences or makes a difference to a decision maker, but the two terms can be distinguished. A decision not to disclose certain information may be made, say, because investors have no need for that kind of information (it is not relevant) or because the amounts involved are too small to make a difference (they are not material). Magnitude by itself, without regard to the nature of the item and the circumstances in which the judgment has to be made, will not generally be a sufficient basis for a materiality judgment. The FASB's present position is that no general standards of materiality can be formulated to take into account all the considerations that enter into an experienced human judgment. Quantitative materiality criteria may be given by the Board in specific standards in the future—as in the past, as appropriate.

SFAC No. 2 is generally regarded as the most well-liked of the concepts statements. Miller et al., in a critique of the FASB, wrote "[*SFAC No. 2*] provides a set of definitions that the Board and its constituents can and do use to communicate with each other. The definitions bring more rigor to the due process and possibly to the thought processes of the participants."[53] Nevertheless, a study of the views of twenty-six former members of the ABP and FASB concluded that the respondents felt that most of the qualitative characteristics could not be operationalized and that there was considerable disagreement on their relative importance. As a result, the authors concluded that the statement failed to meet its objectives, which casts doubt on the ability of the qualitative characteristics to facilitate accounting policy making.[54]

Statement of Financial Accounting Concepts No. 5: "Recognition and Measurement in Financial Statements of Business Enterprises"

In *SFAC No. 5*, the FASB attempted to broaden the scope of the measurements of the operating results of business enterprises by introducing the definition of *comprehensive income* as follows:

> Comprehensive income is the change in equity (net assets) of an entity during a period from transactions and events and circumstances from

---

53. Paul B. W. Miller, Rodney J. Redding, and Paul R. Bahnson, *The FASB: The People, the Process, and the Politics* (Burr Ridge, IL: Irwin/McGraw-Hill, 1998), 110.

54. Edward J. Joyce, Robert Libby, and Shyam Sunder, "Using the FASB's Qualitative Characteristics in Accounting Policy Choices," *Journal of Accounting Research* 20, no. 2, Pt. II (1982): 654–75.

non-owner sources. It includes all changes in equity during a period except those resulting from investments by owners and distributions to owners.[55]

This approach represents the FASB's attempt to tie together the capital maintenance approach and the traditional accounting transactions approach to income measurement. Under the capital maintenance approach, *net income* is defined as the maximum amount of a firm's resources that can be distributed to owners during a given period (exclusive of new owner investments) and still leave the business enterprise as well off at the end of that period as it was in the beginning. However, the FASB attempted to allay fears that the concept of comprehensive income was a radical shift toward using current value measurements by stating that the measurement of most assets and liabilities would not differ under the concept of comprehensive income. Yet other FASB pronouncements, such as *SFAS No. 115* (see FASB ASC 320), which requires the use of market values to measure investments in common stock, *SFAS No. 144* (see FASB ASC 360), requiring the use of present value measurements, and SFAS No. 157 outlining the measurement of fair value (see FASB ASC 820) provide evidence that the FASB is making a shift toward current-value accounting.

SFAC No. 5 did not suggest major changes in the current structure and content of financial statements. However, it did propose that a statement of cash flows should replace the statement of changes in financial position that was required when *SFAC No. 5* was released and it provided the impetus for requiring the statement of cash flows (discussed in Chapter 7). *SFAC No. 5* attempted to set forth recognition criteria and guidance on what information should be incorporated into financial statements and when this information should be reported. According to *SFAC No. 5*, a full set of financial statements for a period should show

1. Financial position at the end of the period
2. Earnings for the period
3. Comprehensive income for the period
4. Cash flows during the period
5. Investments by and distributions to owners during the period

The statement of financial position should provide information about an entity's assets, liabilities, and equity and their relationship to one another at a moment in time. It should also delineate the entity's resource structure—major classes and amounts of assets—and its financing structure—major classes and amounts of liabilities and equity. The statement of financial position is not intended to show the value of a business, but it should provide information to users wishing to make their own estimates of the enterprise's value.

Earnings are a measure of entity performance during a period. This value measures the extent to which asset inflows (revenues and gains) exceed asset outflows. The concept of earnings provided in *SFAC No. 5* is similar to net income for a period determined under the transactions approach. It is expected that the

---

55. *Statement of Financial Accounting Concepts No. 5*, "Recognition and Measurement in Financial Statements of Business Enterprises" (Stamford, CT: FASB, 1984), para. 39.

concept of earnings will continue to be subject to the process of gradual change that has characterized its development.

SFAC No. 5 defined comprehensive income as a broad measure of the effects of transactions and other events on an entity. It comprises all recognized changes in equity of the entity during a period from transactions except those resulting from investments by owners and distributions to owners. Under the *SFAC No. 5* definition, the relationship between earnings and comprehensive income is illustrated as follows.

Revenues	Earnings
Less: Expenses	Plus or minus cumulative accounting adjustments
Plus: Gains	Plus or minus other nonowner changes in equity
Less: Losses	
= Earnings	= Comprehensive income

The statement of cash flows should directly or indirectly reflect an entity's cash receipts, classified by major source; and its cash payments, classified by major uses during a period. The statement should include cash-flow information about its operating, financing, and investing activities.

A statement of investments by and distributions to owners reflects an entity's capital transactions during a period. That is, it reflects the extent to which and in what ways the equity of the entity increased or decreased from transactions with owners. In addition to the issue of comprehensive income, *SFAC No. 5* addresses certain measurement issues that are closely related to recognition. Accordingly, an item and information about it should meet four recognition criteria and should be recognized at the time these criteria are met (subject to the cost-benefit and materiality constraints).

1. *Definitions.* The item meets the definition of an element contained in *SFAC No. 6.*

2. *Measurability.* It has a relevant attribute, measurable with sufficient reliability.

3. *Relevance.* The information about the item is capable of making a difference in user decisions.

4. *Reliability.* The information is representationally faithful, verifiable, and neutral.

These recognition criteria are consistent with and in fact drawn from *SFAC Nos. 1, 2,* and *6. SFAC No. 5* provides guidance in applying the recognition criteria in those cases when enterprise earnings are affected by the recognition decision. This guidance is consistent with the doctrine of conservatism. In other words, recognition of revenues and gains is based on the additional tests of their (1) being realized or realizable and (2) being earned before recognized as income. Guidance for recognizing expenses and losses is dependent on either consumption of benefit or loss of future benefit.

One of the major gaps in *SFAC No. 5* is its failure to define the term *earnings.*[56] Moreover, it does not resolve the debate over current value versus historical cost. This failure was apparently due to the Board's position of accepting *decision useful-ness* as the overriding objective of financial reporting.

56. Ibid.

This document is disappointing to those who had hoped it would provide a formula or set of formulas from which solutions to specific accounting problems could be derived. In other words, some accountants and financial statement users would prefer a document that answers questions about when, if at all, a specific event should be recognized and what amount best measures that event.

Although *SFAC No. 5* did not suggest any radical changes in the structure and content of financial statements, it did provide the impetus for the change to a statement of cash flows from the statement of changes in financial position that was previously required. In addition, the scope of the measurement of the operating results of business enterprises was broadened by the definition of comprehensive income. Additionally, although the text of *SFAS No. 5* was limited to a discussion of recognition and measurement, the statement also provided a framework for the building blocks to disclosure outside the actual financial statements. This framework will be discussed in Chapter 17.

The future development of accounting theory will use the concepts defined in *SFAC No. 5* as operational guidelines. They should serve as broad boundaries in the development of responses to controversial accounting issues.

If *SFAC No. 2* was the most well-liked of the concepts statements, *SFAC No. 5* was the most vilified. The major criticisms were that the FASB had failed to select a single measurement attribute and that *SFAC No. 5* did little more than describe current practice.[57] *SFAC No. 5* defended this approach by maintaining that the recognition criteria contained in the statement were consistent with current practice and that change should be should be gradual and evolutionary. However David Solomons, a member of the Wheat Commission, called this approach a "cop-out" and opined that a listing of alternative practices might be appropriate for a discussion memorandum but not for a concepts statement.[58]

Statement of Financial Accounting Concepts No. 6: "Elements of Financial Statements of Business Enterprises"

SFAC No. 6 (discussed in more detail in Chapters 5 and 6) defines the ten elements of financial statements that are used to measure the performance and financial position of economic entities. These ten elements—assets, liabilities, equity, investments by owners, distributions to owners, comprehensive income, revenues, expense, gains, and losses—represent the building blocks used to construct financial statements. The definitions of the elements can be used to determine the content of financial statements.

Statement of Financial Accounting Concepts No. 7: "Using Cash Flow Information and Present Value in Accounting Measurements"

SFAC No. 7 provides a framework for using future cash flows as the basis for accounting measurements at the time of the initial recognition of assets or fresh-start

57. Reed K. Storey and Sylvia Storey, *The Framework of Financial Accounting Concepts and Standards* (Norwalk, CT: FASB, 1998), 159.

58. David Solomons, "The FASB's Conceptual Framework: An Evaluation," *Journal of Accountancy* 161, no. 6 (1986): 122.

measurements, and for the interest method of amortization. Additionally, it provides general principles that govern the use of present value, especially when the amount of future cash flows, their timing, or both are uncertain and there is a common understanding of the objective of present value in accounting measurements. *SFAC No. 7* does not deal with recognition issues or specify when fresh-start measurements are appropriate. The events and circumstances that prompt a fresh-start measurement were seen as varying from one situation to the next. The FASB expects to decide whether a particular situation requires fresh-start measurement on a project-by-project basis.

Accounting measurement is a very broad topic. Consequently, the FASB focused on a series of questions relevant to measurement and amortization conventions that employ present-value techniques. Among these questions are the following:

1. What are the objectives of using present value in the initial recognition of assets and liabilities? And do these objectives differ in subsequent fresh-start measurements of assets and liabilities?

2. Does the measurement of liabilities at present value differ from the measurement of assets?

3. How should the estimates of cash flows and interest rates be developed?

4. What are the objectives of present value when used in conjunction with the amortization of assets and liabilities?

5. How should present-value amortizations be used when the estimates of cash flows change?

The FASB indicated that the purpose of present-value measurements is to capture the economic difference between sets of future cash flows. For example, each of the following assets with a future cash flow of $25,000 has an economic difference:

a. An asset with a certain, fixed contractual cash flow due in one day of $25,000.

b. An asset with a certain, fixed contractual cash flow due in ten years of $25,000.

c. An asset with a certain, fixed contractual cash flow due in one day of $25,000. The actual amount to be received may be less but not more than $25,000.

d. An asset with a certain, fixed contractual cash flow due in 10 years of $25,000. The actual amount to be received may be less but not more than $25,000.

e. An asset with expected cash flow of $25,000 in 10 years with a range of $20,000 to $30,000.

These assets are distinguished from one another by the timing and uncertainty of their future cash flows. Measurements based on undiscounted cash flows would have the result of recording each at the same amount. Since they are economically different, their expected present values are different. A present-value measurement that fully captures the economic differences between the five assets should include the following elements:

a. An estimate of future cash flows

b. Expectations about variations in the timing of those cash flows

c. The time value of money represented by the risk-free rate of interest

d. The price for bearing the uncertainty

e. Other, sometimes unidentifiable, factors including illiquidity and market imperfections

Two approaches to present value were discussed in *SFAC No. 7:*

- *Traditional.* A single cash flow and a single interest rate as in a 12 percent bond due in 10 years. Cases (a) and (b) above are examples of the use of the traditional approach.

- *Expected cash flow.* A range of possible cash flows with a range of likelihoods. Cases (c), (d), and (e) above are examples of the expected cash-flow approach.

To further illustrate the expected cash-flow approach, assume that a business is faced with a liability to be measured. No market information exists about prices for comparable obligations. The most likely payment amount is $2 million in 10 years. However, under the best-case scenario, the liability might be settled for $1 million in five years; and under the worst-case scenario, the company might be required to pay $50 million in 25 years. Assuming a 5 percent risk-free discount rate and a flat yield curve, the present-value computation with unknown probabilities is as follows:

	Years	Amount	PV
Best case	5	$ 1,000,000	$ 783,526
Most likely	10	2,000,000	1,227,826
Worst case	25	50,000,000	2,953,028
			$ 4,964,380
		Divided by 3	$ 1,654,794

However, the fact that the three cases are equally likely is counterintuitive. Assume instead that management has estimated that the most likely case is twice as likely as the best case and that the worst case is only a third as likely as the best case. These estimations result in probabilities of 30, 60, and 10 percent, respectively, for the best, most likely, and worst cases. Incorporating these probabilities into the analysis results in the following expected present value:

Years	PV	P	Extension
5	$ 783,526	.30	$ 235,058
10	1,227,826	.60	736,696
25	2,953,028	.10	295,303
	Expected present value		$ 1,267,057

It should be emphasized that the probability of the outcomes significantly affects the expected present value, and assigning different probabilities to the three possible outcomes will result in different expected present values. In the previous example, if we change the probabilities to 35 percent, 45 percent, and 20 percent, an expected present value of $1,060,567 will result.

The objective is to estimate the value of the assets required currently to settle the liability with the holder, or to transfer the liability to an entity with a comparable credit standing. To estimate the fair value of an entity's notes or bonds payable, it is necessary to estimate the price at which other entities are willing to acquire the entity's liabilities as assets. For example, the proceeds from a loan are the price that a lender paid to acquire the borrower's promise of future cash flows as an asset, or the value of a bond payable is the price at which that security trades in the marketplace. On the other hand, some liabilities are owed to individuals who do not usually sell their rights as they might sell other assets. For example, entities may sell products with an accompanying warranty. In estimating the fair value of such liabilities, it is necessary to estimate the price a company would have to pay a third party to assume the liability. (Notice that this will include a provision for a profit.)

The most relevant measure of a liability must incorporate the credit standing of the entity obligated to pay. When a liability is incurred in exchange for cash, the role of credit standing is easily determined. Thus, an entity with a strong credit standing will receive more cash than an entity with a weak credit standing. For example, if two entities both promise to pay $500 in five years, the entity with the strong credit standing may receive about $374 (assuming a 6 percent interest rate), whereas the entity with the weak credit standing may receive only about $284 (assuming a 12 percent interest rate). The effect of credit standing on the measurement of an entity's liabilities is usually captured in an adjustment to the interest rate, which is similar to the traditional approach of incorporating risk and uncertainty in the measurement of cash flows. This approach is well suited for liabilities with contractual cash flows, but an expected cash-flow approach may be more effective when measuring the effect of credit standing on other liabilities. For example, a liability may present the entity with a range of possible cash outflows ranging from very low to high amounts. There may be little chance of default if the amount is low, but a high chance if the amount is high. In such situations, the effect of credit standing may be more effectively incorporated in the computation of expected cash flows.

The FASB noted that the purpose of all accounting allocations is to report changes in the value, utility, or substance of assets and liabilities over time. Accounting allocations attempt to relate the change in the recorded value of an asset or liability to some observable real-world phenomenon. For example, straight-line depreciation relates that change to the estimated useful life of an asset. The interest method of allocation associates changes in the recorded amount with changes in the present value of a set of future cash inflows or outflows. Under current GAAP, the interest method of allocation is considered more relevant than other methods when it is applied to assets containing one or more of the following characteristics:

a. The transaction giving rise to the asset or liability involves borrowing or lending.

b. A particular set of estimated future cash flows is closely associated with the asset or liability.

c. The measurement at initial recognition was based on present value.

Changes from the original estimate of cash flows, in either timing or amount, can be accommodated in the interest amortization scheme or included in a fresh-start measurement of the asset or liability. If the amount or timing of estimated cash flows changes and the item is not remeasured, the interest amortization scheme must be altered to incorporate the new estimate of cash flows. The FASB noted that the following methods have been used to address changes in estimated cash flows:

- *Prospective*. Computes a new effective interest rate based on future cash flows.
- *Catch-up*. Adjusts carrying amount to the present value of the revised cash flows.
- *Retrospective*. Computes a new interest rate based on to-date cash flows and expected future cash flows.

The FASB stated a preference for the catch-up method when recording changes in estimated future cash flows because it is consistent with the present-value approach. If conditions change, a change in estimate is recorded and the new information is incorporated.

Principles-Based versus Rules-Based Accounting Standards

During the early 2000s, the FASB noted that concerns were being expressed about the quality and transparency of accounting information.[59] One of the main concerns was the increasing complexity of FASB standards and the development of rule-based accounting standards. Harvey Pitt, former chairman of the SEC in testimony before the SEC, highlighted this issue by stating: "The development of rule-based accounting standards has resulted in the employment of financial engineering techniques designed solely to achieve accounting objectives rather than to achieve economic objectives."[60] For example, *SFAS No. 13*, "Accounting for Leases," identifies four criteria that cannot be violated if a lease is to be recorded as an operating lease (see FASB ASC 840-10-25-1).[61] As a consequence, leasing companies and prospective lessees attempt to structure lease contracts so as not to violate these criteria.

The Sarbanes-Oxley Act of 2002 attempted to address this concern by requiring the SEC to examine the feasibility of a principles-based accounting system. In 2003 the SEC published its study on the adoption of a principles-based system. The study noted that imperfections can exist when standards are established on either a rules-based or a principles-only basis. That is, principles-only standards may present enforcement difficulties because they provide little guidance or structure for preparers and auditors to exercise professional judgment. Rules-based standards often provide a vehicle for circumventing the intention of the standard. However,

59. Barth and Schipper have defined financial reporting transparency as "the extent to which financial reports reveal an entity's underlying economics in a way that is readily understandable by those using the financial reports." Mary E. Barth and Katherine Schipper, "Financial Reporting Transparency," *Journal of Accounting, Auditing & Finance* 23, no. 2 (Spring 2008): 173–90.

60. Harvey L.Pitt, "Written Testimony Concerning Accounting and Investor Protection Issues Raised by Enron and OtherPublic Companies," Before the Committee on Banking, Housing andUrban Affairs United States Senate (March 21, 2002), http://www.sec.gov/news/testimony/032102tshlp.htm.

61. Discussed in Chapter 14.

the study recommended that those involved in the standard-setting process more consistently develop standards on a principles-based or objectives-oriented basis.[62]

To illustrate the difference between rules-based and principles-based standards, the standard-setting process can be viewed as a continuum ranging from highly rigid standards on one end to general definitions of economics-based concepts on the other end. For example, consider accounting for the intangible asset of goodwill. An example of the extremely rigid end of the continuum is the previously acceptable practice:

Goodwill is to be amortized over a period not to exceed 40 years.

This requirement leaves no room for judgment or disagreement about the amount of amortization expense to be recognized. Comparability and consistency across firms and through time is virtually assured under such a rule. However, the requirement lacks relevance because it does not reflect the underlying economics of the reporting entity, which differ across firms and through time.

At the opposite end of the continuum is the FASB ASC's 350-20-35-1 rule:

Goodwill shall not be amortized. Instead, goodwill shall be tested for impairment at a level of reporting referred to as a reporting unit.

This requirement necessitates the application of judgment and expertise by both managers and auditors. The goal is to record the economic deterioration of the asset, goodwill. To further illustrate the difference between a principles-based set of standards, the following table summarizes what are commonly identified as some of the benefits of each of these approaches.

Principles-Based Set of Standards	Rules-Based Set of Standards
• Better able to cope with speed of change of business environment	• More workable in large, complex economies and countries
• Less voluminous	• Less room for interpretation
• Encourages use of professional judgment with a focus on what is right	• Provides more guidance for practical implementation
• Seen as possibly discouraging financial engineering	• Less need for explanation in financial statements

The FASB issued an invitation to comment on this issue and posed the following questions:[63]

1. Do you support the Board's proposal for a principles-based approach to U.S. standard setting? Will that approach improve the quality and transparency of U.S. financial accounting and reporting?

---

62. SEC, Study Pursuant to Section 108(d) of the Sarbanes-Oxley Act of 2002 on the Adoption by the United States Financial Reporting System of a Principles-Based Accounting System. Submitted to Committee on Banking, Housing, and Urban Affairs of the United States Senate and Committee on Financial Services of the United States House of Representatives. July 25, 2003.

63. Ibid., 10–11.

2. Should the Board develop an overall reporting framework as in *IAS No. 1* and, if so, should that framework include a true and fair override?

3. Under what circumstances should interpretive and implementation guidance be provided under a principles-based approach to U.S. standard setting? Should the Board be the primary standard setter responsible for providing that guidance?

4. Will preparers, auditors, the SEC, investors, creditors, and other users of financial information be able to adjust to a principles-based approach to U.S. standard setting? If not, what needs to be done and by whom?

5. What are the benefits and costs (including transition costs) of adopting a principles-based approach to U.S. standard setting? How might those benefits and costs be quantified?

6. What other factors should the Board consider in assessing the extent to which it should adopt a principles-based approach to U.S. standard setting?

An American Accounting Association Committee was appointed to address this invitation to comment. It responded as follows:

> We believe that the economic substance, not the form, of any given transaction should guide financial reporting and standard setting, and that concepts-based standards represent the best approach for achieving this objective.[64]

The committee listed the characteristics that concepts-based standards should possess. These characteristics were described as follows:

1. In a concepts-based standard, the economic substance, not the form, of a given transaction should guide its *financial* reporting. The FASB's Conceptual Framework defines the classification and measurement of economic transactions and, accordingly, should serve as the foundation for financial reporting that reflects the economic substance of a transaction.

2. A concepts-based standard should include a description of the particular transaction that is the subject of the standard. This description should include the underlying economics of the transaction in order to provide a common, explicit understanding of these economics.

3. A concepts-based standard should include a general discussion of the mapping between the economics of a transaction and the *financial* statements, using the Conceptual Framework to guide classification and measurement issues associated with this mapping.

4. A concepts-based standard may include implementation guidance, most likely in the form of examples that illustrate application of the standard's general principles to typical transactions covered by the standard. In these implementation examples, it may be necessary to make choices that are based on practicality rather than explicitly on the concepts. We believe this is acceptable, but should be noted as such in the discussion of the example.

---

64. Laureen A. Maines, Eli Bartov, Patricia Fairfield, D. Eric Hirst, Teresa E. Iannaconi, Russell Mallett et al., "Evaluating Concepts-Based vs. Rules-Based Approaches to Standard Setting," *Accounting Horizons* 17, no. 1 (March 2003): 73.

5. In a concepts-based standard, the Board should be careful when creating "names" for concepts, even if they enhance the readability of the standard. The names may already have connotations for readers that differ from the concept that the Board has in mind. If it is unavoidable to use such names, the Board should articulate their definitions.

6. Concepts-based standards should include disclosure requirements related to a description of the economics of the transaction being reported, the assumptions made in the reporting, and any supporting information that will facilitate understanding both the economics and the reporting.[65]

Despite the strength of these arguments, not all accountants agree that the FASB's standards are extremely rule based. For example, Katherine Schipper, an accounting professor and member of the FASB at that time, stated:

> U.S. financial reporting standards are in general based on principles, derived from the FASB's Conceptual Framework, but they also contain elements—such as scope and treatment exceptions and detailed implementation guidance—that make them also appear to be rules-based.[66]

In 2003, the SEC staff submitted a study to Congress addressing this issue that included the following recommendations to the FASB:

1. The FASB should issue objectives-oriented standards.

2. The FASB should address deficiencies in the conceptual framework.

3. The FASB should be the only organization setting authoritative accounting guidance in the United States.

4. The FASB should continue its convergence efforts.

5. The FASB should work to redefine the GAAP hierarchy.

6. The FASB should increase access to authoritative literature.

7. The FASB should perform a comprehensive review of its literature to identify standards that are more rules based and adopt a transition plan to change those standards.[67]

In July 2004, the FASB responded to the study's recommendations and noted that a number of its recommendations were already being implemented. The Board said it had discussed the comments it received on its invitation to comment and decided to pursue a number of initiatives aimed at improving the quality of FASB standards as well as the standard-setting process.[68] The FASB's specific responses to the recommendations are summarized in the following paragraphs.

65. Ibid., 79–80.

66. Katherine Schipper, "Principles-Based Accounting Standards," *Accounting Horizons* (March 2003): 72.

67. Study Pursuant to Section 108(d) of the Sarbanes Oxley Act of 2002 on the Adoption by the United States Financial Reporting System of a Principles-Based Accounting System (Washington, DC: SEC, July 2003).

68. FASB Response to SEC Study on the Adoption of a Principles-Based Accounting System (Norwalk, CT: FASB, July 2004).

Issuing Objectives-Oriented Standards

The FASB observed that the objectives-oriented approach outlined in the SEC study was similar to the one described in the Board's invitation to comment. After reviewing the comments received on its proposal, the Board concluded that its conceptual framework needed to be improved. The Board also agreed with the SEC that the objectives of its standards need to be more clearly defined, implementation guidance needs to be improved, scope exceptions need to be reduced, and the asset-liability approach to standard setting should be retained.

Conceptual Framework

The FASB noted that it had several projects on its agenda that address how the trade-offs among relevance, reliability, and comparability should be made. It also is addressing the inconsistencies between the earnings process found in *SFAC No. 5* and the definitions of the elements of the financial statements found in *SFAC No. 6*.

The Board also indicated that it was embarking on a joint project with the IASB (discussed below) to develop an internally consistent conceptual framework that would be used by both boards. This project will specifically address what are termed "crosscutting issues"—troublesome, unresolved issues that continue to reappear in different projects, such as the definition of the term *probable*.

One U.S. Standard Setter

The FASB has acted to become the only designated standard setter in the United States by reaching an agreement with the AICPA to allow it to have direct control over the standard-setting process. It also acted to require all EITF decisions to be ratified by the FASB before they become effective.

GAAP Hierarchy

The SEC study criticized the GAAP hierarchy's placement of industry practices above the conceptual framework. At the time, the FASB was working on a project that proposed to reduce the number of levels in the GAAP hierarchy and move it into the FASB literature.

Access to Authoritative Literature

The SEC study also observed that a source of frustration of accounting professionals was the lack of a single, searchable database of all authoritative guidance. The FASB agreed with the overall objective of creating such a database, but noted that its development would require the resolution of numerous conceptual, financial, and logistical issues that could take several years to resolve. This process has been completed and resulted in the FASB ASC.

Comprehensive Review of Literature

The Board disagreed with this recommendation because of resource limitations and stated: "the areas needing more attention are those areas that either have no guidance or have guidance that is not functional, not those areas that have existing rules-based standards that are functional."[69]

The comment period for the proposal ended in January 2003; however, no action has since been taken. These issues will be incorporated into the FASB-IASB convergence project discussed below.

International Convergence

At a joint meeting in Norwalk, Connecticut, on September 18, 2002, the FASB and the IASB both acknowledged their commitment to the development of high-quality, compatible accounting standards that could be used for both domestic and cross-border financial reporting (the Norwalk Agreement). The two boards pledged to use their best efforts to (1) make their existing financial reporting standards fully compatible as soon as is practicable; and (2) coordinate their future work programs to ensure that once achieved, compatibility is maintained. The international convergence project has three major aspects: (1) the Financial Statement Presentation Project, (2) the Conceptual Framework Project, and (3) the Standards Update Project.

The FASB IASB Financial Statement Presentation Project

The purpose of the financial statement presentation project is to establish a standard that will guide the organization and presentation of information in the financial statements. The boards' goal is to improve the usefulness of the information provided in an entity's financial statements to help users make decisions in their capacity as capital providers Accordingly, as a part of the Norwalk Agreement, the FASB and IASB committed to (1) undertake a short-term project aimed at removing a variety of individual differences between U.S. GAAP and International Financial Reporting Standards (IFRSs, discussed in Chapter 3); (2) remove other differences between IFRSs and U.S. GAAP that remained at January 1, 2005, through coordination of their future work programs; that is, through the mutual undertaking of discrete, substantial projects that both boards would address concurrently; (3) continue progress on the joint projects that they are currently undertaking; and (4) encourage their respective interpretative bodies to coordinate their activities.

Later in April 2004, the FASB and IASB decided to combine their respective projects on the reporting and classification of items of revenue, expense, gains, and losses. This project was undertaken to establish a common, high-quality standard for the presentation of information in financial statements, including the classification and display of line items and the aggregation of line items into subtotals and totals. The goal is to present information in individual financial statements (and among financial statements) in ways that improve the ability of investors, creditors, and other financial statement users to

1. Understand an entity's present and past financial position
2. Understand the past operating, financing, and other activities that caused an entity's financial position to change and the components of those changes

69. Ibid., 14.

3. Use that financial statement information, along with information from other sources, to assess the amounts, timing, and uncertainty of an entity's future cash flows

The project is being conducted in three phases. Phase A addresses what constitutes a complete set of financial statements and requirements to present comparative information.

Phase B addresses the more fundamental issues for presentation of information on the face of the financial statements, including

1. Developing principles for aggregating and disaggregating information in each financial statement
2. Defining the totals and subtotals to be reported in each financial statement (which might include categories such as business and financing)
3. Deciding whether components of other comprehensive income/other recognized income and expense should be recycled to profit or loss and, if so, the characteristics of the transactions and events that should be recycled and when recycling should occur
4. Reconsidering *SFAS No. 95*, "Statement of Cash Flows," and IAS 7, *Cash Flow Statements*, including whether to require the use of the direct or indirect method

Some preliminary decisions regarding the presentation of the financial statements have been published by the FASB. These decisions are discussed and illustrated in Chapters 6 and 7.

Phase C addresses the presentation and display of interim financial information in U.S. GAAP, including

1. Which financial statements, if any, should be required to be presented in an interim financial report
2. Whether financial statements required in an interim financial report should be allowed to be presented in a condensed format, and if so, whether guidance should be provided related to how the information may be condensed
3. What comparative periods, if any, should be required to be allowed in interim financial reports and when, if ever, should 12 month-to-date financial statements be required or allowed to be presented in interim financial reports
4. Whether guidance for nonpublic companies should differ from guidance for public companies

The boards completed their deliberations on Phase A in December 2005. On March 16, 2006, the IASB published its Phase A exposure draft, "Proposed Amendments to IAS 1 Presentation of Financial Statements: A Revised Presentation." The FASB decided to consider phases A and B issues together and, therefore, did not publish an exposure draft on phase A. After considering the responses to its exposure draft, the IASB issued a revised version of *IAS No. 1* in September 2007 (see Chapter 3 for a discussion of *IAS No. 1*). The revisions to *IAS No. 1* affected the presentation of changes in equity and the presentation of comprehensive income, bringing *IAS No. 1* largely into line with *FASB Statement No. 130, Reporting Comprehensive Income* (FASB ASC 220).

Previously, in February 2006, the two boards reaffirmed their commitment to the process of convergence in a Memorandum of Understanding (MOU) and voiced the shared objective of developing high-quality, common accounting standards for use in the world's capital markets. The MOU outlines a "road map" for the elimination of the reconciliation requirement for non-U.S. companies that use IFRSs and are registered in the United States (discussed in Chapter 3). The MOU maintains that trying to eliminate differences between standards is not the best use of resources; rather, new common standards should be developed. Convergence will proceed as follows: First, the boards will reach a conclusion about whether major differences in focused areas should be eliminated through one or more short-term standard-setting projects, and, if so, the goal was to complete or substantially complete work in those areas by 2008. Second, the FASB and the IASB will seek to make continued progress in other areas identified by both boards where accounting practices under U.S. GAAP and IFRSs are regarded as candidates for improvement. Later, in November 2009 the IASB and the FASB published a progress report describing their plans for completing the major projects on the MOU. This plan included milestone targets for each project. In order to provide transparency and accountability regarding those milestones, the two boards committed to reporting quarterly on the progress on convergence projects and to making those reports available on their respective websites. Additionally, they committed to hosting monthly joint board meetings and to provide quarterly updates on their progress on convergence projects. These milestones are discussed within their topic areas throughout the text.

In an effort to comply with the goals of the Norwalk Agreement, the FASB issued four new statements to bring U.S. GAAP into consistency with IFRSs (*SFAS No.151* (Superseded), SFAS No. 153 (Superseded), *SFAS No. 154* (FASB ASC 250-10), and *SFAS No. 163* (FASB ASC 944). Additionally, it issued a revised *SFAS No. 141* (FASB ASC 805). The IASB published new standards on borrowing costs (*IAS No. 23* revised) and segment reporting (*IFRS No. 8*). Each of these new or revised statements is discussed under the relevant topics later in the text.

Phase B is being conducted with the following principles in mind:

Financial statements should present information in a manner that

1. Portrays a cohesive financial picture of an entity
2. Separates an entity's financing activities from its business and other activities
3. Helps a user access the liquidity of an entity's assets and liabilities
4. Disaggregates line items if that disaggregation enhances the usefulness of that information in predicting future cash flows
5. Helps a user understand

   - how assets and liabilities are measured.
   - the uncertainty and subjectivity in measurements of individual assets and liabilities.
   - what causes a change in reported amounts of individual assets and liabilities.

The project has adopted cohesiveness as a standard for assessing its ability to attain these principles. That is, each financial statement should contain the same sections and categories, and the classification of assets and liabilities will drive the classification of the related changes in the statement of cash flows and comprehensive income statements. This process is expected to obtain more clarity in the relationships between statements and to facilitate financial analysis.

The Statements of Comprehensive Income, Financial Position, and Cash Flows will each contain a Business Section that reports operating activities and investing activities of the specific statement. For example, in the Statement of Comprehensive Income, the Business Section will contain operating income and expenses as well as investing income and expenses; in the Statement of Financial Position, the Business Section will report operating assets and liabilities and investing assets and liabilities. In addition to the Business Section, in three of the four statements (excluding the Changes in Equity Statement), a Financing Section is provided as well as a section on taxes and discontinued operations (net of taxes). Each financial statement will contain the following two primary sections: (1) *business*, and (2) *financing*. The following guidelines were adopted for displaying the items in each section:

1. The **business section** *should* have two defined categories: operating and investing. These categories require an entity to make a distinction between business activities that are part of an entity's day-to-day business activities (and the business activity generates revenue through a process that requires the interrelated use of the net resources of the entity) [operating category] and business activities that generate non-revenue income (and no significant synergies are created from combining assets) [investing category].

2. The **financing section** will include items that are part of an entity's activities to obtain (or repay) capital and consist of two categories: debt and equity (a change from their decisions in September).

   a. The debt category will include liabilities where the nature of those liabilities is a borrowing arrangement entered into for the purpose of raising (or repaying) capital.

   b. The equity category will include equity as defined in either IFRS or U.S. GAAP.

Illustrations of draft financial statements incorporating these guidelines are presented in Chapters 6 and 7.

Conceptual Framework Project

In October 2004, the FASB and IASB decided to add to their agendas a joint project to develop an improved and common conceptual framework that is based on and builds on their existing frameworks; that is, the IASB's *Framework for the Preparation and Presentation of Financial Statements* (discussed in Chapter 3) and the FASB's Conceptual Framework Project (CFP). The goal of this project is to create a sound foundation for future accounting standards that are principles based, internally consistent, and internationally converged. The boards also intend to improve some parts of the existing frameworks, such as recognition and measurement, as well as to fill some gaps in the frameworks. For example, neither framework includes a robust concept of a reporting entity.

The project:

1. Focuses on changes in the environment since the original frameworks were issued, as well as omissions in the original frameworks, in order to efficiently and effectively improve, complete, and converge the existing frameworks.

2. Gives priority to addressing and deliberating those issues within each phase that are likely to yield benefits to the boards in the short term; that is, crosscutting issues that affect a number of their projects for new or revised standards. Thus work on several phases of the project will be conducted simultaneously, and the boards expect to benefit from work being conducted on other projects.

3. Initially considers concepts applicable to private sector business entities. Later, the boards will jointly consider the applicability of those concepts to private sector not-for-profit organizations. Representatives of public sector (governmental) standard-setting boards are monitoring the project and, in some cases, are considering what the consequences of private sector deliberations might be for public sector entities.

The project is being developed in eight phases. Each of the first seven phases are expected to involve planning, research, and initial board deliberations on major aspects of the boards' frameworks and to result in an initial document that will seek comments on the boards' tentative decisions for that phase. This will be followed by a period of redeliberations—the boards' consideration of constituents' comments and redeliberations of the tentative decisions. While the boards may seek comments on each phase separately, they did not preclude seeking comments on several phases concurrently. An eighth phase will be used to address any remaining issues.

The eight phases of the CFP are as follows:

A. Objectives and qualitative characteristics
B. Definitions of elements, recognition and derecognition
C. Measurement
D. Reporting entity concept
E. Boundaries of financial reporting, and presentation and disclosure
F. Purpose and status of the framework
G. Application of the framework to not-for-profit entities
H. Remaining issues, if any

The objectives and summary of the decisions reached for each phase of the project at the time this text was published are outlined in the following paragraphs.

Objectives and Qualitative Characteristics Phase

The aim of the Objectives and Qualitative Characteristics phase of Financial Reporting is to consider the following issues:

- The objective of financial reporting
- The qualitative characteristics of financial reporting information

- The trade-offs among qualitative characteristics and how they relate to the concepts of materiality and cost-benefit relationships

In July 2006, the first publication from the CFP was released. This document, which addressed Phase A of the CFP, was titled "Preliminary Views Conceptual Framework for Financial Reporting: Objective of Financial Reporting and Qualitative Characteristics of Decision-Useful Financial Reporting Information" (PV) and is quite similar to *SFAC Nos. 1* and *2*.

Finally, in May 2008, the FASB and IASB jointly published an exposure draft (ED) of Chapters 1 and 2 of the CFP. This document updated PV to reflect the comments received on the initial document and stated:

> The Conceptual Framework for Financial Reporting establishes the concepts that underlie financial reporting. The framework is a coherent system of concepts that flow from an objective. The objective of financial reporting is the foundation of the framework. The other concepts provide guidance on identifying the boundaries of financial reporting; selecting the transactions, other events, and circumstances to be represented; how they should be recognized, measured, and disclosed; and how they should be summarized and communicated in financial reports.[70]

The ED indicated that the objective of general-purpose financial reporting is to provide financial information about the reporting entity that is useful to present and potential equity investors, lenders, and other creditors in making decisions in their capacity as capital providers. Capital providers were defined as the primary users of financial reporting. The ED also indicated that in order to accomplish the defined objective, financial reports should communicate information about an entity's economic resources, claims to those resources, and the transactions and other events and circumstances that change them.

The ED noted that the degree to which that financial information is useful will depend on its qualitative characteristics. Qualitative characteristics were defined as the attributes that make financial reporting information useful. Additionally, the qualitative characteristics were defined as complementary concepts that each contribute to the usefulness of financial reporting information.

The exposure draft maintains that two fundamental qualitative characteristics, *relevance* and *faithful representation*, distinguish useful financial reporting information from information that is not useful or is misleading. Relevant information was seen as capable of making a difference in decision making by virtue of its predictive or confirmatory value. Financial reporting information is viewed as faithfully representative if it depicts the substance of an economic phenomenon completely, neutrally, and without material error.

The ED suggests that financial reporting information may have varying degrees of usefulness to different capital providers and that certain enhancing qualitative characteristics (EQCs) distinguish more useful information from less useful information. These EQCs augment the decision usefulness of financial reporting information that is relevant and faithfully represented. The EQCs were

---

70. "Conceptual Framework for Financial Reporting: The Objective of Financial Reporting and Qualitative Characteristics and Constraints of Decision-Useful Financial Reporting Information" (Norwalk, CT: FASB, 2008).

defined as *comparability, verifiability, timeliness,* and *understandability*. The ED maintains that these enhancing qualitative characteristics should be maximized to the extent possible. Nevertheless, the boards maintained that the EQCs, either individually or in concert with each other, cannot make information useful for decisions if that information is irrelevant or not faithfully represented. The enhancing qualitative characteristics were defined as follows:

1. *Comparable information* enables users to identify similarities in and differences between two sets of economic phenomena.

2. *Verifiable information* lends credibility to the assertion that financial reporting information represents the economic phenomena that it purports to represent.

3. *Timeliness* provides information to decision makers when it has the capacity to influence decisions.

4. *Understandability* is the quality of information that enables users to comprehend its meaning.

Finally, the ED maintains that providing useful financial reporting information is limited by two pervasive constraints, *materiality* and *cost*. Information was defined as material if its omission or misstatement could influence the decisions that users make on the basis of an entity's financial information. With respect to cost, the ED indicates that the benefits of providing financial reporting information should justify the costs of providing that information.

Definitions of Elements, Recognition and Derecognition Phase

The objectives of the Elements and Recognition phase are to refine and converge the boards' frameworks in the following manner:

1. *Revise and clarify the definitions of asset and liability.* The boards have agreed that the FASB and IASB definitions of these elements have several shortcomings and have tentatively agreed on the following working definitions:

   a. An *asset* of an entity is a present economic resource to which the entity has a right or other access that others do not have.

   b. A *liability* of an entity is a present economic obligation for which the entity is the obligor.

2. *Resolve differences regarding other elements and their definitions.* The FASB Concepts Statements presently identify more elements than does the IASB Framework, and the two frameworks define differently those elements that are common. The boards' approach will focus initially on converging and defining only those key elements that are defined today in the FASB and IASB Frameworks. Additionally, the boards will need to consider how to define elements that are not currently defined, such as comprehensive income.

3. *Revise the recognition criteria concepts to eliminate differences and provide a basis for resolving issues such as derecognition and unit of account.* Each board's current framework describes specific recognition criteria, some of which are similar and some of which are different. Neither board's frameworks contain criteria to determine when an item should be derecognized. The boards plan to revise their recognition criteria concepts to eliminate those differences and

provide a framework for resolving derecognition issues. The boards' current frameworks provide little or no guidance on how the unit of account should be determined. A discussion paper is expected to be issued in late 2010.

Measurement Phase

The objective of the Measurement phase is to provide guidance for selecting measurement bases that satisfy the objectives and qualitative characteristics of financial reporting. It consists of the following "milestones":

- *Milestone I* will inventory and defines a list of measurement basis candidates that might be used as a basis for measurement on financial statements;
- *Milestone II* will evaluate the basis candidates identified in Milestone I; and
- *Milestone III* will draw conceptual conclusions from Milestones I and II while addressing practical issues.

During its deliberations of Milestone I, the boards addressed the following five issues:

1. **What are the measurement basis candidates?** The boards agreed to a list of nine candidates: *past entry price, past exit price, modified past amount, current entry price, current exit price, current equilibrium price, value in use, future entry price,* and *future exit price.*

2. **How are the measurement bases defined?** The boards agreed to provide two definitions for each candidate—one from the perspective of an asset and one from the perspective of a liability. They further decided to focus on the concepts behind entry and exit prices, without respect to the way they are measured.

3. **What are the basic properties of the measurement bases?** The boards concluded that most candidates are either prices or values, and that each candidate provides information primarily about a specific time frame.

4. **Are the measurement issues appropriate for both assets and liabilities?** The boards concluded that all the candidates were appropriate for use with assets and liabilities.

5. **Should any measurement basis candidates be eliminated from consideration for evaluation in Milestone II?** The boards agreed not to eliminate any of the nine candidates identified at the end of Milestone I. However, they did eliminate some other candidates in the earlier stages of Milestone I deliberations.

A discussion paper is expected to be released in 2010.

Reporting Entity Concept Phase

The objective of the Reporting Entity phase is to determine what constitutes a reporting entity for the purposes of financial reporting. The FASB has authorized its staff to prepare an exposure draft. The IASB had not formally addressed this issue at the time this text was published, but a final draft is expected by the end of 2010.

On March 11, 2010, the boards issued an exposure draft titled *Conceptual Framework for Financial Reporting: The Reporting Entity* (ED). This document notes that the objective of general-purpose financial reporting is to provide financial information about reporting entities that is useful in making decisions about providing resources to the entity and in assessing whether the management and the corporate officers of that entity have made efficient and effective use of the resources provided. The ED defines a reporting entity as a circumscribed area of economic activities whose financial information has the potential to be useful to existing and potential equity investors, lenders, and other creditors who cannot directly obtain the information they need in making decisions about providing resources to the entity and in assessing whether management and the corporate officers of that entity have made efficient and effective use of the resources provided.

The ED noted that a reporting entity has three features:

1. Economic activities of an entity are being conducted, have been conducted, or will be conducted.

2. Those economic activities can be objectively distinguished from those of other entities and from the economic environment in which the entity exists.

3. Financial information about the economic activities of that entity has the potential to be useful in making decisions about providing resources to the entity and in assessing whether the management has made efficient and effective use of the resources provided.

As a result, identifying a reporting entity in a specific situation requires consideration of the boundary of the economic activities that are being conducted, have been conducted, or will be conducted. The existence of a legal entity is neither necessary nor sufficient to identify a reporting entity. A reporting entity can include more than one entity, or it can be a portion of a single entity.

The ED also notes a single legal entity that conducts economic activities and does not control any other entity is likely to qualify as a reporting entity and that most, if not all, legal entities have the potential to be reporting entities. However, a single legal entity may not qualify as a reporting entity if, for example, its economic activities are commingled with the economic activities of another entity and there is no basis for objectively distinguishing their activities. But a portion of an entity could qualify as a reporting entity if the economic activities of that portion can be distinguished objectively from the rest of the entity and financial information about that portion of the entity has the potential to be useful in making decisions about providing resources to that portion of the entity. For example, a potential equity investor could be considering a purchase of a branch or division of an entity. Comments on this exposure draft were to be received by July 11, 2010.

Boundaries of Financial Reporting, and Presentation and Disclosure Phase

An objective of the Presentation and Disclosure, including Financial Reporting Boundaries, phase is to determine the concepts underlying the display and disclosure of financial information and to identify the boundaries of such information that will achieve the objective of general-purpose financial reporting. This phase is currently inactive. The boards have not yet deliberated or made decisions regarding concepts for financial presentation and disclosure of financial information.

Purpose and Status of the Framework Phase

The objective of the Purpose and Status of the Framework phase is to consider the framework's authoritative status in the GAAP hierarchy. The goal is to develop a framework that is of comparable authority for the use of both boards in the standard-setting process.

At present, there are differences in the status of the boards' existing frameworks. For an entity preparing financial statements under International Financial Reporting Standards, the IASB's *Framework* provides guidance when there is no standard or interpretation that specifically applies to a transaction or other event or condition, or that deals with a similar and related issue. In those situations, the entity's management is required to consider the definitions, recognition criteria, and measurement concepts for assets, liabilities, income, and expenses in the *Framework*. Under U.S. GAAP, the FASB's Concepts Statements have a much lower status—they are ranked no higher than accounting textbooks, handbooks, and articles and are ranked below widely recognized and prevalent general or industry practices.

The FASB has decided that the authoritative status of the framework within the U.S. GAAP hierarchy should be considered once the framework is more substantially complete. However, for the purposes of providing comments on documents issued by the boards, respondents will be asked to assume that the framework's authoritative status will be elevated in the U.S. GAAP hierarchy to have a status comparable to the IASB's current *Framework*.

The FASB and the IASB agreed that each board, within the context of its current GAAP hierarchy, will finalize the common framework as parts are completed and that later parts may include consequential amendments to earlier parts. The boards noted that the decision of how to finalize the joint framework may need to be readdressed when the boards discuss the placement of the framework within the IASB and FASB hierarchies. This phase of the Conceptual Framework Project is currently inactive.

Application of the Framework to Not-for-Profit Entities Phase

The objective of this phase of the Conceptual Framework Project is to consider the applicability of the concepts developed in earlier phases to not-for-profit entities in the private sector. This phase is currently inactive. The boards have not yet deliberated or made decisions regarding the applicability of particular concepts to not-for-profit entities.

Remaining Issues, If Any Phase

The objective of the Remaining Issues phase is to consider remaining issues that have not been addressed by the previous seven phases. This phase is currently inactive. The boards will not deliberate or make decisions regarding final issues until the first seven phases are complete.

Standards Update Project

The FASB and IASB are also working on a number of individual standard issues, such as discontinued operation, financial instruments, fair value measurements, comprehensive income, consolidations, leases, revenue recognition, earnings per share, income taxes, and postretirement benefits. The overall objective of the standards update project is to make FASB and IASB standards more comparable. On June 2, the FASB and the IASB issued a joint statement[71] on their convergence work in response to expressed concerns about the ability to provide high-quality input on the large number of major Exposure Drafts planned for publication in the second quarter of this year.

The boards are in the process of developing a modified strategy to address these concerns that would:

1. Prioritize the major projects in the Memorandum of Understanding (MoU) to permit a sharper focus on issues and projects that will bring about significant improvement and convergence between US GAAP and IFRS.

2. Stagger the publication of Exposure Drafts and related outreach (such as public round-table meetings) to enable more effective participation in the due process that is critically important to the quality of accounting standards. Accordingly, the boards plan to limit the number of significant or complex Exposure Drafts issued in any one quarter.

3. Issue a separate document seeking feedback about effective dates and transition methods.

The modified strategy retains the target completion date of June 2011 for many of the projects where a converged solution is urgently required. The target completion dates for a few projects will extend into the second half of 2011.

Security and Exchange Commission (SEC) Chairman Schapiro responded with a statement[72] confirming that the delay announced by the FASB and IASB will not negatively impact the SEC's Work Plan. The SEC's Work Plan, will consider in 2011 whether and how to incorporate IFRS into the US financial system. The objectives and current status of each of these projects are discussed in the appropriate chapters throughout the text.

Cases

• Case 2-1 SFAC No. 2

The FASB has been working on a conceptual framework for financial accounting and reporting and has issued seven *Statements of Financial Accounting Concepts*. These *SFACs* are intended to set forth objectives and fundamentals that will be the basis for developing financial accounting and reporting standards. The objectives identify the goals and purposes of financial reporting. The fundamentals are the underlying concepts of financial accounting—concepts that guide the selection of transactions, events, and circumstances to be accounted for; their recognition and measurement; and the means of summarizing and communicating them to interested parties.

The purpose of *SFAC No. 2*, "Qualitative Characteristics of Accounting Information," is to examine the characteristics that make accounting information

---

71. http://www.fesb.org/cs/ContentServer?c=Document_C&pagename=FASB%2FDoc ument_C%2FDocumentPage&cid=1176156919319

72. Chairman Schapiro Statement on FASB-IASB Decision to Modify Timing of Certain Convergence Projects http://www.sec.gov/news/press/2010/2010-96.htm

useful. The characteristics or qualities of information discussed in *SFAC No. 2* are the ingredients that make information useful and the qualities to be sought when accounting choices are made.

Required:

a. Identify and discuss the benefits that can be expected to be derived from the FASB's conceptual framework study.

b. What is the most important quality for accounting information as identified in *SAFC No. 2*? Explain why it is the most important.

• Case 2-2 The Theoretical Foundation of Accounting Principles

During the past several years, the FASB has attempted to strengthen the theoretical foundation for the development of accounting principles. Two of the most important results of this attempt are the Conceptual Framework Project and the Emerging Issues Task Force. During this same period, the FASB has been criticized for imposing too many standards on the financial reporting process, the so-called standards overload problem.

Required:

a. Discuss the goals and objectives of
    i. the Conceptual Framework Project
    ii. the Emerging Issues Task Force

b. Discuss the standards overload problem.

• Case 2-3 Quantification

Sprouse and Moonitz proposed that quantification is an element of the economic environment that is relevant for accounting.

Required:

a. Explain why Sprouse and Moonitz say that quantification is relevant.

b. Discuss how the Sprouse and Moonitz discussion of quantification is similar to
    i. The definition of accounting found in *ASOBAT*
    ii. The decision-usefulness approach used by the FASB in *SFAC No. 1*

• Case 2-4 Continuity

Continuity is often cited as a basic accounting postulate that affects how a company presents information in published financial statements.

Required:

a. How did Sprouse and Moonitz describe continuity?

b. Given the presumption of continuity, if you are planning to buy a business, would the historical cost of the company's assets be relevant to your decision to invest? Explain. If your answer is no, what asset values would be relevant to your decision to invest?

c. If a company is bankrupt and plans to liquidate its assets, can continuity still be presumed? Explain. If your answer is no, how do you think the lack of continuity should affect the measurement of assets reported in a company's balance sheet?

• Case 2-5 Definition of Assets

Your company owns a building that is fully paid for. Explain how the building meets the definition of an asset under each of the following scenarios.

Required:

a. Your company is using the building as a plant that is producing automobiles.

b. Your company is not using the building, but plans to sell it. Explain how the building meets the definition of an asset.

c. Your company is not using the building, but plans to remodel it so that it can be used as a plant to produce automobiles.

• Case 2-6 Measurement and Reporting

Gabel Company spent money to train its employees so that they can be productive workers. Such expenditures are often referred to as investments in human capital.

Required:

a. Do you think that Gabel Company's trained employees meet the definition of an asset? Explain. In your answer, discuss the characteristics of an asset and whether you think they meet each of those characteristics.

b. Most accountants would say that human capital is valuable, but that it is difficult, or even impossible, to measure the value of human capital. Given that you cannot determine an amount to place a value on the Gabel Company's employees, but you think that they are assets, what would *SFAC No. 5* tell you to do? Should you report them as an asset in the company's balance sheet? Explain.

c. If a value can be estimated for Gabel Company's trained employees,

   i. Would that value be more relevant or more reliable to a prospective investor? Explain.

   ii. Would the company's assets reported in its balance sheet be more representationally faithful if they include the human capital than they would be without reporting an amount for the employees? Explain.

• Case 2-7 Relevance versus Reliability

Good Company purchased a used machine by issuing 1,000 shares of its common stock to the seller. Good's stock is traded on the NYSE. On the date of purchase, its price was quoted at $42 per share, making the value of the stock issued to purchase the machine equal to $42,000 (1,000 shares × $42). Good had the machine appraised. The appraiser estimates its value at $50,000.

According to *SFAC No. 2*, amounts reported in published financial statements should satisfy the qualitative characteristics of relevance and reliability. You are an investor trying to decide whether to invest in Good common stock. Which value—$42,000 or $50,000—is more relevant to your decision to invest? Which is more reliable? Explain your answers to both questions. In your answer, describe what *relevance* and *reliability* mean and how each valuation is thus more relevant or more reliable than the other.

• Case 2-8 SFAC No. 7

Company A and Company B each have a $10,000 bond outstanding.

Required:

a. If both companies' bonds are due in ten years, what factor(s) might make the bond market value the Company A bond at an amount greater than the Company B bond? If so, would Company A have a higher credit rating than Company B? If so, would the market rate of the Company A bond be higher than the market rate of the Company B bond? Explain your answers to this question, referring to the guidance found in *SFAC No. 7*.

b. If both companies have the same credit rating, what factor(s) might make the bond market value the Company A bond at an amount greater than the Company B bond? Explain.

FASB ASC Research

For each of the following research cases, search the FASB ASC database for information to address each questions. Cut and paste the FASB requirements that support your responses. Then summarize briefly what your responses are, citing the pronouncements and paragraphs used to support your responses.

• FASB ASC 2-1 Use of Present Value

SFAC No. 7 provides a framework for using future cash flows as the basis for an accounting measurement.

Required:
Find, cite and copy the FASB ASC guidance on using present value measurements.

• FASB ASC 2-2 Conceptual Framework

The conceptual framework is not a part of the FASB's ASC; however, it is mentioned under one topic. Find the conceptual framework citation, cite it, and copy the citation.

• FASB ASC 2-3 Decision-Maker Concept

The decision-maker concept is a component of several FASB ASC topics. Find, cite, and copy the relevant sections of those topics.

- ## FASB ASC 2-4 Understandability Concept

The "understandability" concept is a component of several FASB ASC topics. Find, cite, and copy the relevant sections of those topics.

- ## FASB ASC 2-5 Relevance Concept

The "relevance" and "reliability" concepts are components of two FASB ASC topics. Find, cite, and copy the appropriate sections of those topics.

- ## FASB ASC 2-6 Recognition and Measurement Guidance

The FASB ASC provides recognition and measurement guidance for several of its topics. Find three topics that provide such guidance and then cite and copy those topics.

- ## FASB ASC 2-7 Comprehensive Income

Find the definition and objective of reporting comprehensive income. Cite and copy the sources of the definition and objectives of comprehensive income.

- ## FASB ASC 2-8 Using Present Value

Using present-value measurements is discussed under many FASB ASC topics Find three FASB ASC topics that provide such guidance, cite, and copy those standards.

Room for Debate

- ## Debate 2-1 A Question of Materiality

Roper Corporation purchased 100 storage boxes for the office. The boxes cost $15 each and should last at least ten years. Each team's arguments should be grounded on the Conceptual Framework, emphasizing the Objectives of Financial Reporting and the qualitative characteristics of accounting information.

Team Debate:

Team 1:   Argue for the capitalization of the boxes.

Team 2:   Argue against the capitalization of the boxes.

- ## Debate 2-2 The Need for a Universally Accepted Theory of Accounting

Team Debate:

Team 1:   Argue that a universally accepted theory of accounting is needed.

Team 2:   Argue that a universally accepted theory of accounting is *not* needed.

International

Accounting

Financial accounting is influenced by the environment in which it operates. Nations have different histories, values, cultures, and political and economic systems, and they are also in various stages of economic development. These national influences interact with each other and, in turn, influence the development and application of financial accounting practices and reporting procedures. Multinational corporations operating in many countries may earn more than half of their revenues outside of the United States. Because of national differences, the financial accounting standards applied to the accounting data reported by these multinational companies often vary significantly from country to country. This has necessitated the demand for global financial reporting to improve multinational commerce.

Companies prepare financial reports that are directed toward their primary users. In the past, most users were residents of the same country as the corporation issuing the financial statements. However, the emergence of multinational corporations and organizations such as the European Union (EU), the General Agreement on Tariffs and Trade (GATT), and the North American Free Trade Agreement (NAFTA) has made transnational financial reporting more commonplace. Transnational financial reporting requires users to understand the accounting practices employed by the company, the language of the country in which the company resides, and the currency used by the corporation to prepare its financial statements. If investors and creditors cannot obtain understandable financial information about companies that operate in foreign countries, they are not likely to invest in or lend money to these companies. As a result, there is a move to harmonize accounting standards among countries.

The move toward the harmonization of international accounting standards rapidly accelerated during the first decade of the twenty-first century. In 2002, the FASB and the International Accounting Standards Board (IASB) announced their joint commitment to the development of accounting standards that could be used for both domestic and cross-border financial reporting. The two bodies also promised to strive to make their existing financial reporting standards compatible as soon as practicable and to coordinate their future work programs to maintain compatibility. In 2004, as discussed in Chapter 2, the FASB and IASB announced two other joint projects: the first is a project to develop an improved and common conceptual framework, and the second project was undertaken to establish a common, high-quality standard for the presentation of information in financial statements Later, in 2005, the chief accountant of the SEC described a "roadmap" for arriving at a common set of high-quality global standards and announced that the SEC was examining the possibility of the removal of the need for the reconciliation requirement for non-U.S. companies that use International Financial Reporting Standards (IFRSs) issued by the IASB and are registered to issue securities in the United States. Also in 2005, the European Union (EU) countries adopted IFRSs. In 2007, the SEC voted to accept financial statements from foreign private issuers prepared in accordance with IFRSs without reconciliation to generally accepted accounting principles, and the SEC is exploring the possibility of allowing U.S. companies to adopt IFRSs. Finally, the FASB and IASB are also working on a number of individual standard issues in order to make FASB and IASB standards more comparable. The two boards expect to have most of these projects completed by the end of 2011.

One of the major problems currently facing U.S. corporations is their ability to compete in a global economy with transnational financial reporting. The following sections discuss the preceding issues in more depth and present several issues that must be addressed by multinational corporations.

International Business Accounting Issues

A company's first exposure to international accounting frequently occurs because of a purchase or sale of an item of merchandise with a foreign entity. Dealing with foreign companies presents some unique problems. First, there is the possibility of foreign exchange gains and losses (discussed in more detail in Chapter 16) between the time an order is given or received and the time of payment. That is, changes in the relative values of currencies give rise to exchange gains and losses. Also, it is difficult to obtain international credit information, and evaluating the company's liquidity and solvency from its financial statements may be complicated by the use of a different language and/or different accounting principles.

As a company's foreign trade increases, it may be necessary to create an international division. It may also become necessary to develop international accounting expertise. Finally, the company may wish to raise capital in foreign markets. If so, the company may be required to prepare its financial statements in a manner that is acceptable to the appropriate foreign stock exchange.

The Development of Accounting Systems

The culture of a country influences not only its business practices but also its accounting procedures. Hofstede provided a widely accepted definition of *culture* as "the collective programming of the mind that distinguishes one category of people from another."[1] He later categorized eight separate cultures: Occidental, Muslim, Japanese, Hindu, Confucian, Slavic, African, and Latin American. However, classifying accounting practices by culture alone is too simplistic because many nations contain more than one cultural group, and many countries use accounting systems that were developed during previous colonial relationships.

The level of development of a country's accounting system is also affected by environmental forces such as overall level of education, type of political system, type of legal system, and extent of economic development. For example, the development of accounting standards in the United States was affected by the industrial revolution and the need to obtain private sources of capital. Consequently, financial accounting information was needed to provide investors and creditors with information on profitability and stewardship. On the other hand, accounting standards in Russia have been in transition over the past two decades. Originally, the Russian economy was centrally planned and as a result required uniform accounting standards. Later, as a country with an emerging market economy, Russia found those accounting standards no longer useful, and new standards were necessary. The impact of various environmental factors on the development of accounting standards is discussed in the following paragraphs.

Level of Education

There tends to be a direct correlation between the level of education obtained by a country's citizens and the development of the financial accounting reporting practices in that country. The characteristics comprising these environmental factors include (1) the degree of literacy in a country; (2) the percentage of the population that has completed grade school, high school, and college; (3) the orientation of the educational system (vocational, professional, etc.); and (4) the appropriateness of the educational system to the country's economic and social needs. Countries with better-educated populations are associated with more advanced financial accounting systems.

Political System

The type of political system (socialist, democratic, totalitarian, etc.) can influence the development of accounting standards and procedures. The accounting system in a country with a centrally controlled economy will be different from the accounting system in a market-oriented economy. For example, companies in a socialist country may be required to provide information on social impact and cost-benefit analysis in addition to information on profitability and financial position.

Legal System

The extent to which a country's laws determine accounting practice influences the strengths of that country's accounting profession. When governments prescribe accounting practices and procedures, the authority of the accounting profession is usually weak. Conversely, the nonlegalistic establishment of accounting policies by professional organizations is a characteristic of common-law countries.

---

1. G. Hofstede, "The Cultural Relativity of Organizational Practices and Theories," *Journal of International Business Studies* (Fall 1983): 25–89.

TABLE 3.1 *Influences on the Development of Financial Reporting*

Type of economy	Agricultural
	Resource based
	Tourist based
	Manufacturing
Legal system	Codified
	Common law
Political system	Democratic
	Totalitarian
Nature of business ownership	Private enterprise
	Socialist
	Communist
Size and complexity of business firms	Conglomerates
	Sole traders
Social climate	Consumerism
	Laissez-faire
Stability of currency	
Sophistication of management	
Sophistication of financial community	
Existence of accounting legislation	
Growth pattern of the economy	Growing
	Stable
	Declining
Education system	

Economic Development

The level of a country's economic development influences both the development and application of its financial reporting practices. Countries with low levels of economic development will have relatively less need for a sophisticated accounting system than countries with high levels of economic development.

Table 3.1 lists some potential social, cultural, political, and legal influences on the development of national financial reporting standards and practices.

Preparation of Financial Statements for Foreign Users

A company issuing financial reports to users in foreign countries may take one of several approaches in the preparation of its financial statements:

1. Send the same set of financial statements to all users (domestic or foreign).

2. Translate the financial statements sent to foreign users into the language of the foreign nation's users.

3. Translate the financial statements sent to foreign users into the foreign nation's language and currency.

4. Prepare two sets of financial statements, one using the home country's language, currency, and accounting principles, the second using the language, currency, and accounting principles of the foreign country's users.

5. Prepare one set of financial statements based on worldwide accepted accounting principles.

The International Accounting Standards Committee

The preparation of financial statements for foreign users under option five above is being increasingly advocated for transnational financial reporting. The International Accounting Standards Committee (IASC) was formed in 1973 to develop worldwide accounting standards. It was an independent private sector body whose objective was to achieve uniformity in accounting principles that are used for worldwide financial reporting. The original members of the IASC were the accounting bodies of nine countries: Australia, Canada, France, Japan, Mexico, The Netherlands, the United Kingdom, the United States, and West Germany. Since 1983, the IASC's members have included all of the professional accounting bodies that are members of the International Federation of Accountants. Most of these organizations are professional associations of licensed public accountants; consequently, the membership of the IASC comprised a narrower range of organizations than the FASB did. In 2001 the IASC was replaced by the IASB (discussed later in the chapter). The IASB immediately voted to retain all of the IASC's pronouncements and positions unless they were replaced by new pronouncements. Consequently, all IASC pronouncements immediately became IASB pronouncements and are referred to as such in the remainder of this and succeeding chapters.

The IASB's *Agreement and Constitution* gives it the authority to promulgate standards for the presentation of financial statements that are audited by its member organizations. The constitution of the IASB also establishes its role in promoting worldwide acceptance of IASB standards. This requirement had arisen because many countries did not have a program of developing accounting standards and because of the need to harmonize differences among national standards.[2] Many observers consider harmonization desirable because of the perceived need to increase the reliability of foreign financial statements. Improved decision making would occur because it would no longer be necessary to interpret foreign financial statements and because comparability would be improved.

Although many differences in worldwide financial reporting practices can be explained by environmental differences between countries, some cannot. The IASB is attempting to harmonize the differences that cannot be explained by environmental differences. The aim of the IASB is to formulate and publish accounting standards that are to be observed in the presentation of financial statements and to promote their worldwide acceptance and observance. The members of the IASB agree to support the standards and to use their best endeavors to ensure that published financial statements comply with the standards, to ensure that auditors enforce the standards, and to persuade governments, stock exchanges, and other bodies to back the standards.

The IASC's original intention was to avoid complex details and concentrate on basic standards. As a result, the IASB's standards are more "principles based" than the FASB's standards. The standard-setting process of the IASB is similar to that followed by the FASB and includes the following six stages.

2. J. A. Hepworth, "International Accounting Standards," *Chartered Accountant in Australia* 48, no. 2 (August 1977): 17–19.

Stage 1: Setting the Agenda

The IASB evaluates the merits of adding a potential item to its agenda mainly by reference to the needs of investors. In making this decision, the IASB considers:

a. The relevance to users of the information and the reliability of the information that could be provided

b. Existing available guidance

c. The possibility of increasing convergence

d. The quality of the standard to be developed

e. Resource constraints

Stage 2: Project Planning

The board decides whether to conduct the project alone or jointly with another standard setter, and a project team is selected.

Stage 3: Development and Publication of a Discussion Paper

The board normally publishes a discussion paper as its first publication on any major new topic as a vehicle to explain the issue and solicit early comment from constituents. A discussion paper includes a comprehensive overview of the issue, possible approaches in addressing the issue, the preliminary views of its authors or the IASB, and an invitation to comment.

Stage 4: Development and Publication of an Exposure Draft

An exposure draft is the IASB's main vehicle for consulting the public. Unlike a discussion paper, an exposure draft sets out a specific proposal in the form of a proposed standard (or amendment to an existing standard).

Stage 5: Development and Publication of an International Financial Reporting Standard

After resolving issues arising from the exposure draft, the IASB considers whether it should expose its revised proposals for public comment, for example, by publishing a second exposure draft.

In considering the need for reexposure, the IASB:

- Identifies substantial issues that emerged during the comment period on the exposure draft that it had not previously considered

- Assesses the evidence that it has considered

- Evaluates whether it has sufficiently understood the issues and actively sought the views of constituents

- Considers whether the various viewpoints were aired in the exposure draft and adequately discussed and reviewed in the basis for conclusions on the exposure draft

When the IASB is satisfied that it has reached a conclusion on the issues arising from the exposure draft, it instructs the staff to draft the IFRS. After the due process is completed, all outstanding issues are resolved, and at least nine of the fourteen IASB members have voted in favor of publication, the IFRS is issued.

Stage 6: Procedures After an IFRS Is Issued

After an IFRS is issued, the staff and the IASB members hold regular meetings with interested parties, including other standard-setting bodies, to help understand unanticipated issues related to the practical implementation and potential impact of its proposals. The IFRS[3] Foundation also fosters educational activities to ensure consistency in the application of IFRSs.

In contrast to standards issued by the FASB, International Accounting Standards (IASs) sometimes permitted two accounting treatments for accounting transactions and events. In such cases, the preferable treatment was termed the *benchmark treatment*, whereas the other was termed the *alternative treatment*. Originally, the IASB did not explain the distinction between these two types of treatments; however, in the December 1995 issue of *IASB Insight*, it provided the following explanation:

> The Board has concluded that it should use the term "benchmark" instead of the proposed term "preferred" [as proposed in *IAS No. 32*, p. 2] in those few cases where it continues to allow a choice of accounting treatment for like transactions and events. The term "benchmark" more closely reflects the Board's intention of identifying a point of reference when making its choice between alternatives.

Later, in 2003, the IASB removed some of the existing alternative accounting treatments. Where an IAS retains alternative treatments, the IASB removed references to "benchmark treatment" and "allowed alternative treatment," instead using descriptive references, such as "cost model" and "revaluation model." The Improvements Project standards (discussed later in the chapter) became effective for annual periods beginning on or after January 1, 2005.

Restructuring the IASC

In 1998 the IASC embarked on a new effort aimed at addressing standard-setting issues. To this end, the IASC formed the Strategy Working Party to consider what the IASC's strategy and structure should be to meet its new challenges. In December 1998 this group issued a discussion paper, titled "Shaping the IASB for the Future," which set out its proposals for changing the IASC's structure. During early 1999, comments on the proposal were received and a final report was issued. In March 2000, the IASB Board unanimously approved a new constitution for restructuring the IASC. The following is a summary of the key points addressed in this document.

Several factors have contributed to the need for new approaches to international standard setting. These factors include the following:

1. A rapid growth in international capital markets, combined with an increase in cross-border listings and cross-border investment. These issues have led to efforts by securities regulators to develop a common "passport" for cross-border securities listings and to achieve greater comparability in financial reporting.

2. The efforts of global organizations (such as the World Trade Organization) and regional bodies (such as the European Union, NAFTA, MERCOSUR [the southern common market countries of Argentina, Brazil, Paraguay, and Uruguay], and Asia-Pacific Economic Cooperation) to dismantle barriers to international trade.

3. A trend toward the internationalization of business regulation.

---

3. On July 1, 2010 the IASC foundation's name was changed to the International Financial Reporting Standards Foundation.

4. The increasing influence of international accounting standards on national accounting requirements and practice.

5. The acceleration of innovation in business transactions.

6. Users' increasing demands for new types of financial and other performance information.

7. New developments in the electronic distribution of financial and other performance information.

8. A growing need for relevant and reliable financial and other performance information both in countries in transition from planned economies to market economies and in developing newly industrialized economies.

As a result, a demand has arisen for high-quality global accounting standards that provide transparency and comparability. In its early years, the IASC acted mainly as a harmonizer—a body that selected an accounting treatment that already existed at the national level in some countries and then sought worldwide acceptance of that treatment, perhaps with some modifications. Later, it began to combine that role with the role of a catalyst—a coordinator of national initiatives and an initiator of new work at the national level. In the future, its successor the IASB's role as catalyst and initiator should become more prominent. It is important for the IASB to focus objectives more precisely, as follows:

1. To develop international accounting standards that require high-quality, transparent, and comparable information that will help participants in capital markets and others make economic decisions

2. To promote the use of international accounting standards by working with national standard setters

The IASB, in partnership with national standard setters, is making every effort to accelerate convergence between national accounting standards and international accounting standards. The goal of this convergence is for enterprises in all countries to report high-quality, transparent, and comparable information that will help participants in capital markets and others make economic decisions. To this end, the IASB should continue to use an agreed-upon conceptual framework (the Framework for the Preparation and Presentation of Financial Statements, discussed in the following section). The IASB's short-term aim should be to effect the convergence of national accounting standards and international accounting standards around high-quality solutions. However, its aim in the longer term should be global uniformity—a single set of high-quality accounting standards for all listed and other economically significant business enterprises around the world.

The changes in the IASC's environment meant that structural changes were needed, so that the IASC could anticipate the new challenges facing it and meet those challenges effectively. The following were identified as issues that needed to be addressed:

1. *Partnership with national standard setters.* The IASC should enter into a partnership with national standard setters so that IASC can work together with them to accelerate convergence between national standards and international accounting standards around solutions requiring high-quality, transparent, and comparable information that will help participants in capital markets and others to make economic decisions.

2. *Wider participation in the IASC Board.* A wider group of countries and organizations should take part in the IASC Board without diluting the quality of the Board's work.

3. *Appointment.* The process for appointments to the IASC Board and key IASC committees should be the responsibility of a variety of constituencies, while ensuring that those appointed are competent, independent, and objective.

On April 1, 2001, the IASC transferred the responsibility for international standards setting to the IASB. The structure of the IASC Foundation is described in the following paragraphs.

The IFRS Foundation

The IFRS Foundation consists of twenty-two trustees. The constitution requires an appropriate balance of professional backgrounds, including auditors, preparers, users, academics, and other officials serving the public interest. Two will normally be senior partners of prominent international accounting firms. The constitution of the IFRS Foundation provides for the following geographic balance in the selection of the trustees:

- Six from North America
- Six from Europe
- Six from the Asia-Oceania region
- Four from any area, subject to establishing overall geographical balance

The trustees' duties include the following:

1. Appointing the members of the Board, including those who will serve in liaison capacities with national standard setters, and establishing their contracts of service and performance criteria

2. Appointing the members of the Standing Interpretations Committee and the Standards Advisory Council

3. Reviewing annually the strategy of the IASB and its effectiveness

4. Approving annually the budget of the IASB and determining the basis for funding

5. Reviewing broad strategic issues affecting accounting standards, promoting IASB and its work, and promoting the objective of rigorous application of International Accounting Standards, provided that the trustees shall be excluded from involvement in technical matters relating to accounting standards

6. Establishing and amending operating procedures for the Board, the Standing Interpretations Committee, and the Standards Advisory Council (SAC)

7. Approving amendments to this constitution after following a due process, including consultation with the SAC and publication of an exposure draft for public comment.

The International Accounting Standards Board

The IASB currently consists of fifteen individuals (The Board membership is scheduled to increase to 16 members in 2012) appointed by the trustees. The key qualification for membership is technical expertise. The trustees also must ensure that the Board is not dominated by any particular constituency or regional interest; consequently, the following guidelines have been established:

1. A minimum of five will have a background as practicing auditors.
2. A minimum of three will have a background in the preparation of financial statements.
3. A minimum of three will have a background as users of financial statements.
4. At least one member will have an academic background.
5. Seven of the full-time members will be expected to have formal liaison responsibilities with national standards setters in order to promote the convergence of national accounting standards with IASB standards.

International accounting standards issued by the Board are now called International Financial Reporting Standards (IFRSs), replacing the term *IAS*s, which were issued by its predecessor, the IASC. The Board's principal responsibilities are to develop and issue IFRS and exposure drafts and approve interpretations developed by the International Financial Reporting Interpretations Committee (IFRIC). Standards are adopted after consultation with the SAC and national standard setters. Before issuing a final standard, the Board must publish an exposure draft for public comment. Normally it will also publish a draft statement of principles or other discussion document for public comment on major projects. It also considers whether to hold a public hearing or conduct field tests.

The IASB has full discretion over its technical agenda. It may outsource detailed research or other work to national standard setters or other organizations. The Board is responsible for establishing the operating procedures for reviewing comments on exposure drafts and other documents. The Board will normally form steering committees or other types of specialist advisory groups to give advice on major projects. The Board is required to consult the SAC on major projects, agenda decisions, and work priorities. The Board will normally issue bases for conclusions with international accounting standards and exposure drafts. Although there is no requirement to hold public hearings or to conduct field tests for every project, the Board must, in each case, consider the need to do so.

The Standards Advisory Council

The Standards Advisory Council has approximately fifty members and provides a forum for organizations and individuals with an interest in international financial reporting to participate in the standard-setting process. Members are appointed for a renewable term of three years and have diverse geographic and functional backgrounds.

The Council normally meets three times each year at meetings open to the public to advise the IASB on priorities in the Board's work, inform the Board of the implications of proposed standards for users and preparers of financial statements, and give other advice to the Board or to the trustees.

International Financial Reporting Interpretations Committee

The IASC originally did not issue interpretations of its standards. However, after noting criticism, in 1997 it began issuing interpretations of its standards. Later the IASB established the International Financial Reporting Interpretations Committee (IFRIC).

The role of the IFRIC has evolved and was clarified by the publication of the IFRIC handbook in 2007. The IFRIC is comprised of fourteen members, appointed by the trustees of the IASB for renewable terms of three years. The trustees appoint a member of the IASB, the director of technical activities or another senior member of the IASB staff, or another appropriately qualified individual, to chair the committee. The chair has the right to speak about the technical issues being considered but not to vote. The trustees also may appoint as nonvoting observers representatives of regulatory organizations, who have the right to attend and speak at meetings.

The committee meets as required, and nine voting members present in person or by telecommunications constitute a quorum. One or two IASB members are designated by the IASB to attend meetings as nonvoting observers; other members of the IASB may also attend and speak at the meetings. On exceptional occasions, members of the committee may be allowed to send nonvoting alternates, at the discretion of the chair of the committee. Members wishing to nominate an alternate member for a meeting seek the consent of the chair beforehand.

Meetings of the committee are open to the public, but certain discussions (normally only about selection, appointment, and other personnel issues) may be held in private at the committee's discretion. Members must vote in accordance with their own views, not as representatives voting according to the views of any firm, organization, or constituency with which they may be associated.

Approval of a draft or final Interpretations requires that not more than three voting members vote against the draft or final Interpretation. The committee (1) interprets the application of International Accounting Standards (IASs) and International Financial Reporting Standards (IFRSs) and provides timely guidance on financial reporting issues not specifically addressed in IASs and IFRSs, in the context of the IASB Framework, and undertakes other tasks at the request of the IASB; (2) in carrying out its work under (1) above, it must have regard to the IASB's objective of working actively with national standard setters to bring about convergence of national accounting standards and IASs and IFRSs to high-quality solutions; (3) publishes after clearance by the IASB the draft Interpretations for public comment and consider comments made within a reasonable period before finalizing an Interpretation; and (4) reports to the IASB and obtains its approval for final Interpretations.

The structure of the IASB is outlined in Figure 3.1 on page 89.

Revising the IASB's Constitution

In November 2003, the IASC Foundation[4] announced that it had initiated a review of the organization's constitution. At this time the trustees also published a consultation paper, "Identifying Issues for the IASC Foundation Constitution Review," that invited respondents to suggest issues for the committee to review. The comment period ended February 11, 2004, and on March 22, 2004, the Constitution Committee outlined ten key issues to be reviewed. The issues are listed below in order of their appearance in the constitution (which may not reflect their relative importance to the committee).

1. *Whether the objectives of the IASC Foundation should expressly refer to the challenges facing small and medium-sized entities (SMEs).* Comments on the need

---

4. We refer to all previous discussions of the IASC foundation by its original name for historical accuracy.

FIGURE 3.1 *Structure of the International Accounting Standards Board*

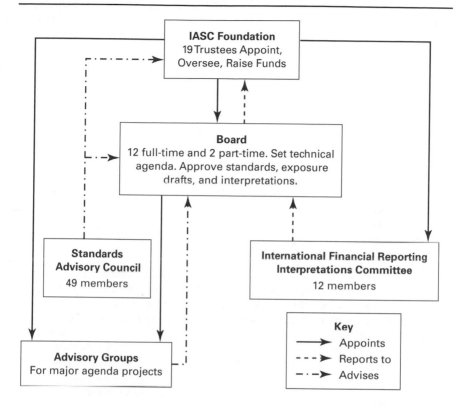

for such a provision in the constitution were mixed, and the committee will need to decide whether the language of the constitution adequately addresses the position of SMEs and emerging economies.

2. *Number of trustees and their geographical and professional distribution.* Some respondents argued for greater representation from Asia-Oceania as well as emerging economies; many respondents referred to what was felt to be the overrepresentation of certain regions. One possibility raised would be to provide for equal numbers of trustees from Asia-Oceania, Europe, and North America. The trustees will also need to consider the appointment process for choosing new trustees, including the chairman.

3. *The oversight role of the trustees.* There is a view that the trustees should strengthen the language regarding their oversight (particularly over the IASB's deliberative procedures) and demonstrate more clearly how they are fulfilling this function. The committee has not reached conclusions on this matter, but the suggestions of establishing an internal compliance committee and holding additional direct consultations with the SAC were raised.

4. *Funding of the IASC Foundation.* The committee or another group of the trustees will need to examine the funding structure of the IASC Foundation. It is noted that a long-term funding committee of the trustees has already been established and is examining options.

5. *The composition of the IASB.* The committee has not taken a position on the geographical background of IASB members, but it noted that the majority of respondents called for the committee to examine the issue. The committee will need to analyze further the questions of the mix of professional backgrounds and full-time versus part-time members.

6. *The appropriateness of the IASB's existing formal liaison relationships.* The committee needs to assess the appropriateness of the existing formal liaison relationships and determine whether more guidance is needed in the constitution regarding the role that liaison relationships play.

7. *Consultative arrangements of the IASB.* The committee will need to examine the IASB's consultative arrangements, including the mandatory steps of the IASB's due process. The committee notes that it may not be desirable to enshrine in the constitution detailed steps regarding due process. The IASB at its own initiative will release a document on its website that sets out proposed interim improvements in its consultative arrangements, and the committee and the other trustees will monitor the response to that document.

8. *Voting procedures of the IASB.* The approval of a standard requires the assent of nine of the fourteen members of the IASB.

9. *Resources and effectiveness of the International Financial Reporting Interpretations Committee (IFRIC).* The committee has not had the opportunity to address issues related to the IFRIC raised by respondents. The IFRIC is already conducting an internal review of its procedures, and recommendations will be made to the trustees. However, given the likely increase in demand for IFRIC Interpretations, the committee will need to decide whether the present constitutional arrangements for the IFRIC are adequate. Members of the SAC noted a tension that possibly exists between an IFRIC that responds to the growing demand for timely guidance and the desire to maintain a principles-based approach to standard setting.

10. *The composition, role, and effectiveness of the SAC.* The responses showed that there was a widespread belief that the IASC Foundation and the IASB could make better use of the SAC. The committee has asked the SAC to make recommendations on its role and operations. The committee has agreed to examine whether an independent chairman of the SAC is needed and whether that chairman would need to commit a significant amount of time to the role.[5]

The Uses of International Accounting Standards

International accounting standards are used in a variety of ways. The IASB noted that its standards are used:[6]

1. As national requirements

2. As the basis for some or all national requirements

---

5. IASB, "Next Steps for the Constitution Review following Initial Consultation," International Accounting Standards Committee Foundation, Invitation to Comment Web page (March 22, 2004), http://www.iasb.org/current/invitation.asp.

6. *International Accounting Standards 1996* (London: International Accounting Standards Committee, 1996), 12.

3. As an international benchmark for those countries that develop their own requirements

4. By regulatory authorities for domestic and foreign companies

5. By companies themselves

In addition, the International Organization of Securities Commissions (IOSCO) looks to the IASB to provide International Accounting Standards that can be used in multinational securities offerings. Currently, several stock exchanges in different countries require or allow issuers to prepare financial statements in accordance with International Accounting Standards.

The IASB has no enforcement authority and must rely on the "best endeavors" of its members. However, the influence of professional accounting bodies in the formation of accounting rules varies from country to country. In some countries, such as France and Germany, the strength and detail of company law leave little room for influence by accounting bodies. On the other hand, in the United Kingdom, Canada, and Australia, accounting standards are set by professional bodies. In the United States, the two bodies directly concerned with standard setting, the FASB and the SEC, are not members of the IASB.

The IASB's charter and actions do not accommodate national differences. That is, each nation has its own group of financial information users (owners, lenders, borrowers, employees, government, etc.), all of which operate within the cultural, social, legal, political, and economic environment. The users may also have different relative importance from nation to nation, creating variations in the role of financial accounting from nation to nation.

The IASC issued forty-one standards; and at the time this book was published, the IASB had issued ten IFRSs covering issues such as disclosure of accounting policies; cash-flow statements, depreciation; information to be disclosed; the statement of changes in financial position, unusual items, prior period items, and changes in accounting policies; research and development; income taxes; foreign exchange; business combinations; and related party disclosures. Each of these standards is discussed in this text in chapters covering the appropriate topic.

Current Issues

In the late 1980s, the IASC entered into partnership with the IOSCO to work together to encourage stock exchanges throughout the world to accept financial statements prepared under IASB standards. To achieve this objective, the IASC was required to complete a comprehensive work program that generated new or revised IASs acceptable to the IOSCO. The IOSCO indicated that the successful completion of the IASC's work program would result in the promulgation of a comprehensive core set of standards for cross-border listings. It will also allow the IOSCO to consider endorsing international accounting standards for listing purposes in all global capital markets. The IOSCO had already endorsed the IASC's pronouncement on cash-flow statements and indicated that other IASC standards required no improvement, provided that the other core standards were successfully completed. Among the issues addressed in the work program were financial instruments, income taxes, intangibles, segmental reporting, earnings per share, employee benefit costs, interim reporting, discontinued operations, contingencies, and leases. Originally, a target date of December 1999 was set for completing this program; however, in 1996, the IASC Board advanced this date to March 1999.

At the completion of the project, the IOSCO reviewed the revised standards to determine whether to endorse them and recommend to its members that they be adopted for cross-border capital-raising purposes. The IOSCO identified a number of potential improvements in the standards; as a result, the IASB initiated an Improvements Project to reduce or eliminate alternatives, redundancies, and conflicts within existing standards and to make other improvements to them. The early completion of this project was seen as crucial in that the European Union (EU) countries were to adopt international standards beginning in 2005.

On December 17, 2003, the IASB published thirteen revised International Accounting Standards (IASs), reissued two others, and gave notice of the withdrawal of its standard on price-level accounting. The revised and reissued standards mark the near completion of the IASB's Improvements Project. The project addressed concerns, questions, and criticisms raised by securities regulators and other interested parties about the existing set of IASs.

The Improvements Project is a central element of the IASB's strategy to raise the quality and consistency of financial reporting generally and of the body of existing IASs in particular. In the interests of better reporting through convergence, the project has drawn on best practices from around the world. It removed a number of options contained in IASs, whose existence had caused uncertainty and reduced comparability. The project benefited from input received from a broad range of market participants, including regulators through the International Organization of Securities Commissions, national standard setters, the IASB's Standards Advisory Council, and other commentators. The IASB has also issued ten IFRSs. These new standards and the amendments to the various IASs are discussed in the text chapters dealing with these issues. Subsequently, in 2005, the Technical Committee of IOSCO reaffirmed its support for the development and use of IFRS as a set of high-quality international standards in cross-border offerings and listings. It recommended that its members allow multinational issuers to use IFRS in cross-border offerings and listings, as supplemented by reconciliation, disclosure, and interpretation where necessary to address outstanding substantive issues at a national or regional level.

The IASB Annual Improvements Project

In July 2006, the IASB announced that it was beginning an annual improvements project. The Board stated: "Changes to standards, however small, are time-consuming for the Board and burdensome for others. The IASB has adopted an annual process to deal with non-urgent but necessary amendments to IFRSs."[7] Issues dealt with in this process arise from matters raised by the IFRIC and suggestions from staff or practitioners, and focus on areas of inconsistency in IFRSs or where clarification of wording is required. As a result, the Board evaluates whether an amendment is appropriate to address the identified issue in this project the same way as it evaluates all other technical agenda decisions that require judgment. The adopted improvements are published in a single omnibus exposure draft in the third or fourth quarter of each year.

7. International Accounting Standards Board, "Project History," http://www.iasb.org/ Current+Projects/ IASB+Projects/Annual+Improvements/Project+history.htm.

The Use of IASC Standards

The globalization of business and finance has led more than 12,000 companies in approximately 113 countries to adopt IFRS. As noted above, in 2005 the European Union began requiring companies incorporated in its member states, whose securities are listed on an EU-regulated stock exchange, to prepare their consolidated financial statements in accordance with IFRS.[8] Australia, New Zealand, and Israel have essentially adopted IFRS as their national standards. Canada, which previously planned convergence with U.S. GAAP, now plans to require IFRS for publicly accountable entities in 2011. The Accounting Standards Board of Japan and the International Accounting Standards Board (IASB) plan convergence by 2011, and China recently announced a convergence plan, as a result all major economics except the US will soon be using IFRSs. Figure 3.2 on page 94 illustrates the status of the adoption of IASB standards throughout the world.

To assist the implementation process, the IASB announced in 2006 that it would not require the application of new IFRSs under development or major amendments to existing IFRSs before January 1, 2009. Delaying implementation of new standards until 2009 provided four years of stability in the IFRS platform of standards for those companies that adopted IFRSs in 2005. Additionally, setting January 1, 2009, as the first date of implementation of new standards provided countries yet to adopt IFRSs with a clear target date for adoption. It was also hoped that by 2009, the joint efforts of the FASB and the IASB would permit the removal of the need for the reconciliation requirement for non-U.S. companies that use IFRSs and are registered in the United States.

To assist companies making the change to IFRS, and to enable users of company reports to understand the effect of applying a new set of accounting standards, the IASB issued *IFRS No. 1*, "First-time Adoption of International Financial Reporting Standards" (discussed later in the chapter), which explains how an entity should make the transition to IFRSs from another basis of accounting.

The IASB-FASB Convergence Project

The IASB and the FASB are currently engaged in several efforts to attain a uniform set of international accounting standards. Among these efforts are (1) the FASB's Short-term International Convergence Project, (2) the Norwalk Agreement, and (3) the Roadmap to Convergence.

The FASB's Short-term International Convergence Project

The goal of the FASB's Short-term International Convergence Project is to remove a variety of individual differences between U.S. GAAP and International Financial Reporting Standards that are not within the scope of other major projects. The project's scope is limited to those differences in which convergence around a high-quality solution would appear to be achievable in the short term, usually by selecting between existing IFRS and U.S. GAAP.

---

8. The EU's decision to require the use of IFRS did not come without a cost to the IASB. The EU requires that all new or revised standards and interpretations be reviewed by the European Commission before they can be required for use by listed companies in the EU. This rule, in effect, gives the EU veto power over the adoption of any new IFRSs.

FIGURE 3.2 *The Worldwide IASB Standards Adoption Map*

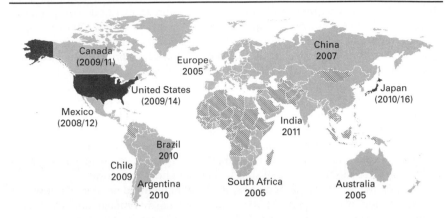

- Current or anticipated requirement or option to use IFRS (or equivalent)
- Adoption under consideration
- No current adoption timetable

Source: United Kingdom: "Ten Lessons from European IFRS Conversion in the Real Estate Industry" (October 30, 2009), Deloitte Real Estate Group, http://www.mondaq.com/article. asp?articleid=88490&login=true.

The FASB intends to analyze each of the differences within the scope and either (1) amend applicable U.S. GAAP literature to reduce or eliminate the difference or (2) communicate to the IASB the Board's rationale for electing not to change U.S. GAAP. Concurrently, the IASB will review IFRS and make similar determinations of whether to amend applicable IFRS or communicate its rationale to the FASB for electing not to change the IASB's GAAP.

The FASB and the IASB commenced deliberating differences identified for resolution in the short-term project in 2003 with the objective of achieving compatibility by identifying common, high-quality solutions. Both boards agreed to use their best efforts to issue exposure drafts of proposed changes to U.S. GAAP or IFRS that reflect common solutions to some, if not all, of the identified differences by the first quarter of 2004. The results of these deliberations are discussed in the chapters impacted by the changes.

The FASB set September 30, 2004, as the target date for issuing final statements covering some, if not all, of the identified differences. This target date was set to allow sufficient time for due process to be completed while providing sufficient time in advance of the 2005 date established by the European Commission for adoption of IAS by all EU-listed companies. It is important to note that the short-term convergence project addressed only differences that meet the criteria for inclusion in the project scope. Differences that are associated with issues requiring comprehensive reconsideration were not addressed by the short-term convergence project and will be addressed over a longer term in the Roadmap to Convergence project.

The Norwalk Agreement

As discussed in Chapter 2, the FASB and the IASB held a joint meeting in Norwalk, Connecticut, on September 18, 2002. Both standard-setting bodies acknowledged their commitment to the development of high-quality compatible accounting standards that can be used for both domestic and cross-border financial reporting. They also promised to use their best efforts to make their existing financial reporting standards compatible as soon as practicable and to coordinate their future work programs to maintain compatibility. To this end, both boards agreed to the following proposals:

1. Undertake a short-term project aimed at removing a variety of differences between U.S. GAAP and IFRSs.

2. Remove any other differences between IFRSs and U.S. GAAP that remained on January 1, 2005, by undertaking projects that both boards would address concurrently.

3. Continue the progress on the joint projects currently under way.

4. Encourage their respective interpretative bodies to coordinate their activities.

The goal of this project is to achieve compatibility by identifying common high-quality solutions.

The Roadmap to Convergence

In 2005, the chief accountant of the SEC described a "roadmap" for arriving at a common set of high-quality global standards and the removal of the need for the reconciliation requirement for non-U.S. companies that use IFRSs and are registered in the United States. Later, in 2008, the SEC voted to publish for public comment a proposed roadmap that could lead to the use of International Financial Reporting Standards by U.S. issuers beginning in 2014. This roadmap included the following seven milestones:

1. *Improvements to accounting standards.* The SEC will determine whether the standards are high in quality and sufficiently comprehensive; whether the standard-setting process is robust and independent with input and consideration of views from investors and other affected parties; and whether the standards, when implemented, are capable of improving the effectiveness of financial reporting and providing financial information useful to investors.

2. *Funding of the International Accounting Standards Committee Foundation.* The SEC will consider the degree to which the Foundation has a secure, stable, and equitable funding mechanism that allows the IASB to function independently of any specific constituent group. The SEC would also consider how effectively regulators oversee the Foundation.

3. *Improved ability to use interactive data for IFRS reporting.* The SEC has proposed rules that would require public companies to provide financial information formatted in the XBRL computer language. The level of detail in the existing IFRS XBRL taxonomy would have to be improved, according to the proposal, in order to realize the benefits of IFRS reporting in XBRL.

4. *Improved education and training in the United States.* A significant investment in preparing investors, management and financial statement preparers,

auditors, audit committees, specialists (such as actuaries and valuation professionals), and regulators would be needed before IFRS is widely understood in the United States. College and university curricula would need to incorporate IFRS, and the CPA and other relevant professional exams would need to cover IFRS.

5. Limited use in a narrow group of companies (i.e., December 31, 2009)

6. SEC to determine in 2011 whether mandatory adoption of IFRS is feasible based on the progress in the first five milestones.

7. *Mandatory use.* If it is decided to go full steam ahead (as discussed in milestone 6) then large accelerated, accelerated, and non-accelerated filers would be required to adopt IFRS beginning with their years ending on or after December 15, 2014, 2015 and 2016, respectively.

The objective of convergence of accounting standards is to have companies in different countries use the same accounting procedures to measure and report their financial position and results of operations. This is a desirable objective because differences in the use of accounting procedures affect the data available for making investment. For example, an individual wishing to invest in pharmaceutical companies might focus on the percentage of earnings reinvested by a company in research and development as a key performance indicator of future growth and might use a ratio of research and development expense as a percentage of revenue to rank various investment opportunities.

If this investor considered only domestic entities, he or she could expect that the financial statements of the pharmaceutical companies would be comparable with both research and development expenditures and revenues measured using the same accounting principles. However, if that investor wished to consider some foreign companies as possible investment opportunities and thus obtains the financial statements of those additional candidates, how useful are comparisons based on the key performance indicators that are derived from information in the financial statements?

For example, if revenue is measured on an accrual basis by domestic companies but one of the foreign candidates uses a cash basis to report revenue, the results are not comparable. Similarly, if the domestic company expenses research and development expenditures as incurred while the foreign company capitalizes them, there is also a lack of comparability.

The roadmap is a step in the direction of solving comparability issues. However, both the FASB and the IASB have noted that removal of the reconciliation requirement will depend on, among other things, the effective implementation of IFRSs in financial statements across companies and jurisdictions, and measurable progress in addressing priority issues on the IASB-FASB convergence program. Therefore, the ability to meet the objectives set out by the roadmap depends on the efforts and actions of many parties—including companies, auditors, investors, standard setters, and regulators.

The FASB and the IASB also recognized that achieving the reconciliation requirement requires measurable progress on the FASB-IASB convergence program. Consequently, both boards affirmed their commitment to making such progress and indicated agreement on the following guidelines:

• Convergence of accounting standards can best be achieved through the development of high-quality, common standards over time.

• Trying to eliminate differences between two standards that are in need of significant improvement is not the best use of the FASB's and the IASB's resources—instead, a new common standard should be developed that improves the financial information reported to investors.

- Serving the needs of investors means that the boards should seek to converge by replacing weaker standards with stronger standards.

At the time this text was published, the SEC was examining the comments it received on the proposed roadmap. Further action was expected in 2010.

The Impact of International versus U.S. GAAP Accounting Standards

In February 2000 the Securities and Exchange Commission voted to ask U.S. companies to comment on whether it should allow foreign companies to list their securities on U.S. stock exchanges under international accounting rules. Previously, foreign companies seeking to list on a U.S. stock exchange must have recast their financial statements to reflect then-current GAAP. This reconciliation was made by filing Form 20-F with the SEC within six months of the company's fiscal year-end. Prior to 2008, only about 1,000 foreign companies were listed on U.S. stock exchanges because of the high cost involved in recasting their financial statements to U.S. GAAP. Previously, the SEC had consistently taken the position that allowing foreign firms to list using other than U.S. GAAP would result in a loss of investor protection and result in a two-tiered disclosure system, one for domestic registrants and another for foreign registrants. There has been little empirical evidence with which to evaluate the SEC's position. One study found mixed evidence in that the Form 20-F reconciliation was found to be value relevant and IAS and U.S. GAAP earnings amounts were valued differently by the marketplace. However, the study did not show that the market valued earnings per share amounts differently.[9]

In 2007, the SEC modified its position on the Form 20-F requirement when it issued the "Acceptance from Foreign Private Issuers of Financial Statements Prepared in Accordance with International Financial Reporting Standards without Reconciliation to GAAP."[10] This rule amends Form 20-F to accept from foreign private issuers in their filings with the SEC financial statements prepared in accordance with International Financial Reporting Standards as issued by the IASB without reconciliation to generally accepted accounting principles as used in the United States. The SEC's rationale for this action was to foster the adoption of a set of globally accepted accounting standards. However, the requirements regarding reconciliation to U.S. GAAP do not change for a foreign private issuer that files its financial statements using a basis of accounting other than IFRSs.

An American Accounting Association committee was given the charge of responding to this proposal and concluded that eliminating the reconciliation requirement was premature. The committee noted that the decision to eliminate

---

9. Mary S. Harris and Karl A. Muller III, "The Market Valuation of IAS versus US–GAAP Accounting Measures Using Form 20-F Reconciliations," *Journal of Accounting and Economics* (1999): 285–312.

10. "Acceptance from Foreign Private Issuers of Financial Statements Prepared in Accordance with International Financial Reporting Standards without Reconciliation to GAAP." (Washington, DC: SEC, 2007).

the Form 20-F reconciliation requirement for a subset of foreign private issuers must be based on at least one of the following premises:

1. U.S. GAAP and IFRS are, at a minimum, informationally equivalent sets of accounting principles, or
2. Investors can reconstruct consistent and comparable U.S.-GAAP-based summary accounting measures from IFRS financial statements.

The committee noted the following points in support of its conclusion:

1. Material reconciling items exist between U.S. GAAP and IFRS and the reconciliation currently reflects information that participants in U.S. stock markets appear to impound into stock prices.
2. In international contexts, U.S. GAAP and IAS/IFRS appear to possess information attributes of high-quality accounting standards (e.g., value relevance or mitigation of information asymmetry); however, U.S. GAAP appears to be preferred by U.S. investors.
3. Cross-country institutional differences will likely result in differences in the implementation of any single set of standards. Thus IFRS may be a high-quality set of reporting standards pre-implementation; but the resulting published financial statement information could be of low quality, given inconsistent cross-border implementation practices.
4. Legal and institutional obstacles inhibit private litigation against foreign firms in the United States, and the SEC rarely undertakes enforcement actions against cross-listed firms. In the absence of a reliable enforcement mechanism, even high-quality accounting standards can yield low-quality financial reporting.
5. Differential implementation of standards across countries and differential enforcement efforts directed toward domestic and cross-listed firms creates differences in financial reporting even with converged standards. Whether the required reconciliation mitigates differences in implementation or improves compliance is an open issue; however, the SEC should understand the role of the reconciliation in mitigating differences in implementation and compliance before it is eliminated.
6. Despite the cost associated with preparing the reconciliation and satisfying the other listing requirements, evidence suggests that non-U.S. firms garner financial benefits from listing on U.S. exchanges and that the net benefits of a U.S. listing have not been eroded in recent years.
7. Harmonization of accounting standards could be beneficial to U.S. investors if it yields greater comparability and if IFRS provides information U.S. investors prefer for their investment decisions. Harmonization appears to be occurring via the joint standard-setting activities of the FASB and the IASB; thus, special, statutory intervention by the SEC appears to be unnecessary.[11]

---

11. American Accounting Association's Financial Accounting and Reporting Section of the Financial Reporting Policy Committee, Response to the SEC Release, "Acceptance from Foreign Private Issuers of Financial Statements Prepared in Accordance with International Financial Reporting Standards without Reconciliation to U.S. GAAP File No. S7–13–07," *Accounting Horizons* 22, no. 2 (2008): 223–40.

The SEC also took another step in the direction of convergence in 2007 when it decided to explore the possibility of allowing U.S. companies to adopt IFRS.[12] In explaining its rationale for this decision, the SEC noted that the movement to IFRS has begun to affect U.S. companies, in particular those with a significant global footprint. That is, under the new rule amending Form 20-F adopted by the SEC, foreign registrants can use either U.S. GAAP or IFRS without reconciling their earnings and shareholders' equity to U.S. GAAP; consequently, it would seem more equitable for U.S. companies, which compete for capital in the same securities market, to also be able to use either U.S. GAAP or IFRS. The comment period on this proposal ended in November 2007, but to date no action has been taken.

Standards Overload

The standards overload issue has also been a concern of the IASB. Over the past several years, there has been increased international demand from both developed and emerging economies for a rigorous and common set of accounting standards for smaller and medium-sized businesses that is much simpler than full IFRSs. As a result, in 2009 the IASB published an IFRS designed for use by small and medium-sized entities (SMEs), which are estimated to represent more than 95 percent of all companies. The aim of the standard is to provide a simplified, self-contained set of accounting principles that are appropriate for smaller, unlisted companies and are based on full IFRSs, developed primarily for listed companies. By removing choices for accounting treatment, eliminating topics that aren't generally relevant to SMEs, and simplifying methods for recognition and measurement, the resulting standard reduces the volume of accounting guidance applicable to SMEs by more than 85 percent when compared with the full set of IFRSs.[13]

This pronouncement has the following effects:

1. Omits topics in IFRS that are not relevant to SMEs
2. Allows the easier option when IFRS permit accounting policy choices
3. Simplifies many principles for the recognition and measurement of assets, liabilities, income and expenses
4. Requires significantly fewer disclosures

Individual companies must decide whether to require or permit the use of *IFRS for SMEs* in place of full IFRS or national requirements and, if so, by which entities. *IFRS for SMEs* is not suitable for publicly traded entities and financial institutions.

This standard becomes another area of difference between U.S. GAAP and IFRS, since no similar standard exists in the United States. However, many private companies in the United States may be able to prepare their financial statements in accordance with *IFRS for SMEs*. A variety of factors will drive that decision, such as the needs of financial statement users and possible regulatory reporting requirements. U.S. companies will need to check with their state boards

---

12. "Concept Release on Allowing U.S. Issuers to Prepare Financial Statements in Accordance with International Financial Reporting Standards" (Washington, DC: SEC, 2007).

13. International Accounting Standards Board,. "IASB publishes draft IFRS for SMEs" (February 2007), http://www.iasb.org/News/Press+Releases/IASB+publishes+draft+IFRS+for+SMEs.htm.

of accountancy to determine the status of reporting on financial statements prepared in accordance with *IFRS for SMEs* within their individual states. Other barriers may arise in the form of unwillingness by a private company's financial statement users to accept financial statements prepared under *IFRS for SMEs*, and a private company's expenditure of money, time and effort to convert to *IFRS for SMEs*.

Framework for the Preparation and Presentation of Financial Statements

In 1989, the IASC issued its conceptual framework titled "Framework for the Preparation and Presentation of Financial Statements." The IASB indicated that the purpose of this pronouncement was to set out the concepts that underlie the preparation and presentation of financial statements for external users by:

1. Assisting the IASB in developing future accounting standards
2. Promoting harmonization of accounting standards
3. Assisting national standard setters
4. Assisting preparers in applying international standards
5. Assisting auditors in forming an opinion as to whether financial statements conform to international standards
6. Assisting users in interpreting financial statements prepared in conformity with international standards
7. Providing interested parties with information about the IASB's approach to the formation of international accounting standards

The framework specifies the following elements:

1. The objective of financial statements
2. The qualitative characteristics that determine the usefulness of information in financial statements
3. The definition, recognition, and measurement of the elements from which financial statements are constructed
4. The concepts of capital and capital maintenance

The framework indicates that companies prepare general-purpose financial statements that are directed toward the information needs of a wide variety of users including investors, employees, lenders, suppliers, and other trade creditors as well as customers, governments and their agencies, and the general public. The framework also indicates that, although the information needs of these users cannot be met solely by the presentation of financial statements, there are needs that are common to all users. In addition, since investors are the providers of risk capital to the enterprise, the preparation of financial statements that meet their needs will also satisfy most of the needs of other users.

The Objective of Financial Statements

The framework indicates that the objective of financial statements is to provide information about the financial position, performance, and changes in financial position of an enterprise that is useful to a wide range of users making economic decisions. It also indicates that financial statements prepared for this purpose will satisfy most user needs, but they do not provide all information that may be needed to make economic decisions because they largely portray past information and do not provide nonfinancial information.

In its discussion of general-purpose financial statements, the framework indicated the following:

1. Users require an evaluation of an enterprise's ability to generate cash and the timing and certainty of this generation.

2. The financial position of an enterprise is affected by the economic resources it controls, its financial structure, its liquidity and solvency, and its capacity to adapt to changes in its environment.

3. Information on profitability is required to assess changes in the economic resources an enterprise controls in the future.

4. Information on the financial position of an enterprise is useful in assessing its investing, financing, and operating activities.

5. Information about financial position is contained in the balance sheet, and information about performance is contained in an income statement.

The framework also indicated that two underlying assumptions for the preparation of financial statements were the *accrual basis* and *going concern*.

Qualitative Characteristics

The framework describes qualitative characteristics as the attributes that make the information provided in financial statements useful. The following four principal qualitative characteristics were defined.

Understandability
Information should be provided so that individuals with a reasonable knowledge of business and economic activities and accounting and a willingness to study the information are capable of using it. Nevertheless, complex information should not be withheld just because it is too difficult for some users to understand.

Relevance
Information is relevant when it influences the economic decisions of users by helping them evaluate past, present, or future events or by confirming or correcting their past evaluations. Relevance is also affected by materiality.

Reliability
Information is reliable when it is free from material error and bias and when users can depend on it to represent faithfully that which it purports to represent. As a consequence, events should be accounted for and presented in accordance with their substance and economic reality, not merely their legal form.

Comparability
Users must be able to compare an enterprise's performance over time and to make comparisons with the performance of other enterprises. The framework also recognized that timeliness and the balance between benefits and costs were constraints on providing both relevant and reliable information.

The Elements of Financial Statements

The framework stated that financial statements portray the financial effects of transactions and other events by grouping them into broad classes according to their economic characteristics. These characteristics are the elements of financial statements. It indicated that the elements directly related to the measurement of financial position in the balance sheet are assets, liabilities, and equity. These elements were defined as follows:

- *Asset.* A resource controlled by an enterprise as a result of past events from which future economic benefits are expected to flow to the enterprise.
- *Liability.* A present obligation of the enterprise arising from past events, the settlement of which is expected to result in an outflow from the enterprise of resources embodying economic benefits.
- *Equity.* The residual interest in the assets of the enterprise after deducting all its liabilities.

The elements directly related to the measurement of performance in the income statement are income and expenses. These elements were defined as follows:

- *Income.* Increases in economic benefits during the accounting period in the form of inflows or enhancement of assets or the decreases in liabilities that result in increases in equity, other than those relating to contributions from equity participants.
- *Expenses.* Decreases in economic benefits during the accounting period in the form of outflows or depletions of assets or incurrences of liabilities that result in decreases in equity, other than those relating to contributions from equity participants.

The framework went on to indicate that recognition is the process of incorporating in the financial statements an item that meets the definition of an element as defined in *SFAC No. 6* and satisfies the following recognition criteria: (1) It is probable that any future economic benefit associated with the item will flow to or from the enterprise; and (2) the item has a cost or value that can be measured with reliability.

Finally, with respect to recognition, the framework defined *measurement* as "the process of determining the monetary amounts at which the elements of the financial statements are to be recognized and carried." It also indicated that a variety of measurement bases are employed in financial statements, including historical cost, current cost, realizable value, and present value.

Concepts of Capital and Capital Maintenance

The final issues addressed in the framework were concepts of capital. Under the financial concept of capital, *capital* was defined as being synonymous with the net assets or equity of the enterprise. Under a physical concept of capital, capital is regarded as the productive capacity of the enterprise. The framework indicated that the selection of the appropriate concept of capital by an enterprise should be based on the needs of the user of its financial statements. As a consequence, a financial concept of capital should be adopted if users are concerned primarily with the maintenance of nominal invested capital or the purchasing power of invested capital. However, if the users' main concern is with the operating capacity of an enterprise, a physical concept of capital should be used. As a result, the following concepts of capital maintenance may be used:

- *Financial capital maintenance.* Profit is earned only if the financial (or money) amount of net assets at the end of the period exceeds the net asset at the beginning of the period excluding any distributions to or contributions from owners.
- *Physical capital maintenance.* Profit is earned only if the physical productive capacity (or operating capacity) of the enterprise exceeds the physical productive capacity at the beginning of the period.

Finally, the framework noted that the selection of the measurement bases and concept of capital maintenance will determine the accounting model used in preparing financial statements. Also, since different accounting models differ with respect to relevance and reliability, management must seek a balance between these qualitative characteristics. At the current time, the IASB does not intend to prescribe a particular model other than for exceptional circumstances, such as for reporting in the currency of a hyperinflationary economy.

Comparison of the IASB's and FASB's Conceptual Frameworks

Both the SEC and FASB have endorsed the IASB, and the convergence of national and international accounting standards is a common objective of these organizations. Understanding the existing differences between individual IFRSs and SFASs is important for this process. However, Campbell et al. maintain that it may be more useful to evaluate the conceptual frameworks upon which these standards are based.[14] That is, both the FASB and IASB conceptual frameworks specify a goal of intending to guide standard setting; therefore, it would be expected that similar conceptual frameworks would result in similar standards. And if the conceptual frameworks are reasonably similar, convergence might be more easily obtained. Campbell et al.'s review of the similarities and differences is summarized in the following paragraphs.

The FASB's conceptual framework for financial reporting consists of the following five Statements of Financial Concepts:

1. *SFAC No. 1.* "Objectives of Financial Reporting by Business Enterprises"
2. *SFAC No. 2.* "Qualitative Characteristics of Accounting Information"
3. *SFAC No. 5.* "Recognition and Measurement in Financial Statements of Business Enterprises"
4. *SFAC No. 6.* "Elements of Financial Statements"
5. *SFAC No. 7.* "Using Cash Flow Information and Present Value in Accounting Measurements"

The IASB's "Framework for the Preparation and Presentation of Financial Statements" consists of six major sections:

1. The objective of financial statements
2. Qualitative characteristics of financial statements
3. The elements of financial statements

14. J. E. Campbell, H. M. Hermanson, and J. P. McAllister, "Obstacles to International Accounting Standards Convergence," *CPA Journal* (May 2002): 20–24.

4. Recognition of the elements of financial statements

5. Measurement of the elements of financial statements

6. Concepts of capital and capital maintenance

The subjects contained in the two frameworks appear to be similar, and apparently they do not create any obstacles for convergence. Nevertheless, the level of detail contained in the two frameworks is seen as a pervasive difference. For example, the FASB's conceptual framework includes a more extensive discussion of the underlying logic for its choices than does the IASC conceptual framework. That is, *SFAC No. 2* (qualitative characteristics) includes 170 paragraphs, while the comparable discussion in the IASB's framework includes only 23 paragraphs, and the difference is reflected mostly in the amount of explanation and analogy. The conceptual framework discussions of the FASB attempt to clarify differences between the qualitative characteristics and provide an underlying rationale. For example, *SFAC No. 2* contains a discussion of traffic laws to highlight the need to impose some minimum or maximum standard while allowing for some flexibility. In contrast, the IASB framework simply states its conventions; the reader is often left to interpret why a certain objective or characteristic was chosen.

As a result, the comparative lack of detail throughout the IASB framework may hamper the ability of the IASB to use its framework in the development of future standards. National standard setters that refer to the IASB framework may not find the conceptual guidance to critically review their existing standards or develop new standards. This lack of detail was not lost on the outgoing IASC Board, which stated in its 2000 annual review:

> IASC's present Framework was written several years ago and, in several sections, the possibility now exists of giving more guidance in the light of more recent experience in developing accounting standards. Equally, recent work has highlighted a number of areas where difficulties exist and the resolution of the difficulties would be helped by further development of the conceptual framework.[15]

This conclusion resulted in the IASB's decision to embark on a review of the "Framework for the Preparation and Presentation of Financial Statements." Differences were also detected in the objectives contained in the two conceptual frameworks. Although both focus on providing information that is useful in making economic decisions, the FASB's conceptual framework establishes the objectives of financial reporting, whereas the IASB's conceptual framework specifies the objectives of financial statements. This difference may gain additional importance given the changing nature of business and corresponding need to improve the information provided to financial statement users. For example, recently there have been suggestions that companies provide more information about their intellectual capital. Given concerns about the reliability of measurements of these assets, their disclosure as supplementary information outside the traditional financial statements and notes may be more appropriate. This treatment would satisfy the FASB's objective but not the IASB's.

Another difference noted was in the form and content of the qualitative characteristics contained in the two conceptual frameworks. The IASB's

---

15. Ibid.

conceptual framework identifies four qualities that make information useful: understandability, relevance, reliability, and comparability. The FASB's framework also identifies these same four characteristics but indicates that they are evident in a hierarchy. Relevance and reliability are considered primary decision-specific qualities, while comparability is considered a secondary and interactive quality and understandability is specified in a separate category because it is a user-specific quality. The FASB indicates that this hierarchy is necessary to improve the usefulness of these qualities when deciding among accounting alternatives. The IASB framework does not prioritize the four principal characteristics, and it indicates that the relative importance of the characteristics in different cases is subject to professional judgment. No guidance is offered regarding the use of the characteristics to make accounting choices.

A difference in the qualitative characteristics concerns reliability. *SFAC No. 2* asserts that an important ingredient of reliability is verifiability; that is, several measurers are likely to obtain the same amount. The IASB framework does not refer to verifiability. Differences in the elements of financial statements are also discovered. The FASB's conceptual framework defines ten elements of financial statements for business enterprises, while the IASB's conceptual framework defines only five; however, the only significant difference is the inclusion of comprehensive income in the FASB's conceptual framework.

Both conceptual frameworks define assets, liabilities, and equity similarly; however, the FASB's framework also defines investments by owners and distributions to owners as separate balance sheet elements. The IASB's conceptual framework does not define these elements separately, but it does refer to them in the section on equity. The FASB's conceptual framework identifies and defines five income statement elements: revenues, expenses, gains, losses, and comprehensive income. The IASB's conceptual framework identifies only two elements: income encompassing both revenues and gains, and expenses encompassing losses.

SFAC No. 6 defines comprehensive income as the change in equity (net assets) of a business enterprise during a period from transactions and other events and circumstances from nonowner sources. The IASB's conceptual framework does not define comprehensive income or its equivalent; however, *IAS No. 1*, "Presentation of Financial Statements," as amended requires that:

> Changes in an entity's equity between balance sheet dates reflect the increase or decrease in net assets during the period. Except for changes resulting from transactions with equity holders acting in their capacity as equity holders, . . . the overall change in equity during a period represents the total amount of income and expenses including gains and losses, generated by the entity's activities during that period (whether those items of income and expenses are recognized in profit or loss or directly as changes in equity).[16]

Consequently, the reporting of comprehensive income is required even though the IASB framework does not acknowledge it as a financial statement element.

---

16. International Accounting Standards Board, *Improvements to International Accounting Standards, IAS No. 1*, "Presentation of Financial Statements" (December 2003), para. 98.

Differences are noted in the area of capital maintenance concepts. *SFAS No. 6* includes a brief discussion of the difference between financial capital maintenance and physical capital maintenance, and asserts that financial capital maintenance is the traditional view and the one used in U.S. GAAP. The IASB's conceptual framework devotes a section to the financial and physical capital maintenance concepts, specifying that the enterprise should select the appropriate concept of capital based on the needs of financial statement users. These approaches are seen as both significantly different and flawed. That is, the FASB's conceptual framework is seen as flawed in that it acknowledges that financial capital maintenance is the traditional view but it does not indicate when it is conceptually acceptable. The IASB framework is viewed as flawed because it suggests that the selection of the capital maintenance to be used be based on users' needs.

Finally, some differences in cash-flow and present-value information are examined. *SFAC No. 7* indicates that present-value techniques should be used to estimate fair value and recommends using an expected cash-flow approach. The IASB's conceptual framework discusses present value only as one of the measurement bases employed in financial statements. The IASB added a present-value project to its agenda in 1998, and it is one of the areas the Board has recommended that the IASB continue to investigate.

Current Developments

In 2005, the IASB and the FASB began a joint agenda project, to revisit their conceptual frameworks for financial accounting and reporting (discussed in more depth in Chapter 2). Currently each Board bases its accounting standards decisions largely on the foundation of objectives, characteristics, definitions, and criteria set forth in their existing conceptual frameworks; and, as discussed above, there are some major differences between these two frameworks. The goals of the new project are to build on the two boards' existing frameworks by refining, updating, completing, and converging them into a common framework that both boards can use in developing new and revised accounting standards.

In announcing this project, the boards noted that a common goal of both the FASB and IASB is for their standards to be principles based. That is, the standards cannot be a collection of conventions but rather must be rooted in fundamental concepts. The standards should result in a coherent financial accounting and reporting system and the fundamental concepts need to constitute a framework that is sound, comprehensive, and internally consistent.

The FASB and IASB also have a common goal of converging their standards. To this end, the boards have been pursuing a number of projects that are aimed at achieving short-term convergence on specific issues, as well as several major projects that are being conducted jointly or in tandem. Moreover, the boards plan to align their agendas more closely to achieve convergence in future standards. The boards will encounter difficulties in converging their standards if they base their decisions on different frameworks.

The IASB-FASB Financial Statement Presentation Project

As noted in Chapter 2, the IASB and the FASB are undertaking a joint project (as a part of the Memorandum of Understanding) to develop a new, joint standard for financial statement presentation. Ultimately, the new standard will replace the existing standards on financial statement presentation: *IAS No. 1*, "Presentation of Financial Statements" (discussed below), and *IAS No. 7*, "Statement of Cash Flows" (discussed in Chapter 7). The main objective of this project is to address fundamental issues relating to presentation and display of information in the financial statements, including

- The relationship between items across financial statements (the cohesiveness objective)
- The disaggregation of information so that it is useful in predicting an entity's future cash flows (the disaggregation objective)
- The provision of information to help users assess an entity's liquidity and financial flexibility (the liquidity and financial flexibility objective)

IAS No. 1 and IFRS No. 1

IAS No. 1, "Presentation of Financial Statements," attempts to address the demand of investors to have transparent information that is comparable over all periods presented, while at the same time giving reporting entities a suitable starting point for their accounting under IFRSs. In developing the standard, the IASB consulted interested parties throughout the world and paid particular attention to the need to ensure that the cost of compliance with the new requirements does not exceed the benefits to users of the financial information. The standard is based on the proposals published as an exposure draft and contains changes that the IASB has made in light of the eighty-three comment letters it received.

In *IAS No. 1*, the IASB discusses the following considerations for preparing financial statements:

1. Fair presentation and compliance with IASB standards
2. Accounting policies
3. Going concern
4. Accrual basis of accounting
5. Consistency of presentation
6. Materiality and aggregation
7. Offsetting
8. Comparative information

IAS No. 1 was one of the thirteen IASs amended by the IASB in 2003. The guidance for applying these considerations was previously less detailed than that provided by U.S. GAAP; however, the revised statement improves disclosure. Some of the most important changes to this statement are as follows:

1. "Presents fairly" is now defined as representing faithfully the effects of transactions and other events in accordance with the definitions and recognition criteria for assets, liabilities, income, and expenses set out in the "Framework for the Preparation and Presentation of Financial Statements." Financial statements that follow IFRS and interpretations of

IFRS, with additional disclosure when necessary, are presumed to achieve a fair presentation.

2. In the extremely rare circumstances when management concludes that compliance with a requirement in an IFRS or an interpretation of a standard would be so misleading that it would conflict with the objective of financial statements set out in the framework:

   • If departure from the requirement is not prohibited by national law, the entity will make that departure and provides specified disclosures.

   • If departure from the requirement is prohibited by national law, the entity must reduce, to the maximum extent possible, the perceived misleading aspects of compliance by providing certain specified disclosures.

3. Standards on the selection of accounting policies currently in *IAS No. 1* are moved to *IAS No. 8*.

4. Disclosure of the following items currently required by *IAS No. 1* is no longer required: an entity's country of incorporation (disclosure of country of domicile is not dropped), the address of its registered office, and the number of its employees.

5. The following accounting policy disclosures are required:

   • Judgments made by management in applying the accounting policies that have the most significant effect on the amounts of items recognized in the financial statements.

   • Key assumptions about the future and other sources of measurement uncertainty that have a significant risk of causing a material adjustment to the carrying amounts of assets and liabilities within the next fiscal year.

6. The Statement of Changes in Equity must now disclose either all changes in equity or changes in equity other than those arising from capital transactions with owners and distributions to owners.

IFRS No. 1, "First Time Adoption of International Reporting Standards," requires an entity to comply with every IASB standard in force in the first year when the entity adopts IFRSs, and with some targeted and specific exceptions after consideration of the cost of full compliance. Under *IFRS No. 1*, entities must explain how the transition to IASB standards affects their reported financial position, financial performance, and cash flows.

IFRS No. 1 requires an entity to comply with each IFRS that has become effective at the reporting date of its first financial statements issued under IASB standards. The following principles apply:

1. Recognize all assets and liabilities whose recognition is required under existing IFRSs.

2. Do not recognize items as assets or liabilities when existing IFRSs do not allow for such recognition.

3. Reclassify assets, liabilities, and equity as necessary to comply with existing IFRSs.

4. Apply existing IFRSs in measuring all recognized assets and liabilities.

Cases

- ## Case 3-1 The Advantages and Disadvantages of Harmonization

The advantages and disadvantages of harmonizing accounting standards were summarized in this chapter.

Required:
Expand on these advantages and disadvantages. [*Hint:* You may wish to consult John N. Turner, "International Harmonization: A Professional Goal," *Journal of Accountancy* (January 1983): 58–59; and Richard K. Goeltz, "International Accounting Harmonization: The Impossible (and Unnecessary?) Dream," *Accounting Horizons* (March 1991), 85–88.]

- ## Case 3-2 The Approaches to Transnational Financial Reporting

Five approaches to transnational financial reporting were identified in the chapter.

Required:
  a. List some of the advantages and disadvantages of each approach.
  b. Which approach do you favor? Why?

- ## Case 3-3 The Purpose and Objectives of the IASB

The International Accounting Standards Committee (IASC) was formed in 1973. In 2001 the IASC was replaced by the International Accounting Standards Board (IASB).

Required:
  a. What was the purpose of the IASB?
  b. How does the IASC attempt to achieve these objectives?

- ## Case 3-4 Qualitative Characteristics Identified by the IASB

The International Accounting Standards Committee's Framework for the Preparation of Financial Statements identifies four primary qualitative characteristics.

Required:
  a. Discuss the four qualitative characteristics identified by the IASB.
  b. Contrast and compare these qualitative characteristics with the qualitative characteristics identified by the FASB in *SFAC No. 2*.

- ## Case 3-5 International versus U.S. Standards

Under U.S. GAAP, property, plant, and equipment are reported at historical cost net of accumulated depreciation. These assets are written down to fair value when it is determined that they have been impaired.

A number of other countries, including Australia, Brazil, England, Mexico, and Singapore, permit the revaluation of property, plant, and equipment to their current cost as of the balance sheet date. The primary argument favoring revaluation is that the historical cost of assets purchased ten, twenty, or more years ago is not meaningful.

A primary argument against revaluation is the lack of objectivity in arriving at current cost estimates, particularly for old assets that either will or cannot be replaced with similar assets or for which no comparable or similar assets are currently available for purchase.

Required:

a. Discuss the qualitative concept of comparability. In your opinion, would the financial statements of companies operating in one of the foreign countries listed above be comparable to a U.S. company's financial statements? Explain.

b. Discuss the concept of reliability. In your opinion, would the amounts reported by U.S. companies for property, plant, and equipment be more or less reliable than the current cost amounts reported by companies in England, Mexico, or elsewhere?

c. Discuss the concept of relevance. In your opinion, would the amounts reported by U.S. companies for property, plant, and equipment be more or less relevant than the current cost amounts reported by companies in England, Mexico, or elsewhere?

• Case 3-6 Accounting Standards

General Motors and Ford use the last-in, first-out (LIFO) method to value their inventories. Honda (of Japan) and Daimler-Benz (manufacturer of Mercedes-Benz of Germany) use the first-in, first-out (FIFO) method. Under LIFO, recent costs are expensed as cost of goods sold; under FIFO, older costs are expensed as cost of goods sold.

Required:

a. Given the income statement effects of LIFO versus FIFO, how will the balance sheet inventory amounts differ between General Motors and Ford versus Honda and Daimler-Benz? In other words, will inventory be reported amounts representing recent costs or older historical costs? In your opinion, which balance sheet amounts would be more useful to financial statement users in making decisions to buy or sell shares of a company's stock?

b. Discuss the concept of conservatism. In your opinion, which is more conservative, General Motors, and Ford or Honda and Daimler-Benz? Explain.

FASB ASC Research

For each of the following research cases, search the FASB ASC database for information to address each questions. Cut and paste the FASB requirements that support your responses. Then summarize briefly what your responses are, citing the pronouncements and paragraphs used to support your responses.

• FASB ASC 3-1 IASB and GAAP

Search the FASB ASC database to determine if International Accounting Board pronouncements are considered GAAP. Cite and copy your answer.

• FASB ASC 3-2 Share-Based Payments

The SEC issued an opinion on the whether there are differences in the measurement provisions for share-based payment arrangements with employees under International Accounting Standards Board International Financial Reporting Standard 2, Share-based Payment (IFRS 2) and Statement 123R (Topic 718)]. Cite and copy this opinion.

Room for Debate

• Debate 3-1 Principles of Consolidation

The IASB framework for preparing and presenting financial statements defines assets as resources controlled by an enterprise as a result of past events from which future economic benefits are expected to flow to the enterprise. This definition is similar to that found in the FASB's conceptual framework.

As discussed in Chapter 15, the IASB requires consolidation of a subsidiary when the parent has the ability to control the subsidiary. In these cases, the subsidiary's assets are added to those of the parent company, and the total is reported in the balance sheet of the parent company. Under *SFAS No. 94*, consolidation is required only for those subsidiaries when the parent company has a majority ownership. The FASB has proposed that U.S. GAAP be changed to require consolidation for subsidiaries when the parent company controls the use of subsidiary assets. One goal of this proposal is harmonization of accounting standards among countries.

Team Debate

Team 1: Assume that you do not believe that control of subsidiary assets implies that those assets are, in substance, parent company assets. Argue for the FASB proposal based on the premise that harmonization of accounting standards among countries should be the paramount consideration. Cite relevant aspects of the U.S. and IASB conceptual frameworks in your argument.

Team 2: Assume that you do not believe that control of subsidiary assets implies that those assets are, in substance, parent company assets. Argue against the FASB proposal based on the premise that harmonization of accounting standards among countries should not be the paramount consideration. Cite relevant aspects of the U.S. and IASB conceptual frameworks.

Research Methodology and Theories on the Uses of Accounting Information

To have a science is to have recognized a domain and a set of phenomena in that domain, and next to have defined a theory whose inputs and outputs are descriptions of phenomena (the first are observations, the second are predictions), whose terms describe the underlying reality of the domain.[1] In Chapter 2, the FASB's Conceptual Framework Project was introduced as the state-of-the-art theory of accounting. However, this theory does not explain how accounting information is used, because very little predictive behavior is explained by existing accounting theory. Over the years, accountants have done a great deal of theorizing, providing new insights and various ways of looking at accounting and its outcomes. A distinction can be made between theorizing and theory construction. Theorizing is the first step to theory construction, but it is frequently lacking because its results are untested or untestable value judgments.[2]

In the following pages, we first introduce several research methods that might be used to develop theories of accounting and its uses. Next we discuss the use of accounting information by investors and a number of theories on the outcomes of the use of accounting information, including fundamental analysis, the efficient market hypothesis, the capital asset pricing model, agency theory, human information processing, and critical perspective research. None of these theories is completely accepted; consequently, each of them is somewhere along the path between theorizing and theory.

1. Peter Caws, "Accounting Research—Science or Methodology," in *Research Methodology in Accounting*, ed. Robert R. Sterling (Lawrence, KS: Scholars Book Co., 1972), 71.

2. Edwin H. Caplan, "Accounting Research as an Information Source for Theory Construction," in Sterling (ed.), *Research Methodology in Accounting*, 46.

Research Methodology

Accounting theory can be developed by using several research methodologies. Among the more commonly identified methodologies are (1) the deductive approach, (2) the inductive approach, (3) the pragmatic approach, (4) the scientific method of inquiry, (5) the ethical approach, and (6) the behavioral approach. In this section we briefly describe each of these research approaches. In addition, we present the scientific method of inquiry, which is essentially a combination of deductive and inductive reasoning, as a guide to research in accounting theory development.

Deductive Approach

The deductive approach to the development of theory begins with establish objectives. Once the objectives are identified, certain key definitions and assumptions must be stated. The researcher must then develop a logical structure for accomplishing the objectives, based on the definitions and assumptions. This methodology is often described as "going from the general to the specific." If accounting theory is to be developed using the deductive approach, the researcher must develop a structure that includes the objectives of accounting, the environment in which accounting is operating, the definitions and assumptions of the system, and the procedures and practices, all of which follow a logical pattern.

The deductive approach is essentially a mental or "armchair" type of research. The validity of any accounting theory developed through this process is highly dependent on the researcher's ability to identify correctly and relate the various components of the accounting process in a logical manner. To the extent that the researcher is in error as to the objectives, the environment, or the ability of the procedures to accomplish the objectives, the conclusions reached will also be in error.

Inductive Approach

The inductive approach to research emphasizes making observations and drawing conclusions from those observations. Thus this method is described as "going from the specific to the general" because the researcher generalizes about the universe on the basis of limited observations of specific situations.

Accounting Principles Board Statement No. 4 is an example of inductive research.[3] The generally accepted accounting principles (GAAP) described in the statement were based primarily on observation of current practice. In addition, the APB acknowledged that the then-current principles had not been derived from the environment, objectives, and basic features of financial accounting. Thus the study was essentially inductive in approach.

Pragmatic Approach

The pragmatic approach to theory development is based on the concept of utility or usefulness. Once the problem has been identified, the researcher attempts to find a utilitarian solution; that is, one that will resolve the problem. This does not suggest that the optimum solution has been found or that the solution will

3. This statement was an attempt by the APB to develop a theory of accounting.

accomplish some stated objective. (Actually, the only objective may be to find a "workable" solution to a problem.) Thus any answers obtained through the pragmatic approach should be viewed as tentative solutions to problems.

Unfortunately in accounting, most of the current principles and practices have resulted from the pragmatic approach, and the solutions have been adopted as GAAP rather than as an expedient resolution to a problem. As noted in Chapter 2, the Sanders, Hatfield, and Moore study, *A Statement of Accounting Principles*, was a pragmatic approach to theory construction. Unfortunately, much subsequent theory development also used this approach. As a result, the accounting profession must frequently admit that a certain practice is followed merely because "that is the way we have always done it," which is a most unsatisfactory reason, particularly when such questions arise in legal suits.

Scientific Method of Inquiry

The scientific method of inquiry, as the name suggests, was developed for the natural and physical sciences and not specifically for social sciences such as accounting. There are some clear limitations on the application of this research methodology to accounting; for example, the influence of people and the economic environment make it impossible to hold the variables constant. Nevertheless, an understanding of the scientific method can provide useful insights as to how research should be conducted.

Conducting research by the scientific method involves five major steps, which may also have several substeps:

1. Identify and state the problem to be studied.
2. State the hypotheses to be tested.
3. Collect the data that seem necessary for testing the hypotheses.
4. Analyze and evaluate the data in relation to the hypotheses.
5. Draw a tentative conclusion.

Although the steps are listed sequentially, there is considerable back-and-forth movement between the steps. For example, at the point of stating the hypotheses, it may be necessary to go back to step 1 and state the problem more precisely. Again, when collecting data, it may be necessary to clarify the problem or the hypotheses, or both. This back-and-forth motion continues throughout the process and is a major factor in the strength of the scientific method.

The back-and-forth movement involved in the scientific method also suggests why it is difficult to do purely deductive or inductive research. Once the problem has been identified, the statement of hypotheses is primarily a deductive process, but the researcher must have previously made some observations in order to formulate expectations. The collection of data is primarily an inductive process, but determining what to observe and which data to collect will be influenced by the hypotheses. Thus the researcher may, at any given moment, emphasize induction or deduction; but each is influenced by the other, and the emphasis is continually shifting so that the two approaches are coordinate aspects of one method.

Unfortunately, the scientific method of inquiry has received only limited attention in accounting research. Those procedures found to have "utility" have become generally accepted regardless of whether they were tested for any relevance to a particular hypothesis.

Other Research Approaches

Various writers have also discussed the ethical and behavioral approaches to research as being applicable to the development of accounting theory. Others view these approaches as supportive rather than as specific methods for research; that is, they can, and should, influence the researcher's attitude but cannot by themselves lead to tightly reasoned conclusions.

The ethical approach, which is attributed to DR Scott,[4] emphasizes the concepts of truth, justice, and fairness. No one would argue with these concepts as guides to actions by the researcher, but there is always the question of fair to whom, for what purpose, and under what circumstances. Because of such questions, this approach may be difficult to use in the development of accounting theory; but it has gained renewed stature due to the emergence of a new school of accounting theory development, "critical perspective" research, which is discussed later in the chapter.

Accounting is recognized as a practice whose consequences are mediated by the human and social contexts in which it operates and the ways in which it intersects with other organizational and social phenomena. As a consequence, both the behavioral and the economic functioning of accounting are now of interest, and questions are being asked about how accounting information is actually used and how it sometimes seems to generate seemingly undesirable and often unanticipated consequences.[5] From this realization has come the school of accounting research and theory development, behavioral accounting research (BAR). BAR is the study of the behavior of accountants or the behavior of nonaccountants as they are influenced by accounting functions and reports,[6] and it is based on research activities in the behavioral sciences. Since the purpose of accounting is to provide information for decision makers, it seems appropriate to be concerned with how preparers and users react to information. BAR has been seen as studying relevant issues but as not having the impact on practice that it should, given the importance of these issues.[7]

The Outcomes of Providing Accounting Information

The development of a theory of accounting will not solve all the needs of the users of accounting information. Theories must also be developed that predict market reactions to accounting information and how users react to accounting data. The following section describes the use of accounting and other information by individuals and presents several theories on how users react to accounting data.

4. DR Scott, "The Basis for Accounting Principles," *The Accounting Review* (December 1941): 341–49.

5. Anthony G. Hopwood, "Behavioral Accounting in Retrospect and Prospect," *Behavioral Research in Accounting* (1989), 2.

6. Thomas R. Hofstedt and James C. Kinard, "A Strategy for Behavioral Accounting Research," *The Accounting Review* (January 1970), 43.

7. Edwin H. Caplan, "Behavioral Accounting—A Personal View," *Behavioral Research in Accounting* (1989), 115.

Fundamental Analysis

Chapter 2 noted that the FASB has indicated that the primary goal of accounting information is to provide investors with relevant and reliable information so they can make informed investment decisions. Individual investors make the following investment decisions:

- Buy—a potential investor decides to purchase a particular security on the basis of available information.
- Hold—an actual investor decides to retain a particular security on the basis of available information.
- Sell—an actual investor decides to dispose of a particular security on the basis of available information.

Individual investors use all available financial information to assist in acquiring or disposing of the securities contained in their investment portfolios that are consistent with their risk preferences and the expected returns offered by their investments. The decision process used by individual investors is termed fundamental analysis. *Fundamental analysis* is an attempt to identify individual securities that are mispriced by reviewing all available financial information. These data are then used to estimate the amount and timing of future cash flows offered by investment opportunities and to incorporate the associated degree of risk to arrive at an expected share price for a security. This discounted share price is then compared to the current market price of the security, thereby allowing the investor to make buy–hold–sell decisions.

Investment analysis may be performed by investors themselves or by security analysts. Because of their training and experience, security analysts are able to process and disseminate financial information more accurately and economically than are individual investors. Security analysts and individual investors use published financial statements, quarterly earnings reports, and the information contained in the Management Discussion and Analysis section of the annual report, particularly those sections containing forward-looking information and the company's plans. Upon review of these information sources, security analysts frequently make their own quarterly earnings estimates for the most widely held companies. Subsequently, as company quarterly information is released, security analysts comment on the company's performance and may make buy–hold–sell recommendations.

Security analysts' estimates and recommendations may affect the market price of a company's stock. For example, on April 17, 2000, IBM released its quarterly earnings report, after the stock market had closed. The report indicated that IBM's first-quarter performance had been better than anticipated. Nevertheless, the company's stock dropped $6.50 from $111.50 to $105 because several security analysts had lowered their ratings on the stock based on IBM's lowered revenue expectations for the second quarter of 2000. The decline in the value of IBM's stock was probably influenced by the fact that the overall stock market also declined on April 18, 2000, but this example illustrates how investor perceptions of future expectations can affect stock prices.

One school of thought, the *efficient market hypothesis*, holds that fundamental analysis is not a useful investment decision tool because a stock's current price reflects the market's consensus of its value. As a result, individual investors are not able to identify mispriced securities. The effect of market forces on the price of securities and the efficient market hypothesis are discussed in the following sections.

The Efficient Market Hypothesis

Economists have argued for many years that in a free market economy with perfect competition, price is determined by (1) the availability of the product (supply) and (2) the desire to possess that product (demand). Accordingly, the price of a product is determined by the consensus in the marketplace. This process is generally represented by the following diagram.

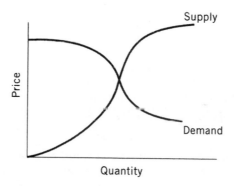

Economists also argue that this model is not completely operational in the marketplace because the following assumptions about the perfectly competitive market are routinely violated by the nature of our economic system.

1. All economic units possess complete knowledge of the economy.
2. All goods and services in the economy are completely mobile and can be easily shifted within the economy.
3. Each buyer and seller must be so small in relation to the total supply and demand that neither has an influence on the price or demand in total.
4. There are no artificial restrictions placed on demand, supply, or prices of goods and services.

The best example of the supply and demand model may be in the securities market, particularly when we consider that stock exchanges provide a relatively efficient distribution system and that information concerning securities is available through many outlets. Examples of these information sources are

- Published financial statements from the companies
- Quarterly earnings reports released by the corporation through the news media
- Reports of management changes released through the news media
- Competitor financial information released through financial reports or the news media
- Contract awards announced by the government or private firms
- Information disseminated to stockholders at annual stockholders' meetings

Under the supply and demand model, price is determined by the consensus of purchasers' knowledge of relevant information about the product. This model has been refined in the securities market to become known as the efficient market hypothesis (EMH). The issues addressed by the EMH are (1) what information about a company is of value to investors, and (2) does the form of the disclosure of various types of corporate information affect the understandability of that information?

Proponents of this theory claim that financial markets price assets at their intrinsic worth, given all publicly available information. Therefore the price of a company's stock accurately reflects the company's value after incorporating the information available on company earnings, business prospects, and other relevant information. Discussions of the EMH in academic literature have defined all available information in three different ways, resulting in three separate forms of the EMH: the *weak form*, the *semistrong form*, and the *strong form*. The EMH holds that an investor cannot make an *excess return* (a return above what should be expected for a group of securities, given market conditions and the risk associated with the securities) by knowledge of particular pieces of information. The three forms of the EMH differ with respect to their definitions of available information.

Weak Form

The weak form of the EMH is essentially an extension of the random walk theory expressed in the financial management literature. According to this theory, the historical price of a stock provides an unbiased estimate of its future price. Several studies have supported this argument.[8] However, the argument that stock prices are random does not mean that fluctuation takes place without cause or reason. On the contrary, it suggests that price changes take place because of investor knowledge about perceived earnings potential or alternative investment opportunities.

According to the weak form of the EMH, an investor cannot make excess returns simply on the basis of knowledge of past prices. For example, suppose a certain group of securities with a known risk yields an average return on investment of 10 percent (this average is composed of returns above and below that figure). According to the weak form of the EMH, the stock market incorporates all information on past prices into the determination of the current price. Therefore the charting of the trends of security prices provides no additional information for the investor. If this form of the EMH is correct, an investor could do just as well by randomly selecting a portfolio of securities as he or she could by charting the past prices of securities and selecting the portfolio on that basis. (It is important to note that the EMH is based on a portfolio of securities and average returns on investments, not on individual purchases of securities.) The implication of the weak form of the EMH is that some of the information provided by security analysts is useless. That is, security analysts have maintained that trends in prices are good indicators of future prices. However, knowledge of this information will not aid an investor, because it has already been incorporated into the price determination process in the marketplace.

---

8. See, for example, E. Fama, "The Behavior of Stock Market Prices," *Journal of Business* (January 1965), 285–99.

Semistrong Form

The difference between the weak, semistrong, and strong forms of the EMH lies in the amount of information assumed to be incorporated into the determination of security prices. Under the semistrong form of the EMH, all publicly available information including past stock prices is assumed to be important in determining security prices. In other words, if this form of the EMH is correct, no investor can make an excess return by use of publicly available information because this information has already been considered by the marketplace in establishing security prices. The implication of the semistrong form of the EMH for accountants is that footnote disclosure is just as relevant as information in the body of financial statements. In addition, it suggests that the accounting procedures adopted by a particular organization will have no effect if an investor can convert to the desired method. The results of studies on this form of the EMH have been generally supportive.

Strong Form

According to the strong form of the EMH, all information, including security price trends, publicly available information, and insider information, is impounded into security prices in such a way as to leave no opportunity for excess returns. The implication of this form of the EMH for accountants is that the marketplace will consider all information available, whether external or internal. That is, as soon as anyone in a corporation knows a piece of information, that information is immediately incorporated into determining a security's price in the market. In effect, the strong form implies that published accounting information is no more valuable than any other type of available information, whether or not publicly available.

Most of the evidence testing this form of the EMH suggests that it is not valid. However, one study of mutual funds, whose managers are more likely to have insider information, indicated that such funds did no better than an individual investor could expect to do if he or she had purchased a diversified portfolio with similar risk. In fact, many did worse than randomly selected portfolios would have done.[9] This study tends to support the strong form of the EMH.

The EMH presents an interesting research challenge for accountants. The market crash of 2008 suggests that the market failed to incorporate some pieces of information such as the "housing bubble" or the unsustainable levels of risk offered by mortgage-backed securities. Research strategies must continue to be designed to test each of the EMH forms so that more solid conclusions can be drawn. This research is important because it provides evidence on the manner in which information about business enterprises is incorporated into the price of corporate securities, and it may allow investor-oriented accounting principles to be developed.

The Implications of Efficient Market Research

The EMH has implications for the development of accounting theory. Some critics of accounting have argued that the lack of uniformity in accounting principles has allowed corporate managers to manipulate earnings and mislead investors.[10]

9. See, for example, J. Williamson, "Measuring Mutual Fund Performance," *Financial Analyst's Journal* (November–December 1972), 78–84.

10. Raymond J. Ball and Philip R. Brown, "An Empirical Evaluation of Accounting Income Numbers," *Journal of Accounting Research* (Autumn 1968): 159–78.

This argument is based on the assumption that accounting reports are a primary source of information on a business organization. The results of EMH research suggest that stock prices are not determined solely by accounting reports. This conclusion has led researchers to investigate how accounting earnings are related to stock prices.

The results of these investigations imply that accounting earnings are correlated with security returns. Other accounting research relies on research findings that support the EMH to test market perceptions of accounting numbers and financial disclosures. This research is based on the premise that an efficient market implies that the market price of a firm's shares reflects the consensus of investors regarding the value of the firm. Thus, if accounting information or other financial disclosures incorporate items that affect a firm's value, they should be reflected in the firm's security price.[11]

An additional issue is the relationship between EMH and the economic consequences argument introduced in Chapter 1. The EMH holds that stock prices will not be influenced by changed accounting practices that do not affect profitability or cash flows. However, history indicates that various stakeholders have attempted to lobby the FASB over such changes. Examples of these efforts include accounting for the investment tax credit and accounting for foreign currency translation (discussed in Chapter 16). Some accountants claim that this is an example of existing theory failing to fully explain current practice and is consistent with steps 3 and 4 of the Kuhnian approach to scientific progress discussed by *SATTA* and reviewed in Chapter 2. If so, an existing paradigm is found to be deficient and the search for a new paradigm begins. These accountants generally maintain that the positive theory of accounting (discussed later in the chapter) provides a better description of existing accounting practice.

The Capital Asset Pricing Model

As indicated earlier in the chapter, investors often wish to use accounting information in an attempt to minimize risk and maximize returns. It is generally assumed that rational individual investors are risk averse. Consequently, riskier investments must offer higher rates of return in order to attract investors. From an accounting standpoint, this means investors need information on both expected risks and returns. The capital asset pricing model (CAPM) is an attempt to deal with both risks and returns. The actual rate of return to an investor from buying a common stock and holding it for a period of time is calculated by adding the dividends to the increase (or decrease) in value of the security during the holding period and dividing this amount by the purchase price of the security, or

$$\frac{\text{Dividends} + \text{increase (or} - \text{decrease) in value}}{\text{Purchase price}}$$

11. Examples of this type of research include G. Peter Wilson, "The Incremental Information Content of the Accrual and Funds Components of Earnings after Controlling for Earnings," *The Accounting Review* (April 1987), 293–321; Thomas L. Stober, "The Incremental Information Content of Financial Statement Disclosures: The Case of LIFO Inventory Liquidations," *Journal of Accounting Research* (Supplement, 1986): 138–60; and Bruce Bublitz and Michael Ettredge, "The Information in Discretionary Outlays: Advertising, Research, and Development," *The Accounting Review* (January 1989), 108–24.

Since stock prices fluctuate in response to changes in investor expectations about the firm's future cash flows, common stocks are considered risky investments. In contrast, U.S. Treasury notes are not considered risky investments, because the expected and stated rates of return are equal (assuming the T-bill is held to maturity). Risk is defined as the possibility that actual returns will deviate from expected returns, and the amount of potential fluctuation determines the degree of risk.

A basic assumption of the CAPM is that risky stocks can be combined into a portfolio that is less risky than any of the individual common stocks that make up that portfolio. This diversification attempts to match the common stocks of companies in such a manner that environmental forces causing a poor performance by one company will simultaneously cause a good performance by another—for example, purchasing the common stock of an oil company and an airline company. Although such negative relationships are rare in our society, diversification will reduce risk.

Types of Risk

Some risk is peculiar to the common stock of a particular company. For example, the value of a company's stock may decline when the company loses a major customer, as when the Ford Motor Company lost Hertz as a purchaser of rental cars. On the other hand, overall environmental forces cause fluctuations in the stock market that affect all stock prices, such as the oil crisis in 1974.

These two types of risk are termed unsystematic risk and systematic risk. *Unsystematic risk* is that portion of a company's particular risk that can be diversified away. *Systematic risk* is the nondiversifiable portion that is related to overall movements in the stock market and is consequently unavoidable. Earlier in the chapter, we indicated that the EMH suggests that investors cannot discover undervalued or overvalued securities because the market consensus will quickly incorporate all available information into a firm's stock price. However, financial information about a firm can help determine the amount of systematic risk associated with a particular stock.

As securities are added to a portfolio, unsystematic risk is reduced. Empirical research has demonstrated that unsystematic risk is virtually eliminated in portfolios of thirty to forty randomly selected stocks. However, if a portfolio contains many common stocks in the same or related industries, a much larger number of stocks must be acquired because the rate of returns on such stocks are positively correlated and will tend to increase or decrease in the same direction. The CAPM also assumes that investors are risk averse; consequently, investors will demand additional returns for taking additional risks. As a result, high-risk securities must be priced to yield higher expected returns than lower risk securities in the marketplace.

A simple equation can be formulated to express the relationship between risk and return. This equation uses the risk-free return (the T-bill rate) as its foundation and is stated as

$$R_s = R_f + R_p$$

where

R_s = the expected return on a given risky security
R_f = the risk-free rate
R_p = the risk premium

Since investors can eliminate the risk associated with acquiring a particular company's common stock by purchasing diversified portfolios, they are not compensated for bearing unsystematic risk. And since well-diversified investors are exposed to systematic risk only, investors using the CAPM as the basis for acquiring their portfolios will be subject only to systematic risk. Consequently, systematic risk is the only relevant type, and investors will be rewarded with higher expected returns for bearing market-related risk that will not be affected by company-specific risk.

The measure of the parallel relationship of a particular common stock with the overall trend in the stock market is termed beta (β). β may be viewed as a gauge of a particular stock's volatility to the total stock market.

A stock with a β of 1.00 has a perfect relationship to the performance of the overall market as measured by a market index such as the Dow-Jones Industrials or the Standard & Poor's 500-stock index. Stocks with a β of greater than 1.00 tend to rise and fall by a greater percentage than the market, whereas stocks with a β of less than 1.00 are less likely to rise and fall than the general market index over the selected period of analysis. Therefore β can be viewed as a stock's sensitivity to market changes and as a measure of systematic risk.

A company's risk premium (the risk adjustment for the amount by which a company's return is expected to exceed that of a risk-free security) is equivalent to its β multiplied by the difference between the market return and the risk-free rate. The risk-return equation can thus be restated to incorporate β, by replacing the risk premium, R_p, with its equivalent, $\beta_s (R_m - R_f)$, as follows:

$$\text{The risk-return equation: } R_s = R_f + R_p$$
$$\text{Restating to incorporate } \beta\text{: } R_s = R_f + \beta_s (R_m - R_f)$$

where

R_s = the stock's expected return

R_f = the risk-free rate

R_m = the expected return on the stock market as a whole

β = the stock's beta, which is calculated over some historical period

The final component of the CAPM reflects how the risk—expected return relationship and securities prices are related. As indicated above, the expected return on a security equals the risk-free rate plus a risk premium. In the competitive and efficient financial markets assumed by the CAPM, no security will be able to sell at low prices to yield more than its appropriate return, nor will a security be able to sell at higher than market price and offer a low return. Consequently, the CAPM holds that a security's price will not be affected by unsystematic risk and that securities offering relatively higher risk (higher βs) will be priced relatively lower than securities offering relatively lower risk.

A major concern over the use of the CAPM is the relationship of past and future Betas. Researchers question whether past Betas can be used to predict future risk and return relationships. In other words, is a company's β stable over time? Much of this concern has now been alleviated because empirical research has supported the contention that past Betas are good predictors of future stock prices.

The CAPM has also been criticized for contributing to the United States' competitiveness problem. According to critics, U.S. corporate managers using the CAPM are forced into making safe investments with predictable short-term returns instead of investing for the long term. This is particularly true when companies with higher Betas attempt to invest in new ventures. Since a high β is seen as evidence of a risky investment, these companies are forced to accept only new projects that promise high rates of return. As a result, researchers have been attempting to develop new models that view the markets as complex and evolving systems that will enable business managers to adopt a more long-range viewpoint.

The CAPM is relevant for accounting theory development because researchers have used it to test hypotheses that rely on the EMH. For example, researchers have estimated the expected returns of firms using CAPM to discern whether the release of accounting information has information content. The expected returns are compared to actual returns, and the residuals (the differences between expected and actual returns) are examined to see if there is a market reaction to the information release. This approach could be used to see if a new FASB pronouncement provides information that was not previously reflected in security prices.

Normative versus Positive Accounting Theory

Financial accounting theory attempts to specify which events to record, how the recorded data should be manipulated, and how the data should be presented. As discussed earlier, accounting theory has developed pragmatically. If a practice or method has been used in the past by a large number of accountants to satisfy a particular reporting need, its continued use is acceptable. As noted in Chapter 2, few attempts to develop a comprehensive theory of accounting were made before World War II. Since then, there has been an increasing demand for a theory of accounting. In recent decades, efforts to satisfy this demand have permeated accounting literature. These efforts rely heavily on theories developed in mathematics, economics, and finance.

Recall from Chapter 1 that there are two basic types of theory: normative and positive. Normative theories are based on sets of goals that proponents maintain prescribe the way things should be. However, no set of goals is universally accepted by accountants. As a consequence, normative accounting theories are usually acceptable only to those individuals who agree with the assumptions on which they are based. Nevertheless, most accounting theories are normative because they are based on certain objectives of financial reporting.

Positive theories attempt to explain observed phenomena. They describe what is without indicating how things should be. The extreme diversity of accounting practices and application has made development of a comprehensive description of accounting difficult. Concurrently, to become a theory, description must have explanatory value. For example, not only must the use of historical cost be observed, but under positive theory that use must also be explained. Positive accounting theory has arisen because existing theory does not fully explain accounting practice. For example, the EMH indicates that knowledge of all publicly available information will not give an investor an advantage, because the market has compounded the information into current security prices. If so, the market should react only to information that reflects or is expected to affect a company's cash flows. Yet, various interest groups continue to lobby the FASB and Congress over accounting policy changes that do not have cash-flow consequences.

Agency Theory

Attempts to describe financial statements and the accounting theories from which they originate, as well as to explain their development based on the economic theories of prices, agency, public choice, and economic regulation, have been categorized as agency theory. *Agency theory* is a positive accounting theory that attempts to explain accounting practices and standards. This research takes the EMH as a given and views accounting as the supplier of information to the capital markets.

The basic assumption of agency theory is that individuals maximize their own expected utilities and are resourceful and innovative in doing so. Therefore the issue raised by agency theory is as follows: What is an individual's expected benefit from a particular course of action? Stated differently, how might a manager or stockholder benefit from a corporate decision? It should also be noted that the interests of managers and stockholders are frequently not the same.

An *agency* is defined as a consensual relationship between two parties, whereby one party (agent) agrees to act on behalf of the other party (principal). For example, the relationship between shareholders and managers of a corporation is an agency relationship, as is the relationship between managers and auditors and, to a greater or lesser degree, that between auditors and shareholders.

An agency relationship exists between shareholders and managers because the owners don't have the training or expertise to manage the firm themselves, have other occupations, and are scattered around the country and the world. Consequently, the stockholders must employ someone to represent them. These employees are agents who are entrusted with making decisions in the shareholders' best interests. However, the shareholders cannot observe all of the actions and decisions made by the agents, so a threat exists that the agents will act to maximize their own wealth rather than that of the stockholders. This is the major agency theory issue—the challenge of ensuring that the manager/agent operates on behalf of the shareholders/principals and maximizes their wealth rather than his or her own.

Inherent in agency theory is the assumption that a conflict of interest exists between the owners (shareholders) and the managers. The conflict occurs when the self-interest of management is not aligned with the interests of shareholders. Shareholders desire to maximize profits on their investment in the company; instead, managers may be maximizing their own utilities at the expense of the shareholders. Under this scenario, shareholder wealth is not maximized. For example, a manager may choose accounting alternatives that increase accounting earnings when a management compensation scheme is tied to those earnings. Because such choices affect only how financial information is measured and thus the amount of reported earnings, they have no real economic effect in and of themselves and thus provide no benefit to the shareholder. At the same time, shareholder wealth declines as management compensation increases.

Agency relationships involve costs to the principals. The costs of an agency relationship have been defined as the sum of (1) monitoring expenditures by the principal, (2) bonding expenditures by the agent, and (3) the residual loss.[12] Watts explains these concepts as follows:

---

12. M. Johnson and W. H. Meckling, "Theory of the Firm: Managerial Behavior, Agency Costs and Ownership Structures," *Journal of Financial Economics* (October 1976): 308.

> Monitoring expenditures are expenditures by the principal to "control" the agent's behavior (e.g., costs of measuring and observing the agent's behavior, costs of establishing compensation policies, etc.). The agent has incentives to make expenditures to guarantee that he will not take certain actions to harm the principal's interest or that he will compensate the principal if he does. These are bonding costs. Finally, even with monitoring and bonding expenditures, the actions taken by the agent will differ from the actions the principal would take himself . . . the wealth effect of this divergence in actions [is defined] as "residual loss."[13]

Examples of monitoring costs are exand internal auditors, the SEC, capital markets including underwriters and lenders, boards of directors, and dividend payments. Examples of bonding costs include managerial compensation, including stock options and bonuses and the threat of a takeover if mismanagement causes a reduction in stock prices.

Since agency theory holds that all individuals will act to maximize their own utility, managers and shareholders would be expected to incur bonding and monitoring costs as long as those costs are less than the reduction in the residual loss. For instance, a management compensation plan that ties management wealth to shareholder wealth will reduce the agency cost of equity, or a bond covenant that restricts dividend payments will reduce the agency costs of debt. Examples of this last type of costs were included in corporate charters as early as the 1600s. According to agency theory, in an unregulated economy, the preparation of financial statements will be determined by the effect of such statements on agency costs. That is, financial statements would tend to be presented more often by companies with many bond covenants (e.g., restrictions on dividends or relatively more outside debt). Similarly, the greater the value of a company's fixed assets, the more likely a charge for maintenance, repair, or depreciation will be included in the financial statements.

The conclusion drawn by agency theory is that multiple methods of accounting for similar circumstances have developed from the desires of various individuals, such as managers, shareholders, and bondholders, to minimize agency costs.

Because private sector regulations and federal legislation help determine the items disclosed in financial statements, the effects of regulation and the political process must be added to the results of agency relationships. However, the regulation process is affected by external pressures. Groups of individuals may have incentives to band together to cause the government to transfer wealth, as in farm subsidies. The justification for these transfers is that they are "in the public interest." In addition, elected officials and special interest groups may use the so-called high profits of corporations to create crises, which are solved by wealth transfers "in the public interest." A prime example is the "windfall profits" tax enacted at the time of the 1974 oil crisis.

The larger a corporation is, the more susceptible it is to political scrutiny and subsequent wealth transfers. Therefore the larger a company is, the more likely it is to choose accounting alternatives that minimize net income; this is termed the

---

13. R. Watts, "Corporate Financial Statements, a Product of the Market and Political Processes," *Australian Journal of Management* (September 1977): 131.

visibility theory of accounting.[14] Conversely, small companies often have incentives to show greater net income in order to increase borrowing potential and available capital. Agency theory holds that these varying desires are a reason for the diversity of acceptable accounting practices.

Agency theory also attributes the preponderance of normative theories of accounting to the influence of the political processes. When a crisis develops, elected officials base their positions on "public interest" arguments. These positions are frequently grounded in the notion that the problem is caused by an inefficiency in the market that can be remedied only by government intervention. Elected officials then seek justification of their position in the form of normative theories supporting that position. They also tend to look for theories prescribing accounting procedures that should be used to increase the information available to investors or make the market more efficient.

The advocates of agency theory maintain that it helps explain financial statements and the absence of a comprehensive theory of accounting. However, the basic assumption that everyone acts to maximize his or her own expected utility causes this theory to be politically and socially unacceptable. Agency theory advocates maintain that this is true regardless of how logically sound the theory may be, or even how well it may stand up to empirical testing. For example, if an elected official supported a theory that explained his or her actions as those that maximize his or her own utility, rather than the public good, the official would not be maximizing his or her own utility.

Agency theory may help explain the lack of a comprehensive accounting theory. It implies that because of the diverse interests involved in financial reporting, a framework of accounting theory cannot be developed. However, there is an even more basic reason that agency theory will have limited direct impact on financial accounting. Agency theory is a descriptive theory in that it helps to explain why a diversity of accounting practices exists. Therefore, even if subsequent testing supports this theory, it will *not* identify the correct accounting procedures to be used in various circumstances; and as a result, accounting practice will not be changed.

Human Information Processing

The annual reports of large corporations provide investors with vast amounts of information. These reports may include a balance sheet, an income statement, a statement of cash flows, numerous footnotes to the financial statements, a five-year summary of operations, a description of the various activities of the corporation, a message to the stockholders from the top management of the corporation, a discussion and analysis by management of the annual operations and the company's plans for the future, and the report of the company's independent certified public accountant.

The disclosure of all this information is intended to aid investors and potential investors in making buy–hold–sell decisions about the company's securities. Studies attempting to assess an individual's ability to use information have been broadly classified as human information processing (HIP) research. The issue

---

14. See, for example, J. R. Hand and T. R. Skantz, "The Economic Determinants of Accounting Choices: The Unique Case of Equity Carve-outs under SAB No. 51," *Journal of Accounting and Economics* 24, no. 2 (1998): 175–203.

addressed by these studies is, how do individuals use available information? Consequently, HIP research can be used to determine how individual investors make decisions.

In general, HIP research has indicated that individuals have a limited ability to process large amounts of information.[15] This finding has three main consequences:

1. An individual's perception of information is quite selective. That is, since people are capable of comprehending only a small part of their environment, their anticipation of what they expect to perceive about a particular situation will determine to a large extent what they do perceive.

2. Since individuals make decisions on the basis of a small part of the total information available, they do not have the capacity to make optimal decisions.

3. Since individuals are incapable of integrating a great deal of information, they process information in a sequential fashion.

In summary, individuals use a selective, stepwise information processing system. This system has limited capacity, and any uncertainty that arises is frequently ignored.[16]

These findings may have far-reaching disclosure implications for accountants. The current trend of the FASB and SEC is to require the disclosure of more and more information. But if the tentative conclusions of the HIP research are correct, these additional disclosures may have an effect opposite to that intended. The goal of the FASB and SEC is to provide all relevant information so that individuals may make informed decisions about a company. However, the annual reports may already contain more information than can be adequately and efficiently processed by individuals.

Research is needed to determine how the selective processing of information by individuals is processed into the marketplace consensus described by the EMH and to determine the most relevant information to include in corporate annual reports. Once these goals have been accomplished, accountants will have taken a giant step in determining what information to disclose about accounting entities.

Critical Perspective Research

Our earlier discussion of EMH, CAPM, agency theory, and HIP includes references to research studies that attempted to test the hypotheses on which these theories were built. Such testing carries the assumptions that knowledge of facts can be gained by observation and that accounting research is completely objective. Critical perspective research rejects the view that knowledge of accounting is grounded in objective principles. Rather, researchers adopting this viewpoint share a belief in the indeterminacy of knowledge claims. Their indeterminacy view rejects the notion that knowledge is externally grounded and is revealed

---

15. See, for example, R. Libby and B. Lewis, "Human Information Processing Research in Accounting: The State of the Art," *Accounting Organizations and Society* 2, no. 3 (1977): 245–68.

16. For a more thorough discussion, see R. M. Hogarth, "Process Tracing in Clinical Judgments," *Behavioral Science* (September 1974), 298–313.

only through systems of rules that are superior to other ways of understanding phenomena. Critical perspective researchers attempt to interpret the history of accounting as a complex web of economic, political, and accidental co-occurrences.[17] They have also argued that accountants have been unduly influenced by one particular viewpoint in economics (utility-based, marginalist economics). The economic viewpoint holds that business organizations trade in markets that form part of a society's economy. Profit is the result of these activities and is indicative of the organization's efficiency in using society's scarce resources. In addition, critical perspective researchers maintain that accountants also take as given the current institutional framework of government, markets, prices, and organizational forms,[18] with the result that accounting serves to aid certain interest groups in society to the detriment of other interest groups.[19]

Critical perspective research views mainstream accounting research as being based on the view that a world of objective reality exists independently of human beings, has a determinable nature, and can be observed and known through research. Consequently, individuals are not seen as makers of their social reality; instead, they are viewed as possessing attributes that can be objectively described (i.e., leadership styles or personalities). The critical perspectivists maintain that mainstream accounting research equates normative and positive theory; that is, what is and what ought to be are the same. They also maintain that mainstream accounting research theories are put forth as attempts to discover an objective reality, and there is an expressed or implied belief that the observed phenomena are not influenced by the research methodology. In summary, this branch of accounting theory, mainstream accounting research, is based on a belief in empirical testability.

In contrast, critical perspective research is concerned with the ways societies, and the institutions that make them up, have emerged and can be understood.[20] Research from this viewpoint is based on three assumptions:

1. Society has the potential to be what it is not.
2. Conscious human action is capable of molding the social world to be something different or better.
3. Assumption 2 can be promoted by using critical theory.[21]

Using these assumptions, critical theory views organizations in both a historic and a societal context. It seeks to detect any hidden meanings that reside in these contexts, and it is concerned with the power of multinational corporations and the resultant distributions of benefits and costs to societies. Critical theory also

---

17. C. Edward Arrington and Jere R. Francis, "Letting the Chat Out of the Bag: Deconstruction, Privilege and Accounting Research," *Accounting, Organizations and Society* (1989), 1.

18. Wai Fong Chua, "Radical Development in Accounting Thought," *The Accounting Review* (October 1986), 610.

19. Anthony M. Tinker, Barbara D. Merino, and Marilyn D. Neimark, "The Normative Origins of Positive Theories, Ideology and Accounting Thought," *Accounting Organizations and Society* (1982), 167.

20. Richard C. Laughlin, "Accounting Systems in Organizational Contexts: A Case for Critical Theory," *Accounting, Organizations and Society* (1987), 482.

21. Ibid., 483.

does not accept the belief of mainstream accounting theories that organizations survive because they are maximally efficient; rather, it maintains that the methods of research are biased in favor of achieving that conclusion.[22]

The Relationship among Research, Education, and Practice

Research is necessary for effective theory development. In most professional disciplines, when research indicates that a preferable method has been found to handle a particular situation, the new method is taught to students, who then implement the method as they enter their profession. Simply stated, research results in education that influences practice. For example, physicians once believed that patients undergoing major surgery needed long periods of bed rest for effective recovery. However, subsequent research indicated that immediate activity and exercise improved recovery rates. Consequently, it is now common practice for doctors to encourage their surgery patients to begin walking and exercising as soon as it is feasible to do so.

The accounting profession has been criticized for not following this model.[23] In fact, before the FASB's development of the conceptual framework, research and normative theory had little impact on accounting education. During this previous period, students were taught current accounting practice as the desired state of affairs, and theoretically preferred methods were rarely discussed in accounting classrooms. As a result, the use of historical cost accounting received little criticism from accounting educators since it was the accepted method of practice, even though it has little relevance to current decision making. Think about where the medical profession might be today if it had adopted a similar policy—doctors might still be using the practice of bloodletting to cure diseases.

The development of the conceptual framework and the refinements of the various theories on the outcomes of accounting are serving to elevate the relationship of research, education, and practice to a more desirable state. For example, historical cost accounting has been openly referred to in a disparaging manner as "once-upon-a-time accounting." Subsequently, *SFAS No. 115* (see FASB ASC 320 and SFAS No. 157) required certain marketable securities to be valued at their market values (see Chapters 7, 8, and 9). The recent highly publicized accounting frauds, such as that perpetrated by Enron, have resulted in new schools of thought, such as those advocated by the critical perspective theorists, and are forcing both educators and practitioners to rethink previously unquestioned practices.[24] Nevertheless, additional progress is still needed, traditions are difficult to overcome, and accountants as a group are not known to advocate a great deal of rapid change.

22. Walter R. Nord, "Toward an Optimal Dialectical Perspective: Comments and Extensions on Neimark and Tinker," *Accounting, Organizations and Society* (1986), 398.

23. See, for example, Robert R. Sterling, "Accounting Research, Education and Practice," *Journal of Accountancy* (September 1973): 44–52.

24. Richard C. Breeden, chairman of the SEC, in testimony before the U.S. Senate Committee on Banking, Housing, and Urban Affairs, September 1990.

Cases

• Case 4-1 Capital Asset Pricing Model

The capital asset pricing model illustrates how risk is incorporated into user decision models.

Required:
Discuss the capital asset pricing model, including systematic and unsystematic risk, beta, the relationship between risk and return, how to avoid risk, and the relationship of beta to stock prices.

• Case 4-2 Supply and Demand

The efficient market hypothesis is an extension of the supply and demand model.

Required:
a. Discuss the assumptions of the supply and demand model inherent in the EMH.
b. Why is the securities market viewed as a good example of the supply and demand model?
c. Discuss the three forms of the EMH.

• Case 4-3 Research Methodology

Various research methodologies are available with which to study the development of accounting theory.

Required:
Discuss the deductive, inductive, and pragmatic research methods. Include in your discussion examples of accounting research that used each method.

• Case 4-4 Agency Theory

Agency theory provides an explanation for the development of accounting theory.

Required:
Discuss agency theory, including its basic assumptions, agency relationships, why the political process affects agency relationships, and why it does or does not explain accounting theory.

• Case 4-5 Human Information Processing

The study of the ability of individuals to interpret information is classified as human information processing research.

Required:
Discuss human information processing research. What is the general finding of this research? What are the consequences of this finding? What impact do these consequences have on accounting?

• Case 4-6 Critical Perspective Research

Critical perspective research views accounting in a manner somewhat different from traditional accounting research.

Required:

  a. What is critical perspective research?
  b. How does it differ from traditional accounting research?
  c. What are the three assumptions of critical perspective research?

• Case 4-7 Economic Consequences

The FASB has issued *SFAS No. 106*, "Employers' Accounting for Postretirement Benefits Other Than Pensions" (see FASB ASC 715), and *SFAS No. 112*, "Employers' Accounting for Postemployment Benefits" (see FASB ASC 712). These pronouncements required companies to change from accounting for benefits, such as health care, that are paid to former employees during retirement on a pay-as-you-go basis to recognizing the expected cost of benefits during employment. As a result, companies must accrue and report expenses today, thereby reducing income and increasing liabilities.

Some have argued that these pronouncements will cause employers to reduce or eliminate postretirement and postemployment benefits. It is not necessary for you to know the particulars of implementing either of these standards to address the issues described below.

Required:

  a. Should financial reporting requirements affect management's decision-making process? Discuss. Should management reduce or eliminate postretirement or postemployment benefits simply because of the new pronouncement? Discuss.
  b. Are there social costs associated with these pronouncements? Explain.
  c. What would critical perspective proponents say about the potential and/or actual impact of these pronouncements?
  d. What would mainstream accounting proponents say about the potential and/or actual impact of these pronouncements?

• Case 4-8 Financial Statement Disclosure

Current accounting for leases requires that certain leases be capitalized. For capital leases, an asset and the associated liability are recorded. Whether or not the lease is capitalized, the cash flows are the same. The rental payments are set by contract and are paid over time at equally spaced intervals.

Required:

  a. If one of the objectives of financial reporting is to enable investors, creditors, and other users to project future cash flows, what difference does it make whether we report the lease as a liability or simply describe its terms in footnotes? Discuss.

b. The efficient market hypothesis states that all available information is impounded in security prices. In an efficient capital market, would it make a difference whether the lease is reported as a liability or simply described in footnotes? Explain.

c. When there are debt covenants that restrict a company's debt to equity ratio and when debt levels rise relative to equity, management may be motivated to structure leasing agreements so that they are not recorded as capital leases. Discuss this motivation in terms of agency theory.

FASB ASC Research

FASB ASC 4-1 Employee Stock Options

According to agency theory, linking management pay to stock price changes through stock option plans and other forms of stock-based compensation should better align management's goals with those of stockholders. At the same time, if stock options are measured at their fair value, an expense would be recorded and any portion of management's bonus that is based on accounting earnings may be negatively affected. Search the FASB ASC database to determine whether companies are required to report an expense for employee stock options measured at the option's fair value. Cut and paste your findings, citing the source. Then write a brief summary of what you found.

Room for Debate

• Debate 4-1 The Efficient Market Hypothesis and Accounting Information

It has been argued that by the time financial statements are issued, the market price of shares already reflects the information contained in them; hence, accounting information is not relevant. The arguments for both debate teams should address all three forms of the EMH.

Team Debate

Team 1: Present arguments that, given the EMH, accounting information is relevant.

Team 2: Present arguments that, given the EMH, accounting information is irrelevant.

• Debate 4-2 Critical Perspective versus Mainstream Accounting

Proponents of critical perspectives research believe that mainstream accounting research relies on assumptions that are considered in a vacuum, which does not mirror reality.

Team Debate:

Team 1: Present arguments supporting critical perspective research.

Team 2: Present arguments supporting traditional, mainstream accounting research.

• Debate 4-3 Positive versus Normative Accounting Theory

A comprehensive theory of accounting has yet to be developed.

Team Debate

Team 1: Present arguments that support reliance on positive theory to develop a general theory of accounting.

Team 2: Present arguments that support reliance on normative theory to develop a general theory of accounting.

CHAPTER 5

Income Concepts

The primary objective of financial accounting is to provide information useful to investors in making predictions about enterprise performance. The emergence of income reporting as the primary source for investor decision making has been well documented, and income reporting aids economic society in a variety of ways.[1] For example, the Study Group on Business Income documented the need for the income concept in society, and Alexander discussed the following uses of income in this work:

1. As the basis of one of the principal forms of taxation.

2. In public reports as a measure of the success of a corporation's operations.

3. As a criterion for determining the availability of dividends.

4. By rate-regulating authorities for investigating whether those rates are fair and reasonable.

5. As a guide to trustees charged with distributing income to a life tenant while preserving the principal for a remainderman.

6. As a guide to management of an enterprise in the conduct of its affairs.[2]

1. Clifford D. Brown, "The Emergence of Income Reporting: An Historical Study," Michigan State University Business Studies (East Lansing, MI: Division of Research, Graduate School of Business Administration, Michigan State University, 1971).

2. Sidney S. Alexander, "Income Measurement in a Dynamic Economy," *Five Monographs on Business Income*, Report by Study Group on Business Income (New York, 1950), 6.

Income determination is also important because a company's value is related to its current and future earnings. The FASB has indicated that the purpose of financial accounting is to provide information to financial statement users that will assist them in assessing the amount, timing, and uncertainty of future cash flows. However, the FASB has also asserted that information about corporate earnings provides a better indicator of performance than does cash-flow information.[3]

During the past three decades, the relationship of accounting information to the value of the enterprise has been of interest to accounting researchers. In Chapter 4, the efficient markets hypothesis (EMH) was introduced. EMH holds that a company's stock price reflects market consensus expectations about a company's future earnings and cash flows while simultaneously incorporating information about the economy and competitor actions. The stock price changes in response to new information that is received periodically, such as quarterly earnings information.

As discussed in Chapter 4, the performance of many large companies is closely followed by financial analysts who provide quarterly earnings estimates. When actual quarterly earnings exceed the financial analysts' consensus estimates, a positive surprise earnings announcement occurs and a company's stock price increases *ceteris paribus*.[4] For a negative surprise, the reverse is true. This issue may be further complicated by the existence of a whisper number for closely followed companies. A *whisper number* occurs when some financial analysts' estimates of a company's quarterly earnings differ from their original estimate as the reporting date approaches. Whisper numbers come from a variety of sources, but it is often an employee or insider who leaks them. They traditionally were meant for the wealthy clients of top brokerages. However, with the advent of the Internet, many websites have sprung up to supply the individual investor with whisper numbers.

The existence of a whisper number can cause additional positive or negative earnings announcement surprises and also can affect the company's stock price. For example, on January 18, 2000, Microsoft's share price rose to $116.50 in anticipation of the company's expected positive earnings surprise announcement the next day (its whisper number). However, when the earnings announcement was made on January 19, the value of Microsoft's shares dropped 8 percent to 107. Microsoft's actual earnings per share for the quarter were $0.44 as opposed to an estimate of $0.42, but analysts attributed much of the drop in price to Microsoft's inability to meet the whisper number of $0.49. However, other factors that might have contributed to this decline were the company's ongoing problems with the U.S. Justice Department and management's expressed concern about the company's ability to meet future revenue expectations. This issue is particularly relevant for the discussions of materiality, earnings quality, and earnings management contained later in the chapter.

Despite the wide use of the income concept in our economy, there is a general lack of agreement as to the proper definition of *income*. Disagreement is most noticeable when the prevailing definitions used in the disciplines of economics and accounting are analyzed. Although there is general agreement that economics and accounting are related sciences and that both are concerned with the activities of

---

3. *Statement of Financial Accounting Concepts No. 1*, "Objectives of Business Reporting by Business Enterprises" (Stamford, CT: Financial Accounting Standards Board, 1978).

4. Assuming all other variables remain unchanged.

businesses and deal with similar variables, there has been a lack of agreement between the two disciplines regarding the proper timing and measurement of income. As a consequence, a good deal of debate has occurred over the relative importance of the balance sheet and the income statement in determining income. Those who adopt the balance sheet viewpoint see income as the increase in net worth (net increase in asset values) that has occurred during a period—the economic approach. Those favoring the income statement approach view income as the result of certain activities that have taken place during a period. They also view the balance sheet as a list of items that remain after income has been determined by matching costs and revenues—the transactions approach. Reconciliation between these two viewpoints requires the following questions to be addressed: What is the nature of income? And, when should income be reported?

The Nature of Income

Income may take various forms; for example, Bedford noted that the literature usually discusses three basic concepts of income:

1. Psychic income—refers to the satisfaction of human wants.

2. Real income—refers to increases in economic wealth.

3. Money income—refers to increases in the monetary valuation of resources.[5]

These three concepts are all important, but each has one or more implementation issues. The measurement of psychic income is difficult because the human wants are not quantifiable and are satisfied on various levels as an individual gains real income.[6] Money income is easily measured but does not take into consideration changes in the value of the monetary unit. Economists generally agree that the objective of measuring income is to determine how much better off an entity has become during some period of time. Consequently, economists have focused on the determination of real income. The definition of the economic concept of income is usually credited to the economist J. R. Hicks, who stated:

> The purpose of income calculation in practical affairs is to give people an indication of the amount which they can consume without impoverishing themselves. Following out this idea it would seem that we ought to define a man's income as the maximum value which he can consume during a week, and still expect to be as well off at the end of the week as he was at the beginning.[7]

The Hicksian definition emphasizes individual income; however, the concept can also be used as the basis for determining business income by changing the word *consume* to *distribute*. *Well-offness* at the beginning and end of each accounting period would be the amount of net assets (assets minus liabilities) available to conduct the affairs of the business entity. Business income would be the change in

5. Norton M. Bedford, *Income Determination Theory: An Accounting Framework* (Reading, MA: Addison-Wesley, 1965), 20.

6. See, for example, Abraham H. Maslow, *Motivation and Personality* (New York: Harper & Brothers, 1954), ch. 5.

7. J. R. Hicks, *Value and Capital* (Oxford: Clarendon Press, 1946), 7.

net assets resulting from business activities during the accounting period. As such, business income would be the change in net assets during the accounting period, exclusive of investments by owners and distributions to owners. This concept of income determination, termed the *capital maintenance* concept by accountants, holds that no income should be recognized until capital (equity, or net assets) has been retained and costs recovered. From a practical standpoint, however, there is disagreement regarding the appropriate measurement of well-offness (the value of net assets). Alternative approaches to implement a capital maintenance approach are discussed in the following section.

Capital Maintenance Concepts

The occurrence of income implies a return on invested capital. A return on invested capital occurs only after the amount invested has been maintained or recovered. Consequently, a concept of capital maintenance is critical to distinguishing between a *return of* and a *return on* invested capital, and thus to the determination of income.

There are two primary concepts of capital maintenance: financial capital maintenance and physical capital maintenance. *Financial capital maintenance* occurs when the financial (money) amount of enterprise net assets at the end of the period exceeds the financial amount of net assets at the beginning of the period, excluding transactions with owners. This view is transactions based. It is the traditional view of capital maintenance employed by financial accountants.

Physical capital maintenance implies that a return on capital (income) occurs when the physical productive capacity of the enterprise at the end of the period exceeds its physical productive capacity at the beginning of the period, excluding transactions with owners. This concept implies that income is recognized only after providing for the physical replacement of operating assets. Physical productive capacity at a point in time is equal to the current value of the net assets employed to generate earnings. *Current value* embodies expectations regarding the future earning power of the net assets.

The primary difference between physical capital maintenance and financial capital maintenance lies in the treatment of holding gains and losses. A holding gain or loss occurs when the value of a balance sheet item changes during an accounting period. For example, when land held by a company increases in value, a holding gain has occurred. Proponents of physical capital maintenance consider holding gains and losses as returns of capital and do not include them in income. Instead, holding gains and losses are treated as direct adjustments to equity. Conversely, under the financial capital maintenance concept, holding gains and losses are considered as returns on capital and are included in income.

Current-Value Accounting

The concept of physical capital maintenance requires that all assets and liabilities be stated at their current values. The most common approaches to current-value measurement are (1) entry price or replacement cost, (2) exit value or selling price, and (3) discounted present value of expected future cash flows. Each of these approaches will be discussed briefly to demonstrate their strengths and weaknesses.

Entry Price or Replacement Cost

When productive capacity is measured using replacement cost, assets are stated at the cost to replace them with similar assets in similar condition. To maintain the entity's physical productive capacity, it must generate enough cash flows to provide for the physical replacement of operating assets. To determine income under this approach, revenues are matched against the current cost of replacing these assets. Consequently, income can be distributed to the owners without impairing the physical capacity to continue operating into the future.[8] As a result, the appropriateness of using the entry value approach relies on the accounting assumption of business continuity.

According to Edwards and Bell, current entry prices allow the assessment of managerial decisions to hold assets by segregating current-value income (holding gains and losses) from current operating income.[9] Under the assumption that operations will continue, this dichotomy allows the long-run profitability of the enterprise to be assessed. The recurring and relatively controllable profits can be evaluated vis-à-vis those factors that affect operations over time but are beyond the control of management. Replacement cost provides a measure of the cost to replace the current operating capacity and, hence, a means of evaluating how much the firm can distribute to stockholders and still maintain its productive capacity.

Nevertheless, numerous measurement problems are encountered in determining replacement cost values. The firm may be able to determine precisely the replacement cost for inventories and certain other assets; for many assets, however, especially the physical plant, there may not be a ready market from which to acquire replacement assets. In such cases, the firm may have to get the assets appraised in order to arrive at an approximation of their current replacement values.

An alternative approach to approximate replacement cost is to use a specific purchasing power index. A specific price index is designed to measure what has happened to the prices of a specific segment of the economy, for example, equipment used in an industry such as steel or mining. Application of a specific purchasing power index should provide a reasonable approximation of replacement cost as long as the price of the asset being measured moves in a manner similar to assets in the industry.

Finally, the relevance of entry values has been questioned. Sterling argued that the entry value of unowned assets is relevant only when asset purchases are contemplated. For owned assets, entry value is irrelevant to what could be realized upon sale of those assets and to their purchase since they are already owned.[10] Moreover, the current replacement cost of a company's assets does not measure

---

8. S. Davidson and R. L. Weil. "Inflation Accounting: The SEC Proposal for Replacement Cost Disclosures," *Financial Analyst Journal* (March/April 1976): 58, 60. Experiments using entry price or replacement cost measurements were first attempted in the 1920s. Renewed interest in this approach to asset valuation and income determination was generated in the 1960s by, among others, E. O. Edwards and P. W. Bell, *Theory and Measurement of Business Income* (Berkeley: University of California Press, 1961), 33–69; Robert T. Sprouse and Maurice Moonitz, "A Tentative Set of Broad Accounting Principles for Business Enterprises," *Accounting Research Study No. 3* (New York: AICPA, 1962); and a committee of the American Accounting Association, *A Statement of Basic Accounting Theory* (Evanston, IL: AAA, 1966).

9. Edwards and Bell, *Theory and Measurement of Business Income*, 73.

10. Robert R. Sterling, *Toward a Science of Accounting* (Houston: Scholars Book Co., 1979), 124.

the capacity, on the basis of present holdings, to make decisions to buy, hold, or sell in the marketplace.[11] In short, the contention is that it does not disclose the entity's ability to adapt to present decision alternatives.

Exit Value or Selling Price

Another approach to determining current value is exit value or selling price.[12] This valuation approach requires the assessment of each asset from a disposal point of view. Each asset—inventory, plant, equipment, and so on—would be valued based on the selling price that would be realized if the firm chose to dispose of it. In determining the cash equivalent exit price, it is presumed that the asset will be sold in an orderly manner, rather than be subject to forced liquidation. This issue has gained additional prominence with the issuance of SFAS No.157, "Fair Value Measurements" (see FASB ASC 820, discussed in Chapter 7).

Because holding gains and losses receive immediate recognition, the exit price approach to valuation completely abandons the realization principle for the recognition of revenues. The critical event for earnings recognition purposes becomes the point of purchase rather than the point of sale.

Chambers and Sterling contend that exit prices have decision relevance. Accordingly, during each accounting period, management decides whether to hold, sell, or replace the assets. It is argued that exit prices provide users with better information to evaluate liquidity and thus the ability of the enterprise to adapt to changing economic stimuli. Because management has the option of selling the asset, exit price provides a means of assessing downside risk. It measures the current sacrifice of holding the asset and thereby provides a guide for evaluating management's stewardship function.

Like entry prices, determining exit values also poses measurement problems. First, there is the basic problem of determining a selling price for assets such as property, plant, and equipment, for which there is no ready market. Second, the notion that exit price should be based on prices arising from sales in the normal course of business, rather than forced liquidation, may be feasible for assets such as inventory but may be impracticable if not impossible for the physical plant, since it would not be disposed of in the normal course of business.

One can argue that replacement costs are more relevant measures of the current value of fixed assets, whereas exit values are better measures of the current value of inventory items. Since management intends to use rather than sell fixed assets, their value in use is what it would cost to replace them. On the other hand, inventory is purchased for resale. Consequently, its value is directly related to its selling price to customers.

Finally, exit value or selling price is inconsistent with the concept of physical capital maintenance. Selling prices generate the cash inflows that must cover the expected cost of replacing operating assets before a return on capital can be distributed to owners. Exit value is a type of opportunity cost. It measures the sacrifice of holding an asset rather than the expected cost of replacing it. Moreover, physical capital maintenance is based on the concept of continuity, not liquidation.

---

11. Raymond J. Chambers, *Accounting Evaluation and Economic Behavior* (Englewood Cliffs, NJ: Prentice-Hall, 1966), 92.

12. Exit price was first advocated by Kenneth MacNeal in "Truth in Accounting" Originally published in 1939; reissued in 1970 by Scholars Book Company, Lawrence, Kansas).

Discounted Present Value

A third approach to the measurement of net asset value is discounted cash flow. According to this concept, the present value of the future cash flows expected to be received from an asset (or disbursed for a liability) is the relevant value of the asset (or liability) that should be disclosed in the balance sheet. Under this method, income is equal to the difference between the present value of the net assets at the end of the period and their present value at the beginning of the period, excluding the effects of investments by owners and distributions to owners. This measurement process is similar to the economic concept of income because discounted present value is perhaps the closest approximation of the actual value of the assets in use—and hence may be viewed as an appropriate surrogate measure of well-offness.

A strong argument can be made for the concept of discounted cash flow. All assets are presumed to be acquired for the future service potential they provide to the firm. Furthermore, there is a presumption that the initial purchase price was paid because of a belief that the asset would generate sufficient revenue in the future to make its acquisition worthwhile. Thus, either implicitly or explicitly, the original cost was related to the present value of expected cash flows. It follows that the continued use of the asset implies that its value in use is related to expected future cash flows. Hence, the change in expected future cash flows and thus present value from one period to the next is decision relevant. Moreover, presumably the present value at the end of the period would approximate what the company would be willing to invest to purchase a similar asset and thereby maintain its physical operating capacity. Consequently, the resulting income measurement is consistent with the physical capital maintenance concept of income.

The use of present-value measurements in accounting gained additional momentum by the FASB's issuance of *SFAC No. 7*, "Using Cash Flow Measurements and Present Value Measurements in Accounting," and *SFAS No. 157* (see FASB ASC 820). Nevertheless, three major measurement problems are associated with the concept of discounted cash flow. First, the concept depends on an estimate of future cash flows by time periods. As a result, both the amounts of the cash flows to be generated in the future and the timing of those cash flows must be determined.

The second problem is selection of an appropriate discount rate. Since a dollar received in the future is not as valuable as a dollar received today, the expected future cash flows must be discounted to the present. Theoretically, the discount rate should be the internal rate of return on the asset. However, this rate can only be approximated, because knowledge of the exact rate of return would require exact knowledge of the amounts and timing of future cash flows expected when the asset was purchased.

The third problem arises because a firm's assets are interrelated. Revenues are generated by the combined use of a company's resources. Therefore, even if the company's future cash flows and the appropriate discount rate could be precisely determined, it would not be practicable to determine exactly how much each asset contributed to those cash flows. As a result, the discounted present value of individual firm assets cannot be determined and summed to determine the present value of a company.

Use of present-value techniques to measure current value can be only as valid as the estimates of the amounts and timing of future cash flow and the appropriateness of the discount factor. To the extent that these estimates approximate reality, the measurement of the present value of future service potential is probably the most relevant measurement to disclose on the balance sheet. In other words, this measurement is relevant in the sense that the balance sheet would provide information about the ability of the assets to produce income in the future.

Current-Value and the Historical Accounting Model

Although the current accounting model relies heavily on historical cost, recent pronouncements and discussion memorandums issued by the FASB indicate a move toward providing more current-value information. One of the first examples of the disclosure of current cost information was *SFAS No. 33* (since superseded by FASB ASC 255) that established guidelines for reporting supplementary current cost information for certain assets by large, publicly traded companies. Additionally, SFAS *115* (see FASB ASC 320, discussed in Chapter 8) requires that investments in certain financial instruments be reported at fair value and *SFAS No. 157*, "Fair Value Measurements" (see FASB ASC 820), specifies how to measure fair value (see Chapter 7).

Income Recognition

In an attempt to overcome the measurement problems associated with using the economic concept of income, accountants originally took the position that a *transactions approach* should be used to account for assets, liabilities, revenues, and expenses. This approach relies on the presumption that the elements of financial statements should be reported when there is evidence of an outside exchange (or an "arm's-length transaction"). Transactions-based accounting generally requires that reported income be the result of dealings with entities external to the reporting unit and gives rise to the realization principle. The *realization principle* holds that income should be recognized when the earnings process is complete or virtually complete and an exchange transaction has taken place. The exchange transaction is the basis of accountability and determines both the timing of revenue recognition and the amount of revenue to be recorded. The resulting financial statements are expressed in terms of financial capital (money) invested in net assets and a return on that investment to stockholders. Consequently, traditional, transactions-based accounting is consistent with the financial capital maintenance concept.

Transactions-based accounting contrasts with the economic concept of income in that accounting income is determined by measuring only the *recorded* net asset values, exclusive of capital and dividend transactions, during a period. The accounting concept of income generally does not attempt to place an expected value on the firm or to report on changes in the expected value of assets or liabilities.

Empirical research has indicated that accounting income is related to market-based measures of income such as stock returns, and security prices respond to the information content in financial statements.[13] Nevertheless, the transactions-based approach to income determination has been criticized for not reporting all relevant information about business entities. Those who favor a more liberal

13. Ray Ball and Philip Brown, "An Empirical Evaluation of Accounting Income Numbers," *Journal of Accounting Research* (Autumn 1968): 159–78.

interpretation of the income concept argue that income should include all gains and losses in assets or liabilities held by an entity during a particular period regardless of whether they are realized or unrealized.[14]

Edwards and Bell suggested that with only slight changes in present accounting procedures, four types of income can be isolated: (1) current operating profit—the excess of sales revenues over the current cost of inputs used in production and sold, (2) realizable cost savings—the increases in the prices of assets held during the period, (3) realized cost savings—the difference between historical costs and the current purchase price of goods sold, and (4) realized capital gains—the excess of sales proceeds over historical costs on the disposal of long-term assets. Edwards and Bell contended that these measures are better indications of well-offness and provide users more information to analyze enterprise results.[15]

Sprouse, in elaborating on the findings of *ARS No. 3*, discussed the concept somewhat more narrowly:

> Because ownership interests are constantly changing hands, we must strive for timely recognition of measurable change, and in so doing we must identify the nature of the changes. As currently reported, income may well be composed of three elements, each of which has considerably different economic significance. Is the gross margin truly the result of operations—the difference between current selling prices of products and current costs of producing products, both measured in today's dollars? How much of the company's income is not the result of its operations but is the result of changes in the value of a significant asset, for example, a large supply of raw material, perhaps a warehouse full of sugar? Such changes are apt to be fortuitous and unpredictable and therefore need to be segregated, if financial statements are to be interpreted meaningfully and if rational investment decisions are to be based on income measurements. And how much of what is now reported as income is not income at all but is merely the spurious result of using a current unit of measurement for revenues and an obsolete unit measurement for costs—particularly depreciation?[16]

The major change advocated by both Edwards and Bell and *ARS No. 3* is the reporting of unrealized (holding) gains or losses in the net assets of the entity during the period. Proponents claim that reporting holding gains and losses would increase the information content of published financial statements. This argument focuses on two main points: (1) windfall gains and losses from holding specific assets and liabilities should be reported as they occur, and (2) changes in the measuring unit should be eliminated from the reporting process; that is, financial statements should be adjusted for the effects of inflation. The effect on income of failing to record holding gains and losses is illustrated by the following example.

---

14. The initial impetus for this broader measure of income is found in Edwards and Bell, *Theory and Measurement of Business Income*; and R. T. Sprouse and M. Moonitz, *A Tentative Set of Broad Accounting Principles for Business Enterprises*, "Accounting Research Study No. 3" (New York: AICPA, 1962).

15. Edwards and Bell, *Theory and Measurement of Business Income*, 111.

16. Robert T. Sprouse, "The Radically Different Principles of Accounting Research Study No. 3," *Journal of Accountancy* (May 1964): 66.

Suppose two individuals, A and B, purchase adjoining 100-acre plots of land for $100,000 on January 1, 2010. Assume that the appraisal value of these plots of land rises to $150,000 on December 31, 2010, and that A sells his land on this date while B retains hers. Traditional accounting practice allows A to recognize a gain of $50,000, whereas B cannot record her gain because it has not been realized by an arm's-length transaction. This difference occurs even though the economic substance of both events is essentially the same. This example illustrates the impact of the transactions approach to income determination.

More recently, the FASB has adopted a balance sheet approach that defines income as the periodic change in net assets. This change was necessary because over time, the FASB had succumbed to pressure from some users of financial statements to endorse the current operating performance approach to income determination (see Chapter 6) by allowing certain changes in assets and liabilities to bypass the income statement. These practices resulted in concerns by academics and investment analysts that centered around two issues: (1) the difficulty that users have in uncovering relevant information that is buried in the income statement and the balance sheet and (2) the importance and impact of these items on equity valuation.[17] In reaction to these concerns, the FASB issued *SFAS No. 130*, "Comprehensive Income" (see FASB ASC 220). *Comprehensive income* is defined as all changes in net assets other than transactions with owners. The major objective of this statement is to give the other comprehensive income items (those changes in assets and liabilities that are not disclosed on the income statement) equal prominence as the net income number within the financial statements. (See Chapter 6 for a further discussion of comprehensive income.)

Measurement

The reporting of business income assumes that all items of revenue and expense are capable of being measured. One requirement of measurement is that the object or event is capable of being ordered or ranked in respect to some property. Measurement is the assigning of numbers to objects or events according to rules. It is also a process of comparison in order to obtain more precise information to distinguish one alternative from another in a decision situation.

The accounting measuring unit in the United States is the dollar; however, the instability of the measuring unit causes major problems. For example, consider the room you are now in. If you were to measure its width in feet and inches today, next week, and next year, accurate measurements would give the same result each time. In contrast, the accounting measurement of sales will undoubtedly differ each year even if exactly the same numbers of units are sold. Much of this difference will be the result of changes in the value of the dollar.

Another factor that complicates accounting measurement is that arbitrary decisions must be made for periodic reporting purposes. Depreciation, depletion, and amortization are all examples of arbitrary and inexact measurement techniques that complicate the measurement process. Because changes in the measurement unit and arbitrary measurements caused by the necessity of periodic presentation persist, the users of accounting information should recognize the inherent limitations in the use of measurement techniques in accounting.

17. D. Beresford, T. Johnson, and C. Reither, "Is a Second Income Needed?" *Journal of Accountancy* (April 1996): 69–72.

Accounting for Inflation

A primary cause of instability in the accounting measuring unit is the effect of inflationary or deflationary forces in the economy as a whole that have a general impact on the purchasing power of the dollar. Sweeney proposed that to be meaningful, financial statement elements should be measured in common-sized dollars that reflect the same level of purchasing power so that they can be properly added together to get a valid result.[18] These measurements are termed *general purchasing power adjustments*. They are not intended to measure the value of assets and liabilities; rather, they are intended to allow for assessing the effects of changes in the general price level. For example, holding receivables during an inflationary period means that when they are collected, the dollars received are worth less than they would have been if the sales had been made for cash. The result is a purchasing power loss. General purchasing power adjustments would result in financial statements that would report gains and losses in purchasing power.

Inflation erodes the purchasing power of net monetary assets (receivables minus payables). Purchasing power losses negatively affect the value of the money capital invested in the firm's net assets. Income measured as the change in price-level-adjusted net assets from the beginning of the period to the end of the period, exclusive of transactions with owners, would reflect the erosion of the monetary capital investment and is therefore consistent with the financial capital maintenance concept of income determination. Proponents of inflation-adjusted financial statements contend that these adjustments are necessary if income is to measure the increase in the well-offness from one period to the next.[19]

Revenue Recognition and Realization

There has been confusion in accounting literature over the precise meaning of the terms *recognition* and *realization*. *Recognition* is the formal process of reporting a transaction or event in a company's financial statements, whereas *realization* is the process of converting noncash assets to cash or claims to cash. Transactions-based accounting recognizes and reports revenues that are realized or realizable. Hence, accounting recognition relies on determining when realization has occurred. Critics of the accounting process favor the economic concept of real income, whereby revenue is earned continuously over time. Accountants contend that it is not practical to record revenues on a continuous basis. Consequently, accountants must choose an appropriate point in time to record the occurrence of revenue. For a manufacturing company, several possibilities exist, including the acquisition of raw materials, the production of the company's product, the sale of the product, the collection of cash, or the completion of after-sale activities such as product warranties.

In 1964, the American Accounting Association Committee on Realization recommended that the concept of realization could be improved if the following criteria were applied: (1) revenue must be capable of measurement, (2) the measurement must be verified by an external market transaction, and (3) the crucial

---

18. Henry W. Sweeney, *Stabilized Accounting* (New York: Harper & Bros., 1936).

19. *FASB ASC 255-10-50-11* requires supplemental disclosures if income from continuing operations on a current cost-constant purchasing power basis would differ significantly from income from continuing operations in the primary financial statements.

event must have occurred.[20] The key element in these recommendations is the third criterion. The crucial-event test states that revenue should be realized on the completion of the most crucial task in the earning process. This test results in the recognition of revenue at various times for different business organizations.

The combined use of the crucial-event test and the transactions approach has resulted in accounting income that measures the difference between sales of the company's product (revenue) and costs incurred in the production and sale of that product (expenses).

The FASB defines revenue as "inflows or other enhancements of assets of an entity or settlements of its liabilities (or a combination of both) during a period from delivering or producing goods, rendering services or other activities that constitute the entity's ongoing operations."[21]

Corporations record revenues, which increase their net assets, as a result of their ongoing activities. These activities vary from company to company, but they generally consist of the following steps for a manufacturing company:

1. Ordering raw materials for production
2. Receiving the raw materials
3. Producing the product
4. Marketing the product
5. Receiving customer orders
6. Delivering the product
7. Collecting cash from customers
8. Paying creditors

These steps generally occur in a sequence, and they tend to recur. That being the case, these steps represent a company's "income-producing activities cycle." Depending on the circumstances, a company may recognize revenue and determine income at various points during the cycle. Accordingly, some guidelines are necessary to determine when to recognize revenues and expenses within a company's income-producing activities cycle.

In general, companies usually recognize revenue at the time they sell their product or service (the point of sale); however, a company may either accelerate or delay revenue recognition within its income-producing activities cycle due to the circumstances associated with a sale. All companies face revenue recognition questions that require them to determine when to recognize revenue. For example, Dell Computer Corporation previously followed a build-to-order business model and still sells some of its products in this manner. It first receives orders from customers, then assembles the products, and finally receives payment from the customer after it ships the goods. The question is, when during this cycle should Dell recognize the revenue it receives from customers? On the other hand, the *New York Times* requires customers to pay for subscriptions in advance. Over

20. American Accounting Association 1964 Concepts and Standards Research Study Committee, "The Matching Concept," *The Accounting Review 40* (April 1965): 318.

21. *Statement of Financial Accounting Concepts No. 6*, "Elements of Financial Statements of Business Enterprises" (Stamford, CT: Financial Accounting Standards Board, 1985), para. 79.

the course of the year, the company must then fulfill its obligation to deliver newspapers to customers. Again the question is, when during its income-producing activities cycle should the *New York Times* recognize its revenue?

The general guideline of recognizing revenue at the point of sale requires some further explanation. It is not enough to state simply that revenue should be recognized at the point of sale, because so many companies' sales activities differ. Under GAAP, revenue should be recognized when both of the following conditions have been satisfied:

1. *The revenue has been earned.* Revenue is considered earned when a company has accomplished all that it must do to be entitled to the benefits represented by the revenues. Whether or not revenue is earned hinges on whether the firm has substantially completed what it must do to be entitled to the revenue, which frequently depends on whether or not the firm has accomplished the crucial event in its earnings process. So, within most income-producing activities cycles, there is a crucial event that the firm must accomplish in order to be entitled to the revenues. Such an event may differ across firms or industries.

2. *The revenue has been "realized" or is "realizable."* *Realization* means that the products or services have been exchanged for cash or claims to cash. Note that the terms *realized* and *realizable* both imply that the revenue can be measured with a reasonable degree of certainty. In other words, the amount of the revenue can be quantified with reasonable assurance of their accuracy. Since the ability to measure the revenue has to occur for it to be realizable, some accountants suggest that measurability and realization are the same thing.

These guidelines are quite broad, and over the years have resulted in many interpretations. Consequently, the FASB and its predecessors have developed a number of more specific guidelines that focus on the reporting practices in specific industries. Companies in industries associated with long-term construction contracts, regulated utilities, franchises, real estate sales, insurance contracts, and, in some cases, entertainment, employ different revenue recognition practices.

Generally speaking, departures from recording revenue at the point of sales arise because of changes in the degree of certainty surrounding cash collection. If cash collections for a particular transaction have a high degree of *certainty*, then the company may accelerate revenue recognition. For example, a corporate farm entering into a preharvesting contract to sell 10,000 bushels of corn to a grain elevator at $1.90 a bushel might record its revenue after it counts the bushels of corn. On the other hand, when a high degree of *uncertainty* of cash collection exists—when a major customer files for bankruptcy, for example—revenue recognition may be delayed.

Recent Developments

In December 2008, the FASB and the IASB jointly issued a discussion paper, *Preliminary Views on Revenue Recognition in Contracts with Customers*, that describes the boards' views on a single, contract-based model for recognizing revenue. The proposed model would provide an asset and liability approach to revenue recognition compared to the earnings approach currently used under U.S. GAAP and International Financial Reporting Standards. The proposed model would apply to essentially all industries and to all contracts with customers, although the boards are still considering whether the model would provide decision-useful information for certain contracts for financial instruments and some nonfinancial instruments, as well as for insurance contracts and leasing contracts.

The discussion paper reflects the boards' mutual goal to develop a model to improve financial reporting and comparability by reducing the number of revenue recognition standards that an entity must refer to and by clarifying the guidance on when an entity should recognize revenue.

The basic concepts included in the proposed model, as compared to existing U.S. GAAP, would collectively have a significant impact on revenue accounting for many entities. Some entities, such as those in the retail sector, would experience minimal changes; others, such as entities that currently apply industry-specific guidance, would experience significant changes.

The discussion paper notes that revenue is an important number to users of financial statements in assessing a company's performance and prospects. However, revenue recognition requirements in U.S. GAAP differ from those in International Financial Reporting Standards, and both are considered in need of improvement. The requirements in U.S. GAAP comprise numerous standards—many are industry specific, and some can produce conflicting results for economically similar transactions. Although IFRSs contain fewer standards on revenue recognition, its two main standards have different principles and can be difficult to understand and apply beyond simple transactions.

The boards' objective is to improve the existing guidance in both IFRSs and U.S. GAAP by developing a single revenue model that can be applied consistently regardless of industry. Applying the underlying principle proposed by the boards, a company would recognize revenue when it satisfies a performance obligation by transferring goods and services to a customer as contractually agreed. That principle is similar to many existing requirements, and the boards expect that many transactions would remain unaffected by the proposals. However, clarifying that principle and applying it consistently to all contracts with customers would improve the comparability and understandability of revenue for users of financial statements.

The comment period ended in June 2009. The boards expect to issue a final standard by 2011.

The SEC previously addressed problems associated with revenue recognition in *Staff Accounting Bulletin (SAB) No. 101*, "Revenue Recognition in Financial Statements," and in a companion document, "Revenue Recognition in Financial Statements— Frequently Asked Questions and Answers." *SAB No. 101* states that if a transaction falls within the scope of specific authoritative literature on revenue recognition, that guidance should be followed; but in the absence of such guidance, the revenue recognition criteria in *SFAC No. 5* (revenue should not be recognized until the crucial event has occurred and it is measurable) should be followed. However, *SAB No. 101* contains additional requirements for meeting the FASB's criteria and reflects the SEC staff's view that the four basic criteria for revenue recognition in *AICPA Statement of Position 97-2*, "Software Revenue Recognition," provide a foundation for all basic revenue recognition principles. These criteria are as follows:

1. Persuasive evidence of an arrangement exists.

2. Delivery has occurred.

3. The vendor's fee is fixed or determinable.

4. Collectability is probable.

As a result of *SAB No. 101,* many companies had to change their revenue recognition criteria. For example, Galaxy Enterprises, Inc., a Nevada company engaged in selling Internet and multimedia products, recorded a $5.26 million change in accounting principle after adopting *SAB No. 101.*

Delayed or Advanced Revenue Recognition

As discussed above, companies usually recognize revenue when they sell their products or services because the sale fulfills the crucial event criterion. But recognition may be advanced or delayed due to circumstances associated with the sale. American Airlines, for example, delays recognizing passenger revenue until the flight is completed, even though the airline usually collects ticket fares in advance. In this case, selling the tickets satisfies the measurability criterion, but the critical event criterion is not satisfied until completion of the scheduled flight. As a result, American initially records its ticket sales as unearned revenue and defers recognizing the revenue from those sales until they're "earned."[22]

All companies must decide when the crucial event and measurability criteria are satisfied. The New York Yankees, for example, must decide when to recognize revenue from season ticket sales. Since the team knows the price it receives from the ticket sales, it easily satisfies the measurability criterion when it sells the tickets, but it doesn't satisfy the crucial-event criterion until after the team plays each individual baseball game.

Consider another example. Sears must decide when to recognize revenue from selling extended warranty contracts on appliances. For these sales, Sears, like the Yankees, satisfies the measurability criterion at the point of sale, but the critical event does not occur until Sears receives warranty claims from its customers. At that point, Sears can measure the amount of warranty expense and then match its expense with its warranty revenues. The requirement to match revenues with the expenses a company incurs to earn them is an important concept that needs to be addressed before turning to special revenue recognition issues. The following section discusses the matching concept; the requirements for recognizing revenue either before or after the point of sale are examined later in the chapter.

Generally, departures from the typical practice of recording revenue at the point of sale occur due to varying degrees of certainty. When a high degree of certainty is associated with realization, revenue recognition may precede the point of sale. Conversely, the greater the level of uncertainty associated with realization,

---

22. The airline revenue recognition process is quite complicated. Each flight coupon is matched against the performance data (uplift data) to determine whether passengers used the tickets they purchased for a particular flight. If so, the sales amount is reported as revenue after the completion of the flight. Otherwise, the airline researches how the flight coupon was actually used by the customer. Flight coupons for each flight are then sent to the accounting department, where they are sorted by flight date and flight origin. To complicate the process further, airlines also generally offer complete routings for their customers, which may contain flights operated by different carriers. Passengers can also rebook at short notice and change the routing. When a customer books flights involving more than one airline, a method for sharing the sales revenue is established in order to properly record revenue.

the greater is the tendency to delay revenue recognition. The degree of certainty criterion results in revenue recognition at various points in the production-sale cycle.

Revenue Recognized during the Production Process

When production of the company's product carries over into two or more periods, the allocation of revenue to the various accounting periods is considered essential for proper reporting. In such cases a method of revenue recognition termed *percentage of completion* may be used. The determination of the percentage completed during an accounting period may be based on predetermined targets, engineering estimates, or the percentage of the expected total costs that were incurred in a particular accounting period. The latter approach requires a known selling price and the ability to estimate reasonably the total costs of the product. It is used in accounting for long-term construction contracts such as roads, shipbuilding, and dams. Because the percentage of completion method recognizes income as it is earned, rather than waiting until the transaction has been completed, the concept of revenue recognition provides income measurements that are closer to the economic concept of income espoused by Hicks.

Revenue Recognized at the Completion of Production

When the company's product can be sold at a determinable price on an organized market, revenue may be realized when the goods are ready for sale. The U.S. gold market formerly was an example of this method in that all gold mined was required to be sold to the government at a fixed price. Some farm products and commodities also meet these conditions. Revenue recognition at the completion of production is defended on the grounds that the event critical to the earnings process (production) has occurred.

Revenue Recognized as Services Are Performed

Three steps are involved in service contracts: (1) order taking, (2) performance of services, and (3) collection of cash. These steps may all be performed in one accounting period or divided between periods. In service contracts, realization should generally be connected with the performance of services, and revenue should be recognized in relation to the degree of services performed. Realization should be tied to services performed because it is the most crucial decision. The signing of the contract results in an executory contract, and the collection of cash may precede or follow the performance of services.

Revenue Recognized as Cash Is Received

In certain circumstances, where the ultimate collectability of the revenue is in doubt, recognition is delayed until cash payment is received. The installment method and the cash recovery method are examples of delaying revenue recognition until the receipt of cash. However, the APB stated that revenue recognition should not be delayed unless ultimate collectability is so seriously doubted that an appropriate allowance for the uncollectible amount cannot be estimated (see FASB ASC 605-10-25-3).

Revenue Recognized on the Occurrence of Some Event

In some cases, where binding contracts do not exist or rights to cancel are in evidence, the level of uncertainty may dictate that revenue recognition be delayed until the point of ratification or the passage of time. For example, some states have passed laws that allow door-to-door sales contracts to be voided within certain periods of time. In such cases, recognition should be delayed until that period has passed.

Matching

Once a company has fulfilled its crucial event and recognized revenue, it must then identify all expenses associated with producing that revenue. This process of associating revenues with expenses is termed the *matching concept*. From a conceptual standpoint, matching revenues with the associated expenses relates efforts to accomplishments.[23] Although it is a relatively easy concept to understand, matching revenues and expenses requires careful consideration in practice. Determining when costs are of no future benefit and should therefore be charged against revenue depends on the definitions of the terms *cost, asset, expense*, and *loss*. We define these terms below.

- *Cost*. The amount given in consideration of goods received or to be received. Costs can be classified as (1) *unexpired* (assets), which are applicable to the production of future revenues, and (2) *expired*, those not applicable to the production of future revenues and thus deducted from revenues or retained earnings in the current period.[24]

- *Expense*. Outflows or other using-up of assets or incurrences of liabilities (or a combination of both) during a period from delivering or producing goods, rendering services, or carrying out other activities that constitute the entity's ongoing major or central operations.[25]

- *Assets*. Probable future economic benefits obtained or controlled by a particular entity as a result of past transactions or events. An asset has three essential characteristics: (1) it embodies a probable future benefit that involves a capacity, singly or in combination with other assets, to contribute directly or indirectly to future net cash inflows; (2) a particular enterprise can obtain the benefit and control others' access to it; and (3) the transaction or other event giving rise to the enterprise's right to or control of the benefit has already occurred.[26]

- *Loss*. Decreases in equity (net assets) from peripheral or incidental transactions of an entity and from all other transactions and other events and circumstances affecting the entity during a period except those that result from expenses or distributions to owners.[27]

In other words, expenses are revenue-producing cost expirations, whereas losses are non-revenue-producing cost expirations. When a company purchases

---

23. W. Paton and A. C. Littleton, *An Introduction to Corporate Accounting Standards*, American Accounting Association Monograph No. 3 (Evanston, IL: AAA, 1940).

24. Committee on Terminology, AICPA, *Accounting Terminology Bulletin No. 1*, "Review and Resume" (New York: AICPA, 1953).

25. *SFAC No. 6*, "Elements of Financial Statements of Business Enterprises" (Stamford, CT: FASB, 1985), paras. 25, 26, 35, 36, and 49.

26. Ibid., para. 80.

27. Ibid., para. 81.

FIGURE 5.1   *Relationships among Cost, Expense, and Loss*

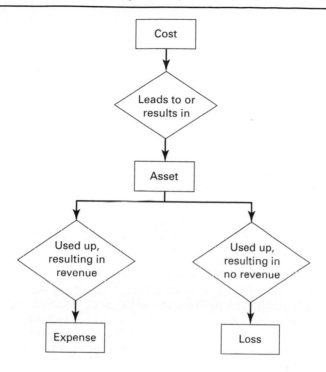

inventory, for example, it purchases an asset. In purchasing the asset, it incurs a cost. As the inventory gets sold (or used up), the cost expires, which results in an expense: cost of goods sold. The company then recognizes an expense because selling or "using up" the inventory contributes to its revenues. On the other hand, suppose the inventory was destroyed in a fire. It still gets used up in a manner of speaking; the cost still "expires," but in this case the using-up of the inventory, or the cost expiration, does not contribute at all to the company's revenue. As a result, this particular cost expiration gives rise to a loss rather than an expense. Figure 5.1 illustrates these relationships.

Consequently, to determine periodic net income, a company must determine the costs that have expired during the current period as well as whether these costs are revenue-producing or non-revenue-producing cost expirations.

Separating expenses into product costs and period costs assists this process. *Product costs* are those cost expirations that can be directly associated with the company's product, such as direct material, direct labor, and direct factory overhead. In addition, it is common practice to arbitrarily assign some costs, such as indirect overhead, to the product even though there is no way to directly associate the cost with a particular product. Ultimately, product costs get charged to expense based on the number of products sold. When an automobile dealer sells a car, for example, the dealer will charge the cost of the car to an expense—cost of goods sold—in the period of sale. The cost of the other, unsold cars remains in inventory until the dealer sells them.

In contrast, *period costs* are those cost expirations that are more closely related to a period of time than to a product, such as administrative salaries or advertising costs. Period costs get charged to expense on the basis of the period of benefit. If the same automobile dealer pays for a radio ad in December 2010 but the ad runs during the first quarter of 2011, then the dealer recognizes the expense associated with the advertisement in 2011 because 2011 is the period of benefit. Losses, too, are associated with periods. When a company determines it has an asset that can no longer provide the expected economic benefit, or its revenue-producing potential has been impaired in some way, it recognizes a loss in that period. The underlying principle is that losses should be written off in the period during which their lack of future economic benefit is determined.

Finally, it should be noted that a company's ability to recognize income is largely dependent on its capability to measure inflows (revenues) and associated outflows (expenses). Recall that the term *measure* means being able to determine the amounts involved with reasonable accuracy. When either inflows or outflows are not measurable, the company must defer income recognition because GAAP requires financial reporting information to be disclosed in units of currency (dollars).

Due to the importance of measurement to revenue recognition, and ultimately income recognition, accounting income represents the efforts and accomplishments of past and present operations. It should also be mentioned that the traditional income statement indicates little in the way of future expectations regarding these efforts and accomplishments. Authoritative accounting pronouncements have generally taken the position that the past is the best indicator of the future and that reporting anticipated gains involves an element of subjectivity that could impair the usefulness of financial statements.

Conservatism

Sterling called *conservatism* the most influential principle of valuation in accounting.[28] Simply stated, conservatism holds that when you are in doubt, it is best to choose the accounting alternative that will be least likely to overstate assets or income.

The principle of conservatism originally gained prominence as a partial offset to the eternal optimism of management and the tendency to overstate financial statements that characterized much of the twentieth century. Conservatism was also seen as overriding the holding gains argument because many accountants believed that the practice of placing the least favorable alternative valuation on the firm was least likely to mislead the users of financial accounting information. In recent years, pressures for more reliable and relevant information have reduced the influence of this concept. Conservative financial statements are usually unfair to present stockholders and biased in favor of prospective stockholders because the net valuation of the firm does not include future expectations. As a consequence, the company's common stock will be priced at a relatively lower value in the marketplace, and analysts' measurements of market to book value will tend to be biased upward.

---

28. Robert R. Sterling, *Theory of the Measurement of Enterprise Income* (Lawrence: University of Kansas Press, 1970), 256.

Materiality

The concept of *materiality* has had a pervasive influence on all accounting activities, even though no all-encompassing definition of the concept exists. Although materiality affects the measurement and disclosure of all information presented on the financial statements, it has its greatest impact on items of revenue and expense.

The concept has both qualitative and quantitative aspects. For example, the private sector organizations empowered to develop GAAP have defined *materiality* both qualitatively and quantitatively. *ARS No. 7* provided the following qualitative definition:

> A statement, fact or item is material, if giving full consideration to the surrounding circumstances, as they exist at the time, it is of such a nature that its disclosure, or the method of treating it, would be likely to influence or to "make a difference" in the judgment and conduct of a reasonable person.[29]

These organizations have also furnished quantitative definitions of materiality. For example, as quantitative requirements were established in *APB Opinion No. 18*, an investment of 20 percent or more in the voting stock of an investee is considered material. In *APB Opinion No. 15*, a reduction of less than 3 percent in the aggregate of earnings per share is not considered material. And most of the SFASs issued prior to the FASB Accounting Standards Codification (ASC) contain this stipulation: "The provisions of this Statement need not be applied to immaterial items."

In *SFAC No. 2*, the FASB made the following statement regarding materiality:

> Those who make accounting decisions and those who make judgments as auditors continually confront the need to make judgments about materiality. Materiality judgments are primarily quantitative in nature. They pose the question: Is this item large enough for users of the information to be influenced by it? However, the answer to that question will usually be affected by the nature of the item; items too small to be thought material if they result from routine transactions may be considered material if they arise in abnormal circumstances.[30]

SFAC No. 2 defined materiality judgments as "screens" or thresholds. Materiality judgments ask this question: When is an item (error or omission) large enough to pass through the threshold that separates material from immaterial items? The more important the item, the finer is the screen that will exist.

The following items are cited as examples:

1. An accounting change in circumstances that puts an enterprise in danger of being in breach of covenant regarding its financial condition may justify a lower materiality threshold than if its position were stronger.

---

29. Paul Grady, *Accounting Research Study No. 7*, "Inventory of Generally Accepted Accounting Principles for Business Enterprises" (New York: AICPA, 1965), 40.

30. *Statement of Financial Accounting Concepts No. 2*, "Qualitative Characteristics of Accounting Information" (Stamford, CT: FASB, May 1980), para. 123.

2. A failure to disclose separately a nonrecurring item of revenue may be material at a lower threshold than would be the case if the revenue turns a loss into a profit or reverses the earnings trend from a downward to an upward trend.

3. A misclassification of assets that would not be material in amount if it affected two categories of plant or equipment might be material if it changed the classification between a noncurrent and a current asset category.

4. Amounts too small to warrant disclosure or correction in normal circumstances may be considered material if they arise from abnormal or unusual transactions or events.[31]

Earnings Quality, Earnings Management, and Fraudulent Financial Reporting

Earnings Quality

Analysts and other financial statement users are keenly interested in a firm's reported earnings because it allows them not only to assess past performance but also to predict future cash flows, which in turn influence security prices. Over the past 20 years, however, research has indicated that, while reported earnings have some effect on security prices, the effect is small.[32] As noted earlier, accounting earnings are influenced by revenue recognition policies and methods, the need to match revenues and expenses in certain time periods, and managers' judgments, all of which may detract from their usefulness. As a result, some security analysts have begun focusing on the "capital maintenance" approach to income, which focuses on the change in net assets resulting from business activities during the accounting period, exclusive of investments by owners and distributions to owners. Therefore the amount of income a company earns is captured by the change in its equity, or net assets, not including any transactions with owners. This view implies that a company doesn't start earning any income until all its costs have been recovered and its capital (i.e., its equity) retained. Because it is broader and more comprehensive in scope, the capital maintenance approach to income represents an economic view of income rather than a strict accounting view.

To counter the drawbacks of reported accounting earnings, and to help align a firm's accounting earnings with its economic earnings, financial statement users should assess the "quality" of a company's earnings. *Earnings quality* is defined as the degree of correlation between a company's accounting income and its economic income. Several techniques may be used to assess earnings quality, including those listed here:

1. Compare the accounting principles employed by the company with those generally used in the industry and by the competition. Do the principles used by the company inflate earnings?

2. Review recent changes in accounting principles and changes in estimates to determine if they inflate earnings.

31. Ibid., para. 128.

32. See, for example, B. Lev, "On the Usefulness of Earnings: Lessons and Directions from Two Decades of Empirical Research," *Journal of Accounting Research* (Supplement, 1989): 153–92.

3. Determine if discretionary expenditures, such as advertising, have been postponed by comparing them to those of previous periods.

4. Attempt to assess whether some expenses, such as warranty expense, are not reflected on the income statement.

5. Determine the replacement cost of inventories and other assets. Assess whether the company generates sufficient cash flow to replace its assets.

6. Review the notes to financial statements to determine if loss contingencies exist that might reduce future earnings and cash flows.

7. Review the relationship between sales and receivables to determine if receivables are increasing more rapidly than sales.

8. Review the management discussion and analysis section of the annual report and the auditor's opinion to determine management's opinion of the company's future and to identify any major accounting issues.

These techniques can help determine whether a company's financial statements have adequately captured the economic substance of the company's operations. One study based on the use of these techniques found that earnings adjusted for nonsustainable gains and losses provided a better explanation of changes in stock prices than did reported income.[33] This result implies that investors and other financial statement users should attempt to adjust the financial statements to reflect economic reality.

There is evidence that investors are becoming more interested in the quality of firms' earnings. In late 1999, American Express, Pitney Bowes, and Tyco International all suffered stock price declines after they reported nonsustainable gains in their quarterly reports. Apparently, the market viewed reporting the gains as an effort to meet earnings expectations.[34] In previous years, investors frequently ignored the components of the reported quarterly income numbers as long income estimates were met. The market's reaction to the reports by American Express and the others may indicate that the market is looking at the components of the income number more skeptically. The SEC has also expressed interest in this issue and has adopted rules that will allow it to consider what might have prompted companies to make, or fail to make, adjustments to their financial statements. These concerns arise because missing expected earnings estimates by even a small amount often has a large impact on a company's stock price. The SEC guidelines indicate that if a company expects an item to have a significant negative impact on its stock price, that item must be reported.

Earnings Management

Earnings management is another aspect of the issue regarding quality of earnings. *Earnings management* is defined as the attempt by corporate officers to influence short-term reported income. During the 1990s many corporate executives faced extreme pressure to attain targeted earnings and to reach financial analysts' earnings projections for their companies. In response, some managers turned to using

33. B. Lev and R. Thiagarajan, "Fundamental Information Analysis," *Journal of Accounting Research* (Autumn 1991): 190–215.

34. Susan Pulliam, "Earnings Management Spurs Selloffs Now," *Wall Street Journal*, 29 October 1999, C1, C2.

aggressive and even fraudulent financial reporting practices. One study found that earnings management occurs for a variety of reasons, including influencing the stock market, increasing management compensation, reducing the likelihood of violating lending agreements, and avoiding intervention by government regulators.[35] Managers may attempt to manage earnings because they believe reported earnings influence investor and creditor decisions. In most cases, earnings management techniques are designed to improve reported income effects and to lower the company's cost of capital. On the other hand, in a move to increase future profits, management may take the opportunity to report more bad news in periods when performance is low.

Some individuals maintain that executive compensation schemes, particularly executive stock option plans, contributed to the earnings management abuses of the 1990s. This view holds that the mix in senior management's compensation between rewards tied directly to performance (e.g., stock options) and personal rewards tied to the scheme's role in the company (e.g., personal salaries) influences its performance on behalf of shareholders. Likewise, the number of people involved in the day-to-day administration of a company influences the extent to which those individuals identify with the management team or with shareholder goals. Generally, the greater the focus on insider benefits to senior management, the higher is the risk of fraud; the greater the political clout of senior management relative to external directors, the higher is the risk of fraud; and the greater the commitment to stock options and benefits that encourage a long-term view, oversight, and balance between the influence of management and the board of directors, the lower is the risk of fraud.

Assessing the appropriateness of an earnings management technique depends on its objectives. In some cases, earnings management does not involve techniques outside the scope of GAAP. Corporate managers often choose accounting policies that maximize earnings and the firm's market value. In general, these techniques involve revenue and expense recognition issues and include estimating bad debt allowances, doing inventory write-downs, estimating the percentage of completion of long-term construction projects, and choosing a depreciation method.

These types of earnings management techniques are considered legitimate; it is illegitimate earnings management and the misrepresentation of earnings that concern the SEC and the investment community. In 1998, Arthur Levitt, the former chair of the SEC, outlined five earnings management techniques that he said threaten the integrity of financial reporting:[36]

1. *Taking a bath*. The one-time overstatement of restructuring charges to reduce assets, which reduces future expenses. The expectation is that the one-time loss is discounted in the marketplace by analysts and investors who will focus on future earnings.

2. *Creative acquisition accounting*. Avoiding future expenses by one-time charges for in-process research and development.

---

35. Paul M. Healy and James Wahlen, "A Review of the Earnings Management Literature and its Implications for Standard Setting," *Accounting Horizons* (December 1999), 366–83.

36. Arthur Levitt, "The Numbers Game," remarks delivered at the New York University Center for Law and Business, September 28, 1998.

FIGURE 5.2 *Distinction between Conservative, Neutral, Aggressive, and Fraudulent Earnings Management Activities*

Conservative accounting	Overly aggressive recognition of loss or reserve provisions Overvaluation of acquired in-process research and development activities
Neutral earnings	Earnings that result from using a neutral perspective
Aggressive accounting	Understating loss or reserve provisions
Fraudulent accounting	Recording sales before they satisfy the earned and measurability criteria Recording fictitious sales
Backdating sales invoices	Overstating inventory

3. *"Cookie jar" reserves.* Overstating sales returns or warranty costs in good times and using these overstatements in bad times to reduce similar charges.

4. *Abusing the materiality concept.* Deliberately recording errors or ignoring mistakes in the financial statements under the assumption that their impact is not significant.

5. *Improper revenue recognition.* Recording revenue before it is earned. It was noted that over half of the SEC's enforcement cases filed in 1999 and 2000 involved improper revenue recognition issues.

Fraudulent Financial Reporting

Many earnings management activities, although aggressive, involve judgments and estimates that are acceptable under GAAP. Earnings manipulations that are intended to deceive investors and creditors, however, constitute financial statement fraud. Figure 5.2, adapted from an article by Dechow and Skinner, depicts the distinction between conservative, neutral, aggressive, and fraudulent earnings management activities.[37]

There are, unfortunately, many examples of fraudulent accounting practices. The Sunbeam case is among the most famous.

The Sunbeam Case

As 1997 neared an end, it was clear that if Sunbeam were going to make the numbers it had promised Wall Street, it would have to find some profits fast. Just how Sunbeam found those profits, and how the auditors resisted and then caved in, provides the most interesting part of the fraud case filed by the Securities

37. P. M. Dechow and D. J. Skinner, "Earnings Management: Reconciling the Views of Accounting Academics, Practitioners and Regulators," *Accounting Horizons* 14 no. 2 (June 2000): 235–50.

and Exchange Commission against Sunbeam's former chief executive, Albert J. Dunlap, who was known as Chainsaw Al for his propensity to fire people. The most creative method of producing profits was the spare-parts gambit. Sunbeam owned a lot of spare parts, used to fix its blenders and grills when they broke. Those parts were stored in the warehouse of a company called EPI Printers, which sent the parts out as needed.

The company came up with a scheme to sell the parts for $11 million to EPI and book an $8 million profit. Unfortunately, EPI thought the parts were worth only $2 million. Sunbeam resolved this disagreement by persuading EPI to sign an "agreement to agree" to buy the parts for $11 million, with a clause allowing EPI to void the agreement in January. In fact, the parts were never sold, but the profit was posted. The partner in charge of the Sunbeam audit concluded the profit was not allowed under GAAP. Sunbeam agreed to reduce it by $3 million but would go no further. Here is where the story becomes really interesting. The audit partner could have said that if such a spurious profit were included, he would not sign off on the audit. But he took a different tack. He decided that the remaining profit was not material. Since the audit opinion says the financial statements "present fairly, in all material respects" the company financial position, he could sign off on them. The part that was not presented fairly was not material. And so it did not matter. In fact, the SEC charged that the chief audit partner allowed the inclusion of items he had challenged totaled 16 percent of Sunbeam's reported annual profits.

Subsequently, after the issue was discovered, the auditors issued a new opinion that dropped all the profits that the SEC claimed were fraudulent. It also paid $110 million to settle a Sunbeam shareholders' suit. But it also stood behind the chief audit partner, saying this case involved not fraud, but "professional disagreements about the application of sophisticated accounting standards."

In the typical accounting fraud case, the auditors say they were fooled. Here, according to the SEC, the auditors discovered a substantial part of what the commission called "sham profits." But they decided the amounts were immaterial, and so investors were not told.

The real importance of this case is that it helped establish a principle: It is material information for investors if a company is trying to report fraudulent profits, regardless of the amount. An auditor who knowingly allows such profits to be reported has failed in his or her duty.

Source: Adapted from Floyd Norris, "Auditors Noticed Sunbeam's Fraud but Ignored It," *New York Times, 18 May 2001.*

Several research studies have developed "red flags" of financial statement fraud. Many of these identified red flags can be uncovered only by external or internal auditors, but others may be discerned by reviewing the published financial statements, the company's SEC 10-K Report, and the financial press. The following list identifies some of the items that raise the potential for fraud:

1. A predominantly insider board of directors
2. Management compensation tied to its stock price
3. Frequent changes of auditors
4. Rapid turnover of key personnel
5. Deteriorating earnings
6. Unusually rapid growth

7. Lack of working capital
8. The need to increase the stock price to meet analysts' earnings projections
9. Extremely high levels of debt
10. Cash shortages
11. Significant off–balance sheet financing arrangements
12. Doubt about the company's ability to continue as a going concern
13. SEC or other regulatory investigations
14. Unfavorable industry economic conditions
15. Suspension or delisting from a stock exchange

These red flags do not necessarily indicate the actual presence of fraud, because some of these conditions may be present in normal business environments. But it is important to note that investigators have frequently found these conditions to be present in fraudulent reporting situations. As a result, the existence of one or more red flags does not necessarily mean the company has engaged in fraudulent activities; it only suggests that the potential for fraud exists.[38]

Cases

• Case 5-1 Income Smoothing

One reason accounting earnings may not be a realistic measure of economic income is the incentive and ability of business managers to manipulate reported profits for their own benefit. This may be particularly true when their company has an incentive compensation plan that is linked to reported net income. The manipulation of earnings, known as *earnings management,* frequently involves income smoothing. *Income smoothing* has been defined as the dampening of fluctuations about some level of earnings that is considered normal for the company. Research has indicated that income smoothing occurs because business managers prefer a stable rather than a volatile earnings trend.

Required:

a. Why do business managers prefer stable earnings trends?
b. Discuss several methods business managers might use to smooth earnings.

• Case 5-2 Earnings Quality

Economic income is considered to be a better predictor of future cash flows than accounting income is. A technique used by security analysts to determine the degree of correlation between a firm's accounting earnings and its true economic income is quality of earnings assessment.

---

38. R. K. Elliott and J. J. Willingham, *Management Fraud: Detection and Deterrence* (New York: Petrocelli Books, 1980).

Required:

a. Discuss measures that may be used to assess the quality of a firm's reported earnings.

b. Obtain an annual report for a large corporation and perform a quality of earnings assessment.

• Case 5-3 Revenue Recognition

Bonanza Trading Stamps, Inc. was formed early this year to sell trading stamps throughout the Southwest to retailers, who distribute the stamps gratuitously to their customers. Books for accumulating the stamps and catalogs illustrating the merchandise for which the stamps may be exchanged are given free to retailers for distribution to stamp recipients. Centers with inventories of merchandise premiums have been established for redemption of the stamps. Retailers may not return unused stamps to Bonanza.

The schedule below expresses Bonanza's expectations as to the percentages of a normal month's activity that will be attained. For this purpose, a *normal month's activity* is defined as the level of operations expected when expansion of activities ceases or tapers off to a stable rate. Bonanza expects to attain this level in the third year and to average $2 million per month in stamp sales throughout the third year.

		Merchandise	
Month	Actual Stamp Sales Percentage	Premium Purchases Percentage	Stamp Redemptions Percentage
6	30%	40%	10%
12	60	60	45
18	80	80	70
24	90	90	80
30	100	100	95

Required:

a. Discuss the factors to be considered in determining when revenue should be recognized in measuring the income of a business enterprise.

b. Discuss the accounting alternatives that should be considered by Bonanza Trading Stamps for the recognition of its revenues and related expenses.

c. For each accounting alternative discussed in (b), give balance sheet accounts that should be used and indicate how each account should be classified.

• Case 5-4 Cost, Expense, and Loss

You are requested to deliver your auditor's report personally to the board of directors of Sebal Manufacturing Corporation and answer questions posed about the financial statements. While reading the statements, one director asks, "What are the precise meanings of the terms *cost, expense,* and *loss*? These terms sometimes seem to identify similar items and other times seem to identify dissimilar items."

Required:

a. Explain the meanings of (1) *cost,* (2) *expense,* and (3) *loss* as used for financial reporting in conformity with GAAP. In your explanation, discuss the distinguishing characteristics of the terms and their similarities and interrelationships.

b. Classify each of the following items as a cost, expense, loss, or other category, and explain how the classification of each item may change:

   i. Cost of goods sold

   ii. Bad debts expense

   iii. Depreciation expense for plant machinery

   iv. Organization costs

   v. Spoiled goods

c. The terms *period cost* and *product cost* are sometimes used to describe certain items in financial statements. Define these terms and distinguish between them. To what types of items does each apply?

• Case 5-5 Revenue Recognition

Revenue is usually recognized at the point of sale. Under special circumstances, however, bases other than the point of sale are used for the timing of revenue recognition.

Required:

a. Why is the point of sale generally used as the basis for the timing of revenue recognition?

b. Disregarding the special circumstances when bases other than the point of sale are used, discuss the merits of each of the following objections to the sales basis of revenue recognition:

   i. It is too conservative because revenue is earned throughout the entire process of production.

   ii. It is not conservative enough because accounts receivable do not represent disposable funds, sales returns and allowances may be made, and collection and bad debt expenses may be incurred in a later period.

c. Revenue may also be recognized (1) during production and (2) when cash is received. For each of these two bases of timing revenue recognition, give an example of the circumstances in which it is properly used and discuss the accounting merits of its use in lieu of the sales basis.

• Case 5-6 Presentation of Financial Statement Information

The FASB has issued *SFAC No. 5,* "Recognition and Measurement in Financial Statements of Business Enterprises." In general, this statement sets recognition criteria and guidance for what information should be incorporated into financial statements and when this information should be reported.

Required:
According to *SFAC No. 5*, five general categories of information should be provided by a full set of financial statements. List and discuss these five categories of information.

• Case 5-7 Matching Concept

The accounting profession has employed the matching concept to determine what to report in the income statement and to determine how to measure items reported in the income statement. This concept implies that expenses should be measured directly, and thus balance sheet measures are residuals. The matching concept is therefore an income statement approach to the measurement and reporting of revenues and expenses.

SFAC No. 5 defined *earnings* as the change in net assets exclusive of investments by owners and distributions to owners, a capital maintenance concept of earnings measurement. Under this concept, asset and liabilities would be measured directly, and changes to them would flow through the income statement. Thus the *SFAC No. 5* definition of earnings represents a balance sheet approach to the measurement and report of revenues and expenses.

Required:
  a. Describe and discuss the matching concept and its importance to income reporting.
  b. Give specific examples of how the matching concept is used in practice.
  c. Describe and discuss the balance sheet approach and its importance to income reporting.
  d. Give specific examples of how balance sheet measurements affect the measurement and reporting of earnings.

• Case 5-8 The Concept of Conservatism

The concept of conservatism has been influential in the development of accounting theory and practice. A major effect of conservatism is that accountants tend to recognize losses but not gains. For example, when the value of an asset is impaired, it is written down to fair value and an unrealized loss is recognized in the income statement. However, when the asset's value appreciates, its value is not written up to fair value. (An exception is current accounting for investments in securities having readily determinable fair values.) Stated differently, accountants tend to recognize holding losses but not holding gains.

Required:
  a. Define *conservatism*.
  b. Why do you believe conservatism has affected financial reporting? Explain.

c. Do you believe that financial statements that recognize losses but not gains provide information that is relevant and representationally faithful? Explain.

d. Do you believe that the concept of conservatism is consistent with the physical capital maintenance concept? Explain.

e. Do you believe that the concept of conservatism is consistent with the financial capital maintenance concept? Explain.

FASB ASC Research

For each of the following research cases, search the FASB ASC database for information to address the issues. Cut and paste the FASB ASC paragraphs that support your responses. Then summarize briefly what your responses are, citing the paragraphs used to support your responses.

• FASB ASC 5-1 Revenue Recognition

Search the FASB ASC current text section to find the paragraphs relating to revenue recognition.

• FASB ASC 5-2 Recognition of Franchise Fee Revenue

Under current GAAP, franchise fee revenue from an individual franchise sale ordinarily shall be recognized, with an appropriate provision for estimated uncollectible amounts, when all material services or conditions relating to the sale have been substantially performed or satisfied by the franchisor. Search the FASB ASC database to determine under what condition(s) substantial performance by the franchisor is deemed to have occurred. Cut and paste your findings, and then write a summary of what you found.

• FASB ASC 5-3 Real Estate Sales

Several FASB statements deal with accounting for real estate sales. Search the FASB ASC database to determine under what conditions profit from real estate sales can be recognized. Cut and paste your findings, and then write a summary of what you found.

• FASB ASC 5-4 Current Value

The FASB ASC has identified an area where current-value financial statements are more useful than historical cost statements. Search the FASB ASC database to find the paragraphs addressing this issue, cite it, and copy the results.

• FASB ASC 5-5 Accounting for Inflation

The general topic of accounting for inflation is outlined in the FASB's ASC. Cite and copy the information on the topic of inflation.

• FASB ASC 5-6 Revenue and Gains

The general topic of revenue recognition is outlined in the FASB ASC. Within that general topic, the concepts of revenue and gains are discussed. Search the codification to find this area, cite it, and copy the results.

• FASB ASC 5-7 Accounting for Long-Term Construction Contracts

The percentage of completion and completed contract methods are described in the FASB ASC. Search the codification to find the paragraphs covering these topics, cite them, and copy the results.

• FASB ASC 5-8 Use of the Installment and Cost Recovery Methods

The use of the installment and cost recovery methods of revenue recognition are outlined in the FASB ASC. Search the FASB ASC database to find paragraphs addressing these topics, cite them, and copy the results.

• FASB ASC 5-9 Matching

The concept of matching is discussed in several places in the FASB ASC. Find three references to matching, cite the paragraph numbers, and copy your findings.

• FASB ASC 5-10 Conservatism

The concept of conservatism is discussed in the FASB ASC in conjunction with quasi reorganizations. Search the codification to find paragraphs addressing this area, cite them, and copy the results.

• FASB ASC 5-11 Materiality

The concept of materiality is discussed in several places in the FASB ASC. Find three references to materiality, cite the paragraphs addressing this issue, and copy your findings.

Room for Debate

• Debate 5-1 Concepts of Capital Maintenance

SFAC No. 5 states that the concept of capital maintenance is critical in distinguishing an enterprise's return on investment from return of its investment. Two concepts of capital maintenance are discussed—physical capital maintenance and financial capital maintenance.

Team Debate:

Team 1:   Present arguments in favor of the physical capital maintenance concept.

Team 2:   Present arguments in favor of the financial capital maintenance concept.

• Debate 5-2 Economic versus Accounting Income

Economists and accountants agree that the concept of income is vitally important. However, the two disciplines disagree on what income is and how it should be measured.

Team Debate:

Team 1:   Present arguments in favor of the economist's view of the concept of income.

Team 2:   Present arguments in favor of the accountant's view of the concept of income.

• Debate 5-3 Current-value Measures

Some accounting theorists believe that entry values should be used to measure current value, while others believe that exit values should be used instead.

Team Debate:

Team 1:   Present arguments in favor of using entry values to measure current value.

Team 2:   Present arguments in favor of using exit values to measure current value.

Financial Statements I:

The Income Statement

The current financial reporting environment in the United States consists of various groups that are affected by and have a stake in the financial reporting requirements of the FASB and the SEC. These groups include investors, creditors, security analysts, regulators, management, and auditors. Investors in equity securities are the central focus of the financial reporting environment. Investment involves forgoing current uses of resources for ownership interests in companies. These ownership interests are claims to uncertain future cash flows. Consequently, investment involves giving up current resources for future, uncertain resources, and investors require information that will help them assess future cash flows from securities.

The Economic Consequences of Financial Reporting

In Chapter 1, we introduced the concept of economic consequences. Income measurement and financial reporting also involve economic consequences, including the following:

- Financial information can affect the distribution of wealth among investors. More informed investors, or investors employing security analysts, may be able to increase their wealth at the expense of less informed investors.

- Financial information can affect the level of risk accepted by a firm. As discussed in Chapter 4, focusing on short-term, less risky projects may have long-term detrimental effects.

- Financial information can affect the rate of capital formation in the economy and result in a reallocation of wealth between consumption and investment within the economy.

- Financial information can affect how investment is allocated among firms.

Since economic consequences may affect different users of information differently, the selection of financial reporting methods by the FASB and the SEC involves trade-offs. The deliberations of accounting standard setters should consider these economic consequences.

Income Statement Elements

The FASB's *Statement of Financial Accounting Concepts (SFAC) No. 1* indicates that the primary purpose of financial reporting is to provide information about a company's performance via measures of earnings. The income statement is of primary importance in this endeavor because of its predictive value, a qualitative characteristic defined in *SFAC No. 2*. Income reporting also has value as a measure of future cash flows, as a measure of management efficiency, and as a guide to the accomplishment of managerial objectives.

The emphasis on corporate income reporting as the vehicle for relaying performance assessments to investors has caused a continuing dialogue among accountants about the proper identification of revenues, gains, expenses, and losses. These financial statement elements are defined in *SFAC No. 6* as follows:

- *Revenues.* Inflows or other enhancements of assets of an entity or settlement of its liabilities (or a combination of both) during a period from delivering or producing goods, rendering services, or other activities that constitute the entity's ongoing major or central operations.

- *Gains.* Increases in net assets from peripheral or incidental transactions of an entity and from all other transactions and other events and circumstances affecting the entity during a period except those that result from revenues or investments by owners.

- *Expenses.* Outflows or other using-up of assets or incurrences of liabilities (or a combination of both) during a period from delivering or producing goods, rendering services, or carrying out other activities that constitute the entity's ongoing major or central operations.

- *Losses.* Decreases in net assets from peripheral or incidental transactions of an entity and from all other transactions and other events and circumstances affecting the entity during a period except from expenses or distributions to owners.[1]

Notice that each of these terms is defined as changes in assets and/or liabilities. This represents a change in emphasis by the FASB from previous definitions provided by the Accounting Principles Board (APB) that stressed inflows and outflows, realization, and the matching concept. Consequently, current recognition and measurement criteria for revenues, expenses, gains, and losses are more closely associated with asset and liability valuation issues, and the balance sheet has become more than a place to store residual values in the income determination process. Although he regarded the new definitions as a distinct improvement, David Solomons, a former member of the Wheat Committee, suggested that they

---

1. Financial Accounting Standards Board, *Statement of Financial Accounting Concepts No. 6,* "Elements of Financial Statements" (Stamford, CT: FASB, 1985), paras. 79–88.

were not sufficiently robust to deal with some of the most difficult accounting problems.[2]

The following are some differences between the changes in assets and/or liabilities and the inflows and outflows definitions of income:

- The changes in assets and/or liabilities approach determines earnings as a measure of the change in net economic resources for a period, whereas the inflows and outflows definition views income as a measure of effectiveness.

- The changes in assets and/or liabilities approach depends on the definition of assets and liabilities to define earnings, whereas the inflows and outflows approach depends on definitions of revenues and expenses and matching them to determine income.

- The inflows and outflows approach results in the creation of deferred charges, deferred credits, and reserves when measuring periodic income; the changes in assets and/or liabilities approach recognizes deferred items only when they are economic resources or obligations.

- Both approaches agree that because investors look to financial statements to provide information from which they can extrapolate future resource flows, the income statement is more useful to investors than is the balance sheet.

- The changes in assets and/or liabilities approach limits the population from which the elements of financial statements can be selected to net economic resources and to the transactions and events that change measurable attributes of those net resources. Under the inflows and outflows approach, revenues and expenses may include items necessary to match costs with revenues, even if they do not represent changes in net resources.[3]

An important distinction between revenues and gains and expenses and losses is whether or not they are associated with ongoing operations. Over the years, this distinction has generated questions concerning the nature of income reporting desired by various financial statement users. Two viewpoints have dominated this dialogue and are termed the *current operating performance concept* and the *all-inclusive concept* of income reporting. These viewpoints are summarized in the following paragraphs.

Statement Format

Proponents of the current operating performance concept of income base their arguments on the belief that only changes and events controllable by management that result from current-period decisions should be included in income. This concept implies that normal and recurring items should constitute the principal measure of enterprise performance. That is, net income should reflect the day-to-day, profit-directed activities of the enterprise, and the inclusion of other items of profit or loss distorts the meaning of the term *net income*.

Alternatively, advocates of the *all-inclusive* concept of income hold that net income should reflect all items that affected the net increase or decrease in

2. David Solomons, "The FASB's Conceptual Framework: An Evaluation," *Journal of Accountancy* 161, no. 6 (1986): 120–21.

3. L. E. Robinson, "The Time Has Come to Report Comprehensive Income," *Accounting Horizons* (June 1991), 110.

stockholders' equity during the period, with the exception of capital transactions. This group believes that the total net income for the life of an enterprise should be determinable by summing the periodic net income figures.

The underlying assumption behind the current operating performance versus all-inclusive concept controversy is that the manner in which financial information is presented is important. In essence, both viewpoints agree on the information to be presented but disagree on where to disclose certain revenues, expenses, gains, and losses. As discussed in Chapters 4 and 5, research indicates that investors are not influenced by where items are reported in financial statements so long as the statements disclose the same information. So, perhaps, the concern over the current operating performance versus the all-inclusive concept of income is unwarranted. The following paragraphs review the history of the issue.

APB Opinion No. 9

One of the first issues the APB studied was what to include in net income. An APB study revealed that business managers were exercising a great deal of discretion in determining which revenues and expenses, and gains and losses, to include on the income statement or on the retained earnings statement. The lack of formal guidelines concerning adjustments to retained earnings resulted in the placement of most items of revenue or gain on the income statement, whereas many expense and loss items that were only remotely related to previous periods were treated as adjustments to retained earnings.

The APB's study of these reporting abuses and its general review of the overall nature of income resulted in the release of *APB Opinion No. 9*, "Reporting the Results of Operations." This opinion took a middle position between the current operating performance and all-inclusive concepts by stating that net income should reflect all items of profit and loss recognized during the period, with the exception of prior period adjustments. In addition, the APB's prescribed statement format included two income figures: net income from operations and net income from operations plus extraordinary items. *APB Opinion No. 9* required preparers of financial statements to determine whether revenues and expenses and gains and losses were properly classified as normal recurring items, extraordinary items, or prior period adjustments according to established criteria. In general, the opinion's provisions specified that all items were to be considered normal and recurring unless they met the stated requirements for classification as either extraordinary items or prior period adjustments (discussed later in the chapter).

Separating the income statement into net income from operations and net income after extraordinary items allowed for the disclosure of most items of revenue and expense and gains and losses on the income statement during any period. It also gave financial statement users the ability to evaluate the results of normal operations or total income according to their needs.

The FASB noted in *SFAC No. 5* that the all-inclusive income statement is intended to avoid discretionary omissions from the income statement, even though "inclusion of unusual or non-recurring gains or losses might reduce the usefulness of an income statement for one year for predictive purposes."[4] The

4. Financial Accounting Standards Board, *Statement of Financial Accounting Concepts No. 5*, "Recognition and Measurement in Financial Statements of Business Enterprises" (Stamford, CT: FASB, 1984), para. 35.

FASB has also stated that because the effects of an entity's activities vary in terms of stability, risks, and predictability, there is a need for information about the various components of income. In the following paragraphs, we examine the elements of the income statement, introduce the accounting principles currently being used in measuring these elements, and discuss how they are disclosed on the income statements of The Hershey Company and Tootsie Roll Industries, Inc., illustrated on pages 171 and 172.

The Hershey Company engages in the manufacture, distribution, and sale of confectionery, snack, refreshment, and grocery products in the United States and internationally. The company sells its products primarily to wholesale distributors, chain grocery stores, mass merchandisers, chain drug stores, vending companies, wholesale clubs, convenience stores, and concessionaires through sales representatives, food brokers, and retail sales merchandisers. Tootsie Roll Industries, Inc., through its subsidiaries, engages in the manufacture and sale of confectionery products. The company's customers include wholesale distributors of candy and groceries, supermarkets, variety stores, dollar stores, chain grocers, drug chains, discount chains, cooperative grocery associations, warehouse and membership club stores, vending machine operators, the U.S. military, and fund-raising charitable organizations. It operates primarily in the United States, Canada, and Mexico, as well as distributing its products through candy and grocery brokers.

The two companies' income statements disclose the aggregate financial results of these activities and include comparative information for the 2008, 2007, and 2006 fiscal years.[5] (see Exhibits 6.1 and 6.2.) The SEC requires all companies to provide three-year comparative income statements and two-year comparative balance sheets. Consequently, most publicly held companies also provide similar data in their annual reports. The components of the traditional income statement exclusive of the elements of other comprehensive income are discussed in the following paragraphs. The elements of other comprehensive income are discussed later in the chapter.

Income from Continuing Operations

The amounts disclosed to arrive at income from continuing operations are the company's normal and recurring revenues and expenses. The resulting income figure represents the amount expected to recur in the future, often referred to as the company's sustainable income. *Sustainable income* is the amount investors should use as a starting point to predict future earnings. In addition, the amount of income tax disclosed in this section of the income statement is the amount of income tax the company would have reported if no nonrecurring income items had been incurred. Hershey's 2008 income statement reports "Income before Income Taxes" of $492,022,000 and income tax on this amount of $180,617,000 the net amount, $311,405,000 is Hershey's income from continuing operations. Similarly, Tootsie Roll's income from continuing operations is reported as the company's "Net Earnings." In 2008 Tootsie Roll reported net earnings of $38,777,000.

---

5. Summary segmental performance information is required to be disclosed by FASB ASC 280-10, as discussed in Chapter 15.

Nonrecurring items of Income

Three nonrecurring items of income may also be incurred by a company. These items are discontinued operations, extraordinary items, and accounting changes. These items are discussed in the following paragraphs.

Discontinued Operations

Study of the results of the application of *APB Opinion No. 9* by various entities disclosed some reporting abuses. For example, some companies were reporting the results of the disposal of segment assets as extraordinary while including the revenue from these segments during the disposal period as ordinary income. In *Opinion No. 30*, the APB concluded that additional criteria were necessary to identify disposed segments of a business. This release required the separate presentation of (1) the results of operations of the disposed segment, and (2) gain or loss on the sale of assets for disposed segments including any operating gains or losses during the disposal period. This information was seen as necessary to users in order to evaluate the past and expected future operations of a business entity. The total

EXHIBIT 6.1 *The Hershey Company Consolidated Statements of Income*

For the years ended December 31	2008	2007	2006
In thousands of dollars except per-share amounts			
Net Sales			
Costs and Expenses:	$5,132,768	$4,946,716	$4,944,230
Cost of sales	3,375,050	3,315,147	3,076,718
Selling, marketing, and administrative	1,073,019	895,874	860,378
Business realignment and impairment charges, net	94,801	276,868	14,576
Total costs and expenses	4,542,870	4,487,889	3,951,672
Income before Interest and Income Taxes	589,898	458,827	992,558
Interest expense, net	97,876	118,585	116,056
Income before Income Taxes	$ 492,022	$ 340,242	$ 876,502
Provision for income taxes	180,617	126,088	317,441
Net Income	$ 311,405	$ 214,154	$ 559,061
Net Income per Share—Basic— Class B Common Stock	$ 1.27	$ .87	$ 2.19
Net Income per Share—Diluted— Class B Common Stock	$ 1.27	$ .87	$ 2.17
Net Income per Share—Basic— Common Stock	$ 1.41	$ .96	$ 2.44
Net Income per Share—Diluted— Common Stock	$ 1.36	$ .93	$ 2.34
Cash Dividends Paid per Share:			
Common Stock	$ 1.1900	$ 1.1350	$ 1.030
Class B Common Stock	1.0712	1.0206	.925

EXHIBIT 6.2 *Tootsie Roll Industries, Inc. and Subsidiaries Consolidated Statements of Earnings, Comprehensive Earnings, and Retained Earnings*

For the year ended December 31	2008	2007	2006
In thousands except per-share data			
Net product sales	$492,051	$492,742	$495,990
Rental and royalty revenue	3,965	4,975	5,150
Total revenue	496,016	497,717	501,140
Product cost of goods sold	333,314	327,695	311,267
Rental and royalty cost	921	1,349	1,312
Total costs	334,235	329,044	312,579
Product gross margin	158,737	165,047	184,723
Rental and royalty gross margin	3,044	3,626	3,838
Total gross margin	161,781	168,673	188,561
Selling, marketing and administrative expenses	95,254	97,821	101,032
Earnings from operations	66,527	70,852	87,529
Other income (expense), net	(10,618)	6,315	7,186
Earnings before income taxes	55,909	77,167	94,715
Provision for income taxes	17,132	25,542	28,796
Net earnings	$ 38,777	$ 51,625	$ 65,919
Net earnings	$ 38,777	$ 51,625	$ 65,919
Other comprehensive earnings (loss)	(3,514)	810	(3,697)
Comprehensive earnings	$ 35,263	$ 52,435	$ 62,222
Retained earnings at beginning of year	$156,752	$169,233	$164,236
Net earnings	38,777	51,625	65,919
Cash dividends ($.32, $.32, and $.32 per share, respectively)	(17,492)	(17,170)	(17,421)
Stock dividends	(35,165)	(46,685)	(43,694)
Cumulative effect of SAB 108	—	—	(58)
Retained earnings at end of year	$142,872	$156,752	$169,233
Earnings per share	$ 0.70	$ 0.91	$ 1.15
Average common and class B common shares outstanding	55,157	56,585	57,405

gain or loss is determined by summing any gains or losses on disposal of segment assets, and gains or losses incurred by the operations of the disposed segment during the period of disposal.

Opinion No. 30 was later amended by *SFAS No. 144*, "Accounting for the Impairment or Disposal of Long-Lived Assets" (see FASB ASC 360). To qualify for treatment as a discontinued operation, an item must meet several criteria. First, the unit being discontinued must be considered a "component" of the business. The definition of component is based on the notion of distinguishable operations and cash flows. Specifically, FASB ASC 205-10-20 defines a component of an entity as comprising operations and cash flows that can be clearly distinguished, operationally and for financial reporting purposes, from the rest of the entity.

> Certain units—segments, operating divisions, lines of business, subsidiaries—are usually considered components. But depending on the business in which an entity operates, other units may be considered components as well.[6]

Assuming the unit to be discontinued is a component of the business, it must meet two additional criteria before the transaction can be reported as a discontinued operation. First, the operations and cash flows of the component being disposed of must be eliminated from the operations and cash flows of the entity as a result of the transaction. The company is not allowed to retain an interest in the cash flows of the operation and still account for it as a discontinued operation. Second, and finally, the entity must retain no significant involvement in the operations of the component after the disposal takes place.

Once management decides to sell a component, its assets and liabilities are classified as "held for sale" on its balance sheet. Then, if a business has a component classified as held for sale, or if it actually disposes of the component during the accounting period, it is to report the results of the operations of the component in that period, and in all periods presented on a comparative income statement, as a discontinued operation. It should report these results directly under the income subtotal "Income from Continuing Operations." These results would be reported net of applicable income taxes or benefit. In the period in which the component is actually sold (or otherwise disposed of), the results of operations and the gain or loss on the sale should be combined and reported on the income statement as the gain or loss from the operations of the discontinued unit.[7] The gain or loss on disposal may then be disclosed on the face of the income statement or in the notes to the financial statements.

6. By employing the "component" concept, the FASB meant to broaden the allowable business units that could be reported as a discontinued operation. Under *APB No. 30*, the discontinued operation had to be a segment before it could qualify for treatment as a discontinued operation.

7. This treatment differs significantly from the treatment afforded to discontinued operations under *APB No. 30*. Under *APB No. 30*, a firm was required to estimate the future income or loss from the operations of the discontinued operation as well as the future gain or loss on disposal, if the sale crossed accounting periods. If the estimated future results of operations and the estimated future gain or loss on the sale resulted in an estimated future net loss, the entity was to report the loss on disposal *in the current period* as a separate line item in the discontinued operations section of the Income Statement. The effect of this treatment was to recognize future operating and disposal losses before they occurred, and to measure the discontinued operation on a net realizable value basis. This treatment has been superseded by *SFAS No. 144* (see FASB ASC 360-10-05), which both simplified the accounting for discontinued operations and made it more consistent with the accounting model for the impairment of long-lived assets.

Accounting for discontinued operations is under continuing review. In September 2008, the FASB issued an Exposure Draft, *Amending the Criteria for Reporting a Discontinued Operations,* the IASB also issued an Exposure Draft, *Discontinued Operations,* which proposes amendments to *IFRS No. 5* (discussed later in the chapter) that parallel those outlined in the FASB proposal. The two boards noted that at that time, the definitions of a discontinued operation in *SFAS No.144* (discussed in Chapter 9) and in *IFRS No. 5* were not convergent. That is, *SFAS No. 144* defined a discontinued operation as a component of an entity that has been disposed of or is classified as held for sale provided that (1) the operations and cash flows of the component have been (or will be) eliminated from the ongoing operations of the entity as a result of the disposal transaction and (2) the entity will have no significant continuing involvement in the operations of the component after the disposal transaction. *SFAS No. 144* indicated that a component of an entity may be a reportable segment or an operating segment, a reporting unit, a subsidiary, or an asset group. *IFRS No. 5* defines a discontinued operation as a component of an entity that either has been disposed of or is classified as held for sale, and (1) represents a separate major line of business or geographical area of operations, (2) is part of a single coordinated plan to dispose of a separate major line of business or geographical area of operations, or (3) is a subsidiary acquired exclusively with a view to resale.

As a part of their joint project on financial statement presentation, the two boards decided to develop a common definition of a discontinued operation and require common disclosures for all components of an entity that have been disposed of or are classified as held for sale. The proposal defines a discontinued operation as a component of an entity that is

a. An *operating segment* (as that term is defined in *SFAS No. 131,* FASB ASC 280-10-20; see Chapter 16) and either has been disposed of or is classified as held for sale; or

b. A *business* (as that term is defined in *SFAS No. 141,* "Business Combinations," (see FASB ASC 805-10-20) that meets the criteria to be classified as held for sale on acquisition (see Chapter 16).

Neither Hershey nor Tootsie Roll disclosed any discontinued operation for the three fiscal years covered by their income statements.

Extraordinary Items

Extraordinary items were originally defined in *APB Opinion No. 9* as events and transactions of material effect that would not be expected to recur frequently and that would not be considered as recurring factors in any evaluation of the ordinary operating processes of the business.[8] This release provided the following examples of these events and transactions: gains or losses from the sale or abandonment of a plant or a significant segment of the business; gains or losses from the sale of an investment not held for resale; the write-off of goodwill owing to unusual events during the period; the condemnation or expropriation of properties; and major devaluations of currencies in a foreign country in which the company was operating.

---

8. Accounting Principles Board, *APB Opinion No. 9,* "Reporting the Results of Operations" (New York: American Institute of Certified Public Accountants, 1966).

The usefulness of the then-prevailing definition of extraordinary items came under review in 1973, and the APB concluded that similar items of revenues and expenses were not being classified in the same manner across the spectrum of business enterprises. The Board also concluded that businesses were not interpreting *APB Opinion No. 9* in a similar manner and that more specific criteria were needed to ensure a more uniform interpretation of its provisions. In *APB Opinion No. 30*, "Reporting the Results of Operations," extraordinary items were defined as events and transactions that are distinguished by both their unusual nature and their infrequency of occurrence. These characteristics were originally defined as follows.

- *Unusual nature.* The event or transaction should possess a high degree of abnormality and be unrelated or only incidentally related to ordinary activities.

- *Infrequency of occurrence.* The event or transaction would not reasonably be expected to recur in the foreseeable future.[9] Question: given the ASC, should we remove footnotes to original sources?

In *APB Opinion No. 30*, several types of transactions were defined as not meeting these criteria. These included write-downs and write-offs of receivables, inventories, equipment leased to others, deferred research and development costs, or other intangible assets; gains or losses in foreign currency transactions or devaluations; gains or losses on disposals of segments of a business; other gains or losses on the sale or abandonment of property, plant, and equipment used in business; effects of strikes; and adjustments of accruals on long-term contracts. The position expressed in *Opinion No. 30* was, therefore, somewhat of a reversal in philosophy; some items previously defined as extraordinary in *APB Opinion No. 9* were now specifically excluded from that classification. The result was the retention of the extraordinary item classification on the income statement. However, the number of revenue and expense items allowed to be reported as extraordinary was significantly reduced.

The separation of extraordinary items from other items on the income statement does not result in a separation of recurring from nonrecurring items. An item that is infrequent but not unusual is classified as nonoperating income in the other gains and losses section of the income statement. Research has indicated that this requirement is not consistent with the FASB's predictive ability criterion. Classifying nonrecurring items tends to increase the variability of earnings per share before extraordinary items and to decrease the predictive ability of earnings.[10] If this evidence is proven correct, the FASB should consider revising income statement reporting practices so that they provide increased predictive ability when nonrecurring items are in evidence. One possible method of achieving this result might be to require footnote disclosure of the effect of nonrecurring items on income and earnings per share. Neither Hershey Company nor Tootsie

9. Accounting Principles Board, *Accounting Principles Board Opinion No. 30*, "Reporting the Results of Operations" (New York: American Institute of Certified Public Accountants, 1973), para. 20.

10. A. B. Cameron and L. Stephens, "The Treatment of Non-Recurring Items in the Income Statement and Their Consistency with the FASB Concept Statements," *Abacus* (September 1991), 81–96.

Roll reported any extraordinary items for the three fiscal years covered by their income statements.[11]

The classification of an event as extraordinary is also affected by the reporting entity's ability to measure it. Consider what happened following the September 11, 2001, terrorist attacks. Shortly after the attacks, the Emerging Issues Task Force (EITF) met to consider the accounting and reporting issues raised by the terrorist attacks. Firms suffering from the attacks had requested guidance from the FASB concerning certain financial reporting issues. At its September 21, 2001, meeting, the EITF tentatively agreed that the losses sustained by companies as a result of the attacks should be considered extraordinary. All the EITF members agreed that the events were both unusual in nature and infrequent. But at the September 28 meeting, the task force decided against treating losses associated with the attack as extraordinary:

> At last week's meeting, the Task Force concluded that, while the events of September 11 were certainly extraordinary, the financial reporting treatment that uses that label would not be an effective way to communicate the financial effects of those events and should not be used in this case. The EITF observed that the economic effects of the events were so extensive and pervasive that it would be impossible to capture them in any one financial statement line item. Any approach to extraordinary item accounting would include only a part—and perhaps a relatively small part—of the real effect of these tragic events. Readers of financial reports will be intensely interested in understanding the whole impact of the events on each company. The EITF concluded that showing part of the effect as an "extraordinary item" would hinder, rather than help, effective communication.[12]

Accounting Changes

The accounting standard of consistency indicates that similar transactions should be reported in the same manner each year. Stated differently, management should choose the set of accounting practices that most correctly presents the resources and performance of the reporting unit and continue to use those practices each year. However, companies may occasionally find that reporting is improved by changing the methods and procedures previously used or that changes in reporting may be dictated by the FASB or the SEC. Even though the results of efficient market research indicate that changes in income due to changed accounting methods do not affect stock prices, when changes in

11. The requirements for reporting an extraordinary item are difficult to meet. In a survey of 600 firms, the AICPA found that only seven (1.17 percent) firms reported an extraordinary item in 2000 that was not associated with the early extinguishment of debt. Until *SFAS No. 145* (which became effective in May 2002, gains or losses from the early extinguishment of debt, if material, were to be classified as extraordinary items. *SFAS No. 145* (see FASB ASC 470-50-45) changed this requirement so that now early debt extinguishment must meet the unusual and infrequent criteria in order to qualify for treatment as an extraordinary item.

12. Financial Accounting Standards Board, "FASB's Emerging Issues Task Force Decides Against Extraordinary Treatment for Terrorist Attack Costs," News release, October 1, 2001.

reporting practices occur, the comparability of financial statements between periods is impaired. The accounting standard of disclosure dictates that the effect of these changes should be reported. The major question surrounding changes in accounting practices is the proper method to use in disclosing them. That is, should previously issued financial statements be changed to reflect the new method or procedure?

The APB originally studied this problem and issued its findings in *APB Opinion No. 20*, "Accounting Changes" (superseded). This release identified three types of accounting changes, discussed the general question of errors in the preparation of financial statements, and defined these changes and errors as follows.

1. *Change in an accounting principle.* This type of change occurs when an entity adopts a GAAP that differs from one previously used for reporting purposes. Examples of such changes are a change from LIFO to FIFO inventory pricing or a change in depreciation methods.

2. *Change in an accounting estimate.* These changes result from the necessary consequences of periodic presentation. That is, financial statement presentation requires estimation of future events, and such estimates are subject to periodic review. Examples of such changes are the life of depreciable assets and the estimated collectability of receivables.

3. *Change in a reporting entity.* Changes of this type are caused by changes in reporting units, which may be the result of consolidations, changes in specific subsidiaries, or a change in the number of companies consolidated.

4. *Errors.* Errors are not viewed as accounting changes; rather, they are the result of mistakes or oversights such as the use of incorrect accounting methods or mathematical miscalculations.[13]

The Board then specified the accounting treatment required to satisfy disclosure requirements in each instance. The basic question was the advisability of retroactive presentation. The following paragraphs summarize the accounting requirements of *APB Opinion No. 20*.

Change in an Accounting Principle

Under the provisions of *APB Opinion No. 20*, when an accounting principle was changed, it was treated currently. That is, the company presented its previously issued financial statements as they were before the change occurred, with the cumulative prior effects of the change shown as a component of net income for the period in which the change occurred. This requirement necessitated determining the yearly changes in net income of all prior periods attributable to changing from one GAAP to another. For example, if a company changed from straight-line to sum-of-year's-digits depreciation, the cumulative effect of this change on all years prior to the change was calculated and disclosed (net of tax) as a separate figure between extraordinary items and net income. The cumulative effect (net of tax) was then disclosed as a separate figure between extraordinary items and net income. In addition, per-share data for all comparative statements included the results of the change as if the change had been consistently applied.

13. Accounting Principles Board, *APB Opinion No. 20*, "Accounting Changes" (New York: AICPA, 1971).

This requirement resulted in the disclosure of additional pro forma, per-share figures for each period presented in which the change affected net income.

The general conclusion of *APB Opinion No. 20* was that previously issued financial statements need not be revised for changes in accounting principles. However, the FASB revisited this issue and in May 2005, it issued *SFAS No. 154*, "Accounting Changes and Error Corrections—A Replacement of APB Opinion No. 20 and FASB Statement No. 3" (see FASB ASC 250). This pronouncement required retrospective application to prior periods' financial statements of changes in accounting principles. *Retrospective application* is defined at FASB ASC 250-10-20 as follows:

> The application of a different accounting principle to one or more previously issued financial statements, or to the statement of financial position at the beginning of the current period, as if that principle had always been used, or a change to financial statements of prior accounting periods to present the financial statements of a new reporting entity as if it had existed in those prior years.

When it is impracticable to determine the period-specific effects of an accounting change on one or more prior periods presented, or to derermine the cumulative effect, FASB ASC 250, requires that the new accounting principle must be applied to the balances of the appropriate assets and liabilities as of the beginning of the earliest period for which retrospective application is practicable and a corresponding adjustment must be made to the opening balance of retained earnings for that period rather than being reported in an income statement. Finally, the guidelines contained at FASB ASC 250 require that a change in depreciation, amortization, or depletion method for long-lived, nonfinancial assets be accounted for as a change in accounting estimate (discussed below) effected by a change in accounting principle.

The guidelines contained at FASB ASC 250 are an example of the effort by the FASB to improve the comparability of cross-border financial reporting by working with the IASB to develop a single set of high-quality accounting standards. As part of that effort, the two bodies identified opportunities to improve financial reporting by eliminating certain narrow differences between their existing accounting standards. Reporting accounting changes was identified as an area in which financial reporting in the United States could be improved by eliminating differences between *Opinion 20* and *IAS 8*, "Accounting Policies, Changes in Accounting Estimates and Errors." FASB ASC 250 (predecessor literature *SFAS No. 154*) was also seen as improving financial reporting because its provisions enhance the consistency of financial information between periods, resulting in more useful financial information that facilitates the analysis and understanding of comparative accounting data.

Change in Estimates

Estimated changes are handled prospectively. They require no adjustments to previously issued financial statements. These changes are accounted for in the period of the change, or if more than one period is affected, in both the period of change and in the future. For example, assume that a company originally estimated that an asset would have a useful service life of 10 years, and after 3 years of service the total service life of the asset was estimated to be only 8 years. The remaining book value of the asset would be depreciated over the remaining useful life of five years. The effects of changes in estimates on operating income, extraordinary items, and the related per-share amounts must be disclosed in the year they occur. As with accounting changes to LIFO, the added disclosures should aid users in their judgments regarding comparability.

Change in Reporting Entities

Changes in reporting entities must be disclosed retroactively by restating all financial statements presented as if the new reporting unit had been in existence at the time the statements were first prepared. That is, previously issued statements are recast to reflect the results of a change in reporting entity. The financial statements should also indicate the nature of the change and the reason for the change. In addition, the effect of the change on operating income, net income, and the related per-share amounts must be disclosed for all comparative statements presented. A change in reporting entity may materially alter financial statements. For example, if a previously unconsolidated subsidiary is consolidated, the investment account is removed and the assets and liabilities of the subsidiary are added to those of the parent company. When this occurs, total assets, debt, and most financial ratios are typically affected. Without retroactive restatement for an accounting change in reporting entity, the investor would find it difficult, if not impossible, to compare company performance before and after the accounting change.

Errors

Errors are defined as prior period adjustments (discussed later in the chapter) by FASB ASC 250. In the period the error is discovered, the nature of the error and its effect on operating income, net income, and the related per-share amounts must be disclosed. In the event the prior period affected is reported for comparative purposes, the corrected information must be disclosed for the period in which it occurred. This requirement is a logical extension of the retroactive treatment required for accounting changes. To continue to report information known to be incorrect would purposefully mislead investors. By providing retroactive corrections, users can better assess the actual performance of the company over time.

The following are examples of errors:

1. A change from an accounting practice that is not generally acceptable to a practice that is generally acceptable
2. Mathematical mistakes
3. The failure to accrue or defer revenues and expenses at the end of any accounting period
4. The incorrect classification of costs and expenses

Earnings per Share

Analysts, investors, and creditors frequently look for some way to condense a firm's performance into a single figure, some quick and efficient way to compare firms' performance. Earnings per share (EPS) serves this purpose, it allows users to summarize the firm's performance in a single number. Additionally, the use of the income statement as the primary source of information by decision makers has resulted in a need to disclose the amount of earnings that accrue to different classes of investors. The amount of earnings accruing to holders of debt and preferred stock (termed senior securities) is generally fixed. Common stockholders are considered residual owners. Their claim to corporate profits is dependent on the levels of revenues and associated expenses. The income remaining after the distribution of interest and preferred dividends is available to common stockholders; it is the focus of accounting income determination. The amount of corporate income accruing to common stockholders is reported on the income statement on a per-share basis.

The basic calculation of EPS is relatively easy. The net income available to common stockholders is divided by the weighted average number of common shares outstanding during the accounting period. A company's net income is already net of interest expense (the claims of debt holders). If the company also has preferred shares outstanding, the claims of these senior securities (dividends) must be subtracted from net income to determine the company's income available to common stockholders. Thus the numerator for basic EPS is net income of the claims of senior securities. Basic EPS is intended to measure the amount that a share of common stock has earned during an accounting period. Because companies often have numerous stock transitions during the accounting period, the denominator is the arithmetic mean of the number of shares outstanding, weighted by time.

Basic EPS is historical. It measures the performance that actually occurred during the accounting period from the perspective of a single share of common stock. However, reporting basic EPS is considered insufficient to meet investor needs because of the potential impact on EPS of a wide variety of securities issued by corporations. For example, many companies have issued stock options, stock warrants, and convertible securities that can be converted into common stock at the option of the holders of the securities. In the event these types of securities are exchanged for common stock, they have the effect of reducing (diluting) the earnings accruing to preexisting stockholders. The exercise of an option or warrant or the conversion of convertible securities to common stock would increase the number of shares of common stock outstanding, thereby having a potentially dilutive effect on EPS. However, the effect on EPS is complicated when a company has convertible securities outstanding because, in addition to issuing new shares of common stock, the amount of the company's reported earnings would also increase. Consequently, the effect of conversion could be either an increase or decrease in reported EPS because the increase in common shares outstanding might be proportionately less than or greater than the accompanying increase in net income.

The APB first discussed the ramifications of these issues in *Opinion No. 9* and developed the residual security and senior security concepts. This release stated:

> When more than one class of common stock is outstanding, or when an outstanding security has participation dividend rights, or when an outstanding security clearly derives a major portion of its value from its conversion rights or its common stock characteristics, such securities should be considered "residual securities" and not "senior securities" for purposes of computing earnings per share.[14]

This provision of *APB Opinion No. 9* was only "strongly recommended" and not made mandatory, but the development of the concept formed the framework for *APB Opinion No. 15*, "Earnings per Share."[15] The latter opinion noted the

---

14. Accounting Principles Board, *APB Opinion No. 9*, para. 23.

15. Accounting Principles Board, *APB Opinion No. 15*, "Earnings per Share" (New York: AICPA, 1969).

importance placed on per-share information by investors and the marketplace and concluded that a consistent method of computation was needed to make EPS amounts comparable across all segments of the business environment.

APB Opinion No. 15 made mandatory the presentation of EPS figures for income before extraordinary items and net income. This requirement was superseded by *SFAS No. 128* (see FASB ASC 260),[16] which requires that EPS figures[17] for income from continuing operations and net income be presented on the face of the income statement. In addition, EPS figures for discontinued operations, extraordinary items, and cumulative effects of accounting changes were required to be disclosed.

Under the provisions of *APB Opinion No. 15*, a company had either a simple or complex capital structure. A *simple capital structure* was comprised solely of common stock or other securities whose exercise or conversion would not in the aggregate dilute EPS by 3 percent or more.

Companies with *complex capital structures* were required to disclose dual EPS figures: (1) primary EPS and (2) fully diluted EPS. *Primary EPS* was intended to display the most likely dilutive effect of exercise or conversion on EPS. It included only the dilutive effects of common stock equivalents. *APB Opinion No. 15* described *common stock equivalents* as securities that are not, in form, common stock, but rather contain provisions that enable the holders of such securities to become common stockholders and to participate in any value appreciation of the common stock. For example, stock warrants, options, and rights were considered common stock equivalents because they exist solely to give the holder the right to acquire common stock. Dual presentation required that EPS be recast under the assumption that the exercise or conversion of potentially dilutive securities (common stock equivalents for primary EPS and all securities for fully dilutive EPS) had actually occurred.

The provisions of *APB Opinion No. 15* were criticized as being arbitrary, too complex, and illogical. Criticisms focused mainly on the requirements for determining whether a convertible security is a common stock equivalent. Under *APB Opinion No. 15* a convertible security was considered a common stock equivalent if, at issuance, its yield was less than two-thirds of the corporate bond yield. This requirement did not reflect the likelihood of conversion in a dynamic securities market. As a result, changes in market prices subsequent to issuance, which may change the nature of convertibles from senior securities to securities that are likely to be converted, were ignored. Thus similar securities issued by different companies were likely to have been classified differently, for common stock equivalency purposes.

In addition, the need for dual presentation as required under *APB Opinion No. 15* was questioned. Companies with complex capital structures were not required to report basic (undiluted) EPS. Critics argued that the extremes, no dilution to full dilution, were endpoints on a continuum of potential dilution and that both endpoints have information content. Moreover, many users contended

---

16. Financial Accounting Standards Board, *SFAS No. 128*, "Earnings per Share" (Stamford, CT: FASB, 1997).

17. Firms with simple capital structures report basic EPS figures. All others report diluted EPS figures. Basic and diluted EPS are discussed later in the chapter.

that basic EPS would be more useful than primary EPS because it displays what actually occurred. Consistent with these views, a research study indicated that primary EPS seldom differs from fully diluted EPS.[18]

In 1991, the FASB issued a plan to make financial statements more useful to investors and creditors by increasing the international comparability of financial information. Subsequently, the FASB undertook a project on the calculation and presentation of EPS information.[19] The International Accounting Standards Committee had begun a similar project in 1989. Both projects were undertaken in response to the criticisms leveled at the complexity and arbitrariness of EPS calculations as described above. While the two bodies agreed to cooperate with each other in sharing information, each issued separate but similar statements: *IAS No. 33* and *SFAS No. 128* (see FASB ASC 260).

The FASB decided to replace primary EPS with basic EPS, citing the following reasons:

1. Basic EPS and diluted EPS data would give users the most factually supportable range of EPS possibilities.

2. Use of a common international EPS statistic is important because of database-oriented financial analysis and the internationalization of business and capital markets.

3. The notion of common stock equivalents does not operate effectively in practice.

4. The computation of primary EPS is complex and may not be well understood or consistently applied.

5. Presenting basic EPS would eliminate the criticisms about the arbitrary determination of whether a security is a common stock equivalent.[20]

FASB ASC 260 requires the presentation of EPS by all companies that have issued common stock or other securities, which upon exercise or conversion would result in the issuance of common stock when those securities are publicly traded. Companies with simple capital structures are to report only basic EPS figures. FASB ASC 260-10-45defines simple capital structures as those companies with only common stock outstanding.[21] All other companies are required to present basic and diluted EPS amounts.

Basic EPS

The objective of *basic EPS* is to measure a company's performance over the reporting period from the perspective of the common stockholder. Basic EPS is

---

18. C. L. DeBerg and B. Murdock, "An Empirical Investigation of the Usefulness of Earnings per Share Information," *Journal of Accounting, Auditing and Finance* (Spring 1994): 249–64.

19. See FASB *Highlights*, "FASB's Plan for International Activities," January 1995, for a discussion of this issue.

20. The sections describing the reasons for issuing standards are not contained in the FASB ASC; they are contained in Financial Accounting Standards Board, *Statement of Financial Accounting Standards No. 128*, "Earnings per Share" (Stamford, CT: FASB, 1997), para. 89.

21. This definition eliminated the *APB Opinion No. 15* 3 percent materiality criterion.

computed by dividing income available to common stockholders by the weighted average number of shares outstanding during the period. That is,

$$\text{Basic EPS} = \frac{\text{Net income} - \text{Preferred dividends}}{\text{Weighted average number of shares outstanding}}$$

Diluted EPS

The objective of *diluted EPS* is to measure a company's pro forma performance over the reporting period from the perspective of the common stockholder as if the exercise or conversion of potentially dilutive securities had actually occurred. This presentation is consistent with the conceptual framework objective of providing information on an enterprise's financial performance, which is useful in assessing the prospects of the enterprise. Basic EPS is historical. It reports what enterprise performance was during the period. Diluted EPS reveals what could happen to EPS if and when dilution occurs. Taken together, these two measures provide users with information to project historical information into the future and to adjust those projections for the effects of potential dilution.

The dilutive effects of *call options and warrants* are reflected in EPS by applying the treasury stock method. The dilutive effects of written *put options*, which require the reporting entity to repurchase shares of its own stock, are computed by applying the reverse treasury stock method. And the dilutive effects of convertible securities are computed by applying the if-converted method. Each of these methods is described below.

Securities whose exercise or conversion is antidilutive (exercise or conversion causes EPS to increase) are excluded from the computation of diluted EPS. Diluted EPS should report the maximum potential dilution. When there is more than one potentially dilutive security, the potential dilutive effect of individual securities is determined first by calculating earnings per incremental share. Securities are then sequentially included in the calculation of diluted EPS. Those with the lowest earnings per incremental share (i.e., those with the highest dilutive potential effect) are included first.

Call Options and Warrants

Call options and warrants give the holder the right to purchase shares of the company's stock for a predetermined option (exercise or strike) price. In the typical exercise of stock options and warrants, the holder receives shares of common stock in exchange for cash. The holders will exercise their options only when the market price of common stock exceeds the option price.[22]

Rather than making complex assumptions regarding how the company might use the cash proceeds from the presumed exercise of call options or warrants, the FASB requires the use of the *treasury stock method* to determine the dilutive effect

---

22. Alternatively, when the option price is higher than the market price of common shares, it would be illogical to presume that dilution would occur. In this case, the options, warrants, or rights are said to be antidilutive. Under FASB ASC 260-10, antidilution occurs when the option price exceeds the average market price during the period.

on EPS.[23] Under this approach, Treasury shares are presumed to be purchased with the proceeds at the average market price occurring during the accounting period.[24] The difference between the number of shares presumed issued upon exercise of the options and the number of treasury shares presumed to have been purchased is termed *incremental shares*. The incremental shares are added to the weighted average number of shares outstanding during the period to determine the dilutive effect of exercising the options or warrants.

Written Put Options

Written put options and forward purchase contracts require the reporting entity to repurchase shares of its own stock at a predetermined price. These securities are dilutive when the exercise price is above the average market price during the period. Hence, their dilutive effect is computed using the *reverse treasury stock method*. This procedure is essentially the opposite of the treasury stock method used for call options and warrants.

Under the reverse treasury stock method, it is presumed that the company issues enough common shares at the average market price to generate enough cash to satisfy the contract. It is then assumed that the proceeds from the stock issuance are used to exercise the put (buy back the shares under contract). The incremental shares (the difference between the number of shares assumed issued and the number of shares that would be received when the put is exercised) are added to the denominator to calculate diluted EPS.

Convertible Securities

Convertible securities are securities (usually bonds or preferred stock) that are convertible into other securities (usually common stock) at a predetermined exchange rate. To determine whether a convertible security is dilutive requires calculation of EPS as if conversion had occurred. The "as-if-converted" figure is then compared to EPS without conversion. If conversion would cause EPS to decline, the security is dilutive. If not, the security would be considered antidilutive, and its pro forma effect of conversion would not be included in diluted EPS.

Under the *if-converted method:*

1. If the company has convertible preferred stock, the preferred dividend applicable to the convertible preferred stock is not subtracted from net income in the EPS numerator. If the preferred stock had been converted,

---

23. For example, if it were assumed that the cash would be spent on operations, the company would have to project the impact of such an investment on revenues and expenses. This would require assumptions regarding such things as the price elasticity of the company's products and services and whether the present physical plant could accommodate the presumed expanded activities.

24. The APB also required the treasury stock approach. As a safeguard against the potential impact that a large repurchase of treasury shares might have on the market price of common shares, the number of treasury shares was limited to 20 percent of the outstanding shares at the end of the period. Excess cash was presumed to have been spent to reduce debt or purchase U.S. government securities. FASB ASC 260-10 imposes no limit on the number of treasury shares assumed repurchased. This is an example of one of the objectives of the original pronouncement, to minimize the computational complexity and arbitrary assumptions of its predecessor, *APB Opinion No. 15*.

the preferred shares would not have been outstanding during the period and the preferred dividends would not have been paid. Hence there would have been no convertible preferred stockholder claim to net income.

2. If the company has convertible debt, the interest expense applicable to the convertible debt net of its tax effect is added to the numerator. If the convertible debt had been converted, the interest would not have been paid to the creditors. At the same time, there would be no associated tax benefit. As a result, net income, and hence income to common stockholders, would have been higher by the amount of the interest expense saved minus its tax benefit.

3. The number of shares that would have been issued upon conversion of the convertible security is added to the denominator.

Contingently Issuable Shares

Contingently issuable shares are those shares whose issuance is contingent upon the satisfaction of certain conditions, such as attaining a certain level of income or market price of the common shares in the future. If all necessary conditions have not been met by the end of the reporting period, FASB ASC 260 requires that contingently issuable shares be included in the computation of diluted EPS based on the number of shares that would be included, if any, if the reporting period were the end of the contingency period. For example, if the shares are issuable once a given level of net income is attained, the company must presume that the current level of earnings will continue until the end of the agreement. Under this presumption, if current earnings are at least as great as the target level of earnings, the contingently issuable shares must be included in diluted EPS if they are dilutive.

The joint FASB-IASB Short-Term International Convergence project is reconsidering some of the more technical aspects of EPS computations relating to the earnings per share treatment of options, warrants, and their equivalents classified as equity, mandatorily convertible instruments, and convertible debt, that are treated differently in *SFAS No. 128* and *IASB No. 33*. At the time this text was published, no amended standard had been issued.

Hershey has a complex capital structure and, consequently, discloses basic as well as diluted EPS on its fiscal 2008 income statements. Tootsie Roll has a simple capital structure and reports only one EPS figure.

Usefulness of Earnings per Share

The overall objective of EPS data is to provide investors with an indication of (1) the value of the firm and (2) expected future dividends. A major theoretical issue surrounding the presentation of EPS is whether this information should be based on historical or forecasted information. Authoritative accounting bodies have generally taken the position that financial information should be based only on historical data. Views formerly expressed by *APB Opinion No. 15* and currently contained at FASB ASC 260 are consistent with this trend.

EPS has been termed a *summary indicator*—a single item that communicates considerable information about an enterprise's performance or financial position. The continuing trend toward complexity in financial reporting has caused many financial statement users to use summary indicators. EPS is especially popular because it is thought to contain information useful in making predictions about future dividends and stock prices, and it is often used as a measure of management efficiency. However, investors' needs might be better satisfied with measures that predict future cash flows (such as current or pro forma dividends per share). As discussed in Chapter 7, cash-flow data may provide more relevant information to investors than earnings data using accrual basis accounting income. Many accountants discourage the use of summary indicators, such as EPS. These individuals maintain that an understanding of a company's performance requires a more comprehensive analysis than a single ratio can provide.

Comprehensive Income

Issues about income reporting have been characterized broadly in terms of a contrast between the current operating performance and the all-inclusive income concepts. Although the FASB generally has followed the all-inclusive income concept, as introduced in Chapter 5, it has made some specific exceptions to that concept. Several accounting standards require that certain items that qualify as components of comprehensive income bypass the income statement. Other components are required to be disclosed in the notes. The rationale for this treatment is that the earnings process is incomplete. Examples of items currently not disclosed on the traditional income statement and reported elsewhere are as follows:

1. Foreign currency translation adjustments (see Chapter 16)

2. Gains and losses on foreign currency transactions that are designated as, and are effective as, economic hedges of a net investment in a foreign entity (see Chapter 16)

3. Gains and losses on intercompany foreign currency transactions that are categorized as long-term investments (that is, settlement is not planned or anticipated in the foreseeable future), when the entities to the transaction are consolidated, combined, or accounted for by the equity method in the reporting entity's financial statements (see Chapter 16)

4. A change in the market value of a futures contract that qualifies as a hedge of an asset reported at fair value unless earlier recognition of a gain or loss in income is required because high correlation has not occurred (see Chapter 16)

5. The excess of the additional pension liability over unrecognized prior service cost (see Chapter 14)

6. Unrealized holding gains and losses on available-for-sale securities (see Chapter 10)

7. Unrealized holding gains and losses that result from a debt security being transferred into the available-for-sale category from the held-to-maturity category (see Chapter 10)

8. Subsequent decreases (if not other-than-temporary impairments) or increases in the fair value of available-for-sale securities previously written down as impaired (see Chapter 10)

In 1996, the FASB initiated a project designed to require the disclosure of comprehensive income by business enterprises. This project was undertaken in response to a variety of concerns, including (1) the increasing use of off–balance sheet financing, (2) the practice of reporting some items of comprehensive income directly in stockholders' equity, and (3) acknowledgment of the need to promote the international harmonization of accounting standards. The result of this project was *SFAS No. 130*, "Reporting Comprehensive Income" (see FASB ASC 220).

The issues considered in this project were organized under five general questions: (1) whether comprehensive income should be reported, (2) whether cumulative accounting adjustments should be included in comprehensive income, (3) how the components of comprehensive income should be classified for disclosure, (4) whether comprehensive income should be disclosed in one or two statements of financial performance, and (5) whether components of other comprehensive income should be displayed before or after their related tax effects.

Comprehensive income is defined as the change in equity [net assets] of a business enterprise during a period from transactions and other events and circumstances from nonowner sources."[25] It includes all changes in equity during a period except those resulting from investments by owners and distributions to owners. The term *comprehensive income* is used to describe the total of all components of comprehensive income, including net income. FASB ASC 220-10-20 uses the term *other comprehensive income* to refer to revenues, expenses, gains, and losses included in comprehensive income but excluded from net income. The stated purpose of reporting comprehensive income is to report a measure of overall enterprise performance by disclosing all changes in equity of a business enterprise that result from recognized transactions and other economic events of the period other than transactions with owners in their capacity as owners.

FASB ASC 220 requires the disclosure of comprehensive income and discusses how to report and disclose comprehensive income and its components, including net income. However, it does not specify when to recognize or how to measure the items that make up comprehensive income. The FASB indicated that existing and future accounting standards will provide guidance on items that are to be included in comprehensive income and its components. When used with related disclosures and information in the other financial statements, the information provided by reporting comprehensive income should help investors, creditors, and others in assessing an enterprise's financial performance and the timing and magnitude of its future cash flows.

In addressing what items should be included in comprehensive income, the main issue was whether the effects of certain accounting adjustments of earlier periods, such as the cumulative effects of changes in accounting principles, should be reported as part of comprehensive income. In reaching its initial conclusions, the FASB considered the definition of comprehensive income originally contained in *SFAC No. 5*, which indicates that the concept includes all recognized changes in equity (net assets), including cumulative accounting adjustments. The Board decided to follow that definition and, therefore, to include cumulative accounting adjustments as part of comprehensive income. Later, in 2005, the FASB reversed this decision and now requires retroactive presentation of the effect of changes in accounting principles.

With respect to the components of comprehensive income, FASB ASC 220 requires companies to disclose an amount for net income that must be accorded equal prominence with the amount disclosed for comprehensive income. When comprehensive income includes only net income, comprehensive income and net income are identical. The standard does not change the components of net income

25. FASB ASC 220-10-20.

or their classifications within the income statement. As discussed earlier, total net income includes income from continuing operations, discontinued operations, and extraordinary items. Items included in other comprehensive income are classified based on their nature. For example, under existing accounting standards, other comprehensive income may be separately classified into foreign currency items, minimum pension liability adjustments, and unrealized gains and losses on certain investments in debt and equity securities.

In reporting comprehensive income, companies are required to use a gross disclosure technique for classifications related to items of other comprehensive income other than minimum pension liability adjustments. For those classifications, reclassification adjustments must be disclosed separately from other changes in the balances of those items so that the total change is disclosed as two amounts. A net disclose technique for the classification related to minimum pension liability adjustments is required (see Chapter 14). For this classification, the reclassification adjustment must be combined with other changes in the balance of that item so that the total change is disclosed as a single amount.

When using the gross disclosure technique, reclassification adjustments may be disclosed in one of two ways. One way is as part of the classification of other comprehensive income to which those adjustments relate, such as within a classification for unrealized securities gains and losses. The other way is to disclose a separate classification consisting solely of reclassification adjustments in which all reclassification adjustments for a period are disclosed.

FASB ASC 220 allows for the reporting of comprehensive income in a financial statement that is displayed with the same prominence as other financial statements. Under this provision the components of other comprehensive income may be displayed below the total for net income in (1) an income statement, (2) a separate statement that begins with net income, or (3) a statement of changes in equity. However, regardless of the display format chosen, the total for comprehensive income is now required to be disclosed in the financial statements. The method of disclosing comprehensive income may be important to investors.

A study by Hirst and Hopkins indicated that financial analysts detected earnings management on selected items only when this information was presented in a separate statement of comprehensive income,[26] Maines and McDaniel found that the corporate performance evaluation of nonprofessional investors (the general public) was affected by the method of presentation.[27] These authors argue that according to their results, nonprofessional investors will use comprehensive income information only if it is included in a separate statement rather than as a component of stockholders' equity. Taken together, these results provide evidence that the presentation format for comprehensive income may influence decision making. These findings are consistent with the FASB's previous contention that the placement of comprehensive income provides a signal to investors about its importance.[28]

---

26. D. Eric Hirst and Patrick Hopkins. "Comprehensive Income Reporting: Financial Analyst's Judgments," *Journal of Accounting Research* (Supplement, 1998): 47–75.

27. Laureen A. Maines and Linda S. McDaniel, "Effects of Comprehensive-Income Characteristics on Nonprofessional Investor Judgments: The Role of Financial-Statement Presentation Format," *The Accounting Review* (April 2000), 179–207.

28. Financial Accounting Standards Board, "Exposure Draft—Reporting Comprehensive Income," 1996, paras. 50 and 63.

The total of other comprehensive income, for elements not reported as part of traditional net income for a period, must be transferred to a separate component of equity in a statement of financial position at the end of an accounting period. A descriptive title such as *accumulated other comprehensive income* is to be used for that component of equity. A company must also disclose accumulated balances for each classification in that separate component of equity on the face of a statement of financial position, in a statement of changes in equity, or in notes accompanying the financial statements. Those classifications must correspond to classifications used for components of other comprehensive income in a statement of financial performance.

On May 26, 2010, the FASB released a proposed Accounting Standards Update (ASU), *Statement of Comprehensive Income* that would require most entities to provide a new primary financial statement, referred to as the statement of comprehensive income. On May 27, 2010, the IASB issued a similar proposed amendment to IAS 1, *Presentation of Financial Statements.* Under these proposals, all components of net income and other comprehensive income would be reflected with equal prominence in one continuous statement of comprehensive income. As a result, the ASU would eliminate the choices now available for the presentation of other comprehensive income. The proposed statement of comprehensive income would have a section for net income and a section for other comprehensive income, with corresponding subtotals.

The ASU retains the existing requirement that allows the option to display the components of other comprehensive income net of related income tax expense or before related income tax effects with one amount shown for the aggregate income tax effects on the face of the continuous statement of comprehensive income. The comment period for the ASU ends September 30, 2010 and a final Accounting Standards Update is expected in the first quarter of 2011.

The overriding question regarding the disclosure of comprehensive income on corporate financial reports is, "Does this amount provide investors with additional information that allows for better predictions?" The evidence so far is mixed. The previously cited study by Hirst and Hopkins found that the presentation of comprehensive income influenced financial analysts' estimates of the value of a company engaged in earnings management.[29] However, Dhaliwal, Subramanyam, and Trezevant did not find that comprehensive income was associated with the market value of a firm's stock or that it was a better predictor of future cash flows than net income.[30] Additional research is needed to further assess this relationship.

Hershey Company discloses changes in other comprehensive income in its consolidated statement of shareholder's equity as a single net amount and elaborates on the individual components of this amount in the footnotes. Tootsie Roll includes the calculation of other comprehensive income on its income statement as shown on p. 000. The disclosure of Hershey Company's items of other comprehensive income is illustrated in Exhibit 6.3.

29. Hirst and Hopkins, "Comprehensive Income Reporting."

30. Dan Dhaliwal K. R. Subramanyam, and Robert Trezevant, "Is Comprehensive Income Superior to Net Income as a Measure of Firm Performance?" *Journal of Accounting and Economics* 26, nos. 1–3 (January 1999): 43–67.

EXHIBIT 6.3   *Hershey Company, Inc. Comprehensive Income as Disclosed in Its Footnotes for the Fiscal Year December 31, 2008*

For the year ended December 31, 2008

	Pre-Tax Amount	Tax (Expense) Benefit	After-Tax Amount
In thousands of dollars			
Net income			$ 311,405
Other comprehensive income (loss):			
Foreign currency translation adjustments	$ (74,563)	$ —	(74,563)
Pension and postretirement benefit plans	(385,482)	150,694	(234,788)
Cash-flow hedges:			
Gains on cash-flow hedging derivatives	17,886	(6,390)	11,496
Reclassification adjustments	(53,297)	19,223	(34,074)
Total other comprehensive loss	$ (495,456)	$ 163,527	(331,929)
Comprehensive loss			$ (20,524)

Prior Period Adjustments

Occasionally, companies make mistakes in their accounting records. Sometimes these "mistakes" occur because of intentional or fraudulent misapplication of accounting rules, principles, or estimates. For example, in the spring of 2002, internal auditors at WorldCom uncovered a massive accounting fraud in which the company capitalized operating expenses and began depreciating them rather than expensing them in the year they occurred.[31] In a case like this, the company will have to restate its financial statements and adjust numerous accounts in order to clean up its books.

Generally, mistakes are unintentional and arise because of errors in arithmetic, double entries, transposed numbers, or failure to record a transaction or adjustment. If the company discovers the mistake in the period when it occurred, an adjustment is made to the accounts affected to correct it. If, however, the mistake is not discovered until a later period, the company will need to make a prior period adjustment. *Prior period adjustments* involve adjusting the beginning retained earnings balance and reporting the adjustment in either the statement of stockholders' equity or in a separate statement of retained earnings. Since the error occurred in a prior period, it does not affect the current income statement, so it is not reported in the income statement in the period of correction. Also, since the prior period's net income was closed to retained earnings at the end of that period, the retained earnings total is misstated in the current period and must be adjusted to remove the effect of the error.

The reporting requirements for disclosing prior period adjustments have evolved over time. The test for classifying an item as a prior period adjustment (adjustment

---

31. The *Wall Street Journal* published an excellent article on how WorldCom's internal auditors uncovered the fraud; see "How Three Unlikely Sleuths Exposed Fraud at WorldCom," *New York Times*, 30 October 2002, 1.

to retained earnings) was originally made quite rigid in *APB Opinion No. 9*. For events and transactions to be classified as prior period adjustments, they must have been:

> . . . specifically identified and directly related to the business activities of particular prior periods, (b) not attributable to economic events occurring subsequent to the date of the financial statements for the prior period, (c) dependent primarily on determination by persons other than management, (d) not susceptible of reasonable estimation prior to such determination.[32]

At the time *Opinion No. 9* was issued, the APB took the position that prior period adjustments that are disclosed as increases or decreases in the beginning retained earnings balance should have been related to events of previous periods that were not susceptible to reasonable estimation at the time they occurred. In addition, since these amounts were material by definition, it is expected that the auditor's opinion would be at least qualified on the financial statements issued when the event or transaction took place. Examples of prior period adjustments under *APB Opinion No. 9* were settlements of income tax cases or other litigations. The category of errors was later added to this classification. Errors would, of course, not result in an opinion qualification because they would not be known to the auditors when the financial statements were released.

In 1976, the SEC released *Staff Accounting Bulletin No. 8*, which concluded that litigation is inevitably an economic event and that settlements of litigation constitute economic events of the period in which they occur. This conclusion created a discrepancy between generally accepted accounting principles and the reporting requirements for companies registered with the SEC. Before the release of *Staff Accounting Bulletin No. 8*, the FASB had undertaken a study of prior period adjustment reporting of 600 companies and also concluded that a clarification of the criteria outlined in *APB Opinion No. 9* was required.

Subsequently, the FASB issued *SFAS No. 16*, "Prior Period Adjustments" (see FASB ASC 250), which indicated that the only items of profit and loss that should be reported as prior period adjustments were

a. Correction of an error in the financial statements of a prior period

b. Adjustments that result from the realization of income tax benefits of pre-acquisition operating loss carry-forwards of purchased subsidiaries[33]

The restrictive criteria for the classification of an item of revenue or expense to be categorized as a prior period adjustment have greatly reduced their inclusion on financial statements. Neither Hershey Company nor Tootsie Roll disclosed any prior period adjustments for the fiscal years covered by their income statements. However, during 2008, Standard Register Company, a leading provider of custom-printed documents and related services, determined that a prior period adjustment was required to properly reflect its capital loss carry-forwards (see Chapter 12) from 2004. As a result, deferred tax assets and income tax benefits were understated by $1,420,000.

---

32. Accounting Principles Board, *APB Opinion No. 9*, para. 23.

33. Financial Accounting Standards Board, *SFAS No. 16*, "Prior Period Adjustments" (Stamford, CT: FASB, 1977), para. 11.

Proposed Format of the Statement of Comprehensive Income

The FASB and the IASB are planning to release a proposal to recast financial statements into a new format. One possible result is the elimination of the current definition of net income. In its place, financial statement users may find a number of profit figures that correspond to different corporate activities. The rationale for the new presentation is that focusing on the net profit number has been seen as one cause for the fraud and stock market excesses that characterize the past several years. That is, many of the major accounting scandals earlier this decade centered on the manipulation of net income. The stock market bubble of the 1990s was the result of investors' assumptions that corporate net profits would grow rapidly for years to come. As a result, beating quarterly earnings estimates became a distraction or worse for companies' managers and investors. While it isn't known whether the new format would reduce attempts to fudge the numbers, companies would be required to give a more detailed breakdown of their activities.

The new proposed income statement has separate categories for the disclosure of a company's operating business, its financing activities, investing activities, and tax payments. Each category also contains an income subtotal. The proposal adopts a single statement of comprehensive income format that combines income statement elements and components of other comprehensive income into a single statement. Items of other comprehensive income are to be presented in a separate section following the income statement elements. This presentation format includes a subtotal of net income and a total of comprehensive income in the period. The boards eliminated the current alternative presentation format that allows items of other comprehensive income to be presented in one of three ways: (1) on a separate statement, (2) on a combined statement of comprehensive income, or (3) on the statement of stockholder's equity. This change was made because research studies suggested that investors and other users' ability to process the information will be enhanced if a uniform format of comprehensive income statement is presented.

According to the proposal, all income and expense items are to be classified into operating, investing, and financing categories. Within those categories, an entity will disaggregate line items by function. Within those functions, an entity should further disaggregate line items by nature when such presentation will enhance the usefulness of the information in predicting future cash flows. *Function* refers to the primary activities in which an entity is engaged. For example, an entity's operating activities consist of selling goods, marketing, or administration. *Nature* refers to the economic characteristics or attributes that distinguish assets, liabilities, and income and expense items that do not respond equally to similar economic events. Examples of disaggregation by nature include disaggregating total sales into wholesale and retail or disaggregating total cost of sales into materials, labor, transport, and energy costs. These desegregations will result in more subtotals than now required on the income statement and therefore facilitate the comparison of the effects of operating, investing and financing activities across financial statements.

The boards agreed on retaining the current intraperiod tax allocation method.[34] The boards did not support allocation of income tax expense or benefit

---

34. See Chapter 12.

to the operating, investing, financing asset, or financing liability categories because they determined that the cost of doing so would exceed the benefit. Similarly, there are no proposed changes in the current reporting format for discontinued operations, extraordinary items, and changes in accounting principles. The exposure draft didn't provide guidance on which items should be included in the comprehensive income, because they are discussed in other exposure drafts. The proposed revisions to the statement of financial position outlined in the FASB-IASB Financial Statement Presentation Project are illustrated in Exhibit 6.4.

EXHIBIT 6.4   *Proposed Statement of Comprehensive Income*

For the year ended

	31 December	
	2012	2011
BUSINESS		
Operating		
Sales—wholesale	$ 2,790,080	$ 2,591,400
Sales—retail	697,520	647,850
Total revenue	*$ 3,487,600*	*$ 3,239,250*
Cost of goods sold		
Materials	(1,043,100)	(925,000)
Labor	(405,000)	(450,000)
Overhead—depreciation	(219,300)	(215,000)
Overhead—transport	(128,640)	(108,000)
Overhead—other	(32,160)	(27,000)
Change in inventory	(60,250)	(46,853)
Pension	(51,975)	(47,250)
Loss on obsolete and damaged inventory	(29,000)	(9,500)
Total cost of goods sold	*(1,969,425)*	*(1,828,603)*
Gross profit	*$ 1,518,175*	*$ 1,410,647*
Selling expenses $		
Advertising	(60,000)	(50,000)
Wages, salaries, and benefits	(56,700)	(52,500)
Bad debt	(23,068)	(15,034)
Other	(13,500)	(12,500)
Total selling expenses	*$ (153,268)*	*$ (130,034)*
General and administrative expenses		
Wages, salaries, and benefits	(321,300)	(297,500)
Depreciation	(59,820)	(58,500)
Pension	(51,975)	(47,250)
Share-based remuneration	(22,023)	(17,000)
Interest on lease liability	(14,825)	(16,500)
Research and development	(8,478)	(7,850)
Other	(15,768)	(14,600)
Total general and administrative expenses	*$ (494,189)*	*$ (459,200)*
Income before other operating items	*$ 870,718*	*$ 821,413*
Other operating income (expense)		
Share of profit of associate A	23,760	22,000
Gain on disposal of property, plant, and equipment	22,650	—

(Continued)

EXHIBIT 6.4   *Proposed Statement of Comprehensive Income (Continued)*

Realized gain on cash-flow hedge	3,996	3,700
Loss on sale of receivables	(4,987)	(2,025)
Impairment loss on goodwill	—	(35,033)
Total other operating income (expense)	*45,419*	*(11,358)*
Total operating income	**$ 916,137**	**$ 810,055**
Investing		
Dividend income	54,000	50,000
Realized gain on available-for-sale securities	18,250	7,500
Share of profit of associate B	7,500	3,250
Total investing income	**$ 79,750**	**$ 60,750**
Total business income	**$ 995,887**	**$ 870,805**
Financing		
Interest income on cash	8,619	5,500
Total financing asset income	**8,619**	**5,500**
Interest expense	(111,352)	(110,250)
Total financing liability expense	**$ (111,352)**	**$ (110,250)**
Total net financing expense	**$ (102,733)**	**$ (104,750)**
Profit from continuing operations		
before taxes and other comprehensive income	*893,154*	*766,055*
Income taxes		
Income tax expense	(333,625)	(295,266)
Net profit from continuing operations	$ *559,529*	$ *470,789*
Discontinued operations		
Loss on discontinued operations	(32,400)	(35,000)
Tax benefit	11,340	12,250
Net loss from discontinued	**$ (21,060)**	**$ (22,750)**
Operations		
Net profit	**$ 538,469**	**$ 448,039**
Other comprehensive income (After Tax)		
Unrealized gain on available-for-sale securities (investing)	17,193	15,275
Revaluation surplus (operating)	3,653	—
Foreign currency translation adjust— consolidated subsidiary	2,094	(1,492)
Unrealized gain on cash-flow hedge (operating)	1,825	1,690
Foreign currency translation adjust— associate A (operating)	(1,404)	(1,300)
Total other comprehensive income	**$ 23,361**	**$ 14,173**
Total comprehensive income	**$ 561,830**	**$ 462,212**
Basic earnings per share	$ 7.07	$ 6.14
Diluted earnings per share	$ 6.85	$ 5.96

Source: Adapted from *Preliminary Views on Financial Statement Presentation* (FASB, October 2008).

The boards expect to release an exposure draft early in 2010 and a final standard by the end of 2010.

The Value of Corporate Earnings

The income statement allows users to evaluate a firm's current performance, estimate its future performance, and predict future cash flows. For analytical purposes, and to evaluate the quality of earnings, it is important for users to understand and be able to identify those revenue and expense items that are likely to continue into the future (sustainable earnings) and those that are not (transitory components). For this reason, the distinction between operating and nonoperating revenues, expenses, gains, and losses is important. It is also important to understand the nature and amounts of special items, as well as those equity items not reflected on the income statement but still appearing in comprehensive income. Some techniques users might employ in conducting these analyses are outlined in the following paragraphs.

The financial analysis of a company's income statement focuses on a company's operating performance by posing questions like these:

1. What are the company's major sources of revenue?
2. What is the persistence of a company's revenues?
3. What is the company's gross profit ratio?
4. What is the company's operating profit margin?
5. What is the relationship between earnings and the market price of the company's stock?

The analysis and interpretation of the operating performance of a company is illustrated by using examples from Hershey Company and Tootsie Roll. The following information has been extracted from the companies' financial statements for the years 2004–2008. (All amounts are stated in thousands of dollars.)

Hershey Company	Sales	Gross Profit	Net Income
2008	$5,132,768	$1,757,718	$311,405
2007	4,946,716	1,631,569	214,154
2006	4,944,230	1,867,512	559,061
2005	4,819,827	1,863,145	488,547
2004	4,416,389	1,743,673	574,637

Tootsie Roll	Sales	Gross Profit	Net Income
2008	$492,051	$161,781	$38,777
2007	492,742	168,673	51,625
2006	495,990	188,561	65,919
2005	487,739	188,056	77,227
2004	420,110	174,539	64,174

Sources of Revenue

Many of the largest corporations are highly diversified, which means that they sell a variety of products. Each of these products has an individual rate of profitability, expected growth patterns, and degree of risk. One measure of the degree of risk is a company's reliance on major customers. If a company's revenues from a single customer are equal to or greater than 10 percent of its total revenues, that fact must be disclosed. The financial analysis of a diversified company requires a review of the impact of various business segments on the company as a whole. Hershey Company reports segmental information for two segments, domestic and international, in its financial statements. Tootsie Roll's segments are identified as United States and foreign.

Persistence of Revenues

The persistence of a company's revenues can be assessed by analyzing the trend of its revenues over time, and by reviewing Management's Discussion and Analysis (MD&A). Exhibit 6.5 contains a revenue trend analysis for Hershey Company and Tootsie Roll for the five-year period beginning with the 2004 fiscal year-end. For purposes of this analysis, year 2004 data are set at 100 percent.

EXHIBIT 6.5   *Revenue Trend Analysis, 2004–2008*

	2004	2005	2006	2007	2008
Hershey Company	100.0%	109.1%	112.0%	112.0%	116.2%
Tootsie Roll	100.0%	116.1%	118.1%	117.3%	117.1%

This analysis shows that both companies experienced similar trends in net revenues from 2004 through 2007. In 2008 Hershey's revenue increased while Tootsie Roll's declined slightly.

Management's Discussion and Analysis

The MD&A section of a company's annual report can provide valuable information on the persistence of a company's earnings and its related costs.[35] The SEC requires companies to disclose any changes or potential changes in revenues and expenses to assist in the evaluation of period-to-period deviations. Examples of these disclosures include unusual events, expected future changes in revenues and expenses, the factors that caused current revenues and expenses to increase or decrease, and trends not otherwise apparent from a review of the company's financial statements. For example, Tootsie Roll indicated that its gross profit percentage decreased in 2008 as compared to 2007 because of increased product, packaging, and energy costs.

Gross Profit Analysis

The analysis of a company's gross profit focuses on explaining variations in sales, cost of goods sold, and their effect on gross profit. This analysis can be enhanced by separating it into product lines. Annual changes in gross profit are caused by: (1) changes in sales volume, (2) changes in unit selling price, and (3) changes in unit costs.

A company's gross profit percentage is calculated as follows:

$$\text{Gross profit percentage} = \frac{\text{Gross profit}}{\text{Net sales}}$$

35. An expanded discussion of the MD&A section of the annual report is contained in Chapter 17.

The gross profit percentages for Hershey Company and Tootsie Roll for the period 2004–2008 are provided in Exhibit 6.6. Hershey's gross profit percentage decreased from 39.5 percent in 2004 to 33.0 percent in 2007; then it rose to 34.2 percent in 2008. Tootsie Roll's gross profit has declined steadily by over 9 percent during the 2004–2008 five-year period. These results indicate that the costs to produce the company's products have risen significantly.

EXHIBIT 6.6 *Gross Profit Percentages, 2004–2008*

	2004	2005	2006	2007	2008
Hershey Company	39.5%	38.7%	37.8%	33.0%	34.2%
Tootsie Roll	41.5%	38.7%	38.0%	34.2%	32.9%

One popular method of analysis compares a company's ratios with industry averages. Industry averages are available from several sources, such as Standard & Poor's *Industry Surveys* or *Reuters Investor*. This comparison asks the question, "Is the company's performance better than that of the industry as a whole?" Hershey and Tootsie Roll are in the sugar and confectionary products (SIC 2160) industry. The five-year average gross profit percentage for this industry in 2008 was 32.07 percent. The two companies' results exceed this average for every year covered by this analysis.

Net Profit Analysis

A company's net profit percentage, an indicator of the effectiveness of its overall performance, is calculated as follows:

$$\text{Net profit percentage} = \frac{\text{Net income}}{\text{Net sales}}$$

The net profit percentages for Hershey Company and Tootsie Roll for the period 2004–2008 are presented in Exhibit 6.7. Although Tootsie Roll's performance measured by its net profit percentage has declined considerably since 2004, it has clearly outperformed Hershey. However, both companies exceeded the five-year industry average of 3.27 percent for every year analyzed.

EXHIBIT 6.7 *Net Profit Percentages, 2004–2008*

	2004	2005	2006	2007	2008
Hershey Company	13.0%	10.1%	11.3%	4.3%	6.1%
Tootsie Roll	15.3%	15.8%	13.3%	10.5%	7.9%

The above net profit percentages used the net income reported on each company's income statement. However, an analyst would probably adjust these figures for any nonrecurring items so that the percentages are more comparable across time and between companies. An examination of Hershey's 2008 annual report reveals that Hershey's cost of goods sold and operating expenses included $94,801,000 of realignment and asset impairment charges. For cross-company comparison, if we adjust net income for the after-tax effect of these charges, Hershey's 2008 net profit percentage increases from 6.0 percent to 7.2 percent.

To get a sense of the company's performance from its core operations, some analysts compute the operating profit percentage (Also termed earnings before interest and taxes, or EBIT). Operating profit is gross margin minus operating (general, selling, and administrative) expenses. Here is the operating profit percentage calculation:

$$\text{Operating profit percentage} = \frac{\text{Operating profit}}{\text{Net sales}}$$

Omitting Hershey's nonrecurring business realignment and impairment, Exhibit 6.8 provides the operating profit percentages for the years 2004–2008.

EXHIBIT 6.8 *Operating Profit Percentages, 2004–2008*

	2004	2005	2006	2007	2008
Hershey Company	19.8%	19.7%	20.4%	14.9%	13.3%
Tootsie Roll	21.4%	18.8%	17.6%	14.4%	13.4%

These percentages reveal a slight improvement in performance for Hershey over the first three years of the analysis and a significant decline in the last two years. Tootsie Roll experienced a steady decline over the five-year period. These results indicate potential erosion in profitability for both companies' recurring core business operations.

In Chapter 5 it was noted that investors are interested in assessing the amount, timing, and uncertainty of future cash flows and that accounting earnings have been found to be more useful than cash-flow information in making this assessment. Future cash-flow and earnings assessments affect the market price of a company's stock. Over the past three decades, accounting researchers have examined the relationship between corporate earnings and a company's stock prices. One measure that has been found useful in assessing this relationship is a company's price-earnings ratio (P/E ratio), which is calculated as follows:

$$\text{P/E ratio} = \frac{\text{Current market price per share}}{\text{Earnings per share}}$$

This ratio provides an earnings multiple at which a company's stock is currently trading. A firm's beta (β) or earnings volatility (as discussed in Chapter 4) will affect its stock price. In addition, research has indicated that the components of earnings income from continuing operations, discontinued operations, extraordinary items, and earnings per share will also be incorporated into the determination of market prices.[36] In other words, all things being equal, a firm that reports only income from continuing operations will be valued more highly than a firm with an equal amount of risk and the same earnings that reports one or more of the other components of income. This occurs because investors are most interested in a company's sustainable earnings, and investors view income components other than income from continuing operations as nonsustainable.

36. Ram T. S. Ramakrishman and Jacob K. Thomas, "Valuation of Permanent, Transitory and Price Irrelevant Components of Reported Earnings," *Journal of Accounting Auditing and Finance* (Summer 1998): 301–36.

The price-earnings ratio for Hershey Company, using the company's market price per share of $34.74 on December 31, 2008, and its basic earnings per share on common stock amount of $1.41, was 26.69:

$$\frac{\$34.74}{\$ \ 1.41} = 24.64$$

The price-earnings ratio for Tootsie Roll, using the company's market price per share of $25.61 on December 31, 2008, and its basic earnings per share from continuing operations amount of $0.70, was 36.59:

$$\frac{\$25.61}{\$ \ 0.70} = 36.59$$

The price-earnings ratios for the two companies over the five-year period covered by our analysis are provided in Exhibit 6.9.

EXHIBIT 6.9 *Price-Earnings Ratios, 2004–2008*

	2004	2005	2006	2007	2008
Hershey Company	23.43	22.10	20.41	41.04	24.64
Tootsie Roll	29.10	20.09	28.43	30.13	36.59

Exhibit 6.9 indicates that the market has alternated between being more impressed with Hershey's potential and then more impressed with Tootsie Roll's. In 2004, 2006, and 2008, Tootsie Roll's P/E ratio was higher than Hershey's; the opposite was true for 2005 and 2007. However, both companies' P/E ratios were consistently higher than the industry average of approximately 20 for all five years of the analysis.

An overall interpretation of the earnings information reveals mixed results. Hershey's revenues have remained at about 2004 levels while Tootsie Rolls' have declined about 10 percent. Both companies' net profit percentages declined significantly. Both companies' P/E ratios have fluctuated over the five-year period of analysis; however, Hershey's declined considerably in 2008 while Tootsie Roll's increased.

International Accounting Standards

In addition to the release of *IAS No. 33* on earnings per share, the International Accounting Standards Board has

1. Defined performance and income in "Framework for the Preparation and Presentation of Financial Statements"
2. Discussed the objective of and the information to be presented on an income statement in *IAS No. 1*, "Presentation of Financial Statements"
3. Discussed some components of the income statement in an amended *IAS No. 8*, now titled "Accounting Policies, Changes in Accounting Estimates and Errors"
4. Defined concept of revenue in *IAS No. 18*, "Revenue"
5. Amended *IAS No. 33*
6. Discussed the required presentation and disclosure of a discontinued operation in *IFRS No. 5*, "Non-Current Assets Held for Sale and Discontinued Operations"
7. Issued a proposed amendment to *IAS No. 1*

In discussing performance, the IASB noted that profit is used to measure performance or as the basis for other measures such as return on investment or earnings per share. The elements relating to the measurement of profit are income and expenses, but the measurements of income and expenses and ultimately profit are dependent on the concepts of capital and capital maintenance used by the enterprise in preparing its financial statements. The concepts of capital maintenance, physical capital maintenance, and financial capital maintenance were defined by the IASB in a manner similar to how they were defined earlier in this chapter.

IAS No. 1 requires an income statement that includes the following line items: revenue, results of operations, finance costs, gains and losses from equity investments, tax expense, profits or losses from ordinary activities, minority interest, and net profit. In addition, expenses must be classified based on either their nature or function, and dividends declared for the period must be disclosed on a per-share basis. In contrast to U.S. GAAP, *IAS No. 1* does not require discontinued operations or accounting changes to be reported as separate components of income. Additionally, the revised *IAS No. 1* does not allow items to be classified as extraordinary. The adoption of the proposed FASB IASC standard on financial statement presentation will significantly change the presentation format of the income statement.

The IASB stated that the goal of *IAS No. 8* is to prescribe the classification, disclosure, and accounting treatment of certain items in the income statement so that all entities prepare and present their income statements in a consistent manner. *IAS No. 8* states that when a standard or an interpretation specifically applies to a transaction, other event, or condition, the accounting policy or policies applied to that item must be determined by applying the standard or interpretation and considering any relevant implementation guidance issued by the IASB for the standard or interpretation. However, in the absence of a standard or an interpretation that specifically applies to a transaction, judgment should be used in developing and applying an accounting policy that results in relevant a nd reliable information. *IAS No. 8* indicates that in making that judgment, the following sources should be considered in descending order:

1. The requirements and guidance in IASB standards and interpretations dealing with similar and related issues
2. The definitions, recognition criteria, and measurement concepts for assets, liabilities, income, and expenses in the Framework for the Presentation of Financial Statements
3. The most recent pronouncements of other standard-setting bodies that use a similar conceptual framework to develop accounting standards
4. Other accounting literature and accepted industry practices, to the extent that these do not conflict with the sources in paragraph

Companies are required to select and apply accounting policies on a consistent basis for similar transactions. Additionally, a company may change an adopted accounting policy only if the change

- Is required by a standard or interpretation; or
- Results in the financial statements providing reliable and more relevant information about the effects of transactions, other events, or conditions on the entity's financial position, financial performance, or cash flows

If a change in accounting policy is required by a new IASB pronouncement, the change should be accounted for by the requirements of the new pronouncement. However, if the new pronouncement does not include specific transition provisions, then the change in accounting policy is applied retroactively. That is, a company adjusts the opening balance of each affected component of equity for the earliest prior period presented and the other comparative amounts disclosed for each prior period presented as if the new accounting policy had always been applied.

Changes in accounting estimates are to be recognized prospectively by including them in profit or loss in the period of the change, if the change affects that period only, or in the period of the change and future periods, if the change affects both.

Errors are defined as mathematical mistakes, mistakes in applying accounting policies, oversights or misinterpretations of facts, and fraud. *IAS No. 8* indicates that all material errors are to be corrected retrospectively in the first set of financial statements authorized for issue after their discovery by restating the comparative amounts for the prior period(s) presented in which the error occurred. Alternatively, if the error occurred before the earliest prior period presented, a company must restate the opening balances of assets, liabilities, and equity for the earliest prior period presented. However, if it is impracticable to determine the period-specific effects of an error on comparative information, a company should restate the opening balances of assets, liabilities, and equity for the earliest period for which retrospective restatement is practicable. Or if it is impracticable to determine the cumulative effect, at the beginning of the current period, of an error on all prior periods, the company should restate the comparative information to correct the error prospectively from the earliest date practicable.

In *IAS No. 18*, the IASB discussed the concept of revenue measurement. It indicated that revenue should be recognized when it is probable that future economic benefit will flow to the enterprise, should be measured at the fair value of the consideration received, and should be recognized from the sale of goods when all of the following conditions have been satisfied:

1. The enterprise has transferred to the buyer the significant risks and rewards of ownership of the goods.

2. The enterprise retains neither continuing managerial involvement to the degree usually associated with ownership nor effective control over the goods sold.

3. The amount of revenue can be measured reliably.

4. It is probable that the economic benefits associated with the transaction will flow to the enterprise.

5. The costs incurred or to be incurred in respect to the transaction can be measured reliably.[37]

The amended *IAS No. 33* incorporated the following additional disclosures and guidelines:

1. Basic and diluted EPS must be presented for (a) profit or loss from continuing operations and for (b) net profit or loss, on the face of the income statement for each class of ordinary shares, for each period presented.

---

37. International Accounting Standards Committee, *International Accounting Standard No. 18,* "Revenue" (London: IASC, 1993), para. 14.

2. Potential ordinary shares are dilutive only when their conversion to ordinary shares would decrease EPS from continuing operations (*IAS No. 33* previously used net income as the benchmark).

3. Contracts that may be settled in cash or shares now includes a rebuttable presumption that the contract will be settled in shares.

4. If an entity purchases (for cancellation) its own preference shares for more than their carrying amount, the excess (premium) should be treated as a preferred dividend in calculating basic EPS (deducted from the numerator of the EPS computation).

5. Guidance is provided on how to calculate the effects of contingently issuable shares; potential ordinary shares of subsidiaries, joint ventures, or associates; participating securities; written put options; and purchased put and call options.

As indicated in Chapter 5, a current FASB-IASB project is addressing the concept of revenue recognition. A new standard is expected to be released in 2011. Two differences between U.S. GAAP and *IAS No. 18* will need to be addressed in this project.

1. IAS No. 18 includes gains in the definition of revenues, and gains are not reported separately on the income statement; under U.S. GAAP, gains are reported separately from revenues, and SFAC No. 6 defines gains as an income statement element.

2. In accounting for long-term construction contracts, IAS No. 18 allows only the percentage-of-completion method. Under U.S. GAAP, the percentage-of-completion method is most commonly used, but the completed-contract method is allowed in certain circumstances.

IFRS No. 5 replaced *IAS No. 35*. The new standard defines discontinued operations as the sum of the post-tax profit or loss of the discontinued operation and the post-tax gain or loss recognized on the measurement of fair value, less cost to sell or fair value adjustments on the disposal of the assets (or disposal group). This amount should be presented as a single amount on the face of the income statement. Detailed disclosure of revenue, expenses, pre-tax profit or loss, and related income taxes is required to be reported either in the notes or on the face of the income statement in a section distinct from continuing operations. Such detailed disclosures must cover both the current and all prior periods presented in the financial statements. *IFRS No. 5* prohibits the retroactive classification as a discontinued operation, when the discontinued criteria are met after the balance sheet date.

In addition, the following disclosures are required:

1. Adjustments made in the current period to amounts disclosed as a discontinued operation in prior periods must be separately disclosed.

2. If an entity ceases to classify a component as held for sale, the results of that component previously presented in discontinued operations must be reclassified and included in income from continuing operations for all periods presented.

Currently, the definitions of a discontinued operation in FASB ASC 360 and in *IFRS No. 5*, "Non-current Assets Held for Sale and Discontinued Operations," are not convergent. FASB ASC 360 defines a discontinued operation as a component of an entity that has been disposed of or is classified as held for sale provided that (1) the operations and cash flows of the component have been (or will be) eliminated from the ongoing operations of the entity as a result of the disposal transaction, and (2) the entity will not have any significant continuing involvement in the operations of the component after the disposal transaction. *IFRS No. 5* defines a discontinued operation as a component of an entity that either has been disposed of or is classified as held for sale, and (1) represents a separate major line of business or geographical area of operations, (2) is part of a single coordinated plan to dispose of a separate major line of business or geographical area of operations, or (3) is a subsidiary acquired exclusively with a view to resale.

In their joint project on financial statement presentation, the FASB and the IASB decided to develop a common definition of a discontinued operation and require common disclosures for all components of an entity that have been disposed of or are classified as held for sale. However, constituents asked the boards to accelerate the issuance of guidance on discontinued operations separately from the joint financial statement presentation project. As a result, the FASB has issued proposed FASB Staff Position (FSP) *No. FAS 144-d,* "Amending the Criteria for Reporting a Discontinued Operation." The intent of this FSP is to develop a definition of a discontinued operation, and disclosure requirements for all components of an entity that have been disposed of or are classified as held for sale, that are convergent with the definition and disclosure requirements of IFRS. Concurrently, the IASB has issued an Exposure Draft, *Discontinued Operations*, which proposes amendments to *IFRS No. 5* that are identical to those proposed in the FASB's FSP. A final FASB Accounting Standards Update is expected to be effective for fiscal periods ending after December 15, 2010.

The IASB's proposed amendment to *IAS No. 1* is similar to the FASB's proposed Accounting Standards Update on the Statement of Comprehensive Income; however, there are some differences. The IASB chose to title the new statement "The Statement of Profit or Loss and other Comprehensive Income". Additionally, since the new guidance would not change those components that are recognized in other comprehensive income under either accounting framework, and the two frameworks differ on the treatment of some of those components, total convergence is not achieved. However, the boards believe that the proposals are an important step in enhancing comparability and providing greater transparency.

Cases

• Case 6-1 Income Recognition in the Motion Picture Industry

The motion picture industry has undergone significant changes during the past four decades. Originally, companies such as Paramount Pictures had to rely solely on domestic and foreign screenings of their movies for their revenues. The birth of the television industry in the 1960s resulted in opportunities for broadcasting rights to networks and individual stations. Moreover, the introduction of cable television in the 1970s opened up substantial new sources of revenue. In addition, the unsaturated demand for new films resulted in a market for made-for-television films. And the invention of the video recorder opened yet another revenue source for these companies.

The production of a film involves four phases:

1. Acquisition of the story rights
2. Preproduction, including script development, set design, cost selection, costume design, and selection of a filming location
3. Actual filming
4. Postproduction, including film editing, adding the musical score, and special effects

Warmen Brothers Production Company has just finished the production of *Absence of Forethought*, a movie that is expected to be successfully distributed to all available markets.

Required:

a. What markets are available to Warmen Brothers for this film?
b. In what order would you suggest Warmen Brothers attempt to enter each market? Why?
c. How should revenues be recognized from each market?
d. How should costs be matched against these revenues?
e. What effect will your decisions have on Warmen Brothers' income statements for the year's revenue?[38]

• Case 6-2 Extraordinary Charges

Goods Company is a major manufacturer of foodstuffs. The company's products are sold in grocery and convenience stores throughout the United States. Goods' name is well known and respected because its products have been marketed nationally for over 50 years.

In April 2010 Goods was forced to recall one of its major products. A total of thirty-five persons in Chicago were treated for severe intestinal pain, and eventually three people died from complications. All of the people had consumed Goods' product.

The product causing the problem was traced to one specific lot. Goods keeps samples from all lots of foodstuffs. After thorough testing, Goods and the legal authorities confirmed that the product had been tampered with after it had left the company's plant and was no longer under the company's control.

The entire product was recalled from the market—the only time a Goods product has been recalled nationally and the only time for reasons of tampering. People who still had the product in their homes, even though it was not from the affected lot, were encouraged to return it for credit or refund. The company designed and implemented a media campaign to explain what had happened and what the company was doing to minimize any chance of recurrence. Goods decided to continue the product with the same trade name and the same wholesale price. However, the packaging was redesigned completely to be tamper resistant and safety sealed. This required the purchase and installation of new equipment.

---

38. You may wish to consult FASB ASC 926-605.

The corporate accounting staff recommended that the costs associated with the tampered product be treated as an extraordinary charge on the 2010 financial statements. Corporate accounting was asked to identify the various costs that could be associated with the tampered product and related recall. These costs ($000 omitted) are as follows.

Credits and refunds to stores and consumers	$30,000
Insurance to cover lost sales and idle plant costs for possible future recalls	6,000
Transportation costs and off-site warehousing of returned product	1,000
Future security measures for other products	4,000
Testing of returned product and inventory	700
Destroying returned product and inventory	2,400
Public relations program to reestablish brand credibility	4,200
Communication program to inform customers, answer inquiries, prepare press releases, and so on	1,600
Higher cost arising from new packaging	700
Investigation of possible involvement of employees, former employees, competitors, and the like	500
Packaging redesign and testing	2,000
Purchase and installation of new packaging equipment	6,000
Legal costs for defense against liability suits	600
Lost sales revenue due to recall	32,000

Goods' estimated earnings before income taxes and before consideration of any of the above items for the year ending December 31, 2010, were $230 million.

Required:

a. Goods Company plans to recognize the costs associated with the product tampering and recall as an extraordinary charge.

   i. Explain why Goods could classify this occurrence as an extraordinary charge.

   ii. Describe the placement and terminology used to present the extraordinary charge in the 2010 income statement.

b. Refer to the fourteen cost items identified by the corporate accounting staff of Goods Company.

   i. Identify the cost items by number that should be included in the extraordinary charge for 2010.

   ii. For any item that is not included in the extraordinary charge, explain why it would not be included in the extraordinary charge.

(CMA adapted)

• Case 6-3 Income Statement Format

Accountants have advocated two types of income statements based on differing views of the concept of income: the *current operating performance* and *all-inclusive* concepts of income.

Required:

   a. Discuss the general nature of these two concepts of income.

   b. How would the following items be handled under each concept?

      i.   Cost of goods sold

      ii. Selling expenses

      iii. Extraordinary items

      iv. Prior period adjustments

• Case 6-4 Accounting Changes

It is important in accounting theory to be able to distinguish the types of accounting changes.

Required:

   a. If a public company desires to change from the sum-of-year's-digits depreciation method to the straight-line method for its fixed assets, what type of accounting change will this be? How would it be treated? Discuss the permissibility of this change.

   b. If a public company obtained additional information about the service lives of some of its fixed assets that showed that the service lives previously used should be shortened, what type of accounting change would this be? Include in your discussion how the change should be reported in the income statement of the year of the change and what disclosures should be made in the financial statements or notes.

   c. Changing specific subsidiaries comprising the group of companies for which consolidated financial statements are presented is an example of what type of accounting change? What effect does it have on the consolidated income statements?

• Case 6-5 Earnings per Share

Progresso Corporation, one of your new audit clients, has not reported EPS data in its annual reports to stockholders in the past. The president requested that you furnish information about the reporting of EPS data in the current year's annual report in accordance with GAAP.

Required:

   a. Define the term *earnings per share* as it applies to a corporation with a capitalization structure composed of only one class of common stock. Then explain how EPS should be computed and how the information should be disclosed in the corporation's financial statements.

b. Explain the meanings of the terms *senior securities* and *residual securities* (terms often used in discussing EPS), and give examples of the types of items that each term includes.

c. Discuss the treatment, if any, that should be given to each of the following items in computing EPS for financial statement reporting:

   i. The declaration of current dividends on cumulative preferred stock

   ii. The acquisition of some of the corporation's outstanding common stock during the current fiscal year (The stock was classified as treasury stock.)

   iii. A two-for-one stock split of common stock during the current fiscal year

   iv. A provision created out of retained earnings for a contingent liability from a possible lawsuit

   v. Outstanding preferred stock issued at a premium with a par value liquidation right

   vi. The exercise at a price below market value but above book value of a common stock option issued during the current year to officers of the corporation

   vii. The replacement of a machine immediately before the close of the current year at a cost 20 percent above the original cost of the replaced machine (The new machine will perform the same function as the old machine, which was sold for its book value.)

• Case 6-6 Accounting Changes

APB Opinion No. 20 was concerned with accounting changes. *SFAS No. 154* (see FASB ASC 250) changes the accounting treatment for some accounting changes.

Required:

a. Define, discuss, and illustrate each of the following in such a way that one can be distinguished from the other:

   i. An accounting change

   ii. A correction of an error in previously issued financial statements

b. Discuss the justification for a change in accounting principle.

c. Discuss the reporting of accounting changes that was required by *APB Opinion No. 20.*

d. Discuss how accounting changes are to be reported under the provisions of FASB ASC 250.

• Case 6-7 Identifying Accounting Changes

Sometimes a business entity may change its method of accounting for certain items. The change may be classified as a change in accounting principle, a change in accounting estimate, or a change in reporting entity. Listed below are three independent, unrelated sets of facts relating to accounting changes.

Situation 1

A company determined that the depreciable lives of its fixed assets were presently too long to fairly match the cost of the fixed assets with the revenue produced.

The company decided at the beginning of the current year to reduce the depreciable lives of all its existing fixed assets by five years.

Situation 2

On December 31, 2010, Gary Company owned 51 percent of Allen Company, at which time Gary reported its investment using the cost method due to political uncertainties in the country in which Allen was located. On January 2, 2011, the management of Gary Company was satisfied that the political uncertainties were resolved and that the assets of the company were in no danger of nationalization. Accordingly, Gary will prepare consolidated financial statements for Gary and Allen for the year ended December 31, 2011.

Situation 3

A company decides in January 2011 to adopt the straight-line method of depreciation for plant equipment. This method will be used for new acquisitions as well as for previously acquired plant equipment for which depreciation had been provided on an accelerated basis.

Required:

For each of the preceding situations, provide the information indicated below. Complete your discussion of each situation before going on to the next situation.

   a. Type of accounting change

   b. Manner of reporting the change under current GAAP, including a discussion, where applicable, of how amounts are computed

   c. Effects of the change on the statement of financial position and earnings statement

   d. Required e disclosures

• Case 6-8 Classification of Accounting Changes

Morgan Company grows various crops and then processes them for sale to retailers. Morgan has changed its depreciation method for its processing equipment from the double-declining-balance method to the straight-line method effective January 1 of this year.

   In the latter part of this year, a large portion of Morgan's crops were destroyed by a hailstorm. Morgan has incurred substantial costs in raising the crops that were destroyed. Severe damage from hailstorms is rare in the locality where the crops are grown.

Required:

   a. How should Morgan calculate and report the effect(s) of the change in depreciation method in this year's income statement?

   b. Where should Morgan report the effects of the hailstorm in its income statement? Why?

   c. How does the classification in the income statement of an extraordinary item differ from that of an operating item? Why?

- ## Case 6-9 Comprehensive Income

Earnings as defined in *SFAC No. 5* are consistent with the current operating performance concept of income. Comprehensive income is consistent with the all-inclusive concept of income.

Required:

a. Discuss the current operating performance concept of income.

b. Explain how earnings, as defined in *SFAC No. 5*, are consistent with the current operating performance concept of income.

c. Discuss the all-inclusive concept of income.

d. Explain how comprehensive income is consistent with the all-inclusive concept of income.

e. Explain how comprehensive income is consistent with the financial capital maintenance concept.

f. What additional changes in reporting practices would have to occur for financial reporting to be consistent with the physical capital maintenance concept? Have some similar changes already occurred? Give an example.

FASB ASC Research

For each of the following FASB ASC research cases, search the FASB ASC database for information to address the issues. Cut and paste the FASB paragraphs that support your responses. Then summarize briefly what your responses are, citing the pronouncements and paragraphs used to support your responses.

- ## FARS 6-1 Extraordinary Items

Several FASB and EITF pronouncements dealt with accounting for extraordinary items. Search the FASB ASC database to identify all of the FASB and EITF pronouncements dealing with extraordinary items and then summarize them.

- ## FARS 6-2 Comprehensive Income

SFAS No. 130 (see FASB ASC 220) establishes the guidelines for reporting comprehensive income. Search the FASB ASC database for the requirements for reporting comprehensive income.

- ## FASB ASC 6-3 Net Income

The definition of net income is contained in the FASB ASC. Find this definition, cite the paragraph, and copy it.

- ## FASB ASC 6-4 APB Opinion No. 9

Several parts of *APB Opinion No. 9* are still GAAP. Find three of these references in the FASB ASC.

• FASB ASC 6-5 Extraordinary Items

The definition of extraordinary items is contained in the FASB ASC. Find this definition, cite the paragraph, and copy it.

• FASB ASC 6-6 Discontinued Operations

The definition of discontinued operations is contained in the FASB ASC. Find this definition, cite the paragraph, and copy it.

• FASB ASC 6-7 Accounting Changes

The topic of accounting changes is discussed in the FASB ASC. Find this discussion, cite the paragraph, and copy it.

• FASB ASC 6-8 Earnings Per Share

The topic of earnings per share is contained in the FASB ASC.

Required:

  a. Find, cite the paragraph, and copy the objectives of earnings per share and the glossary of terms associated with earnings per share.
  b. Find and cite the paragraph, but do not copy the required presentation of earnings per share.

Room for Debate

• Debate 6-1 Comprehensive Income

The FASB requires that financial statements report comprehensive income.

Team Debate:

Team 1:   Defend comprehensive income. Your defense should relate to the conceptual framework and to the concept of capital maintenance where appropriate.

Team 2:   Oppose comprehensive income. Your opposition should relate to the conceptual framework and to the concept of capital maintenance where appropriate.

• Debate 6-2 Income Concepts

The all-inclusive and current operating performance concepts of income represent opposing views regarding the inclusion of items to be reported in earnings on the income statement.

Team Debate:

Team 1:   Defend the all-inclusive concept of income.

Team 2:   Defend the current operating performance concept of income.

CHAPTER 7

Financial Statements II: The Balance Sheet and the Statement of Cash Flows

Financial reports can be divided into two categories. The first category discloses the results of the flow of resources over time and includes the income statement, the statement of retained earnings, and the statement of cash flows. The second category summarizes the status of resources at a particular point in time.

These two categories suggest an important distinction in measurement emphasis between *flows* and *stocks*. Flows are productive services that must be measured over some period of time, whereas stocks are resources that are measured at a particular point in time. The matching concept emphasizes flows. This emphasis previously resulted in the direct measurement of flows and reporting stocks as residuals of the matching process. Alternatively, defining earnings as the change in the net assets from nonowner transactions implies that stocks should be measured directly, making flows the residuals. Recent pronouncements of the FASB are consistent with the latter measurement approach, indicating a shift in emphasis from an income statement to an asset-liability, or balance sheet approach to the measurement of net income.

Accounting is the means by which management reports to various users of financial information. Evaluation of a company's financial position is an important factor in satisfying the needs of creditors, stockholders, management, the government, and other interested parties. Management attempts to satisfy these needs by presenting information on the company's resources, obligations, and equities at periodic intervals.

In this chapter we first describe the balance sheet and the measurement techniques currently used to disclose assets, liabilities, and equity; illustrate the disclosure of financial statement elements on the balance sheets of Hershey and Tootsie Roll; and discuss how to evaluate a company's financial position. In so doing, we do not presume that current stock measurement techniques provide enough relevant information to the users of financial statements. Rather, we believe a thorough examination of these techniques will disclose their inherent limitations. Later in the chapter, we discuss the evolution of the third major financial statement from the statement of changes in financial position to the statement of cash flows, illustrate the disclosure of cash-flow information on Hershey's and Tootsie Roll's statements of cash flows, and discuss how investors can use this information to evaluate a company's performance.

The Balance Sheet

The balance sheet should disclose a company's wealth at a point in time. *Wealth* is defined as the present value of all resources less the present value of all obligations. Although the use of present-value measurements in accounting is increasing, it is not used extensively for all assets and liabilities. As a result, a variety of methods are currently being used to measure changes in the individual components of the elements of the balance sheet. These measurements can be summarized as past oriented—historical; current oriented—replacement amounts; and future oriented—expected amounts.

Over the years, accounting theorists have debated the respective merits of alternative accounting measurement approaches. Those favoring historical cost base their argument on the premise that cost is objective and verifiable. Historical cost is not based on subjective estimations; rather, it is the result of the value buyers and sellers have agreed to in an "arm's-length" transaction. Some accounting theorists have even suggested that historical cost actually represents the present value of expected future cash flows at the time the exchange takes place. It is also argued that accountants serve a stewardship role, and because cost measures the actual resources exchanged, it is relevant to readers of financial statements. Opponents of historical cost maintain that values may change over time and, consequently, that historical cost can lose its relevance as a valuation base.

Zeff has documented the role of the SEC in requiring the use of historical cost.[1] The SEC's position emerged from an investigation of the public utility holding companies that disclosed that flagrant asset write-up policies had been used by these holding companies during the 1920s. The SEC's advocacy of historical cost lasted into the mid-1970s, when the United States was experiencing high inflation. In 1976 the SEC altered its position on historical cost by requiring the supplemental disclosure of replacement cost information by about 1,000 of the largest nonfinancial companies. Currently, the SEC and the FASB both recognize that financial statement disclosers must attempt to more clearly reflect economic reality and that historical costs frequently do not reflect economic reality.

Accounting theorists favoring current cost measurements, rather than historical cost amounts, hold that this value reflects current conditions and therefore represents the current value to the firm. Opponents point out that current value may not be available for all balance sheet elements and that recording current values on the balance sheet would result in recording unrealized gains and losses on the income statement. The latter argument is less valid today, because the unrealized gains and losses can now be reported as a component of other comprehensive income.

1. Stephen A. Zeff, "The SEC Rules Historical Cost Accounting: 1934 to the 1970s," *Accounting & Business Research* (2007 Special Issue): 49–62.

Those favoring expected future value disclosures maintain that this valuation procedure approximates the economic concept of income and is therefore the most relevant value to the users of financial statements. Critics of expected future value point out (as noted in Chapter 5) that the future cash flows associated with the elements of the balance sheet are difficult to estimate, the timing of these cash flows is uncertain, and an appropriate discount rate is difficult to ascertain.

In the following paragraphs, we look more closely at the measurement approaches actually used to value balance sheet elements. This review reveals that no single measurement basis is used for all of the elements; rather, a variety of measurement approaches are currently acceptable, depending on the circumstances and available information.

Balance Sheet Elements

FASB *Statement of Concepts No. 6* defined the elements of the balance sheet as follows:

> **Assets** Assets are probable future economic benefits obtained or controlled by a particular entity as a result of past transactions or events. An asset has three essential characteristics: (1) it embodies a probable future benefit that involves a capacity, singly or in combination with other assets, to contribute directly or indirectly to future net cash inflows; (2) a particular enterprise can obtain the benefit and control others' access to it; and (3) the transaction or other event giving rise to the enterprise's right to or control of the benefit has already occurred.
>
> **Liabilities** Liabilities are probable future sacrifices of economic benefits arising from present obligations of a particular entity to transfer assets or provide services to other entities in the future as a result of past transactions or events. A liability has three essential characteristics: (1) it embodies a present duty or responsibility to one or more other entities that entails settlement by probable future transfer or use of assets at a specified or determinable date, on occurrence of a specified event, or on demand; (2) the duty or responsibility obligates a particular enterprise, leaving it little or no discretion to avoid the future sacrifice; and (3) the transaction or other event obligating the enterprise has already happened.
>
> **Equity** Equity is the residual interest in the assets of an entity that remains after deducting its liabilities. In a business enterprise, the equity is the ownership interest. Equity in a business enterprise stems from ownership rights (or the equivalent). It involves a relation between an enterprise and its owners as owners rather than as employees, suppliers, customers, lenders, or in some other nonowner role.[2]

These definitions form the basis of the FASB's asset-liability approach to the measurement of stocks and flows that is prevalent in many of its standards. They

---

2. *Financial Accounting Standards Board Statement of Concepts No. 6*, "Elements of Financial Statements of Business Enterprises" (Stamford, CT: FASB, 1985), paras. 25, 26, 35, 36, and 49.

represent a departure from previous definitions that viewed the balance sheet as a statement of residual amounts whose values were frequently arrived at through income determination. For example, consider the definitions of assets and liabilities presented by the Accounting Principles Board (APB) in *Statement No. 4:*

> (Assets are) economic resources of an enterprise that are recognized and measured in conformity with generally accepted accounting principles including certain deferred charges that are not resources.[3]

> (Liabilities are) economic obligations of an enterprise that are recognized and measured in conformity with generally accepted accounting principles.[4]

In other words, deferred charges, which result from unexpired costs not charged to expense, are assets, and liabilities are created because of the necessity to record debits.

Even with their limitations, the APB definitions were believed to be significant improvements over previous definitions when they were released. Formerly, assets were defined as debit balances carried forward when the books were closed, and liabilities as credit balances carried forward, except those representing owners' equity.[5]

The preceding *SFAC No. 6* definitions should be examined carefully. They assert that assets are economic resources of an enterprise and that liabilities are economic obligations of an enterprise. These statements probably correspond to most users' understanding of the terms *assets* and *liabilities*, and therefore they are not likely to be misunderstood. However, to properly understand the numbers presented on a balance sheet, the user must be aware of the recognition and measurement procedures associated with generally accepted accounting principles (GAAP). These procedures are a combination of past, present, and future measurement approaches.

In addition, it has been considered more informative to provide subclassifications for each of these balance sheet elements. This classification scheme makes information more easily accessible to the various interested user groups and allows for more rapid identification of specific types of information for decision making. In general, the following classification scheme may be viewed as representative of the typical balance sheet presentation.

Assets

Current assets
Investments
Property, plant, and equipment
Intangible assets
Other assets

---

3. *Accounting Principles Board Statement No. 4,* "Basic Concepts and Accounting Principles Underlying Financial Statements of Business Enterprises" (AICPA, 1970), para. 132.

4. Ibid., para. 132.

5. *Accounting Terminology Bulletin No. 1,* "Review and Resume" (AICPA, 1953), paras. 26–27.

Liabilities
Current liabilities
Long-term liabilities
Other liabilities

Equity
Capital stock
Additional paid-in capital
Retained earnings

In the following paragraphs we examine each of the elements of the balance sheet, introduce the accounting principles currently being used in measuring these elements, and discuss how they are disclosed on the balance sheets of Hershey's and Tootsie Roll illustrated in Exhibits 7.1 and 7.2 on pages 216–218. It is important to recognize that the financial statement elements reported in balance sheets are categorized according to the concept of *managerial intent*—that is, how management intends to use the item in question. Accordingly, virtually every element disclosed under the various balance sheet subsections might be disclosed under a different category under different circumstances. The measurement issues for each of the balance sheet elements are discussed in greater depth in subsequent chapters.

Assets

Current Assets
The Committee on Accounting Procedure has supplied the most commonly encountered definition of current assets. This definition may be summarized as follows: current assets are those assets that may *reasonably be expected* to be realized in cash, sold, or consumed during the normal operating cycle of the business or one year, whichever is longer. The operating cycle is defined as the average time it takes to acquire materials, produce the product, sell the product, and collect the proceeds from customers.[6] Current assets are presented on the balance sheet in the order of their liquidity and generally include these items: cash, cash equivalents, temporary investments, receivables, inventories, and prepaid expenses. Nevertheless, special problems are connected with the valuation procedure for most of these items.

Companies are now required to classify temporary investments in all debt securities and equity securities with readily determinable fair values as trading, available for sale, and (for debt securities only) held to maturity. Temporary investments in equity securities that do not have readily determinable fair values are accounted for under the cost method. All trading and available-for-sale securities are reported in the balance sheet at fair value. Unrealized gains and losses for trading securities are reported in earnings, while unrealized gains and losses for available-for-sale securities are reported as a component of other comprehensive income.

---

6. *Accounting Research Bulletin No. 43*, "Restatement and Revision of Accounting Research Bulletins" (AICPA, 1953), ch. 3, para. 5 (see FASB ASC 210-10-20 and 210-10-45 1 through 4).

EXHIBIT 7.1   *The Hershey Company Consolidated Balance Sheets*

December 31	2008	2007
In thousands		
Current Assets:		
Cash and cash equivalents	$ 37,103	$ 129,198
Accounts receivable—trade	455,153	487,285
Inventories	592,530	600,185
Deferred income taxes	70,903	83,668
Prepaid expenses and other	189,256	126,238
Total current assets	$ 1,344,945	$1,426,574
Property, plant and equipment, net	1,458,949	1,539,715
Goodwill	554,677	584,713
Other intangibles	110,772	155,862
Deferred income taxes	13,815	—
Other assets	151,561	540,249
Total assets	$ 3,634,719	$4,247,113
LIABILITIES, MINORITY INTEREST, AND STOCKHOLDERS' EQUITY		
Current Liabilities:		
Accounts payable	$ 249,454	$ 223,019
Accrued liabilities	504,065	538,986
Accrued income taxes	15,189	373
Short-term debt	483,120	850,288
Current portion of long-term debt	18,384	6,104
Total current liabilities	1,270,212	1,618,770
Long-term debt	1,505,954	1,279,965
Other long-term liabilities	504,963	544,016
Deferred income taxes	3,646	180,842
Total liabilities	3,284,775	3,623,593
Commitments and contingencies	—	—
Minority interest	31,745 3	30,598
Stockholders' Equity:		
Preferred Stock, shares issued: none in 2008 and 2007	—	—
Common Stock, shares issued: 299,190,836 in 2008 and 299,095,417 in 2007	299,190	299,095
Class B Common Stock, shares issued: 60,710,908 in 2008 and 60,806,327 in 2007	60,711	60,806
Additional paid-in capital	352,375	335,256
Retained earnings	3,975,762	3,927,306
Treasury—Common Stock shares, at cost: 132,866,673 in 2008 and 132,851,893 in 2007	(4,009,931)	(4,001,562)
Accumulated other comprehensive loss	(359,908)	(27,979)
Total stockholders' equity	318,199	592,922
Total liabilities, minority interest, and stockholders' equity	$ 3,634,719	$4,247,113

EXHIBIT 7.2 *Financial Position Tootsie Roll Industries, Inc. and Subsidiaries*

December 31	2008	2007
In thousands		
Assets		
Current Assets:		
Cash and cash equivalents	$ 68,908	$ 57,606
Investments	17,963	41,307
Accounts receivable trade, less		
allowances of $1,923 and $2,287	31,213	32,371
Other receivables	2,983	2,913
Inventories:		
Finished goods and work-in-process	34,862	37,031
Raw materials and supplies	20,722	20,371
Prepaid expenses	11,328	6,551
Deferred income taxes	—	1,576
Total current assets	187,979	199,726
Property, Plant, and Equipment, at cost:		
Land	19,307	19,398
Buildings	89,077	88,225
Machinery and equipment	279,100	265,359
Construction in progress	20,701	4,711
	408,185	377,693
Less—Accumulated depreciation	190,557	176,292
Net property, plant and equipment	217,628	201,401
Other Assets:		
Goodwill	73,237	73,237
Trademarks	189,024	189,024
Investments	49,809	65,993
Split dollar officer life insurance	74,808	74,944
Prepaid expenses	10,333	—
Investment in joint venture	9,274	8,400
Total other assets	406,485	411,598
Total assets	$812,092	$812,725
LIABILITIES AND SHAREHOLDERS' EQUITY		
Current Liabilities:		
Accounts payable	$ 13,885	$ 11,572
Dividends payable	4,401	4,344
Accrued liabilities	40,335	42,056
Deferred income taxes	631	—
Total current liabilities	59,252	57,972
Noncurrent Liabilities:		
Deferred income taxes	43,346	35,940
Postretirement health care and life		
insurance benefits	15,468	13,214
Industrial development bonds	7,500	7,500
Liability for uncertain tax positions	19,412	20,056
Deferred compensation and other liabilities	32,344	39,813
Total noncurrent liabilities	118,070	116,523
Shareholder's Equity:		
Common stock, $0.69-4/9 par value—		

(Continued)

EXHIBIT 7.2 (*Continued*)

December 31	2008	2007
Shareholder's Equity:		
Common stock, $0.69-4/9 par value—120,000 shares authorized—35,658 and 35,404, respectively, issued	24,762	24,586
Class B common stock, $0.69-4/9 par value—40,000 shares authorized—19,357 and 18,892, respectively, issued	13,442	13,120
Capital in excess of par value	470,927	457,491
Retained earnings, per accompanying statement	142,872	156,752
Accumulated other comprehensive loss	(15,241)	(11,727)
Treasury stock (at cost)—65 shares and 63 shares, respectively	(1,992)	(1,992)
Total shareholders' equity	634,770	638,230
Total liabilities and shareholders' equity	$812,092	$812,725

Temporary investments in debt securities for which management has a positive intent to hold to maturity are carried in the balance sheet at amortized cost. Amortized cost implies that premiums or discounts, which arose when the purchase price of the debt security differed from face value, are being amortized over the remaining life of the security. Premiums and discounts for debt securities having short terms—for example, U.S. treasury notes are generally not amortized for materiality reasons.

Because they are to be consumed in a relatively short period of time, receivables are typically reported at amounts that "approximate" their expected present values, GAAP dictates that an item should not be valued at an amount in excess of its current value. It is considered appropriate to value receivables at their *expected net realizable value*—the recorded amount less an amount deemed to be uncollectible.

Inventories and prepaid expenses present some additional valuation issues. With the emphasis on net income reporting, the inventory valuation process has become secondary to the matching of expired inventory costs to sales. The use of any of the acceptable inventory flow assumption techniques (e.g., LIFO, FIFO, weighted average discussed in Chapter 8) prescribes the amount that remains on the balance sheet, and each of these flow assumptions likely will result in different inventory valuations in fluctuating market conditions. In addition, the accounting convention of conservatism has resulted in the requirement that a lower of cost or market valuation be used for inventories. In any case, the financial statement user should interpret the inventory figure as being less than its estimated selling price.

Prepaid items are valued at historical cost, and an appropriate amount is charged to expense each year until they are consumed. Prepaid expenses are reported as current assets because it is argued that if these items had not been paid in advance, they would require the use of current funds. However, the same argument might be made for other assets; and even though the lives of many prepaid items encompass several accounting periods, this does not enhance the logic of the argument. It should be noted that prepaid items are not usually material, and perhaps that is where the dispute loses its significance.

As can be seen from the previous discussion, two problems arise when we attempt to classify an asset as current: (1) the period of time over which it is to be consumed, and (2) the proper valuation technique. In many cases historical precedent rather than accounting theory has dictated the inclusion of items as current assets. The valuation procedures associated with each of the items may, when considered by itself, be appropriate; but when all items are summed to arrive at a figure termed *total current assets*, it may be difficult to interpret the result. This total approximates the minimum amount of cash that could be collected during the next fiscal period, but it leaves to the user's imagination the actual amount expected to be realized. The issues associated with the valuation of current assets and current liabilities (i.e., working capital) are explored more fully in Chapter 8.

Hershey's balance sheet discloses total current assets of $1,344,945,000, whereas Tootsie Roll's total current assets are $187,979,000. The two companies' balance sheets contain all of the current assets discussed above.

Investments

Investments may be divided into three categories:

1. Securities acquired for specific purposes, such as using idle funds for long periods or exercising influence on the operations of another company

2. Assets not currently in use by the business organization, such as land held for a future building site

3. Special funds to be used for special purposes in the future, such as sinking funds

When a company has a controlling interest (owns more than 50 percent) in an investee company, the reporting company is considered a parent company and the investee company is considered a subsidiary. In this case, GAAP requires a consolidation of the financial statements of the two companies into a single set of financial statements. As a result, the investments section of the balance sheet will not report the parent company's investment in the subsidiary. If instead, the company acquired the investee company's equity securities to influence that company's operations, GAAP requires that the investment be accounted for by the equity method. The equity method adjusts historical cost for income of the investee and dividends received. As with temporary investments, all other investments in equity securities are accounted for under the cost method when they have no readily determinable fair values. Those equity securities that have readily determinable fair values and debt securities that are not classified as held to maturity are considered available for sale. Long-term available-for-sale securities are treated in the same manner as temporary securities similarly classified. That is, these securities are reported at fair value, and unrealized gains and losses are recognized in stockholders' equity as a component of accumulated other comprehensive income. Debt securities classified as held to maturity—that is, those debt securities that management has positive intent to hold to maturity—are reported at amortized cost.

Hershey does not disclose any investments on its balance sheet, whereas Tootsie Roll discloses long-term investments of $49,809,000 and an investment in a joint venture of $9,274,000 in the other assets section of its balance sheet.

Property, Plant, and Equipment and Intangibles

Although property, plant, and equipment and intangibles are physically dissimilar assets, the valuation procedures associated with them are similar. Except for land, the cost of these assets is allocated to the various accounting periods benefiting from their use. In the case of property, plant, and equipment, the carrying value is disclosed as the difference between cost and accumulated depreciation. However, intangible assets are generally disclosed at the net amount of their cost less amortization.

These valuation procedures are again the result of the emphasis on income reporting. Various methods of depreciation and amortization are available, but there is no attempt to disclose the current value of long-term assets or the expected future cash flows from holding them on the financial statements. Instead, the emphasis is on a proper matching of revenues and expenses, and asset valuation is the residual effect of this process.

Hershey's 2008 balance sheet discloses net property, plant, and equipment of $1,458,949,000. The components of this amount are disclosed in the company's footnotes, which indicate that accumulated depreciation is $1,978,471,000 and the original cost of the assets was $3,437,420,000. Tootsie Roll reported property, plant, and equipment costing $408,185,000 with accumulated depreciation of $190,557,000, resulting in a book value of $217,628,000. The Hershey's balance sheet discloses a goodwill balance of $554,677,000 and other intangibles of $110,772,000. Tootsie Roll's balance sheet discloses goodwill of $73,237,000 and trademarks of $189,024,000.

Other Assets

The preceding asset category captions will usually allow for the disclosure of all assets, but some corporations include a final category: other assets. Items such as fixed assets held for resale or long-term receivables may be included under this category. The valuation of these assets is generally their carrying value on the balance sheet at the time they were originally reported in the other assets category. Since the amounts associated with these items are normally immaterial, it is unlikely that any alternative valuation procedure would result in a significantly different carrying value. Hershey's balance sheet discloses other assets of $151,561,000. Tootsie Roll's other assets including the investments and intangibles discussed above total $406,485,000.

Asset Valuation

The preceding discussion reveals that many different measurement techniques are used when valuing assets on the typical balance sheet. Under almost any measurement scheme devised, it is common practice to add and subtract only like items measured in the same manner. However, the measurement of assets on the balance sheet takes an unusual form when we consider that asset totals are derived from summing subclassifications of assets whose measurement bases may be significantly different.

Consider the following measurement bases that are included in a typical balance sheet presentation of assets:

Asset	Measurement Basis
Cash	Current value
Accounts receivable	Expected future value
Marketable securities	Fair value or amortized cost
Inventory	Current or past value
Investments	Fair value, amortized cost, or the result of applying the equity method
Property, plant, and equipment	Past value adjusted for depreciation

Summing these items is much like adding apples and oranges. Investors need to be aware of these differences when using the balance sheet to evaluate a company's financial position. If assets are truly the firm's economic resources, it seems plausible to conclude that the totals on balance sheets should reflect somewhat more than values arrived at by convention. Presentation of information on the expected future benefits to be derived from holding these items would better satisfy user needs.

Liabilities

Current Liabilities

Current liabilities have been defined as "obligations whose liquidation is reasonably expected to require the use of existing resources properly classified as current assets or the creation of other current liabilities."[7] Notice that, although the operating cycle is not explicitly discussed in this definition, it is implied because the definition of current liabilities depends on the definition of current assets. Examples of current liabilities are short-term payables, the currently maturing portion of long-term debt, income taxes payable, returnable deposits, and accrued liabilities.

Even though the current value of a debt instrument is equal to the present value of its future cash flows, current liabilities are usually measured and reported at liquidation value because their period of existence is relatively short and the satisfaction of these obligations generally involves the payment of cash.

Since current liabilities usually require the use of current funds, it might be considered justifiable to offset them against current assets. However, the principle of disclosure requires that they be shown separately unless a specific right of offset exists. *APB Opinion No. 10* (see FASB ASC 210-20-05-1) emphasized this point in stating: "It is a general principle of accounting that offsetting of assets and liabilities in the balance sheet are improper except where a right of offset exists."[8] Hershey's 2008 balance sheet includes all of the typical items and discloses total current liabilities of $1,270,212,000, whereas Tootsie Roll's are $59,252,000.

Long-Term and Other Liabilities

Long-term liabilities are those obligations that will not require the use of current assets within the current year or operating cycle. These obligations include bonds, notes, mortgages, and capital lease obligations and are originally valued at the amount of consideration received by the entity incurring the obligation. The resulting debt valuation implies that the beginning loan balance is equal to the present value of the debt instrument's future cash flows discounted at the rate charged by the creditor (the market or effective rate of interest). In those cases where the market rate differs from the rate stated on the debt instrument or when there is no stated rate, the debt will be issued at a premium or a discount. GAAP requires that premiums or discounts on long-term obligations should be written off over the life of the obligation to properly reflect the effective interest rate on the debt. In such cases, the conventions of realization and

---

7. Ibid., ch. 3, para. 7 (see FASB ASC 210-10-20 and 210-10-45-5 through 9).

8. *Accounting Principles Board Opinion No. 10*, "Omnibus Opinion—1966" (New York: AICPA, 1966).

matching dictate the balance sheet presentation of long-term liabilities. This is an example of the use of discounted cash-flow techniques to measure a balance sheet element.

The long-term liability section may also include long-term prepayments on contracts, deferred income taxes, and, in some cases, contingent liabilities, each of which has an associated measurement problem. Deferred revenues are measured at historical cost and remain at that amount until the situation that caused them to be recorded has reversed. Such reversals are dictated by the conventions of realization and matching. Contingent liabilities reported in balance sheets are measured as the best approximation of a future loss that the entity believes is forthcoming based on the convention of conservatism. Hershey's 2008 balance sheet discloses three long-term liabilities: long-term debt—$1,505,954,000, other long-term liabilities—$504,963,000, and deferred income taxes—$3,646,000. Tootsie Roll's 2008 balance sheet discloses total noncurrent liabilities of $118,070,000.

Liability Valuation

As with assets, liabilities are measured by a number of different procedures. Most current liability measurements ignore the time value of money. Their typical balance sheet measurement is equal to the amount of resources that it will ultimately take to satisfy the obligation. Conversely, the initial measurement of most long-term liabilities is equivalent to the present value of future payments discounted at the yield rate existing on the date of issue. When there are discounts or premiums on these obligations, they are reported in the balance sheet at amortized cost (net of unamortized premiums or discounts). Yet, a long-term deferred tax liability may be quite significant but is not discounted at all, so it is reported neither at present value nor amortized cost. In all cases, liability valuations are not changed to reflect current changes in the market rates of interest—that is, they are not reported at current value. Failure to consider the current market interest rates may cause the financial statements to be biased in favor of current creditors, particularly when many obligations are of a long-term nature.

Equity

State laws and corporate articles of incorporation make generalizations about the equity section of the balance sheet somewhat difficult. However, certain practices have become widespread enough to discuss several generally accepted standards of reporting.

Common Stock

Common stock is measured at historical cost—the amount received from investors when the stock is issued. Initially, most corporations designate a par or stated value for their stock, and as each share of common stock is sold, an amount equal to the par or stated value is reported in the common stock section of the balance sheet. Any differences between selling price and par value are then reported under the caption "additional paid-in capital." These captions have no particular accounting significance except perhaps to determine an average issue price of common stock if such a computation seems meaningful. Companies may also issue more than one class of common stock. The additional categories such as Class B common generally carry fewer voting rights than Class A shares. For example, one Class A share may be accompanied by five voting rights, while one

Class B share may be accompanied by only one right to vote. A detailed description of each share division of a company is included in its bylaws and charter. Hershey's 2008 balance sheet discloses common stock of $299,190,000, Class B common stock of $60,711,000, and additional paid-in capital of $ 352,375,000. The par value of the company's common stock is $1.00 per share. Tootsie Roll's 2008 balance sheet discloses common stock of $24,762,000. The par value of the company's common stock is 0.69^{4/9}$. The company also discloses Class B common stock of $13,442,000 and additional paid-in capital of $470,927,000.

Preferred Stock
Many companies also issue other classes of stock, known as preferred. These shares generally have preference as to dividends, and a stated amount of dividends must be paid to preferred shareholders before any dividends can be paid to the common stockholders. The measurement basis of preferred stock is similar to that of common stock, with amounts divided between the par value of the shares and additional paid-in capital. Thus the reported balance sheet amounts also represent historical cost. Hershey's fiscal 2008 balance sheet indicates that the company is authorized to issue shares of authorized preferred stock; however, none of these shares had been issued on the balance sheet date. Tootsie Roll does not disclose any information about preferred stock.

Treasury Stock
Corporations may reduce their stockholders' equity by acquiring their shares on the open market. These reacquired shares are termed treasury stock. Hershey discloses the cost of its treasury stock as $4,009,931,000, whereas the cost of Tootsie Roll's treasury stock is $1,992,000.

Retained Earnings and Other Comprehensive Income
Ownership interest in a corporation may be defined as the residual interest in the company's assets after the liabilities have been deducted. The amounts reported in stockholders' equity as retained earnings and accumulated other comprehensive income are associated with the measurement methods used to record specific assets and liabilities. However, these amounts should not be confused with any attempt to measure the owners' current-value interest in the firm. Consequently, the measurement of retained earnings and accumulated other comprehensive income is dependent on the measurement of revenues and cost expirations over the life of the firm.

Most states require that dividends not exceed the balance in retained earnings, and stockholders may wish to have extra dividends distributed when the retained earnings balance becomes relatively large. However, individual entities may have various long-range plans and commitments that do not allow for current distribution of dividends, and firms may provide for the dissemination of this information through an appropriation of retained earnings. A retained earnings appropriation is measured as the amount of retained earnings set aside for the stated purpose. It should be emphasized that retained earnings appropriations do not provide the cash to finance such projects and are presented only to show managerial intent. This intent might just as easily be disclosed through a footnote.

Companies are also now required to disclose the components of other comprehensive income. The amounts of these components (discussed in more detail in Chapter 6) represent all nonowner changes in equity resulting from changes in the valuation of balance sheet items that are not included in net income.

The measurement of equity can be said to be based primarily on the measurement of specific assets and liabilities. The transfer of assets to expense and the incurrence of liabilities determine the measurement of changes in equity. As such, equity does not have a measurement criterion other than a residual valuation.

Hershey's 2008 balance sheet discloses a retained earnings balance of $3,975,762,000 and an accumulated other comprehensive loss of $359,908,000. Tootsie Roll's retained earnings balance at the end of its 2008 fiscal year was $142,872,000 and the accumulated other comprehensive loss was $15,241,000.

Fair Value Measurements Under *SFAS No. 157*

In September 2007 the FASB issued *SFAS No. 157*, "Fair Value Measurements" (see FASB ASC 820). This statement specifies how fair value is to be determined when such measurements are required by existing GAAP. It does not indicate when fair value measurements are to be used. The rationale for *SFAS No. 157* was that previous GAAP contained inconsistent definitions and only limited application guidance for fair value measurements. The most important aspects of *SFAS No. 157* are as follows:

1. A new definition of fair value
2. A fair value hierarchy used to classify the source of information used in fair value measurements (for example, market-based or nonmarket-based)
3. New disclosures of assets and liabilities measured at fair value based on their level in the hierarchy
4. A modification of the presumption that the transaction price of an asset or liability equals its initial fair value

SFAS No. 157 is to be applied to any asset or liability that is measured at fair value under current GAAP. The statement identified sixty-seven previous pronouncements that referred to fair value and are impacted by its provisions. *SFAS No. 157* (Now FASB ASC 820) represents the FASB's current position on the trade-off between reliability and relevance of financial information. It also reflects the FASB's conclusion that investors and creditors find fair value measurement relevant, even in the absence of exact market data. As a result, the trade-off now favors relevance; thus, in order to assess the relative reliability of the fair value measurements provided, financial statement users will need to be made aware of the quality of the information provided through meaningful and transparent disclosures.

Definition of Fair Value

SFAS No. 157 defined *fair value* as "the price that would be received to sell an asset or paid to transfer a liability in an orderly transaction between market participants at the measurement date."[9] This definition is based on *exit price*. For an asset, fair value is the price at which it would be sold. In contrast, an *entry price* for an asset is the price at which it would be bought. The exit price is to be used regardless of

---

9. *Statement of Financial Accounting Standards No. 157*, "Fair Value Measurements" (Norwalk, CT: FASB, 2007), para. 5.

EXHIBIT 7.3   *Hierarchy of the Quality and Reliability of Information Used to Determine Fair Values*

Level and Inputs Information Used to Determine Fair Value	Examples
Level 1—Quoted market prices for *identical* assets or liabilities in *active* markets	Company A common stock traded and quoted on the New York Stock Exchange
Level 2—Observable market-based inputs, other than Level 1 quoted prices (or unobservable inputs that are corroborated by market data)	Company B common stock traded and quoted only on an inactive market in an emerging country
	A privately placed bond of Z whose value is derived from a similar Z bond that is publicly traded
	An over-the-counter interest rate swap, valued based on a model whose inputs are observable, such as LIBOR (London Interbank Offered Rate) forward interest rate curves.
Level 3—Unobservable inputs (that are not corroborated by observable market data)	A long-dated commodity swap whose forward price curve, used in a valuation model, is not directly observable or correlated with observable market data
	Shares of a privately held company whose value is based on projected cash flows

Source: Adapted from *Statement of Financial Accounting Standards No. 157,* "Fair Value Measurements" (Norwalk, CT: FASB, 2007).

whether the entity plans to hold or sell the asset. Additionally, *SFAS No. 157* specified that fair value is *market based* rather than *entity specific*. As a result, fair values must be based on assumptions that market participants would use in pricing the asset or liability.

Fair Value Hierarchy

SFAS No. 157 establishes a hierarchy that ranks the quality and reliability of information used to determine fair values. Exhibit 7.3 provides a description of the levels in the hierarchy and examples.

If the fair value of an asset or liability is based on information from more than one level of the hierarchy, the classification of fair value depends on the lowest-level input with significant effect. For example, if a particular measurement contains both Level 2 and Level 3 inputs and both have a significant effect, then the measurement falls in Level 3.

Disclosures

The disclosure requirements are designed to indicate the relative reliability of fair value measurements. *SFAS No. 157* required separate disclosures of items that are measured at fair value on a recurring basis (e.g., an investment portfolio versus items that are measured at fair value on a nonrecurring basis, such as an impaired asset). Following are the major disclosures required at each annual and interim balance sheet date:

1. For items that are measured on a nonrecurring basis at fair value, a separate table is required for assets and for liabilities. The table displays the balance sheet fair value carrying amount of major categories of assets and of liabilities.

EXHIBIT 7.4 *Illustration of Tabular Disclosures for Assets Remeasured on a Nonrecurring Basis*

($ in millions)		Fair Value Measurements Using			
Description	Year Ended 12/31/XX	Quoted Prices in Active Markets for Inputs Identical 1 Assets (Level 1)	Significant Other Observable (Level 2)	Significant Unobservable Inputs (Level 3)	Total Gains (Losses)
Long-lived assets held and used[a]	$75		$75		$(25)
Goodwill[b]	30			$30	(35)
Long-lived assets held for sale[c]	26		26		(15)
					$(75)

[a]In accordance with the provisions of *Statement 144*, long-lived assets held and used with a carrying amount of $100 million were written down to their fair value of $75 million, resulting in an impairment charge of $25 million, which was included in earnings for the period (this issue is discussed in Chapter 9).

[b]In accordance with the provisions of *Statement 142*, goodwill with a carrying amount of $65 million was written down to its implied fair value of $30 million, resulting in an impairment charge of $35 million, which was included in earnings for the period (this issue is discussed in Chapter 10).

[c]In accordance with the provisions of *Statement 144*, long-lived assets held for sale with a carrying amount of $35 million were written down to their fair value of $26 million, less cost to sell of $6 million (or $20 million), resulting in a loss of $15 million, which was included in earnings for the period (this issue is discussed in Chapter 9).

Source: Adapted from *Statement of Financial Accounting Standards No. 157,* "Fair Value Measurements" (Norwalk, CT: FASB, 2007), para. 36.

Within each table, the assets and liabilities measured at fair value in each major category are separated into the level of the hierarchy on which fair value is based. The table also includes total gains and losses recognized for each major category.

2. For items measured on a recurring basis at fair value, tables similar to those for nonrecurring items are required. These tables must provide additional information regarding fair values based on Level 3 (unobservable) inputs, including a roll-forward analysis of fair value balance sheet amounts and disclosure of the unrealized gains and losses for Level 3 items held at the reporting date.

SFAS No. 157 required disclosures about the fair value measurements in a tabular format for each major category of assets and liabilities measured at fair value on a nonrecurring basis during the period. A table is also required for liabilities measured at fair value on a nonrecurring basis, if any exist. A similar set of disclosures is to be made for assets and liabilities that are remeasured at fair value on a recurring basis.

An illustration of information on assets measured at fair value on a nonrecurring basis is provided in Exhibit 7.4.

Additionally, qualitative information such as a description of the information used to develop the measurements, the valuation technique, and a discussion of any changes to valuation techniques should accompany the table.

Modification of the Transaction Price Presumption

Under previous GAAP, when an item was initially recognized, the transaction or entry price (the price paid for an asset) is presumed to be its fair value absent persuasive evidence to the contrary. Because an exit price is not necessarily equal to the transaction price, *SFAS No. 157* did away with that presumption. Instead, entities should consider whether certain factors, when present, *might* indicate that the transaction price does not represent fair value. When that is the case, a separate determination of fair value is to be made. *SFAS No. 157* cites four examples that might indicate that the transaction price does not represent fair value.

1. The transaction is between related parties.
2. The transaction occurs under duress or the seller is forced to accept the price in the transaction because of urgency.
3. The unit of account represented by the transaction is different from the unit of account for the asset or liability measured at fair value.
4. The market in which the transaction occurs is different from the principal (or most advantageous) market in which the reporting entity would sell or otherwise dispose of the asset or transfer the liability.

FASB Staff Position *FAS No. 157-4*

As noted earlier in Chapter 1, some critics of *SFAS No.157* maintained that it caused or exacerbated the 2007–2008 market crises by forcing a downward spiral of valuations based on distressed institutions. They also raised concerns that as a result of *SFAS No. 157* and *SFAS No. 115* (see Chapter 8), financial institutions were forced to book losses on securities that may have value after the credit market crisis has passed. However, proponents of the standard maintained that suspending or revising *SFAS No. 157* would be a disservice to investors who deserve to know the current value of a reporting entity's assets and liabilities.

As a result of these differing viewpoints, financial institutions, accounting groups, and others requested guidance from the SEC and the FASB on how to determine fair value measurements in the then-current economic climate. On September 30, 2008, the SEC and FASB were granted authority by Congress to study the implications of *SFAS No. 157*.

On October 3, 2008, President Bush signed the Emergency Economic Stabilization Act of 2008 into law. Section 133 of this legislation required the SEC to study fair value accounting and report on its impact. On December 30, 2008, the SEC issued its study on fair value accounting, *Report and Recommendations Pursuant to Section 133 of the Emergency Economic Stabilization Act of 2008: Study on Mark-to-Market Accounting.*[10] This study recommended that existing fair value accounting and mark-to-market standards, including *SFAS No. 157*, should not be suspended.

---

10. Securities and Exchange Commission. *Report and Recommendations Pursuant to Section 133 of the Emergency Economic Stabilization Act of 2008: Study on Mark-to-Market Accounting,* Washington, DC: SEC, 2008).

Nevertheless, the publication of SEC's report did not satisfy the critics of *SFAS No. 157*. The *Wall Street Journal* reported, in its analysis of public filings, that thirty-one financial firms and trade groups had formed a coalition in early 2009 and spent $27.6 million to lobby legislators about the rule and other issues.[11] Later, after some contentious hearings in Congress, where the FASB's standard-setting authority was threatened by some of its members, the FASB amended *SFAS No. 157* by issuing FASB Staff Position (FSP). *FAS 157-4* (see FASB ASC 820-10-65).

FSP *FAS 157-4* provided guidance on how to determine when the volume and level of activity for an asset or liability has significantly decreased and identified the circumstances in which a transaction is not orderly. The factors (which are not intended to be all inclusive) specified that indicate a significant decrease in the volume and level of activity for an asset or liability in relation to normal market activity for the same or similar assets or liabilities include the following:

1. There are few recent transactions.
2. Price quotations are not based on current information.
3. Price quotations vary substantially either over time or among market makers (e.g., some brokered markets).
4. Indexes that previously were highly correlated with the fair values of the asset or liability are demonstrably uncorrelated with recent indications of fair value for that asset or liability.
5. There is a significant increase in implied liquidity risk premiums, yields, or performance indicators (such as delinquency rates or loss severities) for observed transactions or quoted prices when compared with the reporting entity's estimate of expected cash flows, considering all available market data about credit and other nonperformance risks for the asset or liability.
6. There is a wide bid-ask spread or significant increase in the bid-ask spread.
7. There is a significant decline or absence of a market for new issuances (i.e., a primary market) for the asset or liability or similar assets or liabilities.
8. Little information is released publicly.

Subsequently, after considering the significance and relevance of each of the above or other factors, judgment should be used to determine whether the market is active and if a significant adjustment to the transactions or quoted prices may be necessary to estimate fair value. The circumstances identified that may indicate that a transaction is not orderly include, but are not limited to, the following:

1. There was not adequate exposure to the market for a period before the measurement date to allow for marketing activities that are usual and customary for transactions involving such assets or liabilities under current market conditions.
2. There was a usual and customary marketing period, but the seller marketed the asset or liability to a single market participant.
3. The seller is in or near bankruptcy or receivership (i.e., distressed), or the seller was required to sell to meet regulatory or legal requirements (i.e., forced).
4. The transaction price is an outlier when compared with other recent transactions for the same or similar asset or liability.

11. S. Pulliam and T. McGinty, "Congress Helped Banks Defang Key Rule," *Wall Street Journal*, 3 June 2009, http://online.wsj.com/article/SB124396078596677535.html#mod=rss_whats_news_us.

An evaluation of the circumstances is necessary to determine whether the transaction is orderly based on the weight of the evidence is required to estimate fair value in accordance with *SFAS No. 157*.

There were differing opinions on the expected impact of FSP *FAS 157-4*. CNBC financial markets commentator Lawrence Kudlow suggested that it would result in banks reporting improved profitability and that their balance sheets would reveal much more capital than was previously reported under the provisions of *SFAS No. 157*.[12] On the other hand, opponents of the amendment, such as hedge fund manager James Chanos, argued that it "allows banks to substitute their own wishful-thinking judgments of value for market prices."[13]

Although proponents and opponents of the amendment differed on the economic consequences of its adoption, both expected it to have a major impact. The expectation was that it would result in the revaluation upward of troubled assets, especially mortgage-based securities, by lowering their fair value hierarchy measurements from Level 2 to Level 3 and that bank profits might increase by as much as 20 percent.[14] However, as noted earlier in Chapter 1, a subsequent study of the impact of the adoption of FSP *FAS 157-4* on seventy-three of the largest banks in the United States found that a large majority of the banks reported that adoption of the new requirements had no material impact.[15]

Proposed Format of the Statement of Financial Position

The proposed revisions to the statement of financial position outlined in Phase B of the FASB-IASB Financial Statement Presentation Project (discussed in Chapter 2) are illustrated in Exhibit 7.5. This proposal would no longer divide assets and liabilities into separate categories on the balance sheet; rather, it groups assets and liabilities together under the categories of operating, investing, and financing activities while continuing to provide a separate section for stockholders' equity.

The boards propose to further disaggregate assets and liabilities within each category into short-term and long-term based on a one-year time frame that would replace the current distinction between current and noncurrent assets and liabilities that uses a one year or the operating cycle criterion. Assets and liabilities presented within each section would be further analyzed as short-term and long-term, unless presenting assets and liabilities in order of liquidity would provide more relevant information. In a presentation based on liquidity, an entity should present its assets and liabilities in increasing or decreasing order of

12. Lawrence Kudlow, "The AIG Outrage: The Government Shouldn't Run Anything, Because It Cannot Run Anything," *National Review Online* (March 17, 2009), http://article.nationalreview. com /?q=YjA0ODRlOWIyMjU5ZjUxMTBkMTEwYjhkNjQ4OG YwNGU=.

13. Quoted in J. Hughes and J. Chung, "IASB to Consider Changes to Fair Value Rule," *Financial Times* (March 18, 2009), http://www.ft.com/cms/s/0/ef960754-1353-11de-a170-0000779 fd2ac.html?nclick_check=1.

14. I. Katz and J. Westbrook, "Mark-to-Market Lobby Buoys Bank Profits 20% as FASB May Say Yes," *Financial Times* (March 30, 2009), http://www.bloomberg.com/apps/ news?pid= 20601109&sid=awSxPMGzDW38&refer=home.

15. Jack M. Cathey and Richard G. Schroeder, "The Impact of FSP FAS 157-4 on Commercial Banks, Financial Services Institute Symposium Proceedings," St. John's University, September 2009.

EXHIBIT 7.5   *Proposed statement of financial position*

As of 31 December	2012	2011
BUSINESS		
Operating		
Accounts receivable, trade	945,678	541,375
Less allowance for doubtful accounts	(23,642)	(13,534)
Accounts receivable, net	922,036	527,841
Inventory	679,474	767,102
Prepaid advertising	80,000	75,000
Foreign exchange contracts—cash-flow hedge	6,552	3,150
Total short-term assets	*1,688,062*	*1,373,092*
Property, plant, and equipment	5,112,700	5,088,500
Less accumulated depreciation	(2,267,620)	(2,023,500)
Property, plant and equipment, net	2,845,080	3,065,000
Investment in associate A	261,600	240,000
Goodwill	154,967	154,967
Other intangible assets	35,000	35,000
Total long-term assets	*3,296,647*	*3,494,967*
Accounts payable, trade	(612,556)	(505,000)
Advances from customers	(182,000)	(425,000)
Wages payable	(173,000)	(200,000)
Share-based remuneration liability	(39,586)	(21,165)
Current portion of lease liability	(35,175)	(33,500)
Interest payable on lease liability	(14,825)	(16,500)
Total short-term liabilities	*(1,057,142)*	*(1,201,165)*
Accrued pension liability	(293,250)	(529,500)
Lease liability (excluding current portion)	(261,325)	(296,500)
Other long-term liabilities	(33,488)	(16,100)
Total long-term liabilities	*(588,063)*	*(842,100)*
Net operating assets Investing	**3,339,504**	**2,824,795**
Available-for-sale financial assets (short-term)	473,600	485,000
Investment in associate B (long-term)	46,750	39,250
Total investing assets	**520,350**	**524,250**
NET BUSINESS ASSETS FINANCING	**3,859,854**	**3,349,045**
Financing assets		
Cash	1,174,102	861,941
Total financing assets	**1,174,102**	**861,941**
Financing liabilities		
Short-term borrowings	(562,000)	(400,000)
Interest payable	(140,401)	(112,563)
Dividends payable	(20,000)	(20,000)
Total short-term financing liabilities	*(722,401)*	*(532,563)*
Long-term borrowings	(2,050,000)	(2,050,000)
Total financing liabilities	**(2,772,401)**	**(2,582,563)**
NET FINANCING LIABILITIES		
DISCONTINUED OPERATIONS	**(1,598,299)**	**(1,720,621)**
Assets held for sale	856,832	876,650
Liabilities related to assets held for sale	(400,000)	(400,000)

(*Continued*)

EXHIBIT 7.5   *proposed statement of financial position (Continued)*

NET ASSETS HELD FOR SALE	456,832	476,650
INCOME TAXES		
Short-term		
Deferred tax asset	4,426	8,907
Income taxes payable	(72,514)	(63,679)
Long-term		
Deferred tax asset	39,833	80,160
NET INCOME TAX ASSET (LIABILITY)	**(28,255)**	**25,388**
NET ASSETS	*2,690,132*	*2,130,462*
EQUITY		
Share capital	(1,427,240)	(1,343,000)
Retained earnings	(1,100,358)	(648,289)
Accumulated other comprehensive income, net	(162,534)	(139,173)
TOTAL EQUITY	**(2,690,132)**	**(2,130,462)**
Total short-term assets	**4,197,021**	**3,605,591**
Total long-term assets	**3,383,231**	**3,614,377**
Total assets	**7,580,252**	**7,219,968**
Total short-term liabilities	**(2,252,057)**	**(2,197,406)**
Total long-term liabilities	**(2,638,063)**	**(2,892,100)**
Total liabilities	**(4,890,120)**	**(5,089,506)**

Source: Adapted from "Preliminary Views on Financial Statement Presentation," FASB, October 2008.

liquidity, and it should include in the notes to its financial statements information about the maturities of its short-term contractual assets and liabilities. Additionally, entities should present information about the maturities of their long-term contractual assets and liabilities in the notes to financial statements.

The boards also propose that cash equivalents be considered similar to short-term investments and presented separately from cash. As discussed earlier in the chapter, cash equivalences currently are aggregated with cash since both FASB and IASB have considered that cash equivalents are highly liquid and are essentially the same as cash. However, the boards concluded that excluding cash equivalents from the amount of cash presented in the statement of financial position would better achieve the liquidity and financial flexibility objective,[16] since short-term investments do not have all the characteristics of currency on hand and are subject to some risk of price change (e.g., those attributable to sudden changes in the credit environment, as occurred in 2007–2008).

Evaluating a Company's Financial Position

Investors and security analysts monitor company performance by using financial ratios. Financial ratios evaluate the relationships between financial statement elements and are most useful when compared to previous years' results, competitor

16. See the discussion of the objectives of financial statement presentation on page 47.

company results, industry averages, or benchmarks. The return on assets (ROA) ratio measures the percentage return on the asset employed by a company and is computed as follows:[17]

$$\text{ROA} = \frac{\text{Net income}}{\text{Average total assets}}$$

Hershey's ROA for fiscal years 2008 and 2007 are computed as follows (all calculations in thousands of dollars):[18]

2008	2007
$311,405	$214,154
($3,634,719 + 4,247,113)/2	($4,247,113 + 4,157,565)/2
= 7.90%	= 5.10%

Tootsie Roll's ROA for fiscal years 2008 and 2007 are computed as follows:

2008	2007
$38,777	$51,625
($812,092 + 812,725)/2	($812,725 + 791,639)/2
= 4.77%	= 6.44%

The five-year average return on assets for the Candy and Other Confectionary Products industry in 2008 was 3.43 percent. This calculation indicates that both Hershey and Tootsie Roll outperformed the industry during 2008. However, Hershey's performance, as measured by ROA, increased from 2007 to 2008 while Tootsie Roll's declined. Hershey's 2008 ROA is 1.66 times that of Tootsie Roll's, so this multiple increased from 0.79 in 2007 and indicates an increasing relative ROA performance.

In recent years, financial analysts have suggested that adjustments be made to both the numerator and denominator of the ROA ratio to improve its use in evaluating profitability. The adjustments suggested include the following:

1. Determination of sustainable income by removing the after-tax effects of nonrecurring (transitory) items from net profit (Examples of these types of items are asset impairment charges, discontinued operations, and extraordinary items.)

2. Elimination of interest expense after tax to improve interfirm comparability by removing the impact of capital structure on the ratio[19]

3. Adjustments that incorporate the effects of off–balance sheet financing (discussed in Chapter 11)

17. The return on assets ratio is an overall measure of firm performance that can be used by all investors. Additional ratios that are used by various investor groups are discussed in subsequent chapters. The average total assets is computed as current year total assets + previous year total assets /2.

18. From the Statement of Operations contained in Chapter 6 and the company's Form 10-K contained on the text's web page.

19. A company that uses relatively more debt to finance its operations than a competitor does will report a relatively higher amount of interest expense and a relatively lower net profit figure (see Chapter 11 for a further discussion).

Hershey included net (after tax) business realignment charges of $94,801,000 in 2008 and $276,868,000 in 2007; these charges are considered transitory items in that they are not expected to recur. The impact of this nonrecurring item is eliminated by adding its effect to the numerator of the ROA ratio.[20] In addition, the impact of capital structure on Hershey's ROA is removed by adding the after-tax amount of interest expense incurred of $99,678,000[21] or $63,096,000[22] to net income for 2008. This results in an adjusted profit figure of $469,302,000 and a ROA of 11.91 percent. When calculating Hershey's ROA for 2007, the after-tax effects of the $121,066,000 interest expense or $76,151,000 and the realignment charges are added to the 2008 net income amount of $214,154,000, resulting in an adjusted ROA of 13.5 percent.

Tootsie Roll's 2008 and 2007 income statements disclosed no transitory items; therefore, the only adjustments necessary are the interest expense charges of $378,000 in 2008 and $535,000 in 2007. The after-tax effects of these charges are $262,000 in 2008 and $358,000 in 2007; they are added to the ROA numerator, resulting in an adjusted ROA of 4.81 percent in 2008 and 6.48 percent in 2007.

A review of these adjusted ROAs reveals a somewhat different picture. Hershey's performance over the two years has declined slightly but is 7.15 percent better than Tootsie Roll's, rather than only 3.13 percent better, as indicated by the unadjusted ROA measures. These results indicate that Tootsie Roll needs to improve its ROA.

ROA can be broken into two components: the profit margin ratio (PMR) and the asset turnover ratio (ATR). A company can improve its return on assets ratio by increasing either of these two ratios. A company's PMR is calculated as:

$$PMR = \frac{\text{Net income}}{\text{Net sales}}$$

Hershey's 2008 PMR after eliminating the impact of nonrecurring items and capital structure for fiscal is calculated as:

$$= \frac{\$469,302}{\$5,132,768} = 0.0914$$

It indicates that every dollar of net sales adds approximately 91 cents to Hershey's adjusted bottom line.

20. The restructuring charges are stated on Hershey's income statement on an after-tax basis.

21. Hershey discloses net interest expense of $97,876,000 for 2008 and $118,585,000 for 2007 on its income statements. A review of its footnotes reveal that its interest expense for fiscal 2008 was $99,678,000, and in fiscal 2007 it was $121,066,000. The company's effective tax rate in 2008 was 36.7 percent while in 2007 the effective tax rate was 37.1 percent. Tootsie Roll reported net other expense of $10,618,000 in 2008 and net other income of $6,315,000 in 2007. The interest expense components of these amounts were $378,000 and $535,000, respectively. The average tax rates were 32.3 percent and 33.2 percent.

22. A company's effective tax rate is disclosed in its income tax footnote to the financial statements.

A company's ATR is evaluated by calculating its asset turnover ratio as follows:

$$\text{ATR} = \frac{\text{Net sales}}{\text{Average total assets}}$$

Hershey's 2008 ATR is calculated as:

$$= \frac{\$5,132,768}{(\$3,634,719 + 4,247,113)/2} = 1.30$$

Tootsie Roll's PMR after eliminating the impact of the nonrecurring items and of capital structure for fiscal is calculated as:

$$= \frac{\$39,039}{\$492.051} = 0.0793$$

Tootsie Roll's 2008 ATR is calculated as:

$$= \frac{\$492,051}{(\$812,092 + 812,725)/2} = 0.606$$

As stated above, these two ratios (PMR and ATR) are actually components of the ROA, as indicated by the following:

$$\frac{\text{Net income}}{\text{Net sales}} \times \frac{\text{Net sales}}{\text{Average total assets}}$$

Eliminating net sales from both the numerator and denominator leaves:

$$\frac{\text{Net income}}{\text{Average total assets}}$$

Following is a comparison of the two companies' adjusted ratios for fiscal year 2008:

	Hershey	Tootsie Roll
Return on assets	11.91%[a]	4.81%
Profit margin ratio	9.14%	7.93%
Asset turnover ratio	1.30	0.606

[a]Difference due to rounding

These results indicate that Hershey's relatively higher ROA is caused by a larger asset turnover ratio than Tootsie Roll's. Additionally, Hershey's profit margin ratio is slightly higher than Tootsie Roll's.

One final method of analysis that might be used is to compare the return on assets ratio with an established benchmark. Investing in corporate stocks carries an associated degree of risk that varies by company. That is, a company may be unprofitable and go out of business, resulting in a loss of the amount originally invested. Consequently, investors wish to be compensated for assuming risk. The benchmark for risk-free rate of return is the yield (or actual interest rate) on long-term government securities. During 2008 the average interest rate on government securities was approximately 3.98 percent. Hershey's return on assets indicates that during fiscal 2008, investors were compensated an additional 7.93 percent for assuming the risk associated with the company's stock, while Tootsie Roll's investors were compensated an additional 0.83 percent.

As indicated in Chapter 4, the risk of investing in a company's stock may be measured by calculating its beta (β). A stock with a β of 1.0 is considered to offer an average amount of risk. During fiscal year 2008, Hershey's β was approximately 0.5 and Tootsie Roll's was 0.9. During that same year, the industry average β is 0.5. Consequently, an investment in the average company in the Candy and Other Confectionary Products industry is viewed as less risky than an average investment. Hershey's β is the same as the average company in the industry, whereas Tootsie Roll's β is somewhat higher than the industry average, indicating it is viewed as a relatively riskier investment. We also know from Chapter 6 that at the end of fiscal year 2008, Hershey's stock was selling at about 24.64 times earnings while Tootsie Roll's was selling for 36.59 times earnings. Taken together, these results indicate that during fiscal year 2008, Hershey was earning a ROA that was above the current risk-free rate, the risk associated with investing in the company was low, and investor perceptions of the future outlook for the company were somewhat optimistic. For Tootsie Roll, the company's fiscal 2008 results indicated that the ROA was above the industry average; the risk associated with the company, although moderate in comparison to the total market average, was higher than both Hershey's and the industry average. Nevertheless, investor perceptions of the future outlook for Tootsie Roll were positive.

The Statement of Cash Flows

Evolution of the Statement of Cash Flows

Before 1971, the income statement and the balance sheet were the only financial statements required under GAAP. However, many large firms were including additional financial statements to disclose relevant information needed to make economic decisions. These disclosures were in response to investors, creditors, and others who voiced the desire to receive information on the financing and investing activities of business organizations. A number of companies responded by issuing a *funds statement.* This statement reported on the resources provided and the uses to which these resources were put during the reporting period.

Funds statements were not uniformly prepared initially, and the method of reporting sources and application of resources depended on the concept of funds preferred by the reporting entity. In general, the concepts of funds used can be categorized as (1) cash, (2) working capital, and (3) all financial resources. Other concepts of funds, such as quick assets or net monetary assets, may also have been encountered.

Statements using the cash concept of funds summarize all material changes in the cash balance. These funds statements became, in effect, statements of cash receipts and disbursements, and they reported the impact of these receipts and disbursements on all other accounts.

Under the working capital definition of funds, all material transactions that result in a change in working capital (current assets minus current liabilities) are reported. Under this concept, *funds* is defined as the net amount of increases and/or decreases in cash, receivables, inventories, payables, and other current items.

Finally, if the all-financial-resources concept is used, the entity reports on the effect of all transactions with outsiders. This concept of funds must be used in conjunction with another concept of funds (e.g., cash, working capital) and includes all items that affect the financing and investing activities of the enterprise. An example of an all-financial-resources transaction is the purchase of assets by issuing stock. In this case, an investing activity (the purchase of assets) is coupled with a financing activity (issuing stock), but neither activity affected cash or working capital. The advantage of the all-financial-resources concept is its inclusion of all transactions that are important items in the financial administration of the entity. A disadvantage is that although the investing and financing activities wash out and have no effect on determining the amount of the change in funds, an investor may be confused by the inclusion of transactions that do not affect the change being measured (e.g., cash or working capital).

Accounting Principles Board *Opinions No. 3* and *No. 19*

In 1963, the APB noted the increased attention that had been given to flow of funds analysis and issued *Opinion No. 3* (since superseded). This release suggested that funds statements should be presented as supplemental information in financial reports but did not make such disclosures mandatory.[23]

By 1971, the APB had noted that regulatory agencies were requiring the preparation of funds statements and that a number of companies were voluntarily disclosing funds statements in their annual reports. As a result, the Board issued *APB Opinion No. 19* (since superseded), which stated that information usually contained on the funds statement was essential to financial statement users and that such a statement should be presented each time a balance sheet and an income statement were reported. In addition, the Board stated that the funds statement should be prepared in accordance with the all-financial-resources concept and that the statement should be titled "Statement of Changes in Financial Position."[24]

APB Opinion No. 19 prescribed the format of the statement as follows:

1. The statement may be prepared in such a manner as to express the financial position in terms of cash, cash and temporary assets, quick assets, or working capital so long as it utilizes the all-financial-resources concept and gives the most useful portrayal of the financing and investing activities of the entity.

2. In each case the statement should disclose the net change in the cash, cash and temporary investments, quick assets or working capital, depending on the form of presentation.

3. The statement should disclose outlays for long-term assets, net proceeds from the sale of long-term assets, conversion of long-term debt or preferred stock to common stocks, issuances and repayments of debts, issuances or repurchases of capital stock and dividends.[25]

23. *APB Opinion No. 3*, "The Statement of Source and Application of Funds" (New York: AICPA, 1963).

24. *APB Opinion No. 19*, "Reporting Changes in Financial Position" (New York: AICPA, 1971).

25. Ibid.

The statement of changes in financial position was designed to enable financial statement users to answer questions like these:

1. Where did the profits go?
2. Why weren't dividends larger?
3. How was it possible to distribute dividends in the presence of a loss?
4. Why are current assets down when there was a profit?
5. Why is extra financing required?
6. How was the expansion financed?
7. Where did the funds from the sale of securities go?
8. How was the debt retirement accomplished?
9. How was the increase in working capital financed?

Although definitive answers to these questions are not readily obtainable from a casual inspection of the statement, usual practice was to elaborate on the presentation in the footnotes. In addition, comparative analyses covering several years of operations enable the user to obtain useful information on past methods and practices and the contribution of funds derived from operations to the growth of the company.

The statement of changes in financial position was designed to report on the company's financial operations and to disclose the results of the company's financial management policies. It was also designed to improve the predictive decision-making ability of users.

Cash-Flow Information

The cash inflows and outflows of a business are of primary importance to investors and creditors. The presentation of cash-flow information by a business enterprise should enable investors to (1) predict the amount of cash that is likely to be distributed as dividends or interest in the future and (2) evaluate the potential risk of a given investment.

The FASB has emphasized the importance of cash-flow information in its deliberations. *SFAC No. 1* states that effective financial reporting must enable investors, creditors, and other users to (1) assess cash-flow prospects; and (2) evaluate liquidity, solvency, and flow of funds.

The presentation of cash-flow data is necessary to evaluate a firm's liquidity, solvency, and financial flexibility. *Liquidity* is the firm's ability to convert an asset to cash or to pay a current liability. It is referred to as the "nearness to cash" of an entity's economic resources and obligations. Liquidity information is important to users in evaluating the timing of future cash flows; it is also necessary to evaluate solvency and financial flexibility.

Solvency refers to a firm's ability to obtain cash for business operations. Specifically, it refers to a firm's ability to pay its debts as they become due. Solvency is necessary for a firm to be considered a "going concern." Insolvency may result in liquidation and losses to owners and creditors. In addition, the threat of insolvency may cause the capital markets to react by increasing the cost of capital in the future; that is, the amount of risk is increased.

Financial flexibility is the firm's ability to use its financial resources to adapt to change. It is the firm's ability to take advantage of new investment opportunities or to react quickly to a "crisis" situation. Financial flexibility comes in part from quick access to the company's liquid assets. However, liquidity is only one part of financial flexibility. Financial flexibility also stems from a firm's ability to generate cash from its operations, contributed capital, or sale of economic resources without disrupting continuing operations.

The presentation of cash-flow data is intended to enable investors to make rational decisions by providing them with useful information. *SFAC No. 2* identifies *relevance* and *reliability* as the primary ingredients that make accounting information useful. A statement of cash flows undoubtedly allows for the presentation of useful information to investors and creditors because it enables users to predict the probability of future returns and evaluate risk.

In 1987 the FASB issued *SFAS No. 95*, "Statement of Cash Flows" (see FASB ASC 230). This statement established standards for cash-flow reporting. It superseded *APB Opinion No. 19*, "Reporting Changes in Financial Position." As a result, all business enterprises are now required to present a statement of cash flows in place of the statement of changes in financial position as part of the full set of financial statements.

SFAS No. 95

The format required by *SFAS No. 95* for presentation of the statement of cash flows evolved over a number of years. In 1980 the FASB issued a discussion memorandum titled *Reporting Funds Flows, Liquidity, and Financial Flexibility* as a part of its conceptual framework project. Major questions raised in this discussion memorandum included the following:

1. Which concept of funds should be adopted?
2. How should transactions not having a direct impact on funds be reported?
3. Which of the various approaches should be used for presenting funds flow information?
4. How should information about funds flow from operations be presented?
5. Should funds flow information be separated into outflows for (a) maintenance of operating capacity, (b) expansion of operating capacity, and (c) nonoperating purposes?

Later, in 1981, the FASB issued an exposure draft titled *Reporting Income, Cash Flows, and Financial Position of Business Enterprises*. This exposure draft concluded that funds-flow reporting should focus on cash rather than working capital. However, a final statement was not issued at that time, and the FASB decided to consider the subject of cash-flow reporting in connection with a study of recognition and measurement concepts.

In 1984 the FASB issued *SFAC No. 5*, "Recognition and Measurement in Financial Statements of Business Enterprises." Included in this statement is the conclusion that a cash-flow statement should be part of a full set of financial statements. Concurrently, the Financial Executives Institute (FEI) was reviewing the issue of cash-flow reporting. In 1984 the FEI published *The Funds Statement: Structure and Use*, a study that pointed out several areas of diversity inherent in the Statement of Changes in Financial Position. For example, *APB Opinion No. 19* allowed different definitions of funds, different definitions of cash and cash flow from operations, and different forms of presentation of the statement of changes in financial position.

During 1985 and 1986, the FASB organized a task force on cash-flow reporting and issued an exposure draft that proposed standards for cash-flow reporting. The FASB was concerned that the divergence in practice affected the understandability and usefulness of the information presented to investors, creditors, and other users of financial statements. In addition, some financial statement users were contending that accrual accounting had resulted in net income not reflecting the underlying cash flows of business enterprises. They argued that too many arbitrary allocation procedures, such as deferred taxes and depreciation, resulted in a net income figure that was not necessarily related to the earning power of an enterprise. As a result, *SFAS No. 95* was issued in 1987.

Purposes of the Statement of Cash Flows

The primary purpose of the statement of cash flows is to provide relevant information about the cash receipts and cash payments of an enterprise during a period. This purpose is consistent with the objectives and concepts delineated in *SFAC Nos. 1* and *5*.

SFAC No. 1 stressed that financial reporting should provide information to help present and potential investors assess the amount, timing, and uncertainty of prospective cash receipts from interest, dividends, sale of securities, and proceeds from loans. These cash flows are seen as important because they may affect an enterprise's liquidity and solvency. *SFAC No. 5* indicated that a full set of financial statements should show cash flows for the period. *SFAC No. 5* also described the usefulness of cash-flow reporting in assessing an entity's liquidity, financial flexibility, profitability, and risk.

These objectives and concepts delineated in *SFAC Nos. 1* and *5* led the FASB to conclude that the statement of cash flows should replace the statement of changes in financial position as a required financial statement. The statement of cash flows is intended to help investors, creditors, and others assess future cash flows, provide feedback about actual cash flows, evaluate the availability of cash for dividends and investments as well as the enterprise's ability to finance growth from internal sources, and identify the reasons for differences between net income and net cash flows. An additional reason for the focus on cash rather than working capital is the questionable usefulness of working capital in evaluating liquidity. That is, a positive working capital balance does not necessarily indicate liquidity, and a negative working capital balance may not indicate a lack of liquidity. More information is needed on receivable and inventory financing to evaluate the overall liquidity of a business enterprise.

Statement Format

The statement of cash flows reports changes during an accounting period in cash and cash equivalents from the following activities: (1) cash flows from operating activities, (2) cash flows from investing activities, and (3) cash flows from financing activities. *Cash equivalents* are defined as highly liquid investments that are both readily convertible to known amounts of cash and so near to maturity that they present insignificant risk changes in value because of changes in interest rates. In general, only investments with original maturities of three months from the date of purchase will qualify as cash equivalents. The Hershey and Tootsie Roll statements of cash flows are presented in Exhibits 7.6 and 7.7 on pages 240 and 241. These exhibits indicate that during fiscal year 2008, Hershey's activities resulted in a net decrease in cash and cash equivalents

EXHIBIT 7.6 *The Hershey Company Consolidated Statements of Cash Flows*

For the years ended December 31	2008	2007	2006
In thousands			
Cash Flows Provided from (Used by) Operating Activities			
Net income	$ 311,405	$ 214,154	$ 559,061
Adjustments to reconcile net income to net cash provided from operations:			
Depreciation and amortization	249,491	310,925	199,911
Stock-based compensation expense, net of tax of $13,265, $10,634 and $14,524, respectively	23,583	18,987	25,598
Excess tax benefits from exercise of stock options	(1,387)	(9,461)	(9,275)
Deferred income taxes	(17,125)	(124,276)	4,173
Business realignment and impairment charges, net of tax of $61,553, $144,928 and $4,070, respectively	119,117	267,653	7,573
Contributions to pension plans (32,759) (15,836) (23,570)			
Changes in assets and liabilities, net of effects from business acquisitions and divestitures:			
Accounts receivable—trade	31,675	40,467	(14,919)
Inventories	7,681	45,348	(12,461)
Accounts payable	26,435	62,204	(13,173)
Other assets and liabilities	(198,555)	(31,329)	275
Net Cash Provided from Operating Activities	519,561	778,836	723,193
Cash Flows Provided from (Used by) Investing Activities			
Capital additions	(262,643)	(189,698)	(183,496)
Capitalized software additions	(20,336)	(14,194)	(15,016)
Proceeds from sales of property, plant and equipment 82,815	—	—	—
Business acquisitions	—	(100,461)	(17,000)
Proceeds from divestitures	1,960	—	—
Net Cash (Used by) Investing Activities	(198,204)	(304,353)	(215,512)
Cash Flows Provided from (Used by) Financing Activities			
Net change in short-term borrowings	(371,393)	195,055	(163,826)
Long-term borrowings	247,845	—	496,728
Repayment of long-term debt	(4,977)	(188,891)	(234)
Cash dividends paid	(262,949)	(252,263)	(235,129)
Exercise of stock options	36,996	50,497	37,111
Excess tax benefits from exercise of stock options	1,387	9,461	9,275
Repurchase of Common Stock	(60,361)	(256,285)	621,648)
Net Cash (Used by) Financing Activities	(413,452)	(442,426)	(477,723)
(Decrease) Increase in Cash and Cash Equivalents	(92,095)	32,057	29,958
Cash and Cash Equivalents as of January 1	129,198	97,141	67,183
Cash and Cash Equivalents as of December 31	$ 37,103	$ 129,198	$ 97,141
Interest Paid	$ 97,364	$ 126,450	$ 105,250
Income Taxes Paid	197,661	253,977	325,451

EXHIBIT 7.7 *Consolidated Statements of Cash Flows Tootsie Roll Industries, Inc. and Subsidiaries*

For the years ended December 31	2008	2007	2006
In thousands			
Cash Flows from Operating Activities:			
Net earnings	$ 38,777	$ 51,625	$ 65,919
Adjustments to reconcile net earnings to net cash provided by operating activities:			
Depreciation	17,036	15,859	15,816
Excess of (earnings) loss from joint venture over dividends received	477	—	(921)
Return on investment in joint venture	—	1,419	—
Other than temporary impairment of investment	5,140	—	—
Amortization of marketable securities	396	521	909
Purchase of trading securities	(491)	(84)	(749)
Changes in operating assets and liabilities:			
Accounts receivable	(261)	2,591	(4,368)
Other receivables	(33)	7	(4,125)
Inventories	1,352	6,506	(8,451)
Prepaid expenses and other assets	(15,139)	283	(1,912)
Accounts payable and accrued liabilities	967	(3,234)	(3,688)
Income taxes payable and deferred	8,642	13,481	(3,984)
Postretirement health care and life insurance benefits	3,394	1,272	971
Deferred compensation and other liabilities	(2,385)	(12)	382
Other	(830)	(170)	(143)
Net cash provided by operating activities	57,042	90,064	55,656
Cash Flows from Investing Activities:			
Proceeds from sale of real estate and other assets	—	434	1,343
Decrease in restricted cash	—	—	22,330
Return of investment in joint venture	—	1,206	—
Capital expenditures	(34,355)	(14,767)	(39,207)
Purchase of available for sale securities	(33,977)	(59,132)	(35,663)
Sale and maturity of available for sale securities	61,258	28,914	62,223
Net cash provided by (used in) investing activities	(7,074)	(43,345)	11,026
Cash Flows from Financing Activities:			
Repayment of bank loan	—	—	(32,001)
Shares repurchased and retired	(21,109)	(27,300)	(30,694)
Dividends paid in cash	(17,557)	(17,542)	(17,264)
Net cash used in financing activities	(38,666)	(44,842)	(79,959)
Increase (decrease) in cash and cash equivalents	11,302	1,877	(13,277)
Cash and cash equivalents at beginning of year	57,606	55,729	69,006
Cash and cash equivalents at end of year	$ 68,908	$ 57,606	$ 55,729
Supplemental cash-flow information:			
Income taxes paid	$ 12,728	$ 11,343	$ 29,780
Interest paid	$ 252	$ 537	$ 733
Stock dividend issued	$ 35,042	$ 46,520	$ 43,563

of $92,095,000, whereas Tootsie Roll reported a net increase in cash and cash equivalents of $11,302,000.

Cash Flow from Operating Activities   Cash flows from operating activities are generally the cash effect from transactions that enter into the determination of net income exclusive of financing and investing activities. Among the cash inflows from operations are the following:

1. Receipts from sales of goods and services and collections on accounts or notes from customers
2. Receipts of interest and dividends
3. All the receipts that are not the result of transactions defined as investing or financing activities (e.g., amounts received to settle lawsuits or insurance settlements)

   Cash outflows from operations include the following:

1. Cash payments to acquire materials for manufacture or goods for resale, and cash payments to reduce payables and notes to creditors
2. Cash payments to other suppliers and employees
3. Cash payments to governments for taxes, duties, fines, and fees or penalties
4. Cash payments to lenders and creditors for interest
5. All other payments that are not the result of transactions defined as investing or financing activities. Examples of such transactions are payments to settle lawsuits and cash contributions to charities

SFAS No. 95 encouraged companies to report operating activities by reporting major classes of gross cash receipts, major classes of gross cash payments, and the difference between them—the net cash flow from operating activities. Reporting gross cash receipts and payments is termed the *direct method*, and it includes reporting the following classes of operating cash receipts and payments:

1. Cash collected from customers
2. Interest and dividends received
3. Other operating cash receipts
4. Cash paid to employees and other suppliers of goods and services
5. Interest paid
6. Income taxes paid
7. Other operating cash payments

One criticism of the computation of cash flows from operating activities is the treatment of dividends and interest received and interest paid. This treatment separates investment returns and interest payments from the sources of these activities, the purchase and sale of investments that are disclosed as investing activities, and the sale and retirement of debt that are disclosed as financing activities.

A company that chooses not to use the direct method for reporting operating cash-flow information must report the same amount of operating cash flow by adjusting net income to reconcile it with operating cash flow. This method of reporting is termed the *indirect method*. The required adjustments include the effect of past deferrals of operating cash receipts and payments; accruals of expected operating cash receipts and payments; and the effect of items related to investing and financing activities such as depreciation, amortization of goodwill, and gains or losses on the sale of property, plant, and equipment.

A company that uses the direct method must reconcile net income to net cash flow from operating activities in a separate schedule. If the indirect method is used, the reconciliation is reported within the statement of cash flows. Consequently, it is sometimes referred to as the *reconciliation method.*

The operating sections of both Hershey's and Tootsie Roll's fiscal 2008 statements of cash flows are both prepared using the indirect method and disclose net cash provided of $519,561,000 and $57,042,000 respectively.

Cash Flow from Investing Activities   Investing activities include making and collecting loans; acquiring and disposing of debt or equity securities of other companies; and acquiring and disposing of property, plant, and equipment as well as other productive resources. Examples of cash inflows from investing activities are as follows:

1. Receipts from the collection or sales of loans made to other entities
2. Receipts from the collection or sale of other companies' debt instruments
3. Receipts from the sales of other companies' equity instruments
4. Receipts from the sales of property, plant, and equipment and other productive assets
   Examples of cash outflows from investing activities are as follows:
1. Disbursement for loans made by the enterprise to other entities
2. Payments to acquire other companies' debt instruments
3. Payments to acquire other companies' equity instruments
4. Payments to acquire property, plant, and equipment and other productive assets

The investing section of Hershey's fiscal 2008 statement of cash flows indicates that investing activities resulted in a net use of cash of $198,204,000, whereas Tootsie Roll's statement disclosed net cash used of $7,074,000.

Cash Flows from Financing Activities   Financing activities result from obtaining resources from owners, providing owners with a return of and a return on their investment, borrowing money and repaying the amount borrowed, and obtaining and paying for other resources from long-term creditors. Cash inflows from financing activities include (1) proceeds from issuing equity instruments and (2) proceeds from issuing debt instruments or other short- or long-term borrowings. Cash outflows from financing activities include (1) payments of dividends or other distributions to owners and (2) repayments of amounts borrowed.

Although loans to or investments in other companies are classified as investing activities and repayments of amounts borrowed are classified as a financing activity, cash receipts from dividends and interest and cash payments for interest are classified as operating activities. The financing section of Hershey's fiscal 2008 statement of cash flows indicates that net cash used from financing activities of $413,452,000 and Tootsie Roll disclosed a net use of cash of $38,666,000.

Proposed Format of the Statement of Cash Flows

The proposed revisions to the statement of cash flows outlined in Phase B of the FASB-IASB Financial Statement Presentation Project (discussed in Chapter 2) are illustrated in Exhibit 7.8. The presentation suggested is an expanded version of the direct method with additional disclosures for each of the statement categories.

In proposing the requirement to use the direct method, the boards noted that it is more consistent than the indirect method with the proposed objectives of financial statement presentation. The operating cash receipts and payments that an entity presents using a direct method are consistent with the cohesiveness objective.[26] Presenting cash receipt and cash payment line items in the operating category helps achieve the disaggregation objective because that information can be of significant help to users in assessing the amount, timing, and uncertainty of an entity's future operating cash flows. Information about the relationships of operating cash receipts and payments is useful in assessing an entity's ability to generate sufficient cash from operations to pay debts, reinvest in operations, and make distributions to owners. Therefore, a direct method of presenting operating cash flows provides information that is consistent with the liquidity and financial flexibility objective.

The major deficiency of the indirect method is that it derives the net cash flow from operating activities without separately presenting any of the operating cash receipts and payments. For example, envision an income statement that begins with the change in shareholders' equity for the period and then reverses any changes in equity that did not affect profit or loss or net income such as dividends, issuance of shares, and repurchases of shares. That income statement format would arrive at the net income amount for the period too, but the statement would not be useful.

The boards received comments that the indirect method provides a helpful link between income from continuing operations, changes in some line items in the statement of financial position, and net operating cash flows. The boards propose to satisfy this criticism by requiring an entity to prepare a new schedule to be included in the notes to financial statements that reconciles cash flows to comprehensive income.

Under its current format, the statement of cash flows reports changes during an accounting period in cash and cash equivalents from operating, investing, or financing activities. The new proposed format will have the same sections and categories as the statement of financial position and the statement of comprehensive income. That is, an entity will present the statement of cash flows by providing a section titled "Business" with the categories "Operating" and "Investing," followed by sections titled "Financing," "Income Taxes," "Discontinued Operations," and "Equity."

The classification of cash flows into the operating, investing, and financing categories in the proposed presentation model is based on the classification of the related asset or liability. Therefore some differences may occur in how an entity classifies its cash flows using existing guidance from how it would classify its cash flows using the proposed format. For example, cash flows from investing in operating assets under current U.S. GAAP are classified as investing cash flows, whereas under the proposed format they would be classified as operating cash flows.

26. See the earlier discussion on the objectives of financial statement presentation in Chapter 6.

EXHIBIT 7.8 *Statement of Cash Flows—Proposed*

For the year ended 31 December	2012	2011
BUSINESS		
Operating		
Cash received from wholesale customers	2,108,754	1,928,798
Cash received from retail customers	703,988	643,275
Total cash collected from customers	*2,812,742*	*2,572,073*
Cash paid for goods		
Materials purchases	(935,544)	(785,000)
Labor	(418,966)	(475,313)
Overhead—transport	(128,640)	(108,000)
Pension	(170,100)	(157,500)
Overhead—other	(32,160)	(27,000)
Total cash paid for goods	*(1,685,409)*	*(1,552,813)*
Cash paid for selling activities		
Advertising	(65,000)	(75,000)
Wages, salaries, and benefits	(58,655)	(55,453)
Other	(13,500)	(12,500)
Total cash paid for selling activities	*(137,155)*	*(142,953)*
Cash paid for general and administrative activities		
Wages, salaries, and benefits	(332,379)	(314,234)
Contributions to pension plan	(170,100)	(157,500)
Capital expenditures	(54,000)	(50,000)
Lease payments	(50,000)	—
Research and development	(8,478)	(7,850)
Settlement of share-based remuneration	(3,602)	(3,335)
Other	(12,960)	(12,000)
Total cash paid for general and administrative activities	*(631,519)*	*(544,919)*
Cash flow before other operating activities	*358,657*	*331,388*
Cash from other operating activities		
Disposal of property, plant, and equipment	37,650	—
Investment in associate A	—	(120,000)
Sale of receivable	8,000	10,000
Settlement of cash-flow hedge	3,402	3,150
Total cash received (paid) for other operating activities	*49,052*	*(106,850)*
Net Cash from Operating Activities	**407,709**	**224,538**
Investing		
Purchase of available-for-sale financial assets	—	(130,000)
Sale of available-for-sale financial assets	56,100	51,000
Dividends received	54,000	50,000
Net Cash from Investing Activities	**110,100**	**(29,000)**
Net Cash from Business Activities	**517,809**	**195,538**
Financing		
Interest received on cash	8,619	5,500
Total Cash from Financing Assets	**8,619**	**5,500**
Proceeds from issue of short-term debt	162,000	150,000
Proceeds from issue of long-term debt	—	250,000
Interest paid	(83,514)	(82,688)
Dividends paid	(86,400)	(80,000)
Total Cash from Financing Liabilities	**(7,914)**	**237,312**

(Continued)

EXHIBIT 7.8   *Statement of Cash Flows—Proposed* (*Continued*)

Net Cash from Financing Activities	**705**	**242,812**
Change in cash from continuing operations before		
taxes and equity	*518,514*	*438,350*
Income Taxes		
Cash taxes paid	(281,221)	(193,786)
Change in cash before discontinued operations		
and equity	*237,293*	*244,564*
Discontinued Operations		
Cash paid from discontinued operations	(12,582)	(11,650)
Net Cash from Discontinued		
Operations	**(12,582)**	**(11,650)**
Change in cash before equity	*224,711*	*232,914*
Equity		
Proceeds from reissue of treasury stock	84,240	78,000
Net Cash from Equity	**84,240**	**78,000**
Effect of foreign exchange rates on cash	3,209	1,027
Change in Cash	**312,161**	**311,941**
Beginning Cash	**861,941**	**550,000**
Ending Cash	**1,174,102**	**861,941**

Source: Adapted from "Preliminary Views on Financial Statement Presentation," FASB, October 2008.

Because cash in the statement of financial position will no longer include cash equivalents, the boards propose not including cash equivalents in the statement of cash flows. However, the boards suggest permitting the net presentation of cash and cash equivalent flows for the following items:

1. Receipts and payments on behalf of customers if the cash and cash equivalent flows reflect the activities of the customer rather than those of the entity
2. Receipts and payments for items in which the turnover is quick, the amounts are large, and the maturities are short

Financial Analysis Of Cash-flow Information

A major objective of accounting is to present data that allows investors and creditors to predict the amount of cash that will be distributed in the form of dividends and interest, and to allow an evaluation of risk. Net income is the result of changes in assets and liabilities: some current, and some noncurrent; consequently, net income cannot be equated with a change in cash. The statement of cash flows discloses the effects of earnings activities on cash resources, how assets were acquired, and how they were financed. The ability of an enterprise to generate cash from operations is an important indicator of its financial health and the degree of risk associated with investing in the firm.

The investors and creditors of a firm anticipate a return that is at least equal to the market rate of interest for investments with equal risk. Or, stated differently, investors expect to receive a discounted present value of future cash flows that is equal to or greater than their original investment. The past cash flows from a firm are the best available basis for forecasting future cash flows.

The FASB stressed the importance of cash flows to investors when it stated: "financial reporting should provide information to help investors, creditors, and others assess the amounts, timing and uncertainty of prospective cash inflow to the related enterprise."[27]

The ability to predict returns to investors and creditors is somewhat complex because management may decide to use cash in a variety of manners, and the uses of cash are interrelated. For example, available cash may be reinvested in assets, or used to expand facilities and markets, retire debt and equity, or pay dividends. Accounting researchers are interested in determining the relationship between accounting information and decision making. Empirical research has indicated that cash-flow data has incremental information content over accrual earnings data and that cash-flow data is superior to changes in working capital information.[28] These findings support the FASB's position on the disclosure of cash-flow data because they provide evidence that such information may result in better decisions. They also indicate that even given the uncertainties surrounding the alternate uses of available cash by firms, knowledge of past cash-flow information allows investors and creditors to make better predictions of future cash flows and assessments of risk.

One method of analyzing a company's statement of cash flows is to determine the amount of annual financing needed to sustain annual activities. A company's *free cash flow* is the amount of cash generated from operating activities less capital expenditures and dividends. As a result, it is an indicator of a company's ability to pay off its debt and maintain growth. A positive free cash-flow amount is frequently a precursor to increased earnings. A negative amount indicates that the company found or will find it necessary to acquire funds from external financing sources to maintain operations or to grow. Free cash flow is calculated as:

net cash provided (used) by operating activities − net cash used in acquiring property, plant, and equipment − cash dividends paid.

Hershey's free cash flows for 2008 and 2007 are calculated as $519,561,000 − 262,643,000 − 262,949,000 = ($6,031,000) and $778,836,000 − 189,698,000 − 252,263,000 = $336,875,000. Tootsie Roll's free cash flows for 2008 and 2007 are calculated as $57,042,000 − 34,355,000 − 17,557,000 = $5,130,000 and $90,064,000 − 14,767,000 − 17,542,000 = $57,755,000. These results indicate that Hershey went from a positive free cash-flow position in 2007 to a negative position in 2008. On the other hand, Tootsie Roll's free cash position deteriorated during 2008, but it still remained positive.

International Accounting Standards

The International Accounting Standards Board (IASB) has

1. Discussed the Statement of Financial Position and the various measurement bases used in financial statements, and defined assets, liabilities, and equity in its "Framework for the Preparation and Presentation of Financial Statements"

2. Discussed the information to be disclosed on the balance sheet and statement of cash flows in a revised *IAS No. 1*

3. Discussed the presentation of the statement of cash flows in *IAS No. 7*

---

27. *Statement of Financial Accounting Concepts No. 1*, "Objectives of Financial Reporting by Business Enterprises." (New York: FASB, 1978), para. 37.

28. Robert M. Bowen, David Burgstahler, and Lane A. Daley, "The Incremental Information Content of Accruals versus Cash Flows," *The Accounting Review* (October 1987), 723–47.

In discussing the statement of financial position in "Preparation and Presentation of Financial Statements," the IASB indicated that economic decisions taken by users of financial statements require an evaluation of an enterprise's ability to generate cash. Consequently, the financial position of an enterprise is affected by the economic resources it controls, its financial structure, its liquidity and solvency, and its capacity to adapt to changes in the environment in which it operates. Information about the economic resources controlled by the enterprise and its capacity in the past to modify these resources is useful in predicting the ability of the enterprise to generate cash in the future.[29] The measurement bases used in the elements of financial statements included historical cost, current cost, realizable (settlement) value, and present value. The IASB also indicated that the most commonly used measurement basis is historical cost. The definitions of assets, liabilities, and equity are similar to those contained in *SFAC No. 6* and embody the concepts of resources, present obligations, and residual interest, respectively.

The IASB's overall considerations for preparing the financial statement contained in *IAS No. 1*, "Presentation of Financial Statements," were discussed in Chapter 3. The recommended disclosures for the balance sheet are similar to those required under U.S. GAAP with some minor exceptions. Originally, the IASC took the position that each enterprise could determine, based on the nature of its operations, whether or not to present current assets and current liabilities as separate classifications, and did not require that assets and liabilities be presented in order of their liquidity. The revised *IAS No. 1* requires assets to be classified as current and noncurrent unless a liquidity presentation provides more relevant and reliable information and recognizes that the differences in the nature and function of assets, liabilities, and equity are so fundamental that they should be presented on the face of the balance sheet. The new standard also requires the following categories to be disclosed:

Property, plant, and equipment
Investment property
Intangible assets
Financial assets
Equity method investments
Biological assets
Receivables
Inventories
Cash and cash equivalents
Trade and other payables
Financial liabilities
Provisions
Liabilities and assets for current tax
Deferred tax liabilities and assets
Equity capital and reserves
Minority interest
Issued capital and reserves attributable to equity holders of the parent

29. "Preparation and Presentation of Financial Statements," International Accounting Standards Committee, paras. 15–16.

Additional line items are to be presented based on materiality and the nature and function of each item. Monetary and nonmonetary items are to be presented separately, as well as operating and financial items and balances with other affiliated enterprises. As noted in Chapter 3, the adoption of the proposed FASB IASC standard on financial statement presentation will significantly change the presentation format of the balance sheet.

In *IAS No. 7*, "Cash Flow Statements," the IASB outlined the required disclosures and presentation format for the statement of cash flows. As with U.S. GAAP, the statement reports cash flows from operating, investing, and financing activities. In addition, cash flows from operating activities may be reported by using either the direct or indirect method, but the IASB stated a preference for the direct method. Cash flows from extraordinary items are required to be disclosed separately as operating, investing, or financing activities under *IAS No. 7*. Also, the aggregate cash flow arising from the acquisition or disposal of subsidiaries is required to be presented separately and disclosed as an investing activity under the provisions of *IAS No. 7*. Adoption of the proposed FASB IASC standard on financial statement presentation will also significantly change the presentation format of the statement of cash flows.

Cases

• Case 7-1 Alternate Financial Statement Treatments

The following financial statement was prepared by employees of your client, Linus Construction Company.

Linus Construction Company Statement of Financial Position December 31, 2000

Current Assets:			
Cash		$182,200	
Accounts receivable (less allowance of $14,000 for doubtful accounts)		220,700	
Materials, supplies, labor, and overhead charged to construction		2,026,000	
Materials and supplies not charged to construction		288,000	
Deposits made to secure performance of contracts		360,000	$3,076,900
Less Current Liabilities:			
Accounts payable to subcontractors		$141,100	
Payable for materials and supplies		65,300	
Accrued payroll		8,260	
Accrued interest on mortgage note		12,000	
Estimated taxes payable		66,000	292,660
Net working capital			$2,784,240

Property, Plant, and Equipment (at cost):			
	Cost	*Depreciation*	*Value*
Land and equipment	$983,300	$310,000	$673,300
Machinery and equipment	905,000	338,000	567,000
Payments made on leased equipment	230,799	230,699	1
	$2,119,000	$878,699	$1,240,301

Deferred Charges:		
Prepaid taxes and other expenses	11,700	1
Points charged on mortgage note	10,800	1,262,801
Total net working capital and noncurrent assets		$4,047,041
Less Deferred Liabilities:		
Mortgage note payable	300,000	
Unearned revenue on work in progress	1,898,000	2,198,000
Total net assets		$1,84,0411
Stockholders' Equity:		
6% preferred stock at par value	$400,000	
Common stock at par value	800,000	
Paid-in surplus	210,000	
Retained earnings	483,641	
Treasury stock at cost (370) shares	(44,000)	
Total stockholders' equity		$1,849,041

The statement is not accompanied by footnotes, but you have discovered the following:

- The average completion period for the company's jobs is 18 months. The company's method of journalizing contract transactions is summarized in the following pro forma entries.

- Linus both owns and leases equipment used on construction jobs. Typically, its equipment lease contracts provide that Linus may return the equipment upon completion of a job or may apply all rentals in full toward purchase of the equipment. About 70 percent of lease rental payments made in the past have been applied to the purchase of equipment. While leased equipment is in use, rents are charged to the account *payments made on leased equipment* (except for $1 balance) and to jobs on which the equipment has been used. In the event of purchase, the balance in the *payments made on leased equipment* account is transferred to the *machinery and equipment* account, and the depreciation and other related accounts are corrected.

- Management is unable to develop dependable estimates of costs to complete contracts in progress.

Required:

a. Identify the weaknesses in the financial statement.
b. For each item identified in part (a), indicate the preferable treatment and explain why the treatment is preferable.

• Case 7-2 The Use of Current Value

The argument among accountants and financial statement users over the proper valuation procedures for assets and liabilities resulted in the release of *SFAS No. 115* (see FASB ASC 320-19). The statement requires current-value disclosures for all investments in debt securities and for investments in equity securities that have readily determinable fair values and for which the investor does not have significant influence. The chairman of the Securities and Exchange Commission termed historical cost valuations "once-upon-a-time accounting." Historical cost accounting also has been criticized as contributing to the savings and loan crisis of the 1980s. During that period, these financial institutions continued to value assets at historical cost when they were billions of dollars overvalued. Critics of current-value accounting point out that objective market values for many assets are not available, current values cannot be used for tax purposes, using current values can cause earnings volatility, and management could use current value to "manage earnings."

Required:

a. Determine how current values might be determined for investments, land, buildings, equipment, patents, copyrights, trademarks, and franchises.

b. How might the use of current values in the accounting records cause earnings volatility?

c. Discuss how management might manage earnings using current cost data.

d. How do the requirements originally established by *SFAS No. 157* affect the use of fair value measurement in financial statements?

• Case 7-3 Analysis of a Statement of Cash Flows

Obtain a copy of a large corporation's annual report and refer to the statement of cash flows.

Required:

a. Did the company use the direct method or the indirect method of disclosing cash flows?

b. Comment on the relationship between cash flows from operations and net income for the year of the statement and the previous year.

c. What were the most significant sources of cash from operating activities during the period covered by the statement? What percentage of total cash inflows do these sources represent? Answer the same question for the previous period.

d. Was the cash from operations more than or less than dividends during the period covered by the statement and the previous period?

e. What were the firm's major investing activities during the period covered by the statement and the previous period? Were cash flows from operations more or less than cash flows from investing activities for the company in question?

f. What were the most significant cash flows from financing activities during the year of the statement and the previous year?

g. Review the management discussion and analysis sections of the financial statements to determine if any additional information is available concerning the company's investment or financing strategy.

• Case 7-4 Measurement Techniques

The measurement of assets and liabilities on the balance sheet is frequently a secondary goal to income determination. As a result, various measurement techniques are used to disclose assets and liabilities.

Required:

Discuss the various measurement techniques used on the balance sheet to disclose assets and liabilities.

• Case 7-5 The Statement of Cash Flows

Presenting information on cash flows has become an important part of financial reporting.

Required:

a. What goals are attempted to be accomplished by the presentation of cash-flow information to investors?

b. Discuss the following terms as they relate to the presentation of cash-flow information.

    i. Liquidity

    ii. Solvency

    iii. Financial flexibility

• Case 7-6 The Usefulness of the Balance Sheet

The recent emphasis on capital maintenance concepts of income as seen in the FASB's support for "comprehensive income" implies that balance sheet measurement should determine measures of income. That is, accrual accounting is to focus on measurements in the balance sheet, and because financial statements are articulated, measurements in the income statement are residual in nature.

Required:

a. Do you think this focus implies that the balance sheet is more important than the income statement? Explain.

b. How is the balance sheet useful to investors? Discuss.

c. What is meant by the phrase "financial statements are articulated"?

d. Which measurements currently reported in balance sheets are consistent with the physical capital maintenance concept? Give examples.

e. Which measurements currently reported in balance sheets are not consistent with the physical capital maintenance concept? Give examples.

• Case 7-7 Alternative Treatments of Items of the Statement of Cash Flows

The statement of cash flows is intended to provide information about the investing, financing, and operating activities of an enterprise during an accounting period. In a statement of cash flows, cash inflows and outflows for interest expense, interest revenue, and dividend revenue and payments to the government are considered operating activities.

Required:

a. Do you believe that cash inflows and outflows associated with nonoperating items, such as interest expense, interest revenue, and dividend revenue, should be separated from operating cash flows? Explain.

b. Do you believe that the cash flows from investing activities should include not only the return of investment but also the return on investment—that is, the interest and dividend revenue? Explain.

c. Do you believe that the cash flows from the sale of an investment should also include the tax effect of the sale? Explain. Do you believe that cash flows from sales of investments should be net of their tax effects, or do you believe that the tax effect should remain an operating activity because it is a part of "payments to the government"? Explain.

• Case 7-8 Evolution of the Statement of Cash Flows

SFAS No. 95 (see FASB ASC 230) requires companies to prepare a statement of cash flows.

Required:
Describe how the FASB's Conceptual Framework eventually led to the requirement that companies issue statements of cash flows.

FASB ASC Research

For each of the following FASB ASC research cases, search the FASB ASC database for information to address the issues. Cut and paste the FASB paragraphs that support your responses. Then summarize briefly what your responses are, citing the pronouncements and paragraphs used to support your responses.

• FASB ASC 7-1 Classification of Savings Accounts by Credit Unions

If you have a savings account, it is an asset. In the past, some credit unions reported savings accounts (often called member share accounts) as equity while others reported them as liabilities. Search the FASB ASC database to see whether the Emerging Issues Task Force (EITF) has responded to this issue, and if so, what their conclusion is. Cut and paste what you find, and write a summary of what it means in your own words.

• FASB ASC 7-2 Statement of Cash Flows

Several FASB pronouncements and the EITF addressed the presentation of the statement of cash flows. Identify the pronouncements that addressed the preparation of the statement of cash flows, and summarize your findings.

• FASB ASC 7-3 Historical Cost

Historical cost has been the most commonly used measurement attribute for assets. Find the places in the FASB ASC that cite historical cost.

• FASB ASC 7-4 Current Cost

The concept of current cost is discussed in the FASB ASC. Find three references to current cost in the FASB ASC. Cite and copy these references.

• FASB ASC 7-5 Fair Value

Find the discussion of *SFAS No. 157* in the FASB ASC. Summarize what you find.

• FASB ASC 7-6 Statement of Cash Flows

Search the FASB ASC to find the discussion of the statement of cash flows.

1. What is the stated objective of the statement?
2. How should the information provided help investors and others?

Room for Debate

• Debate 7-1 Usefulness of the Statement of Cash Flows versus the Income Statement

According to *SFAC No. 1*, financial statements should provide information that is useful for investor decision making. Paragraph 37 of *SFAC No. 1* states that financial reporting should provide information to help users assess the amounts, timing, and uncertainty of prospective cash flows. Paragraph 43 of *SFAC No. 1* states that the primary focus of financial reporting is providing information about an enterprise's performance based on measures of earnings and earnings components.

Team Debate:

Team 1: Present arguments that the statement of cash flows, not the income statement, is the most important financial statement to prospective investors.

Team 2: Present arguments that the income statement, not the statement of cash flows, is the most important financial statement to prospective investors.

• Debate 7-2 Use of Fair Value Information

Recent pronouncements of the FASB indicate that the FASB is moving away from historical cost accounting toward the use of current, or fair, value. In your debate on this issue, support your position with references to the conceptual framework and to concepts of capital maintenance where appropriate.

Team Debate:

Team 1: Present arguments that historical cost is more relevant than current value.

Team 2: Present arguments that current value is more relevant than historical cost.

CHAPTER 8

Working Capital

A company's *working capital* is the net short-term investment needed to carry on day-to-day activities. The measurement and disclosure of working capital on financial statements has been considered an appropriate accounting function for decades, and so the usefulness of this concept for financial analysis is accepted almost without question. This is not to say that the concept does not present some serious problems, namely (1) inconsistencies in the measurements of the various components of working capital, (2) differences of opinion over what should be included as the elements of working capital, and (3) a lack of precision in the meaning of certain key terms involved in defining the elements of working capital, such as *liquidity* and *current*. This chapter examines the foundation of the working capital concept; reviews the concept and its components as currently understood; illustrates how the adequacy of a company's working capital position can be evaluated; and discusses how the concept might be modified to add to its usefulness.

Development of the Working Capital Concept

The concept of working capital originated with the distinction between fixed and circulating capital at the beginning of the twentieth century. As noted in Chapter 1, at that time accounting was in its adolescent stage, and such concepts as asset, liability, income, and expense were not clearly understood.[1] The impetus for the fixed and circulating capital definitions came from court decisions on the legality

---

1. For a complete documentation of the history of the working capital concept, see William Huizingh, *Working Capital Classification* (Ann Arbor: Bureau of Business Research, Graduate School of Business Administration, University of Michigan, 1967).

of dividends in Great Britain. As first defined, *fixed capital* was money expended that was sunk once and for all, while *circulating capital* was defined as items of stock in trade, which are parted with and replaced by similar items in the ordinary course of business.

These definitions were not readily accepted by members of the accounting profession, some of whom feared that the general public would misinterpret the distinction. Soon thereafter, British and American accountants began to examine the valuation bases of various assets and gave increased attention to a method of accounting termed the *double-account system*. This system divided the balance sheet horizontally into two sections. The upper portion contained all the long-lived assets, the capital, the debt, and a balancing figure that represented the difference between capital and long-term liabilities and long-lived assets. The lower section contained all other assets, current liabilities, and the balancing figure from the top section.

During this same period, the notion of *liquidity* was becoming established as a basis for the classification of assets on the financial statements. Liquidity classification schemes were intended to report on the short-run solvency of the enterprise; however, criticisms arose suggesting that such schemes conflicted with the going-concern concept. Nevertheless, the liquidity concept continued to gain acceptance among accountants and financial statement users and was included by Paton when he wrote about the distinction between fixed and current assets.[2] Paton noted that length of life, rate of use, and method of consumption were important factors in distinguishing between fixed and current assets. He elaborated on these factors as follows: A fixed asset will remain in the enterprise two or more periods, whereas current assets will be used more rapidly; fixed assets may be charged to expense over many periods, whereas current assets are used more quickly; and fixed assets are used entirely to furnish a series of similar services, whereas current assets are consumed.[3]

During the first three decades of the twentieth century, most users in the United States viewed the balance sheet as the principal financial statement. During this period, financial statements were prepared on the basis of their usefulness to creditors, and investors were left to make their decisions on whatever basis they felt was applicable. In 1936 the AICPA attempted to modify this viewpoint by acknowledging the different viewpoints of the creditor and investor:

> As a rule a creditor is more particularly interested in the liquidity of a business enterprise and the nature and adequacy of its working capital; hence the details of the current assets and current liabilities are to him of relatively more importance than details of long-term assets and liabilities. He also has a real interest in the earnings, because the ability to repay a loan may be dependent upon the profits of the enterprise. From an investor's point of view, it is generally recognized that earning capacity is of vital importance and that the income account is at least as important as the balance sheet.[4]

2. William A. Paton, *Accounting Theory* (New York: Ronald Press, 1922).

3. Ibid., 215–16.

4. *Examination of Financial Statements by Independent Public Accountants* (New York: AICPA, 1936), 4.

By the 1940s, the concept of working capital as a basis for determining liquidity had become well established, even though there was some disagreement as to its exact meaning. The confusion centered on how to identify current assets and whether the classification should be based on those items that *will be* converted into cash in the short run or those that *could be* converted into cash. At this time, the one-year rule as the basis for classifying assets as current or noncurrent was fairly well established. But Anson Herrick, who was an active member of the AICPA, began to point out some of the fallacies of the one-year rule.

Herrick focused on the differences in preparing statements for credit and investment purposes and noted some inconsistencies in the then-current practice, such as including inventories under the current classification when their turnover might take more than a year while excluding trade receivables due more than a year after the balance sheet date.[5] His thoughts are summarized in the following statement:

> It is not logical to adopt a practice which may result in substantial difference between the reported amount of net current assets . . . and the amount which would be shown if the statement were to be prepared a few days earlier or later.[6]

In lieu of the one-year rule, Herrick proposed the *operating cycle* as the basis for classifying assets as current. This distinction was based on the contrast of the assets' economic substance as either *fixed* or *circulating* capital.[7]

In 1947, while Herrick was a committee member, the Committee on Accounting Procedure issued *Accounting Research Bulletin (ARB) No. 30*. This release defined current assets as "cash or other resources commonly identified as those which are reasonably expected to be realized in cash or sold or consumed during the normal operating cycle of the business." Current liabilities were defined as "debts or obligations, the liquidation or payment of which is reasonably expected to require the use of existing resources properly classifiable as current assets or the creation of other current liabilities."[8] The operating cycle was then defined as "the average time intervening between the acquisition of materials or services . . . and the final cash realization." The committee also established one year as the basis for classification when the operating cycle was shorter than one year.[9] Although this distinction was slightly modified by *ARB No. 43*, it has stood essentially intact and was recently reaffirmed in *No. 115* (see FASB ASC 330), as discussed later in the chapter.

Current Usage

The working capital concept provides useful information by giving an indication of an entity's liquidity and the degree of protection given to short-term creditors. Specifically, the presentation of working capital can be said to add to the flow of

5. Anson Herrick, "Current Assets and Current Liabilities," *Journal of Accountancy* (January 1944): 48–55.

6. Ibid., 49.

7. Ibid., 50.

8. *Accounting Research Bulletin No. 30*, 248–49.

9. Ibid., 247, 249.

information to financial statement users by (1) indicating the amount of margin or buffer available to meet current obligations, (2) presenting the flow of current assets and current liabilities from past periods, and (3) presenting information on which to base predictions of future inflows and outflows. In the following sections, we examine the measurement of the items included under working capital.

Components of Working Capital

The *ARB No. 43* definitions of current assets and current liabilities (see FASB ASC 210-10-45) include examples of each classification as follows:

Current Assets

1. Cash available for current operations and items that are the equivalent of cash

2. Inventories of merchandise, raw materials, goods in process, finished goods, operating supplies, and ordinary maintenance materials and parts

3. Trade accounts, notes, and acceptances receivable

4. Receivables from officers, employees, affiliates, and others if collectible in the ordinary course of business within a year

5. Installment or deferred accounts and notes receivable if they conform generally to normal trade practices and terms within the business

6. Marketable securities representing the investment of cash available for current operations

7. Prepaid expenses, such as insurance, interest, rents, taxes, unused royalties, current paid advertising service not yet received and operating supplies[10]

Current Liabilities

1. Obligations for items that have entered into the operating cycle, such as payables incurred in the acquisition of materials and supplies to be used in the production of goods or in providing services to be offered for sale

2. Collections received in advance of the delivery of goods or performance of services

3. Debts that arise from operations directly related to the operating cycle, such as accruals for wages, salaries and commission, rentals, royalties, and income and other taxes

4. Other liabilities whose regular and ordinary liquidation is expected to occur within a relatively short period of time, usually 12 months, are also intended for inclusion, such as short-term debts arising from the acquisition of capital assets, serial maturities of long-term obligations, amounts required to be expended within one year under sinking fund provisions, and agency obligations arising from the collection or acceptance of cash or other assets for the account of third persons[11]

   These items will now be examined in more detail.

---

10. *Accounting Research Bulletin No. 43*, "Restatement and Revision of Accounting Research Bulletins," (New York: AICPA, 1953), ch. 3A, para. 4.

11. Ibid.

Current Assets

Cash

The accurate measurement of cash is important not only because cash represents the amount of resources available to meet emergency situations but also because most accounting measurements are based on actual or expected cash inflows and outflows. The ability to project future cash flows is essential to investors, creditors, and management to enable these groups to determine (1) the availability of cash to meet maturing obligations, (2) the availability of cash to pay dividends, and (3) the amount of idle cash that can safely be invested for future use. Measuring cash normally includes counting not only the cash on hand and in banks but also formal negotiable paper, such as personal checks, cashier's checks, and bank drafts.

The amount of cash disclosed as a current asset must be available for current use and is not subject to any restrictions. For example, sinking fund cash should not be reported as a current asset because it is intended to be used to purchase long-term investments or to repay long-term debt.

It has also become commonplace for banks to require a portion of amounts borrowed to remain on deposit during the period of the loan. These deposits are called *compensating balances*. This type of agreement has two main effects: (1) it reduces the amount of cash available for current use, and (2) it increases the effective interest rate on the loan. In 1973, the SEC issued *Accounting Series Release (ASR) No. 148*, which recommended that compensating balances against short-term loans be shown separately in the current assets section of the balance sheet. Compensating balances on long-term loans may be classified as either investments or other assets.[12]

Cash Equivalents

Firms frequently invest cash in excess of immediate needs in short-term, highly liquid investments. Whether cash is on hand, on deposit, or invested in a short-term investment that is readily convertible to cash is irrelevant to financial statement users' assessments of liquidity and future cash flows. The investment of idle funds in cash equivalents to earn interest is a part of the firm's cash management policy. This policy is in contrast to investing capital in the hope of benefiting from favorable price changes that may result from changes in interest rates or other factors. To distinguish between cash management and investment policies, *SFAS No. 95* (see FASB ASC 230-10-20) defines cash equivalents as short-term investments that satisfy the following two criteria: (1) readily convertible into a known amount of cash and (2) sufficiently close to its maturity date so that its market value is relatively insensitive to interest rate changes.

Generally, only investments purchased within three months of their maturity value will satisfy these criteria. Examples of cash equivalents are short-term investments in U.S. Treasury bills, commercial paper, and money market funds. The purchase and sale of these investments are viewed as part of the firm's cash management activities rather than part of its operating, financing, and investing

---

12. "Amendments to Regulation S-X and Related Interpretations and Guidelines Regarding the Disclosure of Compensating Balances and Short-Term Borrowing Agreements," *Accounting Series Release No. 148* (Washington, DC: SEC, November 13, 1973).

activities. In addition, the FASB noted that different types of firms in different industries might pursue different cash management and investing strategies. Consequently, each firm must disclose its policy for treating items as cash equivalents, and any change in that policy must be treated as a change in accounting principle that requires the restatement of prior years' financial statements.

Temporary Investments

In the event that the cash and cash equivalent balances are larger than necessary to provide for current operations, it is advisable to invest idle funds until they are needed. Investments classified as current assets should be readily marketable and intended to be converted into cash within the operating cycle or a year, whichever is longer. Short-term investments are generally distinguished from cash equivalents by relatively longer investment perspectives, at relatively higher rates of return.

In theory, the procedures used to report the value of temporary investments on the balance sheet should provide investors with an indication of the resources that will be available for future use, that is, the amount of cash that could be generated from the disposal of these securities. Most temporary investments are unlike other assets in that an objectively determined measurement of their value is available from day to day in the securities market. Therefore accountants have been divided over the proper methods to use to value temporary investments. Three alternative methods for reporting temporary investments have been debated: *historical cost, market value,* and *the lower of cost or market.*

The *historical cost* method reports temporary investments at their acquisition cost until disposal. Advocates of historical cost believe that an objectively verified purchase price provides the most relevant information about investments to decision makers. They also argue that current market prices do not provide any better information on future prices than does original cost and that only realized gains and losses should be reported on the income statement.

Investments reported at *market value* are adjusted to reflect both upward and downward changes in value, and these changes are reported as either gains or losses on the income statement. Advocates of the market-value method state that current amounts represent the current resources that would be needed to acquire the same securities now as well as the amount that would be received from sale of the securities. In addition, they note that fair value is as objectively determined as historical cost for most investments, and it also presents more timely information on the effect of holding investments.

The *lower of cost or market* (LCM) method, as originally defined, reports only downward adjustments in the value of temporary investments. Proponents of this method believe that it provides users with more conservative balance sheet and income statement valuations. They argue that conservative valuations are necessary to avoid misleading investors.

The accounting treatment for temporary investments in marketable securities has evolved over time. The FASB first studied accounting for temporary investments when their value falls below cost in response to stock market conditions in 1973 and 1974. During that period, the stock market declined substantially from previous levels and then made a partial recovery. The general movement in stock prices during this period had two main effects on financial reporting for investments:

1. Some companies used the historical cost method and did not write their investments down to reflect market prices; they were therefore carrying their portfolios of investments at amounts above current market prices.

2. Some companies used the LCM method, valued their investments at market values, and wrote their investments down to current prices when the stock market reached its lowest level. The partial recovery experienced by the stock market then could not be reflected on these companies' financial statements, which resulted in the companies carrying their investments at an amount below both cost and current market.

Subsequently, the FASB issued *SFAS No. 12*, "Accounting for Certain Marketable Securities" (later superseded), which attempted to alleviate this problem.[13]

According to the provisions of *SFAS No. 12*, marketable equity securities classified as current assets were valued at their aggregate cost or market value, whichever was lower on each balance sheet date. This determination was made by comparing the total cost of the entire portfolio of temporary investments in equity securities against its total market value. Losses and subsequent recoveries (up to historical cost) in market value were included as income. When market on the balance sheet date was less than cost, the difference was reported on the balance sheet by way of a valuation account offset against the temporary investment account.

If all or any part of the portfolio was sold, a gain or loss was recognized on the sale by comparing the original cost of the securities sold with the proceeds from the sale. The valuation account was not affected by the sale of securities. Changes in the valuation account were recorded on the balance sheet date by comparing the cost of the remaining securities with their market value to determine the required balance in the valuation account. If no securities remained, the entire valuation account was eliminated.

It was anticipated that the provisions of *SFAS No. 12* would allow investors to evaluate the management of the temporary investment portfolio. For example, it might be possible to compare the yearly change in the market value of the portfolio to the overall trend in the stock market to assess the effect of management's temporary investment strategy.

SFAS No. 12 referred only to marketable equity securities and did not alter the accounting treatment required for other types of temporary investments, such as short-term investments in debt securities (e.g., notes). Under traditional GAAP, other temporary investments would have been reported by using either the cost or the LCM methods. However, under the cost method, losses were recognized only when there had been a permanent impairment in value. Subsequent recoveries in market value for permanently impaired securities were not recognized.

Later, concerns began to be expressed about the different accounting treatments allowed for investments in equity versus debt securities. Questions were raised about reporting diminished values, but not reporting appreciations. In addition, the issue of gains trading was raised. *Gains trading* is the practice of selling securities that appreciate in value in order to recognize a gain, while holding securities with unrealized losses that were not reported under the cost

13. Financial Accounting Standards Board, *Statement of Financial Accounting Standards No. 12*, "Accounting for Certain Marketable Securities" (Stamford, CT: FASB, 1975).

As a result of such concerns, the FASB undertook a project to address accounting for both equity and debt securities. This project was limited in scope because not all financial assets were included (e.g., receivables), and current accounting requirements for financial liabilities were not changed. The result of this project was the release of *SFAS No. 115*, "Accounting for Certain Investments in Debt and Equity Securities" (see FASB ASC 320).

FASB ASC 320-10-25 requires companies to classify equity and debt securities into one of the following three categories:

1. *Trading securities*. Securities held for resale.
2. *Securities available for sale*. Securities not classified as trading securities or held-to-maturity securities.
3. *Securities held to maturity*. Debt securities for which the reporting entity has both the positive intent and ability to hold until they mature.

Trading securities are reported at fair value, and all unrealized holding gains and losses are recognized in earnings. Available-for-sale securities are reported at fair value. However, unrealized holding gains and losses for these securities are not included in periodic net income; rather, they are reported as a component of other comprehensive income. Held-to-maturity securities are reported at amortized cost, whereby discounts and premiums are amortized over the remaining lives of the securities.

All trading securities are reported as current assets on the balance sheet. Individual held-to-maturity and available-for-sale securities are reported as either current assets or investments as appropriate. The appropriate classification is to be based on the definition of current assets provided in *ARB No. 43*, discussed earlier.

The transfer of a security between investment categories is accounted for at fair value. At the date of the transfer, the security's unrealized holding gain or loss is accounted for as follows:

1. For a security transferred from the trading category, the unrealized holding gain or loss will already have been recognized in earnings, so no additional recognition is required.
2. For a security transferred into the trading category, the unrealized holding gain or loss at the date of the transfer is immediately recognized in earnings.
3. For a debt security transferred into the available-for-sale category from the held-to-maturity category, the unrealized holding gain or loss is recognized in other comprehensive income.
4. For a debt security transferred into the held-to-maturity category from the available-for-sale category, the unrealized holding gain or loss shall continue to be reported in accumulated other comprehensive income, but shall be amortized over the remaining life of the security as an adjustment to interest in a manner similar to the amortization of a premium or discount.

These requirements were adopted to further deter gains trading. If all transfers could be made at fair value and all holding gains and losses could be recognized immediately in earnings, the possibility of discretionary transfers to recognize earnings would be left open. The approach adopted is similar to recognizing holding gains and losses in a manner consistent with the category into which the security is being transferred.

Receivables

The term *receivables* encompasses a wide variety of claims held against others. Receivables are classified into two categories for financial statement presentation: (1) trade receivables and (2) nontrade receivables.

The outstanding receivables balance often constitutes a major source of cash inflows to meet maturing obligations; therefore, the composition of this balance must be carefully evaluated so that financial statement users are not misled. For an item to be classified as a receivable, both the amount to be received and the expected due date must be subject to reasonable estimation.

Ideally, each enterprise would make only cash sales; however, given the nature of our economic society, most firms must extend various types of credit. Businesses sell on credit to increase sales, but when credit is extended, losses from nonpayments invariably occur. Once a business decides to sell on credit, it may record bad debts by one of the following procedures:

1. Bad debts are recorded as the loss is discovered (the direct write-off method).
2. Bad debts are estimated at the end of the accounting period (the estimation, or allowance method).

Under the *direct write-off* method, a loss is recorded when a specific customer account is determined to be uncollectible. Frequently, this determination may not be made until an accounting period subsequent to the year of sale. The problem with this approach is that the amount reported as receivable at the balance sheet date is overstated because it includes amounts that the company does not expect to receive; thus, income for the period is also overstated. *SFAS No. 5* (see FASB ASC 450-20-25) provides a resolution to this issue by requiring estimated losses to be accrued when it is probable that an asset has been impaired or a liability has been incurred, and the amount of the loss can be estimated. Since these conditions are usually satisfied for uncollectible accounts, most companies estimate bad debts.

Two approaches may be used to estimate expected losses from nonpayment of outstanding accounts receivable: (1) the estimated loss is based on annual sales; and (2) the estimated loss is based on the outstanding accounts receivable balance. When the estimated loss is based on annual sales, the matching process is enhanced because expenses are directly related to the revenues that caused the expenses. On the other hand, a more precise measure of anticipated losses can usually be made by reviewing the age and characteristics of the various accounts receivable. When the amount of loss is based on the outstanding accounts receivable, the net balance of the asset account closely resembles the expected amount to be collected in the future (*net realizable value*). With the increased emphasis on the income statement as the primary financial statement, most accountants now recommend estimating losses on the basis of sales and thus providing a better measure for working capital. However, where sales and credit policies are relatively stable, it is unlikely that use of either method of estimation will materially affect reported bad debt expense.

Some accountants have also suggested that receivables should be carried at their present value by applying a discount factor. But others have argued that this treatment is not usually considered necessary due to the relatively short collection (or discount) period involved for most accounts receivable. The FASB's embrace of the asset and liability approach has also had implications for these issues. Under the provisions of *SFAS No. 114*, "Accounting by Creditors for the Impairment of a Loan" (see FASB ASC 310-10-35), creditors must now evaluate the probability that receivables will be collected. If it is determined that amounts will probably not be collected, the present value of the expected future cash payments must be calculated. When this present value is less than the recorded value of the amount due, a loss is recognized and charged to bad debt expense, and the receivable is reduced through a valuation allowance. Alternatively, loss impairments may be measured based on the fair market value of the receivable, or if collateralized, the fair market value of the collateral. The definition of a probable loss is that a future event is likely to occur, which is consistent with the definition provided in *No. 5*, "Accounting for Contingencies" (see FASB ASC 450-20-25). (See Chapter 11 for a discussion of accounting for contingencies.)

Inventories

The term *inventory* was originally defined in *APR No. 43* (see FASB ASC 330-10-20) as follows:

> ...designate[s] the aggregate of those items of tangible personal property which: (1) are held for sale in the ordinary course of business, (2) are in process of production for such sale, or (3) are to be currently consumed in the production of goods or services to be available for sale.[14]

The valuation of inventories is of major importance, for two reasons. First, inventories generally constitute a major portion of current assets; consequently, they have a significant impact on working capital and a company's current position. Second, inventory valuation has a major and immediate impact on the reported amount of net profit.

Inventory valuation procedures differ from the valuation procedures associated with cash, cash equivalents, temporary investments, and receivables. The amounts disclosed for cash, cash equivalents, temporary investments, and receivables approximate the amount of funds expected to be received from these assets. The amount of inventory disclosed on the financial statements does not represent the future cash receipts expected to be generated. Rather, it represents the acquisition value of a cost expected to generate future revenues.

The proper valuation of inventories rests on answers to the following questions:

1. What amount of goods is on hand?
2. What cost-flow assumption is most reasonable for the enterprise?
3. Has the market value of the inventory declined since its acquisition?

Inventory Quantity   The inventory quantity question posed above involves determining the amount of goods on hand by (1) an actual count, (2) perpetual records, or (3) estimating procedures.

Businesses that issue audited financial statements are usually required to *actually count* all items of inventory at least once a year, unless other methods

---

14. *Accounting Research and Terminology Bulletin No. 43*, "Restatement and Revision of Accounting Research Bulletins" (New York: AICPA, 1953), ch. 4, para. 2.

provide reasonable assurance that the inventory figure is correct. When the inventory count is used to determine ending inventory, as in a *periodic inventory system*, the expectation is that all goods not on hand were sold. However, other factors, such as spoilage and pilferage, must be taken into consideration.

When quantity is determined by the *perpetual records method*, all inventory items are tabulated as purchases and sales occur. The resulting amount contained in the accounting records and the amount of inventory on hand should be equal. However, the perpetual inventory count will not reflect accounting errors or depletions of inventory due to pilferage, spoilage, and so on; thus, it is necessary to verify the perpetual record by an actual count of inventory at least once a year. Accounting control over inventories is increased by the use of a perpetual system because the difference between the physical count and the count supplied by the perpetual records provides the company with valuable information not only to track their inventories but also to notice significant differences between actual and expected inventory levels. But a perpetual system should be used only when the benefits derived from maintaining the records are greater than the cost of keeping the records. Given today's advances in technology, such as the use of bar codes, increasing numbers of businesses can now afford to use perpetual inventories; in the past, this method of inventory control was often reserved for only high-priced, low-volume items, such as automobiles.

Estimation methods are used when it is impossible or impractical to count or keep perpetual records for the inventory. Two methods may be used to estimate inventories: (1) the gross profit method and (2) the retail method. The *gross profit* method computes the ending inventory on a dollar basis by subtracting the estimated cost of sales from the cost of goods available. This method is especially useful in estimating inventories for interim financial statements or in computing losses from casualties, such as fire or theft.

The *retail method* is used most frequently where merchandise is available for sale directly to customers, such as in department or discount stores (Hershey uses the retail method for some of its inventory items). With this method, the retail value of inventory is computed by subtracting the retail price of goods sold from the retail price of goods available. Inventory at cost is then computed by applying a markup percentage to the ending inventory at retail.

Both the gross profit and retail methods, although approximating balance sheet values, fail to provide management with all available information concerning the quantity and unit prices of specific items of inventory. Since both methods estimate the ending inventory based on sales records, neither method ensures that the computed balance of the inventory is physically there. For this reason, an actual count of goods on hand should be made annually.

Flow Assumptions   Historically, the matching of costs with associated revenues has been the primary objective in inventory valuation. Even though cost of goods sold is residual because it results from determining the cost of the ending inventory, balance sheet valuation was often viewed as secondary to income determination. Each of the flow assumptions discussed below necessarily requires a trade-off between asset valuation and income determination. Four generally accepted methods are used to account for the flow of goods from purchase to sale: (1) specific identification; (2) first in, first out; (3) last in, first out; and (4) averaging.

If an exact matching of expenses and revenues is the primary objective of inventory valuation, then *specific identification* of each item of merchandise sold may be the most appropriate method. However, even this method has low informational content to balance sheet readers because the valuation of inventories at original cost generally has little relation to future expectations. With the specific identification method, the inventory cost is determined by keeping a separate record for each item acquired and totaling the cost of the inventory items on hand at the end of each accounting period. Most companies find that the cost of the required record keeping associated with the procedure outweighs any expected benefits, and so they turn to other methods. Specific identification is most feasible when the volume of sales is low and the cost of individual items is high, for example, with items like jewelry, automobiles, and yachts.

The *first in, first out* (FIFO) *method* is based on assumptions about the actual flow of merchandise throughout the enterprise; in effect, it is an approximation of specific identification. In most cases this assumption conforms to reality because the oldest items in the inventory are the items management wishes to sell first, and where perishables are involved, the oldest items must be sold quickly or they will spoil.

The FIFO flow assumption satisfies the historical cost and matching principles since the recorded amount for cost of goods sold is similar to the amount that would have been recorded under specific identification if the actual flow of goods were on a FIFO basis. Moreover, the valuation of the unsold inventory reported on the balance sheet more closely resembles the replacement cost of the items on hand and thereby allows financial statement users to evaluate future working capital flows more accurately. However, the effects of inflation have caused accountants to question the desirability of using FIFO. Including older and lower unit costs in cost of goods sold during a period of inflation causes an inflated net profit figure that may mislead financial statement users. This inflated profit figure could also result in the payment of additional income taxes. However, since most companies turn their inventory over fairly rapidly, this argument may be moot in many instances.

The *last in, first out* (LIFO) *method* of inventory valuation is based on the assumption that current costs should be matched against current revenues. Most advocates of LIFO cite the matching principle as the basis for their stand and argue that decades of almost uninterrupted inflation require that LIFO be used to more closely approximate actual net income. These arguments are also based on the belief that price-level changes should be eliminated from financial statements. LIFO is, in effect, a partial price-level adjustment (see Chapter 17 for a further discussion of price-level adjustments).

LIFO liquidations result in distortions of earnings. LIFO liquidation occurs when normal inventory levels are depleted. That is, if inventory levels fall below the normal number of units in any year, the older, usually much lower, cost of these items is charged to cost of goods sold and matched against current sales revenue dollars, resulting in an inflated net income amount that is not sustainable. When a material LIFO liquidation occurs, the SEC requires it to be disclosed in the company's 10-K report. This information is also usually included in the company's annual report to stockholders. For example, Vulcan Materials Company reported that during 2008 and 2007, reductions in LIFO inventory layers resulted in liquidations of LIFO inventory layers carried at lower costs prevailing in prior years as compared with the cost of current-year purchases. The effect of the LIFO liquidation on 2008 results was to decrease cost of goods sold by $2,654,000; increase earnings from continuing operations by $1,605,000; and increase net earnings by

$1,605,000. The effect of the LIFO liquidation on 2007 results was to decrease cost of goods sold by $85,000; increase earnings from continuing operations by $52,000; and increase net earnings by $52,000.

An added impetus to the use of LIFO in external financial reports is the Internal Revenue Service requirement enacted by Congress in the late 1930s that this method must be used for reporting purposes when it is used for income tax purposes. LIFO can result in substantial tax savings, to the extent that cost of goods sold under LIFO and FIFO differ. This tax benefit is calculated as the difference in cost of goods sold times the company's marginal tax rate. As a consequence, many companies that might not otherwise use LIFO for reporting purposes do so because of income tax considerations.

Nevertheless, some accountants maintain that the LIFO conformity rule forces managers to mislead stockholders in either the financial statements or the tax return. These individuals claim that financial reporting would provide more useful information, and the economy would be more productive and prosperous if the rule was eliminated. They hold that the flaw of LIFO is its incomplete description of operating results and its distorted description of financial position, which creates a dilemma for corporate managers. If they want to minimize taxes by choosing LIFO, the conformity rule forces them to publish financial statements that report misleading results. That is, specific identification of sold inventory items matches their acquisition cost with sales price and FIFO is a good approximation of specific identification. If they want statements that describe the results of both inventory purchasing and marketing decisions more completely, they will choose first-in, first-out (FIFO), but only by requiring the corporation to pay more taxes.

Accounting Trends and Techniques recently reported that 213 of 783 companies surveyed used LIFO for some portion of their inventory valuation. However, the use of LIFO has been declining in recent years as inflation has become a less significant factor.[15]

LIFO and FIFO provide the two extremes for inventory valuation. The inventory values of all other inventory costing methods fall in between the LIFO and FIFO values. Because of the potential for significantly different inventory and cost of goods sold values between these two methods, the SEC requires companies using LIFO to provide the financial statement reader with the amount of their LIFO reserve (the difference between LIFO and FIFO), so that investors can convert financial statement numbers from LIFO to FIFO and thus make better comparisons across companies. For example, the investor can convert a balance sheet from LIFO to FIFO by adding the LIFO reserve to the current assets of a company that uses LIFO and then compare that company's working capital to that of another company that uses FIFO.

Averaging techniques are, in effect, a compromise position between FIFO and LIFO. When averaging is used, each purchase affects both inventory valuation and cost of goods sold. Therefore, averaging does not result in either a good match of costs with revenues or a proper valuation of inventories in fluctuating market conditions. Proponents of averaging base their arguments on the necessity of periodic presentation. That is, all the transactions during an accounting period are

15. AICPA, "Presenting and Analyzing Financial Reporting Practices," *Accounting Trends and Techniques*, 62nd ed. (New York: AICPA, 2008), sec. 2.68.

viewed as reflective of the period as a whole rather than as individual transactions. The advocates of averaging maintain that financial statements should reflect the operations of the entire period as a whole rather than as a series of transactions.

When the averaging method used is a weighted or moving weighted average, a claim can be made that the cost of goods sold is reflective of the total period's operations; however, the resulting inventory valuation is not representative of expected future cash flows. If the simple average method is used, the resulting valuations can result in completely distorted unit prices when lot sizes and prices are changing.

Market Fluctuations   Many accountants have advocated valuing inventories at market because they believe that current assets should reflect current values. This might add to the information content of working capital, but to date the doctrine of conservatism has been seen as overriding the advantages claimed by current valuation advocates. Nevertheless, when inventories have declined in value, current GAAP maintains that the future selling price will move in the same direction and that anticipated future losses should be reported in the same period as the inventory decline. In other words, companies should use the lower of cost or market (LCM) method to value inventories.

The AICPA has provided the following definitions to use in applying the LCM rule to inventories:

> As used in the phrase *lower of cost or market* the term *market* means current replacement cost (by purchase or reproduction, as the case may be) except that:

1. market should not exceed the net realizable value (i.e., estimated selling price in the ordinary course of business less reasonably predictable costs of completion and disposal), and
2. market should not be less than net realizable value reduced by an allowance for an approximately normal profit margin.[16]

Use of the LCM rule for inventories is consistent with the qualitative characteristics of accounting information contained in *SFAC No. 2* and the definitions of assets and losses contained in *SFAC No. 6*. That is, when the cost of inventory exceeds its expected benefit, a reduction of the inventory to its market value is a better measure of its expected future benefit.

The major criticism of the LCM rule is that it is applied only for downward adjustments. Therefore holding losses are recognized, and holding gains are ignored. As noted earlier, this criticism has not been considered as important as maintaining conservative financial statements, and the importance of the concept of conservatism was reaffirmed by the FASB in *SFAC No. 5*. Additionally, the application of the LCM rule results in inventory being reported at an *expected utility* value and in the reporting of a "normal profit" when the inventory is sold. The result is that expenses are understated in the period of sale, which may give rise to misinterpretations by external users.

16. Ibid., ch. 4, para 7.

Prepaids

Prepaid items result from recording expected future benefits from services to be rendered. They do not represent current assets in the sense that they will be converted into cash, but rather in the sense that they would require the use of current assets during the operating cycle if they were not in existence.

The measurement of prepaids is generally the residual result of charging the expiration of their cost to expense, and little attention is given to balance sheet valuations. Two main cost expiration methods are used in the measurement of prepaids: (1) specific identification and (2) time. Specific identification is used where the items are consumed, as with office supplies, and time is used where no tangible asset exists and rights are in evidence over a certain period, such as with unexpired insurance or prepaid rent.

In most cases, the amortization method is of little consequence because of the relative immateriality of these items. However, where substantial prepayments occur, care should be exercised to ensure that the allocation method is reasonable under the circumstances.

Current Liabilities

Liability recognition frequently results from the necessity to recognize an asset or an expense where the focus of attention is not on the liability. However, the recognition of short-term liabilities may significantly affect the working capital position of the enterprise. The most frequently encountered current liabilities are payables, deferrals, and current maturities of long-term debt.

Payables

The measurement of payables typically presents no particular difficulty, because the amount of the obligation is usually fixed by a transaction and involves a promise to pay at a subsequent date. As with receivables, recording discounts from face value is not considered necessary because the period of debt is generally short. However, where interest is not specifically stated on notes payable, *APB Opinion No. 21*, "Interest on Receivables and Payables" (see FASB ASC 835-30), requires that interest be calculated for certain types of notes[17] (see Chapter 11). In addition to notes and accounts payable, dividends and taxes represent payables requiring the use of current funds.

Deferrals

Deferrals are liabilities whose settlement requires the performance of services rather than the payment of money. Examples of deferrals include magazine subscriptions collected in advance, advance-purchase airline tickets, and unearned rent. They are similar to prepaid expenses in that they are generally the residual result of measuring another amount. In this case the amount measured is revenue, whereas it is an expense in the case of prepaids.

The placement of deferrals in the current liability section of the balance sheet has been criticized on the grounds that they are liabilities that lack a claimant. But, unless they are unusually large, it is unlikely that recording deferrals as liabilities will have much impact on financial statement presentation. Care should be taken to ensure that the company is not reporting deferrals as revenue before

---

17. Accounting Principles Board, *APB Opinion No. 21*, "Interest on Receivables and Payables" (New York: AICPA, 1971).

they are actually earned and to determine that the deferral accounts are not being used as an additional allowance for uncollectible accounts.

Current Maturities

Unlike most assets, liabilities may be transferred from the long term to the current classification with the passage of time. When the payment of long-term debt in the current period requires the use of current funds, GAAP dictates that this amount be classified as current. On the other hand, not all current maturities are classified as current liabilities. When the long-term liability is to be retired out of a special fund or by issuing additional long-term debt, the obligation should not be classified as current.

The proper classification of current maturities is important because of the effect it can have on the working capital presentation. When adequate provision has not previously been made to retire current maturities, a company may find itself in a weak working capital position and future capital sources may evaporate.

Financial Analysis of a Company's Working Capital Position

The evaluation of a company's working capital position and current operating cycle can highlight possible liquidity problems. Liquidity problems can arise from the failure to convert current assets into cash in a timely manner or from excessive bad debt losses. Several ratios, in addition to working capital, are available to assist in evaluating a company's liquidity. Hershey and Tootsie Roll report some bad debt losses, but most of their sales are to other large corporations, which limits the amount of necessary credit analysis. However, a large retailer such as the Nordstrom department store chain has more difficulty in choosing its customers. Nordstrom purchases merchandise on credit from various manufacturers such as Bally shoes, Tommy Hilfiger clothes, and Giorgio cosmetics. Nordstrom's merchandise is first shipped to the chain's warehouses and later to various stores throughout the country, where it is displayed and sold to customers. Many of Nordstrom's sales are made on Nordstrom credit cards. The company must carefully evaluate each credit application in order to minimize bad debt losses because liquidity problems can arise when customer payments on account are not received in a timely manner.

The ratios used to evaluate a company's liquidity include its working capital, the current ratio, the acid test (quick) ratio, the cash flow from operations to current liabilities ratio, the accounts receivable turnover ratio, the inventory turnover ratio, and the accounts payable turnover ratio. The calculation and analysis of each of these ratios are illustrated by using the information contained in the Hershey Company and Tootsie Roll Incorporated balance sheets, income statements, and statements of cash flows that are found in Chapters 6 and 7. Each of the ratios is computed for both 2008 and 2007 for comparative purposes.

The working capital (current assets minus current liabilities) for Hershey and Tootsie Roll for the two years 2008 and 2007 is ($000 omitted) as follows:

	Hershey			Tootsie Roll		
	Current Assets	Current Liabilities	Working Capital	Current Assets	Current Liabilities	Working Capital
2008	$1,344,945 −	1,270,212 =	$ 74,733	$187,979 −	59,252 =	$128,727
2007	$1,426,574 −	1,618,770 =	($192,196)	$199,726 −	57,972 =	$141,754

Management of a company's working capital is important for any business. This analysis indicates that Hershey's working capital went from negative $192,196,000 in 2007 to positive $74,733,000 in 2008, an increase of $266,929,000. Tootsie Roll's working capital decreased by $13,027,000 from $141,754,000 in 2007 to $128,727,000 in 2008.

Nevertheless, calculating the amount of working capital provides limited information because it does not allow for easy comparisons with benchmarks, industry standards, or other companies. In other words, it is an absolute amount that does not take into consideration the size of a company. Moreover, an amount that is adequate for one company may be inadequate for a larger company.

To overcome this deficiency, financial analysts compute the current ratio and the acid test (quick) ratio. The current ratio is calculated as follows.

$$\frac{\text{Current assets}}{\text{Current liabilities}}$$

The current ratios for Hershey and Tootsie Roll for 2008 and 2007 are calculated ($000 omitted):

	Hershey	Tootsie Roll
2008	$\dfrac{\$1,344,945}{\$1,270,212} = 1.06{:}1$	$\dfrac{\$187,979}{\$\ 59,252} = 3.17{:}1$
2007	$\dfrac{\$1,426,574}{\$1,618,770} = 0.88{:}1$	$\dfrac{\$199,726}{\$\ 57,972} = 3.45{:}1$

The average current ratio for companies in the Candy and Other Confectionary Products industry is 1.69. These calculations indicate that Hershey's liquidity position improved during fiscal 2008 but is below the industry average. Tootsie Roll's current ratio declined somewhat in fiscal 2008.

When evaluating a company's liquidity and working capital position, an additional concern is the composition of its current assets. As a rule, current liabilities are satisfied through the payment of cash, so the analysis should consider which of a company's current assets might be used to repay its current debt. The acid test (quick) ratio provides a more rigid analysis of a company's ability to pay its current obligations as they become due because it includes only those current assets that can easily be converted into cash in the numerator. The acid test (quick) ratio is computed as:

$$\frac{\text{Cash} + \text{Marketable securities} + \text{Receivables}}{\text{Current liabilities}}$$

The acid test (quick) ratios for Hershey and Tootsie Roll for 2008 and 2007 are calculated ($000 omitted) as:

	Hershey	Tootsie Roll
2008	$\dfrac{\$37,103 + 455,153}{\$1,279,212} = 0.39{:}1$	$\dfrac{\$68,908 + 17,963 + 31,213}{\$59,252} = 1.99{:}1$
2007	$\dfrac{\$129,198 + 487,285}{1,618,770} = 0.38{:}1$	$\dfrac{\$57,606 + 41,307 + 32,371}{\$57,972} = 2.26{:}1$

The industry average acid test (quick) ratio is 1.25. This analysis indicates that Hershey's quick liquidity was static over the period of analysis, and it is significantly below the industry average. Tootsie Roll's quick position is higher than the industry average, but it declined during 2008.

One final measure that may be used to evaluate a company's liquidity is the cash flow from operations to current liabilities ratio. This ratio indicates a company's ability to repay current liabilities from current operations. The cash flow from operations to current liabilities ratio is calculated as:

$$\frac{\text{Net cash provided from operating activities}}{\text{Average current liabilities}}$$

Notice that this ratio is calculated by using average current liabilities in the denominator. This results in the use of a consistent numerator and denominator since the net cash provided from operating activities represents the flow of cash over the year.

The cash flow from operations to current liabilities ratios for Hershey and Tootsie Roll for 2008 and 2007 are calculated as ($000 omitted):

	Hershey	Tootsie Roll
2006	$\frac{\$519,561}{(\$1,270,212 + 1,618,770)/2} = 0.36:1$	$\frac{\$57,042}{\$59,252 + 57,972} = 0.97:1$
2007	$\frac{\$778,836}{(\$1,618,770 + 1,453,538)/2} = 0.51:1$	$\frac{\$90,064}{(\$57,972 + 62,211)/2} = 1.50:1$

These ratios indicate that both companies' cash flow positions deteriorated during fiscal year 2008, but the Hershey deterioration is sufficient to cause concern. Still, both companies have positive cash flows that are greater than the increases in their accounts payable, which is an indication that operations generated enough cash to cover their respective cost of goods manufactured during the year.

Taken together, the above three ratios indicate that Tootsie Roll is far more liquid than Hershey and that Hershey appears to be experiencing a significant decline in its liquidity position.

The preceding ratios are used to evaluate a company's liquidity. Other ratios are available that assist in evaluating how efficient a company is in using its current assets and managing its current liabilities. The accounts receivable turnover ratio measures a company's ability to collect its receivables on a timely basis. The accounts receivable turnover ratio is computed as:

$$\frac{\text{Net credit sales}[18]}{\text{Average gross accounts receivable}}$$

18. The sales figure contained on most companies' income statement is the combined amount of cash and credit sales. Most companies make the greatest majority of their sales on credit, so the sales figure on the income statement can be used to approximate credit sales. However, if a company makes a large amount of cash sales, the result may be misleading. Additionally, the numerator in this calculation is gross rather than net accounts receivable because the company is attempting to collect all of its accounts receivables. Hershey's balance sheet does not disclose the amount of the allowance for uncollectibles; however, the footnotes to Hershey's 2008, 2007 and 2006 financial statements reported allowances for uncollectibles of $16,700,000, $17,800,000 and $18,700,000 respectively. Tootsie Roll's 2006 balance sheet disclosed an allowance for uncollectibles of $2,322,000.

Note that this ratio also uses an average amount in the denominator to provide consistency with the numerator.

The accounts receivable turnover ratios for Hershey and Tootsie Roll for 2008 and 2007 are calculated as ($000 omitted):

	Hershey	Tootsie Roll
2008	$\dfrac{\$5,132,768}{(\$455,153 + 16700 + 487,285 + 17,800)/2} = 10.51$	$\dfrac{\$492,051}{(\$31,213 + 1,923 + 32,371 + 2,287)/2} = 14.52$
2007	$\dfrac{\$4,946,716}{(\$487,285 + 17,800 + 584,033 + 18,700)/2} = 8.93$	$\dfrac{\$492,742}{(\$32,371 + 2,287 + 41211 + 2,322)/2} = 12.60$

These ratios indicate that Hershey's accounts receivable was paid off by customers an average of almost 11 times in fiscal 2008 and approximately 9 times in fiscal 2007, whereas Tootsie Roll's was paid off approximately 15 times and 13 times in fiscal 2008 and 2007, respectively. These ratios are both well above the industry average of 1.41. To add perspective to the company's efficiency in collecting accounts receivable, financial analysts calculate the number of days in receivables as follows:

$$\frac{365}{\text{Accounts receivable turnover}}$$

The number of days in receivables ratios for Hershey and Tootsie Roll for 2008 and 2007 are calculated as:

	Hershey	Tootsie Roll
2008	$\dfrac{365}{10.51} = 34.73$	$\dfrac{365}{14.52} = 25.14$
2007	$\dfrac{365}{8.93} = 40.87$	$\dfrac{365}{12.60} = 28.97$

The calculation of average days in receivables allows a company to evaluate its ability to collect its accounts receivable within its normal credit period. These calculations indicate that Hershey is having a little difficulty collecting its receivables when considering that normal trade credit policies generally require payment within 30 days. Tootsie Roll apparently has more efficient credit policies in that its average collection period is about ten days less than Hershey's.

Another issue to consider when evaluating the collectibility of a company's accounts receivable is the potential impact of a bankruptcy of a major customer. Hershey reported that McLane Company, a wholesale distributor, accounted for more than 20 percent of the company's sales, and Tootsie Roll sells over 24 percent of its output to Wal-Mart. Neither of these amounts are believed to be of major concern.

A company's efficiency in managing its inventory can be similarly analyzed by computing the inventory turnover ratio. This ratio is calculated as:

$$\frac{\text{Cost of goods sold}}{\text{Average inventory}}$$

The inventory turnover ratios for Hershey and Tootsie Roll for 2008 and 2007 are calculated as ($000 omitted):

	Hershey	Tootsie Roll
2008	$\dfrac{\$3,375,050}{(\$592,530 + 600,185)/2} = 5.66$	$\dfrac{\$333,314}{(\$34,862 + 20,722 + 37,031 + 20,371)/2} = 5.90$
2007	$\dfrac{\$3,315,147}{(\$600,185 + 648,820)/2} = 5.31$	$\dfrac{\$3,27,695}{(\$37,031 + 20,371 + 63,957)/2} = 5.40$

The average inventory turnover ratio for the Candy and Other Confectionary Products industry was 0.78 in 2008, indicating that both Hershey and Tootsie Roll turned their inventory more frequently than the industry as a whole.

This ratio can be further analyzed by calculating the average days in inventory as follows:

$$\frac{365}{\text{Inventory turnover ratio}}$$

The average number of days in inventory for Hershey and Tootsie Roll for 2008 and 2007 are calculated as:

	Hershey	Tootsie Roll
2008	$\dfrac{365}{5.66} = 64.49$	$\dfrac{365}{5.90} = 61.86$
2007	$\dfrac{365}{5.31} = 68.74$	$\dfrac{365}{5.40} = 67.59$

These ratios indicate that for both Hershey and Tootsie Roll, the ability to manage inventory improved somewhat. Care must be exercised in evaluating these ratios because they are highly industry dependent. For example, a grocery chain like Safeway sells many perishables and would be expected to have a high inventory turnover ratio, but for defense contractors such as Boeing, this ratio would be relatively lower.

The analysis of a company's working capital, current ratio, and inventory turnover ratios can be misleading for companies using LIFO inventory costing. In such cases, the amount of working capital and the current ratio will be understated because the average inventory amounts used in calculating these ratios will usually be much lower than if they had been computed using FIFO. As discussed earlier in the chapter, this difference is termed the *LIFO reserve*. On the other hand, the inventory turnover ratio will generally be overstated because the average inventory amounts used in the denominator will be lower than if FIFO had been used.

A company's inventory costing method is disclosed in its summary of significant accounting policies. Financial statement users should exercise care in interpreting the amount of working capital, the current ratio, and the inventory turnover ratio for companies using LIFO. For comparative purposes, the reported amount of LIFO inventory should be adjusted by the amount of the LIFO reserve.[19] Both Hershey and Tootsie Roll use LIFO to value most of their inventories. In 2008, Hershey reported LIFO reserves of $137,781,000 and $86,615,000 respectively, for 2008 and 2007. For the same two years, Tootsie Roll reported LIFO reserves of $12,432,000 and $11,284,000. Following are the adjusted

---

19. This amount, or the replacement cost of the inventory, is a recommended disclosure by an AICPA task force and is reported by most companies that use LIFO.

working capital, the current ratio, and the inventory turnover ratio for the two companies after adjusting for the amount of the LIFO reserve.

	Hershey	Tootsie Roll
Working Capital	$74,733 + 137,781 = $212,514	$128,727 + 12,432 = $141,159
Current Ratio	$\dfrac{\$1,344,945 + 137,781}{\$1,279,212} = 1.16:1$	$\dfrac{\$187,979 + 12,432}{\$59,252} = 3.38:1$
Inventory Turnover	$\dfrac{\$3,375,050 - 137,781 + 86,615^{20}}{(\$592,530 + 600,185 + 137,781 + 86,615)/2} = 4.69$	$\dfrac{\$333,314 - 12,432 + 11,284}{(\$34,862 + 20,722 + 37,031 + 20,371 + 12,432 + 11,284)/2} = 4.86$
Days in Inventory	77.83	75.10

These calculations increase the previously computed working capital and current ratios while decreasing the inventory ratio.

One final ratio helps evaluate a company's pattern of payments to suppliers by analyzing its accounts payable. A company's accounts payable turnover ratio is calculated as:

$$\frac{\text{Inventory purchases}^{21}}{\text{Average accounts payable}}$$

The accounts payable turnover ratios for Hershey and Tootsie Roll for 2008 and 2007 are calculated as ($000 omitted):

	Hershey	Tootsie Roll
2008	$\dfrac{\$3,375,050 - 7,655}{(\$249,454 + 223,019)/2} = 14.25$	$\dfrac{\$333,314 - 1,818}{(\$13,885 + 11,572)/2} = 26.04$
2007	$\dfrac{\$3,315,147 - 48,635}{(\$223,019 + 155,517)/2} = 17.26$	$\dfrac{\$3,27,695 - 6,555}{(\$11,572 + 13,102)/2} = 26.03$

This ratio can also be used to calculate the average days that payables are outstanding as follows:

$$\frac{365}{\text{Accounts payable turnover ratio}}$$

For Hershey and Tootsie Roll, these amounts for 2008 and 2007 are as follows:

	Hershey	Tootsie Roll
2008	$\dfrac{365}{14.25} = 25.61 \text{ days}$	$\dfrac{365}{26.04} = 14.01 \text{ days}$
2007	$\dfrac{365}{17.26} = 21.15 \text{ days}$	$\dfrac{365}{26.03} = 14.02 \text{ days}$

20. Since cost of goods sold is calculated as beginning inventory plus purchases minus ending inventory, the numerator must also be adjusted to incorporate the beginning and ending effects of the LIFO reserve.

21. This amount is not usually disclosed on corporate financial statements but can be estimated by cost of goods sold plus increases or minus decreases in inventory during the year.

These ratios indicate that the two companies' payable balances are being satisfied in a timely manner in that normal trade policy is for payables to be repaid within 30 days. The comparative analysis also indicates that Hershey's average days outstanding increased over the two-year period while Tootsie Roll's stayed about the same.

A comprehensive analysis of Hershey's working capital position would combine the results of the above calculations. This analysis for fiscal 2008 indicates that

- Customers pay accounts receivable in approximately 35 days.
- Inventory remains on hand for approximately 64 days.
- Current operations are generating sufficient cash to repay current liabilities.
- Accounts payable are being satisfied in approximately 26 days.

  This same analysis for Tootsie Roll for fiscal 2008 indicates that

- Customers pay accounts receivable in approximately 25 days.
- Inventory remains on hand for approximately 62 days.
- Current operations are generating sufficient cash to repay current liabilities.
- Accounts payable are being satisfied in approximately 14 days.

These analyses indicate that both companies are maintaining adequate liquidity positions; however, Hershey's failure to generate enough cash to maintain current operations is a concern.

International Accounting Standards

The IASB has issued pronouncements on the following issues affecting working capital:

1. The presentation of current assets and current liabilities in a revised *IAS No. 1*, "Presentation of Financial Statements"
2. Accounting for Financial Assets and Liabilities in *IAS No. 39*, "Financial Instruments: Recognition and Measurement" (discussed in Chapters 9 and 10)
3. Accounting for inventories in a revised *IAS No. 2*, "Inventories"

The IASB does not deal with the valuation issues discussed earlier in the chapter in its discussion of the presentation of current assets and current liabilities, However, the Board noted that some financial statement users see the classification of assets and liabilities into current and noncurrent as providing a means to measure an enterprise's liquidity, whereas others regard this classification as the identification of the enterprise's circulating resources and obligations. The IASB indicated that since these two concepts are somewhat contradictory, it has led to the classification of items as current or noncurrent based on convention rather than on any one concept. *IAS No. 1* originally allowed companies to determine whether or not to separately present current assets and current liabilities. This decision was apparently based on the Board's inability to agree on the usefulness of the concept because of the limitations noted earlier in this chapter. The revised *IAS No. 1* now requires assets and liabilities to be classified as current or noncurrent unless a liquidity presentation provides more relevant information.

In *IAS No. 2*, the IASB held that the objective of inventory reporting is to determine the proper amount of cost to recognize as an asset and carry forward until the related revenues are recognized. The Board stated a preference for the specific identification method of inventory valuation when the items are inter-changeable or are produced and segregated for specific projects. This method was viewed as inappropriate when large numbers of interchangeable items are present. In these cases, the IASB stated a preference for either FIFO or weighted aver-age methods; however, LIFO was an allowed alternative. Under the revised *IAS No. 2*, the use of LIFO is no longer allowed. Additionally, *IAS No. 2* requires inven-tory to be written down to net realizable value (floor) on an item-by-item basis, but allows write-downs to occur by groups of similar products in special circum-stances. This process contrasts to U.S. GAAP, under which write-downs are nor-mally determined either on an item-by-item, group, or categorical basis. Also, *IAS No 2* allows previous inventory write-down reversals to be recognized in the same period as the write-down; however, any inventory write-downs under U.S. GAAP cannot subsequently be reversed.

As the FASB and the IASB move toward convergence of accounting stan-dards, the LIFO issue will need to be resolved. Although the process of converg-ing U.S. GAAP with international GAAP has made a great deal of progress, many issues remain to be addressed, including the fate of the LIFO method. For over a decade, FASB and IASB have had an ongoing agenda of projects, the objective of which is to move the process of convergence forward. For the period 2006–2008, numerous convergence-related issues were identified as either being on an active agenda or on a research agenda before being added to an active agenda. However, the issues of LIFO and inventory valuation in general were not included on the active research agenda of either board at the time this text was published.

Cases

• Case 8-1 Accounting for Investments

FASB ASC 320 requires companies to assign their portfolio of investment securi-ties into (1) trading securities, (2) securities available for sale, and (3) held-to-maturity securities.

Required:

a. Define each of these categories of securities and discuss the accounting treatment for each category.

b. Discuss how companies are required to assign each category of securities into its current and noncurrent portions.

c. Some individuals maintain that the only proper accounting treatment for all marketable securities is current value. Others maintain that this treatment might allow companies to "manage earnings." Discuss the arguments for each position.

• Case 8-2 Cost-Flow Assumptions

Cost for inventory purposes should be determined by the inventory cost-flow method most clearly reflecting periodic income.

Required:

a. Describe the fundamental cost-flow assumptions of the average cost, FIFO, and LIFO inventory cost-flow methods.

b. Discuss the reasons for using LIFO in an inflationary economy.

c. Where there is evidence that the utility of goods, in their disposal in the ordinary course of business, will be less than cost, what is the proper accounting treatment, and under what concept is that treatment justified?

• Case 8-3 Inventory Cost and Income

Steel Company, a wholesaler that has been in business for two years, purchases its inventories from various suppliers. During the two years, each purchase has been at a lower price than the previous purchase.

Steel uses the lower of FIFO cost or market method to value inventories. The original cost of the inventories is above replacement cost and below the net realizable value. The net realizable value less the normal profit margin is below the replacement cost.

Required:

a. In general, what criteria should be used to determine which costs should be included in inventory?

b. In general, why is the lower of cost or market rule used to report inventory?

c. At what amount should Steel's inventories be reported on the balance sheet? Explain the application of the lower of cost or market rule in this situation.

d. What would have been the effect on ending inventories and net income for the second year had Steel used the lower of average cost or market inventory method instead of the lower of FIFO cost or market inventory method? Why?

• Case 8-4 Uncollectible Accounts

Anth Company has significant amounts of trade accounts receivable. Anth uses the allowance method to estimate bad debts. During the year, some specific accounts were written off as uncollectible, and some that were previously written off as uncollectible were collected.

Anth also has some interest-bearing notes receivable for which the face amount plus interest at the prevailing rate of interest is due at maturity. The notes were received on July 1, 2008, and are due on June 30, 2009.

Required:

a. What are the deficiencies of the direct write-off method?

b. What are the two basic allowance methods used to estimate bad debts, and what is the theoretical justification for each?

c. How should Anth account for the collection of the specific accounts previously written off as uncollectible?

d. How should Anth report the effects of the interest-bearing notes receivable on its December 31, 2008, balance sheet and its income statement for the year ended December 31, 2008? Why?

• Case 8-5 Lower of Cost or Market Valuation of Inventories

Accountants generally follow the lower of cost or market (LCM) basis of inventory valuations.

Required:

a. Define *cost* as applied to the valuation of inventories.

b. Define *market* as applied to the valuation of inventories.

c. Why are inventories valued at the lower of cost or market? Discuss.

d. List the arguments against the use of the LCM method of valuing inventories.

• Case 8-6 Accounting for Bad Debt Expense under the Allowance Method

On December 31, 2008, Carme Company had significant amounts of accounts receivables as a result of credit sales to its customers. Carme uses the allowance method based on credit sales to estimate bad debts. Based on experience, 1 percent of credit sales normally will not be collected. This pattern is expected to continue.

Required:

a. Discuss the rationale for using the allowance method based on credit sales to estimate bad debts. Contrast this method with the allowance method based on the balance in the trade receivables accounts.

b. How should Carme Company report the allowance for bad debts account on its balance sheet at December 31, 2008? Also, describe the alternatives, if any, for presentation of bad debt expense in Carme's 2008 income statement.

• Case 8-7 Accounting for Trading and Available-for-Sale Securities

At the end of the first year of operations, Key Company had a current equity securities portfolio classified as available-for-sale securities with a cost of $500,000 and a fair value of $550,000. At the end of its second year of operations, Key had a current equity securities portfolio classified as available-for-sale securities with a cost of $525,000 and a fair value of $475,000. No securities were sold during the first year. One security with a cost of $80,000 and a fair value of $70,000 at the end of the first year was sold for $100,000 during the second year.

Required:

a. How should Key Company report the preceding facts in its balance sheets and income statements for both years? Discuss the rationale for your answer.

b. How would your answer differ if the security had been classified as trading securities?

• Case 8-8 Alternate Inventory Valuations

Specific identification is sometimes said to be the ideal method for assigning cost to inventory and to cost of goods sold.

Required:

   a. List the arguments for and against the foregoing statement.

   b. FIFO, weighted average, and LIFO methods are often used instead of specific identification. Compare each of these methods with the specific identification method. Include in your discussion analysis of the theoretical propriety of each method in the determination of income and asset valuation. (Do not define the methods or describe their technical accounting procedures.)

• Case 8-9 Net Realizable Value of Accounts Receivable

The theoretical valuation of receivables is the present value of expected future cash flows. However, trade receivables are not discounted due to materiality considerations; hence, their net realizable value is the closest practical approximation to the theoretical valuation.

Required:

   a. Define net realizable value.

   b. The allowance method of accounting for bad debts may use an income statement or a balance sheet approach.

   i. Which approach provides the best estimate of net realizable value? Explain.

   ii. Working capital is intended to provide a measure of liquidity. Which approach provides a better measure of liquidity? Explain.

   iii. Which approach is consistent with the matching concept? Explain.

   iv. Which approach is consistent with the definition of comprehensive income? Explain.

   v. Which approach is more consistent with the concept of financial capital maintenance? Explain.

   vi. Which approach is more consistent with the concept of physical capital maintenance? Explain.

• Case 8-10 Accounting for Prepaids and Deferrals

Short-term deferrals (prepaids and unearned revenues) are classified as current assets and current liabilities. As such, they are included in working capital.

Required:

   a. Some argue that prepaids will not generate cash and hence are not liquid assets.

   i. Why do accountants include short-term prepaids as current assets? Do they meet the definition of assets found in the conceptual framework? Do they provide working capital? Explain.

ii. Present arguments for excluding prepaids from current assets. Do they provide liquidity? Explain.

b. Some argue that deferred liabilities will not be "paid."

i. Why do accountants include short-term unearned revenues as current liabilities? Do they meet the definition of liabilities found in the conceptual framework? Do they affect working capital? Explain.

c. Present arguments for excluding unearned revenues from current liabilities. Do they affect liquidity? Explain.

FASB ASC Research

• FASB ASC Research

For each of the following FASB ASC research cases, search the FASB ASC database for information to address the issues. Cut and paste the FASB paragraphs that support your responses. Then summarize briefly what your responses are, citing the pronouncements and paragraphs used to support your responses.

• FASB ASC 8-1 Current Assets and Current Liabilities

Over the years, many official pronouncements have been issued regarding current liabilities. These sources include APB Opinions, FASB Statements, FASB Technical Bulletins, and EITF releases. Search the FASB ASC database to find the pronouncements on current assets and liabilities, list these sources, and summarize your findings.

• FASB ASC 8-2 Offsetting Assets and Liabilities

Accounts receivable is presented on the balance sheet at net realizable value. This amount is calculated by offsetting the allowance for doubtful accounts against accounts receivable. Search the FASB ASC database to determine the rule for offsetting assets and liabilities. List the official pronouncements related to this issue.

• FASB ASC 8-3 Inventory

Search the FASB ASC database to determine the accounting objective of accounting for inventory, and cite the paragraph number. Cite the original pronouncement that stated this objective. Find, cite, and copy the following definitions:

1. Current assets
2. Current liabilities
3. Operating cycle
4. Working capital

• FASB ASC 8-4 Examples of Current Assets

Search the FASB ASC to find the items classified as current assets. Cite and copy the relevant paragraph.

- ## FASB ASC 8-5 Classification of Current Liabilities

Search the FASB ASC to find information on the classification of current liabilities. Cite and copy the relevant paragraph.

- ## FASB ASC 8-6 Compensating Balances

An SEC Staff Bulletin on compensating balances is found in the FASB ASC. Find and cite the paragraph and then copy the relevant information.

- ## FASB ASC 8-7 *SFAS No. 115*

Find and cite the material on *SFAS No. 115* in the FASB ASC. Cite the relevant paragraphs.

- ## FASB ASC 8-8 *ARB No. 43* and Inventory

Sections of *ARB No. 43* on accounting for the cost of inventory are still considered GAAP. Find this information. Cite the paragraphs and copy the relevant information.

Room for Debate

- ## Debate 8-1 LIFO versus FIFO

MVP Corp uses LIFO to value its inventory. The 20×8 inventory records disclose the following:

Beginning Inventory	Units	Unit Cost
First layer	10,000	$15
Second layer	22,000	18
Purchases	250,000	20

At December 26, 20×8, the company had a special, nonrecurring opportunity to purchase 40,000 units at $17 per unit. The purchase can be made and the units delivered on December 30, or it can be delayed until the first week of January 20×9. The company plans to make the purchase, due to the obvious cost savings involved. Sales for 20×8 totaled 245,000 units.

Team Debate:

Team 1:   Describe the financial statement effects of making the purchase in 20×8 as opposed to 20×9. Argue for making the purchase during 20×8. Defend the use of LIFO. Use the matching concept in your defense.

Team 2:   Given the financial statement effects of the decision to purchase in 20×8, argue against the use of LIFO and in favor of FIFO. Base your arguments on the conceptual framework, for example, representational faithfulness and neutrality. Use the matching concept in your argument.

• Debate 8-2 Components of Working Capital

In the following debate, take the position of an investor who wants to evaluate the liquidity of a company.

Team Debate:

Team 1:   Argue for including inventory, prepaids, and deferrals in working capital.

Team 2:   Argue against including inventory, prepaids, and deferrals in working capital.

• Debate 8-3 Capitalization versus Expense

Entre Preneur found a site for his new haute cuisine restaurant. The site has a vacant gasoline station. He purchased the property for $900,000 and had the station demolished at a cost of $30,000. A government regulation required that he spend $40,000 to remove and dispose of three underground tanks and $30,000 to refine the soil. The restaurant was constructed for $1,800,000. Avoidable interest during construction totaled $22,000.

Team Debate:

Team 1:   Present arguments for capitalizing all of the above costs. Your arguments should utilize the conceptual framework definitions and concepts.

Team 2:   Criticize capitalization of the cost to remove the tanks and refine the soil and the capitalization of interest during construction. Do they provide added service potential? Your arguments should use the conceptual framework definitions and concepts.

Long-Term Assets I: Property, Plant, and Equipment

The evolution of the circulating and noncirculating capital distinction of assets and liabilities into the working capital concept has been accompanied by the separate classification and disclosure of long-term assets. In this chapter we examine one of the categories of long-term assets—property, plant, and equipment. Long-term investments and intangibles are discussed in Chapter 10.

Property, Plant, and Equipment

The items of property, plant, and equipment generally are a major source of future service potential to the enterprise. These assets represent a significant commitment of economic resources for companies in capital-intensive industries, such as Ford in the automobile manufacturing industry, Boeing in the airplane manufacturing industry, and Exxon Mobil in the oil exploration and refining industry. Such companies may have as much as 75 percent of their total assets invested in property, plant, and equipment. The valuation of property, plant, and equipment assets is of interest to financial statement users because it indicates the physical resources available to the firm and may also give some indication of future liquidity and cash flows. These valuations are particularly important in capital-intensive industries because property, plant, and equipment constitutes a major component of the company's total assets. The objectives of plant and equipment accounting are as follows:

1. Reporting to investors on stewardship
2. Accounting for the use and deterioration of plant and equipment
3. Planning for new acquisitions, through budgeting

4. Supplying information for taxing authorities
5. Supplying rate-making information for regulated industries

Accounting for Cost

Many businesses commit substantial corporate resources to acquire property, plant, and equipment. Investors, creditors, and other users rely on accountants to report the extent of corporate investment in these assets. The initial investment, or cost to the enterprise, represents the sacrifice of resources given up in the past to accomplish future objectives. Traditionally, accountants have placed a great deal of emphasis on the principle of objective evidence to determine the initial valuation of long-term assets. Cost (the economic sacrifice incurred) is the preferred valuation method used to account for the acquisition of property, plant, and equipment because, as discussed in Chapter 4, cost is more reliable and verifiable than other valuation methods such as discounted present value, replacement cost, or net realizable value. There is also a presumption that the agreed-upon purchase price represents the future service potential of the asset to the buyer in an arm's-length transaction.

Despite the reliability and verifiability of the purchase price as the basis for initially recording property, plant, and equipment, the assignment of cost to individual assets is not always as uncomplicated as might be expected. When assets are acquired in groups, when they are self-constructed, when they are acquired in nonmonetary exchanges, when property contains assets that are to be removed, or when there are expected future costs associated with decommissioning an asset, certain accounting issues arise. These issues are discussed in the following sections.

Group Purchases

When a group of assets is acquired for a lump-sum purchase price, such as the purchase of land, buildings, and equipment for a single purchase price, the total acquisition cost must be allocated to the individual assets so that an appropriate amount of cost can be charged to expense as the service potential of the individual assets expires. The most frequent, though arbitrary, solution to this allocation problem has been to assign the acquisition cost to the various assets on the basis of the weighted average of their respective appraisal values. Where appraisal values are not available, the cost assignment may be based on the relative carrying values on the seller's books. Since no evidence exists that either of these values is the relative value to the purchaser, assignment by either of these procedures would seem to violate the objectivity principle, but the use of these methods is usually justified on the basis of expediency and the lack of acceptable alternative methods.

Self-Constructed Assets

Self-constructed assets give rise to questions about the proper components of cost. Although it is generally agreed that all expenses directly associated with the construction process should be included in the recorded cost of the asset (material, direct labor, etc.), there are controversial issues regarding the assignment of fixed overhead and the capitalization of interest. The fixed-overhead issue has two aspects: (1) should any fixed overhead be allocated? and (2) if so, how much fixed overhead should be allocated? This problem has further ramifications. If a plant is operating at less than full capacity and fixed overhead is assigned to a self-constructed asset, charging the asset with a portion of the fixed overhead will cause the profit margin on all other products to increase during the period of construction. Three approaches are available to resolve this issue:

1. Allocate no fixed overhead to the self-construction project.
2. Allocate only incremental fixed overhead to the project.
3. Allocate fixed overhead to the project on the same basis as it is allocated to other products.

Some accountants favor the first approach. They argue that the allocation of fixed overhead is arbitrary and therefore only direct costs should be considered. Nevertheless, the prevailing opinion is that the construction of the asset required the use of some amount of fixed overhead; thus, fixed overhead is a proper component of cost. Consequently, no allocation is seen as a violation of the historical cost principle.

When the production of other products has been discontinued to produce a self-constructed asset, allocation of the entire amount of fixed overhead to the remaining products will cause reported profits on these products to decrease. (The same amount of overhead is allocated to fewer products.) Under these circumstances, the third approach seems most appropriate. On the other hand, it seems unlikely that an enterprise would discontinue operations of a profitable product to construct productive facilities except in unusual circumstances.

When operations are at less than full capacity, the second approach is the most logical. The decision to build the asset was probably connected with the availability of idle facilities. Increasing the profit margin on existing products by allocating a portion of the fixed overhead to the self-construction project will distort reported profits.

A corollary to the fixed overhead allocation question is the issue of the capitalization of interest charges during the period of the construction of the asset. During the construction period, extra financing for materials and supplies will undoubtedly be required, and these funds will frequently be obtained from external sources. The central question is the advisability of capitalizing the cost associated with the use of these funds. Some accountants have argued that interest is a financing rather than an operating charge and should not be charged against the asset. Others have noted that if the asset were acquired from outsiders, interest charges would undoubtedly be part of the cost basis to the seller and would be included in the sales price. In addition, public utilities normally capitalize both actual and implicit interest (when their own funds are used) on construction projects because future rates are based on the costs of services. Charging existing products for the expenses associated with a separate decision results in an improper matching of costs and revenues. Therefore a more logical approach is to capitalize incremental interest charges during the construction period. Once the new asset is placed in service, interest is charged against operations.

The misapplication of this theory resulted in abuses during the early 1970s, when many companies adopted the policy of capitalizing all interest costs. However, in 1974 the SEC established a rule preventing this practice.[1] Later, in 1979,

---

1 *Accounting Series Release No. 163*, "Capitalization of Interest by Companies Other Than Public Utilities" (Washington, DC: Securities and Exchange Commission, 1974).

the FASB issued *SFAS No. 34*, "Capitalization of Interest Costs"[2] (see FASB ASC 835-20). In this release, the FASB maintained that interest should be capitalized only when an asset requires a period of time to be prepared for its intended use.

The primary objective of the guidance contained at FASB ASC 835-20 is to recognize interest cost as a significant part of the historical cost of acquiring an asset. The criteria for determining whether an asset qualifies for interest capitalization are that the asset must not yet be ready for its intended purpose, and it must be undergoing activities necessary to get it ready. Qualified assets are defined as (1) assets that are constructed or otherwise produced for an enterprise's own use, and (2) assets intended for sale or lease that are constructed or otherwise produced as discrete projects. The FASB ASC 835-20-15-6 guidance excludes interest capitalization for inventories that are routinely manufactured or otherwise produced in large quantities on a repetitive basis. Assets that are in use or are not being readied for use are also excluded.

An additional issue addressed is the determination of the proper amount of interest to capitalize. The FASB ASC 835-20-30 guidance indicates that the amount of interest to be capitalized is the amount that could have been avoided if the asset had not been constructed. Two interest rates may be used: the weighted average rate of interest charges during the period and the interest charge on a specific debt instrument issued to finance the project. The amount of avoidable interest is determined by applying the appropriate interest rate to the average amount of accumulated expenditures for the asset during the construction period. The specific interest is applied first; then, if there are additional average accumulated expenditures, the average rate is applied to the balance. The capitalized amount is the lesser of the calculated "avoidable" interest and the actual interest incurred. In addition, only actual interest costs on present obligations may be capitalized, not imputed interest on equity funds.

Removal of Existing Assets

When a firm acquires property containing existing structures that are to be removed, a question arises concerning the proper treatment of the cost of removing these structures. Current practice is to assign removal costs less any proceeds received from the sale of the assets to the land, since these costs are necessary to put the site in a state of readiness for construction.

Assets Acquired in Noncash Transactions

In addition to cash transactions, assets may also be acquired by trading equity securities, or one asset may be exchanged in partial or full payment for another (trade-in). When equity securities are exchanged for assets, the cost principle dictates that the recorded value of the asset is the amount of consideration given. This amount is usually the market value of the securities exchanged. If the market value of the securities is not determinable, cost should be assigned to the property on the basis of its fair market value. This procedure is a departure from the cost principle and can be viewed as an example of the use of replacement cost in current practice.

When assets are exchanged—for example, in trade-ins—additional complications arise. Accountants have long argued the relative merits of using the fair market value versus the book value of the exchanged asset. In 1973, the APB

---

2 Financial Accounting Standards Board, *Statement of Financial Accounting Standards No. 34*, "Capitalization of Interest Costs" (Stamford, CT: FASB, 1979), para. 9.

released *Opinion No. 29*, "Accounting for Nonmonetary Transactions" (see FASB ASC 845), which maintains that fair value should (generally) be used as the basis of accountability.[3] Therefore the cost of an asset acquired in a straight exchange for another asset is the fair market value of the surrendered asset.

This general rule was originally subject to one exception. The original APB guidance stated that exchanges should be recorded at the book value of the asset given up when the exchange is not the culmination of the earning process. Two examples of exchanges that do not result in the culmination of the earning process were defined as follows:

1. Exchange of a *product or property held for sale* in the ordinary course of business (inventory) for a product or property to be sold in the same line of business to facilitate sales to customers other than parties to the exchange

2. Exchange of a *productive asset* not held for sale in the ordinary course of business for a *similar* productive asset or an equivalent interest in the same or similar productive asset[4]

That is, if the exchanged assets were dissimilar, the presumption was to be that the earning process was complete, and the acquired asset was recorded at the fair value of the asset exchanged including any gain or loss. This requirement existed for straight exchanges and for exchanges accompanied by cash payments (also known as *boot*). For example, if Company G exchanges cash of $2,000, and an asset with a book value of $10,000 and a fair market value of $13,000, for a dissimilar asset, a gain of $3,000 should be recognized ($13,000 − $10,000), and the new asset is recorded at $15,000.

On the other hand, accounting for the exchange of *similar productive assets* originally took a somewhat different form. According to the original provisions of *APB Opinion No. 29*, losses on the exchange of similar productive assets are always recognized in their entirety whether or not boot (cash) is involved. However, gains were never recognized unless boot was received. In 2004, the FASB issued *SFAS No. 153*, "Exchanges of Nonmonetary Assets an Amendment of APB Opinion No. 29"[5] (see FASB ASC 845-10). This amendment eliminated the exception for nonmonetary exchanges of similar productive assets and replaced it with a general exception for exchanges of nonmonetary assets that do not have commercial substance. A nonmonetary exchange has commercial substance if the future cash flows of the entity are expected to change significantly as a result of the exchange. For these exchanges, the book value of the asset exchanged is to be used to measure the asset acquired in the exchange. Thus, no gains are to be recognized; however, a loss should be recognized if the fair value of the asset exchanged is less than its book value (i.e., an impairment is evident). The resulting amount initially recorded for the acquired asset is equal to the book value of the exchanged asset (adjusted to its fair value, when there is an apparent impairment) plus or minus any cash (boot) paid or received.

3. Accounting Principles Board, *APB Opinion No. 29*, "Accounting for Nonmonetary Transactions" (New York: AICPA, 1973).

4. Ibid., para. 21.

5. *Statement of Financial Accounting Standards No. 153*, "Exchanges of Nonmonetary Assets an Amendment of APB Opinion No. 29" (Norwalk, CT: FASB, 2004).

Donated and Discovery Values

Corporations sometimes acquire assets as gifts from municipalities, local citizens' groups, or stockholders as inducements to locate facilities in certain areas. For example, in 1992 BMW automobile company announced it would build a plant in the Greenville-Spartanburg area of South Carolina after the state offered several incentives, including $70.7 million in reduced property taxes, $25 million to buy land for the plant and lease it to BMW for $1 per year, and $40 million to lengthen the local airport runway so that it could accommodate wide-body cargo aircraft. The cost principle holds that the recorded values of assets should be equal to the consideration given in return, but since donations are nonreciprocal transfers, strict adherence to this principle will result in a failure to record donated assets at all. On the other hand, failure to report values for these assets on the balance sheet is inconsistent with the full disclosure principle.

Previous practice required donated assets to be recorded at their fair market values, with a corresponding increase in an equity account termed *donated capital*. Recording donated assets at fair market values is defended on the grounds that if the donation had been in cash, the amount received would have been recorded as donated capital, and the cash could have been used to purchase the asset at its fair market value.

SFAS No. 116 (see FASB ASC 605-10-15-3), requires that the inflow of assets from a donation be considered revenue (not donated capital).[6] If so, the fair market value of the assets received represents the appropriate measurement. However, the characterization of donations as revenues may be flawed. According to *SFAC No. 6*, revenues arise from the delivery or production of goods and the rendering of services. If the contribution is a nonreciprocal transfer, then it is difficult to see how revenue has been earned. Alternatively, it may be argued that the inflow represents a gain. This latter argument is consistent with the conceptual framework definition of a gain, as resulting from peripheral or incidental transactions and with the definition of comprehensive income as the change in net assets resulting from nonowner transactions. Under this approach, the asset and gain would be recorded at the fair market value of the asset received, thereby allowing full disclosure of the asset in the balance sheet.

Similarly, valuable natural resources may be discovered on property subsequent to its acquisition, and the original cost may not provide all relevant information about the nature of the property. In such cases, the cost principle is modified to account for the appraisal increase in the property. A corresponding increase is reported as an unrealized gain in accumulated other comprehensive income. An alternative practice consistent with the conceptual framework definition of comprehensive income would be to recognize the appraisal increase as a gain.

Financial Analysis of Property, Plant, and Equipment

In Chapter 6 we discussed analyzing a company's profitability by computing the return on assets (ROA) ratio. The sustainability of earnings is a major consideration in this process. For capital-intensive companies, a large portion of their asset base will be investments in property, plant, and equipment, and a major question

---

6 *Statement of Financial Accounting Standards No. 116*, "Accounting for Contributions Received and Contributions Made" (Stamford, CT: Financial Accounting Standards Board, 1993), para. 8.

for investors analyzing such companies is their asset replacement policy. A company with a large investment in property, plant, and equipment that fails to systematically replace those assets will generally report an increasing return on assets over the useful life of its asset base. This occurs because the ROA denominator will decrease by the amount of the company's annual depreciation expense, resulting in an increasing return percentage for stable amounts of earnings. In addition, the general pattern of rising prices will tend to increase the selling price of the company's product, resulting in a further upward bias for the ROA percentage.

An examination of a company's investing activity helps in analyzing the earnings sustainability of its ROA percentage. For example, Hershey's statement of cash flows, contained in Chapter 7, reveals that the company acquired $262,643,000 and $189,698,000 of property, plant, and equipment assets in 2008 and 2007, respectively. These amounts are 7.6 percent and 5.3 percent, respectively, of the gross property, plant, and equipment assets. Tootsie Roll's statement of cash flows reveals that the company acquired approximately $34,355,000 and $14,767,000 of property, plant, and equipment assets in 2008 and 2007, respectively, amounting to 8.4 percent and 3.9 percent of the purchase price of its property, plant, and equipment assets. Both of these computations provide evidence that the companies' ROA percentages are not being distorted by a failure to systematically replace their long-term assets.

Cost Allocation

Capitalizing the cost of an asset implies that the asset has future service potential. Future service potential indicates that the asset is expected to generate or be associated with future resource flows. As those flows materialize, the matching concept (discussed in Chapter 5) dictates that certain costs no longer have future service potential and should be charged to expense during the period the associated revenues are earned. Because the cost of property, plant, and equipment is incurred to benefit future periods, it must be spread, or allocated, to the periods benefited. The process of recognizing, or spreading, cost over multiple periods is termed *cost allocation*. For items of property, plant, and equipment, cost allocation is referred to as *depreciation*. As the asset is depreciated, the cost is said to expire—that is, it is expensed (see Chapter 5 for a discussion of the process of cost expiration).

As discussed earlier, balance sheet measurements should theoretically reflect the future service potential of assets at a moment in time. Accountants generally agree that cost reflects future service potential at acquisition. However, in subsequent periods, expectations about future resource flows may change. Also, the discount rate used to measure the present value of the future service potential may change. As a result, the asset may still be useful; but because of technological changes, its future service potential at the end of any given period may differ from what was originally anticipated. Systematic cost allocation methods do not attempt to measure changes in expectations or discount rates. Consequently, no systematic cost allocation method can provide balance sheet measures that consistently reflect future service potential.

The historical cost accounting model presently dominant in accounting practice requires that the costs incurred be allocated in a systematic and rational manner. Thomas, who conducted an extensive study of cost allocation, concluded that all allocation is based on arbitrary assumptions and that no one method of cost allocation is superior to another.[7] At the same time, it cannot be concluded that the present accounting model provides information that is not useful for investor decision making. A number of studies document an association between accounting income numbers and stock returns. This evidence implies that historical cost-based accounting income, which employs cost allocation methods, has information content (see Chapter 4 for further discussion of this issue).

Depreciation

Once the appropriate cost of an asset has been determined, the reporting entity must decide how to allocate its cost. At one extreme, the entire cost of the asset could be expensed when the asset is acquired; at the other extreme, cost could be retained in the accounting records until disposal of the asset, when the entire cost would be expensed. However, neither of these approaches provides for a satisfactory measure of periodic income, because cost expiration would not be allocated to the periods in which the asset is in use and thus would not satisfy the matching principle. Thus the concept of depreciation was devised in an effort to satisfy the need to allocate the cost of property, plant, and equipment over the periods that receive benefit from use of long-term assets.

The desire of financial statement users to receive periodic reports on the result of operations necessitated allocating asset cost to the periods receiving benefit from the use of assets classified as property, plant, and equipment. Because depreciation is a form of cost allocation, all depreciation concepts are related to some view of income measurement. A strict interpretation of the FASB's comprehensive income concept would require that changes in service potential be recorded in income. Economic depreciation has been defined as the change in the discounted present value of the items of property, plant, and equipment during a period. If the discounted present value measures the service potential of the asset at a point in time, the change in service potential interpretation is consistent with the economic concept of income.

As discussed in Chapter 5, recording cost expirations by the change in service potential is a difficult concept to operationalize. Consequently, accountants have adopted a transactions view of income determination, in which they see income as the end result of revenue recognition according to certain criteria, coupled with the appropriate matching of expenses with those revenues. Thus most depreciation methods emphasize the matching concept, and little attention is directed to balance sheet valuation. Depreciation is typically described as a process of systematic and rational cost allocation that is not intended to result in the presentation of asset fair value on the balance sheet. This point was first emphasized by the Committee on Terminology of the AICPA as follows:

> Depreciation accounting is a system of accounting which aims to distribute the cost or other basic value of tangible capital assets, less salvage value (if any), over the estimated useful life of the unit (which may be a group of assets) in a systematic and rational manner. It is a process of allocation, not valuation[8] [See FASB ASC 360-10-35-4.]

7. Arthur L. Thomas, "The Allocation Problem in Financial Accounting Theory," *Studies in Accounting Research No. 3* (Evanston, IL: American Accounting Association, 1969).

8. *Accounting Terminology Bulletin No. 1*, "Review and Resume" (New York: AICPA, 1953), ch. 9C, para. 5.

The AICPA's view of depreciation is particularly important to an understanding of the difference between accounting and economic concepts of income, and it also provides insight into many misunderstandings about accounting depreciation. Economists see depreciation as the decline in the real value of assets. Other individuals believe that depreciation charges and the resulting accumulated depreciation provide the source of funds for future replacement of assets. Still others have suggested that business investment decisions are influenced by the portion of the original asset cost that has been previously allocated. Accordingly, new investments cannot be made, because the old asset has not been fully depreciated. These views are not consistent with the stated objective of depreciation for accounting purposes. Moreover, we do not support the view that business decisions should be affected by accounting rules. In the following section, we examine the accounting concept of depreciation more closely.

The Depreciation Process

The depreciation process for long-term assets comprises three separate factors:

1. Establishing the depreciation base
2. Estimating the useful service life
3. Choosing a cost apportionment method

Depreciation Base   The depreciation base is that portion of the cost of the asset that should be charged to expense over its expected useful life. Because cost represents the future service potential of the asset embodied in future resource flows, the theoretical depreciation base is the present value of all resource flows over the life of the asset, until disposition of the asset. Hence, it should be cost minus the present value of the salvage value. In practice, salvage value is not discounted; and as a practical matter, it is typically ignored. Proper accounting treatment requires that salvage value be taken into consideration. For example, rental car agencies normally use automobiles for only a short period; the expected value of these automobiles at the time they are retired from service would be material and should be considered in establishing the depreciation base.

Useful Service Life   The useful service life of an asset is the period of time the asset is expected to function efficiently. Consequently, an asset's useful service life may be less than its physical life, and factors other than wear and tear should be examined to establish the useful service life.

Various authors have suggested possible obsolescence, inadequacy, supersession, and changes in the social environment as factors to be considered in establishing the expected service life. For example, jet airplanes have replaced most of the airlines' propeller-driven planes, and ecological factors have caused changes in manufacturing processes in the steel industry. Estimating such factors requires a certain amount of clairvoyance—a quality difficult to acquire.

Depreciation Methods   Most of the controversy in depreciation accounting revolves around the question of the appropriate method that should be used to allocate the depreciation base over its estimated service life. Theoretically, the expired cost of the asset should be related to the value received from the asset in each period; however, it is extremely difficult to measure these amounts. Accountants have, therefore, attempted to estimate expired costs by other methods, namely: (1) straight line, (2) accelerated, and (3) units of activity.

1. *Straight line.* The straight-line method allocates an equal portion of the depreciable cost of an asset to each period the asset is used. Straight-line depreciation is often justified on the basis of the lack of evidence to support other methods. Since it is difficult to establish evidence that links the value received from an asset to any particular period, the advocates of straight-line depreciation accounting argue that other methods are arbitrary and therefore inappropriate. Use of the straight-line method implies that the asset is declining in service potential in equal amounts over its estimated service life.

2. *Accelerated.* The sum-of-the-year's-digits and the fixed-percentage-of-declining-base (declining balance) are the most frequently encountered methods of accelerated depreciation.[9] These methods result in larger charges to expense in the earlier years of asset use, although little evidence supports the notion that assets actually decline in service potential in the manner suggested by these methods. Advocates contend that accelerated depreciation is preferred to straight-line because as the asset ages, the smaller depreciation charges are associated with higher maintenance charges. The resulting combined expense pattern provides a better matching against the associated revenue stream. Accelerated depreciation methods probably give balance sheet valuations that are closer to the actual value of the assets in question than straight-line methods do, since most assets lose their value more rapidly during the earlier years of use. But since depreciation accounting is not intended to be a method of asset valuation, this factor should not be viewed as an advantage of using accelerated depreciation methods.

3. *Units of activity.* When assets (e.g., machinery) are used in the actual production process, it may be possible to determine an activity level, such as the total expected output to be obtained from these assets. Depreciation may then be based on the number of units of output produced during an accounting period. The activity measures of depreciation assume that each product produced during the asset's existence receives the same amount of benefit from the asset. This assumption may or may not be realistic. In addition, care must be exercised in establishing a direct relationship between the measurement unit and the asset. For example, when direct labor hours are used as a measure of the units of output, a decline in productive efficiency in the later years of the asset's use may cause the addition of more direct labor hours per product, which would result in charging more cost per unit.

Disclosure of Depreciation Methods

Most U.S. companies use straight-line depreciation, as shown by the 2006 edition of *Accounting Trends and Techniques*, which reported that 592 of the 600 firms

9 Since 1954, the Internal Revenue Code has specified various accelerated depreciation methods to be used to determine taxable income. The current acceptable method to use is termed the Modified Accelerated Cost Recovery System. This method is not acceptable for financial reporting purposes (see FASB ASC 360-10-35-9).

surveyed used straight-line depreciation for at least some of their assets.[10] Both Hershey and Tootsie Roll use straight-line depreciation for financial reporting purposes. The following is excerpted from Tootsie Roll's summary of significant accounting policies:

> **Property, plant and equipment:**
> Depreciation is computed for financial reporting purposes by use of the straight-line method based on useful lives of 20 to 35 years for buildings and 5 to 20 years for machinery and equipment. Depreciation expense was $17,036,000, $15,859,000 and $15,816,000 in 2008, 2007, and 2006, respectively.

Capital and Revenue Expenditures

The purchase and installation of plants and equipment does not eliminate expenditures associated with these assets. Almost all productive facilities require periodic maintenance that should be charged to current expense. The cost of the asset to the enterprise includes the initial cost plus all costs associated with keeping the asset in working order. However, if additional expenditures give rise to an increase in future service potential, these expenditures should not be charged to current operations. Expenditures that increase future service potential should be added to the remaining unexpired cost of the asset and be charged to expense over the estimated remaining period of benefit.

In most cases, the decision to expense or capitalize plant and equipment expenditures subsequent to acquisition is fairly simple and is based on whether the cost incurred is "ordinary and necessary" or "prolongs future life." But frequently this decision becomes more complicated, and additional rules have been formulated that assist in determining whether an expenditure should be recorded as a capital improvement. If the asset's life is increased, the efficiency provided is increased; or if output is increased, its service potential has increased, and the cost of an expenditure should be capitalized and written off over the expected period of benefit. All other expenditures made subsequent to acquisition should be expensed as incurred.

Recognition and Measurement Issues

Accounting depreciation methods are objective because they use historical cost. Moreover, once selected, the resulting depreciation charges are generally reliable. Nevertheless, all accounting depreciation methods have similar recognition and measurement problems. Given that fixed assets are intended to provide service potential over multiple future years, each cost allocation method requires estimates of salvage value and useful life, and given the rapidly changing competitive environment, revisions of these estimates may be required each accounting period.

One can argue that accounting depreciation methods do not provide relevant information for users. Users desire information that is useful in predicting future

10 Yury Lofe and Matthew C. Calderisi, eds., *Accounting Trends and Techniques*, 60th ed. (New York: AICPA, 2006), sec. 3.101.

cash flows. Users are also aware that management makes a decision each period either to reinvest in available long-term assets or to replace existing long-term assets with new ones. Consequently, a current-value approach to depreciation may be more consistent with investor needs.

Using a current-value balance sheet approach to report depreciation would require knowledge of the reinvestment value of each long-term asset at the end of each accounting period. Such a determination may be impracticable or even impossible. The assets in question may be old, or they may be so specialized that there is no readily determinable market value. Alternative discounted present-value techniques require estimates of future cash flows that may be unreliable. And appraisal values may not be realistic. Hence, there is no simple answer to the determination of the most appropriate approach to depreciation. This determination depends, to a large extent, on an individual's perception of the necessary trade-off between relevance and reliability.

Impairment of Value

The *SFAC No. 6* definition of assets indicates that assets have future service potential and consequently value to the reporting entity. Having future service potential implies that the asset is expected to generate future cash flows. When the present value of future cash flows decreases, the value of the asset to the firm declines. If the decline in value over the life of the asset is greater than the accumulated depreciation charges, the book value of the asset is overstated, and the value of the asset is said to be impaired. Yet accountants have been reluctant to apply the lower of cost or market (LCM) rule to account for property, plant, and equipment.

The FASB, noting divergent practices in the recognition of impairment of long-lived assets, originally issued *SFAS No. 121,*[11] now superseded, which addressed the matter of when to recognize the impairment of long-lived assets and how to measure the loss. This release ignored current value as a determinant of impairment. Rather, it stated that impairment occurs when the carrying amount of the asset is not recoverable. The recoverable amount is defined as the sum of the future cash flows expected to result from use of the asset and its eventual disposal. Under this standard, companies were required to review long-lived assets (including intangibles) for impairment whenever events or changes in circumstances indicate that book value may not be recoverable. Examples indicating potential impairment included the following:

1. A significant decrease in the market value of an asset
2. A significant change in the extent or manner in which an asset is used
3. A significant adverse change in legal factors or in business climate that affects the value of assets
4. An accumulation of significant costs in excess of the amount originally expended to acquire or construct an asset
5. A projection or forecast that demonstrates a history of continuing losses associated with the asset

11 *Statement of Financial Accounting Standards No. 121,* "Accounting for the Impairment of Long-Lived Assets to Be Disposed Of" (Stamford, CT: FASB, 1995).

Although fair value was not used to determine impairment, *SFAS No. 121* required that when an impairment occurred, a loss was to be recognized for the difference between the carrying value of an asset and its current value less estimated cost to dispose of the asset. The resulting reduced carrying value of the asset became its new cost basis and was to be depreciated over the remaining useful life of the asset.

Later in 2001, the FASB issued *SFAS No. 144*, "Accounting for the Impairment or Disposal of Long-Lived Assets"[12] (see FASB ASCs 360-10-35-15 to 49). The FASB stated that the new standard was issued because *SFAS No. 121* did not address accounting for a segment of a business accounted for as a discontinued operation, as originally required by *APB Opinion 30*. Consequently, two accounting models existed for disposing of long-lived assets. The Board decided to establish a single accounting model, based on the framework established in *SFAS No. 121*, for long-lived assets to be disposed of by sale.

The guidance at FASB ASC 360-10-40 applies to all dispositions of long-term assets; however, it excludes current assets, intangibles, and financial instruments because they are covered in other releases. According to its provisions, assets are to be classified as follows:

1. Long-term assets held and used
2. Long-lived assets to be disposed of other than by sale
3. Long-lived assets to be disposed of by sale

Long-term assets held and used are to be tested for impairment using the original *SFAS No. 121* criteria if events suggest there may have been impairment. The impairment is to be measured at fair value by using the present-value procedures outlined in *SFAC No. 7* (see Chapter 2). To illustrate, consider the following scenario. Baxter Company owns a manufacturing facility with a carrying value of $80 million that is tested for recoverability.[13] Two courses of action are under consideration—sell in two years, or sell at the end of its remaining useful life of 10 years. The company develops the probability of a range of possible estimated future cash flows for each possibility, considering various future sales levels and future economic conditions as follows.

Course of Action	Cash Flow Estimate (000,000)	Probability	Probability Weighted Cash Flows (000,000)
Sell in 2 years	$ 76	20%	$ 15.2
	82	50	41.0
	86	30	25.8
			$ 82.0
Sell in 10 years	$ 74	20%	$ 14.8
	98	50	49.0
	112	30	33.6
			$ 97.4

12 *Statement of Financial Accounting Standards No. 144*, "Accounting for the Impairment or Disposal of Long-Lived Assets" (Norwalk, CT: FASB, 2001).

13 This and the following example were adapted from *SFAS No. 144*, Appendix A.

Next, the probability of each of the courses of action must be determined. If the probability of the first course of action is 60 percent and the second 40 percent, the total present value is $88.2 [($82.0×.6) + ($97.4×.4)].

For long-term assets held and used, it might be necessary to review the original depreciation policy to determine if the useful life is still as originally estimated. Next, the assets are grouped at the lowest level for which identifiable cash flows are independent of cash flows from other assets and liabilities, and losses are allocated pro rata to the assets in the group. Any losses are disclosed in income from continuing operations.

To illustrate grouping, assume that Alvaraz Company owns a manufacturing facility that is one of the groups of assets that is tested for recoverability. In addition to long-term assets, the asset group includes inventory and other current liabilities not covered by FASB ASC 360. The $5.5 million aggregate carrying amount of the asset group is not fully recoverable and exceeds its fair value by $1.2 million. How is the impairment loss allocated?

Asset Group	Carrying Amount (000,000)	Pro Rata	Loss Allocation (000,000)	Adjusted Carrying Value (000,000)
Current assets	$ 800			$ 800
Liabilities	(300)			(300)
Long-term assets				
A	1,180	24%	$ (288)	892
B	1,560	31	(372)	1,188
C	1,900	38	(456)	1,444
D	360	7	(84)	276
Total	$5,500	100%	$(1,200)	$4,300

Long-lived assets to be disposed of other than by sale, such as those to be abandoned, exchanged for a similar productive asset, or distributed to owners in a spin-off, are to be considered held and used until disposed of. Additionally, to resolve implementation issues, the depreciable life of a long-lived asset to be abandoned was to be revised in accordance with the criteria originally established in *APB Opinion No. 20*, "Accounting Changes" (since rescinded).

The accounting treatment for long-lived assets to be disposed of by sale is used for all long-lived assets, whether previously held and used or newly acquired (FASB ASC 360-10-35). That treatment retains the requirement originally outlined in *SFAS No. 121* to measure a long-lived asset classified as held for sale at the lower of its carrying amount or fair value less cost to sell and to cease depreciation (amortization). As a result, discontinued operations are no longer measured on the basis of net realizable value, and future operating losses are no longer recognized before they occur.

In summary, *SFAS No. 144* retained the requirements of *SFAS No. 121* to recognize an impairment loss only if the carrying amount of a long-lived asset is not recoverable from its undiscounted cash flows. This loss is measured as the difference between the carrying amount and fair value of the asset (see FASB ASC 360-10-35-17).

In 2008, Hershey disclosed the following information regarding a business realignment initiative that included an asset impairment:

> As a result of our annual impairment tests of intangible assets with useful lives determined to be indefinite, we recorded total impairment charges of $45.7 million in the fourth quarter of 2008. Certain trademarks, primarily the *Mauna Loa* brand, were determined to be impaired as a result of a decrease in the fair value of the brands resulting from reduced expectations for future sales and cash flows compared with the valuations of these trademarks at the acquisition dates.

Accounting for Asset Retirement Obligations

In February 1994, Edison Electric Institute asked the FASB to add a project to its agenda to address accounting for nuclear decommissioning and other similar costs. Later, the FASB issued an exposure draft to include a broader project for all asset retirement obligations. This exposure draft became *SFAS No. 143*, "Accounting for Asset Retirement Obligations"[14] (see FASB ASC 410-20).

At the time *SFAS No. 143* was issued, the FASB noted that existing practice was inconsistent; consequently, the objective of this release was to provide accounting requirements for all obligations associated with the removal of long-lived assets. FASB ASC 410-20 applies to all entities that face existing legal obligations associated with the retirement of tangible long-lived assets.

FASB ASC 410-20 provides the following definitions associated with the issue:

1. *Asset retirement obligation*. The liability associated with the ultimate disposal of a long-term asset

2. *Asset retirement cost*. The increase in the capitalized cost of a long-term asset that occurs when the liability for an asset retirement obligation is recognized

3. *Retirement*. An other than temporary removal of a long-term asset from service by sale, abandonment, or other disposal

4. *Promissory estoppel*. A legal concept holding that a promise made without consideration may be enforced to prevent injustice

For each asset retirement obligation, a company is required to initially record the fair value (present value) of the liability to dispose of the asset when a reasonable estimate of its fair value is available. Companies are required to use *SFAC No. 7* criteria for recognition of the liability, which is the present value of the asset at the credit-adjusted rate. This amount is defined as the amount a third party with a comparable credit standing would charge to assume the obligation.

Subsequently, the capitalized asset retirement cost is allocated in a systematic and rational manner as depreciation expense over the estimated useful life of the asset. Additionally, the initial carrying value of the liability is increased each year by use of the interest method using the credit adjusted rate and is classified as accretion expense and not interest expense. In the event any of the original assumptions change, a recalculation of the obligation and the subsequent associated expenses is to be recorded as a change in accounting estimate.

---

14 *Statement of Financial Accounting Standards No. 143*, "Accounting for Asset Retirement Obligations" (Norwalk, CT: FASB, 2001).

To illustrate, consider the following example.[15] Gulfshores Oil Company completes construction and places into service an offshore oil platform on January 1, 2008. The company is legally required to dismantle and remove the platform at the end of its useful life, which is estimated to be 10 years. FASB ASC 410-20 requires the company to recognize a liability for an asset retirement obligation that is capitalized as a part of the asset's cost. The company estimates this liability by using its estimated present value and the following additional information.

1. Labor costs required to dismantle the platform are based on the best estimates of future costs and are assigned the following probabilities:

Cash Flow Estimate	Probability	Expected Cash Flow
$200,000	.25	$ 50,000
250,000	.50	125,000
350,000	.25	87,500
		$262,500

2. Overhead is allocated at 75 percent of labor cost. This amount is based on the company's current overhead application rate.

3. A contract for removal will include a profit to the contractor. The profit margin is estimated to be 25 percent of labor and overhead.

4. The company wishes to contract now for the asset removal. A contractor will normally require a risk premium to cover future uncertainties. The market risk premium for "locking in" is assumed to be 5 percent of the inflation-adjusted cash flows.

5. The assumed inflation rate is 2 percent.

6. The risk-free interest rate is 2 percent, and the adjusted credit standing rate is 4 percent.

The initial measurement of the liability is as follows:

	Expected Cash Flow
	1/1/08
Labor costs	$262,500
Allocated overhead (75%)	196,875
Profit margin	114,844
Expected cash flow before inflation	$574,219
Inflation adjustment (2% for 10 years)	1,2190
Expected cash flow	$699,973
Market risk premium (5%)	34,999
Adjusted expected cash flow	$734,972
Present value (Credit-adjusted rate of 6% for 10 years or 0.5584)	$410,408

15 Adapted from *SFAS No. 143*, Appendix C.

These calculations will result in Gulfshores' recording the following entry on January 1, 2008:

Asset (asset retirement obligation)	$410,408	
ARO liability		$410,408

As a result, the company will record annual depreciation expense of $41,041 for the next 10 years, and it will increase the value of the ARO liability by 6.0 percent each year as illustrated:

Year	Beginning Liability Balance	Accretion	Ending Liability Balance
2008	$410,408	$ 24,624	$435,032
2009	435,032	26,102	461,134
2010	461,134	27,688	488,802
2011	488,802	29,328	518,131
2012	518,131	31,088	549,218
2013	549,218	32,953	582,172
2014	582,172	34,930	617,102
2015	617,102	37,026	654,128
2017	654,128	39,248	693,376
2018	693,376	41,596[16]	734,972

On December 30, 2018, Gulfshores will settle the asset retirement obligation by using its own workforce at a total cost of $710,000. It is necessary to compare the settlement cost with the book value of the asset retirement obligation on the date of retirement to determine if a gain or loss has occurred as follows:

Total costs incurred	$710,000
ARO liability	734,972
Settlement gain	$ 24,972

On the settlement date, the liability is removed from the book, the costs associated with the restoration are recorded, and the gain is recognized.

International Accounting Standards

The IASB has issued pronouncements on the following issues affecting items of property, plant, and equipment:

1. The overall issues associated with accounting for property, plant, and equipment assets in a revised *IAS No. 16*, "Property, Plant and Equipment"
2. The capitalization of interest costs on acquired assets in *IAS No. 23*, "Borrowing Costs"
3. The accounting treatment for impairment of assets in *IAS No. 36*, "Impairment of Assets"

---

16 This amount was rounded.

4. The accounting treatment for assets held for disposal in *IFRS No. 5*, "Non-Current Assets Held for Sale and Discontinued Operations"

5. Accounting for mineral resources in *IFRS No. 6*, "Exploration for and Evaluation of Mineral Resources"

The issues in *IAS No. 16* are the timing of recognition of assets, the determination of their carrying amounts, and the associated depreciation charges to be recognized. The revised *IAS No. 16* did not change the fundamental approach to accounting for property, plant, and equipment. The Board's purpose in revising the standard was to provide additional guidance on selected matters. The original standard permits differences from U.S. GAAP in that items of property, plant, and equipment are allowed (but not required) to be periodically revalued to current market values. The standard also requires depreciation to be calculated in a manner that more closely resembles the actual decline in service potential of the assets.

IAS No. 16 indicates that items of property, plant, and equipment should be recognized as assets when it is probable that the future economic benefit associated with these assets will flow to the enterprise and that their cost can be reliably measured. Under these circumstances, the initial measurement of the value of the asset is defined as its cost. Subsequently, the stated preferred treatment is to depreciate the asset's historical cost; however, an allowed alternative treatment is to periodically revalue the asset to its fair market value. When such revaluations occur, increases in value are to be recorded in stockholders' equity unless a previously existing reevaluation surplus exists, whereas decreases are recorded as current-period expenses. In the event a revaluation is undertaken, the statement requires that the entire group of assets to which the revalued asset belongs also be revalued. Examples of groups of property, plant, and equipment assets are land, buildings, and machinery. Finally, the required disclosures for items of property, plant, and equipment include the measurement bases used for the assets, as well as a reconciliation of the beginning and ending balances to include disposals and acquisitions and any revaluation adjustments.

IAS No. 16 also requires companies to periodically review the carrying amounts of items of property, plant, and equipment to determine whether the recoverable amount of the asset has declined below its carrying amount. When such a decline has occurred, the carrying amount of the asset must be reduced to the recoverable amount, and this reduction is recognized as an expense in the current period. *IAS No. 16* also requires write-ups when the circumstances or events that led to write-downs cease to exist. This treatment contrasts to the requirements of *SFAS No. 144* (see FASB ASC 360-10), which prohibits recognition of subsequent recoveries.

With respect to depreciation, *IAS No. 16* indicated that the periodic charge should be allocated in a systematic basis over the asset's useful life and that the depreciation method selected should reflect the pattern in which the asset's economic benefits are consumed. Finally, the standard requires periodic review of the pattern of economic benefits consumed, and when a change in the pattern of benefits is in evidence, the method of depreciation must be changed to reflect this new pattern of benefits. Such changes in depreciation methods are to be accounted for as changes in accounting principles. This treatment differs substantially from U.S. GAAP, where the depreciation method selected is required only to be systematic and rational, and changes in depreciation methods are allowed only in unusual circumstances.

The major clarifications outlined in the revised *IAS No. 16* were as follows:

1. A components approach is required for depreciation. Under a components approach, each material component of a composite asset with different useful lives or different patterns of depreciation is accounted for separately for the purpose of depreciation and accounting for subsequent expenditure (including replacement and renewal).

2. The acquisition cost of property, plant, and equipment should include the amount of an *IAS No. 37* provision for the estimated cost of dismantling and removing the asset and restoring the site, including both provisions recognized when the asset is acquired and incremental provisions recognized while the asset is used. However, after a provision is recognized, an increase to the provision resulting from accretion of interest or a change in the discount rate will be charged to expense, not added to the asset cost.

3. Accounting for incidental revenue (and related expenses) during construction or development of an asset will depend on whether the incidental revenue is a necessary activity in bringing the asset to the location and working condition necessary for it to be capable of operating in the manner intended by management (including those to test whether the asset is functioning properly):

   i. Net sales proceeds received during activities necessary to bring the asset to the location and working condition necessary for it to be capable of operating properly are deducted from the cost of the asset.

   ii. Revenue and related expenses should be separately recognized for operations that occur in connection with construction or development of an asset but that are not necessary to bring the asset to the location and working condition necessary for it to be capable of operating properly.

4. Measurement of residual value is defined as the current prices for assets of a similar age and condition to the estimated age and condition of the asset when it reaches the end of its useful life.

5. Exchanges of similar items of property, plant, and equipment will be recorded at fair value, and gain or loss will be recognized, unless neither the fair value of the asset given up nor the fair value of the asset acquired can be measured reliably, in which case the cost of the acquired asset would be the carrying amount of the asset given up.

6. Subsequent expenditure is added to the carrying amount of an asset only if the expenditure increases the asset's future economic benefits above those reflected in its most recently assessed level of performance.

IAS No. 23 defines borrowing costs as interest on bank overdrafts and borrowings, amortization of discounts or premiums on borrowings, amortization of ancillary costs incurred in the arrangement of borrowings, finance charges on finance leases, and exchange differences on foreign currency borrowings where they are regarded as an adjustment to interest costs. The original standard allowed companies to choose between two methods of accounting for borrowing costs. Under the benchmark treatment, companies were required to recognize interest costs in the period in which they were incurred. Under the allowed alternative treatment, interest costs that are directly attributable to the acquisition, construction, or production of a qualifying asset are capitalized as part of that asset. The interest costs that were to be capitalized were the costs that could be avoided if the expenditure for the qualifying asset had not been made. In 2007, the IASB revised *IAS No. 23* as a result of its joint short-term convergence project with the FASB to reduce differences between IFRSs and U.S. GAAP. This revision removed a major difference between the original pronouncement and *SFAS No. 34*. The main change in the revised *IAS No. 23* is the removal of the option of immediately recognizing all borrowing costs as an expense, which was previously the benchmark treatment. The revised standard requires that an entity capitalize borrowing costs directly attributable to the acquisition, construction, or production of a qualifying asset as part of the cost of that asset, which was a permitted alternative treatment under the original *IAS 23*.

The purpose of *IAS No. 36* is to make sure that assets are carried at no more than their recoverable amount and to define how the recoverable amount is calculated. *IAS No. 36* requires an impairment loss to be recognized whenever the recoverable amount of an asset is less than its carrying amount (its book value). The recoverable amount of an asset is the higher of its net selling price and its value in use. Both are based on present-value calculations.

Net selling price is defined as the amount obtainable from the sale of an asset in an arm's-length transaction between knowledgeable willing parties, less the costs of disposal. *Value in use* is the amount obtainable from use of an asset until the end of its useful life and from its subsequent disposal. Value in use is calculated as the present value of estimated future cash flows. The discount rate should be a pretax rate that reflects current market assessments of the time value of money and the risks specific to the asset.

An impairment loss should be recognized as an expense in the income statement for assets carried at cost and treated as a revaluation decrease for assets carried at a revalued amount. An impairment loss should be reversed (and income recognized) when there has been a change in the estimates used to determine an asset's recoverable amount since the last impairment loss was recognized.

In determining value in use, an enterprise should use these two methods:

1. Cash flow projections based on reasonable and supportable assumptions that reflect the asset in its current condition and represent management's best estimate of the set of economic conditions that will exist over the remaining useful life of the asset (Estimates of future cash flows should include all estimated future cash inflows and cash outflows, except for cash flows from financing activities and income tax receipts and payments.)

2. A pretax discount rate that reflects current market assessments of the time value of money and the risks specific to the asset (The discount rate should not reflect risks for which the future cash flows have been adjusted.)

If an asset does not generate cash inflows that are largely independent of the cash inflows from other assets, an enterprise should determine the recoverable amount of the cash-generating unit to which the asset belongs. A cash-generating unit is the smallest identifiable group of assets that generates cash inflows that are largely independent of the cash inflows from other assets or group of assets.

Impairment losses recognized in prior years should be reversed if, and only if, there has been a change in the estimates used to determine recoverable amount since the last impairment loss was recognized. However, an impairment loss should be reversed only to the extent that the reversal does not increase the carrying amount of the asset above the carrying amount that would have been determined for the asset (net of amortization or depreciation) had no impairment loss been recognized. An impairment loss for goodwill should be reversed only if the specific external event that caused the recognition of the impairment loss reverses. A reversal of an impairment loss should be recognized as income in the income statement for assets carried at cost and treated as a revaluation increase for assets carried at revalued amount.

IFRS No. 5 establishes the accounting treatment for discontinued operations and long-term assets held for sale. The *IFRS No. 5* definition of discontinued operations is quite similar to the definition of discontinuing operations in originally contained in *IAS No. 35*. However, the timing of the classification now depends on when the discontinued operation satisfies the criteria to be classified as held for sale. The same requirement applies to noncurrent assets held for sale. Further, *IFRS No. 5* requires the results of discontinued operations to be presented as a single amount on the face of the income statement.

IFRS No. 5 also achieves substantial convergence with the accounting requirements originally outlined in *SFAS No. 144*, "Accounting for the Impairment or Disposal of Long-Lived Assets," with respect to the timing of the classification of operations as discontinued operations and their disclosure. With respect to long-lived assets that are not being disposed of, the impairment recognition and measurement standards in *SFAS No. 144* are significantly different from those in *IAS No. 36*, "Impairment of Assets." These differences are not currently being addressed in the short-term convergence project.

The following principles apply to measurement:

1. At the time of classification as held for sale. Immediately before the initial classification of the asset as held for sale, the carrying amount of the asset will be measured in accordance with applicable IFRSs.

2. After classification as held for sale. Noncurrent assets or disposal groups that are classified as held for sale are measured at the lower of carrying amount and fair value less costs to sell.

3. An impairment loss is recognized in the profit or loss for any initial and subsequent write-down of the asset or disposal group to fair value less costs to sell.

4. Assets carried at fair value before initial classification. For such assets, the requirement to deduct costs to sell from fair value will result in an immediate charge to profit or loss.

5. Subsequent increases in fair value. A gain for any subsequent increase in fair value less costs to sell of an asset can be recognized in the profit or loss to the extent that it is not in excess of the cumulative impairment loss that has been recognized in accordance with *IFRS No. 5* or previously in accordance with *IAS No. 36*.

Assets classified as held for sale, and the assets and liabilities included within a disposal group classified as held for sale, must be presented separately on the face of the balance sheet and are not depreciated.

The following disclosures are required:

1. Noncurrent assets classified as held for sale and the assets of a disposal group classified as held for sale must be disclosed separately from other assets in the balance sheet.

2. The liabilities of a disposal group classified as held for sale must also be disclosed separately from other liabilities in the balance sheet.

3. There are also several other additional disclosures, including a description of the nature of assets held and the facts and circumstances surrounding the sale.

Under the provisions of *IFRS No. 6*, exploration and evaluation assets are required to be measured initially at cost. The expenditures to be included in the cost of these assets are determined by the entity as a matter of accounting policy and should be applied consistently. In making this determination, the entity should consider the degree to which the expenditures can be associated with finding specific mineral resources. *IFRS No. 6* cites the following as examples of expenditures that might be included in the initial measurement of exploration and evaluation assets: acquisition of rights to explore; topographical, geological, geochemical, and geophysical studies; exploratory drilling; trenching; sampling; and activities in relation to evaluating the technical feasibility and commercial viability of extracting a mineral resource. Where an entity incurs obligations for removal and restoration as a consequence of having undertaken the exploration for and evaluation of mineral resources, those obligations are to be recognized in accordance with the requirements of *IAS No. 37*, "Provisions, Contingent Liabilities, and Contingent Assets."

After initial recognition, entities can apply either the cost model or the revaluation model to exploration and evaluation assets. Where the revaluation model is selected, the rules of *IAS No. 16* are applied to exploration and evaluation assets classified as tangible assets, and the rules of *IAS No. 38*, "Intangible Assets," are applied to those classified as intangible assets.

Additionally, because of the difficulty in obtaining the information necessary to estimate future cash flows from exploration and evaluation assets, *IFRS 6* modifies the rules of *IAS No. 36* as regards the circumstances in which such assets are required to be assessed for impairment. A detailed impairment test is required in two circumstances:

1. When the technical feasibility and commercial viability of extracting a mineral resource become demonstrable, at which point the asset falls outside the scope of *IFRS No. 6* and is reclassified in the financial statements

2. When facts and circumstances suggest that the asset's carrying amount may exceed its recoverable amount

Cases

• Case 9-1 Donated Assets

The City of Martinsville donated land to Essex Company. The fair value of the land was $100,000. The land had cost the city $45,000.

Required:

a. Describe the current accounting treatment for the land. Include in your answer the amount at which the land would be valued by Essex Company and any other income statement or balance sheet effect.

b. Under the recommendations outlined in *SFAS No. 116* (see FASB ASC 720), the FASB required that donated assets be recorded at fair value and that revenue be recognized equivalent to the amount recorded for a donation.

   i. Defend the FASB's position. In your answer, refer to the conceptual framework.

   ii. Criticize the FASB's position. In your answer, refer to the conceptual framework.

c. Assume that immediately before the donation, Essex had assets totaling $800,000 and liabilities totaling $350,000. Compare the financial statement effects of the FASB requirement with previous practice. For example, how would EPS or ratios such as debt to equity be affected?

• Case 9-2 Purchase of Assets

On October 10, 2010, Mason Engineering Company completed negotiations on a contract for the purchase of new equipment. Under the terms of the agreement, the equipment may be purchased now or Mason may wait until January 10, 2011, to make the purchase. The cost of the equipment is $400,000. It will be financed by a note bearing interest at the market rate. Straight-line depreciation over a 10-year life will be used for book purposes. A double-declining balance over seven years will be used for tax purposes. (One-half year of depreciation will be taken in the year of purchase regardless of the date of purchase.)

Required:

a. Discuss the financial statement impacts of postponing the purchase of the equipment. Would the market price of the firm's common stock be affected by any or all of these impacts? Do not assume in your discussion that the postponement will affect revenues or any operating costs other than depreciation.

b. Discuss any cash flow impacts related to postponing the purchase of the equipment.

c. Efficient markets assume that stockholder wealth is affected by the amount and timing of cash flows. Which alternative is more favorable to them: purchasing before year-end or waiting until January? Explain your answer.

• Case 9-3 Depreciation Accounting

Depreciation continues to be one of the most controversial, difficult, and important problem areas in accounting.

Required:

a. Explain the conventional accounting concept of depreciation accounting.

b. Discuss its conceptual merit with respect to

i. the value of the asset

ii. the charge(s) to expense

iii. the discretion of management in selecting the method

c. Explain the factors that should be considered when applying the conventional concept of depreciation to the determination of how the value of a newly acquired computer system should be assigned to expense for financial reporting purposes (ignore income tax considerations).

d. What depreciation methods might be used for the computer system? Describe the advantages and disadvantages of each.

• Case 9-4 Self-Constructed Assets

Jay Manufacturing, Inc. began operations five years ago producing the probo, a new type of instrument it hoped to sell to doctors, dentists, and hospitals. The demand for probos far exceeded initial expectations, and the company was unable to produce enough probos to meet that demand. Jay was manufacturing probos on equipment it built at the start of its operations, but it needed more efficient equipment to meet demand. Company management decided to design and build the equipment, because no equipment currently available on the market was suitable for producing probos.

In 2010, a section of the plant was devoted to development of the new equipment and a special staff of personnel was hired. Within six months, a machine was developed at a cost of $170,000 that increased production and reduced labor cost substantially. Sparked by the success of the new machine, the company built three more machines of the same type at a cost of $80,000 each.

Required:

a. In addition to satisfying a need that outsiders cannot meet within the desired time, what other reasons might cause a firm to construct fixed assets for its own use?

b. In general, what costs should be capitalized for a self-constructed asset?

c. Discuss the appropriateness (give pros and cons) of including these charges in the capitalized cost of self-constructed assets:

   i. The increase in overhead caused by the self-construction of fixed assets

   ii. A proportionate share of overhead on the same basis as that applied to goods manufactured for sale (Consider whether the company is at full capacity.)

d. Discuss the proper accounting treatment of the $90,000 ($170,000 − $80,000) by which the cost of the first machine exceeded the cost of the subsequent machines.

• Case 9-5 Accounting for Land

Your client found three suitable sites, each having certain unique advantages, for a new plant. To thoroughly investigate the advantages and disadvantages of each site, one-year options were purchased for an amount equal to 5 percent of the contract price of each site. The costs of the options cannot be applied against the contracts. Before the options expire, one of the sites was purchased at the contract price of $60,000. The option on this site had cost $3,000. The two options not exercised had cost $3,500 each.

a. $60,000

b. $63,000

c. $70,000

• Case 9-6 Depreciation Accounting

Property, plant, and equipment (plant assets) generally represent a material portion of the total assets of most companies. Accounting for the acquisition and usage of such assets is therefore an important part of the financial reporting process.

Required:

a. Distinguish between revenue and capital expenditures, and explain why this distinction is important.

b. Briefly define depreciation as used in accounting.

c. Identify the factors that are relevant in determining the annual depreciation, and explain whether these factors are determined objectively or whether they are based on judgment.

d. Explain why depreciation is shown as an adjustment to cash in the operations section on the statement of cash flows.

• Case 9-7 Accounting for Land and Plant Assets

A company may acquire plant assets (among other ways) for cash, on a deferred payment plan, by exchanging other assets, or by a combination of these ways.

Required:

a. Identify six costs that should be capitalized as the cost of the land. For your answer, assume that land with an existing building is acquired for cash and that the existing building is to be removed in the immediate future so that a new building can be constructed on the site.

b. At what amount should a company capitalize a plant asset acquired on a deferred payment plan?

c. In general, at what amount should plant assets received in exchange for other nonmonetary assets be recorded? Specifically, at what amount should a company record a new machine acquired by exchanging an older, similar machine and paying cash? Would your answer be the same if cash were received?

• Case 9-8 Acquisition and Sale of Plant Assets

George Company purchased land for use as its corporate headquarters. A small factory that was on the land when it was purchased was torn down before construction of the office building began. Furthermore, a substantial amount of rock blasting and removal had to be done to the site before construction of the building foundation began. Because the office building was set back on the land far from the public road, George had the contractor construct a paved road from the public road to the parking lot of the office building.

Three years after the office building was occupied, George added four stories to the office building. The four stories had an estimated useful life of five years more than the remaining estimated life of the original building.

Ten years later, the land and buildings were sold at an amount more than their net book value, and George had a new office building constructed in another state for use as its new corporate headquarters.

Required:

a. Which of the preceding expenditures should be capitalized? How should each be depreciated or amortized? Discuss the rationale for your answers.

b. How would the sale of the land and building be accounted for? Include in your answer how to determine the net book value at the date of sale. Discuss the rationale for your answer.

• Case 9-9 Accounting for Property, Plant, and Equipment

Among the principal topics related to the accounting for the property, plant, and equipment of a company are acquisitions and retirements.

Required:

a. What expenditures should be capitalized when equipment is acquired for cash?

b. Assume the market value of equipment is not determinable by reference to a similar purchase for cash. Describe how the acquiring company should determine the capitalized cost of equipment purchased by exchanging it for each of the following:

   i. Bonds having an established market price

   ii. Common stock not having an established market price

   iii. Similar equipment not having a determinable market price

c. Describe the factors that determine whether expenditures relating to property, plant, and equipment already in use should be capitalized.

d. Describe how to account for the gain or loss on the sale of property, plant, or equipment.

• Case 9-10 Environmental Costs

Joe Mason acquired land on which he will construct a new restaurant. A chemical plant had once occupied the site. Government regulations require Mason to clean up the chemical residue before building. The cost of the cleanup is material.

Required:

a. Under current GAAP, an asset is charged with historical cost, which includes the purchase price and all costs incident to getting the asset ready for its intended use. Defend the historical cost principle. Use the conceptual framework concepts and definitions in your defense.

b. How should Joe treat the cost of the cleanup? Is it a land cost, a building cost, or an expense? Explain.

• Case 9-11 Cost Allocation

Keeping an asset implies reinvestment in the asset. Finance theory is consistent with the notion that reinvestment is at current value, or replacement cost. Such a decision is presumably based on comparing expected future cash flows that will be generated by the asset and the cost of replacing it with a new one that may generate the same or different cash flows.

According to the conceptual framework, the purpose of financial statements is to provide information regarding performance. Investment or reinvestment decisions are a part of that performance. Yet, the historical cost of fixed assets is retained and allocated over subsequent accounting periods.

Required:

a. Present arguments in favor of cost allocation.

b. Does cost allocation provide relevant information?

c. Would a current-value approach to measurement of fixed assets be preferable? Why?

d. Would a current-value approach be consistent with the physical capital maintenance concept? Explain.

e. What problems and limitations are associated with using replacement cost for fixed assets?

FASB ASC Research

For each of the following research cases, search the FASB ASC database for information to address the issues. Cut and paste the FASB paragraphs that support your responses. Then summarize briefly what your responses are, citing the pronouncements and paragraphs used to support your responses.

• FASB ASC 9-1 Depreciation

Several pronouncements by authoritative accounting bodies deal with depreciation. List the pronouncements dealing with depreciation. What is the FASB's current definition of depreciation?

• FASB ASC 9-2 Asset Impairment Obligations

Several FASB statements dealt with the topic of asset impairments. List the FASB statements that dealt with asset impairments and summarize them. Several EITF documents provide additional guidance on implementing the FASB standards. List the implementation issues discussed in the EITF releases.

• FASB ASC 9-3 Asset Retirement Obligations

SFAS No. 144 dealt with asset retirement obligations. Provide a summary of this statement. Additionally, list the implementation issues addressed by the EITF for asset retirement obligations.

• FASB ASC 9-4 Disclosure of Depreciation

The FASB ASC requires the disclosure of certain information pertaining to depreciation. Search the FASB ASC to find these requirements. Cite the appropriate paragraphs and summarize your finding.

• FASB ASC 9-5 Overhaul Costs in the Airline Industry

Overhaul costs are a significant aspect of accounting for property, plant, and equipment in the airline industry. Search the FASB ASC to find a definition of overhaul cost in the airline industry. What two methods of accounting for overhaul cost are defined in the FASB ASC? Be sure to cite the appropriate FASB ASC paragraphs.

Room for Debate

• Debate 9-1 Capitalization of Interest

According to *SFAS No. 34*, interest on self-constructed assets should be capitalized.

Team Debate:

Team 1: Present arguments in favor of capitalizing interest. Tie your arguments to the concepts and definitions found in the conceptual framework.

Team 2: Criticize the provisions of *SFAS No. 34*. Present arguments against capitalizing interest. Tie your arguments to the concepts and definitions found in the conceptual framework. (Finance theory would say that interest is a return to the capital provider, the lender. Finance theory may assist you in your argument.)

• Debate 9-2 Donated Assets

Under current GAAP, assets that have been donated to a company are recorded at fair value.

Team Debate:

Team 1:   Argue that donated assets should not be reported in a company's balance sheet. Base your arguments on the conceptual framework. You might find the historical cost principle useful in your discussion.

Team 2:   Argue in favor of the current GAAP treatment for donated assets. Base your arguments on the conceptual framework, where appropriate

Long-Term Assets II:

Investments and

Intangibles

Companies invest in the securities of other business entities for a variety of reasons such as obtaining additional income, creating desirable relationships with suppliers, obtaining partial or full control over related companies, or adding new products. The decision to classify these investments as long term rather than as current assets is based on the concept of *managerial intent*. When management intends to use the securities for long-term purposes, they are separately classified on the balance sheet as long-term investments rather than as temporary investments.

As discussed in Chapter 6, the balance sheet category of investments includes investments in equity and debt securities of other business entities, assets not currently in use, and special funds. This chapter discusses investments in equity and debt securities. Detailed discussion of equity investments is to those that do not result in consolidated financial statements. The topic of intangible assets is also addressed.

Investments in Equity Securities

The term *equity security* is defined in *SFAS No. 115* (see FASB ASC 320-10-20) as:

> Any security representing an ownership interest in an enterprise (for example, common, preferred, or other capital stock) or the right to acquire (for example, warrants, rights, and call options) or dispose of (for example, put options) an ownership interest in an enterprise at fixed or determinable prices.[1]

Equity securities do not include redeemable preferred stock or convertible bonds.

---

1. *Statement of Financial Accounting Standards No. 115*, "Accounting for Certain Investments in Debt and Equity Securities" (Stamford, CT: Financial Accounting Standards Board, 1993), para. 137.

Equity securities may be acquired on an organized stock exchange, over the counter, or by direct sale. In addition, warrants, rights, and options may be attached to other securities (bonds or preferred stock), or they may be received from the issuer, cost free, to enable the acquiring company or individual investor to maintain its present proportionate share of ownership.[2] The recorded cost of investments in equity securities includes the purchase price of the securities plus any brokerage fees, transfer costs, or taxes on transfer. When equity securities are obtained in a nonmonetary transaction, the recorded cost is based on the fair market value of the consideration given. If the fair market value of the consideration is unavailable, cost is based on the fair market value of the marketable equity security received.

Subsequent to acquisition, six methods of accounting and financial statement presentation are used under current generally accepted accounting principles (GAAP) for the various types of equity securities: (1) consolidation, (2) the equity method, (3) the cost method, (4) fair value accounting under *SFAS No. 115* (see FASB ASC 320), (5) the market value method, and (6) the fair value option under *SFAS No. 159* (see FASB ASC 825-10-10). Except for the fair value option, these methods are not alternatives for recording investments in equity securities. As a general rule, they are applied on the basis of the investee's percentage of ownership, taking into consideration the surrounding circumstances. Each method and the circumstances under which it is applicable are described in the following paragraphs. The fair value option may be selected for all equity investments except those that must be accounted for as consolidations. In addition to the above six accounting methods, we discuss the theoretical merits of another method that was required in the past: lower of cost or market.

Consolidation

Consolidated financial statements are required when an investor owns enough common stock to obtain control over the investee. *Control* was defined in *SFAS No. 94* as ownership of a majority voting interest (over 50 percent) unless the parent company is precluded from exercising control or unless control is temporary.[3] *Consolidation* requires that at the balance sheet date, the investment account (accounted for during the year under the equity method described below) be replaced by the assets and liabilities of the investee company. In the consolidation process the investee's assets, liabilities, and income statement accounts are consolidated with (added to) those of the controlling parent company. Consolidated financial statements are discussed in detail in Chapter 16.

The Equity Method

The *equity method* is used when an investor has the ability to significantly influence the financing and operating decisions of an investee, even though that investor holds less than 50 percent of the voting stock. Ability to exercise significant influence can be determined in a number of ways, including

- Representation on the board of directors
- Participation in policymaking processes

2. Allowing investors to maintain their proportionate share of ownership is one of the basic rights of common stock ownership. This is referred to as the preemptive right.

3. *Statement of Financial Accounting Standards No. 94*, "Consolidation of All Majority-Owned Subsidiaries" (Stamford, CT: FASB, 1988), para. 13.

- Material intercompany transactions
- Interchange of managerial personnel
- Technological dependency
- The percent of ownership the investor has in relation to other holdings[4]

Under the *equity method*, adjustments are made to the recorded cost of the investment to account for the profits and losses of the investee and for distributions of earnings. These adjustments are based on the investor's percentage of ownership of the investee. For example, if the investee reports a profit, the investor will report as income its pro rata ownership share of the investee profit and simultaneously increase the carrying value of the investment account by the same amount. Conversely, dividends received decrease in the carrying value of the investment account for the amount of the dividend received or receivable. Dividends are not reported as income, because the investor reports the income of the investee as the investee earns it. In other words, under the equity method, dividends are viewed as distributions of accumulated earnings. Because the accumulation of earnings increases the investment account, the distribution of earnings decreases the investment account. Consequently, the investment account represents the investee's equity in the investment.

The Committee on Accounting Procedure (CAP) originally described the equity method[5] in *ARB No. 51*, stating that it is the preferred method to account for unconsolidated subsidiaries.[6] In 1971, the Accounting Principles Board (APB) reported its conclusions on a study of accounting for long-term investments in stocks by issuing *APB Opinion No. 18*, "The Equity Method of Accounting for Investments in Common Stock"[7] (see FASB ASC 323). This opinion clarified the applicability of the equity method to investments of common stock in subsidiaries; however, it noted that the equity method is not a valid substitute for consolidation.[8]

Additionally, the Board noted that determining the investor's ability to influence the investee is not always clear; and "in order to achieve a reasonable degree of uniformity in application,"[9] an investment of 20 percent or more of the voting stock of the investee is deemed to constitute evidence of a presumption of the ability to exercise significant influence. Conversely, ownership of less than 20 percent of the voting stock leads to the presumption that the investor does not have significant influence unless an ability to exercise significant influence can be demonstrated.[10] Thus the APB concluded that significant influence is normally attained when an investor holds 20 percent or more of the voting stock of an investee unless the surrounding circumstances indicate otherwise.

4. Accounting Principles Board, *Opinion No. 18*, "The Equity Method of Accounting for Investments in Common Stock" (New York: AICPA, 1971). Para. 17 (see FASB ASC 323-10-15-6).

5. *ARB No. 51* did not refer to the equity method by name.

6. Committee on Accounting Procedure, *Accounting Research Bulletin No. 51*, "Consolidated Financial Statements" (New York: AICPA, 1959), para. 19. The APB reiterated this position in *APB Opinion No. 10*, "Omnibus Opinion of 1966" (para. 3), and referred to the procedure described in *ARB No. 51* as the equity method.

7. Accounting Principles Board, *Opinion No. 18*.

8. Ibid., para. 14.

9. Ibid.

10. Ibid.

On the other hand, not all investments of 20 percent or more are accounted for by using the equity method. *FASB Interpretation No. 35* (see FASB ASC 323-10-15-10) suggested that the following facts and circumstances might preclude an investor from using the equity method even if an investment of 20 percent or more is held:

- Opposition by the investee, such as litigation or complaints to governmental regulatory authorities, challenges the investor's ability to exercise significant influence.
- The investor and investee sign an agreement under which the investor surrenders significant rights as a shareholder.
- Majority ownership of the investee is concentrated among a small group of shareholders who operate the investee without regard to the views of the investor.
- The investor needs or wants more financial information to apply the equity method than is available to the investee's other shareholders (e.g., the investor wants quarterly financial information from an investee that publicly reports only annually), tries to obtain that information, and fails.
- The investor tries and fails to obtain representation on the investee's board of directors.[11]

The APB's decision to embrace the equity method was based on the objectives of accrual accounting—reporting transactions when they occur rather than as cash is collected or paid. When the investor can exercise significant influence over the investee, the results of operating decisions better reflect the periodic outcomes resulting from making the investment, rather than distributions of the investor's share of accumulated profits (which, in and of themselves, may be unrelated to performance). The Board apparently believed that the cash flow needs of investors and other users of financial information can be satisfied by the significant influence test and that reporting needs are of primary importance.

Despite some speculation at the time *APB Opinion No. 18* was issued that it might require fair value, *APB Opinion No. 18* did little to add to the acceptability of this approach. The use of fair value is a departure from the historical cost principle. The APB apparently was not prepared to take the radical step of endorsing a departure from historical cost even though the information needed to determine the fair values for most investments is readily available. However, the FASB reversed this position in *SFAS No. 115* (see FASB ASC 320) at least for certain equity investments, and now the fair value option may be selected under *SFAS No. 159* (see FASB ASC 825-10-10). The specifics of when and how to apply fair value accounting to investments are discussed later in the chapter.

The Cost Method

When there is a lack of significant influence or control, investments in common stocks may be accounted for under either the cost method or a fair value method. When the fair value option is not selected, or when there is no readily determinable market price for equity securities and neither the equity method nor consolidation is required, the cost method must be used.

11. *Interpretation No. 35*, "Criteria for Applying the Equity Method of Accounting for Investments in Common Stock" (Stamford, CT: FASB, 1981), para. 4.

Under the cost method, an investment in equity securities is carried at its historical cost. Dividends received or receivable are reported as revenue. The cost method can be criticized because it does not measure current fair value. Historical cost provides information relevant for determining recovery when the securities are acquired. Current fair market value would provide a similar measure for the current accounting period. If the purpose of financial statements is to provide investors, creditors, and other users with information useful in assessing future cash flows, the current assessment of recoverable amounts (current market values) would be relevant. Even for those equity securities that are not actively traded, an estimate of current fair value may be more relevant than cost.

The Lower of Cost or Market Method

In 1975, the FASB issued *SFAS No. 12* (since superseded). This release required that equity securities having readily determinable market values that were not accounted for under the equity method or consolidation be accounted for by applying lower of cost or market (LCM). Under *SFAS No. 12*, marketable equity securities were separated into current and long-term portfolios. Each portfolio was carried on the balance sheet at the lower of that portfolio's aggregate cost or market value. For temporary investments in marketable equity securities, unrealized losses in market value as well as any subsequent recoveries of those losses were recognized in the income statement. In contrast, for long-term investments in marketable equity securities, the cumulative effect of unrealized losses and loss recoveries was reported as negative stockholders' equity.

The FASB's advocacy of the LCM method in *SFAS No. 12* was not a strict departure from historical cost. Rather, it was simply further evidence of the overriding concern for conservatism (see Chapter 5 for a discussion of the concept of conservatism). LCM for marketable *equity* securities can be defended on the grounds that the recording of cost implies recovery of that cost. It is reasonable to assume that management would not invest in assets that are not recoverable. By the same token, when recovery has declined temporarily through decline in market value, it is reasonable to reduce the book value of assets to the lower market value.

The LCM method was criticized because it did not result in consistent treatment of all marketable equity securities. Gains were treated differently from losses, and temporary investments were treated differently from long-term investments with no rational explanation. Furthermore, it is inconsistent to recognize market value increases up to cost, but not to market. Opponents of *SFAS No. 12* argued that the consequent recognition of unrealized gains is so arbitrary that no recognition of these gains would be preferable.

Finally, the determination of LCM on an aggregate basis may be deceptive. Unrealized losses are offset against unrealized gains. In a subsequent period when a security was sold, prior cumulative unrecognized gains and losses were recognized, causing a mismatching of gain and loss recognition for the period in which it actually occurred.

The Fair Value Method under *SFAS No. 115*

SFAS No. 115, "Accounting for Certain Investments in Debt and Equity Securities" (see FASB ASC 320), describes the current GAAP for equity securities that have readily determinable fair values and that are not subject to the equity method under *APB Opinion No. 18* or to consolidation.[12] It has been modified by *SFAS No. 159* (see FASB ASC 825-10-10) as described in the subsequent section. According to *SFAS No. 115*, the fair value of an equity security is readily determinable if

- The sales prices or bid-ask quotations are currently available on a securities exchange registered with the Securities and Exchange Commission (SEC) or in the over-the-counter market when they are publicly reported by the National Association of Securities Dealers Automated Quotations systems or by the National Quotation Bureau.
- The security is traded only in foreign markets, and if the foreign market is of a breadth and scope comparable to one of the U.S. markets mentioned above.
- The investment is in a mutual fund that has a fair value per share (unit) that is published and is the basis for current transactions.[13]

Under the *SFAS No. 115* fair value method, at acquisition, equity securities are classified as either trading or available for sale. As discussed in Chapter 8, *trading securities* are defined as "securities that are bought and held principally for the purpose of selling them in the near term (thus held for only a short period of time)."[14] Trading securities are actively and frequently bought and sold, generally with the objective of generating profits from short-term price movements. *Available-for-sale securities* are those equity securities having readily determinable market prices that are not considered trading securities.[15] All trading securities are classified as current assets. Available-for-sale securities are classified as current or long term depending on whether they meet the *ARB No. 43* definition of current assets. Accordingly, these securities should be classified as current if they are reasonably expected to be realized in cash or sold or consumed during the normal operating cycle of the business or one year, whichever is longer. All other available-for-sale securities should be classified as long-term investments.

At each balance sheet date, current and long-term equity securities subject to the *SFAS No. 115* provisions are reported at fair value. Unrealized holding gains and losses for available-for-sale securities are excluded from earnings. The cumulative unrealized holding gains and losses for these securities should be reported as a separate component of accumulated other comprehensive income. Dividend income for available-for-sale securities will continue to be included in earnings.

When an equity security is transferred from the trading to the available-for-sale category or vice versa, the transfer is accounted for at the security's fair value on the date of transfer. In these cases, the treatment of unrealized holding gains is as follows:

- For a transfer from trading to available for sale, the unrealized holding gain or loss is recognized in income up to the date of transfer. It is not reversed.
- For a transfer from available for sale to trading, the unrecognized holding gain or loss at the date of transfer is reported immediately in earnings.[16]

---

12. *Statement of Financial Accounting Standards No. 115*, "Accounting for Certain Investments in Debt and Equity Securities" (Stamford, CT: FASB, 1993). (See FASB ASC 320-10-20.)

13. Ibid., para. 3 (see FASB ASC 320-10-20).

14. Ibid., para. 12 (see FASB ASC 320-10-20).

15 Ibid. (see FASB ASC 320-10-20).

16. Ibid., para. 15 (see FASB ASC 320-10-35-10).

The FASB's primary impetus for requiring fair value accounting for investments in equity securities is relevance. The advocates of fair value accounting for investments in equity securities believe that fair value is useful in assisting investors, creditors, and other users in evaluating the performance of the accounting entity's investing strategies. According to *SFAC No. 1*, users of financial information are interested in assessing the amount, timing, and risk associated with expected net cash inflows to the enterprise. These assessments aid users in evaluating the potential outcome of their own personal investing strategies because the expected cash flows to the enterprise are the main source of expected cash flows from the enterprise to them. Fair value is market determined. It reflects the market consensus regarding the expected future resource flows of a security discounted by the current interest rate adjusted for the risk associated with that security.

In addition, the fair value method partially eliminates the inequitable treatment that *SFAS No. 12* afforded to gains and losses. All unrealized gains and unrealized losses are now treated the same for asset valuation purposes. For trading securities, the gains and losses are recognized in the periods when they occur; for these assets, the method is consistent with other accrual accounting requirements. It is also consistent with the *SFAC No. 6* definition of comprehensive income, because comprehensive income is based on changes in net assets and would include changes in the market values of assets. For trading securities, no further masking of gains against losses that occurred under the aggregate valuation approach of *SFAS No. 12*.

However, inconsistent income statement treatment for equity securities will continue. Unrealized gains and losses for available-for-sale securities are not recognized in earnings until they are reclassified as trading securities and sold. Thus, for these securities, there is no accrual accounting-based matching of market gains and losses in the period when they are incurred. The result is a distortion of reported earnings.

Finally, the readily determinable criterion precludes fair value accounting for those securities that are not actively traded—a criticism that is alleviated when investors elect the fair value option offered by *SFAS No. 159*. Some advocates of fair value argue that for securities not included within the scope of *SFAS No. 115*, reporting other estimates of fair value would be more meaningful than historical cost. Nevertheless, by limiting the scope of fair value accounting for investments in equity securities to those whose fair values are readily determinable in the securities market, the market-based measures provided under *SFAS No. 115* are reliable. They do not rely on imprecise measures that subjective judgments regarding market values would entail.

The Market Value Method

SFAS No. 115 excludes investments that are already accounted for using the market value method. As with the fair value method, the market value method follows the cost method by recognizing income when dividends are received. However, under the market value method, all equity securities that are neither consolidated nor reported as equity method investments are treated the same way with respect to reporting unrealized gains and losses. All unrealized gains and losses are recognized in earnings; none are included as a component of other comprehensive income. As with trading securities, all upward and downward changes in market value of the investment shares are reported as income or losses, and changes in the market value of the investment require adjustment to the carrying value of the investment.

Thus, the market value method is analogous to the fair value method for trading securities described above. It has become accepted industry practice for certain industries, such as mutual funds, where it has attained the status of GAAP.

Exhibit 10.1 summarizes the approaches that are considered current GAAP for investments in equity securities.

EXHIBIT 10.1   *Accounting for Investments in Equity Securities*

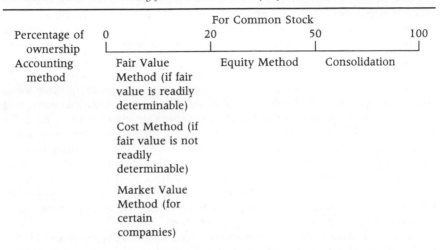

Recent Developments

On May 26, 2010, the FASB issued a proposed Accounting Standards Update, *Accounting for Financial Instruments and Revisions to the Accounting for Derivative Instruments and Hedging Activities (PASU)*, outlining a proposed approach to financial instrument classification and measurement based on their characteristics and how assets are used in the business. The PASC would require

- Classification to be determined at acquisition or issuance; with reclassification not permitted.

- Financial assets that have variable cash flows or that are regularly traded to be accounted for at fair value, with value changes reflected in net income (regardless of business strategy). This would include all derivatives.

- Changes in the fair value of equity securities, certain hybrid instruments, and financial instruments that can be contractually prepaid in such a way that the holder would not recover substantially all of its investment to be recognized in net income each reporting period (regardless of business strategy).

- For financial assets that are held for the collection of cash:
  - Both amortized cost and fair value measures would be presented in the balance sheet.
  - Fair value changes arising from interest accruals, credit impairments and reversals, and realized gains and losses would be recognized in net income.
  - Other FV changes would be recognized in other comprehensive income.

Financial assets for which other comprehensive income treatment or amortized cost is elected would be subject to a single credit impairment model. A credit impairment would be recognized in net income when an entity does not expect to collect all of the contractually promised cash flows. An entity no longer would wait for a probable event to recognize a loss; instead, it would need to consider the impact of past events and existing conditions on the collectability of contractual cash flows over the remaining life of the asset(s) without regard to the probability threshold. The proposal provides latitude in measuring credit impairment, including whether on an individual asset or pooled basis. An entity would determine its best estimate of the amount of credit impairment at the end of each reporting period.

The Fair Value Option

SFAS No. 159, "The Fair Value Option for Financial Assets and Financial Liabilities," permits companies to measure most financial assets and liabilities that are recognized in financial statements at fair value. Companies may not opt for fair value reporting for the following financial items: investments that must be consolidated, assets and obligations representing postretirement benefits, leases, demand deposits reported by banks, and financial instruments classified as components of stockholder's equity. The objective of the fair value option is "to improve financial reporting by providing entities with an opportunity to mitigate volatility in reported earnings caused by measuring related assets and liabilities differently without having to apply complex hedge accounting."[17] However, since the pronouncement is not limited to related assets and liabilities, it is apparent that the FASB is attempting to broaden the use of fair value accounting to areas where it was not previously allowed, most notably to liabilities.

The long-standing GAAP rule under the historical cost model has been to capitalize as historical cost all costs associated with the acquisition of an asset. Moreover, GAAP for debt instruments has been to defer up-front costs associated with their issuance. *SFAS No. 159* changed these rules for those assets and liabilities within its scope. It requires that up-front cost related to items for which the fair value option is elected be expensed as incurred and not deferred.

The election to opt for fair value reporting may be applied by instrument. It may be elected for a single eligible debt or equity security without electing it for other identical items. Moreover, the option need not be applied to all instruments issued or acquired in a single transaction. An exception to being able to apply by instrument is that when electing fair value for an investment that would otherwise be accounted for under the equity method, the investor must apply fair value to all financial interests in the same entity, including its eligible debt and equity instruments.

Election to opt for fair value for a reporting must be made only on one of the following election dates:[18]

- The investor first recognizes the eligible item.
- Financial assets that are reported at fair value under specialized accounting rules cease to quality for the specialized accounting.
- The accounting treatment for the financial instrument changes, such as an investment that becomes subject to the equity method.
- The date of the adoption of *SFAS No. 159*.

17. *SFAS No. 159*, para. 1.

18. Eligible items also include firm commitments and insurance company riders, which are not discussed here (see FASB ASC 825-10-25-4).

Once the fair value option has been made for a financial instrument, it is irrevocable unless a new election date occurs.

After making the fair value election, all subject items are reported in the balance sheet at fair value. Fair value is to be measured using exit prices on the balance sheet date. *SFAS No. 159* defined fair value as the price that the reporting entity would receive to sell an asset or pay to transfer a liability in an orderly transaction between market participants. All unrealized holding gains and losses are to be reported in earnings.

The reporting entity must separately disclose assets and liabilities pursuant to electing fair value in a manner that clearly separates them from the carrying values of other assets and liabilities, either parenthetically by a single line that includes both values or on separate lines in the balance sheet. Moreover, if the fair value option is elected for available-for-sale and/or held-to-maturity securities when *SFAS No. 159* (see FASB ASC 825-10) is adopted, these investments are to be reported as trading securities. The cumulative effect of the gains and losses for these securities is to be reported as an adjustment to retained earnings.

Investments in Debt Securities

Investments in debt securities, such as bonds or government securities, for which the fair value option is not elected are initially recorded at cost, including up-front cost to acquire the securities. Typically, the purchase price of a debt instrument differs from its face value. This difference reflects the fluctuations in market interest rates that have occurred since the time the debt instrument was initially offered for sale to the present. Thus, debt instruments are usually sold at a premium or discount (for a detailed discussion of how the amount of a bond premium or discount is determined and how this affects interest, see Chapter 11). The *SFAS No. 115* accounting guidelines also apply to all investments in debt securities. Before the issuance of *SFAS No. 115*, all debt securities that were classified as long term were accounted for by amortizing the premium or discount over the term of the bond, regardless of the intent or ability of the investing entity to hold the investment to maturity or whether the investment had a readily determinable fair value. Regulators and others expressed concerns that the recognition and measurement of investments in debt securities, particularly those held by financial institutions, should better reflect the intent of the investor to hold, make available to sell, or trade these securities. Moreover, the provisions of *SFAS No. 12* did not apply to investments in debt securities. Some companies applied LCM debt securities; others accounted for them under the cost method. The result was that the accounting treatment for these securities was inconsistent from one entity to the next, thus making it difficult to compare their performance across companies.

SFAS No. 115 required that at acquisition, individual investments in debt securities be classified as trading, available for sale, or held to maturity (see FASB 320-10-25-1). Debt securities classified as trading or available for sale are to be treated in the same manner as equity securities that are similarly classified. That is, the fair value method described above for trading and available-for-sale equity securities also applies to trading and available-for-sale debt securities. Thus, the discussion that follows is limited to those debt securities classified as held to maturity.

Debt instruments must be classified as *held to maturity* "only if the reporting enterprise has the positive intent and ability to hold those securities to maturity."[19]

---

19. Ibid., para. 7 (see FASB 320-10-25-3).

Debt securities that are classified as held to maturity must be measured at *amortized cost*. When these debt securities are sold at a premium or discount, the total interest income to the investing enterprise over the life of the debt instrument from acquisition to maturity is affected by the amount of the premium or discount. Measurement at amortized cost means that the premium or discount is amortized each period to calculate interest income (Chapter 11 illustrates how a premium or discount affects interest over the life of a bond). Amortization of the premium or discount is treated as an adjustment to interest income and to the investment account.

Two methods of debt premium or discount amortization are considered GAAP: straight-line and effective interest. Under the *straight-line* method, the premium or discount is divided by the number of periods remaining in the life of the debt issue. In each subsequent period, an equal amount of premium or discount is written off as an interest income adjustment. The rationale underlying the use of the straight-line method is its ease of computation and the belief that its use results in premium or discount amortization amounts that are not materially different from the amounts resulting from the use of other measurement methods.

When the *effective interest* method is used to measure interest income, the market rate of interest on the debt instrument at the time the investment is acquired is applied to the carrying value of the investment at the beginning of each interest period. This step determines the amount of interest income for that period. Using the effective interest method reflects the fact that the investor earns a uniform rate of return over the life of the investment. Thus, the use of this method is based on the belief that the investment was acquired at a certain yield and that the financial statements issued in subsequent periods should reflect the effects of that decision.

When it is evident that the investor has changed intent to hold a debt security to maturity, the security is transferred to either the trading or the available-for-sale category. The transfer is accounted for at fair value. If the security is transferred to the trading category, the unrealized gain or loss at the date of transfer is recognized in income. If the security is transferred to the available-for-sale category, the unrealized gain or loss at the date of transfer is recognized as a component of other comprehensive income. When a change from the available-for-sale category to the held-to-maturity category occurs, the amount of accumulated unrealized holding gains and losses that exists at the date of transfer will continue to be included as a component of other comprehensive income, which is reported in the stockholders' equity section of the balance sheet, and that amount will be amortized over the remaining life of the debt security as an adjustment to interest income. The effect of this treatment is that interest income each period will be what it would have been under the amortized cost method, but the carrying value of the debt security on the balance sheet in subsequent periods will reflect the amortized market value at the date of transfer, rather than amortized cost.

According to *SFAS No. 115*, a change in circumstances may result in the change of intent to hold a debt security to maturity, but it may not call into question the classification of other debt as held to maturity if the change in circumstances is caused by one or more of the following:

1. Evidence of significant deterioration in the issuer's creditworthiness

2. A tax law change that eliminates or reduces the tax-exempt status of interest on the debt security

3. A major business combination or disposition (such as sale of a segment of the business) that necessitates the sale or transfer of the debt security in order to maintain the enterprise's existing interest rate risk position or credit risk policy

4. A change in statutory or regulatory requirements that significantly modifies either what constitutes a permissible investment or the maximum level of investment that the enterprise can hold in certain kinds of securities

5. A change in regulatory requirements that significantly increases the enterprise's industry capital requirements that causes the enterprise to downsize

6. A significant increase in the risk weights of debt securities used for regulatory risk-based capital purposes[20]

A debt security should not be classified as held to maturity if the enterprise intends to hold the security for an indefinite period. An indefinite holding period is presumed if, for example, the debt security would be available to be sold in response to these conditions:

1. Changes in market interest rates and related changes in the security's prepayment risk

2. Needs for liquidity (e.g., for financial institutions, the withdrawal of deposits or the increased demand for loans; and for insurance companies, the surrender of insurance policies or the payment of insurance claims)

3. Changes in the availability and yield on alternative investments

4. Changes in funding sources and terms

5. Changes in foreign currency risk[21]

SFAS No. 115 addressed issues concerning the relevance of fair value to investors, creditors, and other users. However, in allowing the continued use of amortized cost for debt securities that are intended to be held to maturity, it did not address concerns that the use of the amortized cost method permits the recognition of holding gains through the selective sale of appreciated debt instruments recorded at amortized cost at the date of sale. This affords management the opportunity to engage in gains trading and to selectively manage reported earnings. Moreover, it did not address the criticism that accounting for debt securities is based on management's plan for holding or disposing of the investment, rather than on the characteristics of the asset itself. In allowing three distinct categories, the same company could conceivably give three different accounting treatments to three otherwise identical debt securities. Critics argue that these issues can be resolved only by reporting all debt and equity securities that have determinable fair values at fair value and by including all unrealized gains and losses in earnings as they occur.

The FASB countered that the procedures outlined in *SFAS No. 115* reflect the economic consequences of events and transactions. The FASB's logic for this contention is as follows. The reporting requirements better reflect the manner in which enterprises manage their investments and the impact of economic events on the overall enterprise. Moreover, the following disclosure requirements should provide fair value information that should prove useful to investor decision making in addition to the reporting requirements outlined above. For securities classified as available for sale and separately for securities classified as held to maturity, the enterprise is to report:

- Aggregate fair value
- Gross unrealized holding gains

---

20. Ibid., para 8 (see FASB ASC 320-10-25-6).
21. Ibid., para. 9 (see FASB ASC 320-10-25-4).

- Gross unrealized holding losses
- The amortized cost basis by major security type

Permanent Decline in Fair Value

When a decline in the fair value of a long-term investment that is classified as available for sale is determined to be other than temporary, an *other-than-temporary impairment* is considered to have occurred. In this case the investment account balance for the security is written down to fair value, a loss is included in earnings, and a new cost basis is established. The new cost basis for recognition of gain or loss on reclassification or sale will not be adjusted for subsequent recoveries of the recognized loss. All subsequent increases in fair value will be reported as components of other comprehensive income, in the same manner as subsequent unrealized losses.[22] Similar treatment is given for other-than-permanent declines in investments in debt securities that are classified as held to maturity.

Impairment of Investments in Unsecuritized Debt

Investments in unsecuritized debt, for example mortgages, are subject to the provisions of *SFAS No. 114*, "Accounting by Creditors for Impairment of Loans."[23] Loans are "impaired when, based on current information and events, it is probable that a creditor will be unable to collect all amounts due according to the contractual terms of the loan agreement," including interest.[24] To reiterate, in these cases, impairment is measured based on the present value of expected future cash flows discounted at the loan's effective interest rate as determined at the origin or acquisition of the loan. Alternatively, impairment may be measured using the market price for the loan or, if the loan is collateralized, the fair value of the collateral. If the resulting measurement of impairment is less than the carrying value of the loan (including interest and unamortized loan fees, premium or discount), the impairment is recognized by creating a valuation allowance and making a corresponding charge to bad debt expense.

In subsequent accounting periods, for those impairments that were calculated by discounting cash flows, impairment is remeasured to reflect any significant changes (positive or negative) in the cash-flow expectations used to calculate the original loan impairment. For those impairments that were measured using fair values, similar remeasurements are made to reflect subsequent significant changes in fair value. However, the loan carrying value may not be written up to a value that exceeds the recorded investment in the loan. For balance sheet purposes, the changes are reflected in the valuation allowance account.

For income statement purposes, changes in the present value of the expected future cash flows of an impaired loan may be treated in one of two ways:

1. Increases that are attributable to the passage of time are reported as interest income; the balance of the change in present value is an adjustment to bad debt expense.
2. The entire change in present value is reported as an adjustment to bad debt expense.[25]

---

22. Ibid., para. 16 (see FASB ASC 320-10-35-30).
23. *Statement of Financial Accounting Standards No. 114*, "Accounting by Creditors for Impairment of a Loan" (Stamford, CT: FASB, 1993). (See FASB ASC 310-10-35.)
24. Ibid., para. 8 (see FASB ASC 310-10-35-2.)
25. Ibid., para. 17 (see FASB ASC 310-10-35-40).

At each balance sheet date, the following disclosures are required:

1. The recorded investment in the impaired loans
2. The beginning and ending balance in the allowance account and the activity occurring during the period in that account
3. The income recognition policy, including the amount of interest income recognized due to changes in the present value of the impaired loan[26]

SFAS No. 114 is intended to address whether present-value measures should be used to measure loan impairment. The pronouncement clarifies present GAAP for loan impairments by specifying that both principal and interest receivable should be considered when calculating loan impairment. The prescribed measurement methods should reflect the amount that is expected to be recovered by the creditor so that investors, creditors, and other users can better assess the amount and timing of future cash flows. The initial present value recorded for the loan reflected the expectations at that time regarding expected future cash flows. Because the loan was originally recorded at a discounted amount, ongoing assessment for impairment should be treated in a similar manner. The added uncertainty associated with expectations regarding the future cash flows from impaired loans should not preclude the use of discounted cash flows. The impairment represents deterioration in quality as reflected in the change in cash-flow expectations. Thus the impairment itself does not indicate that a new loan has replaced the old one. Rather, the old loan is continuing, but expectations about future cash flows have changed; consequently, the contractual effective interest rate is the appropriate rate to discount those cash flows.

Critics argue that the effect of impairment is a change in the character of the loan that should be measured directly. If so, the contractual effective interest rate is no longer relevant. The most desirable direct measure of an impaired loan is fair value. If no market value exists, the creditor should discount the expected future cash flows using an interest rate that is commensurate with the risk involved. Moreover, allowing the use of a fair value alternative is inconsistent with requiring the original loan interest rate to be used when the discounting alternative is selected. To be consistent in approach, the discounting should require an interest rate commensurate with the risk associated with the current status of the loan; such a rate is implicit in the fair value of the loan. In addition, *SFAS No. 114* allows three alternative measures of loan impairment with no guidance on when to use one method over the other. Allowing alternatives in this manner enables companies to use the provisions of this pronouncement to manage their financial statements.

Transfers of Financial Assets

Financial assets include investments in debt and equity securities. Accounting for financial assets was first outlined in *SFAS No. 125*,[27] which was superseded by *SFAS No. 140*.[28] This statement adopts a financial consequences approach, which

---

26. Ibid., para. 20 17 (see FASB ASC 310-10-50).

27. *Statement of Financial Accounting Standards No. 125*, "Accounting for Transfers and Servicing of Financial Assets and Extinguishments of Liabilities" (Stamford, CT: FASB, 1996).

28. *Statement of Financial Accounting Standards No. 140*, "Accounting for Transfers and Servicing of Financial Assets and Extinguishments of Liabilities—A Replacement of FASB Statement No. 125" (Stamford, CT: FASB, 2000), 17 (see FASB ASC 860-10-05).

requires an entity to recognize the financial assets it controls and the liabilities it has incurred, and to derecognize financial assets when control has been surrendered and to derecognize financial liabilities when they are extinguished.

According to *SFAS No. 140*, the investor transfers or surrenders control over transferred assets if and only if all of the following conditions are met:

1. The transferred assets have been isolated from the transferor—put beyond the transferor's reach as well as the reach of its creditors.

2. Each transferee (or, if the transferee is a qualifying special-purpose entity, each holder of its beneficial interests) has the right to pledge or exchange the assets (or beneficial interests) it received, and no condition both constrains the transferee (or holder) from taking advantage of its right to pledge or exchange and provides more than a trivial benefit to the transferor.

3. The transferor does not maintain effective control over the transferred asset by having an agreement that obligates it to repurchase or redeem the asset before maturity or by having an agreement that allows it to repurchase or redeem assets that are not readily obtainable.[29]

A transfer of financial assets is accounted for as a sale to the extent that consideration other than beneficial interests in the transferred asset is received in exchange. Liabilities and derivatives incurred in a transfer of financial assets are initially measured at their fair market values. Servicing assets and liabilities[30] are measured by amortization over the period of servicing income or loss, and assessment for asset impairment or increased obligation is based on their fair market values. Liabilities are derecognized only when repaid or when the debtor is legally relieved of the obligation. That is, in-substance defeasance is not permitted.

Intangibles

It is difficult to define the term *intangibles* adequately. Kohler defined intangibles as capital assets having no physical existence and whose value depends on the rights and benefits that possession confers to the owner.[31] However, Paton had previously noted that the lack of physical existence test was not particularly helpful and suggested that intangibles are assets more closely related to the enterprise as a whole than to any components.[32] It should also be noted that many intangibles

29. Ibid., para. 9 (see FASB ASC 860-10-40-5).

30. Servicing of financial assets typically includes the following: collecting principal, interest and escrow payments from borrowers, paying taxes and insurance from escrowed funds, monitoring delinquencies, executing foreclosures, if necessary, temporarily investing funds pending distributions, remitting fees to guarantors, trustees and others providing services and accounting for and remitting principal and interest payments to the holders of beneficial interests in the financial assets. FASB ASC 850-50-30 requires the recording of a servicing asset when the benefits of servicing are expected to be more than adequate compensation to a servicer for performing the servicing; however, if the benefits of servicing are not expected to adequately compensate a servicer for performing the servicing, a servicing liability is recorded.

31. Eric L. Kohler, *A Dictionary for Accountants*, 3rd ed. (Englewood Cliffs, NJ: Prentice-Hall, 1963), 269.

32. William A. Paton and William A. Paton, Jr., *Asset Accounting* (New York: Macmillan, 1952), 485–90.

convey a sort of monopolistic right to their owners. Examples of intangibles are patents, copyrights, franchises, leaseholds, and goodwill.

Intangible assets derive their value from the special rights and privileges they convey, and accounting for these assets involves the same problems as accounting for other long-term assets. Specifically, an initial carrying amount must be determined and then systematically and rationally allocated to the periods that receive benefit. Companies must also account for the effects of impairment. These problems are magnified in the case of intangibles because their very nature makes evidence elusive. Both the value and the useful lives of intangibles are difficult to determine.

These issues were initially addressed by the APB, which noted that intangible assets might be classified on several bases.

1. *Identifiability.* Assets may be separately identifiable or may lack specific identification.

2. *Manner of acquisition.* Assets may be acquired singularly, in groups, or in business combinations, or developed internally.

3. *Expected period of benefit.* The period of benefit for an asset may be limited by law or contract, related to human or economic factors, or have indefinite or indeterminate duration.

4. *Separability from an entire enterprise.* The rights to an asset may be transferable without title, salable, or inseparable from the enterprise or a substantial part of it.[33]

Today, the cost of internally developed intangibles, such as patents, are considered costs of research and development and are expensed as incurred under *SFAS No. 2* (discussed later in the chapter).

The foregoing definitions suggest that intangibles may be classified according to whether they are *externally acquired* (purchased from outsiders) or *internally developed*. Additionally, they may be classified as *identifiable* or *unidentifiable*. These last two classifications, which relate to the Type (a) and Type (b) classifications originally identified in ARB No. 43, are discussed later in the chapter.

Accounting for Cost

The initial valuation process for intangible assets generally follows the same standards employed for other long-lived assets. Cost includes all expenditures necessary to acquire an individual asset and make it ready for use. When intangibles are purchased from outsiders, assigning cost is fairly easy, and the methods used in allocating cost to groups of assets and by exchanges of other assets are similar to those discussed for tangible fixed assets.

However, companies frequently develop intangible assets internally. The APB addressed the problems inherent in accounting for internally developed intangibles in *Opinion No. 17*. The Board's conclusions were based on the identifiability characteristic defined earlier:

> A company should record as assets the costs of intangible assets acquired from other enterprises or individuals. Costs of developing, maintaining, or restoring intangible assets which are not specifically

33. Accounting Principles Board, *APB Opinion No. 17*, "Intangible Assets" (New York: AICPA, 1970) (Superseded.)

identifiable, have indeterminate lives, or are inherent in a continuing business and related to the enterprise as a whole—such as goodwill—should be deducted from income when incurred.[34]

The identifiability criterion alleviated much of the problem in accounting for the cost of intangible assets and is yet another example of the APB's attempts to narrow alternatives. Where a specific cost could be assigned to a specific asset, intangibles were carried forward at recorded values. Where either a specific asset or specific amount was indeterminable, no attempt was made to carry values forward. As stated above, internally developed intangibles are no longer reported as assets under *SFAS No. 2*.

Amortization

The matching principle dictates that the cost of intangible assets be apportioned to the expected periods of benefit. In *ARB No. 43*, it was noted that this process involved two separate types of intangibles.

1. Those having a term of existence limited by law, regulation, or agreement, or by their nature (such as patents, copyrights, leases, licenses, franchises for a fixed term, and goodwill as to which there is evidence of limited duration)

2. Those having no such term of existence and as to which there is, at the time of acquisition, no indication of limited life (such as goodwill generally, going value, trade names, secret processes, subscription lists, perpetual franchises, and organization costs)[35]

This release resulted in the adoption of a classification scheme that identified intangibles as either (1) Type (a) or (2) Type (b), and these terms became widely used in discussing the issues associated with recording and amortizing intangible assets. In *APB Opinion No. 17*, the terms *Type (a)* and *Type (b)* were not specifically used; the terms *identifiable* and *unidentifiable* were substituted. In this release, the APB noted that then-current practices allowed for the following variations in treatment of unidentifiable intangibles: (1) retention of cost until a reduction of value was apparent, (2) amortization over an arbitrary period, (3) amortization over estimated useful life with specified minimum and maximum periods, and (4) deduction from equity as acquired.[36]

In *Opinion No. 17*, the APB concluded that intangible assets should be amortized by systematic charges to income over the estimated period to be benefited. The Board also suggested that the following factors should be considered in estimating the useful lives of intangibles:

1. Legal, regulatory, or contractual provisions may limit the maximum useful life.

2. Provisions for renewal or extension may alter a specific limit on useful life.

3. Effects of obsolescence, demand, competition, and other economic factors may reduce a useful life.

34. Ibid., para. 24.

35. *Accounting Research Bulletin No. 43*, "Restatement and Revision of Accounting Research Bulletins" (New York: AICPA, 1953), 6019 (Superseded.)

36. *APB Opinion No. 17*.

4. A useful life may parallel the service life expectancies of individuals or groups of employees.

5. Expected actions of competitors and others may restrict present competitive advantages.

6. An apparently unlimited useful life may in fact be indefinite and benefits cannot be reasonably projected.

7. An intangible asset may be a composite of many individual factors with varying effective lives.[37]

APB Opinion No. 17 indicated that the period over which the cost of intangibles is amortized should be determined from a review of the foregoing factors, but it should not exceed 40 years. The straight-line method of amortization was required to be used unless another method could be demonstrated to be more appropriate.

As noted earlier, the release of *APB Opinion No. 17* narrowed the accounting treatment available for similar transactions; however, whether or not it created the desired result is subject to question. *APB Opinion No. 17* was criticized by some because it placed values on the balance sheet that relate to future expectations (for example, purchased goodwill), and others disagreed with the Board's conclusions because it assigned costs to arbitrary periods where there is no evidence that costs have expired (for example, perpetual franchises). Further evidence of the lack of acceptability of this pronouncement lies in the fact that originally it was part of *APB Opinion No. 16*, "Business Combinations"; however, since enough members of the APB objected to various provisions of both opinions, it was necessary to separate the provisions to obtain the required majority for passage. In 2001, the FASB issued *SFAS No. 142*, "Goodwill and Other Intangible Assets" (see FASB ASC 350), which changed the method of accounting for intangible assets.[38]

Under *SFAS No. 142*, intangible assets other than goodwill are divided into two groups: those with indefinite lives and those with finite lives. *SFAS No. 142* does not presume that intangibles are wasting assets. An acquired intangible asset's useful life is determined by reviewing various factors such as its expected use, related assets, legal regulatory or contractual provisions, the effects of obsolescence, and the level of required maintenance. If no legal, regulatory, contractual, or other factor limits the useful life of an intangible asset, it is considered to have an indefinite life. Intangible assets that are not amortized must be tested for impairment at least annually by comparing the fair values of those assets with their recorded amounts and/or amortized over their remaining useful lives. Intangible assets that have finite useful lives will continue to be amortized over their useful lives. *SFAS No. 142* did not change the accounting treatment for internally developed intangibles or research and development activities.

Goodwill

The topic of goodwill has been of interest for many years. As initially conceived, goodwill was viewed as good relations with customers. Such factors as a convenient location and habits of customers were viewed as adding to the value of the business. Yang described goodwill as everything that might contribute to the

---

37. Ibid., para. 27.

38. *Statement of Financial Accounting Standards No. 142*, "Goodwill and Other Intangible Assets" (Norwalk, CT: FASB, 2001).

advantage an established business possessed over a business to be started anew.[39] Since that time, the concept of goodwill has evolved into an earning power concept in which its value is approximated by attributing to goodwill all future earnings that are expected to be in excess of those that a similar company would generate and then discounting the expected excess earnings stream to its present value.

Catlett and Olson summarized the characteristics of goodwill that distinguish it from other elements of value:

1. The value of goodwill has no reliable or predictable relationship to costs that may have been incurred in its creation.
2. Individual intangible factors that may contribute to goodwill cannot be valued.
3. Goodwill attaches only to a business as a whole.
4. The value of goodwill may, and does, fluctuate suddenly and widely because of the innumerable factors that influence that value.
5. Goodwill is not utilized or consumed in the production of earnings.
6. Goodwill appears to be an element of value that runs directly to the investor or owner in a business enterprise.[40]

In theory the value of goodwill is equal to the discounted present value of expected superior earnings (expected future earnings less normal earnings for the industry). Thus the process of estimating the value of goodwill involves forecasting future earnings and choosing an appropriate discount rate.

Forecasting future earnings is a risky proposition. Since the best indicator of the future is the past, prior and current revenue and expense figures are typically used. However, the following points are relevant to this process:

1. The use of too few or too many years may distort projections.
2. Trends in earnings should be considered.
3. Industry trends are important.
4. Overall economic conditions can be significant.

In choosing the discount rate to be used in making goodwill calculations, the objective is to approximate the existing cost of capital for the company. This approximation must take into consideration existing and expected risk conditions as well as earnings potential.

Although goodwill may exist at any time, in practice goodwill is recognized for accounting purposes only when it is acquired through the purchase of an existing business.[41] Only then is the value of goodwill readily determinable, because the purchase embodies an arm's-length transaction wherein assets, often cash or marketable securities, are exchanged. The value of the assets exchanged indicates a total fair value for the business entity acquired. The excess of total fair value over the fair value of identifiable net assets is considered goodwill. This

---

39. J. M. Yang, *Goodwill and Other Intangibles* (New York: Ronald Press, 1927), 29.

40. George R. Catlett, and Norman O. Olson, *Accounting for Goodwill* (New York: AICPA, 1968), 20–21.

41. In certain cases, goodwill is recognized when a new partner is admitted to a partnership or when a partner leaves a partnership.

practice fulfills the stewardship function of accounting and facilitates the accountability of management to stockholders.

When goodwill is recorded, it is considered an intangible asset. Under *APB Opinion No. 17*, goodwill was amortized over its useful life or 40 years, whichever came first.[42] The case for amortization was based on accrual accounting. That is, the company had paid for the goodwill, and it will presumably generate future earnings; thus, its cost should be matched against those future earnings as they arise. However, in the case of goodwill, it is difficult if not impossible to estimate what that useful life will be. If goodwill measures excess earning power, how long can it be expected to last? An economist would say that it would not last very long, because competition would drive it away. If so, it should be written off over a relatively short period. On the other hand, if the goodwill is attributable to some ability associated with the enterprise, its employees, or management that would be difficult for others to duplicate, then it may have an indefinite useful life. In that case, it may be inappropriate to amortize goodwill at all.

Some accountants have argued that goodwill should be written off when it is acquired because it would then receive the same treatment as inherent goodwill (goodwill that exists but is not paid for in a business combination). There are costs associated with developing inherent goodwill. These costs are written off as they are incurred. Moreover, when goodwill is acquired, further costs will be incurred to continue excess earnings ability. Hence, to amortize the cost of goodwill acquired over future periods represents a double counting of cost. The immediate write-off of purchased goodwill could be treated as an extraordinary item because it represents a transaction outside the normal trading activity of the acquiring or investee enterprise.

Opponents of immediate write-off of goodwill contend that the purchase of goodwill implies future profitability; thus, it is inconsistent and perhaps misleading to investors to write off the cost of goodwill because it represents an asset having future service potential. This is particularly true for investments in people-intensive companies, for example, in service industries. For these investments, the amount of goodwill acquired relative to other assets is high; thus, the immediate write-off would be material and would have a major and misleading impact on financial ratios, particularly debt to equity and return on investment. Moreover, future profits would be inflated because they would not be matched against the cost of the investment.

SFAS No. 142

In 1996, the FASB put the issue of accounting for business combinations and the related topic of goodwill on its agenda in response to growing concerns voiced by constituents about the need for improved standards to account for business combinations. In September 1999, the FASB published an exposure draft titled "Business Combinations and Intangible Assets." The exposure draft proposed that the pooling of interests method be eliminated in favor of the purchase method for business combinations (see Chapter 16) and that goodwill should be amortized over no more than 20 years, in contrast to the previously required amortization period of up to 40 years.

The two proposals drew considerable interest and some vocal opposition, which resulted in a series of meetings between the FASB and its constituents as

---

42. The Revenue Reconciliation Act of 1993 allows goodwill to be written off over a 15-year period for income tax purposes. Consequently, a new income tax temporary difference was created by this legislation, and the previous permanent difference has been eliminated. See Chapter 12 for a discussion of this issue.

well as testimony before committees of the U.S. House of Representatives and Senate. The opposition was based on the contention that recording large amounts of goodwill and subsequently amortizing goodwill over a 20-year period would result in a large drain on reported earnings. Subsequently, the Board issued a revised exposure draft, "Business Combinations and Intangible Assets—Accounting for Goodwill," in early 2001; this draft proposed that goodwill not be amortized, but rather that it be tested for impairment.

In June 2001, the FASB issued *SFAS No. 141*, "Business Combinations"[43] (see FASB ASC 805), and *SFAS No. 142*, "Goodwill and Other Intangible Assets"[44] (see FASB ASC 350). These statements changed the accounting for business combinations and goodwill. *SFAS No. 141* now requires that the purchase method of accounting be used for all business combinations.[45] *SFAS No. 142* changes the accounting treatment for goodwill from an amortization period not to exceed 40 years to an approach that requires, at a minimum, annual testing for impairment. The goodwill impairment test is to be performed at the reporting unit level, which is defined as an operating segment or one level below an operating segment (also known as a component).[46]

Under the provisions of *SFAS No. 142*, the test for goodwill impairment is a two-step process:

1. Compare the fair value of the reporting unit to its carrying value. In the event fair value exceeds carrying value, no further testing is required. However, if the carrying value of the reporting unit exceeds its fair value, step 2 is required.

2. Calculate the implied fair value of goodwill by measuring the fair value of the net assets other than goodwill and subtracting this amount from the fair value of the reporting unit.

In determining fair value, the FASB noted that the fair value of a reporting unit is the amount at which the whole unit could be bought or sold in a current transaction. As a result, quoted market prices in active markets were described as the best evidence of fair value. The FASB further indicated that if quoted market prices are not available, fair value should be based on the best available information, such as the present value measurements outlined in *SFAC No. 7*. These procedures now fall under the guidance provided at FASB ASC 820 for measuring fair value.

In determining whether to record an impairment loss, the FASB stated that certain indications suggest when an impairment exists, including significant under-performance relative to historical or projected future operating results, significant changes in the manner of the company's use of underlying assets, and significant adverse industry or market economic trends. The goodwill impairment test requires companies to assess whether the cash flows their reporting units are expected to generate can support the values assigned to those units. If the carrying value of assets is determined to be unrecoverable, the company must estimate the fair value

43. *Statement of Financial Accounting Standards No. 141*, "Business Combinations" (Norwalk, CT: FASB, 2001).

44. *Statement of Financial Accounting Standards No. 142*, "Goodwill and Other Intangible Assets" (Norwalk, CT: FASB, 2001).

45. This issue is discussed in Chapter 16.

46. See FASB ASC350-20-20.

of the assets of the reporting unit and record an impairment charge for the excess of the carrying value over the fair value. The estimate of fair value requires management to make a number of assumptions and/or projections, such as future revenues, future earnings, and the probability of outcomes in contingency situations.

A company can identify reporting units in many ways. Possibilities include categorizing operations by products, operating units, geographical area, legal entity, and significant customers. Prior guidance had been provided in *SFAS No. 131*, "Segment Reporting" (see FASB ASC 280), which defined segments through a "management approach" to segment reporting.[47] Under this approach, management reports segment information based on the way segments are organized within the company for internal decision-making purposes and assessing performance. If, for example, management makes decisions on and assesses the performance of certain product lines, then it must report segment information based on those product lines.

Specifically, *SFAS No. 131* defined an operating segment as a component of an enterprise:

1. That engages in business activities that earn revenues and incur expenses
2. Whose operating results are regularly reviewed by the organization's chief operating decision maker, who makes decisions about resource allocation and assesses its performance
3. For which discrete financial information is available

Since many firms have different operations and operate in multiple geographical areas, financial statement users often need specific information concerning the operating units or geographic segments to help them better assess financial performance or prospects for future cash flows. By providing specific information about various segments, companies can help users make better-informed judgments about the firm as a whole. Since *SFAS No. 142* required the goodwill analysis to be performed at the reporting unit level, the standard gave companies the option to offer more transparent financial information, that is, how well a company and its acquisitions have been performing as well as which of the individual reporting units have been able to meet their own expectations. In addition, *SFAS No. 142* required companies to provide specific information on the facts and circumstances that led to the recorded impairment. The guidance provided at FASB ASC 350 retains these features.

Disclosure Requirements of *SFAS No. 142*   The disclosure requirements of *SFAS No. 142* include the following (see FASB ASC 350-20-50):

1. The total aggregative amount of goodwill is to be disclosed as a separate line item on the balance sheet.
2. Any transitory impairment loss is to be reported as a change in accounting principle.
3. Any annual impairment loss is to be disclosed as a separate line item on the income statement.
4. A description of the impaired asset and the facts and circumstances that led to the impairment is to be disclosed.
5. The amount of the impairment loss and a description of the method used to determine the fair value of its reporting units are to be disclosed.

47. FASB ASC 280-10-50 (see Chapter 16 for a further discussion of this issue).

Research and Development Costs

Large corporations are continually attempting to improve their product lines, develop new products, improve manufacturing methods, and develop improved manufacturing facilities. Accounting for the cost of the activities of the research department is a complicated process because some costs may never result in future benefits. For those costs that will provide future benefit, an asset exists; but due to the uncertainty surrounding the present determination of which costs will result in future benefits and over what periods those future benefits will be realized, many accountants view such determinations as too subjective and unreliable. In the past, many corporations recognized the importance of developing accounting procedures to allow such costs to be capitalized and amortized on a reasonable basis. For example, one study suggested that such costs might be classified as follows:

1. *Basic research.* Experimentation with no specific commercial objective
2. *New product development.* Experimental effort toward previously untried products
3. *Product improvement.* Effort toward improving quality or functional performance of current product lines
4. *Cost and/or capacity improvement.* Development of new and improved processes, manufacturing equipment, etc., to reduce operations costs or expand capacity
5. *Safety, health, and convenience.* Improvement of working conditions generally for purposes of employee welfare, community relations, and so forth.[48]

This classification scheme would make it easier to identify the costs that should be deferred and those that should be expensed. The authors of this study suggest that categories 1, 2, and 3 should generally be deferred and amortized, whereas 4 and 5 should be charged to expense because of the difficulty in determining the future periods expected to receive benefit.

APB Opinion No. 17 required the immediate expensing of intangible assets that are not specifically identifiable, because these costs do not specifically generate revenue and have dubious future service potential. This provision was adopted to discourage the manipulation of research and development expenses. (Many companies were capitalizing research and development costs in low-profit years and writing them off in a lump sum in high-profit years.)

Later the FASB restudied the issue of research and development (R&D) costs and issued *SFAS No. 2* (see FASB ASC 730). This release requires all R&D costs to be charged to expense as incurred. To distinguish R&D costs from other costs, the SFAS No. 2 provided the following definitions.

> *Research* is planned search or critical investigation aimed at discovery of new knowledge with the hope that such knowledge will be useful in developing a new product or service or new process or technique or in bringing about a significant improvement to an existing product or process.
>
> *Development* is the translation of research findings or other knowledge into a plan or design for a new product or process or for a significant

---

48. Donald L. Madden, Levis D. McCullers, and Relmond P. Van Daniker, "Classification of Research and Development Expenditures: A Guide to Better Accounting," *CPA Journal* (February 1972): 139–42.

improvement to an existing product or process whether intended for sale or use. It includes the conceptual formulation, design and testing of product alternatives, construction of prototypes, and operation of pilot plants. It does not include routine or periodic alterations to existing products, production lines, manufacturing processes, and other ongoing operations even though these alterations may represent improvements and it does not include market research or market testing activities.[49]

Since many costs may have characteristics similar to R&D costs, *SFAS No. 2* also listed activities that would and would not be included in the category of R&D costs as follows:

Research and Development Activities	Activities Not Considered Research and Development
Laboratory research aimed at discovery of a new knowledge	Engineering follow-through in an early phase of commercial production
Searching for applications of new research findings	Quality control during commercial production including routine testing
Conceptual formulation and design of possible product or process alternatives	Troubleshooting breakdowns during production
Testing in search for or evaluation of product or process alternatives	Routine, ongoing efforts to refine, enrich, or improve the qualities of an existing product
Modification of the design of a product or process	Adaptation of an existing capability to a particular requirement or customer's need
Design, construction, and testing of preproduction prototypes and models	Periodic design changes to existing products
Design of tools, jigs, molds, and dies involving new technology	Routine design of tools, jigs, molds, and dies
Design, construction, and operation of a pilot plant not useful for commercial production	Activity, including design and construction engineering, related to the construction, relocation, rearrangement, or start-up of facilities or equipment
Engineering activity required to advance the design of a product to the manufacturing stage	Legal work on patent applications, sale, licensing, or litigation

The disclosure of R&D costs in annual reports was the subject of a research study. Entwistle (1999)[50] found that only 1 percent of the firms he surveyed made R&D disclosures in the financial statements and that such disclosures were located throughout the annual report. Following is Hershey's discussion of its R&D activities:

> We expense research and development costs as incurred. Research and development expense was $28.1 million in 2008, $28.0 million in

49. *Statement of Financial Accounting Standards No. 2*, "Accounting for Research and Development Costs" (Stamford, CT: FASB, 1974), para. 8 (see FASB ASC 730-10-20).

50. Gary M. Entwistle, "Exploring the R & D Disclosure Reporting Environment," *Accounting Horizons* 14, no. 4 (December 1999): 323–41.

2007 and $27.6 million in 2006. Research and development expense is included in selling, marketing and administrative expenses

Tootsie Roll did not report material amounts of research and development activities.

Financial Analysis of Investments and Intangibles

There are no specific financial analysis issues associated with investments and intangibles. As noted in Chapter 6, Hershey does not disclose any long-term investments on its balance sheet but discloses a goodwill net balance of $554,677,000 and other intangibles of $110,772,000, Tootsie Roll discloses long-term investments of $49,809,000, goodwill of $73,237,000, and trademarks of $189,024,000 in the other assets section of its balance sheet.

International Accounting Standards

The International Accounting Standards Board (IASB) has issued pronouncements on the following issues:

1. Accounting for investments in associates in a revised *IAS No. 28*, "Accounting for Investments in Associates."
2. Accounting for financial assets in *IAS No. 32*, "Financial Instruments: Presentation."
3. Accounting for intangibles in *IAS No. 38*, "Intangible Assets."
4. The recognition and measurement of financial assets in a reissued *IAS No. 39*, "Financial Instruments: Recognition and Measurement."
5. Accounting for goodwill in *SFRS No. 3*, "Business Combinations," which replaced *IAS No. 22*.
6. The disclosure of information on financial instruments in *IFRS No. 7*, "Financial Instruments: Disclosures."
7. Accounting for financial assets in *IFRS No. 9*, "Financial Instruments," as a first step in its project to replace *IAS No. 39*.

IAS No. 28 applies to all investments in which an investor has significant influence but not control or joint control except for investments held by a venture capital organization, mutual fund, unit trust, and similar entity that are designated under *IAS No. 39* to be at fair value with fair value changes recognized in profit or loss. In the revised *IAS No. 28*, the IASB did not change the fundamental accounting for associates in using the equity method. The Board's main objective for the revision was to reduce alternatives. The original *IAS No. 28* addressed accounting for investments where the investor does not own a majority interest but has the ability to significantly influence the investee. The reporting requirements contained in this statement are quite similar to U.S. GAAP discussed in *APB Opinion No. 18*.

The major changes in the revised *IAS No. 28* were as follows:

1. It added additional guidance and disclosures for when it is appropriate to overcome the presumption that an investor has significant influence if it holds 20 percent or more of the voting power. An example would be when an investee is in legal reorganization or bankruptcy or operating under severe long-term restrictions on its ability to transfer funds to the investor.

2. It required the investor and equity method associates to use uniform accounting policies for like transactions and events in similar circumstances.

3. It required additional disclosures, including the fair values of investments in associates for which there are published price quotations, summarized financial information of associates, reasons for a departure from the 20 percent presumption of significant influence, differences in reporting dates, restrictions on an associate's ability to transfer funds, unrecognized losses of an associate, and the investor's contingent liabilities with respect to the associate.

The title of *IAS No. 32* was originally "Financial Instruments Disclosure and Presentation," but its disclosure provisions were replaced by *IFRS No. 7* in 2007. *IAS No. 32* main objectives are to provide additional guidance on selected matters such as the measurement of the components of financial statements on initial recognition and the classification of derivatives based on an entity's own shares; it also aimed to put all disclosures relating to financial instruments in one standard. The fundamental approach to the presentation and disclosure of financial statements was not changed in the revision. Under *IAS No. 32*, financial assets are defined as cash, a right to receive cash or other financial assets from another enterprise, or a contractual right to exchange financial assets with another enterprise under potential favorable conditions or equity instruments of other enterprises.

IAS No. 38, "Intangible Assets," applies to all intangible assets that are not specifically dealt with in other International Accounting Standards. It specifically applies to expenditures for advertising, training, start-up, and research and development (R&D) activities. Specifically, *IAS No. 38* indicates that an intangible asset should be recognized initially, at cost, in the financial statements if it meets these three conditions:

1. The asset meets the definition of an intangible asset. Particularly, there should be an identifiable asset that is controlled and clearly distinguishable from an enterprise's goodwill.

2. It is probable that the future economic benefits that are attributable to the asset will flow to the enterprise.

3. The cost of the asset can be measured reliably.

These requirements apply whether an intangible asset is acquired externally or generated internally. If an intangible item does not meet both the definition and the criteria for the recognition of an intangible asset, it is expensed when incurred. All expenditures on research are to be immediately recognized as expenses, and internally generated intangibles such as goodwill cannot be recognized as assets.

After initial recognition in the financial statements, *IAS No. 38* indicates that an intangible asset should be measured under one of the following two treatments:

1. *Benchmark treatment.* Historical cost less any amortization and impairment losses

2. *Allowed alternative treatment.* Revalued amount (based on fair value) less any subsequent amortization and impairment losses. The main difference from the treatment for revaluations of property, plant, and equipment under *IAS No. 16* is that revaluations for intangible assets are permitted only if fair value can be determined by reference to an active market. Active markets are expected to be rare for intangible assets.

The statement requires intangible assets to be amortized over the best estimate of their useful life, and it includes the presumption that the useful life of an intangible asset will not exceed 20 years from the date when the asset is available for use. In rare cases, where persuasive evidence suggests that the useful life of an intangible asset will exceed 20 years, an enterprise should amortize the intangible asset over the best estimate of its useful life as well as perform these steps:

1. Test the intangible asset for impairment at least annually in accordance with *IAS No. 36*, "Impairment of Assets."

2. Disclose the reasons why the presumption that the useful life of an intangible asset will not exceed 20 years is rebutted and also the factor(s) that played a significant role in determining the useful life of the asset.

With respect to goodwill, *SFRS No. 3* requires goodwill to be recognized by the acquirer as an asset from the acquisition date and to be initially measured as the excess of the cost of the business combination over the acquirer's share of the net fair values of the acquiree's identifiable assets, liabilities, and contingent liabilities. *SFRS No. 3* prohibits the amortization of goodwill. Instead, goodwill must be tested for impairment at least annually in accordance with *IAS No. 36*, "Impairment of Assets."

If the acquirer's interest in the net fair value of the acquired identifiable net assets exceeds the cost of the business combination, that excess (referred to as negative goodwill) must be recognized immediately in the income statement as a gain. Before concluding that negative goodwill has arisen, however, *SFRS No. 3* requires that the acquirer reassess the identification and measurement of the acquiree's identifiable assets, liabilities, and contingent liabilities and the measurement of the cost of the combination. These requirements bring international accounting standards in line with U.S. GAAP.

The IASB indicated that its main objective in reissuing *IAS No. 39* was to provide additional guidance on selected matters such as when financial assets and financial liabilities may be measured at fair value, how to assess impairment, how to determine fair value, and some aspects of hedge accounting.[51] *IAS No. 39* indicates that an entity should recognize a financial asset or its statement of financial position when, and only when, the entity becomes a party to the contractual provisions of the instrument.

All financial assets are to be recognized on the balance sheet. They are initially measured at cost, which is the fair value of whatever was paid or received to acquire the financial asset. An entity records normal purchases of financial assets on either the trade date or settlement date, and certain value changes between trade and settlement dates are recognized if settlement date accounting is used. Transaction costs are to be included in the initial measurement of all financial instruments.

Subsequently, most financial assets and liabilities are to be measured at fair value, except for the following, which should be carried at amortized cost:

1. Loans and receivables originated by the enterprise and not held for trading

2. Other fixed maturity investments, such as debt securities and mandatorily redeemable preferred shares, that the enterprise intends and is able to hold to maturity

51. The discussion of accounting for financial liabilities under *IAS No. 39* is contained in Chapter 11.

3. Financial assets whose fair value cannot be reliably measured (generally limited to some equity securities with no quoted market price and forwards and options on unquoted equity securities)

Fair value is the amount for which an asset could be exchanged, or a liability settled, between knowledgeable, willing parties in an arm's-length transaction.

Additionally, an entity is required to assess, at each balance sheet date, whether there is objective evidence of asset impairments. Any impairment losses are measured as the difference between the asset's carrying amount and the present value of estimated cash flows discounted at the financial asset's original effective interest rate.

If, in a subsequent period, the amount of the impairment loss relating to a financial asset carried at amortized cost or a debt instrument carried as available for sale decreases due to an event occurring after the impairment was originally recognized, the previously recognized impairment loss is reversed; however, impairments relating to investments in available-for-sale equity instruments are not reversed.

If an entity has neither retained nor transferred substantially all of the risks and rewards of a financial asset, then the entity must assess whether it has relinquished control of the financial asset or not. If the entity does not control the financial asset, then derecognition is appropriate; however, if the entity has retained control of the asset, then the entity continues to recognize the asset to the extent to which it has a continuing involvement in the asset.

If an asset is to be derecognized, the entity must first determine whether the asset under consideration for derecognition is:

*   An asset in its entirety
*   Specifically identified cash flows from an asset
*   A fully proportionate share of the cash flows from an asset
*   A fully proportionate share of specifically identified cash flows from a financial asset

The steps to determine if derecognition is appropriate are summarized in Figure 10.1 as a decision tree.

In 2008 the IASB issued a revised *IFRS No. 3*. Among the changes was an option to permit an entity to recognize 100 percent of the goodwill of an acquired entity, not just the acquiring entity's portion of the goodwill, with the increased amount of goodwill also increasing the noncontrolling interest (minority interest) in the net assets of the acquired entity. This is termed the *full goodwill method*. Noncontrolling interest is to be reported as a part of consolidated equity. The full goodwill option may be elected on a transaction-by-transaction basis.

The primary objective of *IFRS No. 7* is to provide risk management and financial instrument disclosures that enable users to evaluate the significance of financial instruments to an entity's financial position and performance. Specifically, *IFRS No. 7* requires the following disclosures:

1. The significance of an entity's financial instruments entity
2. The nature and extent of risks arising from financial instruments to which an entity is exposed and how those risks have been managed.

The following balance sheet and income statement disclosures are required to provide information about the significance of an entity's assets:

FIGURE 10.1 *Derecognition Decision Tree*

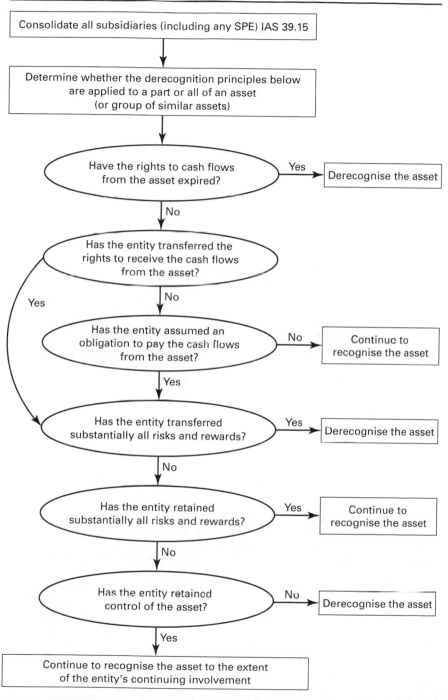

Source: Adapted from *IAS No. 39*, "Financial Instruments: Recognition and Measurement. Technical Summary," IASC Foundation Education, http://www.iasb.org/NR/rdonlyres/339C384D-045B-47D7-AA8E-8D26DFA726FB/0/IAS39.pdf.

- Financial assets measured at fair value
- Held-to-maturity investments
- Loans and receivables
- Available-for-sale assets

IFRS No. 7 requires quantitative disclosures that are to be based on information provided internally to key management personnel as defined in *IAS No. 24*, "Related Party Disclosures." These disclosures include

- Risk exposures for each type of financial instrument
- Management's objectives, policies, and processes for managing those risks
- Changes from the prior period
- Summary quantitative data about exposure to each risk at the reporting date

IFRS No. 7 also seeks to provide risk-based disclosures from an entity's perspective and requires an entity to communicate the nature and extent of risks, the significance of financial instruments, and how it manages financial risks to its stakeholders by explaining its risk objectives, policies, and processes. These disclosures include

- Maximum amount of exposure, a description of any collateral, information about the credit quality of its financial assets that are neither past due nor impaired, and information about credit quality of financial assets whose terms have been renegotiated
- Certain analytical disclosures for financial assets that are past due or impaired
- Information about collateral or other credit enhancements obtained or called

On November 12, 2009, the IASB issued *IFRS No. 9*, "Financial Instruments," as the first step in a project to replace *IAS No. 39*. This project was undertaken in response to vicious concerns expressed by the European Commission (The council of the European Union) over the impact of *IAS No. 39*.

IFRS No. 9 introduces new requirements for classifying and measuring financial assets that must be applied January 1, 2013, with early adoption permitted. The IASB intends to expand *IFRS No. 9* during 2010 to add new requirements for classifying and measuring financial liabilities, derecognition of financial instruments, impairment, and hedge accounting. By the end of 2010, *IFRS No. 9* will be a complete replacement for *IAS No.39*. The requirements of *IFRS No. 9* relating to financial assets are summarized in the following paragraphs.

All financial assets are initially measured at fair value plus, in the case of a financial asset not at fair value through profit or loss, transaction costs. Subsequently, *IFRS No. 9* divides all financial assets that are currently under the scope of *IAS No. 39* into two classifications:

1. Those measured at amortized cost
2. Those measured at fair value

This classification is made at the time the financial asset is initially recognized; that is, when an entity becomes a party to the contractual provisions of the instrument.

A financial asset debt instrument that meets the following two conditions is to be measured at amortized cost (net of any write-down for impairment):

1. *Business model test.* The objective of the entity's business model is to hold the financial asset to collect the contractual cash flows (rather than to sell the instrument before its contractual maturity to realize its fair value changes).

2. *Cash flow characteristics test.* The contractual terms of the financial asset give rise on specified dates to cash flows that are solely payments of principal and interest on the principal outstanding.

All other debt instruments must be measured at fair value through profit or loss (FVTPL). However, even if an instrument meets the two amortized cost tests, *IFRS No. 9* contains an option to designate a financial asset as measured at FVTPL if doing so eliminates or significantly reduces a measurement or recognition inconsistency (sometimes referred to as an *accounting mismatch*) that would otherwise arise from measuring assets or liabilities or recognizing the gains and losses on them on different bases. These requirements eliminate the *IAS No. 39* available for sale and held-to-maturity categories.

All equity investments that fall under the scope of *IFRS No. 9* are to be measured at fair value on the balance sheet. Fair value changes are recognized as income, except for those equity investments for which the entity has elected to report fair value changes in other comprehensive income. If an equity investment is not held for trading purposes, an entity can make an irrevocable election at initial recognition to measure it at fair value through other comprehensive income (FVTOCI) with only dividend income recognized in profit or loss.

All derivatives, including those linked to unquoted equity investments, are to be measured at fair value. Fair value changes are recognized as income unless the entity has elected to treat the derivative as a hedging instrument in accordance with *IAS No. 39*, in which case the requirements of *IAS No. 39* apply. The embedded derivative concept of *IAS No. 39* is not included in *IFRS No. 9*. Consequently, embedded derivatives that under *IAS No. 39* would have been separately accounted for at FVTPL because they were not closely related to the financial host asset will no longer be separated. Instead, the contractual cash flows of the financial asset are assessed in their entirety, and the asset as a whole is measured at FVTPL if any of its cash flows do not represent payments of principal and interest.

A debt instrument may be reclassified between FVTPL and amortized cost, or vice versa, if and only if the entity's business model objective for its financial assets changes so its previous model assessment would no longer apply. If reclassification is appropriate, it must be done prospectively from the reclassification date. An entity does not restate any previously recognized gains, losses, or interest.

Cases

• Case 10-1 Investment Classification

Qtip Corp. owns stock in Maxey Corp. The investment represents a 10 percent interest, and Qtip is unable to exercise significant influence over Maxey.

The Maxey stock was purchased by Qtip on January 1, 2002, for $23,000. The stock consistently pays an annual dividend to Qtip of $2,000. Qtip classifies the stock as available for sale. Its fair value at December 31, 2009, was $21,600. This amount was properly reported as an asset in the balance sheet. Due to the development of a new Maxey product line, the market value of Qtip's investment rose to $27,000 at December 31, 2010.

The Qtip management team is aware of the provisions of *SFAS No. 115*. The possibility of changing the classification from available for sale to trading is discussed. This change is justified, the managers say, because they intend to sell the security at some point in 2011 so that they can realize the gain.

Required:

a. Discuss the role that managerial intention plays in the accounting treatment of equity securities that have a readily determinable fair value under *SFAS No. 115*.

b. What income statement effect, if any, would the change in classification have for Qtip?

c. Discuss the ethical considerations of this case.

d. Opponents of *SFAS No. 115* contend that allowing a change in classification masks effects of unrealized losses and results in improper matching of market-value changes with accounting periods. Describe how the accounting treatment and the proposed change in classification would result in this sort of mismatching.

• Case 10-2 Income Effects of Investments

Victoria Company has both current and noncurrent equity securities portfolios. All of the equity securities have readily determinable fair values. Those equity securities in the current portfolio are considered trading securities. At the beginning of the year, the market value of each security exceeded cost.

During the year, some of the securities increased in value. These securities (some in the current portfolio and some in the long-term portfolio) were sold. At the end of the year, the market value of each of the remaining securities was less than original cost.

Victoria also has investments in long-term bonds, which the company intends to hold to maturity. All of the bonds were purchased at face value. During the year, some of these bonds were called by the issuer before maturity. In each case the call price was in excess of par value. Three months before the end of the year, additional similar bonds were purchased for face value plus 2 months' accrued interest.

Required:

a. How should Victoria account for the sale of the securities from each portfolio? Why?

b. How should Victoria account for the marketable equity securities portfolios at year-end? Why?

c. How should Victoria account for the disposition before their maturity of the long-term bonds called by their issuer? Why?

d. How should Victoria report the purchase of the additional similar bonds at the date of acquisition? Why?

• Case 10-3 Equity Method and Disclosures

On July 1, 2010, Dynamic Company purchased for cash 40 percent of the out-standing capital stock of Cart Company. Both Dynamic and Cart have a December 31 year-end. Cart, whose common stock is actively traded in the over-the-counter market, reported its total net income for the year to Dynamic and also paid cash dividends on November 15, 2010, to Dynamic and its other stockholders.

Required:

a. How should Dynamic report the foregoing facts in its December 31, 2010, balance sheet and its income statement for the year then ended? Discuss the rationale for your answer.

b. If Dynamic should elect to report its investment at fair value, how would its balance sheet and income statement differ from your answer to part (a)?

• Case 10-4 Research and Development

The Thomas Company is in the process of developing a revolutionary new product. A new division of the company was formed to develop, manufacture, and market this product. As of year-end (December 31, 2010), the product has not been manufactured for resale; however, a prototype unit was built and is in operation.

Throughout 2010 the division incurred certain costs. These costs include design and engineering studies, prototype manufacturing costs, administrative expenses (including salaries of administrative personnel), and market research costs. In addition, $500,000 in equipment (estimated useful life, 10 years) was purchased for use in developing and manufacturing the preproduction prototype and will be used to manufacture the product. Approximately $200,000 of this equipment was built specifically for the design and development of the product; the remaining $300,000 of equipment will be used to manufacture the product once it is in commercial production.

Required:

a. What is the definition of *research* and *development* as defined in *Statement of Financial Accounting Standards No. 2*?

b. Briefly indicate the practical and conceptual reasons for the conclusion reached by the FASB on accounting and reporting practices for R&D costs.

c. In accordance with *SFAS No. 2*, how should the various costs of Thomas just described be reported in the financial statements for the year ended December 31, 2010?

• Case 10-5 Trading versus Available-for-Sale Securities

The FASB issued *SFAS No. 115* to describe the accounting treatment that should be afforded to equity securities that have readily determinable market values that are not accounted for under the equity method or consolidation. An important part of the statement concerns the distinction between trading securities and available-for-sale securities.

Required:

a. Compare and contrast trading securities and available-for-sale securities.

b. How are the trading securities and available-for-sale securities classified in the balance sheet? In your answer, discuss the factors that should be considered in determining whether a security is classified as trading or available for sale and as current or noncurrent.

c. How do the above classifications affect the accounting treatment for unrealized losses?

d. Why does a company maintain an investment portfolio containing current and noncurrent securities?

e. If a company elects to adopt fair value accounting for securities that are classified as available for sale simultaneously with the adoption of *SFAS No. 159*, what effect would the election have on its financial statements?

• Case 10-6 Accounting for Investments

Presented below are four unrelated situations involving equity securities that have readily determinable fair values.

Situation 1

A noncurrent portfolio with an aggregate market value in excess of cost includes one particular security whose market value has declined to less than half of the original cost. The decline in value is considered to be other than temporary.

Situation 2

The balance sheet of a company does not classify assets and liabilities as current and noncurrent. The portfolio of marketable equity securities includes securities normally considered to be trading securities that have a net cost in excess of market value of $2,000. The remainder of the portfolio is considered noncurrent and has a net market value in excess of $5,000.

Situation 3

A marketable equity security, whose market value is currently less than cost, is classified as a noncurrent security that is available for sale but is to be reclassified as a trading security.

Situation 4

A company's noncurrent portfolio of marketable equity securities consists of the common stock of one company. At the end of the prior year the market value of the security was 50 percent of original cost, and the effect was properly reflected in the balance sheet. However, at the end of the current year the market value of the security had appreciated to twice the original cost. The security is still considered noncurrent at year-end.

Required:

Determine the effect on classification, carrying value, and earnings for each of the preceding situations. Complete your response to each situation before proceeding to the next situation.

• Case 10-7 Equity Securities: GAAP versus IASB Standards

SFAS No. 115 prescribes the accounting treatment for investments in equity securities having readily determined fair values for which the equity method and consolidation do not apply. *IAS No. 39* prescribes international accounting practice for similar securities.

Required:

a. Compare and contrast U.S. GAAP for investments in equity securities under *SFAS No. 115* with the provisions of *IAS No. 39*.

b. Discuss whether U.S. GAAP under *SFAS No. 115* or the requirements of *IAS No. 25* are more consistent with the following concepts:

   i. Conservatism

   ii. Comparability

   iii. Relevance

   iv. Neutrality

   v. Representational faithfulness

   vi. Physical capital maintenance

• Case 10-8 Accounting for Goodwill

Kallus Corp. is an industry leader in the manufacture of toys. Each year, its design staff comes up with new ideas that are a great success. As a result, Kallus sales and profits consistently exceed those of other toy manufacturers. Over the past 10 years, Kallus has earned average net profits of $189 million compared to $122 million for the typical company in the toy industry.

Required:

Answer the following questions:

a. Does Kallus have goodwill? Explain.

b. Is goodwill an asset? Explain. (Does it meet the definition of an asset found in *SFAS No. 6*?)

c. If you believe Kallus has goodwill, how would you go about measuring it? Explain.

d. Should Kallus Corp. report goodwill in the balance sheet? Why or why not?

FASB ASC Research

For each of the following research cases, search the FASB ASC database for information to address the issues. Cut and paste the FASB paragraphs that support your responses. Then summarize briefly what your responses are, citing the pronouncements and paragraphs used to support your responses.

• FASB ASC 10-1 Debt and Equity Investments

A variety of authoritative accounting pronouncements have addressed accounting for debt and equity investments.

1. Summarize the current accounting treatment for investments in debt and equity securities.
2. The EITF has addressed many implementation issues for accounting for investments in debt and equity securities. List five of these issues.

• FASB ASC 10-2 Research and Development

In addition to the FASB's statement on accounting for research and development activities, the EITF has addressed three implementation issues. List and briefly summarize each of these issues.

• FASB ASC 10-3 Best-Efforts Basis, Research and Development Cost-Sharing Arrangements

The FASB ASC provides guidance on accounting for best-efforts basis, research and development cost-sharing arrangements by federal government contractors. Find, cite, and copy that guidance.

• FASB ASC 10-4 Direct-Response Advertising

The FASB ASC contains guidance on accounting for direct-response advertising that may result in reported assets. Search the FASB ASC and find answers to the following questions:

1. How are such assets to be measured initially?
2. How will the amounts ascribed to such assets be amortized?
3. How can the realizability of such assets be assessed?
4. What financial statement disclosures will be made about advertising?

(Be sure to cite the appropriate FASB ASC paragraph in answering each question).

• FASB ASC 10-5 Accumulated Losses on Equity Method Investments

The FASB ASC contains guidance on how to account for equity investments when accumulated losses by the investee have resulted in the investment account of the investor being reduced to zero. Find, cite, and copy that guidance.

Room for Debate

• Debate 10-1 *SFAS No. 115*

SFAS No. 115 (see FASB ASC 320) was issued in response to concerns by regulators and others regarding the recognition and measurement of investments in debt securities. For the following debate, you may consider tying your arguments to theories of capital maintenance and/or the conceptual framework.

Team Debate:

Team 1: Present arguments supporting the provisions of *SFAS No. 115*, now contained in FASB ASC 320.

Team 2: Present arguments describing the deficiencies of *SFAS No. 115*, now contained in FASB ASC 320.

• Debate 10-2 Goodwill

Under current GAAP, goodwill is recorded when purchased. For the following debate, you may consider tying your arguments to theories of capital maintenance and/or the conceptual framework.

Team Debate:

Team 1: Present arguments in favor of the capitalization of "purchased" goodwill.

Team 2: Present arguments against the capitalization of "purchased" goodwill.

• Debate 10-3 The Fair Value Option

Under current GAAP, companies may opt to report financial assets and liabilities at fair value.

Team Debate:

Team 1: Present arguments in favor of the fair value option for financial assets and liabilities.

Team 2: Present arguments against the fair value option for financial assets and liabilities.

Long-Term Liabilities

The importance of short-term liabilities as an element of working capital was discussed in Chapter 8. In this chapter we examine the nature of long-term liabilities. The emphasis is on recognition and measurement of transactions and events as liabilities, with specific attention to some of the more troublesome aspects, and on analysis of the risk associated with a company's use of long-term debt.

Investors, creditors, and other users view the separation of liabilities into current and noncurrent classifications as important because their decision models use the working capital concept, current ratios, and projections of expected future cash flows to analyze and compare the performance of firms. The amount of long-term debt relative to equity is also relevant because the debt-to-equity ratio is directly related to the risk associated with investing in the firm's stock.[1] As the debt-to-equity ratio of a firm increases, the market's perception of the riskiness of investing in the firm's stock also rises. Thus it is important that accountants have criteria to appropriately classify liabilities as short term or long term, so that decision makers can reliably evaluate the firm's ability to meet current needs and to determine the level of riskiness inherent in projections of future cash flows over time.

1. See Robert S. Hamada, "The Effect of the Firm's Capital Structure on the Systematic Risk of Common Stocks," *Journal of Finance* (March 1969), 13–31; and Mark E. Rubinstein, "A Mean-Variance Synthesis of Corporate Financial Theory," *Journal of Finance* (May 1973), 167–81.

The Definition of Liabilities

SFAC No. 6 describes the elements comprising the balance sheet as assets, liabilities, and equity. Assets have future economic benefit. Liabilities and equity provide resources (capital) for the acquisition of assets. The amount of liabilities a firm has relative to equity is termed the firm's capital structure.

In current accounting practice, liabilities and equity are treated as separate and distinct elements of the firm's capital structure. This distinction is apparent in the fundamental accounting equation

$$\text{assets} = \text{liabilities} + \text{equity}$$

Accordingly, liabilities and equity are both claimants to enterprise assets; but equity represents an ownership interest, whereas liabilities are creditor claims. These interests are different, and their separate disclosure is relevant to decision makers who rely on published financial information.[2]

Theories of equity postulate how the balance sheet elements are related, and they have implications for the definitions of both liabilities and equity. The two prominent theories of equity—entity theory and proprietary theory—imply unique relationships between assets, liabilities, and equity.

The *entity theory* depicts the accounting equation as

$$\text{assets} = \text{equities}$$

According to the entity theory, there is no fundamental difference between liabilities and owners' equity.[3] Both provide capital to the business entity and receive income in return in the form of interest and dividends. Under entity theory, liabilities and equity would require separate line disclosure in the balance sheet, but there would be no subtotals for total liabilities or total equity, and no need for separate or distinct definitions for each.

The *proprietary theory* views the net assets of the firm as belonging to the owners.[4] Under this theory, equity is equal to the net worth of the owners. The proprietary theory relationship is articulated as

$$\text{assets} - \text{liabilities} = \text{equity}$$

Although the AICPA, APB, and FASB have not formally described this relationship as the theory underlying the elements of financial statements, the APB defined liabilities and owners' equity in *Statement No. 4* and stated that the approach implicit in their definitions is that assets minus liabilities equals owners' equity.[5]

2. See Myrtle W. Clark, "Entity Theory, Modern Capital Structure Theory, and the Distinction between Debt and Equity," *Accounting Horizons* (September 1993), 14–31.

3. William A. Paton, *Accounting Theory* (New York: Ronald Press, 1922), 73.

4. Henry Rand Hatfield, *Accounting: Its Principles and Problems* (New York: D. Appleton & Co., 1927), 171, 221.

5. Accounting Principles Board, *APB Statement No. 4*, "Basic Concepts and Accounting Principles Underlying Financial Statements of Business Enterprises" (New York: AICPA, 1970), para. 132.

In addition, *SFAC No. 6* has defined liabilities and equities in a manner that is also consistent with proprietary theory as follows:

- *Liabilities.* Probable future sacrifices of economic benefits arising from present obligations of a particular entity to transfer assets or provide services to other entities in the future as a result of past transactions or events
- *Equities.* The residual interest in the assets of an entity that remains after deducting its liabilities. In a business enterprise, the equity is the ownership.[6]

Recognition and Measurement of Liabilities

According to *SFAC No. 5*, for an item to be recognized as a liability in financial statements, it must meet the definition of liabilities found in *SFAC No. 6*, and it must be measurable. Theoretically, liabilities should be measured at the present value of their future cash flows, discounted at the market rate of interest. The discounted present value measures the initial fair market value of a liability. For example, the selling price of a bond is equal to the sum of the present value of the interest payments and maturity value, discounted at the market rate of interest on the date it is sold. Discounting is often ignored for current liabilities because the undiscounted value is not materially different from the discounted present value.

Liabilities are measured at the amount established in an exchange—initial fair value. But, under the traditional historical cost accounting model, liabilities are not adjusted to fair value at the end of each subsequent accounting period. Alternatively, under *SFAS No. 159* (see FASB ASC 825, discussed in Chapter 10), companies may opt to report many financial assets and liabilities at fair value. If this alternative is elected, the liabilities for which the election was made are revalued at each reporting date. Their fair values are reported in the balance sheet, and changes in fair value are included in earnings. This measurement and reporting approach is consistent with the theoretical valuation of liabilities.

The classification and measurement of items as liabilities is not always straightforward. For example, the present value of postretirement benefits, such as health care for retired employees, are recognized as liabilities, even though the benefits may not be paid for many years in the future and there is a great deal of uncertainty surrounding projections of future cash flows. The FASB supports this kind of recognition by referring to the *SFAC No. 6* definition of liabilities. Postretirement benefits represent sacrifices of future resources resulting from employees having earned those future benefits during present and prior accounting periods.

Unfortunately, the definitions in *SFAC No. 6*, like those in *APB Statement No. 4*, leave many unresolved questions. In the following section we examine some of these questions and attempt to develop more specific criteria for the proper classification of items as liabilities.

Debt versus Equity

The preceding definitions require the classification of all items on the right-hand side of the balance sheet into their liability or equity components. This requirement presumes that all financial interests in the enterprise are liability or equity

6. *Statement of Financial Accounting Concepts No. 6*, "Elements of Financial Statements" (Stamford, CT: Financial Accounting Standards Board, 1985), paras. 35, 49.

interests, and it further presumes that these distinctions are readily apparent to whoever is preparing financial statements. There are at least two fallacies in these assumptions: (1) the wide variety of securities issued by the modern, complex corporation does not readily lend itself to classification schemes; and (2) to date there are no authoritative guidelines to use in applying the classification schemes. What one individual may view as debt, another may view as equity.

An example of a security presenting this type of dilemma is redeemable preferred stock. Until the issuance of *SFAS No. 150* (see FASB ASC 480, discussed later in this chapter), GAAP considered redeemable preferred stock as equity, or as a so-called mezzanine item disclosed between liabilities and equity on the balance sheet, even though it must be repaid. Additionally, the SEC mandated that future cash obligations attached to preferred stock subject to mandatory redemption or whose redemption is outside the issuer's control should be highlighted to distinguish it from permanent capital.[7] Accordingly, these securities were not included in stockholders' equity. Moreover, under the SEC ruling they were not to be included in total liabilities either. The SEC had in effect created a separate "temporary" equity balance sheet category. Yet, *SFAC No. 6* does not recognize such a category as an element of financial statements. Later, in 2003, the FASB issued *SFAS No. 150*, "Accounting for Certain Financial Instruments with Characteristics of Both Liabilities and Equity" (see FASB ASC 480). This guidance requires companies to record and report mandatorily redeemable preferred stock (MRPS) as a liability on their balance sheets, and the dividends on these securities as interest expense.

As long as accountants feel that the present distinction between debt and equity should be continued, such examples point to the need for accountants to develop additional criteria to aid in classifying items on the right-hand side of the accounting equation as either debt or equity. The following section discusses some of the decision factors that may be used.

Consolidated Set of Decision Factors

The following set of thirteen factors is presented as a guide to assist in determining the classification of items on the right-hand side of the accounting equation as either debt or equity. (The sequence in which the factors are presented is not intended to reflect any judgment about their relative importance.)

Maturity Date
Debt instruments typically have a fixed maturity date, whereas equity instruments do not mature. Because they do mature, debt instruments set forth the redemption requirements. One of the requirements may be the establishment of a sinking fund to ensure that funds will be available for the redemption.

Claim on Assets
In the event the business is liquidated, creditors' claims take precedence over those of the owners. There are two possible interpretations of this factor. The first is that all claims other than the first priority are equity claims. The second is that

7. Securities and Exchange Commission, *Accounting Series Release No. 268*, Presentation in Financial Statements of "Redeemable Preferred Stocks," in *SEC Accounting Rules* (Chicago: Commerce Clearing House, 1983).

all claims other than the last are creditor claims. The problem area includes all claims between these two interpretations: those claims that are subordinated to the first claim but take precedence over the last claim.

Claim on Income

A fixed dividend or interest rate has a preference over other dividend or interest payments. That it is cumulative in the event it is not paid for a particular period is said to indicate a debt security. On the other hand, a security that does not provide for a fixed rate, one that gives the holder the right to participate with common stockholders in any income distribution, or one whose claim is subordinate to other claims may indicate an ownership interest.

Market Valuations

As long as a company is solvent, market valuations of its liabilities are unaffected by company performance. Conversely, the market price of equity securities is affected by the earnings of the company as well as by investor expectations regarding future dividend payments.

Voice in Management

A voting right is the most frequent evidence of a voice in the management of a corporation. This right is normally limited to common stockholders, but it may be extended to other investors if the company defaults on some predetermined conditions. For example, if interest is not paid when due or profits fall below a certain level, voting rights may be granted to other security holders, thus suggesting that the security in question has ownership characteristics.

Maturity Value

A liability has a fixed maturity value that does not change throughout its life. An ownership interest does not mature, except in the event of liquidation; consequently, it has no maturity value.

Intent of Parties

The courts have determined that the intent of the parties is one factor to be evaluated in ruling on the debt or equity nature of a particular security. Investor attitude and investment character are two sub-factors that help in making this determination. Investors may be divided into those who want safety and those who want capital growth, and the investments may be divided into those that provide either safety or an opportunity for capital gains or losses. If the investor was motivated to make a particular investment on the basis of safety and if the corporation included in the issue those features normally equated with safety, then the security may be debt rather than equity. However, if the investor was motivated to acquire the security by the possibility of capital growth and if the security offered the opportunity of capital growth, the security would be viewed as equity rather than debt.

Preemptive Right

By law, common stockholders have a preemptive right (the right to purchase common shares in a new stock offering by the corporation). If a security offers its holder a preemptive right, it may be considered to have an equity characteristic. Securities not carrying this right may be considered debt.

Conversion Features

A security that may be converted into common stock has at least the potential to become equity if it is not currently considered equity. Thus the security, or perhaps its conversion feature, may be considered equity. A historical study of eventual conversion or liquidation may be useful in evaluating this particular factor.

Potential Dilution of Earnings per Share

This factor might be considered as a sub-factor of *conversion* because the conversion feature of a security is the most likely cause of dilution of earnings per share, other than a new issue of common stock. In any event, a security that has the potential to dilute earnings per share is assumed to have equity characteristics.

Right to Enforce Payments

From a legal point of view, creditors have the right to receive periodic interest at the agreed-upon date and to have the maturity value paid at the maturity date. The enforcement of this right may result in the corporation being placed in receivership. Owners have no such legal right; therefore, the existence of the right to enforce payment is an indication of a debt instrument.

Good Business Reasons for Issuing

Determining what constitutes good business reasons for issuing a security with certain features rather than one with different features presents a difficult problem. Two relevant sub-factors are the alternatives available and the amount of capitalization. Securities issued by a company in financial difficulty or with a low level of capitalization may be considered equity on the grounds that only those with an ownership interest would be willing to accept the risk, whereas securities issued by a company with a high level of capitalization may be viewed as debt.

Identity of Interest between Creditors and Owners

When the individuals who invest in debt securities are the same individuals, or family members, who hold the common stock, an ownership interest is implied.

Recognizing that these problems exist, the FASB resurrected a discussion memorandum titled "Distinguishing between Liability and Equity Instruments and Accounting for Instruments with Characteristics of Both."[8] The impetus for the discussion memorandum is the increasing use of *complex financial instruments*, which have both debt and equity characteristics. In late 2000 the FASB issued an exposure draft of a proposed statement, "Accounting for Financial Instruments with Characteristics of Liabilities, Equity, or Both," and a proposed amendment to *SFAC No. 6* that would revise the definition of liabilities.[9]

The Board's tentative conclusions have led to the development of an approach based on the characteristics of liabilities and equity. The first step in this approach is to determine whether the component includes an obligation. An

8. FASB Discussion Memorandum, "Distinguishing between Liability and Equity Instruments and Accounting for Instruments with Characteristics of Both" (Stamford, CT: FASB, August 20, 1990).

9. FASB Exposure Draft, "Accounting for Financial Instruments with Characteristics of Liabilities, Equity, or Both" (Stamford, CT: FASB, October 27, 2000).

obligation is a contractual provision that requires the issuer to perform by transferring to the holder cash, other assets, or the issuer's stock. Those financial instrument components that embody obligations that require settlement by a transfer of cash or other assets are classified as liabilities because they do not give rise to the possibility of establishing an ownership interest by the holder. Obligations permitting or requiring settlement by the issuance of stock give rise to liability-equity classification questions. These components should be classified as equity if they convey the risks and rewards of ownership to the holder. If the relationship is that of a debtor or creditor, the component should be classified as liability. The proceeds from issuing a compound financial instrument that includes both liability and equity components should be allocated to its liability and equity components using their relative fair value unless such an allocation is impracticable. Interest, dividends, gains, and losses relating to financial instrument components classified as liabilities are reported in income. Similar amounts related to equity components are reported in equity.

The FASB has not yet resolved the issues raised by the existence of complex financial instruments. In its 2003 issuance of *SFAS No. 150*, "Accounting for Certain Financial Instruments with Characteristics of both Liabilities and Equity" (see FASB ASC 480), the Board has, however, used the definitions of obligations and equity found in the "components" approach to certain financial instruments. *SFAS No. 150* required that the following freestanding financial instruments be classified as liabilities:

- A mandatorily redeemable financial instrument, such as mandatorily redeemable preferred stock

- A financial instrument that (at inception) embodies an obligation to repurchase the issuer's equity shares, or is indexed to such an obligation, and that requires or may require the issuer to settle the obligation by transferring assets, such as a written put option on the issuer's common stock

- A financial instrument that embodies an obligation (unconditional or conditional) that requires or may require the issuer to settle by issuing a variable number of shares of its equity securities, if, at inception, the financial instrument's monetary value is based (solely or predominantly) on any of the following:

  - A fixed monetary amount

  - Variations in the value of something other than the fair value of the issuer's equity securities—for example, a financial instrument indexed to the S&P 500

  - Variations inversely related to changes in the fair value of the issuer's equity shares, for example, a written put that could be net share settled

Mandatorily redeemable financial instruments meet the definition of a liability because they embody unconditional obligations for the issuer to redeem them by transferring assets at a specified or determinable date or dates, or upon an event that is certain to occur. Freestanding written put options and forward contracts on the issuer's equity shares that require physical settlement are classified as liabilities because the issuer must repurchase equity shares by transferring assets. Finally, obligations that are to be settled by the issuance of a variable number of equity shares are considered liabilities when the number of shares issued in settlement is determined by a monetary amount fixed at the date they are issued.

Such settlements are tantamount to a settlement by transferring assets because the settlements made are equivalent in value to a known amount that was pre-determined at the obligation's inception.

Long-Term Debt Classification

Once a liability has been identified and measured, it is reported as either a current or a long-term liability. The classification of an item as a long-term liability is based on the one-year or current operating cycle rule. If the settlement of an existing obligation is not expected to use an asset properly classified as current or to be replaced by another current liability, it is classified as a long-term liability. The most frequently encountered long-term liabilities are bonds, long-term notes, lease obligations, pension obligations, deferred taxes, other long-term deferrals, and, occasionally, contingent liabilities. Leases, pensions, and deferred taxes are discussed separately in the following chapters. In this section we examine the reporting requirements for bonds, notes, deferrals, and contingencies.

Bonds Payable

When additional funds are needed to finance current operations or to expand the business, a corporation has the choice of issuing debt or equity securities. There are four basic reasons why a corporation may wish to issue debt rather than equity securities:

- *Bonds may be the only available source of funds.* Many small and medium-sized companies may appear too risky for investors to make a permanent investment.
- *Debt financing has a lower cost.* Since bonds have lower investment risk than stock, they traditionally have paid relatively low rates of interest. Investors acquiring equity securities generally expect a greater return to compensate for higher investment risk.
- *Debt financing offers a tax advantage.* Interest payments to debt holders are deductible for income tax purposes, whereas dividends paid on equity securities are not.
- *The voting privilege is not shared.* Stockholders wishing to maintain their present percentage of ownership in a corporation must purchase the current ownership proportion of each new common stock issue. Debt issues do not carry ownership or voting rights; consequently, they do not dilute voting power. Where the proportion of ownership is small and holdings are widespread, this consideration is probably not very important.

The use of borrowed funds is known as *financial leverage*. The customary reason for using borrowed funds is the expectation of investing them in a capital project that will provide a return in excess of the cost of the acquired funds. The stockholders' investment serves as protection for the bondholders' principal and income, and the strength of current earnings and the debt-to-equity relationship both influence the rate of interest required by the debt holder. When using debt financing, it should be recognized that financial leverage increases the rate of return to common stockholders only when the return on the project is greater than the cost of the borrowed funds. Earnings (less their related tax effect) in excess of interest payments will increase earnings per share. However, if the return on the investment project falls below the stipulated bond interest rate, earnings per share will decline. The assessment of a company's use of financial leverage is discussed later in the chapter.

Bond Classifications

Bonds frequently are classified by the nature of the protection offered by the company. Bonds that are secured by a lien against specific assets of the corporation are known as *mortgage bonds*. In the event the corporation becomes bankrupt and is liquidated, the holders of mortgage bonds have first claim against the proceeds from the sale of the assets that secured their debt. If the proceeds from the sale of secured assets are not sufficient to repay the debt, mortgage bondholders become general creditors for the remainder of the unpaid debt.

Debenture bonds are not secured by any property or assets, and their marketability is based on the corporation's general credit. A long period of earnings and continued favorable predictions are necessary for a company to sell debenture bonds. Debenture bondholders become general creditors of the corporation in the event of liquidation.

Bond Selling Prices

Bonds are generally sold in $1,000 denominations and carry a stated amount of interest. The *stated interest rate* is printed on the *bond indenture* (contract). It determines the amount of interest that will be paid to the investor at the end of each interest period. The stated rate will approximate the rate that management believes necessary to sell the bonds, given the current state of the economy and the perceived risk associated with the bonds. A bond issued with a relatively low amount of perceived risk will offer a lower interest rate than a bond issued with a relatively higher amount of risk.

The decision to issue bonds and their subsequent sale may take place over a relatively long period of time. From the time the bonds are authorized until they are issued, economic conditions affecting interest rates are likely to change. As a result, at issuance the stated interest rate may differ from the *market rate* for bonds of similar perceived risk. The investor will be unwilling to invest in a bond yielding interest at a rate less than the market rate. Similarly, the issuing company will be unwilling to issue a bond yielding an interest rate that is higher than the market rate. Because the stated rate is predetermined and cannot be changed, the market price of the bond is adjusted so that the *effective rate* of interest is equal to the market rate.

The market rate of interest necessary to sell a bond issue is also known as the *yield rate* on the bonds. The amount investors are willing to invest is the amount that will yield the market rate of interest, given the amount and timing of the stated interest payments and the *maturity value* of the bonds. Thus the issue price of the bond is equal to the sum of the present values of the principal and interest payments, discounted at the yield rate. If investors are willing to accept the interest rate stated on the bonds, they will be sold at their *face value*, or *par*, and the yield rate will equal the stated interest rate. When the market rate of interest exceeds the stated interest rate, the bonds will sell below face value (at a *discount*), thereby increasing the effective interest rate. Alternatively, when the market rate of interest is less than the stated interest rate, the bonds will sell above face value (at a *premium*), thereby lowering the effective interest rate.

To illustrate, assume that the XYZ Corporation issued $100,000 of 10 percent, 10-year bonds on January 1, 2010. Interest on these bonds is to be paid annually each December 31. If these bonds are actually sold to yield 9 percent, the bond selling price will be calculated as follows:

Present value of maturity value	
$100,000 × 0.422411*	$ 42,241.10
Present value of interest payments	
$10,000 × 6.417658**	64,176.58
	$106,417.68

*Present value of $1: $i = 0.09$, $n = 10$.
**Present value of an ordinary annuity of $1: $i = 0.09$, $n = 10$.

Since investors must accept an interest rate lower than the rate stated on the bonds, the bond selling price will be higher than the face value of the bonds. The increased selling price has the effect of lowering the yield rate. That is, the amount of interest stipulated on the bonds will be the amount paid to investors each interest payment date, but the actual cash amount invested has increased. The result is that total interest expense over the life of the bonds will be less than the stated amount of interest by the amount of the premium.

Total interest paid	
$10,000 × 10	$100,000.00
Principal payment at maturity	
	100,000.00
Total paid by the borrower	$200,000.00
Issue price	106,417.68
Total interest expense	$ 93,582.32
Premium on the bonds	$ 6,417.68

On the other hand, assume that the rate of interest required by investors is 12 percent. The bond selling price will be reduced to achieve a higher yield rate as follows:

Present value of maturity value	
$100,000 × 0.321973*	$32,197.30
Present value of interest payments	
$10,000 × 5.650223**	56,502.23
	$88,699.53

*Present value of $1: $i = 12$, $n = 10$.
**Present value of an ordinary annuity of $1: i = 12, $n = 10$.

In this case, the yield rate is higher than the stated rate because the cash payment to investors remains the same while the amount borrowed has decreased.

The total interest expense over the life of the bonds will exceed the total interest payments by the amount of the discount, $11,300.47 ($100,000 − $88,699.53).

When bonds are issued between interest payment dates, because interest payments are fixed by the bond indenture, investors will receive the full amount of the interest payment on the interest payment date, even though the bonds have not been held for the entire interest period. To compensate the issuer, the investor pays interest accrued from the contract date to the date of issuance. The *accrued interest* will be repaid to the investor on the next interest payment date and therefore is a current liability to the issuing corporation. The issue price is determined by discounting the maturity value and interest payments from the contract date to maturity plus the return on the bond from the contract date to the date of issuance minus the amount of accrued interest paid.

Bond Issue Costs

The costs to issue bonds may be substantial. The issuing corporation incurs attorney's fees, costs to print the bonds, the cost of preparing the bond prospectus, and sales brokerage commissions. Under *APB Opinion No. 21* (see FASB ASC 470-35-10-2), *bond issue costs* were treated as a deferred charge and shown on the balance sheet as an asset. The asset is amortized from the date of issue to the maturity date of the bonds. The rationale for this treatment is that the costs were incurred to derive benefit from the issuance of the bonds because the debt proceeds contribute to the earnings process. Consequently, they represent future service potential and are assets.

In contrast, debt issue costs were cited by *SFAC No. 6* as an expenditure that does not meet the definition of an asset.[10] The FASB argued that these costs reduce the proceeds of borrowing, resulting in a higher effective interest rate. Consequently, they have no future benefit. This argument provides a basis for subtracting unamortized bond issue costs from the initial carrying value of the debt and allowing it to affect the calculation of periodic interest expense. Alternatively, the FASB stated that because they provide no future benefit, debt issue costs may be treated as an expense of the period of borrowing.[11]

Alternatively, when a company elects to measure a financial obligation using the *SFAS No. 159* (see FASB ASC 825-10-25) fair value option, all up-front costs and fees are expensed as incurred. They are not deferred. A rationale for this treatment is that the market does not factor in up-front costs when setting the issue price of the debt (the debt's fair value) and thus the amount borrowed by the debtor on the date of issuance. Because these costs neither affect the debt's fair value nor meet the definition of an asset, as discussed above, they are logically an expense.

Bond Interest Expense

Interest is the cost of borrowing, and because debt is borrowed over a period of time, it should be allocated to the periods over which the debt is owed. As shown above, the total interest over the life of the bond issue is affected by the presence of a premium or discount. In these cases, the calculation of *interest expense* involves amortization of the premium or discount. There are two methods of allocating

10. *SFAC No. 6*, para. 237.
11. Ibid.

interest expense and the associated premium or discount over the life of the bond issue: (1) the straight-line method and (2) the effective interest method. Under the *straight-line method,* the total discount or premium is divided by the total number of interest periods to arrive at the amount to be amortized each period. This method gives an equal allocation per period and results in a stable interest cost per period.

The assumption of a stable interest cost per interest period is not realistic, however, when a premium or discount is involved. The original selling price of the bonds was set to yield the market rate of interest. Therefore the more valid assumption is that the yield rate should be reflected over the life of the bond issue. The *effective interest method* satisfies this objective by applying the yield rate to the beginning carrying value of the bonds in each successive period to determine the amount of interest expense to record. When using the effective interest method, the premium or discount amortization is determined by finding the difference between the stated interest payment and the amount of interest expense for the period.

The effective interest method is theoretically preferable because it results in a stable interest rate per period and discloses a liability balance on the balance sheet equivalent to the present value of the future cash flows discounted at the original market rate of interest. In addition, *APB Opinion No. 21* (see FASB ASC 835-30-25) required use of the effective interest method unless the results obtained from use of the straight-line method are not materially different. Some companies use the straight-line method because it is easy to calculate and because the difference between income statement and balance sheet values reported under the two methods from period to period are relatively minor.

However, one could argue that the effective interest method does not yield balance sheet amounts that are relevant to users of financial statements. The resulting balance sheet amount is the amount that it would take to satisfy the obligation under its original terms. The fair value option may provide greater relevance because under this option, fair value is equal to the exit value of the financial liability and thus would reveal the amount that it would take to extinguish the debt on the balance sheet date. Moreover, reporting changes in the fair value of unextinguished debt in earnings provides a measure of the opportunity cost or gain resulting from management's decision to carry the debt rather than retire it.

Zero Coupon Bonds

A *zero coupon* or *deep discount bond* is a bond that does not carry a stated rate of interest; thus, the borrower makes no interest payments to the investor. As a result, zero coupon bonds are sold at considerably less than face value (i.e., at a deep discount). Because there are no interest payments, the interest cost to the issuer is equal to the difference between the maturity value and the issue price of the bond. The resulting periodic interest expense is equal to the amount of the discount amortized for the accounting period. For example, if a $100,000 zero coupon bond with a life of 10 years is issued to yield 12 percent, the issue price will be $32,197 and the unamortized discount will be $67,803. Interest expense should be calculated using the effective interest method. For the first year, interest expense will be $3,864 (12% × $32,197). The bond's carrying value will then increase by the amount of the discount amortized ($3,864), resulting in an increase in interest expense incurred for year two. This pattern is repeated until the carrying value of the bond has increased to its face value.

Many accountants have questioned the logic of investing in zero coupon bonds because of the Internal Revenue Code regulation that requires investors to include the yearly discount amortization as income prior to the time the cash interest is actually received. However, zero coupon bonds became popular with pension funds because (1) they usually do not contain a call provision, and therefore the stated return is guaranteed until maturity; and (2) they offer *reinvestment return*, which means that all the interest is reinvested at the same rate of return over the life of the issue. In addition, the income from pension investments is tax deferred. No tax is paid until distributions are made during retirement.

Call Provisions

Long-term debt is issued under the prevailing market conditions at the time it is issued. When market conditions are unfavorable, it may be necessary to pay unusually high interest rates or to include promises in the *bond indenture* (the agreement between the issuing corporation and the bondholders) that inhibit the financial operation of the company. For example, the indenture may include restrictions (debt covenants) on dividends, a promise to maintain a certain working capital position, or the maintenance of a certain debt-equity relationship.

Most companies protect themselves from the inability to take advantage of future favorable changes in market conditions by including a call provision in the bond indenture. This provision allows the company to recall debt at a prestated percentage of the issue price (the call price).

The recall, or *early extinguishment*, of debt may take two forms: (1) the borrowed funds may no longer be needed and the debt is therefore canceled, which is termed *debt retirement*; or (2) the existing debt may be replaced with another debt issue, termed *debt refunding*.

The cancellation of existing debt poses no particular accounting problem. Any gain or loss resulting from the difference between the carrying value and the call price is treated as a gain or loss in the year the extinguishment takes place. The theory behind this treatment is that the recall of the debt was a current decision, and its effects should therefore be reflected in current income.

The argument is not quite so convincing in the case of refunding transactions. In *ARB No. 43*, three methods of accounting for the gain or loss from a refunding transaction were discussed.

- Make a direct write-off of the gain or loss in the year of the transaction.
- Amortize the gain or loss over the remaining life of the original issue.
- Amortize the gain or loss over the life of the new issue.[12]

Some accountants favor recognizing the gain or loss over the remaining life of the old issue because they view this as the period of benefit; that is, a higher interest cost would have been incurred during this period if the old issue had not been refunded. Those who favor recognizing the gain or loss over the life of the new issue base their argument on the matching concept; that is, the lower interest rates obtained by the refunding should be adjusted to reflect any refunding gain or loss. Finally, those accountants favoring immediate write-off argue that this method is the most logical because the value of the debt has changed over time, and paying the call price is the most favorable method of eliminating the debt.

---

12. Accounting Principles Board, *Accounting Research Bulletin No. 43*, "Restatement and Revision of Accounting Research Bulletins" (New York: AICPA, 1953).

ARB No. 43 stated a preference for the first method and allowed the second. Later, *APB Opinion No. 6* (superseded) allowed the use of the third method under certain circumstances.[13] In effect, these two releases frequently permitted a company to use any one of three available methods.

After a subsequent reexamination of the topic, the APB issued *Opinion No. 26*, "Early Extinguishment of Debt"[14] (see FASB ASC 470-50). In this release the Board maintained that all early extinguishments were fundamentally alike (whether retirements or refundings) and that they should be accounted for in the same manner. Since the accounting treatment of retirements was to reflect any gain or loss in the period of recall, it was concluded that any gains or losses from refunding should also be reflected currently in income. Thus options two and three are no longer considered acceptable under GAAP.

In the mid-1970s, because of pressure from the SEC, the FASB undertook a study of the reporting requirements for gains and losses arising from early extinguishment of debt. Prevailing market conditions in 1973 and 1974 allowed several companies to reacquire long-term debt at prices well below face value. For example, in 1973 United Brands was able to realize a $37.5 million gain by exchanging $12.5 million in cash and $75 million in 9⅛ percent debentures for $125 million of 5½ percent convertible subordinated debentures. This entire gain was reported as ordinary income.

Upon completion of its study, the FASB issued *SFAS No. 4*, "Reporting Gains and Losses from Extinguishment of Debt"[15] (superseded).This release required that gains and losses on all extinguishments, whether early or at scheduled maturity, be classified as extraordinary items without regard to the criteria of "unusual nature" or "infrequency of occurrence." However, recently the FASB revisited this issue and reached a different conclusion. The Board noted that when *SFAS No. 4* was originally issued, its provisions represented a "practical and reasonable solution to the question regarding income statement classification of gains or losses from extinguishment of debt until such time as the broader issues involved can be addressed."[16] In the ensuing years, the use of debt extinguishment became part of the risk management strategy of many companies. As a result, the FASB concluded that debt extinguishments that are used as a part of an entity's risk management strategy do not meet the criteria for classification as extraordinary items and therefore should not be classified as extraordinary.[17]

In 1983, *APB Opinion No. 26* was amended by *SFAS No. 76*, "Extinguishment of Debt" (superseded). This release made the provisions of *APB Opinion No. 26* applicable to all debt extinguishments, whether early or not, except those specifically

---

13. Accounting Principles Board, *Accounting Principles Board Opinion No. 6*, "Status of Accounting Research Bulletins" (New York: AICPA, 1965).

14. Accounting Principles Board, *Accounting Principles Board Opinion No. 26*, "Early Extinguishment of Debt" (New York: AICPA, 1972).

15. *Statement of Financial Accounting Standards No. 4*, "Reporting Gains and Losses from Extinguishment of Debt" (Stamford, CT: FASB, 1975).

16. Ibid., para. 15.

17. *Statement of Financial Accounting Standards No. 145*, "Rescission of FASB Statements No. 4, 44, and 64, Amendment of FASB Statement No. 13, and Technical Corrections" (Norwich, CT: FASB, 2002; see FASB ASC 470-50).

exempted by other pronouncements (e.g., debt restructurings). Debt was considered to be extinguished in the following circumstances:

- The debtor has paid the creditor and is relieved of all obligations regardless of whether the securities are canceled or held as Treasury bonds by the debtor.
- The debtor is legally released from being the primary obligor by the creditor, and it is probable that no future payment will be required (*legal defeasance*).
- The debtor places cash or other essentially risk-free securities (such as government securities) in a trust used solely for satisfying both the scheduled interest payments and principal of a specific obligation, and the possibility of future payments is remote (*in-substance defeasance*).

Under the third situation, known as in-substance defeasance, the debt was considered extinguished even though the debtor was not legally released from being the primary obligor of the debt. *SFAS No. 76* allowed the debt and the assets placed into the irrevocable trust to be derecognized. This practice was criticized as being inconsistent with economic reality. It was argued that the transaction does not have sufficient economic substance to justify derecognition or gain recognition. Moreover, it allowed management to manipulate income by reporting a gain even though the debtor had not been legally released from the obligation.

The FASB reviewed in-substance defeasance as part of its project on financial instruments and off–balance sheet financing (discussed later in this chapter). The Board subsequently issued *SFAS No. 125* (superseded), which eliminated the reporting of "in-substance defeasance" transactions as early extinguishments of debt.[18] This release indicated that a debt should be extinguished if and only if the following two conditions are met:

1. The debtor pays the creditor and is relieved of its obligation. Payment may be in the form of cash, other financial assets, goods, or services or reacquisition of debt securities.

2. The debtor is legally released from being the primary obligor.

It was argued that an in-substance defeasance transaction does not meet the conditions necessary for derecognition of a liability or an asset because it lacks the following essential characteristics:

1. Placing the assets in a trust does not release the debtor from the debt. If the assets should prove insufficient, the debtor must make up the difference.

2. The lender is not limited to the cash flows generated by the trust.

3. The lender does not have the ability to dispose of the assets or to terminate the trust.

4. If the assets in the trust exceed the amounts necessary to meet scheduled interest and principal payments, the debtor can remove the assets.

5. The lender is not a contractual party to establishing the trust.

6. The debtor does not surrender control of the benefits of the assets. The debtor continues to derive benefit because the assets are being used to extinguish the debt.

18. *Statement of Financial Accounting Standards No. 125*, "Accounting for Transfers and Servicing of Financial Assets and Extinguishments of Liabilities" (Norwalk, CT: FASB, 1996).

The FASB recently replaced *SFAS No. 125* with *SFAS No. 140*, "Accounting for Transfers and Servicing of Financial Assets and Extinguishments of Liabilities—A Replacement of FASB Statement No. 125" (see FASB ASC 860). However, the provisions of *SFAS No. 125* that related to the issue of debt extinguishment were retained.

Convertible Debt

Senior securities (bonds or preferred stock) that are convertible into common stock at the election of the bondholder play a frequent role in corporate financing. There is rather widespread agreement that firms sell convertible securities for one of two primary reasons: either the firm wants to increase equity capital and decides that convertible securities are the most advantageous way, or the firm wants to increase its debt or preferred stock and discovers that the conversion feature is necessary to make the security sufficiently marketable at a reasonable interest or dividend rate. In addition, several other factors may, at one time or another, motivate corporate management to decide to issue convertible debt. Among these are

1. Avoiding the downward price pressures on the firm's stock that placing a large new issue of common stock on the market would cause
2. Avoiding dilution of earnings and increased dividend requirements while an expansion program is getting under way
3. Avoiding the direct sale of common stock when the corporation believes that its stock is currently undervalued in the market
4. Penetrating that segment of the capital market that is unwilling or unable to participate in a direct common stock issue
5. Minimizing the flotation cost (costs associated with selling securities)

The remainder of this section concentrates on convertible debt. Convertible preferred stock is discussed in Chapter 15.

Accounting for *convertible debt* has been the subject of controversy for a number of years. Convertible debt is a *complex financial instrument*. Complex financial instruments combine two or more fundamental financial instruments. Convertible debt combines debt with the option to convert. This combination raises questions regarding the nature of convertible debt and as a result raises questions regarding its appropriate accounting treatment.

There is no question regarding the nature of straight-debt issues. These bonds are liabilities and nothing more. Convertible debt, however, can be viewed in a number of ways. One possibility is to ignore the conversion feature and treat convertible debt like a straight-debt issue. This is the currently required treatment under *APB Opinion No. 14* (see FASB ASC 470-20). This approach is defended on the basis that the bond and conversion option are not separable. Thus the conversion feature itself, regardless of its nature, has no marketable valuation. Opponents of the current requirement argue that it results in an understatement of interest expense and an overstatement of bond indebtedness.[19]

A second view holds that the conversion feature is equity, and as such, its value should be separated from the bond and included in stockholders' equity

---

19. It should be noted that *APB Opinion No. 14* was issued before the availability of the Black-Scholes options pricing model (discussed in Chapter 15). Use of the Black-Scholes model allows for separating the debt and equity portions of convertible bonds.

.as additional paid-in capital. Proponents of this view argue that the conversion feature has value that is a function of the price of the stock, not the bond. Investors are willing to pay for the option to convert. Moreover, due to the flexibility to convert or hold the bond, they may also accept a lower interest rate on the debt than would otherwise be obtainable. Therefore, the valuation of the equity component would be the difference between the price at which the bonds might have been sold and the price at which they were sold. This position was initially embraced by the APB in *Opinion No. 10*,[20] but shortly after, due to widespread opposition by corporate management, it was superseded by *APB Opinion No. 12*.[21]

A third view is that convertible debt should be classified according to its governing characteristic.[22] The governing characteristic is based on whether the instrument satisfies the definition of a liability or equity at the date of issuance. The FASB has described four alternative approaches by which the governing characteristic might be determined. The first three would classify convertible debt as a liability. The approaches are as follows:

1. Classify based on the contractual terms in effect at issuance. Without conversion, interest and maturity payments must be made; therefore convertible debt should be classified as a liability.

2. Classify as a liability if the instrument embodies an obligation to transfer financial instruments to the holder if the option were exercised.

3. Classify in accordance with the fundamental financial instrument having the highest value.

4. Classify based on the most probable outcome. A convertible bond would be classified as an equity security if conversion were deemed to be the more probable outcome.[23]

Another view is based on alternative 2 above. This view considers the bond and the option to be two distinct liabilities that warrant separate disclosure.[24] Because the option obligates the corporation to transfer stock to the bondholder upon conversion, the option itself may be considered a liability. The corporation may satisfy the obligation at any time before exercise by buying the bond in the open market or by exercising a call. When the bond is converted, because the corporation could have sold the stock that the bond was converted into at market value, the difference between the market value and the cost to the investor to purchase the bond represents compensation to the investor—a cost to the issuing company. That is, common stock is used in lieu of cash. An exercise of the option to convert would typically occur when the market price of the stock is high enough

20. Accounting Principles Board, *Accounting Principles Board Opinion No. 10*, "Omnibus Opinion—1966" (New York: AICPA, 1966).

21. Accounting Principles Board, *Accounting Principles Board Opinion No. 12*, "Omnibus Opinion—1967" (New York: AICPA, 1967).

22. FASB Discussion Memorandum, "Distinguishing between Liability and Equity Instruments and Accounting for Instruments with Characteristics of Both" (Stamford, CT: FASB, 1990), para. 287.

23. Ibid., paras. 289–90.

24. Clark, "Entity Theory, Modern Capital Structure Theory, and the Distinction between Debt and Equity."

to motivate conversion. Thus, at exercise the corporation would receive less than it would have received had the stock transaction occurred at market price. Consequently, the decision to allow the bonds to be converted causes the corporation to suffer a loss. Since equity transactions are between the corporation and stockholders acting as owners, such a loss is inconsistent with the definition of equity. Finally, if the option to convert is never exercised, the initial value received for the conversion feature cannot be equity because the bondholder never acted in an ownership capacity and has never been anything but a debt holder.

Long-Term Notes Payable

Long-term notes payable are similar to bonds in that they represent future obligations to repay debt. And, the promise to pay is generally accompanied by a provision for interest on the borrowed funds. The amount of interest charged will depend on such factors as the credit standing of the borrower, the amount of current debt, and usual business customs.

During the early 1970s, the APB studied accounting for notes receivable and payable. The study disclosed a rather unusual occurrence in that some note transactions were being conducted without an accompanying interest charge. These transactions were apparently being carried out for such purposes as maintaining favorable customer relations, maintaining current suppliers, or ensuring future services. After reviewing these practices, the Board issued *Opinion No. 21*, "Interest on Receivables and Payables"[25] (see FASB ASC 835-30), which provided guidelines for cases in which no rate of interest was stipulated on notes or the rate stipulated was clearly inappropriate.

The provisions of *APB Opinion No. 21* are summarized as follows (see FASB ASC 835-30-25):

1. Notes exchanged solely for cash are assumed to have a present value equal to the cash exchanged.

2. Notes exchanged for property, goods, and services are presumed to have an appropriate rate of interest.

3. If no interest is stated or the amount of interest is clearly inappropriate on notes exchanged for property, goods, and services, the present value of the note should be determined by (whichever is more clearly determinable):

   a. Determining the fair market value of the property, goods, and services exchanged.

   b. Determining the market value of the note at the time of the transaction.

4. If neither 3a nor 3b is determinable, the present value of the note should be determined by discounting all future payments to the present at an imputed rate of interest. The imputed rate should approximate the rate of similar independent borrowers and lenders in arm's-length transactions.[26] In this case, the imputed rate should approximate the rate that the borrower would have to pay to obtain additional funds. So, it is often referred to as the incremental borrowing rate.

25. Accounting Principles Board, *Accounting Principles Board Opinion No. 21*, "Interest on Receivables and Payables" (New York: AICPA, 1971).

26. Ibid., paras. 11–13.

Accounting for notes is similar to accounting for bonds. When the face value of the note differs from its present value, the difference is a premium or discount on the face value of the note and is amortized over the life of the note by the *effective interest method* in such a manner as to reflect a constant rate of interest. The amortization is subtracted from the premium or discount each year, as discussed earlier for bond discount and premiums, in such a manner that at the time of repayment the face value and carrying value are equal.

Although *APB Opinion No. 21* was designed to require the recording of interest on most notes receivable and payable, it specifically *exempted* the following types of transactions (see FASB ASC 835-30-15-3):

- Normal trade transactions not exceeding a year
- Amounts that will be applied to the purchase of property, goods, and services
- Security deposits
- Customary activities of financial institutions
- Transactions where the rate is affected by the regulations of government agencies
- Transactions between parent and subsidiaries and between subsidiaries of a common parent

Short-Term Debt Expected to Be Refinanced

Some corporations have attempted to improve their liquidity position by excluding that portion of short-term debt from current liabilities that was expected to be refinanced on a long-term basis. This treatment resulted in disclosure variations between companies and led to the issuance of *SFAS No. 6*, "Classification of Short-Term Obligations Expected to Be Refinanced" (see FASB ASC 470-10-45). In this release, the FASB took the position that short-term obligations cannot be disclosed as long-term liabilities unless the following conditions exist: (1) there is an intention to refinance current liabilities on a long-term basis, and (2) the corporation demonstrates the ability to refinance such liabilities. The intent of the company to refinance current obligations means that working capital will not be reduced by satisfaction of the obligation. The ability to refinance means that the company has an agreement to refinance the obligations on a long-term basis with a qualified creditor.

A company may refinance short-term debt on a long-term basis by replacing a current liability with long-term debt or ownership securities. In addition, refinancing may be demonstrated if the current liability is extended, renewed, or replaced by other short-term debt.

A short-term obligation that is excluded from the current liability section of the balance sheet requires disclosure in the financial statement footnotes. This disclosure must include a general description of the financing agreement and the terms of any new obligation incurred or expected to be incurred, or equity securities issued or expected to be issued, as a result of the refinancing.

Deferred Credits

Deferred credits are not liabilities in the usual sense of the word, in that they will not normally be satisfied by the payment of funds but rather by the performance of services. They result from the double-entry accounting system, which requires a credit for every debit. The most frequently encountered deferred credits are (1) income received in advance, for example, airline tickets sold in advance; and (2) unrealized gross profit on installment sales (usually no longer appropriate). These items represent anticipated future revenues (unearned income). But there is no assurance that all deferrals will ultimately be included in earnings.

Although unearned revenues fit the definition of liabilities found in *SFAC No. 6*, deferred gross profit on installment sales does not.[27] Unearned revenues reflect liabilities to perform future services resulting from transactions for which the company was compensated in advance. Deferred gross profits arise from prior performance of services, the compensation for which has not yet been received and the future receipt of which is in doubt. The corporation has no further obligation to the customer or client; rather, it is the customer or client who is obligated to the corporation. Because the deferred gross profit resulted from recognition of a receivable that continues to reflect unrecovered cost, the deferred gross profit is conceptually an asset valuation and should be shown as a contra to the receivable on the balance sheet.[28]

Reporting deferred credits on the balance sheet is grounded in the principle of conservatism. As discussed in Chapter 5, this principle requires that revenue recognition be postponed until there is assurance that it is earned, but expenses are to be recorded as incurred.

Contingencies

A contingency is a possible future event that will have some impact on the firm. Although *APB Statement No. 4* required the disclosure of contingencies, it made no effort to define or give examples of them.[29] Among the most frequently encountered contingencies are

- Pending lawsuits
- Income tax disputes
- Notes receivable discounted
- Accommodation endorsements

The decision to report contingencies should be based on the principle of disclosure. That is, when the disclosure of an event adds to the information content of financial statements, it should be reported. Some authors have argued for basing this decision on expected value criteria. If a potential obligation has a high probability of occurrence, it should be recorded as a liability, whereas potential obligations with low probabilities are reported in the footnotes to the financial statements.

On the other hand, reporting some types of contingencies may result in a self-fulfilling prophecy. For example, a frequently encountered contingency problem is the question of including the possible loss from a lawsuit. The dollar value of the loss can generally be estimated by applying the expected value criteria, but placing expected liability on the balance sheet may supply the plaintiff with additional evidence of the company's guilt. Here the corporation is faced with the

---

27. *SFAC No. 6*, para. 233.

28. Ibid., para. 234.

29. *APB Statement No. 4*,

dilemma of conflicting responsibilities to its financial statement users to disclose all pertinent information while at the same time minimizing losses.

The FASB reviewed the nature of contingencies in *SFAS No. 5*, "Accounting for Contingencies"[30] (see FASB ASC 450). This release defines two types of contingencies—gain contingencies (expected future gains) and loss contingencies (expected future losses).

With respect to gain contingencies, the Board held that they should not usually be reflected currently in the financial statement because to do so might result in revenue recognition before realization. Adequate disclosure should be made of all gain contingencies while exercising due care to avoid misleading implications as to the likelihood of realization.

The criteria established for reporting loss contingencies require that the likelihood of loss be determined as follows:

- *Probable.* The future event is likely to occur.
- *Reasonably possible.* The chance of occurrence is more than remote but less than likely.
- *Remote.* The chance of occurrence is slight.

Once the likelihood of a loss is determined, contingencies are charged against income and a liability is recorded if both of the following conditions are met:

1. Information available before the issuance of the financial statements indicates that it is probable that an asset had been impaired or a liability had been incurred at the date of the financial statements.
2. The amount of the loss can be reasonably estimated.

If a loss is not accrued because one or both of these conditions has not been met, footnote disclosure of the contingency should be made when there is at least a reasonable possibility that a loss may have been incurred.

SFAS No. 5 provided evidence of the FASB's preference for the conservatism convention because probable losses are recognized while probable gains are not. Thus, this statement results in the application of separate standards for the reporting of revenues and expenses. The provisions of *SFAS No. 5* might cause one company to record a liability without a corresponding asset being recorded by the claimant company. So, even though two parties are affected by the same transaction or event, their respective financial statements would indicate otherwise. These procedures are not conducive to the development of a general theory of accounting and are further evidence of the need to establish a broad framework within which to establish consistent accounting principles.

An examination of the Hershey and Tootsie Roll balance sheets and footnotes did not reveal any potential contingencies.

Other Liability Measurement Issues

During the past several years, some additional measurement issues relating to liabilities have arisen. Among the most important of these are the disclosure of "off–balance sheet" financing arrangements and derivatives.

30. *Statement of Financial Accounting Standards No. 5*, "Accounting for Contingencies" (Stamford, CT: FASB, 1975).

Off–Balance Sheet Financing

The proportion of debt in a firm's capital structure is perceived as an indicator of the level of risk associated with investing in that company. Some companies have utilized innovative financing arrangements that are structured in such a manner that they do not satisfy liability recognition criteria. These arrangements are termed *off–balance sheet financing*. Their principal goal is to keep debt off the balance sheet. For example, several oil companies may form a joint venture to drill for off-shore oil and may agree to make payments to support the venture over time, or a company may engage in a lease agreement that does not require it to capitalize the cost of acquiring a productive asset.[31] In such cases, neither their share of the assets nor their obligation to expend future resources will appear on the balance sheet. In essence, the companies have acquired the use of economic resources (assets) without recording the corresponding economic obligation (liabilities).

The FASB has an off–balance sheet financing project on its agenda. The objective of this project is to develop broad standards of financial accounting and reporting about financial instruments and related transactions. Due to the complexity of these issues, the FASB has decided to give the widest possible exposure to proposed statements before their release. As an interim step, the Board determined that improved disclosure of certain information is necessary. Subsequently, the FASB completed two disclosure phases, which resulted in the issuance of *SFAS No. 105*, "Disclosure of Information about Financial Instruments with Off–Balance Sheet Risk and Financial Instruments with Concentrations of Credit Risk," in 1990, and the issuance of *SFAS No. 107*, "Disclosures about Fair Value of Financial Instruments" (see FASB ASC 825), in 1991. *SFAS No. 105* was later superseded by *SFAS No. 133* (see FASB ASC 815), which is discussed in the next section.

FASB ASC 825 requires the disclosure of the fair value of financial instruments for which an estimate of fair value is practicable. The methods and assumptions used to estimate fair value also must be disclosed. The fair value of a financial instrument is defined as "the amount at which the instrument could be exchanged in a current transaction between willing parties, other than in a forced or liquidation sale."[32] A quoted market price is cited as the best evidence of fair value.

These disclosure requirements apply to financial instruments regardless of whether they are assets or liabilities or whether or not they are reported in the balance sheet. The following items are exempt from the FASB ASC 825 requirements. Many of them already have extensive disclosure requirements.

1. Deferred compensation arrangements such as pensions, postretirement benefits, and employee stock option and purchase plans
2. Debt extinguished and the related assets removed from the balance sheet in cases of in-substance defeasance (no longer applicable)
3. Insurance contracts, other than financial guarantees and investment contracts
4. Leases
5. Warranty obligations and rights
6. Unconditional purchase obligations

---

31. This is termed an operating lease. Accounting for leases is discussed in Chapter 14.

32. *Statement of Financial Accounting Standards No. 107*, "Disclosures about Fair Value of Financial Instruments" (Stamford, CT: FASB, 1991), para. 5 (see FASB ASC 825-10-20).

7. Investments accounted for under the equity method

8. Minority interest

9. Equity investments in consolidated subsidiaries

10. Equity instruments classified in stockholders' equity[33]

  SFAS No. 133 (see FASB ASC 815, discussed in the next section) amended *SFAS No. 107* to include the footnote disclosure provisions relating to credit risk contained in *SFAS No. 105.*

Derivatives

A derivative is a transaction, or contract, whose value depends on the value of an underlying asset or index. (That is, its value is derived from an underlying asset or index.) In such a transaction, a party with exposure to unwanted risk can pass some or all of that risk on to a second party.[34] When derivatives are employed, the first party can (1) assume a different risk from the second party, (2) pay the second party to assume the risk, or (3) use some combination of these approaches.

  The rise in the use of derivatives can be traced to the abandonment of currencies fixed against the value of gold, whereby most currencies have been allowed to float to exchange levels determined by market forces. In addition, most governments now allow interest rates to fluctuate more freely than they did in the past, and exposure to exchange risk has increased due to the growth of international commerce.

  All derivative transactions stem from two types of transactions—forwards and options. A *forward* transaction obligates one party to buy and another to sell a specified item, such as 10,000 euros (€), at a specified price on a specified future date. On the other hand, an *option* gives its holder the right, but not the obligation, to buy or sell the specific item, such as the €10,000, at a specified price on a specified date in the future. The major difference between the two types of transactions is that a forward requires performance, whereas an option will be exercised only if it is financially advantageous to do so. But in either case, the future price is fixed in advance.

  The participants in derivative transactions can be categorized as dealers and end users. There are only a small number of dealers (less than 200) worldwide. Dealers are generally banks, although some are independent brokers. The number of end users is constantly increasing as business and government organizations become involved in international financial transactions. End users include businesses, banks, securities firms, mutual and pension funds, governmental units, and even the World Bank.

  The goals of end users vary. Some use derivatives so that the risk of financial operations can be controlled, whereas others attempt to manage foreign exchange rate fluctuation exposure. Speculators may seek profits from simultaneous price differentials in different foreign markets. Or others may attempt to hedge exposure to currency rate changes.

  Five types of derivatives that transfer elements of risk can be identified: forward contracts, futures, options, asset swaps, and hybrids. Each carries an associated risk; however, although the associated risk is not unique to derivatives, they

33. FASB ASC 825-10-50-8.

34. Risk is defined in this case as the possibility that the actual return from holding a security will deviate from the original expected return when the security was acquired.

TABLE 11.1   *Types of Derivatives*

Type	Market	Purpose	Type of Contract	Definition
Forward	Over-the-counter	Transfer risk	Negotiated on a case-by-case basis.	Obligates the holder to buy or sell specified amount of currency at a specified price on a specified date in the future
Future	Organized exchange	Transfer risk	Fixed as to face value, period, and point of settlement	Obligates the holder to buy or sell specified amount of currency at a specified price on a specified date in the future
Option	Over-the-counter or organized exchange	Transfer risk	Either negotiated or fixed period	Grants the purchaser the right, but not the obligation, to buy or sell a specific amount of currency at a specified price within a specified period
Swap	Over-the-counter	Transfer risk	Negotiated on a case-by-case basis	Agreement between the parties to make periodic payments to each other during the swap period
Hybrid	Over-the-counter	Transfer risk	Negotiated on a case-by-case	Incorporates various provisions of any or all of the above types

are difficult to manage because derivative products are complex. Moreover, there is difficulty in measuring the actual risk associated with the various types of derivatives. These five types of derivatives are summarized in Table 11.1.

Each of these derivatives carries risk that can be identified as market, credit, operational, legal, and systems. *Market risk* is the exposure to the possibility of financial loss resulting from an unfavorable movement in interest rates, exchange rates, stock prices, or commodity prices. Estimating the market value of a derivative at any point is difficult because it is influenced by a variety of factors such as exchange rates, interest rates, and time until settlement. *Credit risk* is the exposure to the possibility of financial loss resulting from the other party's failure to meet its financial obligations. *Operational risk* is the exposure to the possibility of financial loss resulting from inadequate internal controls, fraud, or human error. *Legal risk* is the exposure to the possibility of financial losses resulting from an action by a court, regulatory agency, or legislative body that invalidates all or part of an existing derivative contract. *Systems risk* is the exposure to the possibility of financial losses resulting from the disruption at a firm, in a market segment, or to a settlement system, that in turn could cause difficulties at other firms, in other market systems, or in the financial system as a whole.

The FASB first addressed the question of derivatives in *SFAS No. 105* (superseded) and defined these securities under the broad category of financial instruments. This category includes not only traditional assets and liabilities such as notes receivable and bonds payable but also innovative financial instruments such as forward contracts, futures, options, and asset swaps discussed above. Disclosure of the fair value of these financial instruments (whether or not recognized) was subsequently required by *SFAS No. 107* (see FASB ASC 825) when it was practicable to estimate fair value. Finally, in *SFAS No. 119*, "Disclosure about Derivative Financial Instruments and Fair Values of Financial Instruments" (superseded), companies were required to disclose information about derivative financial instruments and change the methods of disclosure of such information.

In 1998, the FASB issued SFAS *No. 133*, "Accounting for Derivative Instruments and Hedging Activities"[35] (see FASB ASC 815). This statement established accounting and reporting standards for derivative financial instruments and similar financial instruments. It requires that an entity recognize all derivatives as either assets or liabilities in the statement of financial position, measured at fair value. If certain conditions are met, a derivative may be specifically designated as (1) a hedge of the exposure to changes in the fair value of a recognized asset or liability or a firm commitment, (2) a hedge of the exposure to variable cash flows of a forecasted transaction, or (3) a hedge of the foreign currency exposure of a net investment in a foreign operation.

The accounting for changes in the fair value of a derivative (that is, gains and losses) depends on the intended use of the derivative and the resulting designation.

1. For a derivative designated as a hedge of the exposure to changes in the fair value of a recognized asset or liability or a firm commitment (referred to as a fair value hedge), the gain or loss is recognized in earnings in the period of change together with the offsetting loss or gain on the hedged item. The effect of this accounting treatment is to adjust the basis of the hedged item by the amount of the gain or loss on the hedging derivative to the extent that the gain or loss offsets the loss or gain experienced on the hedged item.

2. For a derivative designated as a hedge of the exposure to variable cash flows of a forecasted transaction (referred to as a cash-flow hedge), the gain or loss is reported as a component of other comprehensive income (outside of earnings) and recognized in earnings on the projected date of the forecasted transaction.

3. For a derivative designated as a hedge of the foreign currency exposure of a net investment in a foreign operation, the portion of the change in fair value equivalent to a foreign currency transaction gain or loss is reported in other comprehensive income (outside of earnings) as part of the cumulative translation adjustment; any remaining change in fair value is recognized in earnings.

4. For a derivative not designated as a hedge, the gain or loss is recognized in earnings in the period of change.

35. *Statement of Financial Accounting Standards No. 133*, "Accounting for Derivative Instruments and Hedging Activities" (Norwalk, CT: FASB, 1998).

At the date of initial application of *SFAS No. 133*, companies were required to measure all derivatives at fair value and recognize them in the statement of financial position as either assets or liabilities. They also recognized offsetting gains and losses on hedged assets, liabilities, and firm commitments by adjusting their carrying amounts at that date. The transition adjustments that resulted from adopting this statement were reported in net income or other comprehensive income, as appropriate, as the effect of a change in accounting principle and were presented in a manner similar to the cumulative effect of a change in accounting principle.

Whether the transition adjustments were reported in net income or other comprehensive income was based on the hedging relationships, if any, that existed for the related derivatives and was the basis for accounting under GAAP before the date of initial application. Transition adjustments reported as a cumulative-effect-type adjustment of other comprehensive income are subsequently recognized in earnings on the date on which the forecasted transaction had been projected to occur.

The FASB thus recognized the emergence of derivative securities and their complexity, and it responded with pronouncements designed to require published financial statements to present a more accurate disclosure of the risks borne by firms using derivative financial instruments.

In addition to the FASB, the SEC also addressed the issue of accounting for derivatives in new required disclosure rules in an amendment to Regulation S-X. This release requires the disclosure of qualitative and quantitative information about market risk by all companies registered with the SEC for annual periods ending after June 15, 1998, and is discussed in more depth in Chapter 17 under the topic "Management Discussion and Analysis." Market risk is defined as the risk of loss arising from adverse changes in market rates and prices from such items as interest rates, currency exchange rates, commodity prices, and equity prices. The required disclosures are designed to provide investors with forward-looking information about a company's exposures to market risk, such as the risks associated with changes in interest rates, foreign currency exchange rates, commodity prices, and stock prices. It is anticipated that the information provided will indicate the market risk a company faces and how the company's management views and manages its market risk.

Troubled Debt Restructurings

Corporations occasionally experience difficulty repaying their long-term debt obligations. These difficulties frequently result in arrangements between debtor and creditor that allow the debtor to avoid bankruptcy. For example, in 2007, Haights Cross Communications, Inc., a developer and publisher of products for the K–12 education and library markets located in Delaware, consummated a recapitalization agreement whereby the holders of previously outstanding Preferred A, Preferred B, and Preferred C stock converted their shares into shares of common stock. The company recorded a gain of $115.5 million on troubled debt restructuring in the year ended December 31, 2007, based on the difference in carrying value of the Preferred B compared to the fair value of the common shares exchanged.

Accountants and financial statement users became concerned over the lack of GAAP by which to account for these agreements. Consequently, the FASB began a study of agreements of this type, termed *troubled debt restructurings*. This study focused on three questions: (1) Do certain kinds of troubled debt restructurings require reductions in the carrying amounts of debt? (2) If they do, should the effect of the reduction be reported as current income, deferred to a future period, or reported as contributed capital? (3) Should contingently payable interest on the restructured debt be recognized before it becomes payable?

The issues underlying each of these questions relate to the recognition of liabilities and holding gains. A liability should be recorded at the amount of the probable future sacrifice of economic benefits arising from present obligations. A holding gain occurs when the value of the liability decreases. The result of the review of these questions was the release of *SFAS No. 15*, "Accounting by Debtors and Creditors for Troubled Debt Restructurings"[36] (see FASB ASC 310-40 and FASB ASC 470-60).

According to FASB ASC 470-60-20, a troubled debt restructuring occurs when "the creditor for economic or legal reasons related to the debtor's financial difficulties grants a concession to the debtor that it would not otherwise consider." A troubled debt restructuring may include, but is not limited to, one or any combination of the following:

1. Modification of terms of a debt such as one or a combination of:
   a. Reduction of the stated interest rate for the remaining original life of the debt
   b. Extension of the maturity date or dates at a stated interest rate lower than the current market rate for new debt with similar risk
   c. Reduction of the face amount or maturity amount of the debt as stated in the instrument or other agreement
   d. Reduction of accrued interest

2. Issuance or other granting of an equity interest to the creditor by the debtor to satisfy fully or partially a debt unless the equity interest is granted pursuant to existing terms for converting the debt into an equity interest

3. A transfer from the debtor to the creditor of receivables from third parties, real estate, or other assets to satisfy fully or partially a debt

Modification of Terms

A restructuring agreement involving a modification of terms is accounted for on a prospective basis and results in one of the two following situations:

1. The amount of principal and interest to be repaid is greater than the current carrying value of the liability; therefore, the debtor recognizes no gain.

2. The amount of principal and interest to be repaid is less than the current carrying value of the liability; therefore, the debtor recognizes a gain.

In the event it is determined that the total amount to be repaid exceeds the carrying value of the debt on the date of the restructuring agreement, no adjustment is made to the original carrying value of the liability. However, it is necessary to determine the effective interest rate that equates the total future payments

---

36. *Statement of Financial Accounting Standards No. 15*, "Accounting by Debtors and Creditors for Troubled Debt Restructurings" (Stamford, CT: FASB, 1977), para. 2 (see FASB ASC 310 and 470).

with the current carrying value. This rate is then applied to the carrying value of the obligation each year to determine the amount of interest expense. The difference between the recorded amount of interest expense and any cash payment reduces the carrying value of the liability.

If the total future cash payments are determined to be less than the carrying value of the obligation, the amount of the liability is reduced to the total amount of the cash to be repaid. The debtor then recognizes an extraordinary gain for the amount of this adjustment, and all future payments are recorded as reductions in the amount of the liability. That is, the debt is treated as though there were no interest rate.

Under *SFAS No. 15*, a creditor treated a troubled debt restructuring resulting in a modification of terms in a manner similar to the debtor. No loss was recognized when the total amount receivable from the debtor under the modified arrangement was greater than the current carrying value of the receivable. Similarly, when the total future cash flows under the modified terms were less than the current carrying value, a loss was recognized for the difference.

This practice was criticized because the creditor would recognize a loss only when the total future cash flows were less than the current carrying value of the loan. The loss recognized would result in a carrying value of the impaired loan equal to the total future cash flows. Consequently, no interest income could be recorded over the term of the new agreement. In the case where no loss was recognized, the current loan amount was presumed to be the amount borrowed, forcing the interest rate on the modified loan arrangement to be unrealistically low. These results were inconsistent with other reporting requirements for similar financial instruments. Initially, the restructured financial instruments were not recorded at fair value, nor was interest calculated using the market rate implied in the loan agreement.

As a part of its financial instruments project, the FASB addressed the issue of whether a creditor should measure an impaired loan based on the present value of the future cash flows related to the loan. The Board concluded that it would be inappropriate to continue to ignore the time value of money and issued *SFAS No. 114*, "Accounting by Creditors for Impairment of a Loan"[37] (see FASB ASC 310-10-35).

FASB ASC 310-10-35 requires creditors to measure impaired receivables, including those that result from a troubled debt restructure involving a modification of terms, at the present value of expected future cash flows discounted at the loan's effective interest rate.[38]

A bad debt loss is recognized and a valuation allowance is credited for the difference between the restructured measurement and the current carrying value of the loan. The effective interest rate used to discount the expected future cash flows must be the effective interest rate on the original contractual agreement rather than the rate specified in the restructuring agreement. The rationale for use of the original loan rate is that the restructure represents continuing efforts to recover the original loan.

As a practical expedient, the creditor may alternatively value the impaired receivable based on the loan's observable market price. If the receivable is collateralized, it may be valued at the fair value of the collateral.

---

37. *Statement of Financial Accounting Standards No. 114*, "Accounting by Creditors for Impairment of a Loan" (Stamford, CT: FASB, 1993; see FASB ASC 310).

38. Ibid., para. 13 (see FASB ASC 310-10-35).

Income over the life of the restructured loan may be recognized in one of two ways:

1. Changes in the present value of expected future cash flows that are due to the passage of time are reported as interest income, whereas those changes attributable to changes in expectations regarding future cash flows are reported as bad debt expense.
2. All changes in the present value of expected future cash flows are treated as adjustments to bad debt expense.

The guidance contained at FASB ASC 310-10-35 may be criticized because its requirements are inconsistent with the intent of the pronouncement. The resulting restructured loan measurements will not provide the fair value of the restructured loan, because the interest rate used to discount the expected future cash inflows is based on prior conditions; and because the borrower is unable to honor the original debt agreement, it does not reflect current conditions or the risk inherent in the restructured cash flows.

Satisfaction of the Debt through an Asset or Equity Swap

When a debtor exchanges an asset or an equity interest in satisfaction of a liability, the transfer is recorded on the basis of the fair market value of the asset or equity interest transferred. Market value is determined at the time of the exchange by the fair market value of the asset or equity exchanged unless the fair market value of the debt satisfied is more clearly evident. An extraordinary gain is recognized for the excess of the recorded liability over the fair market value of the asset transferred. The creditor records a corresponding bad debt loss (not an extraordinary item). In the case of asset exchanges, it is also necessary to record a gain or loss on disposition of the assets to the extent of any difference between the asset's fair market value and its carrying value.

Equity for debt swaps can increase reported income by the amount of the extraordinary gain on debt restructure and by reduced interest expense. Also, debt is removed from the balance sheet and replaced by equity, thereby improving the financial position of the company and its debt-to-equity ratios. For example, in 1990, Financial Corp. of Santa Barbara swapped $50 million of equity for debt and recognized an extraordinary gain of $36.5 million.[39] The common shares issued replaced preferred stock, subordinated debentures, and notes.

Financial Analysis of Long-Term Debt

The financial analysis of a company's long-term debt includes assessing its liquidity, solvency, and financial flexibility as well as assessing the risk associated with its use of financial leverage. Liquidity refers to a company's ability to generate cash for short-term needs. The assessment of a company's liquidity was discussed in Chapter 8.

Solvency refers to a company's ability to pay its debts when they become due. Several ratios may be used to evaluate a company's solvency, including the long-

---

39. "Financial Corp. of Santa Barbara's Net Jumps Sevenfold," *Wall Street Journal*, 24 April 1990, C22.

term debt-to-assets ratio, the interest coverage ratio, and the debt service coverage ratio. The long-term debt-to-assets ratio provides information on the extent to which a company is using financial leverage and its accompanying solvency risk. A high ratio value indicates that a company is using a great deal of financial leverage to acquire its assets and, consequently, has a higher risk of insolvency than a company with a low ratio value. The long-term debt-to-assets ratio is calculated as:

$$\frac{\text{Long-term debt}}{\text{Total assets}}$$

The calculation of the long-term debt-to-assets ratio is illustrated for Hershey and Tootsie Roll for their 2008 and 2007 fiscal years. Their financial statements are provided in Chapters 6 and 7.

Hershey's long-term debt-to-assets ratio is calculated as follows ($000 omitted; all amounts in these and succeeding calculations are in thousands of dollars):

	Hershey		Tootsie Roll	
2008	$\dfrac{\$1,505,954 + 504,963 + 3,646}{\$3,634,719}$	$= 55.43\%$	$\dfrac{\$118,070}{\$812,092}$	$= 14.54\%$
2007	$\dfrac{\$1,279,965 + 544,016 + 180,842}{\$4,247,113}$	$= 47.20\%$	$\dfrac{\$116,523}{\$812,725}$	$= 14.34\%$

These analyses indicate that Hershey is making more extensive use of financial leverage; and as a result, its risk of insolvency is relatively greater than Tootsie Roll's. However, further analysis is warranted. When using the long-term debt-to-assets ratio, adjustments should be made to both the numerator and denominator in order to obtain more reliable results. For example, a company engaging in extensive off–balance sheet financing arrangements may have unrecorded liabilities that need to be considered. Similarly, a company disclosing a large amount of intangible assets may distort the ratios because of the difficulty in determining the reliability of the values of those assets. An analysis of the footnotes to Hershey's and Tootsie Roll's financial statements indicates that neither company made extensive use of leases. In the event large operating lease commitments are in evidence, the discounted present value of the amounts of these future commitments should be added to the ratio numerator to obtain a more realistic evaluation of the company's solvency.[40] Both companies do disclose relatively large intangible asset balances, which raises the possibility of overstated total asset values. The interest coverage (or times interest earned) ratio provides information about a company's ability to generate sufficient sustainable income to pay its interest obligation. This ratio is calculated as:

$$\frac{\text{Operating income before interest and taxes}}{\text{Interest expense}}$$

---

40. A rough approximation of the discounted present value of operating leases can be found by taking the average lease payment due over the average lease commitment period and discounting it back to the present at an assumed interest rate. The analysis of a company's operating leases is discussed in more detail in Chapter 13.

The interest coverage ratios for Hershey and Tootsie Roll for 2008 and 2007 are calculated as follows ($000 omitted):

Interest Coverage Ratios

	Hershey	Tootsie Roll
2008	$\dfrac{\$589,898 + 189,700^{41}}{\$99,678^{42}} = 7.82$	$\dfrac{\$66,527}{378} = 176.00$
2007	$\dfrac{\$458,827 + 412,600}{\$121,066} = 7.20$	$\dfrac{\$70,852}{535} = 132.43$

These ratios indicate that both companies are generating enough income to cover their debt service payments, although Tootsie Roll's ratio is significantly higher. This analysis should also be expanded to include debt repayment amounts for a company expecting to retire a portion of its long-term debt during the next annual period. An examination of Hershey's footnotes indicates that most of its long-term debt is payable after 2012. A similar examination of Tootsie Roll's footnotes indicated that most of the company's long-term debt consists of deferred income taxes and deferred compensation expenses (options). These amounts generally are not settled with cash payments.

A criticism of the interest coverage ratio is that it does not consider the cash-flow effects of net income. That is, interest payments require a cash outflow, and the ratio does not consider the cash effects of the company's income-generating ability. The debt service coverage ratio attempts to overcome this criticism by using cash flow from operating activities in the numerator and is calculated as:

$$\frac{\text{Cash flow from operating activities before interest and taxes}}{\text{Interest expense}}$$

The debt service ratios for Hershey and Tootsie Roll for 2008 and 2007 are calculated as follows ($000 omitted):

	Hershey	Tootsie Roll
2008	$\dfrac{\$519,561 + 97,364 + 197,661}{\$99,678} = 8.17$	$\dfrac{\$57,042 + 252 + 12,728}{\$378} = 185.24$
2007	$\dfrac{\$778,836 + 126,450 + 253,977}{\$121,066} = 9.58$	$\dfrac{\$90,064 + 537 + 11,343}{\$535} = 190.55$

41. Calculated earnings before interest and taxes plus gross realignment charge. Hershey footnotes to its 2008 financial statements revealed that the before-tax amounts of the realignment charges for 2008 and 2007 were $189,700 and $412,600, respectively.

42. Hershey discloses net interest expense of $97,876,000 for 2008 and $118,585,000 for 2007 on its income statements. A review of its footnotes revealed that its interest expense for fiscal 2008 was $99,678,000 and for fiscal 2007 was $121,066,000. Tootsie Roll reported net other expense of $10,618,000 in 2008 and net other income of $6,315,000 in 2007. The interest expense components of these amounts were $378,000 and $535,000, respectively.

An examination of the results of these calculations indicates that both Hershey's and Tootsie Roll's ability to generate sufficient cash to service their debt declined considerably during 2008. Additionally, Hershey's debt service position should be closely monitored to determine if it continues to decline.

A final method of solvency analysis involves assessing a company's financial flexibility; in other words, its ability to react to changing economic conditions. This assessment is made by attempting to prepare pro forma financial statements that are subsequently evaluated in light of a company's ability to react to various scenarios such as economic downturns or rising interest rates.

International Accounting Standards

The IASB addressed the following issues relating to long-term liabilities:

1. Accounting for financial liabilities and debt and equity classifications in *IAS No. 32*, "Financial Instruments: Presentation"
2. Contingencies in *IAS No. 37*, "Provisions, Contingent Liabilities, and Contingent Assets"
3. Financial instruments in *IAS No. 39*, "Financial Instruments Recognition and Measurement"
4. The disclosure of information on financial instruments in *IFRS No. 7*, "Financial Instruments: Disclosures"
5. The presentation of gains and losses on liabilities designated under the fair value option in an exposure draft, *Fair Value Option for Financial Liabilities.*

The title of *IAS No. 32* was originally "Financial Instruments Disclosure and Presentation," but its disclosure provisions were replaced by *IFRS No. 7* in 2007. The stated objective of *IAS No. 32* is to enhance financial statement users' understanding of the significance of financial instruments to an entity's financial position, performance, and cash flows. *IAS No. 32* defines financial liabilities as contractual obligations to deliver cash or another financial asset to another enterprise, or to exchange financial instruments with another enterprise under conditions that are potentially unfavorable. Equity instruments are defined as contracts that evidence a residual interest in the assets of an enterprise after deducting all of its liabilities.

IAS No. 32 states that a financial instrument should be classified as either a financial liability or an equity instrument according to the substance of the contract, not its legal form. The enterprise must make the classification decision at the time the instrument is initially recognized, and this classification may not be subsequently changed based on changed circumstances.

A financial instrument is to be recorded as an equity instrument only under these conditions: (1) if the instrument includes no contractual obligation to deliver cash or another financial asset to another entity, and (2) if the instrument will or may be settled in the issuer's own equity instruments, it is either:

- A nonderivative that includes no contractual obligation for the issuer to deliver a variable number of its own equity instruments; or
- A derivative that will be settled only by the issuer exchanging a fixed amount of cash or another financial asset for a fixed number of its own equity instruments

With respect to compound financial instruments, *IAS No. 32* indicates that some financial instruments have both a liability and an equity component. In such case, *IAS No. 32* requires that the component parts be accounted for and presented separately according to their substance based on the definitions of liability and equity. The split is made at issuance and not revised for subsequent changes in market interest rates, share prices, or other event that changes the likelihood that the conversion option will be exercised.

In accounting for treasury stock, *IAS No. 32* indicates that the cost of an entity's own equity instruments that it has reacquired is to be deducted from equity. Any gain or loss is not recognized on the purchase, sale, issue, or cancellation of treasury shares. The gain or loss treatment differs from U.S. GAAP: when using the cost method, proceeds in excess of the purchase price are generally credited to a specific paid-in capital account from treasury stock, while subsequent losses are reduced from the paid-in capital account (to the extent of its balance) and then any residual is deducted from retained earnings.

IAS No. 32 also prescribes rules for the offsetting of financial assets and financial liabilities. It specifies that a financial asset and a financial liability should be offset and the net amount reported when, and only when, an enterprise

- Has a legally enforceable right to set off the amounts; and
- Intends either to settle on a net basis or to realize the asset and settle the liability simultaneously

The objective of *IAS No. 37* is to ensure that appropriate recognition criteria and measurement bases are applied to provisions, contingent liabilities, and contingent assets and that sufficient information is disclosed in the notes to the financial statements to enable users to understand their nature, timing, and amount. The key principle established by the standard is that a provision should be recognized only when there is a liability (i.e., a present obligation resulting from past events).

IAS No. 37 indicated that provisions should be recognized in the balance sheet when an enterprise has a present obligation (legal or constructive) as a result of a past event. It is probable that an outflow of resources will be required to settle the obligation and a reliable estimate can be made of the amount of the obligation. Balance sheet measurements should be based on the best estimate of the expenditure required to settle the obligation at the balance sheet date. This amount should not be reduced by gains from the expected disposal of assets or by expected reimbursements. When it is virtually certain that reimbursement will be received if the enterprise settles the obligation, the reimbursement should be recognized as a separate asset. A provision should be used only for expenditures for which it was originally recognized and should be reversed if an outflow of resources is no longer probable. A financial liability should be removed from the balance sheet when, and only when, it is extinguished; that is, when the obligation specified in the contract is either discharged, canceled, or expired. Where there has been an exchange between an existing borrower and lender of debt instruments with substantially different terms, or where there has been a substantial modification of the terms of an existing financial liability, this transaction is accounted for as an extinguishment of the original financial liability and the recognition of a new financial liability. A gain or loss from extinguishment of the original financial liability is recognized in the income statement.

IAS No. 39 discusses the recognition of two classes of financial liabilities:

1. Financial liabilities that are measured at fair value
2. Other financial liabilities that are measured at amortized cost by using the effective interest method

The category of financial liability at fair value through profit or loss has two subcategories:

1. *Designated.* A financial liability that is designated by the entity as a liability at fair value upon initial recognition
2. *Held for trading.* A financial liability classified as held for trading, such as an obligation for securities borrowed in a short sale, which have to be returned in the future

IAS No. 39 requires recognition of a financial liability when, and only when, the entity becomes a party to the contractual provisions of the instrument. *IAS No. 39* permits hedge accounting provided that the hedging relationship is formally designated and documented, including the entity's risk management objective and strategy for undertaking the hedge, identification of the hedging instrument, the hedged item, the nature of the risk being hedged, and how the entity will assess the hedging instrument's effectiveness. Hedge accounting is expected to be highly effective in achieving offsetting changes in fair value or cash flows attributable to the hedged risk as designated and documented, and effectiveness must be reliably measured on a prospective basis and on a retrospective basis where actual results are within a range of 80 to 125 percent. All hedge ineffectiveness is recognized immediately in the income statement (including ineffectiveness within the 80 to 125 percent window).

IAS No. 39 describes three types of hedging relationships:

1. *Fair value hedge.* A hedge of the exposure to changes in the fair value of a recognized asset or liability or an unrecognized firm commitment, or an identified portion of such an asset, liability or firm commitment, that is attributable to a particular risk and could affect profit or loss
2. *Cash-flow hedge.* A hedge of the exposure to the variability in cash flows that (a) is attributable to a particular risk associated with a recognized asset or liability (such as all or some future interest payments on variable-rate debt) or a highly probable forecast transaction, and (b) could affect profit or loss
3. *Hedge of a net investment in a foreign operation.* A hedge of the exposure of the amount of the reporting entity's interest in the net assets of that operation.

A hedge that satisfies the conditions for being designated as a fair value hedge during the period is accounted for as follows:

1. The gain or loss from remeasuring the hedging instrument at fair value (for a derivative hedging instrument) or the foreign currency component of its carrying amount is recognized in income.
2. The gain or loss on the hedged item attributable to the hedged risk shall adjust the carrying amount of the hedged item and is recognized in income. Recognition of the gain or loss attributable to the hedged risk in income also applies if the hedged item is an available-for-sale financial asset.

A hedge that satisfies the conditions for being designated as a cash-flow hedge during the period is accounted for as follows:

1. The portion of the gain or loss on the hedging instrument that is determined to be an effective hedge is recognized in other comprehensive income.
2. The ineffective portion of the gain or loss on the hedging instrument is recognized in income.

Hedges of net investments in foreign operations, including hedges of monetary items that are accounted for as part of the net investment, are accounted for in a manner similar to cash-flow hedges:

1. The portion of the gain or loss on the hedging instrument that is determined to be an effective hedge is recognized in other comprehensive income.
2. The ineffective portion is recognized in income.

A financial liability should be derecognized and removed from the balance sheet when, and only when, it is extinguished; that is, when the obligation specified in the contract is either discharged, canceled, or expired. Where there has been an exchange between an existing borrower and lender of debt instruments with substantially different terms, or there has been a substantial modification of the terms of an existing financial liability, this transaction is accounted for as an extinguishment of the original financial liability and the recognition of a new financial liability. Any gain or loss from extinguishment of the original financial liability is recognized in the income statement or both) on initial recognition as one(s) to be measured at fair value, and changes in fair value are recognized in profit or loss. To impose discipline on this categorization, an entity is precluded from reclassifying financial instruments into or out of this category. The IASB expects to amend the provision of *IAS No 39* relating to financial liabilities through its *IFRS No. 9* project by the end of 2010.

As noted in Chapter 10, *IFRS No. 7* requires disclosure of

- The significance of an entity's financial instruments
- The nature and extent of risks arising from financial instruments to which an entity is exposed and how those risks have been managed

The balance sheet and income statement disclosures required for financial liabilities by *IFRS No. 7* are

- Financial liabilities at fair value
- Financial liabilities measured at amortized cost

The following quantitative disclosures relating to financial liabilities are required by *IFRS No. 7*:

- Disclosures about credit risk, liquidity risk, and market risk as further described below
- Concentrations of risk

Finally, *IFRS No. 7* requires the following risk-based disclosures regarding its financial liabilities:

- A maturity analysis of financial liabilities
- A description of the entity's approach to risk management
- A sensitivity analysis of each type of market risk to which the entity is exposed

In May, 2010 the IASB published an exposure draft *Fair Value Option for Financial Liabilities* (ED). This proposal outlines the IASB's deliberations on the presentation of gains and losses on liabilities designated under the fair value option. The ED is part of the IASB's plan to improve and simplify the accounting for financial instruments. The proposed treatment would require entities that have designated financial liabilities at fair value through profit or loss under the fair value option to no longer present in profit or loss a gain from deterioration in their own credit risk or loss from an improvement in their own credit risk. Instead, gains and losses arising from changes in an entity's own credit risk will be presented in other comprehensive income. The IASB issued this ED in response to criticisms voiced by many constituents that recognizing the effects of changes in an entity's own credit risk in profit or loss does not provide useful information and is counter-intuitive, as an entity will recognize gains that it has limited ability to realize at times when its performance is worsening.

The ED is limited in its impact in that focuses only on the following two areas:

1. The presentation of the effects of changes in an entity's own credit risk. The ED distinguishes between financial liabilities held for trading and financial liabilities designated as at fair value through profit or loss using the fair value option. Financial liabilities held for trading would continue to be measured at fair value with all changes being recognized in profit or loss.

2. The elimination of the cost exception for derivative liabilities to be settled by delivery of unquoted equity instruments. The ED proposes to change the presentation of the effects of changes in the credit risk of a financial liability designated at fair value through profit or loss using the fair value option. In an effort to increase transparency, the ED proposes a 'two-step approach' in recognizing those changes. As a first step, an entity would present the full change in fair value in profit or loss. In the second step, the portion relating to changes in an entity's own credit risk would be presented as an offsetting entry in profit or loss and presented in OCI.

Cases

• Case 11-1 Reporting Bond Liabilities

On January 1, 2010, Plywood Homes, Inc. issued 20-year, 4 percent bonds having a face value of $1 million. The interest on the bonds is payable semiannually on June 30 and December 31. The proceeds to the company were $975,000 (i.e., on the day they were issued the bonds had a market value of $975,000). On June 30, 2010, the company's fiscal closing date, when the bonds were being traded at $98\frac{1}{2}$, each of the following amounts was suggested as a possible valuation basis for reporting the bond liability on the balance sheet.

1. $975,625 (proceeds, plus six months' straight-line amortization)
2. $1 million (face value)
3. $1,780,000 (face value plus interest payments)

Required:

a. Distinguish between nominal and effective interest rates.

b. Explain the nature of the $25,000 difference between the face value and market value of the bonds on January 1, 2010.

c. Between January 1 and June 30, the market value of the company's bonds increased from $975,000 to $985,000. Explain. Discuss the significance of the increase to the company.

d. Evaluate each of the three suggested alternatives for reporting the bond liability on the balance sheet, giving arguments for and against each alternative. Your answer should take the investor and the reporting company into consideration.

• Case 11-2 Debt Restructuring

Whiley Company issued a $100,000, five-year, 10 percent note to Security Company on January 2, 2009. Interest was to be paid annually each December 31. The stated rate of interest reflected the market rate of interest on similar notes.

Whiley made the first interest payment on December 31, 2009. Due to financial difficulties, the firm was unable to pay any interest on December 31, 2010.

Security agreed to the following terms:

1. The $100,000 principal would be payable in five equal installments, beginning December 31, 2011.

2. The accrued interest at December 31, 2010, would be forgiven.

3. Whiley would be required to make no other payments.

Because of the risk associated with the note, it has no determinable fair value. The note is secured by equipment having a fair value of $80,000 at December 31, 2010. The present value of the five equal installments discounted at 10 percent is $75,815.

Required:

a. Under current GAAP, at which amount would Whiley report the restructured liability at December 31, 2010? Explain. How much gain would Whiley recognize in its income statement for 2010? Explain. How much interest expense would Whiley recognize in 2011? Explain.

b. Under current GAAP, what alternatives does Security have for reporting the restructured receivable? Explain. How would each alternative affect the 2010 income statement and future interest revenue? Explain.

c. Discuss the pros and cons of the alternatives in (b) and compare them to the prior GAAP treatment (treatment that was reciprocal to the debtor).

d. If debtors were allowed to record the restructuring agreement in a manner similar to creditors, what would be the incremental effect (difference between what would be reported in this case and current GAAP for debtors) on Whiley's financial statements, debt-to-equity ratio, and EPS for 2010 and 2011? Explain.

• Case 11-3 Alternative Financing Decision

Baker Company needs $1 million to expand its existing plant. Baker management is considering the following two alternative forms of financing:

1. At the beginning of 2011, issue $1 million of convertible, 10-year, 10 percent bonds. Each $1,000 bond can be converted into 20 shares of Baker $10 par value common stock. The conversion may take place any time after three years.

2. At the beginning of 2011, issue 10,000 shares of $100 par value, $10, redeemable preferred stock. The preferred is redeemable at $102 ten years from the date of issue.

Baker's management is concerned about the effects of the two alternatives on cash flows, their financial statements, and future financing for other planned expansion activities. Also, existing debt covenants restrict the debt-to-equity ratio to 2:1; $1 million in new debt would cause the debt-to-equity ratio to be close to 2:1. Baker believes that either the bonds or the preferred stock could be sold at par value. Their income tax rate is 34 percent.

Baker Company common stock is currently selling for $45 per share.

Required:

a. Discuss the theoretical and current GAAP treatments for convertible bonds.

b. Discuss the current GAAP treatment for redeemable preferred stock.

c. Compare the effects of the two financing alternatives on Baker Company's balance sheet, income statement, and cash flows under current GAAP. Your comparison should consider 2011 and future years, the potential conversion of the bonds, and the debt covenant restrictions.

d. If the FASB were to decide to recognize the value for conversion (conversion feature) as equity, would this have an impact on Baker Company's decision? How would Baker's financial statements be affected if it chose the convertible bond alternative? Would the decision to select convertible bonds versus redeemable preferred stock be affected, especially in light of the concern regarding the debt covenant restrictions?

• Case 11-4 Effective Interest Amortization of Premiums and Discounts

The appropriate method of amortizing a premium or discount on issuance of bonds is the effective interest method.

Required:

a. What is the effective interest method of amortization, and how is it different from or similar to the straight-line method of amortization?

b. How are interest and the amount of discount or premium amortization computed using the effective interest method, and why and how do amounts obtained using the effective interest method differ from amounts computed under the straight-line method?

c. Generally, the effective interest method is defended on the grounds that it provides the appropriate amount of interest expense. Does it also provide an appropriate balance sheet amount for the liability balance? Why or why not?

• Case 11-5 Early Extinguishment of Debt

Gains or losses from the early extinguishment of debt that is refunded can theoretically be accounted for in three ways:

1. Amortized over the life of old debt
2. Amortized over the life of the new debt issue
3. Recognized in the period of extinguishment

Required:

a. Discuss the supporting arguments for each of the three theoretical methods of accounting for gains and losses from the early extinguishment of debt.

b. Which of the three methods would provide a balance sheet measure that reflects the present value of the future cash flows discounted at the interest rate that is commensurate with the risk associated with the new debt issue? Why?

c. Which of the three methods is generally accepted, and how should the appropriate amount of gain or loss be shown in a company's financial statements?

• Case 11-6 Contingencies

Angela Company is a manufacturer of toys. During the year, the following situations arose:

1. A safety hazard related to one of its toy products was discovered. It is considered probable that liabilities have been incurred. Based on past experience, a reasonable estimate of the amount of loss can be made.

2. One of the firm's small warehouses is located on the bank of a river and can no longer be insured against flood losses. No flood losses occurred after the date the insurance became unavailable.

3. This year, Angela began promoting a new toy by including a coupon, redeemable for a movie ticket, in each toy's carton. The movie ticket, which cost Angela $2, is purchased in advance and then mailed to the customer when Angela receives the coupon. Based on past experience, Angela estimated that 60 percent of the coupons would be redeemed. Forty percent of the coupons would be actually redeemed this year, and the remaining 20 percent of the coupons were expected to be redeemed next year.

Required:

a. How should Angela report the safety hazard? Why? Do not discuss deferred tax implications.

b. How should Angela report the uninsured flood risk? Why?

c. How should Angela account for the toy promotion campaign in this year?

• Case 11-7 Accounting for Notes Payable

Business transactions often involve the exchange of property, goods, or services for notes on similar instruments that may stipulate no interest rate or an interest rate that varies from prevailing rates.

Required:

a. When a note is exchanged for property, goods, or services, what value should be placed on the note:

   i. If it bears interest at a reasonable rate and is issued in a bargained transaction entered into at arm's length? Explain.

   ii. If it bears no interest and/or is not issued in a bargained transaction entered into at arm's length? Explain.

b. If the recorded value of a note differs from the face value,

   i. How should the difference be accounted for? Explain.

   ii. How should this difference be presented in the financial statements? Explain.

• Case 11-8 Accounting for Bonds Payable

On April 1, 2011, Janine Corporation sold some of its five-year, $1,000 face value, 12 percent term bonds dated March 1, 2011, at an effective annual interest rate (yield) of 10 percent. Interest is payable semiannually, and the first interest payment date is September 1, 2011. Janine uses the interest method of amortization. Bond issue costs were incurred in preparing and selling the bond issue.

On November 1, 2011, Janine sold directly to underwriters, at lump-sum price, $1,000 face value, 9 percent serial bonds dated November 1, 2011, at an effective interest rate (yield) of 11 percent. Of these serial bonds, a total of 25 percent is due on November 1, 2011; a total of 30 percent is due on November 1, 2012; and the rest is due on November 1, 2013. Interest is payable semiannually, and the first interest payment date is May 1, 2011. Janine uses the interest method of amortization. Bond issue costs were incurred in preparing and selling the bond issue.

Required:

a. How would the market price of the term bonds and the serial bonds be determined?

   i. How would all items related to the term bonds, except for bond issue costs, be presented in a balance sheet prepared immediately after the term bond issue was sold?

   ii. How would all items related to the serial bonds, except for bond issue costs, be presented in a balance sheet prepared immediately after the serial bond issue was sold?

b. What alternative methods could be used to account for the bond issue costs for the term bonds in 2011? Which method(s) is (are) considered current GAAP? Which method(s), if any, would affect the calculation of interest expense? Why? (For this question, do not assume that Janine opts to use the fair value method to account for the bonds.)

c. How would the amount of interest expense for the term bonds and the serial bonds be determined for 2011?

• Case 11-9 Accounting Concepts and Contingencies

The two basic requirements for the accrual of a loss contingency are supported by several basic concepts of accounting. Four of these concepts are periodicity (time periods), measurement, objectivity, and relevance.

Required:

Discuss how the two basic requirements for accrual of a loss contingency relate to the four concepts listed above.

• Case 11-10 Reporting Contingencies

The following three independent sets of facts relate to (1) the possible accrual or (2) the possible disclosure by other means of a loss contingency.

Situation 1

A company offers a one-way warranty for the product that it manufactures. A history of warranty claims has been compiled, and the probable amount of claims related to sales for a given period can be determined.

Situation 2

Following the date of a set of financial statements, but before the issuance of the financial statements, a company enters into a contract that will probably result in a significant loss to the company. The amount of the loss can be reasonably estimated.

Situation 3

A company has adopted a policy of recording self-insurance for any possible losses resulting from injury to others by the company's vehicles. The premium for an insurance policy for the same risk from an independent insurance company would have an annual cost of $2,000. During the period covered by the financial statements, no accidents involving the company's vehicles resulted in injury to others.

Required:

Discuss the accrual of a loss contingency and/or type of disclosure necessary (if any) and the reason(s) why such a disclosure is appropriate for each of the three independent sets of facts above. Complete your response to each situation before proceeding to the next situation.

FASB ASC Research

For each of the following research cases, search the FASB ASC database for information to address the issues. Cut and paste the FASB paragraphs that support your responses. Then summarize briefly what your responses are, citing the pronouncements and paragraphs used to support your responses.

• FASB ASC 11-1 Disclosure of Liabilities by Not-for-Profit Entities

Financial accounting standards normally address the reporting practices of for-profit business entities. Search the FASB ASC database to discover what the FASB reporting requirements are (if any) for the reporting by not-for-profit entities of their outstanding liabilities. Cut and paste your findings, cite your source(s), and write a brief summary of your findings.

• FASB ASC 11-2 Indirect Guarantees

FASB ASC 450 addresses accounting for loss contingencies, including those that represent a right to proceed against an outside party in the event that the guarantor is called upon to satisfy the guarantee—for example, a guarantee to pay the debts of another entity. Search the FASB ASC database to determine the requirement for reporting or not reporting such guarantees. Then search for a FASB interpretation (FIN) that was issued to clarify this issue. Cut and paste your findings and, in your own words, write a summary of what the findings mean.

• FARS 11-3 Accounting for Derivatives

SFAS No. 133 was one of the most complex standards ever issued by the FASB. As a result, numerous implementation guidelines have been issued. Search the FASB ASC database to find three issues addressed by the EITF concerning accounting for derivatives. Cite and briefly summarize these issues.

• FASB ASC 11-4 The Fair Value Option and Health Care Businesses

The FASB ASC indicates that not-for-profit, business-oriented health-care entities shall report unrealized gains and losses on items for which the fair value option has been elected within the performance indicator or as a part of discontinued operations, as appropriate. Find cite and copy the FASB ASC's definition of performance indicator as it relates to not-for-profit businesses.

• FASB ASC 11-5 Use of Zero Coupon Bonds in a Troubled Debt Restructuring

The FASB ASC provides guidance on accounting for the use of zero coupon bonds in a troubled debt restructuring. Find, cite, and copy that guidance.

• FASB ASC 11-6 Accounting for Loss Contingencies by Regulated Entities

The FASB ASC provides an exception for the guidance on accounting for loss contingencies for entities with regulated operations. Find, cite, and copy that guidance.

• FASB ASC 11-7 Hedging and Gas-Balancing Arrangements

The FASB ASC indicates that the terms of a gas-balancing arrangement should be analyzed to determine whether they meet the definition of a derivative instrument. Search the FASB ASC to find the definition of a gas-balancing arrangement. Find, cite, and copy that definition.

Room for Debate

• Debate 11-1 Liabilities versus Equity

In the discussion memorandum, "Distinguishing between Liability and Equity Instruments and Accounting for Instruments with Characteristics of Both," the FASB addressed the issue of whether redeemable preferred stock is debt or equity. *SFAS No. 150* (see FASB ASC 480) requires mandatorily redeemable preferred stock to be classified as debt.

For the following debate, your arguments should take into consideration definitions of the elements of financial statements in *SFAS No. 6* and any other relevant aspects of the conceptual framework, as well as implications regarding the usefulness of financial statement information to investors.

Team Debate:

Team 1: Present arguments in favor of presenting redeemable preferred stock as debt.

Team 2: Present arguments in favor of presenting redeemable preferred stock as equity.

• Debate 11-2 Fair Value Option

SFAS No. 159 (see FASB 825) allows companies to value financial liabilities at fair value. If not elected, financial liabilities will continue to be accounted for under the historical cost model.

Team Debate:

Team 1: Present arguments in favor of measuring liabilities at fair value.

Team 2: Present arguments against measuring liabilities at fair value.

• Debate 11-3 Convertible Debt

Should we separate the debt and equity features of convertible debt?

Team Debate:

Team 1: Pro Separation. Present arguments in favor of separating the debt and equity features of convertible debt.

Team 2: Against Separation. Present arguments against the separation of the debt and equity features of convertible debt.

CHAPTER 12

Accounting for

Income Taxes

Most accountants now agree that corporate income tax is an expense. Treating income tax as an expense is required under current GAAP. This treatment is consistent with proprietary theory because the earnings that accrue to owners are reduced by corporate obligations to the government. Also, because the income tax does not result from transactions with owners, expensing corporate income tax is consistent with the *SFAC No. 6* definition of comprehensive income. Thus, on the surface, accounting for income taxes would appear to be a nonissue.

Yet accounting for income taxes has been a most controversial financial accounting topic for many years. The controversy centers on a number of reporting and measurement issues. This chapter traces the historical development of GAAP for income taxes. It examines the theoretical accounting issues as well as the reporting requirements of *APB Opinion No. 11*, *SFAS No. 96*, and the current authoritative pronouncement originally issued as *SFAS No. 109* (see FASB ASC 740).

Historical Perspective

Accounting for income taxes became a significant issue in the 1940s when the Internal Revenue Code (IRC) permitted companies to depreciate the cost of emergency facilities considered essential to the war effort over a period of 60 months.[1] For a five-year period, businesses were able to reduce taxable income below what it would have been under the accounting method of depreciation.

1. Frank R. Rayburn, "A Chronological Review of the Authoritative Literature on Interperiod Tax Allocation: 1940–1985," *Accounting Historians Journal* (Fall 1986): 91.

The total depreciation charge over the life of the asset was the same for financial accounting income as it was for taxable income, but the allocation of cost to financial accounting income in each accounting period differed significantly from the allocation to taxable income. Before this IRC regulation existed, accounting practitioners expensed income tax as it was incurred per the corporate tax return. Some accountants argued that when accelerated tax depreciation is allowed, expensing the amount of the tax liability incurred in each period results in material distortions of periodic earnings. For example, when pretax financial accounting income is the same in each accounting period, tax expense fluctuates and reported earnings are not normalized.

The initial question raised by imposing a tax on corporate profits was whether income taxes were an expense or a distribution of a company's profits to the government. The Committee on Accounting Procedure resolved this issue in *ARB No. 23*, "Accounting for Income Taxes" (since superseded), by taking the position that income taxes are an expense that should be allocated to income in a manner similar to the way a company's other expenses are allocated.[2] *ARB No. 23* subsequently became Chapter 10, Section B of the AICPA's consolidated set of accounting procedures, *ARB No. 43*.[3] This release stated:

> Income taxes are an expense that should be allocated, when necessary and practicable, to income and other accounts, as other expenses are allocated. What the income statement should reflect ... is the expense properly allocable to the income included in the income statement for the year.[4]

It follows that items reported in the income statement have tax consequences. These tax consequences are expenses and should be treated in a manner similar to other expenses reported in the income statement. Accrual accounting requires the recognition of revenues and expenses in the period incurred, without regard to the timing of cash receipts and payments. Consequently, the tax effects of business transactions should be recorded in a similar manner. That is, income tax should be allocated to periods so that the items reported on the income statement are matched with their respective tax consequences. The allocation of income taxes to accounting periods is termed *interperiod tax allocation*.

ARB No. 23 did not apply to those cases where "differences between the tax return and the income statement will recur regularly over a comparatively long period of time."[5] A debate ensued as to whether the tax consequences of all items resulting in tax treatment that differs from accounting treatment should be allocated. In addition, *ARB No. 23* did not provide clear guidance on how to measure specific tax consequences. The nature of income taxes was subsequently studied by the APB, which issued *APB Opinion No. 11*, "Accounting for Income Taxes"[6]

2. American Institute of Accountants, Committee on Accounting Procedure, "Accounting for Income Taxes," *Accounting Research Bulletin No. 23* (New York: AIA, 1944).

3. Committee on Accounting Procedure, "Restatement and Revision of Accounting Research Bulletins," *Accounting Research Bulletin No. 43* (New York: AIA, 1953).

4. Ibid., sec. B, para. 4.

5. Ibid., sec. B, para. 1.

6. Accounting Principles Board, *Opinion No. 11*, "Accounting for Income Taxes" (New York: AICPA, 1967).

(since superseded). This release extended interperiod tax allocation to all items resulting in differences due to the timing of revenue and expense recognition in the income statement and the tax return. It required the deferred method, which measures the effects of future tax consequences using today's tax rates, an income statement approach that stresses the matching concept. As such, it is consistent with the recommendations outlined in *ARB No. 43*. Yet, *APB Opinion No. 11* was widely criticized. Opponents argued that the use of current tax rates resulted in balance sheet amounts that did not reflect the future tax consequences of economic events and transactions, because when those future consequences actually occur, the tax rates are likely to have changed. In response, the FASB issued *SFAS No. 96*, "Accounting for Income Taxes," which proscribed a balance sheet approach to allocating income taxes among accounting periods.[7] But *SFAS No. 96* did not silence the critics of accounting for income taxes, and some of its provisions were so controversial that the FASB was compelled to delay the effective date of the pronouncement twice. Subsequently, *SFAS No. 96* was superseded by *SFAS No. 109*, "Accounting for Income Taxes"[8] (see FASB ASC 740).

The Income Tax Allocation Issue

According to *SFAC No. 1*, the objective of financial reporting is to provide information that is useful in predicting the amounts and timing of future cash flows.[9] GAAP guides the reporting and measurement of economic events and transactions to meet this goal.

Most economic events and transactions have tax cash-flow consequences. These consequences are reported on tax returns in accordance with the IRC. The IRC is enacted by Congress, and its goal is to provide revenue, in an equitable manner, to operate the federal government. On occasion the IRC may also be used to regulate the economy. The same economic events that give rise to taxable income are also reported in published financial statements by following GAAP. In general, revenue becomes taxable when taxpayers receive cash, or expenses are deductible when cash is paid (the ability-to-pay criterion). Consequently, income tax accounting is more closely associated with cash basis accounting than is financial accounting. Because the IRC is based on an ability-to-pay criterion, the IRC's reporting requirements differ from the reporting requirements for financial accounting as defined by GAAP. As a result, the taxes paid in a given year may not reflect the tax consequences of events and transactions that are reported in the income statement for that same year.

When the IRC requires that revenues and expenses be recognized in different accounting periods from GAAP, taxable income is temporarily different from pretax financial accounting income. In a subsequent period, the event that caused the difference will reverse itself. Originating and reversing temporary differences cause an accounting problem that is termed the *income tax allocation issue*.

7. Financial Accounting Standards Board, *Statement of Financial Accounting Standards No. 96*, "Accounting for Income Taxes" (Stamford, CT: FASB, 1987).

8. *Statement of Financial Accounting Standards No. 109*, "Accounting for Income Taxes" (Stamford, CT: FASB, 1992).

9. *Statement of Financial Accounting Concepts No. 1*, "Objectives of Financial Reporting by Business Enterprises" (Stamford, CT: FASB, 1978), para. 37.

The objectives of accounting for income taxes are to recognize the amount of taxes payable or refundable for the current year and to recognize the future tax consequences of temporary differences as well as net operating losses (NOLs) and unused tax credits. To facilitate discussion of the issues raised by the concept of interperiod tax allocation, we first examine the nature of differences among pretax financial income, taxable income, and NOLs.

Permanent and Temporary Differences

Differences between pretax financial accounting income and taxable income may be either permanent differences or temporary differences. Temporary differences between pretax financial accounting income and taxable income affect two or more accounting periods and thereby involve the allocation of income taxes between accounting periods. Permanent differences do not have income tax consequences. Thus only temporary differences result in deferred income tax assets and liabilities.

Permanent Differences

Certain events and transactions cause differences between pretax accounting income and taxable income to be permanent. Most *permanent differences* between pretax financial accounting income and taxable income occur when specific provisions of the IRC exempt certain types of revenue from taxation or prohibit the deduction of certain types of expenses. Others occur when the IRC allows tax deductions that are not expenses under GAAP. Permanent differences arise because of federal economic policy or because Congress may wish to alleviate a provision of the IRC that falls too heavily on one segment of the economy. There are three types of permanent differences:

1. *Revenue recognized for financial accounting reporting purposes that is never taxable.* Examples include interest on municipal bonds and life insurance proceeds payable to a corporation upon the death of an insured employee.

2. *Expenses recognized for financial accounting reporting purposes that are never deductible for income tax purposes.* An example is life insurance premiums on employees where the corporation is the beneficiary.

3. *Income tax deductions that do not qualify as expenses under GAAP.* Examples include percentage depletion in excess of cost depletion and the special dividend exclusion.[10]

Permanent differences affect pretax financial accounting income or taxable income, but not both. A corporation that has nontaxable revenue or additional deductions for income tax reporting purposes will report a relatively lower taxable income compared to pretax financial accounting income than it would have if these items were not present, whereas a corporation with expenses that are not tax deductible will report a relatively higher taxable income.

Temporary Differences

Most *temporary differences* between pretax financial accounting income and taxable income arise because the timing of revenues, gains, expenses, or losses in financial

---

10. Corporations are allowed to deduct between 80 and 100 percent of the dividends received from other corporations, depending on their percentage of ownership, in computing their taxable income.

accounting income occurs in a different period from taxable income. These timing differences result in assets and liabilities having different bases for financial accounting purposes than for income tax purposes at the end of a given accounting period. Additional temporary differences occur because specific provisions of the IRC create different bases for depreciation or for gain or loss recognition for income tax purposes than are used for financial accounting purposes. Since many of these additional temporary differences relate to more complex provisions of the tax laws, only timing differences are discussed in detail here.

When a temporary difference occurs, it causes current pretax accounting income to be either greater than or less than current taxable income. A temporary difference that causes current pretax accounting income to be greater than current taxable income will cause future taxable income to be greater than future pretax accounting income. The resulting future differences become taxable in those accounting periods when they occur; thus, the excess of the future taxable income over pretax accounting income is termed a *taxable amount*. The opposite occurs for temporary differences that cause current taxable income to exceed current pretax accounting income. These temporary differences result in future *deductible amounts*.

Temporary differences that result in future taxable amounts result from the postponement of tax payments to future accounting periods. Proponents of the balance sheet approach to measuring and reporting deferred income taxes argue that because these temporary differences result from a prior transaction or event (an originating temporary difference) that will reverse and thus result in the probable future outflow of economic resources (future tax consequences), the future tax consequences of these temporary differences meet the conceptual framework definition of liabilities and should be reported as deferred tax liabilities. Conversely, they argue that timing differences that result in future deductible amounts represent future tax benefits and thereby meet the conceptual framework definition of assets. As a result, the future tax consequences of these temporary differences are deferred tax assets. Examples of both types of temporary differences are given below.[11]

Current Financial Accounting Income Exceeds Current Taxable Income

1. *Revenues or gains are included in financial accounting income before they are included in taxable income.* For example, gross profit on installment sales is included in financial accounting income at the point of sale but may be reported for tax purposes as the cash is collected.

2. *Expenses or losses are deducted to compute taxable income before they are deducted to compute financial accounting income.* For example, a fixed asset may be depreciated by MACRS depreciation for income tax purposes and by the straight-line method for financial accounting purposes.[12]

---

11. *SFAS No. 109* described these temporary differences in paragraph 11 (see FASB ASC 740-10-25-20).

12. The modified accelerated cost recovery system (MACRS) is the only allowable accelerated depreciation method allowed under the IRC. It usually results in relatively higher depreciation amounts than straight-line depreciation in the early years of an asset's life.

Current Financial Accounting Income Is Less than Current Taxable Income

1. *Revenues or gains are included in taxable income before they are included in financial accounting income.* For example, rent received in advance is taxable when it is received, but it is reported in financial accounting income under as it is earned.

2. *Expenses or losses are deducted to compute financial accounting income before they are deducted to determine taxable income.* For example, product warranty costs are estimated and reported as expenses when the product is sold for financial accounting purposes, but they are deducted as actually incurred in later years to determine taxable income.

APB Opinion No. 11 limited the scope of temporary differences to timing differences. *Timing differences* occur when taxable revenues or gains, or tax-deductible expenses or losses, are recognized in one accounting period for financial accounting reporting purposes and in a different accounting period for income tax purposes. *SFAS No. 109* broadened the scope of temporary differences by including all "events that create differences between the tax bases of assets and liabilities and their amounts for financial reporting."[13] For example, an asset donated to a business has a zero basis for tax purposes but is recorded at its fair market value for financial accounting purposes. This creates a temporary difference that will reverse either through depreciation or sale of the asset. Thus these additional temporary differences also result in tax consequences that affect two or more accounting periods. The following additional temporary differences are noted in *SFAS No. 109.*[14]

Additional Temporary Differences

1. *A reduction in the tax basis of depreciable assets because of tax credits.* The amounts received on future recovery of the amount of the asset for financial accounting purposes will be taxable when the asset is recovered. For example, the IRC formerly allowed taxpayers to reduce the depreciation basis of assets by half of the amount of the investment tax credit (ITC) taken for the asset. As a result, future taxable incomes exceeded future pretax financial accounting income by the amount of the tax basis reduction. Hence, the basis reduction is a temporary difference that creates a future taxable amount. The future taxable amount was equivalent to the amount needed to recover the additional financial accounting asset cost basis.[15]

2. *The ITC accounted for by the deferred method.* Recall from our discussion in Chapter 1 that the preferred treatment of accounting for the ITC is to reduce the cost of the related asset by the amount of the ITC. If this method is used, the amounts received on future recovery of the reduced cost of the asset for financial accounting purposes will be less than the tax basis of the asset. The difference will be tax deductible when the asset is recovered.

13. *SFAS No. 109*, para. 3 (see FASB ASC 740-10-25-19).

14. These temporary differences were also described in *SFAS No. 109*, para. 11 (see FASB ASC 740-10-25-20).

15. The investment tax credit is used to stimulate the economy. It has been phased in and out of the IRC, depending on the state of the economy, since the early 1960s. At the present time it is not in effect.

3. *Foreign operations for which the reporting currency is the functional currency.* The provisions of *SFAS No. 52*, "Foreign Currency Translation"[16] (see FASB ASC 830) require certain assets to be remeasured from the foreign currency to U.S. dollars using historical exchange rates when the reporting currency is the functional currency.[17] If exchange rates subsequently change, there will be a difference between the foreign tax basis and the U.S. dollar historical cost of assets and liabilities. That difference will be taxable or deductible for foreign tax purposes when the reported amounts of the assets and liabilities are recovered and settled, respectively.

4. *An increase in the tax basis of assets because of indexing for inflation.* The tax law may require adjustment of the tax basis of a depreciable asset for the effects of inflation. The inflation-adjusted basis of the asset will then be used to compute future tax deductions for depreciation, or the gain or loss on the sale of the asset. Amounts received on future recovery of the remaining cost of the asset recorded for financial accounting purposes will then be less than the remaining tax basis of the asset, and the difference will be tax deductible when the asset is recovered.

5. *Business combinations accounted for by the purchase method.* There may be differences between the assigned value and the tax basis of the assets and liabilities recognized in a business combination accounted for as a purchase.[18] These differences will result in taxable or deductible amounts when the recorded amounts of the assets are recovered or the recorded amounts of the liabilities are settled.

GAAP requires published financial statements to reflect the tax consequences of economic events and transactions reported in those financial statements. Since GAAP and the IRC do not always agree on the timing of recognition of revenues and expenses, creating temporary differences, the current period's income tax expense must include the current period effects resulting from the recognition of future tax consequences. The effects of these future tax consequences are reported as deferred tax assets and deferred tax liabilities. Stated differently, the expected cash flows of future tax consequences resulting from temporary differences between pretax financial accounting income and taxable income reflect anticipated future tax benefits (*deferred tax assets*) or payables (*deferred tax liabilities*). The result is that income tax expense is equal to the amount of income taxes currently payable, adjusted for changes in deferred tax assets and liabilities.

16. *Statement of Financial Accounting Standards No. 52*, "Foreign Currency Translation" (Stamford, CT: FASB, 1981).

17. *SFAS No. 52* (see FASB ASC 830-10-20) defines the functional currency as the currency of the primary economic environment in which an entity operates. See Chapter 15 for a discussion of foreign currency translation.

18. Under the purchase method of accounting for business combinations now termed the acquisitions method, which is now the only acceptable method of accounting for business combinations, the assets and liabilities acquired are recorded at their fair market values, not their previous book values. See Chapter 16 for a discussion of business combinations.

Net Operating Losses (NOLs)

An NOL occurs when the amount of total tax deductions and tax-deductible losses is greater than the amount of total taxable revenues and gains during an accounting period. The IRC allows corporations reporting NOLs to carry these losses back and forward to offset other reported taxable income (currently back 2 years and forward 20 years).

An NOL carry-back is applied to the taxable income of the two preceding years in the order in which they occurred, beginning with the older year first. If unused NOLs are still available, they are carried forward for up to 20 years to offset future taxable income.[19] NOL carry-backs result in the refund of prior taxes paid. Thus the tax benefits of NOL carry-backs are currently realizable and for financial accounting purposes are reported as reductions in the current-period loss. A receivable is recognized on the balance sheet, and the associated benefit is shown on the current year's income statement.

Whether to recognize the potential benefit of an NOL carry-forward has added controversy to the income tax accounting debate. The APB argued that the benefit of an NOL carry-forward is generally not assured in the loss period.[20] Nevertheless, *APB Opinion No. 11* allowed the recognition of anticipated benefit to be realized from an NOL carry-forward in the unusual circumstances when realization is assured beyond any reasonable doubt.[21] *SFAS No. 96* did not allow the potential tax benefits of NOL carry-forwards to be treated as assets. This position was based on the following argument:

> Incurring losses or generating profits in future years are future events that are not recognized in financial statements for the current year and are not inherently assumed in financial statements for the current year. Those future events shall not be anticipated, regardless of probability, for purposes of recognizing or measuring . . . [income taxes] . . . in the current year.[22]

SFAS No. 109 liberalizes the policies for recognizing tax assets (as discussed later) and, thus, for the financial accounting treatment of NOL carry-forwards.

Conceptual Issues

The primary income tax allocation issue involves whether and how to account for the tax effects of temporary differences between taxable income, as determined by the IRC, and pretax financial accounting income as determined under GAAP. Some accountants believe it is inappropriate to give any accounting recognition to the tax effects of these differences. Others believe that recognition is appropriate but disagree on the method to use. There is also disagreement on the appropriate tax rate to use and whether reported future tax effects should

---

19. A company may choose not to use the carry-back provisions and only carry forward net operating losses. Such an election might occur if Congress were expected to increase tax rates in the near future.

20. *APB Opinion No. 11*, para. 43.

21. Ibid.

22. Ibid., para. 15.

be discounted to their present values. Finally, there is a lack of consensus over whether interperiod tax allocation should be applied comprehensively to all differences or only to those expected to reverse in the future. Each of these conceptual issues is examined in more detail in the following paragraphs.

Allocation versus Non-allocation

Although authoritative pronouncements have consistently required interperiod tax allocation, opponents maintain that the amount of income tax expense reported on a company's income statement should be the same as the income taxes payable for the accounting period as determined by the income tax return. Under this approach, there would be no interperiod allocation of income taxes.

Advocates of non-allocation argue as follows:

1. Income taxes result only from taxable income. Whether or not the company has accounting income is irrelevant. Hence, attempts to match income taxes with accounting income provide no relevant information for users of published financial statements.

2. Income taxes are different from other expenses; therefore, allocation in a manner similar to other expenses is irrelevant. Expenses are incurred to generate revenues; income taxes generate no revenues. They are not incurred in anticipation of future benefits, nor are they expirations of cost to provide facilities to generate revenues.

3. Income taxes are levied on total taxable income, not on individual items of revenue and expense. Thus there can be no temporary differences related to these items.

4. Interperiod tax allocation hides an economic difference between a company that employs tax strategies to reduce current tax payments (and is therefore economically better off) and one that does not.

5. Reporting a company's income tax expense at the amount paid or currently payable is a better predictor of the company's future cash outflows because many of the deferred taxes will never be paid, or will be paid only in the distant future.

6. Income tax allocation entails an implicit forecasting of future profits. To incorporate such forecasting into the preparation of financial information is inconsistent with the long-standing principle of conservatism.

7. There is no present obligation for the potential or future tax consequences of present or prior transactions because there is no legal liability to pay taxes until an actual future tax return is prepared.

8. The accounting record keeping procedures involving interperiod tax allocation are too costly for the purported benefits.

On the other hand, the advocates of interperiod tax allocation cite the following reasons to counter the preceding arguments or to criticize non-allocation:

1. Income taxes result from the incurrence of transactions and events. As a result, income tax expense should be based on the results of the transactions or events that are included in financial accounting income.

2. Income taxes are an expense of doing business and should involve the same accrual, deferral, and estimation concepts that are applied to other expenses.

3. Differences between the timing of revenues and expenses do result in temporary differences that will reverse in the future. Expanding, growing businesses experience increasing asset and liability balances. Old assets are collected, old liabilities are paid, and new ones take their place. Deferred tax balances grow in a similar manner.

4. Interperiod tax allocation makes a company's net income a more useful measure of its long-term earning power and avoids periodic income distortions resulting from income tax regulations.

5. Non-allocation of a company's income tax expense hinders the prediction of its future cash flows. For instance, a company's future cash inflows from installment sales collection would usually be offset by related cash outflows for taxes.

6. A company is a going concern, and income taxes that are currently deferred will eventually be paid. The validity of other assets and liabilities reported in the balance sheet depends on the presumption of a viable company and hence the incurrence of future net income.

7. Temporary differences are associated with future tax consequences. For example, reversals of originating differences that provide present tax savings are associated with higher future taxable incomes and therefore higher future tax payments. In this sense, deferred tax liabilities are similar to other contingent liabilities that are currently reported under GAAP. However, one could argue that the recognition and measurement of other contingent liabilities hinges on the probability of their incurrence, whereas probability of future tax consequences is not a consideration.

Comprehensive versus Partial Allocation

Authoritative accounting pronouncements have consistently required the use of in terperiod tax allocation, and they have also consistently required that it be applied to all temporary differences between taxable income and pretax accounting income. This approach is termed "comprehensive" interperiod income tax allocation. An alternative approach, called "partial" interperiod income tax allocation, would result in allocating the tax for only a few temporary differences. This issue revolves around the question of how much income tax should be allocated.

Comprehensive Allocation   Under *comprehensive allocation*, the income tax expense reported in an accounting period is affected by all transactions and events entering into the determination of pretax financial accounting income for that period. Comprehensive allocation results in including the tax consequences of all temporary differences as deferred tax assets and liabilities, regardless of how significant or recurrent they are. Proponents of comprehensive allocation view all transactions and events that create temporary differences as affecting cash flows in the accounting periods when the future tax consequences of temporary differences are realized. Under this view, the future tax consequence of a temporary difference is analogous to an unpaid accounts receivable or accounts payable invoice, which in the future is collected or paid.

Partial Allocation   In contrast, under *partial allocation*, the income tax expense reported in an accounting period would not be affected by those temporary differences that are not expected to reverse in the future. That is, proponents of partial allocation argue that, in certain cases, groups of similar transactions or events may continually create new temporary differences in the future that will offset the realization of any taxable or deductible amounts, resulting in an indefinite postponement of deferred tax consequences. In effect, partial allocationists argue that these types of temporary differences are more like permanent differences. Examples of these types of differences include depreciation for manufacturing companies with large amounts of depreciable assets and installment sales for merchandising companies.

Advocates of comprehensive allocation raise the following arguments:

1. Individual temporary differences do reverse. By definition, a temporary difference cannot be permanent; the offsetting effect of future events should not be assumed. It is inappropriate to look at the effect of a group of temporary differences on income taxes; the focus should be on the individual items comprising the group. Temporary differences should be viewed in the same manner as accounts payable. Although the total balance of accounts payable may not change, many individual credit and payment transactions affect the total.

2. Accounting is primarily historical. It is inappropriate to offset the income tax effects of possible future transactions against the tax effects of transactions that have already occurred.

3. The income tax effects of temporary differences should be reported in the same period as the related transactions and events are reported in pretax financial accounting income.

4. Accounting results should not be subject to manipulation by management. That is, a company's management should not be able to alter the company's results of operations and ending financial position by arbitrarily deciding what temporary differences will and will not reverse in the future.

In contrast, advocates of partial income tax allocation raise these arguments:

1. All groups of temporary differences are not similar to certain other groups of accounting items, such as accounts payable. Accounts payable "roll over" as a result of actual individual credit and payment transactions. Income taxes, however, are based on total taxable income and not on the individual items constituting that income. Therefore consideration of the impact of the *group* of temporary differences on income taxes is the appropriate viewpoint.

2. Comprehensive income tax allocation distorts economic reality. The income tax regulations that cause the temporary differences will continue to exist. For instance, Congress is not likely to reduce investment incentives with respect to depreciation. Consequently, future investments are virtually certain to result in originating depreciation differences of an amount to at least offset reversing differences. Consideration should thus be given to the impact of future as well as historical transactions.

3. Assessment of a company's future cash flows is enhanced by using the partial allocation approach. Since the deferred income taxes (if any) reported on a company's balance sheet under partial allocation should actually reverse rather than continue to grow, partial allocation would better reflect future cash flows.

4. Accounting results should not be distorted by the use of a rigid, mechanical approach, such as comprehensive tax allocation. Furthermore, an objective of the audit function is to identify and deter any management manipulation.

Discounting Deferred Taxes

GAAP requires comprehensive interperiod income tax allocation. Reported deferred tax assets and liabilities reflect anticipated future tax consequences resulting from temporary differences between pretax financial accounting income and taxable income. Specific measurement issues, such as the appropriate method and tax rate to use to calculate deferred tax balances, are discussed in the following sections. This section addresses the issue of whether deferred taxes, regardless of the measurement method used, should be discounted.

Proponents of reporting deferred taxes at their discounted amounts argue that the company that reduces or postpones tax payments is economically better off. It is their belief that by discounting deferred taxes, a company best reflects the operational advantages of its tax strategies in its financial statements. Proponents also feel that discounting deferred taxes is consistent with the accounting principles established for such items as notes receivable and notes payable, pension costs, and leases. They argue that discounted amounts are considered to be the most appropriate indicators of future cash flows.

Critics of discounting counter that discounting deferred taxes mismatches taxable transactions and the related tax effects. That is, the taxable transaction would be reported in one period and the related tax effects over several periods. They also argue that discounting would conceal a company's actual tax burden by reporting as interest expense the discount factor that would otherwise be reported as part of income tax expense. Furthermore, deferred taxes may be considered as interest-free loans from the government that do not require discounting because the effective interest rate is zero. Although this argument has conceptual merit, a plausible counterargument would be that the time value of money is important to the well-being of companies and that because of this aspect, GAAP requires interest to be imputed for non-interest-bearing financial instruments. It follows that the time value of money is enhanced by postponing tax payments; thus, consistency under GAAP would require imputing interest on deferred taxes.

Alternative Interperiod Tax Allocation Methods

Three methods of income tax allocation may be used in conjunction with either the comprehensive or partial allocation approach. These are (1) the deferred method, (2) the asset-liability method, and (3) the net-of-tax method.

The Deferred Method

The *deferred method* of income tax allocation is an income statement approach. It is based on the concept that income tax expense is related to the period in which income is recognized. The deferred method measures income tax expense as though the current-period pretax financial accounting income is reported on the current year's income tax return. The tax effect of a temporary difference is the difference between income taxes computed with and without inclusion of the temporary difference. The resulting difference between income tax expense and income taxes currently payable is a debit or credit to the deferred income tax account.

The deferred tax account balance is reported in the balance sheet as deferred tax credit or deferred tax charge. Under the deferred method, the deferred tax amount reported on the balance sheets is the effect of temporary differences that will reverse in the future and that are measured using the income tax rates and laws in effect when the differences originated. No adjustments are made to deferred taxes for changes in the income tax rates or tax laws that occur after the period of origination. When the deferrals reverse, the tax effects are recorded at the rates that were in existence when the temporary differences originated.

APB Opinion No. 11 required comprehensive interperiod income tax allocation using the deferred method.[23] Like its predecessor, *ARB No. 43*, *APB Opinion No. 11* concluded that "income tax expense should include the tax effects of revenue and expense transactions included in the determination of pretax accounting income."[24] Use of the deferred method caused considerable controversy. The primary criticism was that neither deferred tax charges nor deferred tax credits have the essential characteristics of assets or liabilities. Because the deferred method does not use tax rates that will be in effect when temporary differences reverse, they do not measure probable future benefits or sacrifices; hence, the resulting deferred taxes do not meet the definition of assets or liabilities in *SFAC No. 6*. The deferred tax balances simply represent the cumulative effects of temporary differences waiting to be adjusted in the matching process of some future accounting period.

Arguments in favor of the deferred method of interperiod tax allocation include the following:

1. The income statement is the most important financial statement, and matching is a critical aspect of the accounting process. Thus it is of little consequence that deferred taxes are not true assets or liabilities in the conceptual sense.

2. Deferred taxes are the result of historical transactions or events that created the temporary differences. Since accounting reports most economic events on a historical cost basis, deferred taxes should be reported in a similar manner.

3. Historical income tax rates are verifiable. Reporting deferred taxes based on historical rates increases the reliability of accounting information.

The Asset-Liability Method

The *asset-liability method* of income tax allocation is balance sheet oriented. The intent is to accrue and report the total tax benefit or taxes payable that will actually be realized or assessed on temporary differences when their respective future taxable or deductible amounts are expected to occur. A temporary difference is viewed as giving rise to either a tax benefit that will result in a decrease in future tax payments or a tax liability that will be paid in the future at tax rates that are then current. Theoretically, the future tax rates used should be estimated, based on expectations regarding future tax law changes. However, GAAP requires that the future tax rates used to determine current period deferred tax asset and liability balances be based on currently enacted tax law.[25]

23. *APB Opinion No. 11*, paras. 34 and 35.
24. Ibid., para. 34.
25. *FASB Statement No. 109*, para. 8 (see FASB ASC 740-10-30-2).

Under the asset-liability method, the deferred tax amount reported on the balance sheet measures the future tax consequences of existing temporary differences using the currently enacted tax rates and laws that will be in effect when those tax consequences are expected to occur. At the end of each accounting period, or when the temporary differences that caused the company to report a deferred tax asset or liability no longer exist, companies adjust their deferred tax asset and liability account balances to reflect any changes in the income tax rates. Stated differently, at year-end companies report deferred tax asset and liability balances that measure the future tax consequences of anticipated deductible and taxable amounts that were caused by current and prior period temporary differences. The reported amounts are measured using tax rates that under currently enacted tax law will be in effect in those years when the deductible and taxable amounts are expected to occur. This practice results in reporting deferred tax assets and liabilities at their expected realizable values.

When using the asset-liability method, income tax expense is the sum of (or difference between) the changes in deferred tax asset and liability balances and the current provision for income taxes per the tax return.[26] According to the FASB, deferred taxes under the asset-liability method meet the conceptual definitions of assets and liabilities established in *SFAC No. 6*.[27] For instance, the resulting deferred tax credit balances of an entity can be viewed as probable future sacrifices (i.e., tax payments based on future tax rates) arising from present obligations (taxes owed) as a result of past transactions (originating differences). That is, deferred taxes measure future resource flows resulting from transactions or events already recognized for financial accounting purposes.

Arguments in favor of the asset-liability method of interperiod tax allocation include the following:

1. The balance sheet is becoming a more important financial statement. Reporting deferred taxes based on the expected tax rates when the temporary differences reverse increases the predictive value of future cash flows, liquidity, and financial flexibility.

2. Reporting deferred taxes based on the expected tax rates is conceptually more sound because the reported amount represents either the likely future economic sacrifice (future tax payments) or economic benefit (future reduction in taxes).

3. Deferred taxes may be the result of historical transactions; but, by definition, they are taxes that are postponed and will be paid (or will reduce taxes) in the future at the future tax rates.

4. Estimates are used extensively in accounting. The use of estimated future tax rates for deferred taxes poses no more of a problem regarding verifiability and reliability than using, say, estimated lives for depreciation.

5. Because the tax expense results from changes in balance sheet values, its measurement is consistent with the *SFAC No. 6* and *SFAS No. 130* (see FASB ASC 220) definitions of comprehensive income.

26. Under *SFAS No. 109*, there may also be a valuation allowance for deferred tax assets. Changes in the valuation allowance would also affect income tax expense. The valuation allowance is discussed later in the chapter.

27. *FASB Statement No. 109*, para. 63 (note that the reasoning behind FASB positions is not contained in the FASB ASC).

The Net-of-Tax Method

The *net-of-tax method* is more a method of disclosure than a different method of calculating deferred taxes. Under this method, the income tax effects of temporary differences are computed by applying either the deferred method or the asset-liability method. The resulting deferred taxes, however, are not separately disclosed on the balance sheet. Instead, under the net-of-tax method the deferred charges (tax assets) or deferred credits (tax liabilities) are treated as adjustments of the accounts to which the temporary differences relate. Generally, the accounts are adjusted through the use of a valuation allowance rather than directly. For instance, if a temporary difference results from additional tax depreciation, the related tax effect would be subtracted (by means of a valuation account) from the cost of the asset (along with accumulated depreciation) to determine the carrying value of the depreciable asset. Similarly, the carrying value of installment accounts receivable would be reduced for the expected increase in income taxes that will occur when the receivable is collected (and taxed). Reversals of temporary differences would reduce the valuation allowance accounts.

Two alternatives exist for disclosing the periodic income tax expense on the income statement under the net-of-tax method. Under the first alternative, the tax effects of temporary differences are included in the total income tax expense. Thus the income tax expense is reported in a manner similar to the deferred method or the asset-liability method. Under the second alternative, income tax expense would be reported at the same amount as current income taxes payable, and the tax effects of temporary differences would be combined with the revenue or expense items to which they relate. For instance, the tax effect of additional tax depreciation would be reported as an adjustment to depreciation expense.

The basic argument advocated by those who favor of the net-of-tax method of interperiod tax allocation centers on the notion that all revenue and expense transactions involve changes in specific asset and liability accounts and should be reported accordingly. Accounting for the tax effects of temporary differences should therefore be no different than accounting for changes in specific asset and liability accounts. Because temporary differences are the result of events that affect the future taxability and tax deductibility of specific assets and liabilities, they have future economic consequences that should be reflected in the value of the related assets and liabilities. For instance, when tax depreciation exceeds financial accounting depreciation, income tax expense is higher than current income taxes payable because an excess amount of the cost of the depreciable asset has been charged against taxable income. Thus the excess (temporary difference) has reduced the future tax deductibility of the depreciable asset cost, and the carrying value of the asset should be reduced accordingly.

There are several arguments against the net-of-tax method. The primary argument is that many factors affect the value of assets and liabilities but are not recorded in the accounts. To single out one factor (impact on future taxes) as affecting value is inappropriate. Also, it is not always possible to determine the related asset or liability account.[28] Furthermore, it is argued that the net-of-tax method is too complex to use and distorts traditional concepts for measuring assets and liabilities.

28. Net operating losses (NOLs) create deferred tax asset balances under current GAAP. NOLs do not result from temporary differences caused by any single transaction or event.

FASB Dissatisfaction with the Deferred Method

The deferred method was prescribed by *APB Opinion No. 11*. In 1982 the FASB, prompted by criticisms and concerns voiced in the literature and letters to the Board regarding the deferred method, began to reconsider accounting for income taxes. In *SFAC No. 6*, the FASB indicated that deferred income tax amounts reported on the balance sheet did not meet the newly established definitions for assets and liabilities.[29] Applying the deferred method most frequently resulted in reporting a deferred tax credit balance. Under the deferred method, deferred tax credits result when the payment of income tax is deferred to a later period. However, the tax rate used to measure the deferral may not be in effect when the deferred taxes are actually paid. If deferred income tax credit balances are liabilities, then the amounts reported in balance sheets should reflect the future resource outflows that will be required to settle them. Any changes in tax rates and tax law that would change the future impact of temporary differences on income tax payments should thus be recognized for financial reporting purposes in the period when tax rate and tax law changes are enacted.

Subsequently, the Tax Reform Act of 1986 significantly reduced income tax rates and created additional pressure to consider a change in the method of accounting for temporary differences. After weighing the various arguments in favor of non-allocation and interperiod income tax allocation, the comprehensive and partial income allocation approaches, and the deferred, asset-liability, and net-of-tax methods of applying income tax allocation, in 1987 the FASB released *SFAS No. 96*, which contained the following conclusions:

1. Interperiod income tax allocation of temporary differences is appropriate.
2. The comprehensive allocation approach should be applied.
3. The asset-liability method of income tax allocation should be used.

In addition to accepting the arguments presented earlier in favor of the asset-liability method, the FASB expanded on these arguments and provided the following rationale for its conclusions:

1. The income tax consequences of an event should be recognized in the same accounting period as that event is recognized in the financial statements. Although most events affect taxable income and pretax financial accounting income in the same accounting period, the income tax consequences of some events are deferred. Temporary differences result from events that have deferred tax consequences.

2. Recognition of deferred income taxes is consistent with accrual accounting. Under accrual accounting, there is an assumption that there will be future recovery and settlement of reported amounts of assets and liabilities, respectively. That assumption necessitates the recognition of deferred tax consequences of those temporary differences that will become refundable or payable when the reported amounts of assets and liabilities are recovered and settled, respectively. On the other hand, earning future income and incurring future losses are events that are *not* assumed in the current

---

29. *Statement of Financial Accounting Concepts No. 6*, "Elements of Financial Statements" (Stamford, CT: FASB, 1985), para. 241.

accounting period under accrual accounting; thus, they should not be assumed for income tax accounting.

3. Under the asset-liability method, the deferred tax consequences of temporary differences generally are recognizable liabilities and assets. That is, a deferred tax liability represents the amount of income taxes that will be payable in future years when temporary differences result in taxable income at that time. Similarly, a deferred tax asset represents the amount of income taxes that will be refundable when temporary differences result in tax-deductible amounts in future years.

Note that the FASB emphasized that temporary differences result in future tax consequences, rather than the allocation of tax among accounting periods. Non-allocation, partial allocation, and the deferred and net-of-tax methods were rejected and are *not* GAAP. Furthermore, reporting deferred taxes using a present-value approach was not considered by the FASB and is also *not* acceptable accounting for income taxes. The asset-liability approach presumably measures the future tax consequences for prior events or transactions. The following sections describe the *SFAS No. 96* arguments and conclusions regarding the nature of deferred tax liabilities and deferred tax assets and explain how they should be measured and reported.

Deferred Tax Liability

The three essential characteristics of a liability established by *SFAC No. 6* are that (1) it must embody a present responsibility to another entity that involves settlement by probable future transfer or use of assets at a specified or determinable date, on occurrence of a specified event, or on demand; (2) the responsibility obligates the entity, leaving it little or no discretion to avoid the future sacrifice; and (3) the transaction or event obligating the entity has already happened. The deferred tax consequences of temporary differences that will result in net taxable amounts in future years meet these characteristics.[30] The first characteristic is met by a deferred tax liability because (1) the deferred tax consequences stem from the requirements of tax law and hence are a responsibility to the government, (2) settlement will involve a probable future transfer or use of assets when the taxes are paid, and (3) settlement will result from events specified by the tax law. The second characteristic is met because, based on the government's tax rules and regulations, income taxes definitely will be payable when temporary differences result in net taxable amounts in future years. The third characteristic is met because the past events that created the temporary differences are the same past events that result in the deferred tax obligation.

Deferred Tax Asset

The three essential characteristics of an asset are that (1) it must embody a probable future benefit that involves a capacity to contribute to future net cash inflows, (2) the entity must be able to obtain the benefit and control other entities' access to it, and (3) the transaction or other event resulting in the entity's right to or

---

30. *Statement of Financial Accounting Standards No. 96*, "Accounting for Income Taxes" (Stamford, CT: FASB, 1997), paras. 83–89 (superseded).

control of the benefit must already have occurred. The deferred tax consequences of temporary differences that will result in net deductible amounts in future years that may be *carried back* as permitted by tax law meet these characteristics.[31] The first characteristic is met because a tax benefit is guaranteed. When the future year actually occurs, one of two events will occur. Either the deductible amount will be used to reduce actual income taxes for that year, or the deductible amount will result in a refund of taxes paid in the current or preceding years. The second characteristic is met because the entity will have an exclusive right to the tax benefit resulting from the carry-back. Finally, the third characteristic is met because the entity must have earned taxable income in the current or past years for a carry-back to be considered realizable.

On the other hand, a net deductible amount that cannot be used in the present period or carried back to prior periods, or an unused NOL carry-forward do not have a refund guarantee. These deductions must be carried forward to future years in order to obtain a tax benefit. Consequently, the entity must have future taxable income for a future tax benefit to occur. Since earning income in future years has not yet occurred and is not inherently assumed in preparing financial statements, the third characteristic is *not* met for net deductible amounts that cannot be carried back to obtain a refund of taxes already paid. Nor is it met for NOL carry-forwards. In other words, these items represent gain contingencies that may not be realized.

In summary, the deferred tax consequences of temporary differences that result in net deductible amounts in future years that may be carried back to present and prior years are an asset. But *SFAS No. 96* limited the recognition of benefit of all other net deductible amounts to reductions of deferred tax liabilities. Under this pronouncement, they were not reported as assets—a treatment consistent with the treatment of other gain contingencies.

Business Dissatisfaction with *SFAS No. 96*

After *SFAS No. 96* was issued, and before its mandatory implementation date, many businesses expressed concerns regarding the effect the standard would have on their financial statements and the cost that would be incurred to implement it. These objections became so widespread that the implementation date was first postponed from 1988 to 1989[32] and later from 1989 to 1991.[33]

The major objections to *SFAS No. 96* centered on the cost of scheduling that would be necessary to determine whether a deferred tax asset could be recognized and the loss of some deferred tax assets because of the zero future income assumption. Before the effective date of *SFAS No. 96*, the FASB received (1) requests for about twenty limited-scope amendments to its provisions; (2) many requests to change the criteria for recognition and measurement of deferred tax assets to anticipate, in certain circumstances, the tax consequences of future income; and (3) requests to reduce the complexity of scheduling the future reversals of temporary

31. Ibid., paras. 97–102.

32. *Statement of Financial Accounting Standards No. 100*, "Accounting for Income Taxes—Deferral of the Effective Date of FASB Statement No. 96" (Stamford, CT: FASB, 1988).

33. *Statement of Financial Accounting Standards No. 103*, "Accounting for Income Taxes—Deferral of the Effective Date of FASB Statement No. 96" (Stamford, CT: FASB, 1989).

differences and considering hypothetical tax planning strategies. On June 5, 1991, the Board issued an exposure draft proposing a new standard to supersede *SFAS No. 96*. Later, on June 17, 1991, the Board issued another exposure draft to delay the effective date for the implementation of *SFAS No. 96* for a third time to December 15, 1992 (effective for 1993 statements) to allow time for interested parties to respond to the June 5, 1991, exposure draft. Finally, in early 1992, *SFAS No. 109* was issued.

SFAS No. 109

The FASB was convinced by the critics of *SFAS No. 96* that deferred tax assets should be treated similarly to deferred tax liabilities and that the scheduling requirements of *SFAS No. 96* were often too complex and costly. However, the Board did not want to return to the deferred method and remained committed to the asset-liability approach. *SFAS No. 109* (see FASB ASC 740) responded to these concerns by allowing the separate recognition and measurement of deferred tax assets and liabilities without regard to future income considerations, using the average enacted tax rates for future years. The deferred tax asset is to be reduced by a *tax valuation allowance* if available evidence indicates that it is *more likely than not* (a likelihood of more than 50 percent) that some portion or the entire deferred tax asset will not be realized.[34]

These requirements result in the following more simplified series of steps for determining deferred tax liability and asset balances:

1. Identify temporary differences, NOL carry-forwards, and unused tax credits.
2. Measure the total deferred tax liability by applying the expected tax rate to future taxable amounts.
3. Measure the total deferred tax asset by applying the expected future tax rate to future deductible amounts and NOL carry-forwards.
4. Measure deferred tax assets for each type of unused tax credit.
5. Measure the valuation allowance based on the more-likely-than-not criterion.

The Valuation Allowance

The deferred tax asset measures potential benefits to be received in future years arising from temporary differences, NOL carryovers, and unused tax credits. Because there may be insufficient future taxable income to actually derive a benefit from a recorded deferred tax asset, *SFAS No. 109* (see FASB ASDC 740-10-30) requires a *valuation allowance* sufficient to reduce the deferred tax asset to the amount that is more likely than not to be realized. The more-likely-than-not criterion was a new measurement yardstick for the FASB. Previously, in establishing standards for contingent liabilities, the FASB introduced the terms *probable, reasonably probable*, and *remote*. The use of these terms for deferred tax assets would imply an *affirmative judgment approach* wherein recognition would require probable realization; however, no recognition would be given to deferred tax assets when

---

34. Ibid., para. 17 (see FASB ASC 740-10-30).

the likelihood of realization was less than probable. The Board decided against the use of this approach to solve the income tax issue because it felt that *probable* was too stringent a benchmark for the recognition of deferred tax assets.[35]

The FASB also considered an *impairment approach* that would have required deferred tax asset recognition unless it is probable that the asset will not be realized. The impairment approach was also deemed problematic because it would have resulted in the recognition of a deferred tax asset that is not expected to be realized when the likelihood of its not being realized is less than probable.[36]

The more-likely-than-not criterion was selected because it eliminates any distinction between the affirmative judgment and impairment approaches. As a practical matter, the use of this criterion provides both of the following results:

1. Recognition of a deferred tax asset if the likelihood of realizing the future tax benefit is more than 50 percent (the affirmative judgment approach).

2. Recognition of a deferred tax asset unless the likelihood of not realizing the future tax benefit is more than 50 percent (the impairment approach).[37]

In other words, the FASB chose a middle ground, which in effect embraced both approaches rather than selecting one over the other. Use of the more-likely-than-not criterion allows practitioners to ignore the zero future income assumption. They may assume that there will be sufficient future taxable income to realize deferred tax assets unless evidence indicates that it is more likely than not that it will not be realized.

The Board considered various criteria to determine when impairment might apply but did not come to any definitive conclusions. The realization of future benefit from a deductible temporary difference or carryover ultimately depends on the incurrence of taxable income that is of an appropriate character to use the carryover of a NOL or credit, or against which a deductible amount may be applied. *SFAS No. 109* cited the following as possible sources of taxable income (affirmative evidence) that may enable the realization of deferred tax assets:

1. Future reversals of existing taxable temporary differences.

2. Future taxable income exclusive of taxable temporary differences and carryovers.

3. Taxable income in the current or prior years to which deductible amounts resulting from temporary differences could be carried back.

4. To prevent an NOL or tax credit carryover from expiring, prudent and feasible tax planning strategies that an enterprise ordinarily might not take may be employed to

   a. Accelerate taxable amounts against which to apply carry-forwards

   b. Change the character of taxable or deductible amounts from ordinary income or loss to capital gain or loss

   c. Switch from tax-exempt to taxable investments[38]

---

35. Ibid., para. 95.

36. Ibid.

37. Ibid.

38. Ibid., paras. 21 and 22 (see FASB ASC 740-10-30-18).

SFAS No. 109 stressed that the exercise of judgment is necessary to determine whether a valuation allowance should be reported and, if so, the level of impairment of the deferred tax asset that is more likely than not to occur. On the downside, negative evidence (potential impairment) might include the following:

1. A history of NOL or tax credit carry-forwards expiring unused
2. Anticipated losses (by a presently profitable enterprise)
3. Unsettled circumstances that may adversely affect future operations and profits
4. A carryover period so brief that it would limit realization of deferred tax benefits if (a) a significant deductible temporary difference is expected to reverse in a single year or (b) the business operating cycle is traditionally cyclical[39]

This type of negative evidence should be weighed against positive evidence, such as

1. Existing contracts or sales backlog
2. Significant appreciation of an asset's value over its tax basis
3. A strong earnings history (exclusive of the NOL or deductible temporary differences) coupled with evidence that the loss is an aberration rather than a continuing condition[40]

By relaxing the future income assumption, the necessity of scheduling that was required under *SFAS No. 96* is greatly reduced. If it is assumed that there will be sufficient taxable income in future years to realize the tax benefit of existing deductible amounts, the carry-back and carry-forward provisions of *SFAS No. 96* will not be needed. If, on the other hand, it is not possible to assume sufficient future taxable income, then scheduling may be needed to determine the balance in the valuation allowance account. However, scheduling is no longer required to determine the proper classification of the deferred amount between current and noncurrent. The deferred tax balance is to be classified as current or noncurrent in the same manner as the assets and liabilities to which the deferred taxes relate.

The adoption of the more-likely-than-not approach led the FASB to conclude that a similar approach should be used for NOLs, unused credits, and deductible amounts resulting from temporary differences. Under *SFAS No. 109* (see FASB ASC 740-10-30), NOLs will now result in deferred tax assets unless it is more likely than not that they cannot be applied against future taxable income. This is a significant change in that millions of dollars of potential benefit that have heretofore been unreported are included in the assets of companies.

Shift in Interpretation of Future Tax Consequences: *SFAC No. 6* versus Deferred Tax Assets and Liabilities

The FASB was concerned that by requiring the separate measurement of deferred tax liabilities and deferred tax assets and the reduction of deferred tax assets by the valuation allowance, the resulting balance sheet amounts would not reflect

---

39. Ibid., para. 23 (see FASB ASC 740-10-30-21).
40. Ibid., para. 24 (see FASB ASC 740-10-30-22).

the effects of netting deductible amounts against taxable amounts or the certain guarantee of realization for deferred tax assets that would have occurred under *SFAS No. 96*. In short, the *SFAS No. 109* provisions introduced different levels of certainty regarding expected future cash flows. As a result, the Board reexamined whether the resulting deferred tax liabilities and deferred tax assets fit the definitions of liabilities and assets found in *SFAC No. 6*. The Board concluded that they do and that the information provided is useful, understandable, and no more complex than any other approach to accounting for income taxes. These conclusions are based on the following arguments regarding the *SFAS No. 109* deferred tax liability and deferred tax asset.

Deferred Tax Liability

Because deferred tax assets and deferred tax liabilities must be measured separately, deferred tax liabilities will not measure the effects of net taxable amounts. Nevertheless, the resulting deferred tax liabilities meet all three essential characteristics of liabilities outlined in *SFAC No. 6*. Specifically, the first characteristic of a liability is that it embodies a present obligation of the enterprise to settle by probable future transfer or use of assets upon the occurrence of a specified event, or on demand. This characteristic is met because the deferred tax liability measures an obligation to the government resulting from the deferred tax consequences of taxable temporary differences that stem from the requirements of the tax law.

The second characteristic, that the enterprise is obligated and has little or no discretion to avoid future sacrifice, is also met. It may be possible to delay future reversals of temporary differences by postponing events such as recovery or settlement of assets or liabilities; but, eventually, these temporary differences will become taxable. Hence, the only relevant question is when, not whether, the tax consequences will occur. Finally, the future payment of tax is the result of past transactions or events that created the originating temporary differences. This satisfies the third characteristic of a liability, that the transaction or event that obligates the enterprise has already happened.

Deferred Tax Asset

The FASB concluded that deferred tax assets, reduced by the valuation allowance, meet the *SFAC No. 6* characteristics of assets.[41] The first characteristic of an asset is that it embodies a capacity to contribute directly or indirectly to enterprise future net cash inflows. There is no question that deductible amounts that may be carried back to offset taxable income that has already been incurred embody a probable future benefit because they contribute directly to future net cash inflows. Other deductible amounts and carryovers under the more-likely-than-not criterion, because they may be used to reduce future taxable amounts, will contribute indirectly to future cash flows.

The second characteristic of an asset is that the enterprise can obtain the benefit and can control others' access to it. To the extent that these benefits will occur, the enterprise has an exclusive right to those benefits as they are realized and therefore can control access to them.

The third characteristic of an asset is that the transaction or event that resulted in the enterprise obtaining the right to control the benefit has already occurred.

---

41. Ibid., para. 63.

Because deferred tax asset realization under *SFAS No. 96* was guaranteed, the critical event giving rise to the asset was prior taxable income. However, *SFAS No. 109* allows recognition if the weight of the evidence implies that it is more likely than not that realization will occur. Thus, the existence or absence of future taxable income is critical to deferred tax asset recognition under current GAAP for those deductible amounts and carry-forwards that will not result in a refund of prior taxes paid. "The Board concluded that earning taxable income in future years (a) is the event that confirms the existence of recognizable tax benefit at the end of the current year and (b) is not the prerequisite event that must occur before a tax benefit may be recognized as was the case under the requirements of *SFAS No. 96*."[42]

Financial Statement Disclosure

Several disclosure issues arise in connection with the reporting of income taxes on financial statements.

Income Statement Presentation and Related Disclosures

The portrayal of the effects of taxation on major segments of the income statement and on items carried directly to retained earnings is enhanced by allocating the income tax expense for a period among these items. The allocation of income tax within an accounting period is termed *intraperiod tax allocation*. Intraperiod tax allocation is required under GAAP. Income tax expense (or benefit) is disclosed for net income from continuing operations, gains or losses resulting from the disposal of a segment of a business, and extraordinary items. In addition, the tax effect of any prior period adjustments to and of the retroactive effects of accounting changes on retained earnings must be disclosed.

SFAS No. 109 (see FASB ASC 740-10-50) also requires disclosure of the significant components of income tax attributable to income from continuing operations. These components include

1. The current provision (or benefit) for income taxes
2. Deferred tax expense or benefit (exclusive of items 3–8 listed below)
3. Investment tax credits
4. Government grants (to the extent that they reduce income tax expense)
5. The benefits of operating loss carry-forwards
6. Tax expense that results from allocations of tax benefits to balance sheets in a business combination
7. Adjustments to the deferred tax liability or asset for enacted changes in tax laws or a change in the tax status of the reporting entity
8. Adjustments of the beginning balance of the valuation allowance because of a change in circumstances that causes a change in judgment about the realizability of the related deferred tax asset

Balance Sheet Presentation and Related Disclosures

The current provision (or benefit) is reported in the balance sheet as a current liability or asset. Deferred tax balances are reported as assets and liabilities. They

---

42. Ibid., para. 86.

are classified as (1) the net current amount and (2) the net noncurrent amount. This classification is based on the classification of the related asset or liability that caused the deferred item. That is, a deferred tax asset or liability is related to an asset or liability if a reduction of the asset or liability will cause the temporary difference to reverse. A deferred tax asset or liability that is not related to an asset or liability, including deferred tax assets created by NOL or tax credit carry-forwards, is classified as current or noncurrent according to the expected reversal date of the temporary difference. A net noncurrent deferred tax asset is classified as *other asset*. A noncurrent net deferred tax liability is classified as *long-term liability*. The valuation allowance (and the net change in it) associated with deferred tax assets that do not meet the more-likely-than-not criterion must be disclosed. Also, companies must disclose the approximate tax effect of each item that gives rise to a significant portion of deferred tax liabilities and assets (exclusive of the valuation allowance).

SEC Disclosure Requirements

The SEC has also adopted income tax disclosure requirements for corporations issuing publicly traded securities. The disclosures required include the following (see FASB ASC 235-10-S99):

1. A reconciliation of the difference between income tax expense and the amount of tax expense that would have been reported by applying the statutory rate to reported income for the company. This requirement highlights the special provisions of the tax code that benefited the company.

2. The amount of any temporary difference that is due to the deferral of investment tax credits (when and if the ITC is applicable).

These requirements are intended to provide information to investors and others on the effective tax rates of corporations.

Fin No. 48, "Accounting for Uncertainty in Income Taxes— An Interpretation of FASB Statement No. 109"

An FASB review of compliance with the reporting requirement of the Sarbanes-Oxley Act revealed that many of the problems associated with compliance with its Section 404 provisions[43] were related to tax issues; as a result, numerous financial statement restatements were required. Most specifically, the use of tax contingencies had become too flexible and was used to manipulate income, and the reporting and disclosure of tax positions lacked transparency.

The SEC was also concerned about the reporting of tax contingencies, and many SEC comment letters were released on this issue. Following is an example of a comment letter received by one company.

> Please explain to us and in future filings your accounting policy for recording income tax reserves. As part of your response, clearly explain to us how you established that your accounting meets the criteria of SFAS 5. In addition, provide a roll-forward of your reserve for each period presented.

---

43. See Chapter 17 for a discussion of the Sarbanes-Oxley Act.

In response to the above-voiced concerns, the FASB undertook a project to determine how to account for uncertain tax positions. The result of this project was *FIN No. 48*, which established the proper accounting treatment for uncertain tax positions. The validity of a tax position is a matter of tax law, and it is not controversial to recognize the benefit of a tax position in a firm's financial statements when there is a high degree of confidence that a particular tax position will be sustained after examination by the IRS. However, in some cases, tax law is subject to varied interpretations, and whether a tax position will ultimately be sustained may be uncertain.

The evaluation of a tax position under *FIN No. 48* (see FASB ASC 740-10-25) is a two-step process:

1. *Recognition.* A firm determines whether it is more likely than not that a tax position will be sustained upon examination by the IRS based on the technical merits of the position. In evaluating whether a tax position has merit, a firm is to use a more-likely-than-not recognition threshold. This evaluation should presume that the IRS would have full knowledge of all relevant information.

2. *Measurement.* A tax position that meets the more-likely-than-not recognition threshold is measured to determine the amount of benefit to recognize in the financial statements. The tax position is measured at the largest cumulative amount of benefit that is greater than 50 percent likely of being realized upon ultimate settlement.

To illustrate, Oakley Company takes a deduction that creates a potential tax benefit of $100,000. First, Oakley must establish that there is a greater than 50 percent likelihood of the position being sustained by the IRS before the company can record the benefit. Next, the company must establish probabilities of different outcomes to determine the actual amount of benefit to record. Assume Oakley determines that the probabilities for the position being sustained by the IRS are 30 percent for a $100,000 deduction, 10 percent for an $80,000 deduction, 15 percent for a $60,000 deduction, 30 percent for a $30,000 deduction, and 20 percent for a $20,000 deduction. Oakley will then use a cumulative probability approach to determine the median amount of its deduction. The median amount is $60,000 (30% + 10% + 15% = 55%). The cumulative probability for $60,000 is 55 percent. This is the largest amount of potential benefit with a greater than 50 percent likelihood of being realized. Consequently, the company will report a tax benefit of $60,000.

In addition, *FIN No. 48* (see FASB ASC 740-10-25-8) indicated that tax positions that previously did not meet the more-likely-than-not recognition threshold should be recognized in the first subsequent financial reporting period in which that threshold is met. Previously recognized tax positions that no longer meet the more-likely-than-not recognition threshold should be derecognized in the first subsequent financial reporting period in which that threshold is no longer met.

Financial Analysis of Income Taxes

Research has found that deferred taxes help predict future earnings, which in turn affects the value of the firm as well as security prices,[44] and that the information required to be provided under the provisions of *SFAS No. 109* and the SEC's

---

44. David A. Guenther and Richard C. Sansing, "Valuation of the Firm in the Presence of Temporary Book-Tax Differences: The Role of Deferred Tax Assets and Liabilities," *The Accounting Review* (January 2000): 1–12.

financial statement disclosure requirements allow investors, creditors, and other users of financial information to make better decisions.[45] Additionally, the magnitude of the valuation allowance has been found to vary widely, consistent with the level of managerial discretion allowed by *SFAS No. 109*. However, preliminary evidence suggests that this variation is not the result of earnings management activities.[46] Taken together, the accumulated evidence regarding income tax disclosures suggests these results:

1. The quality of earnings can be assessed because special situations that give rise to one-time earnings are highlighted. For example, an examination of the footnotes to Hershey's and Tootsie Roll's financial statements did not reveal any one-time charges that affected taxes payable.

2. Future cash flows can be more easily assessed because reversals of deferred tax assets and liabilities are highlighted. For example during fiscal year 2008, Hershey's deferred tax net current assets decreased by $12,765,000, its deferred net long-term assets increased by $13,815,000, and its deferred tax net long-term liabilities decreased by $177,196,000. During this same period, Tootsie Roll's deferred tax current assets decreased by $1,576,000 and its deferred tax long-term liabilities increased by $7,406,000. Hershey disclosed valuation allowances of $30,814,000 in 2008 and $28,029,000 in 2007. Tootsie Roll disclosed valuation allowances of $8,506,000 in 2008 and $7,556,000 in 2007, indicating that some of their deferred tax assets might not be realized.

3. Government regulation of the economy is enhanced because it is easier to calculate actual tax rates. For example, Hershey disclosed an effective tax rate of 36.7 percent for its 2008 fiscal year, while Tootsie Roll disclosed an effective tax rate of 30.6 percent for the same period.

The footnotes to a company's financial statements provide additional information that can be used to analyze its income tax amounts. Specifically, most companies will disclose information on the amount of taxes that would be paid at the federal statutory rate and on the amount actually paid, in addition to changes in the deferred tax asset and liability accounts and information concerning income tax carry-backs and carry-forwards.

The financial analysis of income taxes is not without controversy. For example, the issue of partial versus comprehensive allocation has caused some financial analysts to exclude deferred tax liability amounts in assessing future cash flows and sustainable income. That is, those advocating partial allocation maintain that this is a liability that will never be paid; consequently, it has no future cash-flow consequences. To illustrate, both Hershey and Tootsie Roll previously experienced increases in their deferred tax liabilities. Those analysts who advocate partial allocation suggest that when conducting an analysis of a company's future cash-flow

---

45. Benjamin C. Ayers, "Deferred Tax Accounting under SFAS No. 109: An Empirical Investigation of its Incremental Value-Relevance to APB No. 11," *The Accounting Review* (April 1998): 195–212.

46. Gregory S. Miller and Douglas J. Skinner, "Determinants of the Valuation Allowance for Deferred Tax Assets under SFAS No 109," *The Accounting Review* (April 1998): 213–33.

prospects, the direction and size of the deferred tax liability amount should be carefully examined; consequently, partial allocationists would maintain that both companies' deferred tax liabilities are unlikely to be paid in the near future.

Finally, some suggest that the amount of a company's income tax liability can be used to assess how aggressive it is in reporting its financial accounting earnings.[47] The company's *earnings conservatism ratio* is calculated as follows:

$$\frac{\text{Pretax accounting income}_{48}}{\text{Taxable income}}$$

The rationale for this ratio is that, to minimize income taxes, most companies will use the most conservative revenue and recognition criteria for income tax reporting purposes while attempting to maximize their deductible expenses. On the other hand, management is under constant pressure to report favorable financial accounting earnings. As a result, it may choose accounting methods and estimations that maximize financial accounting income. In interpreting the results of this calculation, amounts in excess of 1.0 will indicate that a company is being more aggressive in its use of accounting choices for financial reporting than it is in calculating its income taxes.

When calculating the earnings conservatism ratio, it is necessary to estimate taxable income because current GAAP does not require this amount to be disclosed in corporate annual reports. Fortunately, this estimation is easy given that companies disclose taxes payable as well as effective tax rates. For example, Hershey's 2008 income tax footnote reported current income taxes payable of $180,617,000 and an effective income tax rate of 36.7 percent. This indicates that the $180,617,000 represented 36.7 percent of its taxable income, or $492,144,000 ($180,617,000 ÷ 0.367). An examination of Hershey's 2008 income statement (contained in Chapter 6) revealed that its pretax financial accounting income was $492,022,000. Consequently, the earnings conservatism ratio for the fiscal year 2008 was as follows:

$$\frac{\$492,022,000}{\$492,144,000} = 0.9998$$

This calculation indicates that Hershey is being conservative in its financial reporting practices. To further examine this issue, we review the earnings conservatism ratios of Hershey and Tootsie Roll for the fiscal years 2008, 2007, and

---

47. P. Joos, J. Pratt, and S. Young, "Book-Tax Differences and the Value Relevance of Earnings," Working paper (Bloomington: Indiana University, 1999). Also, Hanlon and Shevlin (2002) suggest that if employee stock option tax benefits are not treated as a book-tax difference, income tax expense is overstated by the amount of the employee stock option benefit tax benefits, and estimates of taxable income are overstated; however, the amount of these differences is difficult to determine for corporate annual reports. M. Hanlon and Terry T. Shevlin, "Accounting for Tax Benefits of Employee Stock Options and Implications for Research," *Accounting Horizons* 16, no. 1 (March 2002): 1–16.

48. In the event a company reports material permanent income tax differences, the amount of these differences adjusts the numerator.

2006. The following information was extracted from the two companies' annual reports (in thousands):

	Pretax Income	Taxes Payable	Tax Rate	Taxable Income
Hershey				
2008	$492,022	$180,617	36.7%	$492,144
2007	340,242	126,088	37.1%	339,860
2006	876,502	317,441	36.2%	876,909
Tootsie Roll				
2008	$ 55,909	$ 17,132	30.6%	$ 55,987
2007	77,167	25,542	33.1%	77,166
2006	94,715	28,796	30.7%	93,798

Consequently, the earnings conservatism ratios for the two companies for 2008, 2007, and 2006 are as follows:

	2008	2007	2006
Hershey	1.00	1.00	1.00
Tootsie Roll	1.00	1.00	1.01

This analysis indicates that neither company's application of GAAP would be considered aggressive and that both companies' earnings conservatism ratios are stable over the three-year period.

The earnings conservatism ratio should also be examined for unusual changes. Consider the case of Harrah's Entertainment, Inc., which operates hotel casinos in Reno, Lake Tahoe, Las Vegas, and Laughlin, Nevada, and in Atlantic City, New Jersey. In its 2000 fiscal year it had an earnings conservatism ratio of 0.04, which rose to 7.58 in 2001. When unusual results such as these arise, the company's footnotes to its financial statements should be analyzed to assess the reasons behind them. An examination of Harrah's Entertainment year 2001 and 2000 footnotes disclosing its income taxes revealed that the company's net deferred tax liability (deferred tax liabilities less deferred tax assets) increased by more than $100 million during 2001. As a result, taxable income fell from $367,551,000 in 2000 to $45,814,000 in 2001. In the previous year the company had recorded a net deferred tax asset in excess of $150,000,000, which resulted in the low earnings conservatism ratio in 2000.

International Accounting Standards

The IASB's discussion of accounting for income taxes is contained in *IAS No. 12*, "Accounting for Taxes on Income." In 1996, this statement was revised to reduce the number of options companies have when accounting for deferred taxes. Previously, companies were allowed to account for income tax timing differences by either the deferred or the liability method. Under the revised standard, only the liability method is allowed. The revised standard is quite similar to U.S. GAAP as outlined in *SFAS No. 109*. The IASB considered some additional issues such as whether the tax consequences of recovering the carrying amount of certain assets and liabilities may depend on the manner of recovery or settlement (e.g., different tax rates on capital gains). If so, deferred tax assets and liabilities will be measured on the basis of the tax consequences that would follow from the expected manner of recovery or settlement.

The issue of uncertain tax provisions falls under the provisions of *IAS No. 37*, "Provisions, Contingent Liabilities, and Contingent Assets." This release indicates that firms should not recognize contingent assets. However, when the realization of income is virtually certain, then the related asset is not a contingent asset and its recognition is appropriate. In contrast to the FASB approach, there is no recognition threshold provided and the amount to be recorded is the expected amount to be realized.

In 2004 the IASB and the FASB added accounting for income tax to the short-term convergence project. At that time, the FASB noted:

> Topic 740 and IAS 12 are founded on similar principles: both take a balance sheet approach to accounting for income taxes. Both account for (1) taxes currently payable (or receivable) arising from current taxable income and (2) future (deferred) taxes payable (or receivable) due to differences in U.S. generally accepted accounting principles (GAAP) (or IFRS) and tax bases of assets and liabilities.[49]

Nevertheless, some differences exist between U.S. GAAP and IFRS that can be categorized:

1. Differences in the exceptions to the application of those similar principles
2. Certain differences in the recognition, measurement, and disclosure criteria
3. Differences resulting from some specific application and implementation guidance that was issued after legacy Statement 109

Both FASB ASC 740 and *IAS No. 12* contain explicit exceptions to the principles enumerated in *FASB Report*. FASB ASC 740 contains six exceptions to these principles, and *IAS No. 12* contains three. Some exceptions involve country-specific issues (for example, the exception related to U.S. steamship entity statutory reserve funds or bad debt reserves of U.S. savings and loan associations) that do not represent a fundamental difference in the overall approach.

There are also differences between FASB ASC 740 and *IAS No. 12* that relate to the recognition and measurement of tax assets and liabilities. These differences relate to tax rates and deferred tax asset recognition. Finally, as a result of subsequently issued implementation guidance, there are differences between U.S. GAAP and IFRS that are not solely the result of differences between *IAS No.12* and FASB ASC 740.

In March 2009, the IASB issued an exposure draft of a revised *IAS No. 12* that attempts to alleviate these differences. The proposed standard retains the basic approach to accounting for income tax—to recognize now the future tax consequences of past events and transactions, rather than waiting until the tax is payable. The main changes contained in the proposed new standard are as follows:

1. A change in the definition of tax basis. Tax basis would be defined as the measurement under applicable substantively enacted tax law of an asset, liability, or other item.

49. Developing Consistent Application of Similar Principles of Accounting for Income Taxes, "FASB Report" (June 30, 2004), http://www.fasb.org/project/tfr_article_06-30-04.pdf.

2. A specification that the tax basis of an asset is determined by the tax deductions that would be available if the entity recovered the carrying amount of the asset by sale.

3. The introduction of an initial step to determine deferred tax assets and liabilities so that no deferred tax arises if there will be no effect on taxable income when the entity recovers or settles its carrying amount.

4. New definitions of tax credit and investment tax credit as follows:

    a. *Tax credit* is a tax benefit that takes the form of an amount that reduces income tax payable.

    b. *Investment tax credit* is a tax credit that relates directly to the acquisition of depreciable assets.

5. Removal of the initial recognition exception in *IAS No. 12.*

6. Changes to the exception in *IAS No. 12* from the temporary difference approach relating to a deferred tax asset or liability arising from investments in subsidiaries, branches, associates, and joint ventures.

7. A proposal to recognize deferred tax assets in full, less (if applicable) a valuation allowance to reduce the net carrying amount to the highest amount that is more likely than not to be realizable against taxable income.

8. A proposal that current and deferred tax assets and liabilities should be measured using the probability-weighted average amounts of possible outcomes assuming that the tax authorities will examine the amounts reported to them by the entity and have full knowledge of all relevant information.

9. Clarification that the term *substantively enacted* as it relates to income tax legislation means that future events required by the enactment process historically have not affected the outcome and are unlikely to do so.

10. A change to the requirements relating to the tax effects of distributions to shareholders. An entity would measure current and deferred tax assets and liabilities using the rate expected to apply when the tax asset or liability is realized or settled, including the effect of the entity's expectations of future distributions.

11. Adoption of the FASB ASC requirements for the allocation of income tax expense to the components of comprehensive income and equity. In particular, some changes in tax effects that were initially recognized outside continuing operations would be recognized in continuing operations.

12. The classification of deferred tax assets and liabilities as either current or noncurrent on the basis of the financial reporting classification of the related non-tax asset or liability.

13. A clarification that indicates the classification of interest and penalties is an accounting policy choice and hence must be applied consistently, and introduction of a requirement to disclose the chosen policy.
    The IASB expects to issue a final standard in 2010.

Cases

• Case 12-1 Income Tax Implication of Capital Investment Decisions

The Whitley Corporation's year-end is December 31. It is now October 1, 2010. The Whitley management team is taking a look at the prior nine months and attempting to make some short-term strategy decisions.

Whitley has experienced steady growth over the five preceding years. The result has been a steadily increasing EPS. Last year Whitley reported an EPS of 1.95.

This year, due to a mild recession, Whitley's sales have fallen off. Management is looking for strategies that may improve the appearance of the financial statements. At the same time, there is a need for new equipment in the plant. Despite the recession, Whitley has enough cash to make the purchase.

Based on the year's performance to date and extrapolation of the results to year-end, management feels that the pretax financial accounting income for the year will be $200,000. Transactions from prior years have resulted in a deferred tax asset of $15,000 and a deferred tax liability of $70,000 at the beginning of 2010. The temporary difference of $37,500 that resulted in the deferred tax asset is expected to completely reverse by the end of 2010. The deferred tax liability resulted totally from temporary depreciation differences. There will be a pretax reversal of $42,500 in this temporary difference during 2010.

Based on presently enacted tax law, the purchase of the equipment will result in a future taxable amount of $50,000. Whitley management feels that it can wait 4 to 6 months to purchase the machine. Whitley's tax rate is 40 percent.

Required:

a. Determine the projected amount of income tax expense that would be reported if Whitley waits until next year to purchase the equipment.

b. Determine the projected amount of income tax expense that would be reported if Whitley purchases the equipment in 2010.

c. Should Whitley wait to purchase the equipment? Your answer should take into consideration the expected financial statement effects, as well as the effect on EPS. Support your conclusions with pro forma data. The number of shares that Whitley will use to calculate EPS is 55,500.

d. What are the ethical considerations of this case?

• Case 12-2 Discounting Deferred Taxes

The FASB has carefully avoided the issue of discounting deferred taxes. *SFAS No. 109*, "Accounting for Income Taxes," states:

> a deferred tax liability or asset should be recognized for the deferred tax consequences of temporary differences and operating loss or tax credit carryforwards. . . . Under the requirements of this Statement: . . . Deferred tax liabilities and assets are not discounted.

Required:

a. Assuming that the firm's deferred tax liabilities exceed its deferred tax assets, select that approach to measurement, discounting, or nondiscounting that is best supported by the qualitative characteristics of *SFAC No. 2* by placing an X in the evaluation matrix under the measurement approach selected. For example, if you feel that discounting has higher representational faithfulness, put an X under column 2 beside *representational faithfulness*. Column 3 is provided for those cases for which a given concept is not applicable.

SFAC No.2 Qualitative Characteristic	Nondiscounting (1)	Discounting (2)	Neither (3)
1. Relevance			
a. Timeliness			
b. Predictive and feedback value			
2. Reliability			
a. Representational faithfulness			
b. Verifiability and neutrality			
3. Understandability			
4. Comparability			

b. Discuss the reasons for your evaluations.

c. Present arguments supporting the discounting of deferred taxes.

d. Present arguments opposing the discounting of deferred taxes.

• Case 12-3 Intraperiod versus Interperiod Income Tax Allocation

Income tax allocation is an integral part of GAAP. The applications of intraperiod income tax allocation (within a period) and interperiod tax allocation (among periods) are both required.

Required:

a. Explain the need for intraperiod income tax allocation.

b. Accountants who favor interperiod income tax allocation argue that income taxes are an expense rather than a distribution of earnings. Explain the significance of this argument. Do not explain the definitions of expense or distribution of earnings.

c. Discuss the nature of the deferred income tax accounts and possible classifications in a company's balance sheet.

d. Indicate and explain whether each of the following independent situations should be treated as a temporary difference or a permanent difference.

   i. Estimated warranty costs (covering a three-year period) are expensed for accounting purposes when incurred.

   ii. Depreciation for accounting and income tax purposes differs because of different bases of carrying the related property. The different bases are a result of a business combination treated as a purchase for accounting purposes and as a tax-free exchange for income tax purposes.

iii. A company properly uses the equity method to account for its 30 percent investment in another company. The investee pays dividends that are about 10 percent of its annual earnings.

e. For each of the above independent situations, determine whether those situations that are treated as temporary differences will result in future taxable amounts or future deductible amounts and whether they will result in deferred tax assets or deferred tax liabilities. Explain.

• Case 12-4 Temporary Differences

SFAS No. 109, "Accounting for Income Taxes," requires interperiod income tax allocation for temporary differences.

Required:

a. Define the term *temporary difference*.
b. List the examples of temporary differences contained in *SFAS No. 109*.
c. Defend interperiod income tax allocation.

• Case 12-5 Asset-Liability Method

SFAS No. 109, "Accounting for Income Taxes," requires companies to use the asset-liability method of interperiod income tax allocation.

Required:

a. Discuss the criteria for recognizing deferred tax assets and deferred tax liabilities under the provisions of *SFAS No. 109*.
b. Compare and contrast the asset-liability method and the deferred method.

• Case 12-6 Methods of Interperiod Tax Allocation

There are three general views regarding interperiod income tax allocation: no allocation, partial allocation, and comprehensive allocation.

Required:

a. Defend the position of no allocation of income taxes.
b. Defend the position of partial allocation of income taxes.
c. Defend the position of comprehensive allocation of income taxes.

• Case 12-7 Accounting for Income Taxes: Different Approaches

Mark or Make is a bourbon distillery. Sales have been steady for the past three years and operating costs have remained unchanged. On January 1, 20×7, Mark or Make took advantage of a special deal to prepay its rent for three years at a substantial savings. The amount of the prepayment was $60,000. The income statement items (excluding the rent) are shown below.

	20×7	20×8	20×9
Gross profit on sales	350,000	349,000	351,000
Operating expense	210,000	210,000	210,000

Assume that the rental is deducted on the corporate tax purposes in 20×7 and that there are no other temporary differences between taxable income and pretax accounting income. In addition, there are no permanent differences between taxable income and pretax accounting income. The corporate tax rate for all three years is 30 percent.

Required:

a. Construct income statements for 20×7, 20×8, and 20×9 under the following approaches to interperiod income tax allocation:

    i. No allocation

    ii. Comprehensive allocation

b. Do you believe that no allocation distorts Mark or Make's net income? Explain.

c. For years 20×7 and 20×8, Mark or Make reported net income applying the concept of comprehensive interperiod income tax allocation. During 20×8 Congress passed a new tax law that will increase the corporate tax rate from 30 to 33 percent. Reconstruct the income statements for 20×8 and 20×9 under the following assumptions:

    i. Mark or Make uses the deferred method to account for interperiod income tax allocation.

    ii. Mark or Make uses the asset-liability approach to account for interperiod income tax allocation.

d. Which of the two approaches used in question (a) provides measures of income and liabilities that are useful to decision makers? Explain.

FASB ASC Research

For each of the following research cases, search the FASB ASC database for information to address the issues. Cut and paste the FASB paragraphs that support your responses. Then summarize briefly what your responses are, citing the pronouncements and paragraphs used to support your responses.

• FASB ASC 12-1 Tax Effect of Translation Adjustment

Companies with foreign subsidiaries report translation adjustments as a component of other comprehensive income. Search the FASB ASC database to find answers to the following questions. For each equation, cut and paste (citing the source) supporting evidence found in the database. Then write a brief summary of your findings.

Since the translation adjustments are not reported in the income statement:

1. Do they create temporary differences between pretax financial income and taxable income, as defined in *SFAS No. 52*? Explain why or why not.

2. If they do not create temporary differences between pretax financial income and taxable income, do they create temporary differences? If so, are they accounted for in the same way as temporary differences related to financial income? Explain.

• FASB ASC 12-2 Interpretations of *SFAS No. 109*

The EITF has issued numerous interpretations of *SFAS No. 109* that are grouped by subject matter.

1. List the general topics covered by these interpretations.
2. Write a brief summary of three of these interpretations.

• FASB ASC 12-3 Undistributed Earnings of a Subsidiary

The undistributed earnings of a subsidiary are normally accounted for as a temporary difference between financial accounting and taxable income. However, the FASB ASC allows them to be accounted for as a permanent difference under certain circumstances. Find, cite, and copy the paragraph that discusses this exception.

• FASB ASC 12-4 Deferred Tax Benefits for the Oil and Gas Industry

The FASB ASC gives an example for the oil and gas industry of an issue that should be considered when assessing whether to record the tax benefit of a deferred tax benefit. Find, cite, and copy that example.

• FASB ASC 12-5 Special Temporary Difference for Steamship Companies

The FASB ASC gives an example of the accounting and reporting for a specific taxable temporary difference related to U.S. steamship entities that may be accounted for differently from the accounting that otherwise requires comprehensive recognition of deferred income taxes for temporary differences. Find, cite, and copy that difference and discuss how it is to be disclosed.

• FASB ASC 12-6 Deferred Taxes in the Casino Industry

The FASB ASC gives examples of special deferred tax items for the casino industry. Find, cite, and copy these differences.

Room for Debate

• Debate 12-1 Deferred Method versus Asset/Liability Method

The APB required comprehensive interperiod income tax allocation under the deferred method. The FASB requires comprehensive interperiod income tax allocation under the asset-liability approach. For the following debate, you may take into consideration the definitions of the elements of financial statements found in *SFAC No. 6* and other theoretical concepts such as relevance, reliability, and matching.

Team Debate:

Team 1: Defend the deferred method of accounting for interperiod income tax allocation.

Team 2: Defend the asset-liability approach of accounting for interperiod income tax allocation.

• Debate 12-2 Discounting Deferred Taxes

The FASB requires that deferred tax assets and liabilities not be discounted.

Team Debate:

Team 1: Present arguments in favor of discounting deferred tax liabilities.

Team 2: Present arguments against discounting deferred tax liabilities.

• Debate 12-3 Income Tax Allocation

The FASB requires comprehensive interperiod income tax allocation using the asset-liability approach. Some feel that there should be only partial interperiod income tax allocation. Others feel that there should be no interperiod income tax allocation.

Team Debate:

Team 1: Present arguments favoring no allocation of income taxes.

Team 2: Present arguments favoring partial allocation of income taxes.

CHAPTER 13

Leases

Businesses generally acquire *property rights* in long-term assets through purchases that are funded by internal sources or by externally borrowed funds. The accounting issues associated with the purchase of long-term assets were discussed in Chapter 9. Leasing is an alternative means of acquiring long-term assets to be used by firms. Leases that are not in-substance purchases provide for the *right to use* property by lessees, in contrast to purchases that transfer property rights to the user of the long-term asset. Lease terms generally obligate lessees to make a series of payments over a future period. As such, they are similar to long-term debt. However, if a lease is structured in a certain way, it enables the lessee to engage in *off–balance sheet financing* (discussed in Chapter 11) because certain leases are not reported as long-term debt on the balance sheet. Business managers frequently wish to use off–balance sheet financing to improve the financial position of their companies. However, as noted earlier in the text, efficient market research indicates that off–balance sheet debt is incorporated into user decision models in determining the value of a company.

Leasing has become a popular method of acquiring property because it has the following advantages:

1. It offers 100 percent financing.
2. It offers protection against obsolescence.
3. It is frequently less costly than other forms of financing the cost of the acquisition of fixed assets.
4. If the lease qualifies as an operating lease, it does not add debt to the balance sheet.

Many long-term leases possess most of the attributes of long-term debt. That is, they create an obligation for payment under an agreement that is noncancelable. The adverse effects of debt are also present in leases in that an inability to pay may result in insolvency. Consequently, even though there are statutory limitations on lease obligations in bankruptcy proceedings, these limits do not affect the probability of the adverse effects of nonpayment on asset values and credit standing in the event of nonpayment of lease obligations. The statutory limitations involve only the evaluation of the amount owed after insolvency proceedings have commenced.

Management's choice between purchasing and leasing should be a function of strategic investment and capital structure objectives, not of leasing's effects on published financial statements. When deciding whether to purchase or lease an asset, management should consider the comparative costs of purchasing versus leasing the asset and the availability of tax benefits, rather than focusing on perceived financial reporting advantages. The tax benefit advantage is a major factor in leasing decisions. From a macroeconomic standpoint, the tax benefits of owning assets may be maximized by transferring them to the party in the higher marginal tax bracket. Firms with lower effective tax rates may engage in more leasing transactions than firms in higher tax brackets since the tax benefits are passed on to the lessor. El-Gazzar et al. found evidence to support this theory; firms with lower effective tax rates were found to have a higher proportion of leased debt to total assets than did firms with higher effective tax rates.[1]

Some lease agreements are in-substance long-term installment purchases of assets that have been structured to gain tax or other benefits to the parties. Since leases may take different forms, accountants must examine the underlying nature of the original transaction to determine the appropriate method of accounting for these agreements. Stated differently, the financial effects of leases should be reported in a manner that describes the intent of the lessor and lessee (i.e., the substance of the agreement) rather than the form of the agreement.

Accounting for Leases

Two methods for allocating lease revenues and expenses to the periods covered by the lease agreement have emerged in accounting practice. One method, termed a *capital lease*, is based on the view that the lease constitutes an agreement through which the lessor finances the acquisition of assets by the lessee. Consequently, capital leases are in-substance installment purchases of assets. The other method is termed an *operating lease* and is based on the view that the lease constitutes a rental agreement between the lessor and lessee.

Two basic accounting questions are associated with leases: (1) What characteristics of the lease agreement require a lease to be reported as an in-substance long-term purchase of an asset? (2) Which characteristics allow the lease to be reported as a long-term rental agreement?

The accounting profession first recognized the problems associated with leases in *Accounting Research Bulletin (ARB) No. 38*. This release recommended that if a lease agreement were in substance an installment purchase of property, the

1. Shamir M. El-Gazzar, Steven Lilien, and Victor Pastena, "Accounting for Leases by Lessees," *Journal of Accounting and Economics* (October 1986): 217–37.

lessee should report it as an asset and a liability. As with many of the ARBs, the recommendations of this pronouncement were largely ignored in practice, and the lease disclosure problem remained an important accounting issue.

Later, in 1964, the APB issued *Opinion No. 5*, "Reporting of Leases in Financial Statements of Lessees" (superseded). *APB Opinion No. 5* required leases that were in-substance purchases to be capitalized on the financial statements of lessees. This conclusion was no match for the countervailing forces against the capitalization of leases that were motivated by the ability to present a more favorable financial structure and patterns of income determination. As a result, relatively few leases were capitalized under the provisions of *APB Opinion No. 5*.

The APB also issued three other statements dealing with accounting for leases by lessors and lessees: *APB Opinion No. 7*, "Accounting for Leases in Financial Statement of Lessors" (superseded), *APB Opinion No. 27*, "Accounting for Lease Transactions by Manufacturers or Dealer Lessors" (superseded), and *APB Opinion No. 31*, "Disclosure of Lease Transactions by Lessees" (superseded). Nevertheless, the overall results of these statements were that few leases were being capitalized and that lessor and lessee accounting for leases lacked symmetry because these four opinions allowed lessees and lessors to report the same lease differently.

In November 1976, the FASB issued *SFAS No. 13*, "Accounting for Leases" (see FASB ASC 840), which superseded *APB Opinion Nos. 5, 7, 27*, and *31*. A major purpose of *SFAS No. 13* was to achieve a greater degree of symmetry of accounting between lessees and lessors. In an effort to accomplish this goal, the statement established standards of financial accounting and reporting for both lessees and lessors. As noted above, one of the problems associated with the four opinions issued by the APB was that they allowed differences in recording and reporting the same lease by lessors and lessees; adherence to *SFAS No. 13* substantially reduces (though does not eliminate) this possibility.

The conceptual foundation underlying *SFAS No. 13* is based on the view that "a lease that transfers substantially all of the benefits and risks inherent in the ownership of property should be accounted for as the acquisition of an asset and the incurrence of an obligation by the lessee and as a sale or financing lease by the lessor."[2] This viewpoint leads immediately to three basic conclusions: (1) The characteristics indicating that substantially all the benefits and risks of ownership have been transferred to the lessee must be identified. These types of leases should be reported as if they involved the purchase and sale of assets (*capital leases*). (2) The same characteristics should apply to both the lessee and lessor; therefore, the inconsistency in accounting treatment that previously existed should be eliminated. (3) Those leases that do not meet the characteristics identified in (1) should be accounted for as rental agreements (*operating leases*).

It has been suggested that the choice of structuring a lease as either an operating or a capital lease is not independent of the original nature of leasing as opposed to buying the asset. As indicated earlier, companies engaging in lease transactions may attempt to transfer the benefits of owning assets to the lease

---

2. Financial Accounting Standards Board, *Statement of Financial Accounting Standards No. 13*, "Accounting for Leases" (Stamford, CT: FASB, 1976), para. 60. This statement was amended in 1980 to incorporate several FASB pronouncements that expanded on the principles outlined in the original pronouncement.

party in the higher tax bracket. In addition, Smith and Wakeman identified eight nontax factors that make leasing more attractive than purchasing:[3]

1. The period of use is short relative to the overall life of the asset.

2. The lessor has a comparative advantage over the lessee in reselling the asset.

3. Corporate bond covenants of the lessee contain restrictions relating to financial policies the firm must follow (maximum debt-to-equity ratios).

4. Management compensation contracts contain provisions expressing compensation as a function of return on invested capital.

5. Lessee ownership is closely held, so that risk reduction is important.

6. The lessor (manufacturer) has market power and can thus generate higher profits by leasing the asset (and controlling the terms of the lease) than by selling the asset.

7. The asset is not specialized to the firm.

8. The asset's value is not sensitive to use or abuse (the owner takes better care of the asset than does the lessee).

Obviously, some of these reasons are not subject to lessee choice but are motivated by the lessor and/or the type of asset involved. However, short periods of use and the resale factor favor the accounting treatment of a lease as operating, whereas the bond covenant and management compensation incentives favor a structuring of the lease as a capital lease. In addition, lessors may be more inclined to seek to structure leases as capital leases to allow earlier recognition of revenue and net income. That is, a lease that is reported as an in-substance sale by the lessor allows for revenue recognition (gross profit on sale) at the time of the original transaction in addition to interest revenue over the life of the lease.

Criteria for Classifying Leases

In *SFAS No. 13*, the FASB outlined specific criteria for classifying leases as either capital or operating leases. If at its inception the lease meets any one of the following four criteria, the lessee will classify the lease as a capital lease; otherwise, it is classified as an operating lease:

1. The lease transfers ownership of the property to the lessee by the end of the lease term. This includes the fixed noncancelable term of the lease plus various specified renewal options and periods.

2. The lease contains a bargain purchase option. This means that when the lessee has the option to purchase the leased asset, at the inception of the lease the stated purchase price is sufficiently lower than the fair market value of the property expected at the date the option will become exercisable such that it appears to be at a bargain price. In this case, exercise of the option appears to be reasonably assured.

3. The lease term is equal to 75 percent or more of the estimated remaining economic life of the leased property, unless the beginning of the lease term

---

3. Clifford Smith Jr. and L. Macdonald Wakeman, "Determinants of Corporate Leasing Policy," *Journal of Finance* (July 1985): pp. 895–908.

falls within the last 25 percent of the total estimated economic life of the leased property.

4. At the beginning of the lease term, the present value of the minimum lease payments (the amounts of the payments the lessee is required to make excluding that portion of the payments representing executory costs such as insurance, maintenance, and taxes to be paid by the lessee) equals or exceeds 90 percent of the fair value of the leased property less any related investment tax credit retained by the lessor. (This criterion is also ignored when the lease term falls within the last 25 percent of the total estimated economic life of the leased property).[4]

The criteria for capitalization of leases are based on the assumption that a lease that transfers to the lessee the risks and benefits of using an asset should be recorded as an acquisition of a long-term asset. However, the criteria are seen as arbitrary because the FASB provided no explanation for choosing a lease term of 75 percent or a fair value of 90 percent as the cutoff points. In addition, the criteria have been viewed as redundant and essentially based on the fourth criterion.[5]

In the case of the lessor (except for leveraged leases, discussed later), if a lease meets any one of the preceding four criteria plus *both* of the following additional criteria, it is classified as a sales type or direct financing lease.

1. Collectibility of the minimum lease payments is reasonably predictable.
2. No important uncertainties surround the amount of unreimbursable costs yet to be incurred by the lessor under the lease.[6]

The latter two criteria are prompted by the concept of conservatism. Accountants are reluctant to report receivables when there is significant uncertainty regarding expected future cash flows.

Accounting and Reporting by Lessees under *SFAS No. 13*

From the lessee's perspective, the primary concern in accounting for lease transactions has historically been the appropriate recognition of assets and liabilities on the balance sheet. This concern has overridden the corollary question of revenue recognition on the part of lessors. Therefore the usual position of accountants has been that when a lease agreement is in substance an installment purchase, lessees should account for the "leased" property as an asset and report a corresponding liability. Failure to do so results in an understatement of assets and liabilities on the balance sheet. Lease arrangements that are not considered installment purchases constitute *off-balance sheet financing* arrangements and should be properly disclosed in the footnotes to financial statements.

As early as 1962, the accounting research division of the AICPA recognized that there was little consistency in the disclosure of leases by lessees and that most companies were not capitalizing leases. It therefore authorized a research study on the reporting of leases by lessees. Among the recommendations of this study were the following:

4. Ibid., para. 7.

5. J. Coughlan, "Regulations, Rents and Residuals," *Journal of Accountancy* 33, no. 2 (Feb. 1980): 63–80.

6. Ibid., para. 8.

To the extent that leases give rise to property rights, those rights and related liabilities should be measured and incorporated in the balance sheet. To the extent that rental payments represent a means of financing the acquisition of property rights which the lessee has in his possession and under his control, the transaction constitutes the acquisition of an asset with a related obligation to pay for it.

To the extent, however, that the rental payments are for services such as maintenance, insurance, property taxes, heat, light, and elevator service, no asset has been acquired, and none should be recorded.

The measurement of the asset value and the related liability involves two steps: (1) determining the part of the rentals that constitutes payment for property rights, and (2) discounting these rentals at an appropriate rate of interest.[7] . . .

The crucial difference in the conclusion of this study and the practice that existed when the conclusion was reached was the emphasis on *property rights* (the right to use property), as opposed to the *rights in property*—ownership of an equity interest in the property.

The APB considered the recommendations of this study and agreed that certain lease agreements should result in the lessee's recording an asset and liability. The Board concluded that the important criterion to be applied was whether the lease was in substance a purchase; that is, rights in property, rather than the existence of property rights. This conclusion indicated that the APB agreed that an asset and liability should be recorded when the lease transaction was in substance an installment purchase in the same manner as other purchase arrangements. The APB, however, did not agree that the rights to use property in exchange for future rental payments give rise to the recording of assets and liabilities, since no equity in property is created.

In *Opinion No. 5*, the APB asserted that a noncancelable lease, or one that is cancelable only on the occurrence of some remote contingency, was probably in substance a purchase if either of the two following conditions exists:

1. The initial term is materially less than the useful life of the property, and the lessee has the option to renew the lease for the remaining useful life of the property at substantially less than the fair rental value.

2. The lessee has the right, during or at the expiration of the lease, to acquire the property at a price that at the inception of the lease appears to be substantially less than the probable fair value of the property at the time or times of permitted acquisition by the lessee.[8]

The presence of either of these two conditions was seen as convincing evidence that the lessee was building equity in the property.

The APB went on to say that one or more of the following circumstances tend to indicate that a lease arrangement is in substance a purchase:

1. The property was acquired by the lessor to meet the special needs of the lessee and will probably be usable only for that purpose and only by the lessee.

7. John H. Myers, *Accounting Research Study No. 4*, "Reporting of Leases in Financial Statements" (New York: AICPA, 1962), 4–5.

8. Accounting Principles Board, *Opinion No. 5*, "Reporting of Leases in Financial Statements of Lessees" (New York: AICPA, 1964), para. 10.

2. The term of the lease corresponds substantially to the estimated useful life of the property, and the lessee is obligated to pay costs such as taxes, insurance, and maintenance, which are usually considered incidental to ownership.

3. The lessee has guaranteed the obligations of the lessor with respect to the leased property.

4. The lessee has treated the lease as a purchase for tax purposes.[9]

In addition, a lease might be considered a purchase if the lessor and lessee were related even in the absence of the preceding conditions and circumstances. In that case, a lease should be recorded as a purchase if a primary purpose of ownership of the property by the lessor is to lease it to the lessee; and (1) the lease payments are pledged to secure the debts of the lessor or (2) the lessee is able, directly or indirectly, to control or influence significantly the actions of the lessor with respect to the lease.[10]

These conclusions caused controversy in the financial community because some individuals believed that they resulted in disincentives to leasing. Those holding this view maintained that noncapitalized leases provide the following benefits:

1. Improved accounting rate of return and debt ratios, thereby improving the financial picture of the company

2. Better debt ratings

3. Increased availability of capital

On the other hand, the advocates of lease capitalization hold that these arguments are, in essence, attempts to deceive financial statement users. That is, a company should fully disclose the impact of all its financing and investing activities and not attempt to hide the economic substance of external transactions. (This issue is discussed in more detail later in the chapter.)

Capital Leases

The views expressed in *APB Opinion No. 5* concerning the capitalization of those leases that are "in-substance installment purchases" are significant from a historical point of view, for two reasons. First, in *SFAS No. 13*, the FASB based its conclusion on the concept that a lease that "Transfers substantially all of the benefits and risks of the ownership of property should be accounted for as the acquisition of an asset and the incurrence of an obligation by the lessee, and as a sale or financing by the lessor." Second, to a great extent, the accounting provisions of *SFAS No. 13* applicable to lessees generally follow *APB Opinion No. 5*.

The provisions of *SFAS No. 13* require a lessee entering into a capital lease agreement to record both an asset and a liability at the lower of the following:

1. The sum of the present value of the *minimum lease payments* at the inception of the lease (see the following discussion)

2. The fair value of the leased property at the inception of the lease

9. Ibid., para. 11.
10. Ibid., para. 12.

The rules for determining minimum lease payments were specifically set forth by the FASB. In summary, those payments that the lessee is obligated to make or can be required to make, with the exception of executory costs, should be included. Consequently, the following items are subject to inclusion in the determination of the minimum lease payments:

1. Minimum rental payments over the life of the lease
2. Payment called for by a bargain purchase option
3. Any guarantee by the lessee of residual value at the expiration of the lease term
4. Any penalties that the lessee can be required to pay for failure to renew the lease[11]

Once the minimum lease payments are known, the lessee must compute their present value. The interest rate to be used in this computation is the smaller of the lessee's incremental borrowing rate or the lessor's implicit rate (if known). The lessee's incremental borrowing rate is the rate that would have been charged, had the lessee borrowed funds to buy the asset with repayments over the same term. If the lessee can readily determine the implicit interest rate used by the lessor, and if that rate is lower than his or her incremental borrowing rate, then the lessee is to use the lessor's implicit interest rate to calculate the present value of the minimum lease payments. If the lessee does not know the lessor's interest rate (a likely situation), or if the lessor's implicit interest rate is higher than the lessee's incremental borrowing rate, the lessee and lessor will have different amortization schedules to recognize interest expense and interest revenue, respectively.

Capital lease assets and liabilities are to be separately identified in the lessee's balance sheet or in the accompanying footnotes. The liability should be classified as current and noncurrent on the same basis as all other liabilities; that is, according to when the obligation must be paid.

Unless the lease involves land, the asset recorded under a capital lease is to be amortized by one of two methods. Leases that meet either criterion 1 or 2 on page 432 are to be amortized in a manner consistent with the lessee's normal depreciation policy for owned assets. That is, when the lease automatically transfers ownership of the leased property or contains a bargain purchase option (capital lease criteria 1 or 2 is met), it is presumed that the lessee will eventually have title to the asset and should amortize the leased asset over its economic life. For all other capital leases, the asset will revert to the lessor at the end of the lease term; thus, those leases that do not meet capital lease criteria 1 or 2 should be amortized in a manner consistent with the lessee's normal depreciation policy, using the lease term as the period of amortization. In conformity with *APB Opinion No. 21*, "Interest on Receivables and Payables" (see FASB ASC 835-30), *SFAS No. 13* requires that each minimum payment under a capital lease be allocated between a reduction of the liability and interest expense. This allocation is to be made in such a manner that the interest expense reflects a constant interest rate on the outstanding balance of the obligation (i.e., the effective interest method). Thus, as with any loan payment schedule, each successive payment allocates a greater amount to the reduction of the principal and a lesser amount to interest expense. This procedure results in the

---

11. *SFAS No. 13*, para. 5.

loan being reflected on the balance sheet at the present value of the future cash flows discounted at the effective interest rate.

Disclosure Requirements for Capital Leases   *SFAS No. 13* also requires the disclosure of additional information for capital leases. The following information must be disclosed in the lessee's financial statements or in the accompanying footnotes:

1. The gross amount of assets recorded under capital leases as of the date of each balance sheet presented by major classes according to nature or function

2. Future minimum lease payments as of the date of the latest balance sheet presented, in the aggregate and for each of the five succeeding fiscal years

3. The total minimum sublease rentals to be received in the future under non-cancelable subleases as of the date of the latest balance sheet presented

4. Total contingent rentals (rentals on which the amounts are dependent on some factor other than the passage of time) actually incurred for each period for which an income statement is presented[12]

Operating Leases

Lessees classify all leases that do not meet any of the four capital lease criteria as operating leases. Failure to meet any of the criteria means that the lease is simply a rental arrangement and, in essence, should be accounted for in the same manner as any other rental agreement, with certain exceptions. The rent payments made on an operating lease are normally charged to expense as they become payable over the life of the lease. An exception is made if the rental schedule does not result in a straight-line basis of payment. In such cases, the rent expense is to be recognized on a straight-line basis, unless the lessee can demonstrate that some other method gives a more systematic and rational periodic charge.

In *Opinion No. 31*, the APB observed that many users of financial statements were dissatisfied with the information being provided about leases. Although many criticisms were being voiced over accounting for leases, the focus of this opinion was on the information that should be disclosed about noncapitalized leases.

The following disclosures are required for operating leases by lessees:

1. For operating leases having initial or remaining noncancelable lease terms in excess of one year:

    a. Future minimum rental payments required as of the date of the latest balance sheet presented in the aggregate and for each of the five succeeding fiscal years

    b. The total of minimum rentals to be received in the future under noncancelable subleases as of the date of the latest balance sheet presented

2. For all operating leases, rental expense for each period for which an income statement is presented, with separate amounts for minimum rentals, contingent rentals, and sublease rentals

---

12. Ibid., para. 16.

3. A general description of the lessee's leasing arrangements including, but not limited to, the following:

    a. The basis on which contingent rental payments are determined

    b. The existence and terms of renewals or purchase options and escalation clauses

    c. Restrictions imposed by lease agreements, such as those concerning dividends, additional debt, and further leasing[13]

The FASB contends that the preceding accounting and disclosure requirements for capital and operating leases by lessees give users information useful in assessing a company's financial position and results of operations. The requirements also provide many specific and detailed rules, which should lead to greater consistency in the presentation of lease information.

Accounting and Reporting by Lessors

The major concern in accounting for leases in the financial statements of lessors is the appropriate allocation of revenues and expenses over the period covered by the lease. This concern contrasts with the lessee's focus on the balance sheet presentation of leases. As a general rule, lease agreements include a specific schedule of the date and amounts of payments the lessee is to make to the lessor. The fact that the lessor knows the date and amount of payment does not necessarily indicate that revenue should be reported in the same period the cash is received. To measure the results of operations more fairly, accrual accounting frequently gives rise to situations in which revenue is recognized in a period other than when payment is received.

The nature of the lease and the rent schedule may make it necessary for the lessor to recognize revenue that is more or less than the payments received in a given period. Furthermore, the lessor must allocate the acquisition and operating costs of the leased property, together with any costs of negotiating and closing the lease, to the accounting periods receiving benefits in a systematic and rational manner consistent with the timing of revenue recognition. The latter point is consistent with the application of the matching principle in accounting; that is, determining the amount of revenue to be recognized in a period and then ascertaining which costs should be matched with that revenue.

Historically, the criterion for choosing between accounting for lease revenue as either a sale, a financing, or as an operating lease was based on the accounting objective of fairly stating the lessor's periodic net income. Whichever approach would best accomplish this objective should be followed. *SFAS No. 13* set forth specific criteria for determining the type of lease as well as the reporting and disclosure requirements for each type.

According to *SFAS No. 13*, if at its inception a lease agreement meets the lessee criteria for classification as a capital lease and if the two additional criteria for lessors contained on page 433 are met, the lessor is to classify the lease either as a *sales-type lease* or a *direct financing lease*, whichever is appropriate. All other leases, except leveraged leases (discussed in a separate section), are to be classified as operating leases.

13. bid., para. 16.

Sales-Type Leases

The lessor should report a lease as a *sales-type lease* when at least one of the capital lease criteria is met, both lessor certainty criteria are met, and there is a manufacturer's or dealer's profit (or loss). This implies that the leased asset is an item of inventory and that the seller is earning a gross profit on the sale. Sales-type leases arise when manufacturers or dealers use leasing as a means of marketing their products.

Table 13.1 depicts the major steps involved in accounting for a sales-type lease by a lessor. The amount to be recorded as gross investment (a) is the total amount of the minimum lease payments over the life of the lease, plus any unguaranteed residual value accruing to the benefit of the lessor. Once the gross investment has been determined, it is to be discounted to its present value (b) using an interest rate that causes the aggregate present value at the beginning of the lease term to be equal to the fair value of the leased property. The rate thus determined is referred to as the interest rate implicit in the lease (the lessor's implicit rate).

TABLE 13.1   *Accounting Steps for Sales-Type Leases*

Gross investment (a)	XX
minus	
Present value of the gross investment (b)	XX
equals	
Unearned income (c)	XX
Gross investment (a)	XX
minus	
Unearned income (c)	XX
equals	
Net investment (d)	XX
Sales (e)	XX
minus	
Cost of goods sold (f)	XX
equals	
Profit or loss (g)	XX

The difference between the gross investment (a) and the present value of the gross investment (b) is to be recorded as unearned interest income (c). The unearned interest income is to be amortized as interest income over the life of the lease using the interest method described in *APB Opinion No. 21* (see FASB ASC 835-30). Applying the interest method results in a constant rate of return on the net investment in the lease. The difference between the gross investment (a) and the unearned interest income (c) is the amount of net investment (d), which is equal to the present value of the gross investment (b). The net investment is classified as a current or noncurrent asset on the lessor's balance sheet in the same manner as all other assets. Income from sales-type leases is thus reflected by two amounts: (1) the gross profit (or loss) on the sale in the year of the lease agreement and (2) interest on the remaining net investment over the life of the lease agreement.

For sales-type leases, because the critical event is the sale, the initial direct costs associated with obtaining the lease agreement are written off when the sale is recorded at the inception of the lease. These costs are disclosed as selling expenses on the income statement.

Direct Financing Leases

When at least one of the capital lease criteria and both lessor certainty criteria are met, but the lessor has no manufacturer's or dealer's profit (or loss), lessors account for the lease as a direct financing lease. Under the direct financing method, the lessor is essentially viewed as a lending institution for revenue recognition purposes. As with a sales-type lease, each payment received for a direct financing lease must be allocated between interest revenue and recovery of the net investment. Because the net receivable is essentially an installment loan, in the early periods of the lease a significant portion of the payment is recorded as interest; but each succeeding payment will result in a decreasing amount of interest revenue and an increasing amount of investment recovery because the amount of the net investment is decreasing.

The FASB adopted the approach of requiring lessors to record the total minimum lease payments for direct financing leases as a gross receivable on the date of the transaction and to treat the difference between that amount and the asset cost as unearned income. Subsequently, as each rental payment is received, the gross receivable is reduced by the full amount of the payment, and a portion of the unearned income is transferred to earned income.

Table 13.2 illustrates the accounting steps for direct financing leases. Gross investment (a) is determined in the same way as in sales-type leases, but unearned income (c) is computed as the difference between gross investment and the cost (b) of the leased property. The difference between gross investment (a) and unearned income (c) is net investment (d), which is the same as (b) in the sales-type lease.

TABLE 13.2   *Accounting Steps for Direct Financing Leases*

Gross investment (a)	XX
minus	
Cost (b)	XX
equals	
Unearned income (c)	XX
Gross investment (a)	XX
minus	
Unearned income (c)	XX
equals	
Net investment (d)	XX
Unearned income (c)	XX
minus	
Initial direct costs (e)	XX
equals	
Unearned income to be authorized (g)	XX

Initial direct costs (e) in financing leases are treated as an adjustment to the investment in the leased asset. Because financing the lease is the revenue-generating activity, *SFAS No. 91* requires that this cost be matched in proportion to the recognition of interest revenue. In each accounting period over the life of the lease, the unearned interest income (c) minus the indirect cost (e) is amortized by the effective interest method. Because the net investment is increased by an amount equal to the initial direct costs, a new effective interest rate must be determined in order to apply the interest method to the declining net investment balance. Under direct financing leases, the only revenue reported by the lessor is disclosed as interest revenue over the lease term. Since initial direct costs increase the amount disclosed as the net investment, the interest income reported represents interest net of the write-off of the initial direct cost.

Disclosure Requirements for Sales-Type and Direct Financing Leases

In addition to the specific procedures required to account for sales-type and direct financing leases, the FASB established certain disclosure requirements. The following information is to be disclosed when leasing constitutes a significant part of the lessor's business activities in terms of revenue, net income, or assets:

1. The components of the net investment in leases as of the date of each balance sheet presented:

   a. Future minimum lease payments to be received with deduction for any executory costs included in payments and allowance for uncollectibles

   b. The unguaranteed residual value

   c. Unearned income

2. Future minimum lease payments to be received for each of the five succeeding fiscal years as of the date of the latest balance sheet presented

3. The amount of unearned income included in income to offset initial direct costs charged against income for each period for which an income statement is presented (for direct financing leases only)

4. Total contingent rentals included in income for each period for which an income statement is presented

5. A general description of the lessor's leasing arrangements[14]

The Board indicated that these disclosures by the lessor, as with the disclosures by lessees, would aid the users of financial statements in their assessment of the financial condition and results of operations of lessors. Note also that these requirements make the information disclosed by lessors and lessees more consistent.

Lessor Operating Leases

Those leases that do not meet the criteria for classification as sales-type or direct financing leases are accounted for as operating leases by the lessor. As a result, the lessor's cost of the leased property is reported with or near other property, plant, and equipment on the lessor's balance sheet and is depreciated following the lessor's normal depreciation policy.

Rental payments are recognized as revenue when they become receivable unless the payments are not made on a straight-line basis. In that case, as with the lessee, the recognition of revenue is to be on a straight-line basis. Initial direct costs associated with the lease are to be deferred and allocated over the lease term in the same manner as rental revenue (usually on a straight-line basis). However, if these costs are not material, they may be charged to expense as incurred.

If leasing is a significant part of the lessor's business activities, the following information is to be disclosed for operating leases:

14. Ibid., para. 23.

1. The cost and carrying amount, if different, of property on lease or held for leasing by major classes of property according to nature or function, and the amount of accumulated depreciation in total as of the date of the latest balance sheet presented

2. Minimum future rentals on noncancelable leases as of the date of the latest balance sheet presented, in the aggregate and for each of the five succeeding fiscal years

3. Total contingent rentals included in income for each period for which an income statement is presented

4. A general description of the lessor's leasing arrangements[15]

Sales and Leasebacks

In a sale and leaseback transaction, the owner of property sells the property and then immediately leases it back from the buyer. These transactions frequently occur when companies have limited cash resources or when the transaction results in tax advantages. Tax advantages occur because the sales price of the asset is usually its current market value, and this amount generally exceeds the carrying value of the asset on the seller's books. Therefore the tax-deductible periodic rental payments are higher than the previously recorded amount of depreciation expense.

Most sales and leaseback transactions are treated as a single economic event, according to the lease classification criteria previously discussed on pages 432 and 433. That is, the lessee-seller applies the *SFAS No. 13* criteria to the lease agreement and records the lease as either a capital or operating lease and the gain on the sale is amortized over the lease term; however, if a loss occurs, it is recognized immediately. Even so, in certain circumstances where the lessee retains significantly smaller rights to use the property, a gain may be immediately recognized. In this case it is argued that two distinctly different transactions have occurred because the rights to use have changed.

Leveraged Leases

A leveraged lease is a special leasing arrangement involving three different parties: (1) the equity holder—the lessor; (2) the asset user—the lessee; and (3) the debt holder—a long-term financer.[16] A leveraged lease may be illustrated as follows:

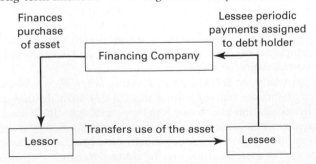

15. Ibid., para. 23.

16. A fourth party may also be involved when the owner-lessor initially purchases the property from a manufacturer.

The major issue in accounting for leveraged leases is whether the transaction should be recorded as a single economic event or as separate transactions. All leveraged leases meet the criteria for direct financing leases. However, a leveraged lease might be accounted for as a lease with an additional debt transaction or as a single transaction. The FASB determined that a leveraged lease should be accounted for as a single transaction, and provided the following guidelines.

The lessee records the lease as a capital lease. The lessor records the lease as a direct financing lease. The lessor's investment in the lease is the net result of several factors:

1. Rentals receivable, net of that portion of the rental applicable to principal and interest on the nonrecourse debt

2. A receivable for the amount of the investment tax credit to be realized on the transaction

3. The estimated residual value of the leased asset

4. Unearned and deferred income consisting of the estimated pretax lease income (or loss), after deducting initial direct costs remaining to be allocated to income over the lease term and the investment tax credit remaining to be allocated to income over the lease term[17]

Once the original investment has been determined, the next step is to project cash receipts and disbursements over the term of the lease and then compute a rate of return on the net investment in those years in which it is positive. Annual cash flow is the sum of gross lease rental and residual value (in the final year), less loan interest payments plus or minus income tax credits or charges, less loan principal payments, plus investment tax credit realized. The rate to be used in the computation is that "which when applied to the net investment in the years in which the net investment is positive will distribute the net income to those years."[18]

In a footnote to an illustration of the allocation of annual cash flow to investment and income, *SFAS No. 13* includes the following comment:

> [The rate used for the allocation] is calculated by a trial and error process. The allocation is calculated based upon an initial estimate of the rate as a starting point. If the total thus allocated to income differs under the estimated rate from the net cash flow the estimated rate is increased or decreased, as appropriate, to devise a revised allocation. This process is repeated until a rate is selected which develops a total amount allocated to income that is precisely equal to the net cash flow. As a practical matter, a computer program is used to calculate [the allocation] under successive iterations until the correct rate is determined.[19]

This method of accounting for leveraged leases was considered to associate the income with the unrecovered balance of the earning asset in a manner consistent

17. *FASB Statement No. 13*, para. 43.
18. Ibid., para. 44.
19. Ibid., para. 123.

with the investor's view of the transaction. Income is recognized at a level rate on net investment in years in which the net investment is positive and is thus identified as "primary" earnings from the lease.

In recent years companies have tried to circumvent *SFAS No. 13*. These efforts are used mainly by lessees who do not wish to report increased liabilities or adversely affect their debt-equity ratios. However, unlike lessees, lessors do not wish to avoid reporting lease transactions as sales-type or direct financing leases. Consequently, the trick is to allow the lessee to report a lease as an operating lease while the lessor reports it as either a sales-type or direct financing lease.

Financial Analysis of Leases

In Chapter 11 we illustrated some procedures that a financial analyst might use to evaluate a company's long-term debt position and indicated that the use of operating leases can affect this type of analysis. The use of leases can also have an impact on a company's liquidity and profitability ratios. That is, a company employing operating leases to acquire its assets will have a relatively better working capital position and relatively higher current and return-on-assets (ROA) ratios than it would if it had recorded the transaction as a capital lease.

To illustrate, Samson Company has the following summarized balance sheet on December 31, 2010, before entering into a lease transaction:

Current assets	$ 50,000
Long-term assets	250,000
Total assets	$300,000
Current liabilities	$ 20,000
Long-term debt	130,000
Stockholders' equity	150,000
Total liabilities and stockholders' equity	$300,000

Assume that the company enters into a lease agreement on December 31, 2010, whereby it promises to pay a lessor $10,000 annually for the next five years for the use of an asset. If the lease is accounted for as an operating lease, neither the asset nor the liability is reported on Samson's balance sheet, and its working capital, current ratio, and return on assets ratios for December 31, 2011, will appear as follows (assume the company earned net income of $25,000 during 2011):

Working capital	= $50,000 − 20,000	= $30,000
Current ratio	= $50,000 ÷ $20,000	= 2.5:1
Return-on-assets ratio	= $25,000 ÷ $300,000[a]	= 8.3%

[a]Assume the company's total assets remained constant throughout the year.

Alternatively, if the lease is recorded as a capital lease, the discounted present values of both the asset and liability are recorded on the company's balance sheet.

In addition, the lease liability is separated into its current and long-term components, and the company's December 31, 2011, balance sheet will now appear as follows (assuming a discount rate of 10 percent):

Current assets	$ 50,000
Long-term assets	250,000
Capital leases	37,908
Total assets	$337,908
Current liabilities	$ 20,000
Current lease obligation	9,091
Long-term debt	130,000
Long-term lease obligation	28,817
Stockholders' equity	150,000
Total liabilities and stockholders' equity	$337,908

The company's working capital, current ratio, and ROA ratio will now become:

Working capital	= $50,000 − 29,091	= $20,909
Current ratio	= $50,000 ÷ $29,091	= 1.7:1
Return-on-assets ratio	= $25,000 ÷ $318,954[a]	= 7.8%

[a]($300,000 + 337,908) ÷ 2

If a company makes extensive use of operating leases, its working capital, current ratio, and quick ratio, illustrated in Chapter 8, and its ROA ratio, illustrated in Chapter 7, are all overstated when the effects of the company's lease financing policy are incorporated into the analysis. The extent of these overstatements can be estimated by discounting the firm's current obligation for one year to arrive at the current portion of its lease obligation and the remaining obligations to arrive at the long-term obligation. The sum of these two amounts is equal to the amount capitalized as a leased asset.[22] For example, Hershey discloses the following information concerning operating leases in the footnotes to its financial statements:

> Future minimum rental payments under noncancelable operating leases with a remaining term in excess of one year as of December 31, 2008, totaled $61.2 million (2009—$14.9 million; 2010—$11.2 million; 2011—$8.9 million; 2012—$8.0 million; 2013—$4.3 million; 2014 and beyond—$13.9 million).

Discounting these amounts at the company's approximate average borrowing rate of 7 percent results in an increase in current liabilities of approximately $13.9 million, an increase in long-term obligations of approximately $35.4 million, and

22. To make this calculation, a discount factor must be assumed, and the annual amounts of the total of payments due after 2011 must be estimated to determine the present value of the long-term obligation and the property under leased assets. The discounted value of the property under leased assets is then added to total assets, which will reduce the company's return-on-assets ratio.

an increase in total assets of approximately $49.3 million. Incorporating these amounts into the calculation of the current ratio results in a decline from the previously calculated amount of 1.06:1 to 1.05:1. The quick ratio also fractionally declined from the previously calculated amount of 0.39:1 to 0.38:1. Adding the discounted value of the lease obligations to Hershey's assets results in a decline in its adjusted ROA from 11.9 to 11.7 percent.

Current Developments

In March 2009, the FASB and IASB announced a joint project on accounting for leases. The boards indicated that the project was needed because the existing accounting model for leases has been criticized for failing to meet the needs of users of financial statements. In particular, many users think that operating leases give rise to assets and liabilities that should be recognized in the financial statements of lessees. Consequently, users routinely adjust current and future obligations in an attempt to recognize those assets and liabilities and reflect the effect of lease contracts in profit or loss. In 2005, the SEC estimated that $1.25 trillion dollars of liabilities had been omitted from balance sheets because of operating lease classifications.[23] However, the information available to users in the notes to the financial statements was viewed as insufficient for them to make reliable estimations to account for these omissions. As a result:

1. The existence of two very different accounting models for leases—the capital lease model (termed the *finance lease model* by the IASB) and the operating lease model—means that similar transactions can be accounted for very differently. This reduces comparability for users.

2. The existing standards provide opportunities to structure transactions so as to achieve a particular lease classification (financial engineering). If the lease is classified as an operating lease, the lessee obtains a source of unrecognized financing that can be difficult for users to understand. As a result, lease structuring to meet various accounting goals has developed into an entire industry.[24]

Preparers and auditors have also criticized the existing lease accounting model for its complexity. In particular, it has proved difficult to define the dividing line between finance leases and operating leases in a principled way. Consequently, the standards use a mixture of subjective judgments and bright-line tests (specific rules) that can be difficult to apply. Some have argued that the existing accounting model is conceptually flawed. In particular:

1. On entering a lease contract, the lessee obtains a valuable right (the right to use the leased item). This right meets the boards' definitions of an asset. Similarly,

---

23. Report and Recommendations Pursuant to Section 401(c) of the Sarbanes-Oxley Act of 2002 on Arrangements with Off-Balance Sheet Implications, Special Purpose Entities, and Transparency of Filings by Issuers, Securities and Exchange Commission, Washington, D.C. (2005), http://www.sec.gov/news/ studies/soxoffbalancerpt.pdf.

24. "Changes to Lease Accounting Standards Are Coming," RSM McGladrey (2009), http://www.rsmmcgladrey.com/Real-Estate/Changes-to-lease-accounting-standards-are-coming.

the lessee assumes an obligation (the obligation to pay rentals) that meets the boards' definitions of a liability. However, if the lessee classifies the lease as an operating lease, that right and obligation are not recognized.

2. There are significant and growing differences between the accounting model for leases and other contractual arrangements. This has led to inconsistent accounting for arrangements that meet the definition of a lease and similar arrangements that do not.

The project is focusing on the accounting for lease arrangements within the scope of existing lease accounting literature and initially is considering only lessee accounting for leases. The scope of the project includes arrangements that are leases in form but in substance are acquisitions of leased assets. At the time this text was published, the boards had decided on an overall approach that would apply the existing finance lease model, adapted where necessary, to all leases—meaning those leases that were capital leases and those that were operating leases under current GAAP. All material leases are to be capitalized. The concepts behind the approach are as follows:

1. A lease contract gives the lessee the right to use an asset and obligates the lessee to pay rent for the term.

2. The rights to use the asset are assets and the obligations to pay rents are liabilities that must be capitalized.

3. The need to account for the whole lease contract rather than its components (like rent, purchase options, renewal options, contingent rents, etc).

The boards decided that a lessee should initially measure both its right-of-use asset and its lease obligation at the present value of the expected lease payments and that a lessee should discount the estimated lease payments using the lessee's incremental borrowing rate for secured borrowings. Subsequently, a lessee should amortize the right-of-use asset systematically over the shorter of the lease term and the economic life of the leased asset. But for leases of items in which it is expected that the lessee will obtain title at the end of the lease term, the amortization period would be the economic life of the leased item. Amortization would be based on the pattern of consumption of economic benefits embodied in the right-of-use asset. Additionally, a lessee would be required to reassess the lease term and its lease obligation using its current assumptions at each reporting date.

International Accounting Standards

The IASB has issued pronouncements on the following items affecting leases:

- *IAS No. 17*, "Accounting for Leases"
- *IAS No. 40*, "Investment Property"

IAS No. 17, "Accounting for Leases," deals with lease accounting issues. This standard, which was slightly revised by the IASB's improvement project, is quite similar to U.S. GAAP as outlined in *SFAS No. 13*. One difference in terminology, however, is that in-substance purchases of assets are termed *financing leases* in

IAS No. 17 rather than capital leases. *IAS No. 17* indicates that a lease is to be classified as a finance lease if it transfers substantially all the risks and rewards incident to ownership. All other leases are classified as operating leases, and this classification is made at the inception of the lease. Whether a lease is a finance lease or an operating lease depends on the substance of the transaction rather than the form. Situations that would normally lead to a lease being classified as a finance lease include the following:

1. The lease transfers ownership of the asset to the lessee by the end of the lease term.

2. The lessee has the option to purchase the asset at a price that is expected to be sufficiently lower than fair value at the date the option becomes exercisable so that, at the inception of the lease, it is reasonably certain that the option will be exercised.

3. The lease term is for the major part of the economic life of the asset, even if title is not transferred.

4. At the inception of the lease, the present value of the minimum lease payments amounts to at least substantially all of the fair value of the leased asset.

5. The lease assets are of a specialized nature such that only the lessee can use them without major modifications being made.

In addition, the terminology *sales-type* and *direct financing* are not used in conjunction with the reporting requirements specified for lessors. Nevertheless, the required accounting treatment for lessors is similar to that outlined in *SFAS No. 13*. The major change in the new standard is that initial direct costs incurred by lessors must now be capitalized and amortized over the lease term. The alternative in the original *IAS No. 17* to expense initial direct costs up front has been eliminated.

IAS No. 40 defined investment property as property (land or a building or part of a building or both) held (by the owner or by the lessee under a finance lease) to earn rentals or for capital appreciation or both. Examples of leased investment property are a building leased out under an operating lease and a vacant building held to be leased out under an operating lease.

In accounting for these properties under *IAS No. 40*, an enterprise must choose one of two models:

1. A fair value model whereby investment property is measured at fair value and changes in fair value are recognized in the income statement.

2. A cost model as described in *IAS No. 16*, "Property, Plant, and Equipment," whereby investment property is measured at depreciated cost (less any accumulated impairment losses). An enterprise that chooses the cost model should disclose the fair value of its investment property.

IAS No. 40 indicates that the model chosen must be used to account for all of its investment properties, and a change from one model to the other model should be made only if the change will result in a more appropriate presentation. The standard states that this is highly unlikely to be the case for a change from the fair value model to the cost model.

Cases

• ## Case 13-1 Capital versus Operating Leases

On January 2, 2008, two identical companies, Daggar Corp. and Bayshore Company, lease similar assets with the following characteristics:

1. The economic life is eight years.
2. The term of the lease is five years.
3. Lease payment of $20,000 per year is due at the beginning of each year beginning January 2, 2008.
4. The fair market value of the leased property is $96,000.
5. Each firm has an incremental borrowing rate of 8 percent and a tax rate of 40 percent.

Daggar capitalizes the lease, whereas Bayshore records the lease as an operating lease. Both firms depreciate assets by the straight-line method, and both treat the lease as an operating lease for federal income tax purposes.

Required:

a. Determine earnings (i) before interest and taxes and (ii) before taxes for both firms. Identify the source of any differences between the companies.
b. Compute any deferred taxes resulting from the lease for each firm in the first year of the lease.
c. Compute the effect of the lease on the 2008 reported cash from operations for both firms. Explain any differences.
d. Compute the effect of the lease on 2008 reported cash flows from investing activities for both firms. Explain any differences.
e. Compute the effect of the lease on 2008 reported cash flow from financing activities for both firms. Explain any differences.
f. Compute the effect of the lease on total 2008 cash flows for both companies. Explain any differences.
g. Give reasons why Daggar and Bayshore may have wanted to use different methods to report similar transactions.

• ## Case 13-2 Lessee and Lessor Accounting for Leases

On January 2, 2011, Grant Corporation leases an asset to Pippin Corporation under the following conditions:

1. Annual lease payments of $10,000 for 20 years.
2. At the end of the lease term, the asset is expected to have a value of $2,750.
3. The fair market value of the asset at the inception of the lease is $92,625.

4. The estimated economic life of the lease is 30 years.

5. Grant's implicit interest rate is 12 percent; Pippin's incremental borrowing rate is 10 percent.

6. The asset is recorded in Grant's inventory at $75,000 just prior to the lease transaction.

Required:

a. What type of lease is this for Pippin? Why?

b. Assume Grant capitalizes the lease. What financial statement accounts are affected by this lease, and what is the amount of each effect?

c. Assume Grant uses straight-line depreciation. What are the income statement, balance sheet, and statement of cash-flow effects for 2011?

d. How should Grant record this lease? Why? Would any additional information be helpful in making this decision?

e. Assume that Grant treats the lease as a sales-type lease and the residual value is not guaranteed by Pippin. What financial statement accounts are affected on January 2, 2011?

f. Assume instead that Grant records the lease as an operating lease and uses straight-line depreciation. What are the income statement, balance sheet, and statement of cash-flow effects on December 31, 2011?

• Case 13-3 Application of *SFAS No. 13*

On January 1, 2010, Lani Company entered into a noncancelable lease for a machine to be used in its manufacturing operations. The lease transfers ownership of the machine to Lani by the end of the lease term. The term of the lease is eight years. The minimum lease payment made by Lani on January 1, 2010, was one of eight equal annual payments. At the inception of the lease, the criteria established for classification as a capital lease by the lessee were met.

Required:

a. What is the theoretical basis for the accounting standard that requires certain long-term leases to be capitalized by the lessee? Do not discuss the specific criteria for classifying a specific lease as a capital lease.

b. How should Lani account for this lease at its inception and determine the amount to be recorded?

c. What expenses related to this lease will Lani incur during the first year of the lease, and how will they be determined?

d. How should Lani report the lease transaction on its December 31, 2010, balance sheet?

• Case 13-4 Lease Classifications

Doherty Company leased equipment from Lambert Company. The classification of the lease makes a difference in the amounts reflected on the balance sheet and income statement of both Doherty and Lambert.

Required:

a. What criteria must be met by the lease so that Doherty Company can classify it as a capital lease?

b. What criteria must be met by the lease so that Lambert Company can classify it as a sales-type or direct financing lease?

c. Contrast a sales-type lease with a direct financing lease.

• Case 13-5 Lease Accounting: Various Issues

On January 1, Borman Company, a lessee, entered into three noncancelable leases for brand-new equipment: Lease J, Lease K, and Lease L. None of the three leases transfers ownership of the equipment to Borman at the end of the lease term. For each of the three leases, the present value at the beginning of the lease term of the minimum lease payments—excluding that portion of the payments representing executory costs such as insurance, maintenance, and taxes to be paid by the lessor and including any profit thereon—is 75 percent of the excess of the fair value of the equipment to the lessor at the inception of the lease over any related investment tax credit retained by the lessor and expected to be realized by the lessor. The following information is peculiar to each lease:

1. Lease J does not contain a bargain purchase option; the lease term is equal to 80 percent of the estimated economic life of the equipment.

2. Lease K contains a bargain purchase option; the lease term is equal to 50 percent of the estimated economic life of the equipment.

3. Lease L does not contain a bargain purchase option; the lease term is equal to 50 percent of the estimated economic life of the equipment.

Required:

a. How should Borman Company classify each of the three leases, and why? Discuss the rationale for your answer.

b. What amount, if any, should Borman record as a liability at the inception of the lease for each of the three leases?

c. Assuming that the minimum lease payments are made on a straight-line basis, how should Borman record each minimum lease payment for each of the three leases?

• Case 13-6 Sales Type versus Direct Financing Leases

Part 1: Capital leases and operating leases are the two classifications of leases described in FASB pronouncements from the standpoint of the lessee.

Required:

a. Describe how a capital lease would be accounted for by the lessee both at the inception of the lease and during the first year of the lease, assuming the lease transfers ownership of the property to the lessee by the end of the lease.

b. Describe how an operating lease would be accounted for by the lessee both at the inception of the lease and during the first year of the lease, assuming the lessee makes equal monthly payments at the beginning of each month of the lease. Describe the change in accounting, if any, when rental payments are not made on a straight-line basis. Do not discuss the criteria for distinguishing between capital leases and operating leases.

Part 2: Sales-type leases and direct financing leases are two of the classifications of leases described in FASB pronouncements, from the standpoint of the lessor.

Required:

Compare and contrast a sales-type lease with a direct financing lease as follows:

a. Gross investment in the lease

b. Amortization of unearned interest income

c. Manufacturer's or dealer's profit

Do not discuss the criteria for distinguishing between the leases described above and operating leases.

• Case 13-7 Lease Issues

Milton Corporation entered into a lease arrangement with James Leasing Corporation for a certain machine. James's primary business is leasing, and it is not a manufacturer or dealer. Milton will lease the machine for a period of three years, which is 50 percent of the machine's economic life. James will take possession of the machine at the end of the initial three-year lease and lease it to another, smaller company that does not need the most current version of the machine. Milton does not guarantee any residual value for the machine and will not purchase the machine at the end of the lease term.

Milton's incremental borrowing rate is 10 percent, and the implicit rate in the lease is $8^1/_2$ percent. Milton has no way of knowing the implicit rate used by James. Using either rate, the present value of the minimum lease payment is between 90 and 100 percent of the fair value of the machine at the date of the lease agreement.

James is reasonably certain that Milton will pay all lease payments, and because Milton has agreed to pay all executory costs, there are no important uncertainties regarding costs to be incurred by James.

Required:

a. With respect to Milton (the lessee), answer the following.

   i. What type of lease has been entered into? Explain the reason for your answer.

   ii. How should Milton compute the appropriate amount to be recorded for the lease or asset acquired?

   iii. What accounts will be created or affected by this transaction, and how will the lease or asset and other costs related to the transaction be matched with earnings?

   iv. What disclosures must Milton make regarding this lease or asset?

b. With respect to James (the lessor), answer the following:

   i. What type of leasing arrangement has been entered into? Explain the reason for your answer.

   ii. How should this lease be recorded by James, and how are the appropriate amounts determined?

iii. How should James determine the appropriate amount of earnings to be recognized from each lease payment?

iv. What disclosures must James make regarding this lease?

• Case 13-8 Lease Capitalization Criteria

On January 1, 2011, Von Company entered into two noncancelable leases for new machines to be used in its manufacturing operations. The first lease does not contain a bargain purchase option; the lease term is equal to 80 percent of the estimated economic life of the machine. The second lease contains a bargain purchase option; the lease term is equal to 50 percent of the estimated economic life of the machine.

Required:

a. What is the theoretical basis for requiring lessees to capitalize certain long-term leases? *Do not discuss the specific criteria for classifying a lease as a capital lease.*

b. How should a lessee account for a capital lease at its inception?

c. How should a lessee record each minimum lease payment for a capital lease?

d. How should Von classify each of the two leases? Why?

FASB ASC Research

For each of the following FASB ASC research cases, search the FASB ASC database for information to address the issues. Cut and paste the FASB paragraphs that support your responses. Then summarize briefly what your responses are, citing the pronouncements and paragraphs used to support your responses.

• FASB ASC 13-1 Initial Direct Cost Incurred by the Lessor

Search the FASB ASC database to address the following questions. For each question, cut and paste your research findings and then write a short summary of your response to each question. Remember to cite your research findings.

1. How does the FASB define initial direct cost associated with leasing?

2. How do lessors account for initial direct costs incurred for a sales-type lease?

3. How do lessors account for initial direct costs incurred for an operating lease?

• FASB ASC 13-2 Interpretations for Lease Accounting

The EITF issued numerous interpretations of lease accounting.

1. List some examples of the topics covered by these interpretations.

2. Write a brief summary of three of these interpretations.

- ## FASB ASC 13-3 Profit on Time-Sharing Transactions

The FASB ASC states that for purposes of recognizing profit on time-sharing transactions, it is necessary that such transfer be nonreversionary. If the title is reversionary, how should the transaction be recorded?

- ## ASB ASC 13-4 Impact of Sale-Leaseback on Rate-Making

Accounting for sale-leaseback transactions in accordance with the FASB ASC guidance may result in a difference between the timing of income and expense recognition required by that subtopic and the timing of income and expense recognition for rate-making purposes. How should companies account for that difference?

- ## FASB ASC 13-5 Definition of Arrangement

The FASB ASC specifies the conditions under which an arrangement qualifies as a lease. What is an arrangement? And, when does it qualify as a lease?

- ## FASB ASC 13-6 Definition of Lease Fiscal Funding Clause

The FASB ASC defines lease fiscal funding clauses. What is a fiscal funding clause? And, how should companies account for fiscal funding clauses?

- ## FASB ASC 13-7 Economic Life of Airport Terminal Facilioties

The FASB ASC indicates that because of special provisions normally present in leases involving terminal space and other airport facilities owned by a governmental unit or authority, the economic life of such facilities for purposes of classifying the lease is essentially indeterminate. Likewise, the concept of fair value is not applicable to such leases. Because such leases also do not provide for a transfer of ownership or a bargain purchase option, they shall be classified as operating leases. Leases of other facilities owned by a governmental unit or authority wherein the rights of the parties are essentially the same as in a lease of airport facilities shall also be classified as operating leases. Examples of such leases may be those involving facilities at ports and bus terminals. The FASB specifies the conditions that must apply to meet this guidance. What are those conditions?

Room for Debate

- ## Debate 13-1 Operating versus Capital Leases

Under *SFAS No. 13,* leases that do not meet one of the four criteria for a capital lease are treated as operating leases.

Team Debate:

Team 1:   Argue for the capitalization of leases that do not meet any of the *SFAS No. 13* criteria for a capital lease. Your argument should take into consideration the conceptual framework definitions of assets and liabilities.

Team 2: Argue against the capitalization of leases that do not meet any of the *SFAS No. 13* criteria for a capital lease. Your argument should take into consideration the matching principle and full disclosure.

• Debate 13-2 Lease Accounting Symmetry

An objective of *SFAS No. 13* is that lessors and lessees should account for leases similarly.

Team Debate:

Team 1: Argue that a lessee should be able to account for a lease as operating leases while lessors may treat the same lease as a sales-type lease.

Team 2: Argue that if the lessor accounts for a lease as a sales-type lease, the lessee should similarly account for the lease as a capital lease.

CHAPTER
14

Pensions and Other

Postretirement

Benefits

For many years, employers have been concerned with providing for the retirement needs of their workforce. This concern resulted in the adoption of pension plans on a massive scale after World War II. Generally, companies provide for pension benefits by making periodic payments to an outside *funding agency*. The agency then assumes responsibility for investing the pension funds and making periodic benefit payments to the recipients.

The two most frequently encountered types of pension plans are defined contribution plans and defined benefit plans. A *defined contribution plan* sets forth a certain amount that the employer is to contribute to the plan each period. For example, the plan may require the employer to contribute 8 percent of the employee's salary each year. However, the plan makes no promises concerning the ultimate benefits to be paid. The retirement benefits actually received by the recipients are determined by the return earned on the invested pension funds during the investment period.

The terms of a *defined benefit plan* specify the amount of pension benefits to be paid out to plan recipients in the future. For example, the retirement plan of a company may promise that an employee retiring at age 65 will receive 2 percent of the average of the highest five years' salary for every year of service. An employee working for this company for 30 years will receive a pension for life equal to 60 percent of the average of his or her highest five salary years. Companies that provide defined benefit pension plans must make sufficient contributions to the funding agency in order to meet benefit requirements when they come due. Although no specific amount is required to be funded each period, the Employee Retirement Income Security Act (ERISA) does impose minimum funding requirements on these plans.

Accounting for defined contribution plans is relatively straightforward. Since the risk for future benefits is borne by the employee, the employer's only cash outflow is the annual contribution to the pension plan fund. Thus periodic pension expense is equal to the amount of promised annual contribution. When a company adopts a defined contribution pension plan, the employer's financial statements should disclose the existence of the plan, the employee groups covered, the basis for determining contributions, and any significant matters affecting comparability from period to period (such as amendments increasing the annual contribution percentage).

On the other hand, accounting for defined benefit plans is much more complex. In these plans, the pension benefits to be received in the future are affected by uncertain variables such as turnover, mortality, length of employee service, compensation levels, and earnings on the pension fund assets. In defined benefit plans, the risks are borne by employers because they must make large enough contributions to meet the pension benefits promised. As a result, the amount of periodic pension expense incurred may not be equal to the cash contributed to the plan.

This issue took on added prominence in the early 2000s. The combination of poor equity markets and low interest rates severely crimped the investment returns of pension plans, causing deterioration in their funded status as pension assets dropped in value while pension obligations remained the same or even increased. Up to 2004, companies were required to fund their plans by a formula that resulted in a cost of up to 120 percent of the weighted average of the 30-year Treasury bond yield. The Treasury Department discontinued the bond in 2001, causing a sharp drop in the bond's rate and artificially inflating pension liabilities. Subsequently, about 20 percent of companies with defined benefit pension plans—the total is now about 32,500—either froze or canceled their plans from 2001 through 2003 because of the costs.[1] In 2004, congressional legislation replaced the Treasury bond index with another index linked to the yield on corporate bonds for a two-year period. During those two years, Congress was to decide whether the new measure should be made permanent or be replaced by another. The subsequent enactment of the Pension Protection Act of 2006 allows long-term funding of underfunded plans by providing a new interest rate assumption based on a modified yield curve formula.[2]

The 2008 credit crisis and stock market crash further exacerbated the problem. The *Wall Street Journal* reported that pension plans at S&P 500 companies suffered large losses during the year, raising the likelihood that corporations will have to make large unplanned cash contributions over the next few years even as global economic growth could reduce profits.[3] The Pension Protection Act of 2006 requires companies to fully fund their pension plans by 2013, which means any company that was short of that goal had five years to close the gap.

Since the future pension benefits are affected by uncertain variables and government actions such as the Pension Protection Act of 2006, employers hire

---

1. Jim Abrams, Associated Press, "House OKs Short-Term Pension Crisis Plan," WashingtonPost.com (October 9, 2003).

2. U.S. Chamber of Commerce, "Defined Benefit Pension Plans," http://www. uschamger.com/issues/index/retirmentpension/definedpension.htm.

3. M. Andrejczak, "Stock Losses Take Heavy Toll on Pension Plans," MarketWatch, *Wall Street Journal* (Oct. 22, 2008), http://www.marketwatch.com/story/stock-market-losses-take-heavy-toll-on-pension-plans.

actuaries to help determine the amount of periodic contributions necessary to satisfy future requirements. The actuary takes into consideration the future benefits promised and the characteristics of the employee group (such as age and sex). He or she makes assumptions about such factors as employee turnover, future salary levels, and the earnings rate on the funds invested and then arrives at the present value of the expected benefits to be received in the future. The employer then determines the funding pattern necessary to satisfy the future obligation.

The employer's actuarial funding method may be either a cost approach or a benefit approach. A *cost approach* estimates the total retirement benefits to be paid in the future and then determines the equal annual payment that will be necessary to fund those benefits. The annual payment necessary is adjusted for the amount of interest assumed to be earned by funds contributed to the plan.

A *benefit approach* determines the amount of pension benefits earned by employee service to date and then estimates the present value of those benefits. Two benefit approaches may be used: (1) the accumulated benefits approach and (2) the benefits/years of service approach. The major difference between these two methods is that under the *accumulated benefits approach*, the annual pension cost and liability are based on existing salary levels, whereas under the *benefits/years of service approach* (also called the *projected unit credit method*), the annual pension cost and liability are based on the estimated final pay at retirement. The liability for pension benefits under the accumulated benefits approach is termed the *accumulated benefits obligation*. The liability computed under the benefits/years of service approach is termed the *projected benefit obligation*.

Even though the actuarial funding approaches have been defined, accounting for the cost of pension plans has caused a great deal of controversy over the years, and several authoritative pronouncements have been issued. In the following sections, we trace the evolution of pension accounting standards.

Historical Perspective

The rapidly increasing number of pension plans adopted by companies immediately after World War II caused accountants to question the treatment of accounting for pension costs. A major concern was that many new pension plans gave employees credit for their years of service before adoption of the plan. The point at issue was the most appropriate treatment of costs associated with this past service. In *Accounting Research Bulletin No. 47*, "Accounting for Costs of Pension Plans" (superseded), the Committee on Accounting Procedure expressed its preference that costs based on current and future service be systematically accrued during the expected period of active service of the covered employees and that costs based on past services be charged off over some reasonable period. The allocation of past service cost was to be made on a systematic and rational basis and was not to cause distortion of the operating results in any one year.

Later, the APB observed that despite *ARB No. 47*, accounting for the cost of pension plans was inconsistent from year to year, both among companies and within a single company. Sometimes the cost charged to operations was equal to the amount paid into the fund during a given year; at other times, no actual funding occurred. Moreover, the amortization of past service cost ranged up to 40 years.

Accounting inconsistencies and the growing importance of pension plan costs prompted the APB to authorize *Accounting Research Study No. 8*, "Accounting for the Cost of Pension Plans." This study was published in 1965, and, after careful examination of its recommendations, the APB issued *Opinion No. 8*, "Accounting for the Cost of Pension Plans" (superseded), in 1966. Since the conclusions of the APB were generally similar to those of the research study, we review only the opinion here.

APB Opinion No. 8

APB Opinion No. 8 identified basic problems associated with accounting for the cost of defined benefit pension plans as (1) measuring the total amount of costs associated with a pension plan, (2) allocating the total pension costs to the proper accounting periods, (3) providing the cash to fund the pension plan, and (4) disclosing the significant aspects of the pension plan on the financial statements.

The APB's conclusions concerning these questions were based to a large extent on two basic beliefs or assumptions. First, the Board believed that most companies will continue the benefits called for in a pension plan even if the plan is not fully funded year to year. Therefore the cost should be recognized annually whether or not the plan is funded. Second, the Board adopted the view that the cost of all past service should be charged against income after the adoption or amendment of a plan and that no portion of such cost should be charged directly to retained earnings. In *APB Opinion No. 8*, several issues were addressed, and various terms were introduced. In the following paragraphs we examine these issues and terms as originally defined by the APB. However, it should be noted that subsequent pronouncements have modified these definitions and/or changed the terminology.

Normal Cost

The current expense provision of pension cost was termed *normal cost* in *APB Opinion No. 8*. This was the amount required to be expensed each year, based on the current number of employees and the actuarial cost method being used. As noted earlier, the actuarial cost method must take into consideration such factors as employee turnover, mortality, and the treatment of actuarial gains and losses. However, the APB did not specify which actuarial cost method to use.

Past Service Cost

When a pension plan is adopted, the employees are usually given credit for previous years of service. These benefits were referred to as *past service cost* and were to be charged to expense in current and future periods. Past service cost was calculated by determining the present value of the amount of future benefits accruing to the current employee group. Before *APB Opinion No. 8* was issued, many companies charged past service costs against retained earnings as prior period adjustments. This policy was based on the theory that the benefits of employee service had been obtained in prior periods; therefore, the cost associated with those benefits should be charged to previous periods. *APB Opinion No. 8* eliminated this treatment of past service costs, and later pronouncements concurred.

Prior Service Cost

Prior service costs were pension costs assigned to years preceding the date of a particular actuarial valuation. Prior service cost arose as a result of an amendment to the original pension agreement or changes in the actuarial assumptions of the pension plan. When the pension agreement is amended or the underlying assumptions change, it becomes necessary to recalculate the expected future benefits accruing to the current employee group. This calculation is similar to the determination of past service cost.

Actuarial Gains and Losses

The pension cost for any period is based on several assumptions. These assumptions frequently do not coincide with actual results. It is therefore necessary to make periodic adjustments so that actual experience is recognized in the recorded amount of pension expense. Under *APB Opinion No. 8*, periodic pension expense included normal cost and amortization of past and prior service costs. These costs were estimated based on actuarial assumptions. If in a subsequent period, the actuary revised his or her assumptions based on new information, a periodic adjustment would be required. *APB Opinion No. 8* termed the deviations between the actuarial assumptions and subsequent changes in assumptions due to actual experience *actuarial gains and losses*.

The amount of any actuarial gain or loss was to be recognized over current and future periods by one of two acceptable methods:

1. *Spreading.* The net actuarial gains and losses were applied to current and future costs through an adjustment to either normal cost or past service cost each year.

2. *Averaging.* An average of the sum of previously expensed annual actuarial gains and losses and expected future actuarial gains and losses was applied to normal cost.

Basic Accounting Method

Before *APB Opinion No. 8* was issued, the Board could not completely agree on the most appropriate measure of cost to be included in each period. Consequently, it was decided that annual cost should be measured by an acceptable actuarial cost method, consistently applied, that produces an amount between a specified minimum and maximum. (In this context, an acceptable actuarial cost method should be rational and systematic and should be consistently applied so that the cost is reasonably stable from year to year.)

The minimum annual provision for pension cost could not be less than the total of:

1. Normal cost (cost associated with the years after the date of adoption or amendment of the plan)

2. An amount equivalent to interest on any unfunded past or prior service cost

3. If indicated, a provision for vested benefits (benefits that are not contingent on the employee continuing in the service of the company)

The maximum annual provision for pension cost could not be more than the total of:

1. Normal cost

2. Ten percent of the past service cost (until fully amortized)

3. Ten percent of the amounts of any increase or decrease in prior service cost arising from amendments of the plan (until fully amortized)

4. Interest equivalents on the difference between pension costs and amounts funded

The Board's disagreement revolved around two differing viewpoints regarding the nature of pension cost. One view held that pensions are a means of promoting efficiency by (1) providing for the systematic retirement of older people and (2) fulfilling a social obligation expected of a business enterprise. Accordingly, pension costs are associated with the plan itself rather than specific employees, and the amount of pension expense is the amount that must be contributed annually to keep the plan in existence indefinitely. The alternative view was that pensions are a form of supplement benefit to the current employee group, so that the amount of pension expense in any period is related to specific employees. This view is rooted in labor economics and is based on the theory that employees contract for wages based on their marginal revenue product. Thus a pension represents payments during retirement of deferred wages that were earned during each year of employment, and the amount of pension expense is established by determining the benefits expected to become payable to specific employees in the future. Under either view, annual pension expense would include normal costs. However, only the second view would include past and prior service costs in the determination of annual pension cost.

By requiring the specified minimum and maximum provisions, *APB Opinion No. 8* did narrow the range of practices previously employed in determining the annual provision of pension cost. However, it should be noted that these minimum and maximum provisions were arbitrarily determined. Thus the only theoretical justification for their use was a higher degree of uniformity. In addition, the Board decided that only the difference between the amount charged against income and the amount funded should be shown in the balance sheet as accrued or prepaid pension cost. The unamortized and unfunded past and prior service cost was not considered to be a liability by the Board and was not required to be disclosed on the balance sheet. This decision caused a great deal of controversy and resulted in many debates among accountants over the proper amount of future pension costs to be disclosed on financial statements.

The Pension Liability Issue

In 1981, the FASB proposed a significant change in the method to account for pension cost. The Board enumerated several reasons for this proposed change. First, the number of pension plans had grown enormously since the issuance of *APB Opinion No. 8* in 1966. A research study performed by Coopers & Lybrand indicated there were 500,000 private pension plans in the United States in 1979, and total plan assets exceeded $320 billion. Also affecting pension plans were significant changes in laws, regulations, and economic factors, not the least of which was double-digit inflation.

Second, the Board contended that pension information was inadequate, despite the increased disclosures mandated by *SFAS No. 36* (discussed later in the chapter). Finally, the flexibility of permitted actuarial methods resulted in a lack of comparability among reporting companies, according to some financial statement users.

The basic issues involved in the FASB's proposal, titled "Preliminary Views," were as follows:

1. Over what period should the cost of pensions be recognized? In 1981, pension costs could be recognized over a period of 30 to 40 years, which is generally longer than the current workforce is expected to continue working.

2. How should pension costs be spread among or allocated to the individual periods? The basic question here was whether the practice of choosing among a variety of acceptable costs and funding methods met the needs of financial statement users.

3. Should information about the status of pensions be included in the statement of changes in financial position? This was undoubtedly the most controversial of the issues considered.

The positions taken in the FASB's "Preliminary Views" would have required an employer sponsoring a defined benefit pension plan to recognize a net pension liability (or asset) on its balance sheet. This disclosure would have comprised the following three components: *the pension benefit obligation* less *the plan's net assets available for benefits* plus or minus *a measurement valuation allowance*. This calculation of pension cost coincides with the view that pension expense should be recognized in the period in which the employees render their services. This view is consistent with the matching principle.

One organization that opposed the position of the "Preliminary View" was the AICPA task force on pension plans and pension costs. This group's opposition was expressed in several general areas:

1. The amounts involved did not meet the definition of assets or liabilities under *SFAC No. 3* (now *SFAC No. 6*).

2. A pension arrangement is essentially an executory contract that under existing GAAP is accounted for only as the covered services are performed.

3. Too much subjectivity is involved in determining the amount of the net pension liability—that is, the number is too "soft" to be reported in basic financial statements.

4. The FASB had not demonstrated the need to amend *APB Opinion No. 8* extensively.

Despite this opposition, the FASB remained steadfast in its determination to change previous pension accounting methods. Under the method originally advocated in "Preliminary Views," the pension benefit obligation would have comprised an accrual for benefits earned by the employees but not yet paid, including prior service credits granted when a plan is initiated or amended. The obligation would include both vested and nonvested benefits and would be measured based on estimates of future compensation levels.

The proposed measure of the pension benefit obligation was called the *actuarial present value of accumulated benefits with salary progression*. As a result, the proposed method would have required a forecast of salary growth for pension plans that defines benefits in terms of an employee's future salary. Since most sponsors use financial pay plans, the salary growth assumption would result in pension benefit obligations larger than those previously being reported.

On the other hand, if plan assets exceeded the benefit obligation, a company would report a net pension asset on its balance sheet. The plan's investment assets available for benefits would be measured at fair value, consistent with *SFAS No. 35*, "Accounting and Reporting for Defined Benefit Pension Plans."[4]

The third component of the net pension liability was to be the measurement valuation allowance. This component was intended to reduce the volatility of the net pension liability inherent in the prediction of events, such as future changes in the pension benefit obligation and the plan assets, due to experience gains and losses or changes in actuarial assumptions.

Under "Preliminary Views," the amount of annual pension expense that an employer would recognize would have been the sum of four factors:

1. The increase in the pension benefit obligation attributable to employee service during the period (conceptually similar to "normal cost").

2. The increase in the pension benefit obligation attributable to the accrual of interest on the obligation (because the obligation is the discounted present value of estimated future payments).

3. The increase in plan assets resulting from earnings on the assets at the assumed rate (reducing the periodic pension expense).

4. The amortization of the measurement valuation allowance, which may either increase or decrease the pension expense. Actuarial gains or losses would be included in the measurement of the valuation allowance.

SFAS No. 87

After deliberating the issues addressed in "Preliminary Views" for several years, the FASB reached a consensus in 1985 and issued *SFAS No. 87*, "Employers' Accounting for Pensions" (see FASB ASC 715). This release was the product of compromises and resulted in several differences from the FASB's original position expressed in "Preliminary Views." *SFAS No. 87* maintained that pension information should be prepared on the accrual basis and retained three fundamental aspects of past pension accounting: (1) delaying recognition of certain events, (2) reporting net cost, and (3) offsetting assets and liabilities.

The delayed-recognition feature results in systematic recognition of changes in the pension obligation (such as plan amendments). It also results in changes in the values of assets set aside to meet those obligations.

The net cost feature results in reporting, as a single amount, the recognized consequences of the events that affected the pension plan. Three items are aggregated to arrive at this amount: (1) the annual cost of the benefits promised, (2) the interest cost resulting from the deferred payment of those benefits, and (3) the result of investing the pension assets.

Offsetting means that the value of the assets contributed to a pension plan and the liabilities recognized as pension cost in previous periods are disclosed as a single net amount in the employer's financial statements.

---

4. In 1980 the FASB issued *SFAS No. 35*, which required companies to disclose the actuarial present value of accumulated plan benefits and the pension plan assets available for those benefits. This pronouncement was later superseded by *SFAS No. 87*.

The FASB members expressed the view that the understandability, comparability, and usefulness of pension information would be improved by narrowing the range of methods available for allocating the cost of an employee's pension to individual periods of service. The Board also stated that the pension plan's benefit formula provides the most relevant and reliable indicator of how pension costs and pension benefits are incurred. Therefore *SFAS No. 87* required three changes in previous pension accounting:

1. A standardized method of measuring net pension cost. The Board indicated that requiring all companies with defined benefit plans to measure net period pension cost, taking into consideration the plan formula and the service period, would improve comparability and understandability.

2. Immediate recognition of a pension liability when the accumulated benefit obligation exceeds the fair value of the pension assets. The accumulated benefit obligation is calculated using present salary levels. Because salary levels generally rise, the amount of the unfunded accumulated benefit obligation represents a conservative floor for the present obligation for future benefits already earned by the employees.

3. Expanded disclosures intended to provide more complete and current information than can be practically incorporated into the financial statements at this time.

Pension Cost

Under the guidelines of FASB ASC 715, the components of net pension cost reflect different aspects of the benefits earned by employees and the method of financing those benefits by the employer. The following components are required to be included in the net pension cost recognized by an employer sponsoring a defined benefit pension plan:

1. Service cost

2. Interest cost

3. Return on plan assets

4. Amortization of unrecognized prior service cost

5. Amortization of gains and losses

6. Amortization of the unrecognized net obligation or unrecognized net asset at the date of the initial application of *SFAS No. 87* (the transition amount)

The *service cost* component is the actuarial present value of the benefits attributed by the pension formula to employee service for that period. This requirement means that one of the benefit approaches discussed earlier must be used as the basis for assigning pension cost to an accounting period. It also means that the benefits/years of service approach should be used to calculate pension cost for all plans that use this benefit approach in calculating earned pension benefits. The FASB position is that the terms of the agreement should form the basis for recording the expense and obligation, and the plan's benefit formula is the best measure of the amount of cost incurred each period. The discount rate to be used in calculating service cost is the rate at which the pension benefits could be settled, such as by purchasing annuity contracts from an insurance company. This rate is termed the *settlement-basis discount rate*.

The *interest cost* component is the increase in the projected benefit obligation due to the passage of time. Recall that the pension liability is calculated on a discounted basis and accrues interest each year. The interest cost component is determined by accruing interest on the previous year's pension liability at the settlement-basis discount rate.

The *return on plan assets* component is the difference between the fair value of these assets from the beginning to the end of the period, adjusted for contributions, benefits, and payments. That is, the interest and dividends earned on the funds actually contributed to the pension fund, combined with changes in the market value of invested assets, will reduce the amount of net pension cost for the period. *SFAS No. 87* allows the use of either the actual return or the expected return on plan assets when calculating this component of pension expense.

Prior service cost is the total cost of retroactive benefits at the date the pension plan is initiated or amended. Prior service cost is assigned to the expected remaining service period of each employee expected to receive benefits. (As a practical matter, the FASB allows for a simplified method of assigning this cost to future periods; the company may assign this cost on a straight-line basis over the average remaining service life of its active employees.)

Gains and losses include *actuarial* gains and losses or *experience* gains and losses. Actuarial gains and losses occur when the actuary changes assumptions, resulting in a change in the projected benefit obligation. For example, if the actuary increases the discount rate, the beginning projected benefit obligation is reduced. This means that prior expense recognition for interest, service cost, and prior service cost was overstated. Thus the amount of the change in the beginning projected benefit obligation is an actuarial gain. Experience gains and losses occur when net pension cost includes the expected, rather than the actual, return on plan assets. The expected return presumes that plan assets will grow to a particular amount by the end of the period. If, for example, the actual return is greater than expected, future pension costs will be defrayed further and an experience gain takes place. The FASB ASC 715 guidelines contain a minimum requirement for the recognition of these gains and losses. At a minimum, the amount of gain or loss to be amortized in a given period is the amount by which the cumulative unamortized gains and losses exceed what the pronouncement termed the *corridor*. The corridor is defined as 10 percent of the greater of the projected benefit obligation or market value of the plan assets. The excess, if any, is divided by the average remaining service period of employees expected to receive benefits. The rationale using the corridor approach is that typically these gains and losses are random errors and should have an expected value of zero. That is, over time, actuarial gains and losses should offset each other. Only extreme values are required to be recognized. The corridor procedure is similar to statistical procedures that are designed to identify outliers.

SFAS No. 87 required significant changes in pension accounting from what was previously required in *APB Opinion No. 8*. As a result, the Board decided to allow for a relatively long transition period. Most companies were not required to follow the provisions of *SFAS No. 87* until the 1987 calendar year. In addition, the minimum liability provision (discussed in the next section) was not required to be reported until calendar year 1989. Since these changes were so significant, an *unrecognized net obligation* or *unrecognized net asset* frequently resulted when changing to the new reporting requirements. Therefore, the provisions of *SFAS No. 87* required companies to determine, on the date the provisions of this statement were first applied, the amount of (1) the projected benefit obligation and (2) the fair value of the plan assets. This resulted in either an unrecognized net obligation or an unrecognized net asset. This amount, termed the *transition amount*, was to be amortized on a straight-line basis over the average remaining service period of employees expecting to receive benefits.

Minimum Liability Recognition

Unlike other expenses that are recognized in the income statement, periodic pension cost is not tied to changes in balance sheet accounts. The FASB ASC 715 guidelines require amortization of prior service cost, gains and losses, and the transition amount, but the unamortized amounts for these items are not recorded. Hence, the *funded status* of the plan (the difference between the projected benefit obligation and the fair value of plan assets) is not recognized in the accounting records. Recall that the FASB's original position on this issue, expressed in "Preliminary Views," was that a liability exists when the projected benefit obligation exceeds the plan assets (i.e., the plan is underfunded) or that an asset exists when the reverse is true. Since agreement on this issue could not be reached, the Board developed a compromise position that requires recognition of a liability, termed the *minimum liability*, when the accumulated benefit obligation exceeds the fair value of the plan assets. Thus, even though future salary levels are used to calculate pension expense, the liability reported on the balance sheet need take into consideration only present salary levels. The result is that the balance sheet and income statements are not articulated a condition that is contrary to the conceptual framework.

The portion of the underfunded pension obligation that is not already recognized in the accounting records occurs because the company has unamortized prior service cost or unamortized gains and losses. Because the minimum liability is based on current salary levels and is therefore likely to be less than the underfunded projected benefit obligation, total unamortized prior service cost and unamortized gains and losses are likely to exceed the amount needed to increase the pension liability to the minimum required. The FASB ASC 715 guidelines require that when an additional liability is recognized to meet the minimum liability requirement, the offsetting debit is to be allocated first to an intangible asset for the unamortized prior service cost. The remainder, if any, is due to unamortized net losses and is reported as an element of other comprehensive income. The minimum liability is reassessed at the end of each accounting period, and necessary adjustments are made directly to the intangible asset or stockholders' equity.

Disclosures

The FASB ASC 715 guidelines require employers to disclose information beyond that previously required. Perhaps the most significant of these added disclosures are the components of net pension cost and the funding status of the plan. Specifically, employers sponsoring defined benefit plans must disclose the following information:

1. A description of the plan, including employee groups covered, type of benefit formula, funding policy, types of assets held, significant non-benefit liabilities (if any), and the nature and effect of significant matters affecting comparability of information for all periods presented

2. The amount of net periodic pension cost for the period showing separately the service cost component, the interest cost component, the actual return on assets for the period, and the net total of other components

3. A schedule reconciling the funded status of the plan with amounts reported in the employer's statement of financial position, showing separately:

   a. The fair value of plan assets

   b. The projected benefit obligation identifying the accumulated benefit obligation and the vested benefit obligation

   c. The amount of unrecognized prior service cost

   d. The amount of unrecognized prior net gain or loss

   e. The amount of any remaining unrecognized transition amount

   f. The amount of any additional liability recognized

   g. The amount of net pension asset or liability recognized in the statement of financial positions (This is the net result of combining the preceding six items.)

   h. The weighted average assumed discount rate and the weighted average expected long-term rate of return on plan assets

The annual pension cost reported by corporations under the FASB ASC 715 guidelines will usually be different from the cost previously disclosed under the provisions of *APB Opinion No. 8*. The magnitude of these differences depends on such factors as the pension plan's benefit formula, employees' remaining service periods, investment returns, and prior accounting and funding policies. Companies that have underfunded pension plans with a relatively short future employee service period may be required to report significantly higher pension expense.

When SFAS No. 87 was released, the Board stated that the pronouncement was a continuation of its evolutionary search for more meaningful and more useful pension accounting information. The Board also stated that while it believes that the conclusions it reached are a worthwhile and significant step in that direction, these conclusions are not likely to be the final step in the evolution.

SFAS No. 87 —Theoretical Issues

The issuance of *SFAS No. 87* (see FASB ASC 715) may have created as many issues as it resolved. Criticism of the pronouncement has been directed at the projected benefits approach, use of the settlement rate to discount projected benefits, allowing alternative measures of return, and the minimum liability requirement.

Projected Benefits Approach

When the benefit formula uses future salary levels, The FASB ASC 715 guidelines require that service cost and the employer's present obligation for future benefits earned to date be measured using projected future salary levels. This measurement can be defended on the basis that employees contract for retirement benefits. These benefits are earned while the employee works; thus, matching would dictate that they be an accrued expense. Also, the projected benefit obligation represents a present obligation to pay the future benefits that employees have already earned. Thus the projected benefit obligation qualifies as a liability under *SFAC No. 6*.

Critics contend that the projected obligation implies that the benefits earned to date will be paid. This is true only for those employees who have vested benefits or who will remain employees until the benefits do vest. Some feel that only vested benefits should be considered a present liability because vested benefits are the only portion that the company has a present legal obligation to pay if the plan were terminated. Others feel that the accumulated benefits approach provides the more appropriate measure because it is a conservative estimate of the present obligation for future benefits and would be the amount that the employer would set aside if the plan were terminated and the employer wanted to provide for all employees who were vested and might vest in the future. Moreover, the accumulated benefits approach does not require subjective projections of future salary levels. At the other extreme, some feel that the projected benefits approach understates the present liability because it does not take into consideration projected years of service.

The Settlement Rate

The FASB ASC 715 guidelines require that the actuarially determined projected benefit obligation be calculated using a discount rate at which the plan could be effectively settled. For example, the rate at which the company could currently obtain an annuity contract to provide the projected future benefits would be an appropriate settlement rate. The FASB felt that the actuary's rate should not be affected by the return expected on funded assets. The projected benefit obligation is a liability. The discount rate selected is chosen to measure the liability and has nothing to do with how the assets that are set aside to satisfy that liability are invested.

Opponents argue that the settlement rate is a short-term current rate and that the pension obligation is not going to be settled currently; rather, it is a long-term phenomenon. The settlement rates fluctuate from period to period, resulting in volatile measures of the projected benefit obligation, service cost, and interest. Some agree with the FASB that the discount rate used need not be the expected return on plan assets but argue that it should be based on a more long-run measure of typical pension fund asset returns over time. Others contend that the fund provides the means by which the company will settle the pension obligation, and thus the return on the plan assets is the relevant rate at which to discount projected benefits.

Return on Plan Assets

The FASB ASC 715 guidelines require that net pension cost include the actual return, or that the actual return be adjusted to the expected return. Allowing these two alternatives represents a compromise. The FASB favors including the actual return. For the most part, the actual return is a realized return. Furthermore, recognition of the actual return is consistent with the comprehensive income concept. Nevertheless, the Board's preference for measuring the return component was criticized because it would produce volatile measures of pension expense from period to period. The FASB conceded by allowing the expected return to be included, instead using the expected rate of return on plan assets applied to the market-related asset value of the plan assets. The market-related asset value is a long-term measure of asset value. Hence, the expected return should allow the smoothing of net periodic pension cost. At the same time, allowing the minimum amortization of actuarial and experience gains and losses should provide further assurance of a smoother, less volatile periodic pension expense.

Reporting the Minimum Liability

One aim of the FASB ASC 715 guidelines is to report the net pension obligation on the balance sheet. However, for many companies, reporting the net obligation measured using projected benefits would dramatically affect total liabilities and debt-to-equity ratios. Moreover, some contended that the projected benefit obligation overstates the pension liability because it does not represent the legal liability or the most likely settlement amount. The Board acquiesced to the concerns and opted for a minimum liability measurement based on the more conservative accumulated benefit obligation. This requirement has been superseded by *SFAS No. 158* (see FASB ASC 715), discussed later in the chapter.

If the projected benefit obligation provides the more appropriate measure, then reporting the minimum liability understates liabilities. Furthermore, it is inconsistent with the measurement of periodic pension expense, which is measured using projected benefits. Such an inconsistency perpetuates the criticism regarding pension reporting under *APB Opinion No. 8*, that pension accounting is contrary to the fundamental notion that the financial statements should be articulated. Empirical research has demonstrated that pension obligations are considered liabilities, but to date there is no conclusive evidence that the market perceives one method of measuring the obligation or pension expense to be better than another.[5]

Accounting for the Pension Fund

Until 1980, accounting practice often relied on the actuary's funding and cash-flow considerations for measuring pension costs and accumulated pension benefits. At that time, *APB Opinion No. 8* stated that accounting for pension expense and related liabilities was separate and distinct from actuarial costing for funding purposes. However, according to *SFAS No. 35*, "Accounting and Reporting by Defined Benefit Pension Plans" (see FASB ASC 960), the status of plans for financial reporting purposes is to be determined by actuarial methodology designed not for funding purposes but rather for financial reporting purposes.

Neither the FASB nor its predecessors had issued authoritative accounting standards specifically applicable to pension plans. Therefore the financial reporting by those plans varied widely. FASB ASC 960 establishes accounting and reporting standards designed to correct this shortcoming.

The primary objective of the FASB ASC 960 guidelines is to provide financial information that is useful in assessing a pension plan's current and future ability to pay benefits when due. In attempting to accomplish this objective, the FASB ASC 960 guidelines require that pension plan financial statements include four basic categories of information:

1. Net assets available for benefits
2. Changes in net assets during the reporting period
3. The actuarial present value of accumulated plan benefits

---

5. See, for example, W. Landsman, "An Empirical Investigation of Pension Fund Property Rights," *Accounting Review* (October 1986): 662–91; and D. S. Dhaliwal, "Measurement of Financial Leverage in the Presence of Unfunded Pension Obligations," *The Accounting Review* (October 1986): 651–61.

4. The significant effects of factors such as plan amendments and changes in actuarial assumptions on the year-to-year change in the actuarial present value of accumulated plan benefits

Information about net assets must be available for plan benefits at the end of the plan year and must be prepared using the accrual basis of accounting.

The FASB ASC 960 guidelines also set standards for information regarding participants' accumulated plan benefits. Accumulated plan benefits are defined as those future benefit payments attributable under the plan's provisions to employees' service rendered to date. Information about accumulated benefits may be presented at either the beginning or the end of the plan year. Accumulated plan benefits are to be measured at their actuarial present value, based primarily on history of pay and service and other appropriate factors.

The Employee Retirement Income Security Act

In 1974, Congress passed the Employee Retirement Income Security Act (ERISA), also known as the Pension Reform Act of 1974. The basic goals of this legislation were to create standards for the operation of pension funds and to correct abuses in the handling of pension funds.

ERISA establishes guidelines for employee participation in pension plans, vesting provisions, minimum funding requirements, financial statement disclosure of pension plans, and the administration of the pension plan. Shortly thereafter, the FASB undertook a study of the impact of ERISA on accounting for pension costs«Xtags error: Missing font». The conclusions of this study were originally contained in *FASB Interpretation No. 3*, which was superseded by *SFAS No. 87* (see FASB ASC 715). In essence, *FASB Interpretation No. 3* stated that ERISA is concerned with pension funding requirements and that accounting for pension costs was not affected by ERISA. The provisions of FASB ASC 715 are also not affected by ERISA. Accounting standards for pension costs are concerned with periodic expense and liability recognition, whereas the provisions of ERISA are concerned mainly with the funding policies of pension plans.

Other Postretirement Benefits

The issue of other postretirement benefits is addressed in *SFAS No. 106*, "Employers' Accounting for Postretirement Benefits Other than Pensions"[6] (see FASB ASC 715). This pronouncement dealt with the accounting for all benefits, other than pension benefits, offered to retired employees; these benefits are commonly referred to as other postretirement benefits (OPRB). Although its provisions apply to a wide variety of postretirement benefits—such as tuition assistance, day care, legal services, and housing subsidies—the most significant OPRBs are retiree health-care benefits and life insurance. Based on the notion that management promises OPRBs in exchange for current services, the Board felt that OPRBs are similar to defined benefit pension plans and as such deserve similar treatment. Consequently, the FASB ASC 715 guidelines require that the cost of OPRBs be accrued over the

---

6. Financial Accounting Standards Board, *Statement of Financial Accounting Standards No. 106*, "Employers' Accounting for Postretirement Benefits Other than Pensions" (Stamford, CT: FASB, 1990).

working lives of the employees expected to receive them. However, due to the controversial nature surrounding measurement and reporting issues related to the employer's obligation for OPRBs, the Board decided not to require minimum liability balance sheet disclosure.

Although on the surface OPRBs are similar to defined benefit pension plans, they have characteristics that necessitate different accounting considerations and that have been the source of considerable controversy:

1. Defined benefit pension payments are determined by formula, whereas the future cash outlays for OPRBs depend on the amount of services, such as medical care, that the employees will eventually receive. Unlike pension plan payments, there is no "cap" on the amount of benefits to be paid to participants. Hence, the future cash flows associated with OPRBs are much more difficult to predict.

2. Unlike defined pension benefits, additional OPRB benefits cannot be accumulated by employees OPRB with each year of service.

3. OPRBs do not vest. That is, employees who leave have no further claim to future benefits. Employees have no statutory right to vested health-care benefits. Defined benefits are covered by stringent minimum vesting, participation, and funding standards, and they are insured by the Pension Benefit Guaranty Corporation under ERISA. Health and other OPRBs are explicitly excluded from ERISA.

The FASB ASC 715 guidelines stipulate that periodic postretirement benefit expenses comprise the same six components as pension expense. Nevertheless, there are measurement differences due to the foregoing differences between the characteristics of OPRBs and those of defined benefit pension plans. The determination of the return on assets and the amortization of gains and losses for OPRBs and defined benefit pension plans are the same. We concentrate on those components that are treated differently.

Service Cost

The service cost component of net periodic pension cost is that portion of the ending projected benefit obligation attributable to employee service during the current period. The basis for computing OPRB *service cost* is the *expected postretirement benefit obligation* (EPBO), which is defined as the actuarial present value of the total benefits expected to be paid assuming full eligibility is achieved.[7] Measurements included in the calculation of the EPBO include estimated effects of medical cost, inflation, and the impact of technological advancements and future delivery patterns. The service cost component for OPRBs is the ratable portion of the EPBO attributable to employee service in the current period.

Interest

Interest is calculated by applying the discount rate by the *accumulated postretirement benefit obligation* (APBO). The APBO is that portion of the EPBO attributable to

---

7. FASB ASC 715-60-35-09.

employee service rendered to the measurement date. Once the employee is fully eligible to receive OPRB benefits, the APBO and the EPBO are equivalent.

Amortization of Prior Service Costs

For OPRBs, *prior service cost* is the increase in the APBO attributed to an increase in benefits to employee service rendered in prior periods. *SFAS No. 106* required that prior service cost be recognized over the life expectancy of the employees when most participants are fully eligible to receive benefits. If employees are not fully eligible, prior service cost is amortized to the date of full eligibility. OPRB gains on decreases in benefits are required to be offset against both unrecognized prior service cost and unrecognized transition obligations.

Amortization of the Transition Obligation

The transition obligation for other postretirement benefits is the difference between the APBO and the fair value of funded OPRB assets. The transition amount may be recognized immediately, or it may be amortized over the average remaining service lives of active participants. The employer may elect a minimum amortization period of 20 years. The amount of amortization allowed is constrained. The cumulative expense recognized as a result of electing to defer recognition of the transition amount may not exceed the cumulative expense that would occur on a pay-as-you-go basis.

Disclosure

The FASB ASC 715 guidelines require the disclosure of plan details, including the funding policy and amounts and types of funded assets, the components of net periodic cost, and a reconciliation of the funded status of the plan with amounts reported in the statement of financial position. Recognizing the sensitivity of the assumptions used to measure OPRB costs, the FASB ASC 715 guidelines also requires disclosure of the following information:

1. The assumed health-care cost trend rates used to measure the EPBO
2. The effects of a one-percentage-point increase in the assumed health-care cost trend rates

Postemployment Benefits

In addition to postretirement benefits, employers often provide benefits to employees who are inactive due to, for example, a layoff or disability, but not retired. *SFAS No. 112*, "Employers' Accounting for Postemployment Benefits" (see FASB ASC 712), indicated that these benefits are compensation for services rendered and as such should be accounted for as a contingency under the provisions of *SFAS No. 5*, "Accounting for Contingencies" (see FASB ASC 450). Hence, a loss contingency should be accrued when the payment of postemployment benefits is probable, the amount of the loss contingency can be reasonably estimated, the employer's obligation is attributable to employee services already rendered, and the employee's rights to postemployment benefits vest or accumulate.

SFAS No. 132

SFAS No. 132, "Employers' Disclosures about Pensions and Other Postretirement Benefits—An Amendment of FASB *Statements No. 87, 88*, and *106*" (see FASB ASC 715-20-50), standardizes the disclosure requirements for pensions and other post-retirement benefits, requires the disclosure of additional information on changes in the benefit obligation and fair value of plan assets in order to facilitate financial analysis, and eliminated certain other disclosure requirements contained in *SFAS Nos. 87, 88*, and *106*. The benefits to financial statement users include the disclosure of disaggregated information on the six components of periodic pension cost and other postretirement benefits and information on changes in the projected benefit obligation and plan assets. The statement suggests a combined format for the presentation of both pensions and other postretirement benefits.

SFAS No. 158

In 2005 the FASB, in conjunction with the IASB, added a two-phase review of accounting for pension plans to its agenda. The objective of the first phase was to address the fact that information about the financial status of a company's defined benefit pension plans (DBPP) and other postretirement benefits plans (OPBP) is reported in the notes to the financial statements but not in the balance sheet. The second phase of the project, which is to begin after completing the first phase, will comprehensively address a broad range of financial accounting and reporting issues in the area of postretirement benefits.

The FASB's phase one review revealed that existing standards on employers' accounting for DBPPs and OPRPs failed to communicate the funded status of those plans in a complete and understandable way. That is, the assets and liabilities of DBPPs and OPBPs were not disclosed on the benefit provider's balance sheet and were reported only in the footnotes. Specifically, current standards allowed an employer to:

1. Delay the recognition of events that affected the costs of providing postretirement benefits, such as changes in plan assets and benefit obligations, and recognize a liability that was sometimes significantly less than the underfunded status of the plan.

2. Recognize an asset in its statement of financial position, in some situations, for a plan that was underfunded.

3. GAAP also allowed for the deferral of actuarial gains and losses that have the potential to fluctuate significantly. Since the procedures outlined in *SFAS Nos. 87* and *106* were designed to smooth the amounts reported for pension plans, financial statements often reported an asset on the balance sheet, giving the impression the plan was overfunded when in fact a funding deficit was reported in the footnotes. The Board concluded that presenting this information in the footnotes made it more difficult for users of financial statements to assess an employer's financial position and ability to satisfy postretirement benefit obligations.

The FASB's phase one review of pension accounting resulted in *SFAS No. 158*, "Employers' Accounting for Defined Benefit Pension and Other Postretirement Plans—an Amendment of FASB *Statements No. 87, 88, 106*, and *132(R)*" (see FASB ASC 715-20-65). The FASB ASC 715-20-65 guidelines require recognition of the overfunded or underfunded status of a DBPP or OPBP as an asset or liability in a company's statement of financial position and to recognize changes in that funded status in the year in which the changes occur through comprehensive income. That is, a company is required to:

1. Recognize the funded status of a benefit plan in its statement of financial position. This amount is to be measured as the difference between plan assets at fair value and the projected benefit obligation

2. Recognize, as a component of other comprehensive income, the net of tax, the gains or losses, and the prior service costs or credits that arise during the period but were not recognized as components of net periodic benefit cost

3. Measure DBPP and OPBP assets and obligations as of the date of the benefit provider's fiscal year-end

4. Disclose in the notes to financial statements additional information about certain effects on net periodic benefit cost for the next fiscal year that arise from delayed recognition of the gains or losses, prior service costs or credits, and transition asset or obligation

These adjustments can result in a reduction of the book value of shareholder equity for many companies that have DBPPs or OPBPs. One study estimated a total reduction in shareholder equity at December, 31, 2006, of $217 billion, or approximately 6 percent.[8]

SFAS No. 158 completed phase one of FASB's two-stage project. It does not affect the income statement. Phase two of the project will reconsider all aspects of accounting for DBPPs or OPBPs, including the measurement of plan assets and plan obligations. In phase two the FASB is considering requiring companies to disclose the *gross* pension assets and gross liabilities on their balance sheets, whereas *SFAS No. 158* requires only disclosure of the *net* difference on the balance sheet at this time. The FASB is currently monitoring the work of the IASB (discussed below) to determine the next steps on the project.

The combined effects of the accounting standards for retirement benefits are to provide investors with additional information about the future cash flows associated with these retirement benefits. The individual components of periodic pension cost have been found to convey different amounts of information to financial statement users. Service cost, interest cost, and the expected return on plan assets have been found to provide information on a company's sustainable information, whereas the other components of pension cost were not found to provide significant additional information.[9] Similarly, the disclosure of the APBO for other postretirement benefits was found to be negatively correlated with the price of a company's stock.[10] However, the implementation of the accounting standard for

8. Merrill Lynch, Investment Strategy, "Market Impact of Pension Accounting Reform" (Oct. 4, 2006), http://rsch1.ml.com/9093/24013/ds/59512817.PDF.

9. M. E. Barth, W. H. Beaver, and W. R. Landsman, "The Market Value Implications of Net Periodic Pension Cost Components," *Journal of Accounting and Economics* (March 1992): 27–62.

10. B. Choi, D. W. Collins, and W. B. Johnson, "Valuation Implications of Reliability Differences: The Case of Non-Pension Postretirement Obligations," *The Accounting Review* (July 1997): 351–83.

postretirement benefits also has had economic consequences. Before that time, employers accounted for OPRBs on a pay-as-you-go basis, postponing any recognition of expense until the postretirement period. Due to the magnitude of these expenditures, particularly in light of rising health-care costs, requiring firms to change from a cash basis to an accrual basis would have had a major impact on financial reporting. A *Wall Street Journal* article described the new standard for accounting for OPRBs as "one of the most significant changes in accounting ever . . . that could cut corporate profits by hundreds of billions of dollars."[11] Because of the pronouncements, some have argued that these benefit provisions may cause management to curtail or even eliminate OPRBs—and in fact, that is what happened.[12] The reduction or elimination of OPRBs could significantly affect an individual's ability to finance future health and life insurance costs. Ultimately, it could also result in additional costs to the federal government, and therefore to the taxpayer, through increased Medicare payments.

Financial Analysis of Pension and Other Postretirement Benefits

The major analysis question concerning pensions and other postretirement benefits is whether they have been adequately funded. Several companies, such as US Airways, have faced reorganizations and even bankruptcy because their pension obligations have not been fully funded. Hershey has a defined benefit pension plan and offers an other postretirement benefit plan.

Disclosure of the information for pensions under the provisions of *SFAS Nos. 87, 132,* and *158* is extracted from the company's footnotes to the fiscal year 2008 financial statements.

> We sponsor a number of defined benefit pension plans. The primary plans are The Hershey Company Retirement Plan and The Hershey Company Retirement Plan for Hourly Employees. These are cash balance plans that provide pension benefits for most domestic employees hired prior to January 1, 2007. We monitor legislative and regulatory developments regarding cash balance plans, as well as recent court cases, for any impact on our plans. We also sponsor two primary postretirement benefit plans. The health care plan is contributory, with participants' contributions adjusted annually, and the life insurance plan is non-contributory.
>
> We fund domestic pension liabilities in accordance with the limits imposed by the Employee Retirement Income Security Act of 1974 and Federal income tax laws. Beginning January 1, 2008, we complied with the funding requirements of the Pension Protection Act of 2006. We fund non-domestic pension liabilities in accordance with laws and regulations applicable to those plans. We broadly diversify

11. "FASB Issues Rule Change on Benefits," *Wall Street Journal* (Dec. 29, 1990), A3.

12. See, for example, Daniel C. Hagen, Jeffrey S. Leavitt, Michael K. Blais, and Gina K. Gunning, "New Pension Funding and Accounting Rules Barrage Employers: Credit Agreement and SEC Disclosure Impact," Jones Day Commentaries (Oct. 2006), http://www.jonesday.com/pubs/pubs_detail.aspx?pubID=033655bc-09d3-4185-a5f4-005e77d814af&RSS=true.

our pension plan assets, consisting primarily of domestic and international common stocks and fixed income securities. Short-term and long-term liabilities associated with benefit plans are primarily determined based on actuarial calculations. These calculations consider payroll and employee data, including age and years of service, along with actuarial assumptions at the date of the financial statements. We take into consideration long-term projections with regard to economic conditions, including interest rates, return on assets and the rate of increase in compensation levels. With regard to liabilities associated with post-retirement benefit plans that provide health care and life insurance, we take into consideration the long-term annual rate of increase in the per capita cost of the covered benefits. In compliance with the provisions of Statement of Financial Accounting Standards No. 87, *Employers' Accounting for Pensions*, and Statement of Financial Accounting Standards No. 106, *Employers' Accounting for Postretirement Benefits Other Than Pensions*, we review the discount rate assumptions and may revise them annually. The expected long-term rate of return on assets assumption ("asset return assumption") for funded plans is by its nature of a longer duration and revised only when long-term asset return projections demonstrate that need.

We adopted the recognition and related disclosure provisions of SFAS No. 158 as of December 31, 2006.

Tootsie Roll also offers a defined benefit pension plan and provides postretirement health care and life insurance benefit plans.

International Accounting Standards

The IASB has issued two standards for retirement benefits: *IAS No. 19*, "Retirement Benefit Costs" and *IAS No. 26*, "Accounting and Reporting by Retirement Benefit Plans."

The objective of *IAS No. 19* is to prescribe the accounting and disclosure for all forms of consideration given by an entity in exchange for service rendered by employees. Consequently, it covers a much wider range of issues than the guidelines contained at FASB ASC 715 and includes such benefits as sabbatical leave, bonuses, and housing allowances. The underlying principle of the standard is that the cost of providing employee benefits should be recognized in the period in which the benefit is earned by the employee, rather than when it is paid or payable. *IAS No. 19*, as amended in 1998, delineates the procedures to account for both defined contribution and defined benefit pension plans. With respect to defined contribution plans, the amount contributed is to be recognized as a current period expense. This treatment is consistent with U.S. GAAP. For defined benefit plans, service cost must be recognized as a current period expense. Past service costs, experience adjustments, the effects of changes in actuarial assumptions, and plan adjustments are generally to be recognized as expenses (or income) in a systematic manner over the remaining working lives of the current employees. The preferred method of determining costs under defined benefit plans is the *accrued benefit valuation method*; however, the *projected benefit valuation method* is an acceptable alternative. This treatment allows for more variation in measuring pension cost than is available under U.S.

GAAP, and *IAS No. 19* does not address the minimum liability issue contained in *SFAS No. 87*.

The IASB is currently engaged in a project to amend *IAS No.19*. In March 2008 it published a discussion paper containing the Board's preliminary views on the subject. After reviewing the responses to that discussion paper, the IASB decided to issue three separate exposure drafts as follows:

1. The appropriate discount rate for measuring employee benefits. *IAS No. 19* requires an entity to determine the rate used to discount employee benefits by reference to market yields on high-quality corporate bonds. The IASB proposal would remove the requirement to use the government bond rate when there is no deep market in high-quality corporate bonds. Instead, an entity would be required to estimate the rate for a high-quality corporate bond using the guidance on determining fair value in *IAS No. 39*.

2. The recognition and presentation of changes in the defined benefit obligation and in plan assets, disclosures, and other issues raised in the comment letters that can be addressed expeditiously.

3. Accounting for contribution-based promises, potentially as part of a comprehensive review of pension accounting.

The IASB expects to issue exposure drafts on the second and third issues shortly and to complete these projects by 2011.

The objective of *IAS No. 26* is to specify the measurement and disclosure principles to be used for reporting the results of retirement benefit plans. It stipulates that all retirement plans should include in their reports a statement of changes in net assets available for benefits, a summary of significant accounting policies, and a description of the plan and the effect of any changes in the plan during the period. *IAS No. 26* establishes separate standards for reporting defined contribution plans and defined benefit plans. For defined contribution plans, the statement indicates that the objective of reporting is to provide information about the plan and the performance of its investments. As a result, information should be provided concerning significant activities affecting the plan, changes relating to the plan, investment performance, and a description of the plan's investment policies. For defined benefit plans, *IAS No. 26* indicates that the objective is to provide information about the financial resources and activities that will be useful in assessing the relationship between plan resources and future benefits. Accordingly, information should be provided concerning significant activities affecting the plan, changes relating to the plan, investment performance actuarial information, and a description of the plan's investment policies. These requirements are similar to U.S. GAAP for reporting on pension plan assets as outlined in *FASB ASC 715*.

Cases

• Case 14-1 Pension Benefits

Pension accounting has become more closely associated with the method of determining pension benefits.

Required:

a. Discuss the following methods of determining pension benefits:
   i. Defined contribution plan
   ii. Defined benefit plan
b. Discuss the following actuarial funding methods:
   i. Cost approach
   ii. Benefit approach

• Case 14-2 Pension Accounting Terminology

SFAS No. 87, "Employers Accounting for Pensions," requires an understanding of certain terms.

Required:

a. Discuss the following components of annual pension cost:
   i. Service cost
   ii. Interest cost
   iii. Actual return on plan assets
   iv. Amortization of unrecognized prior service cost
   v. Amortization of the transition amount
b. Discuss the composition and treatment of the minimum liability provision.

• Case 14-3 Application of *SFAS No. 87*

Carson Company sponsors a single-employer defined benefit pension plan. The plan provides that pension benefits are determined by age, years of service, and compensation. Among the components that should be included in the net pension cost recognized for a period are service cost, interest cost, and actual return on plan assets.

Required:

a. What two accounting problems result from the nature of the defined benefit pension plan? Why do these problems arise?
b. How should Carson determine the service cost component of the net pension cost?
c. How should Carson determine the interest cost component of the net pension cost?
d. How should Carson determine the actual return on plan assets component of the net pension cost?

• Case 14-4 Accounting for Other Postretirement Benefits

Postretirement benefits other than pensions (OPRBs) are similar to defined benefit pension plans in some respects and different in others.

Required:

a. Discuss the characteristics of OPRBs that make them different from defined benefit pension plans.

b. Discuss how the accounting for OPRBs differs from the accounting for defined benefit pension plans.

c. In what respects are OPRBs similar to defined benefit pension plans? Explain.

d. In what respects is the accounting for OPRBs similar to, or the same as, the accounting for defined benefit pension plans? Explain.

• Case 14-5 Pension Funding Status

Penny Pincher Company has a defined benefit pension plan for its employees. The following pension data are available at year end (in millions):

Accumulated benefit obligation	$142
Projected benefit obligation	205
Fair value of plan assets	175

There is no balance in prepaid/accrued pension costs.

Required:

a. Calculate the funded status of the plan (see *SFAS No. 158* for a definition of funded status). Is the plan overfunded or underfunded?

b. If the projected benefit obligation provides the appropriate measure of the company's obligation for pension benefits and the assets in the fund are viewed as satisfying all or part of that obligation, what is Penny Pincher's liability, if any, for the pension plan at year-end? Explain, citing the Conceptual Framework's definition of liabilities in your explanation.

c. What amount will Penny Pincher have to report in its balance sheet? Is it an asset or a liability?

• Case 14-6 Effect of the Settlement Rate on Periodic Pension Cost

Critics of *SFAS No. 87* argue that its requirements result in reporting pension expense that is volatile. One of the factors causing volatility is changing the discount rate used to calculate service cost and the projected benefit obligation. The FASB requires use of the "settlement rate" to discount projected benefits.

Required:

a. What is the settlement rate?

b. Explain why the FASB chose the settlement rate to discount projected benefits.

c. What alternative rate, or rates, might be preferred by opponents of the settlement rate? Why?

d. Why might companies object to increased volatility of pension expense? Discuss.

FASB ASC Research

For each of the following FASB ASC research cases, search the FASB ASC database for information to address the issues. Cut and paste the FASB paragraphs that support your responses. Then summarize briefly what your responses are, citing the pronouncements and paragraphs used to support your responses.

• FASB ASC 14-1 Settlement and Curtailment of a Defined Benefit Pension Plan

Search the FASB ASC database for answers to the following questions. For each question, cut and paste your findings, citing the source. Then write a brief summary response to the question asked.

1. What is the difference between a settlement and a curtailment of a defined benefit pension plan? Give an example of each.
2. Can a settlement and a curtailment occur simultaneously? If so, give an example.
3. How would a company compute the maximum gain or loss to recognize when a settlement occurs?
4. How would a company treat any remaining unrecognized prior service cost under a curtailment?

• FASB ASC 14-2 Interpretations for Pension Accounting

The EITF has issued numerous interpretations of accounting for pensions. Find, cite, and copy three of these interpretations.

• FASB ASC 14-3 Interpretations for Postretirement Benefits Accounting

The EITF has issued numerous interpretations of accounting for postretirement benefits. Find, cite, and copy three of these interpretations.

• FASB ASC 14-4 Discount Rate on Retirement Benefits

The FASB ASC indicates that the discount rate for other postretirement benefits may not be the same as the rate used for pension benefit obligations and discusses the reasons why they might be different. Find, cite, and copy the FASB ASC paragraphs that discuss this issue.

• FASB ASC 14-5 Excess Pension Plan Assets for Contractors

The FASB ASC indicates that contractors should consider disclosing the effect, if any, of the government's rights with respect to any excess pension plan assets in the event of a plan termination. Find, cite, and copy the FASB ASC paragraphs that discuss this issue.

• FASB ASC 14-6 Postretirement Health Benefits for Entities in the Coal Industry

The FASB ASC addresses the accounting and reporting for postretirement health benefits for entities in the coal industry affected by the Coal Industry Retiree Health Benefit Act of 1992. Find, cite, and copy the FASB ASC paragraphs that discuss this issue.

• FASB ASC 14-7 Pension Cost in Regulated Industries

The FASB ASC provides guidance for accounting for the difference between net periodic pension cost and amounts of pension cost considered for rate-making purposes as an asset or a liability created by the actions of the regulator. Find, cite, and copy the FASB ASC paragraphs that discuss this issue.

• FASB ASC 14-8 Postretirement Benefit Cost in Regulated Industries

The FASB ASC provides guidance for accounting for the difference between net periodic postretirement benefit cost and amounts of postretirement benefit cost considered for rate-making purposes as an asset or a liability created by the actions of the regulator. Find, cite, and copy the FASB ASC paragraphs that discuss this issue.

Room for Debate

• Debate 14-1 Articulation of Financial Statements

SFAS No. 87 required that projected benefits be used to measure pension expense, but allowed companies to report a minimum liability on the balance sheet using accumulated benefits. The result was that financial statements were not articulated. For the following debate, relate your arguments to the conceptual framework, where appropriate.

Team Debate:

Team 1: Argue in favor of articulation between the balance sheet and the income statement.

Team 2: Argue against articulation between the balance sheet and the income statement.

• Debate 14-2 Measurement of the Pension Obligation

SFAS No. 158 no longer allows companies to report the *SFAS No. 87* minimum liability in the balance sheet. Instead, the amount reported in the balance sheet is measured using projected benefits rather than accumulated benefits. For the following debate, relate your arguments to appropriate accounting theory, including the conceptual framework and capital maintenance theories. An article you may find helpful in supporting your arguments is "Alternative Accounting Treatments for Pensions," *The Accounting Review* (October 1982), pp. 806–23.

Team Debate:

Team 1: Argue for the use of projected benefits for pension expense and liability purposes.

Team 2: Argue for the use of accumulated benefits for pension expense and liability purposes.

CHAPTER 15

Equity

Equity is the basic risk capital of an enterprise. Equity capital has no guaranteed return and no timetable for the repayment of the capital investment. From the standpoint of enterprise stability and exposure to risk of insolvency, a basic characteristic of equity capital is that it is permanent and can be counted on to remain invested in good times as well as bad. Consequently, equity funds can be most confidently invested in long-term assets, and it is generally thought that equity funds can be exposed to the greatest potential risks.

Investors deciding whether to purchase a company's common stock must balance the existence of the company's debt, which represents a risk of loss of investment, against the potential of high profits from financial leverage. The mix of a company's debt and equity capital is termed its *capital structure*. Over the years, there has been considerable debate over whether a firm's cost of capital varies with different capital structures. Specifically, financial theorists and researchers have espoused theories and examined empirical evidence to discern whether different mixtures of debt and equity in a firm's capital affect the value of the firm. Modigliani and Miller found that an enterprise's cost of capital is, except for the tax deductibility of interest, not affected by the mix of debt and equity.[1] This is true, they asserted, because each individual stockholder can inject his or her own blend of risk into the total investment position.

In this chapter we maintain that the degree of risk associated with an investment in an enterprise as perceived by a potential investor is a given. In the following paragraphs, we review some theories of equity and discuss the theoretical issues associated with recording the various components of equity.

---

1. F. Modigliani and M. Miller. "Cost of Capital, Corporation Finance and the Theory of Investment," *American Economic Review* (June 1958), 261–97.

Theories of Equity

Chapter 11 introduced two theories of equity: the proprietary theory and the entity theory. These and several other theories may provide a frame of reference for the presentation and measurement of information reported in financial statements. When viewing the applicability of the various theories of equity, it is important to remember that the purpose of a theory is to provide a rationale or explanation for some action. The proprietary theory gained prominence because the interests of owners were seen as the guiding force in the preparation of financial statements. However, as the interests of other users became more significant, accountants made changes in financial reporting formats without adopting a particular equity theory.

In the following discussion, the student should keep in mind that the adoption of a particular theory could influence a number of accounting and reporting procedures. The student should also note that the theories represent a point of view toward the firm for accounting purposes that is not necessarily the same as the legal view of the firm.

Proprietary Theory

According to the proprietary theory, the firm is owned by some specified person or group. The ownership interest may be represented by a sole proprietor, a partnership, or a number of stockholders. The assets of the firm belong to these owners, and any liabilities of the firm are also the owners' liabilities. Revenues received by the firm immediately increase the owner's net interest in the firm. Likewise, all expenses incurred by the firm immediately decrease the net proprietary interest in the firm. This theory holds that all profits or losses immediately become the property of the owners, and not the firm, whether or not they are distributed. Therefore the firm exists simply to provide the means to carry on transactions for the owners, and the net worth or equity section of the balance sheet should be viewed as

$$\text{assets} - \text{liabilities} = \text{proprietorship}$$

Under the proprietary theory, financial reporting is based on the premise that the owner is the primary focus of a company's financial statements. The proprietary theory is particularly applicable to sole proprietorships where the owner is the decision maker. When the form of the enterprise grows more complex, and the ownership and management separate, this theory becomes less acceptable. An attempt has been made to retain the concepts of the proprietary theory in the corporate situation; however, many accountants have asserted that it cannot meet the requirements of the corporate form of organization.[2] Nevertheless, we still find significant accounting policies that can be justified only through acceptance of the proprietary theory. For example, the calculation and presentation of earnings per share figures are relevant only if we assume that those earnings belong to the shareholders before the declaration of dividends.

---

2. Ibid.

Entity Theory

The rise of the corporate form of organization (1) was accompanied by the separation of ownership and management, (2) conveyed limited liability to the owners, and (3) resulted in the legal definition of a corporation as though it were a person. This form of organization encouraged the evolution of new theories of ownership. Among the first of these theories was the entity theory. From an accounting standpoint, the entity theory can be expressed as

$$\text{assets} = \text{equities}$$

The entity theory, like the proprietary theory, is a point of view toward the firm and the people concerned with its operation. This viewpoint places the firm, and not the owners, at the center of interest for accounting and financial reporting purposes. The essence of the entity theory is that creditors as well as stockholders contribute resources to the firm, and the firm exists as a separate and distinct entity apart from these groups. The assets and liabilities belong to the firm, not to its owners. As revenue is received, it becomes the property of the entity; and as expenses are incurred, they become obligations of the entity. Any profits belong to the entity and accrue to the stockholders only when a dividend is declared. Under this theory, all the items on the right-hand side of the balance sheet, except retained earnings (these belong to the firm), are viewed as claims against the assets of the firm, and individual items are distinguished by the nature of their claims. Some items are identified as creditor claims, and others are identified as owner claims; nevertheless, they are all claims against the firm as a separate entity.

Goldberg illustrated the difference between the proprietary and entity theories through an example involving a small child in possession of his or her first unit of monetary exchange:

> Suppose that a small child is given, say £1, with which he can do whatever he likes. If (as is most likely) he is not familiar with the idea of ownership, he will think (i) "Here is £1"; and (ii) "This £1 is mine." These thoughts comprise the essence of the proprietary viewpoint and of double entry, for if the child were a born accountant, he would express the same thoughts as (i) "There exists an asset," and (ii) "I have a proprietary interest in that asset." That is to say, the £1 is regarded from two aspects: (i) as something that exists—an asset; and (ii) as belonging to somebody—my asset. Suppose further that, until the child can decide what he will do with the £1, he puts it in a money box. The entity theory can be introduced here by personalizing the money box—it involves adopting the point of view that the money box now has the £1 and owes £1 to the child.[3]

Embedded in this illustration is the fundamental distinction between the proprietary and entity theories—perceptions of the right-hand side of the balance sheet. Individuals who view net income as accruing only to owners will favor the proprietary approach, whereas those taking a broader view of the nature of the beneficiaries of income will favor the entity approach.

---

3. Louis Goldberg, *An Inquiry into the Nature of Accounting* (Sarasota, FL: American Accounting Association, Monograph No. 7, 1963), 126.

Entity theory makes no distinction between debt and equity. Both are considered sources of capital, and the operations of the firm are not affected by the amount of debt relative to equity.[4] Thus, under entity theory, debt-to-equity ratios would not provide relevant information for investor decision making.[5] Yet, present accounting practice makes a sharp distinction between debt and equity. Moreover, the amount of debt relative to equity is generally considered an important indicator of risk.[6] Such a distinction implies that accountants must separately identify and classify liabilities from equities. Nevertheless, complex financial instruments such as convertible bonds may comprise debt and equity components. This means that the components of a given financial instrument may meet the definition of more than one financial statement element. Given the conceptual framework objective that financial statements should report each element in a representationally faithful manner, from a theoretical standpoint, a company should separate a complex financial instrument into its various parts and report each part in accordance with the financial statement element it meets the definition of. At the same time, the reporting requirements of the conceptual framework dictate that an item must not only meet the definition of a financial statement element, it must also be capable of being measured. Yet, it may be difficult or even impossible to separately measure each component of a complex financial instrument. Nevertheless, it is evident from a recent exposure draft and the issuance of *SFAS No. 150* (see FASB ASC 480) that the FASB not only favors the position that balance sheets should distinguish between debt and equity but also intends to make determinations on how to accomplish such distinctions between the components of a complex financial instrument.[7] Later in this chapter, we trace the developments that led to the issuance of *SFAS No. 150* and discuss pending, unresolved issues related to the distinction between debt and equity.

Other Theoretical Approaches

Several authors have noted inadequacies in the entity and proprietary approaches and have developed additional viewpoints, or perspectives, from which to rationalize the recording and reporting of accounting information. The most notable of these alternative viewpoints are the fund theory, the commander theory, the enterprise theory, and the residual equity theory. Each of these theories is considered separately.

Fund Theory
Vatter attacked the proprietary theory as too simplistic for modern corporate reporting.[8] He saw no logical basis for viewing the corporation as a person in the

4. W. A. Paton, *Accounting Theory* (New York: Ronald Press, 1922).

5. M. W. Clark, "Entity Theory, Modern Capital Structure Theory, and the Distinction between Debt and Equity," *Accounting Horizons* (September 1993), 14–31.

6. Ibid.

7. Financial Accounting Standards Board, *Proposed Statement of Financial Accounting Standards*, "Accounting for Financial Instrument with Characteristics of Liabilities, Equity, or Both" (Stamford, CT: FASB, October 27, 2000).

8. William J. Vatter, *The Fund Theory of Accounting and Its Implications for Financial Reports* (Chicago: University of Chicago Press, 1947).

legal sense, and he argued that the corporation is the people it represents. As an alternative, Vatter proposed the fund theory of accounting.

The fund theory would abandon the personal relationship advocated by the proprietary theory and the personalization of the firm advocated by the entity theory. Under the fund approach, the measurement of net income plays a role secondary to satisfying the special interests of management, social control agencies (e.g., government agencies), and the overall process of credit extension and investment. The fund theory is expressed by the following equation:

$$\text{assets} = \text{restrictions on assets}$$

This theory explains the financial reporting of an organization in terms of three features, as follows:

1. *Fund.* An area of attention defined by the activities and operations surrounding any one set of accounting records and for which a self-balancing set of accounts is created

2. *Assets.* Economic services and potentials

3. *Restrictions.* Limitations on the use of assets

These features are applied to each homogeneous set of activities and functions within the organization, thereby providing a separate accounting for each area of economic concern.

The fund theory has not gained general acceptance in financial accounting; it is more suitable to governmental accounting. This theory is a somewhat radical departure from current practices, and the added volume of bookkeeping it would require has inhibited its adoption. Use of the fund approach in government accounting is attributed principally to the legal restrictions typically imposed on each fund, thus requiring a separate accounting for each.

Commander Theory

The entity theory adopts the point of view of the business entity, whereas the proprietary theory takes the viewpoint of the proprietor. But, asks Goldberg, "What of the point of view of the managers—the activity force in a . . . company?"[9] Goldberg argues that this question is of major importance because of the divergent self-interested viewpoints of owners and managers in large-scale corporations. In fact, so relevant is this divergence that "a whole . . . field of study, going under the name of 'management accounting' and an ancillary literature have grown up, in which the emphasis is laid upon accountants for information to enable them (the managers) to carry out their function of control of property with a view to its increase."[10]

The commander approach is offered as a replacement for the proprietary and entity theories because it is argued that the goals of the manager ("commander") are at least equally important to those of the proprietor or entity. The proprietary, entity, and fund approaches emphasize persons, personalization, and funds, respectively; but the commander theory emphasizes control. Everyone who has resources to deploy is viewed as a commander.

9. Goldberg, *An Inquiry into the Nature of Accounting,* 152.

10. Ibid.

The commander theory, unlike the proprietary, entity, and fund approaches, has applicability to all organizational forms (sole proprietorships, partnerships, and corporations). The form of organization does not negate the applicability of the commander view, because the commander can take on more than one identity in any organization. In sole proprietorships or partnerships, the proprietors or partners are both owners and commanders. Under the corporate form, both the managers and the stockholders are commanders in that each maintains some control over resources. (Managers control the enterprise resources, and stockholders control returns on investment emerging from the enterprise.)

A commander theorist would argue that the notion of control is broad enough to encompass all relevant parties to the exclusion of none. The function of accounting, then, takes on an element of stewardship, and the question of where resource increments flow is not relevant. Rather, the relevant factor is how the commander allocates resources to the benefit of all parties. Responsibility accounting is consistent with the commander theory. Responsibility accounting identifies the revenues and costs that are under the control of various so-called commanders within the organization, and the organization's financial statements are constructed to highlight the contributions of each level of control to enterprise profits. The commander theory is not on the surface a radical move from current accounting practices, and it has generated little reaction in accounting circles.

Enterprise Theory

Under the enterprise theory, business units, most notably those listed on national or regional stock exchanges, are viewed as social institutions composed of capital contributors having "a common purpose or purposes and, to a certain extent, roles of common action."[11] Management within this framework essentially maintains an arm's-length relationship with owners and has as its primary responsibilities (1) the distribution of adequate dividends and (2) the maintenance of friendly terms with employees, consumers, and government units. Because this theory applies only to large nationally or regionally traded issues, it is generally considered to have only a minor impact on accounting theory or on the development of accounting principles and practices.

Residual Equity Theory

Staubus defined *residual equity* as "the equitable interest in organization's assets which will absorb the effect upon those assets of any economic event that no interested party has specifically agreed to."[12] Here, the common shareholders hold the residual equity in the enterprise by virtue of having the final claim on income, yet they are the first to be charged for losses. The residual equity holders are vital to the firm's existence in that they are the highest risk takers and provide a substantial volume of capital during the firm's developmental stage.

The residual equity theory is formulated as

$$\text{assets} - \text{specific equities} = \text{residual equities}$$

11. Waino Soujanen, "Enterprise Theory and Corporate Balance Sheets," *The Accounting Review* (January 1958), 56.

12. George J. Staubus, "The Residual Equity Point of View in Accounting," *The Accounting Review* (January 1959), 3.

Under this approach the residual of assets, net of the claim of specific equity holders (creditors and preferred stockholders), accrue to residual owners. In this framework, the role of financial reporting is to provide prospective and current residual owners with information regarding enterprise resource flows so that they can assess the value of their residual claim. Management is in effect a trustee responsible for maximizing the wealth of residual equity holders. Income accrues to the residual owners after the claims of specific equity holders are met. Thus the income to specific equity holders, including interest on debt and dividends to preferred stockholders, would be deducted in arriving at residual net income. This theory is consistent with models that are formulated in the finance literature,[13] with current financial statement presentation of earnings per share, and with the conceptual framework's emphasis on the relevance of projecting cash flows. Again, as with the fund, commander, and enterprise theories, the residual equity approach has gained little attention in financial accounting.

Definition of Equity

SFAC No. 6 defines equity as a residual interest. However, the residual interest described therein is not equivalent to residual equity as defined above. Rather, it is the difference between assets and liabilities.[14] Consequently, under *SFAC No. 6*, the definition and characteristics of equity hinge on the definitions and characteristics of assets and liabilities. *SFAC No. 6* defines equity in total but does not define the attributes of the elements of equity. It does note that enterprises may have more than one class of equity, such as common stock and preferred stock. Equity is defined as the difference between assets and liabilities, and liabilities are described as embodying an obligation to transfer assets or provide services to another entity in the future as the result of some prior transaction or event. Consequently, under the *SFAC No. 6* definitions, the distinguishing feature between liabilities and equities is that equities do not obligate the entity to transfer future resources or provide services. There is no obligation to distribute resources to equity holders until they are declared by the board of directors or unless the entity is liquidated.

According to *SFAC No. 6*, if a financial instrument issued by the enterprise does not fit the definition of a liability, then it must be an equity instrument. A 1990 FASB discussion memorandum questions whether the definition of equity should continue to be governed by the definition of liabilities or whether it should be separately defined.[15] If equity were independently defined, then the liabilities might be the residual outcome of identifying assets and equity. In this case, the equation describing the relationship between financial statement elements could be stated as follows:

$$\text{assets} - \text{equity} = \text{liabilities}$$

13. Clark, "Entity Theory, Modern Capital Structure Theory, and the Distinction between Debt and Equity"

14. *Statement of Financial Accounting Concepts No. 6*, "Elements of Financial Statements" (Stamford, CT: FASB, 1985), para. 60.

15. Financial Accounting Standards Board, *Discussion Memorandum: Distinguishing between Liability and Equity Instruments and Accounting for Instruments with Characteristics of Both* (Stamford, CT: FASB, 1990).

Alternatively, equity might be defined as an absolute residual, as under the residual equity theory, and a third category added to the balance sheet—"quasi-equity." The quasi-equity category might include items such as preferred stock or minority interest. This category would allow accountants to retain the definition of liabilities and treat the quasi-equity category as a residual. If this form of financial statement presentation should emerge, then other issues would have to be addressed, such as the definition of earnings. For example, as stated before, a residual equity definition of equity would imply that preferred dividends would be subtracted in the determination of net income.

FASB ASC 480-10 requires that certain obligations that could be settled by issuance of an entity's equity securities be classified as liabilities. Because these obligations do not meet the *SFAC No. 6* definition of liabilities, they would under the present conceptual framework be considered equity. As a result, the FASB "expects to amend Concepts Statement 6 to eliminate that inconsistency."[16] In effect, the FASB has proposed that the definition of liabilities be broadened to include financial instruments that would otherwise be considered equity because they are not obligations to transfer assets or perform services.

The Distinction between Debt and Equity

The relationship of a company's long-term debt to its equity is relevant because this ratio is directly related to the risk associated with investing in the firm's stock.[17] As the debt-to-equity ratio of a firm increases, the market's perception of the riskiness of investing in the firm's stock also rises. Thus it is important to have criteria to appropriately classify liabilities and equity so that decision makers can reliably evaluate the firm's ability to meet current needs and to determine the level of riskiness inherent in projections of future cash flows over time.

In 1986, the FASB recognized the importance of this issue by adding a project on financial instruments to its agenda. The project initially focused on the disclosure of risk, resulting in 1990 in the issuance of *SFAS Nos. 105* and *107* (*SFAS No. 105* has been superseded, and *SFAS No. 107* is now contained at FASB ASC 825). These pronouncements set forth requirements regarding the footnote disclosures of risks inherent in financial instruments, particularly those with off–balance sheet risk. In the same year, the FASB issued a discussion memorandum (DM), "Distinguishing between Liability and Equity Instruments and Accounting for Instruments with the Characteristics of Both."[18] The DM asks whether the sharp distinction between debt and equity should be continued. In other words, should accounting follow entity theory, or should accounting attempt to identify and separately report the

---

16. *Statement of Financial Accounting Standards No. 150*, "Accounting for Certain Financial Instruments with Characteristics of both Liabilities and Equity" (Stamford, CT: FASB, May 2003).

17. See, for example, Robert S. Hamada, "The Effect of the Firm's Capital Structure on the Systematic Risk of Common Stocks," *Journal of Finance* 27, no. 2 (May 1972): 435–52; Mark E. Rubinstein, "A Mean-Variance Synthesis of Corporate Financial Theory," *Journal of Finance* 28, no. 1 (March 1973): 167–81.

18. Financial Accounting Standards Board, *Discussion Memorandum: Distinguishing between Liability and Equity Instruments and Accounting for Instruments with Characteristics of Both* (Stamford, CT: FASB, 1990).

elements of debt and equity (proprietary theory)? If the distinction is to continue, decisions must be made regarding the nature of fundamental financial instruments and how to appropriately measure and report them.

Following subsequent deliberations that began in 1996, the FASB responded in October 2000 to concerns expressed by accountants, regulators, and others regarding how issuers classify financial instruments on the balance sheet by issuing an exposure draft (ED). Specifically, these concerns focused on three types of financial instruments:

1. Financial instruments that have characteristics of liabilities, but are reported as equity or between liabilities and equity
2. Financial instruments that have characteristics of equity, but are presented between liabilities and equity
3. Financial instruments that have characteristics of both liabilities and equity, but are classified either as liabilities or equity

The ED responded by proposing that (1) an issuer not classify as a liability a financial instrument that does not impose an obligation on the issuer and that (2) if a financial instrument component does impose an obligation on the issuer, the issuer should classify a financial instrument component based on its liability or equity characteristics. According to the ED, the classification of a component as a liability or equity depends on whether the component imposes an obligation that must be settled by a transfer of assets or whether the relationship between the issuer and the holder of the instrument is deemed to be an ownership relationship. The proposed pronouncement determined that an ownership relationship exists when the financial instrument does not require settlement by a transfer of assets and when changes in the monetary value of the instrument are attributable to, equal to, or in the same direction as changes in the fair value of the issuer's equity shares.

The ED suggests that complex financial instruments containing at least one equity component and at least one liability component be separated into their equity and liability components. The issue price of the financial instrument would then be allocated between its components based on their relative fair values. If the fair value of one of the components is not readily determinable, then its value would be determined using the with-and-without method. That is, the value of components that can be reliably measured would be determined and subtracted from the issue price of the financial instrument to provide a measure of the apparent fair value of the component that does not have a readily determinable fair value.

Later, in 2003, the FASB issued *SFAS No. 150*, "Accounting for Certain Financial Instruments with Characteristics of Both Liabilities and Equity" (see FASB ASC 480). This guidance requires companies to record and report mandatorily redeemable preferred stock (MRPS) as a liability on their balance sheets and the dividends on these securities as interest expense. Most companies previously disclosed MRPS between the liability and stockholders' equity sections (i.e., the mezzanine section) of the balance sheet.

Redemption provisions on preferred stock are common features of agreements entered into among the owners of closely held businesses. These agreements, which are often referred to as shareholders' or buy-sell agreements, provide for the orderly disposition of the owners' investment in the company upon their separation from the company, usually at retirement, disability, or death. Because there is no market for the equity securities of a closely held company, departing owners or their heirs must rely on the company or the remaining owners to provide them with liquidity. Redemption by the company is usually favored over requiring the remaining owners to fund a buyout, because the remaining owners may not have the necessary financial resources. Prior to the guidance contained at FASB ASC 480, owners' equity that was redeemable pursuant to a buy-sell agreement was accounted for as equity, not debt, and the existence and significant terms of the buy-sell agreement were required to be described in the notes to financial statements.

The provisions of FASB ASC 480 relating to MRPS were seen as potentially devastating to these closely held, nonpublic companies. A large number of such firms, including many public accounting firms, have issued MRPS. As a result, the effect of the standard was seen as potentially eliminating the net worth of the nonpublic companies that have issued MRPS. A comment letter to the FASB from the Financial Executives Institute maintained that the application of this guidance to nonpublic companies would present an overly pessimistic picture of the entity's financial position that might result in its disqualification from bidding on private contracts or the prevention of obtaining bank financing.[19]

The primary effect of the FASB ASC 480 guidance is the reclassification of some amounts previously disclosed as equity to the liability section of the company's balance sheet. Additionally, this reclassification would result in a decrease in reported net income, since distributions to investors previously recorded as dividends must now be recorded as interest expense. While the income statement effect is interesting, the increase in reported liabilities resulting from reclassifying MRPS from equity to debt may restrict the firm's ability to issue additional debt and possibly result in debt covenant violations. The debt levels of a company can be measured by comparing its liabilities to its assets and to its liabilities; accordingly, the debt-to-assets ratio and debt-to-equity ratio are the metrics used in the analysis.

Reporting Equity

The American economy is characterized by three forms of business organization: sole proprietorships, partnerships, and corporations. Although the number of sole proprietorships greatly exceeds the number of partnerships and corporations in the United States, the greatest amount of economic activity is carried out by corporations. This phenomenon is due to the efficiency of corporate production and distribution systems.

Several advantages accrue to the corporate form and help explain its emergence. Among them are the following:

1. *Limited liability.* A stockholder's loss on his or her investment is limited to the amount of the amount invested (unless on the date of acquisition, the purchase price of the shares acquired was less than their par value). Creditors may not look to the assets of individual owners for debt repayments in the event of a liquidation, as is possible in the case of sole proprietorships and partnerships.

19. Philip Ameen, "Comment Letter on Exposure Draft Accounting for Financial Instruments with Characteristics of Liabilities, Equity or Both," May 18, 2001.

2. *Continuity*. The corporation's life is not affected by the death or resignation of owners.

3. *Investment liquidity*. Corporate shares may be freely exchanged on the open market. Many shares are listed on national security exchanges, thereby improving their marketability.

4. *Variety of ownership interest*. Shares of corporate stock usually contain four basic rights: the right to vote for members of the board of directors of the corporation and thereby participate in management, the right to receive dividends, the right to receive assets on the liquidation of the corporation, and the preemptive right to purchase additional shares in the same pro-portion to current ownership interest if new issues of stock are marketed. Shareholders may sacrifice any or all of these rights in return for special privileges. This results in an additional class of stock, termed *preferred stock*, that may have either or both of the following features:

    a. Preference as to dividends

    b. Preference as to assets in liquidation

Traditionally, utilities were the largest issuers of preferred stock because sell-ing preferred shares does not affect a company's debt cost. Recently, banks and other financial institutions have also become more active in preferred stock offer-ings because of new federal requirements. Preferred stock is most often acquired by corporate investors because of the dividend exclusion allowance rule allowed under the Internal Revenue Code.

The corporate form of business organization allows management specialists to be employed. The owners thereby gain an expertise not normally available in sole proprietorships or partnerships. Evidence of the extent of this advantage can be found in the growth of business schools in the major universities. A large per-centage of the students in these programs are in training to obtain employment in large corporations.

As noted earlier, two major types of stock may be found in any corporation, preferred stock and common stock. Preferred stockholders give up one or more of the rights usually accruing to stockholders for preference as to dividends or to assets in liquidation. Common stockholders retain these rights and have a residual claim on both the earnings and assets in liquidation.

The capital section of a corporation's balance sheet is usually subdivided into several components. In addition to disclosing the legal claims that the various ownership groups have against the assets of the corporation, the separation of the components of capital gives information regarding the sources of capital, dividend requirements, and the relative priorities of different types of equity securities in the event of corporate liquidation.

The components of a corporation's capital section are classified by source in the following manner:

I. Paid-in capital (contributed capital)

    A. Legal capital—par, stated value, or entire proceeds if no par or stated value accompanies the stock issue

    B. Additional paid-in capital—amounts received in excess of par or stated value

  II. Earned capital

    A. Appropriated

    B. Unappropriated

 III. Other comprehensive income

Each of these components is discussed in further detail in the following sections.

Paid-in Capital

The limited liability advantage of the corporate form of business organization provides that creditors may look only to the assets of the corporation to satisfy their claims. This factor has caused various states to enact laws that attempt to protect creditors and inform them of the true nature of the assets and liabilities of individual corporations. State laws generally protect creditors by establishing the concept of *legal capital*—the amount of net assets that cannot be distributed to stockholders. These laws vary from state to state, but the par or stated value of the outstanding shares generally constitutes a corporation's legal capital. State laws generally require legal capital to be reported separately from the total amount invested. As a result, ownership interests are classified as capital stock or additional paid-in capital in excess of par value. The classification, *additional paid-in capital*, includes all amounts originally received for shares of stock in excess of par or stated value. In unusual cases, stock may be sold for less than par value. In the event the corporation is liquidated, the holders of securities acquired for less than their par value could be required to pay the corporation the amount of the difference between the original investment and par value in order to protect creditors.

Stock Subscriptions

Large corporations frequently sell entire issues of stock to a group of investment advisors, or *underwriters*, who then attempt to resell the shares to the public. When a corporation sells shares of stock directly to individuals, it is common practice for individuals to contract to purchase shares on an installment basis. These individuals, termed *subscribers*, usually receive the rights of ownership when they contract to purchase the shares on subscription but do not actually receive any shares until the company has received payment for all subscribed shares. That is, each installment received is viewed as a percentage payment on each contracted share, and no shares are issued until all are paid in full. In some states, capital stock subscribed is viewed as part of legal capital, even though the shares are not outstanding. In other states, the subscribed shares are included in legal capital only after they have been fully paid and issued.

When a stock subscription takes place, the corporation has a legally enforceable claim against the subscribers for the balance due on the subscriptions. Therefore, receivables resulting from stock subscriptions embody probable future economic benefits and fit the definition of assets. However, present practice typically follows SEC Regulation S-X, which requires stock subscriptions receivable to be disclosed in stockholders' equity. Proponents of this treatment argue that the enterprise's recourse if the receivable is not collected is not to issue the stock. Moreover, the enterprise may not pursue collection, and therefore these receivables are sufficiently uncertain to qualify them as recognizable assets. It is also argued that stock subscriptions receivable are different from other receivables because they do not result from transferring assets or providing services.

Special Features

Securities other than common stock may contain features that allow (1) the holders of these securities to become common stockholders, (2) the corporation to reacquire these securities, or (3) the rate of return on the securities to fluctuate. Among these features are convertible provisions, call provisions, cumulative provisions, participating provisions, and redemption provisions. These provisions are found most frequently on preferred stock, but some of them may also be found on long-term debt, as discussed in Chapter 10.

Conversion

A conversion feature is included on a preferred stock issue to make it more attractive to potential investors. Usually, a conversion feature is attached to allow the corporation to sell its preferred shares at a relatively lower dividend rate than is found on other securities with the same degree of risk. The conversion rate is normally set above the current relationship of the market value of the common share to the market value of the preferred convertible shares. For example, if the corporation's common stock is selling at $10 per share and the preferred stock has a selling price of $100 per share, the conversion rate might be set at eight shares of common for one preferred. All other things being equal, it would appear to be profitable for the preferred shareholders to convert to common when the value of the common shares rises above $12.50 per share. However, it is normal for the market price of the preferred shares to fluctuate in proportion to the market price of the common; therefore, an investor would not be able to make a profit by simply converting one type of security to another. Convertible stock is attractive to investors because the exchange ratio tends to tie the market price of the preferred stock to the market price of the common stock.

When preferred stock is converted to common stock, the proper accounting treatment is to transfer the par value of the preferred, plus a proportionate share of any additional paid-in capital on the preferred stock, to common stock. If this amount differs from the par or stated value of common stock, it is apportioned between par or stated value and additional paid-in capital on common stock.

The outstanding FASB exposure draft (ED), described previously in this chapter, would require that the issuer of a complex financial instrument allocate the proceeds received at issuance to the instrument's separately classified liability and equity components.[20] The FASB proposal does not explicitly address convertible preferred stock, since the conversion feature and the preferred stock would be separate components of this complex financial instrument. For convertible preferred stock, these components are both equity components; and according to the exposure draft, they could be reported as a single item. However, if the provisions of the proposed standard are fully implemented, each of these features may also be reported as a separate component of equity. According to the ED, the measurement of individual components should be made using the relative fair values of

---

20. *Proposed Statement of Financial Accounting Standards,* "Accounting for Financial Instruments with Characteristics of Liabilities, Equities, or Both" (Stamford, CT: FASB, March 31 2001).

those components. However, the fair value of the conversion feature would not typically be readily determinable. In this case, the measurement for convertible preferred stock would follow the ED's proposed measurement of the conversion feature for convertible bonds. The fair value of the preferred stock (without a conversion feature) would be used to value it, and the remainder of the issue price would be allocated to the option to convert. The resulting separate disclosure of the value received for the conversion feature may have information content.[21]

Call Provisions

Call provisions allow the corporation to reacquire preferred stock at some predetermined amount. Corporations include call provisions on securities because of uncertain future conditions. Current conditions dictate the return on investment that will be attractive to potential investors, but conditions may change so that the corporation may offer a lower return on investment in the future. In addition, market conditions may make it necessary to promise a certain debt-equity relationship at the time of issue. Call provisions allow the corporation to take advantage of future favorable conditions and indicate how the securities may be retired. The existence of a call price tends to set an upper limit on the market price of nonconvertible securities, since investors will not normally be inclined to purchase shares that could be recalled momentarily at a lower price.

Because a call provision conveys benefits to the issuing corporation, it is an asset component of a complex financial instrument. However, the FASB's ED that would require the separate recognition of the liability and equity components of a complex financial instrument does not propose the separate recognition and measurement of the value of the call.[22]

Cumulative Provisions

Preferred shareholders normally have a preference as to dividends. That is, no common dividends may be paid in any one year until all required preferred dividends for that year are paid. Usually, corporations also include added protection for preferred shareholders in the form of a cumulative provision. This provision states that if all or any part of the stated preferred dividend is not paid in any one year, the unpaid portion accumulates and must be paid in subsequent years before any dividend can be paid on common stock. Any unpaid dividend on cumulative preferred stock constitutes a dividend in arrears and should be disclosed in the notes to the financial statements, even though it is not a liability until the board of directors of the corporation actually declares it. Dividends in arrears are important in predicting future cash flows and as an indicator of financial flexibility and liquidity.

Participating Provisions

Participating provisions allow preferred stockholders to share dividends in excess of normal returns with common stockholders. For example, a participating provision might indicate that preferred shares are to participate in dividends on a 1:1 basis with common stock on all dividends in excess of $5 per share. This provision requires that any payments of more than $5 per share to the common stockholder also be made on a dollar-for-dollar basis to each share of preferred.

21. Clark, "Entity Theory, Modern Capital Structure Theory, and the Distinction between Debt and Equity."

22. *FASB No. 18.*

Redemption Provision

A redemption provision indicates that the shareholder may exchange preferred stock for cash in the future. The redemption provision may include a mandatory maturity date or may specify a redemption price. If so, the financial instrument embodies an obligation to transfer assets and would meet the definition of a liability, rather than equity. The SEC requires separate disclosure of manditorily redeemable preferred shares because of their separate nature. FASB ASC 480-10-50-4 requires that a manditorily redeemable financial instrument be classified as a liability unless redemption is required to occur only upon the liquidation or termination of the issuing company.

Stock Options and Warrants

Many corporations have agreements with employees and security holders, that may result in the issuance of additional shares of common stock. These agreements, termed stock options and stock warrants can significantly affect the amount of common stock outstanding, and the method of accounting for them should be carefully evaluated.

Accounting for Stock Option Plans Under *APB Opinion No. 25*   Executive stock option plans have become an important element of the compensation package for corporate officers. These plans allow corporate officials to purchase a stated number of shares of stock at an established price for some predetermined period. In the past, stock option plans were especially advantageous because of income tax regulations that taxed proceeds at the capital gains rate when the securities purchased under stock option plans were sold. Current tax laws have substantially reduced the tax advantage of stock options. Nevertheless, many corporations still use them as part of the total compensation package.

Stock option plans are most valuable when the option price is lower than the market price. For this reason, stock option plans are viewed as an incentive that influences the holders of options to try to increase corporate profits and thereby increase the value of the company's common shares on the stock market. These plans have a potentially dilutive effect on other shareholders, since exercising options results in additional stockholder claims against the same amount of income. The relative effects of this potential dilution versus the effect of management's incentive to increase profits should be examined by current and potential shareholders. Such measurements are, of course, quite difficult.

In 1972 the Accounting Principles Board reviewed the issue of accounting for stock options and issued *APB Opinion No. 25*, "Accounting for Stock Issued to Employees."[23] Two types of plans were defined in this pronouncement: noncompensatory and compensatory.

A *noncompensatory stock option plan* was defined as one not primarily designed as a method of compensation, but rather as a source of additional capital or of more widespread ownership among employees. Four essential characteristics of noncompensatory plans were identified : (1) the participation of all full-time employees, (2) the offering of stock on an equal basis or as a uniform percentage of salary to all employees, (3) a limited time for exercise of the option, and (4) a discount from market price that would not differ from a reasonable offer to

---

23. Accounting Principles Board, *Opinion No. 25*, "Accounting for Stock Issued to Employees" (New York: AICPA, 1972).

stockholders. When these conditions were met, the plan did not discriminate in favor of company employees; thus, the corporation was not required to record any compensation expense.

Compensatory stock option plans, on the other hand, give employees an option that is not offered to all employees or to stockholders. These plans involve the recording of an expense, and the timing of the measurement of this expense can greatly affect its impact on financial reports. The six possible measurement dates to determine the amount of compensation expense associated with a stock option plan originally discussed in *ARB No. 43* were reviewed in Appendix B to *APB Opinion No. 25*. These dates are

1. The date of the adoption of an option plan

2. The date on which an option is granted to a specific individual

3. The date on which the grantee has performed any conditions precedent to exercise of the option

4. The date on which the grantee may first exercise the option

5. The date on which the option is exercised by the grantee

6. The date on which the grantee disposes of the stock acquired[24]

The APB concluded that compensation expense should be measured on the first date on which both the number of shares to be received by a particular individual and the option price are known. In most cases, this would be the date on which the option is granted to a specific individual. The compensation expense is equal to the difference between the market price of the stock on the measurement date and the price the employee is required to pay.

Determination of the measurement date is of primary importance for compensatory stock option plans. In some plans the date of the grant is the measurement date, and therefore the amount of compensation is known. In other plans the measurement date is later than the date of the grant, and the annual compensation expense must be estimated.

Under the provisions of *APB Opinion No. 25*, if the date of the grant and the measurement date were the same, deferred compensation and common stock options were established for the total amount of compensation cost. The deferred compensation cost was offset against the common stock options in the stockholders' equity section and amortized to expense over the period of benefit. In the event the measurement date was later than the date of the grant, total compensation cost could not be precisely measured on the date of the grant. Therefore annual compensation expense was estimated, and common stock options were recorded during each period until the measurement date was reached.

Occasionally, available stock options may not be exercised. In the event an option was not exercised before the expiration date, previously recognized compensation expense was not affected; however, on the expiration date, the value of any previously recorded common stock options was transferred to additional paid-in capital.

The rationale for use of the *APB Opinion No. 25* measurement date was that it coincides with the date that the corporation commits to a specified number

---

24. Ibid., para. 6.

of shares. Because the shares could have been sold in the market rather than set aside for the employees, the difference between the market value of those shares and the option price on the date committed represents the opportunity cost associated with the options and thus the total compensation. An alternative argument, in favor of the *APB Opinion No. 25* measurement date, relies on labor economic theory. From the employee's perspective, the employees contract for services based on the amount of marginal revenue product they provide. Accordingly, the employee accepts the options in lieu of current wages. Consequently, the difference between the current market price and the option of the shares represents employee compensation.

The ultimate value of this investment lies somewhere between zero, when the market price never exceeds the option price, and a very large return—when the market price rises substantially above the option price. Some accountants have advocated recording the value of the option at the expected value that lies between these two extremes. However, this procedure would result in a more subjective valuation. The recording and measurement of common stock option plans will undoubtedly continue to be a controversial issue in the near future. In addition, recent innovations using leverage and preferred stock have added to the complexity of employee stock option plans.

Recording Stock Options under FASB ASC 718   Many accountants believe that the procedures for recognizing common stock options previously required under the provisions of *APB Opinion No. 25* resulted in understated income statement and balance sheet valuations. They maintain that employees accepting stock options are accepting an investment in the firm in lieu of additional cash compensation. For example, in 1984, Walt Disney Company granted stock options to its chairman of the board, Michael Eisner. These options allowed him to purchase shares at approximately $57.44 per share. By 1992, when he exercised most of his options, the split-adjusted value of the shares had risen to approximately $646.00. As a result, Eisner realized a profit of over $126,900,000. However, the accounting rules in place at the time did not require Disney to report any expense at the time the options were granted.[25] As the result of many similar situations, several organizations interested in the development of accounting standards asked the FASB to reconsider the reporting requirements contained in *APB Opinion No. 25*.

Since options are generally given to motivate future performance, the option price is almost always at the market price at the time options are granted with an expiration date of 10 years.[26] As a result, the provisions of *APB Opinion No. 25* seldom resulted in companies recording compensation expense when stock options were granted. This inconsistency and the increasing use of stock option plans as a form of employee compensation caused the FASB to reconsider accounting for stock options.

25. Thomas Barton, William Shenkir, and Frederick Cole, "Other Voices," *Barron's* (November 14, 1994), 65–68.

26. See, for example, S. R. Matsunaga, "The Effects of Financial Reporting Costs on the Use of Employee Stock Options," *Accounting Review* 70, no. 1 (1995): 1–26; "The Relationship between Abnormal Stock Price Performance and Equity Incentive Programs," White Paper (Scottsdale, AZ: Gradient Analytics, Inc, 2005).

The accounting guidance for stock options now contained at FASB ASC 718 has a long and evolutionary history. As far back as 1984, the FASB issued an invitation to comment on the stock option issue; and between that time and 1988, the FASB deliberated the subject. However, even though the Board initially came to an agreement that stock options were a form of employee compensation, it could not agree on how to account for their cost. Later in 1992, the FASB again took up the issue and in 1993 issued an exposure draft reaffirming the Board's position that stock options are a form of employee compensation that should be estimated at fair value.

The FASB received more than 1,700 comment letters on the exposure draft that mainly objected to the proposed new treatment. Opponents claimed that the result would be a dramatic charge against earnings that would have detrimental effects on competitiveness and innovation, and might also have the unintended consequence of companies deciding to discontinue their stock option plans. Subsequently, in 1993, Senator Joseph Lieberman introduced a bill in Congress that would have ordered the SEC to require that no compensation expense be reported on the income statement for stock option plans. This bill could have set a dangerous precedent for interfering in the operations of FASB.

The strong opposition to the FASB's position forced it to compromise. In 1995 the Board released *SFAS No 123*, "Accounting for Stock Based Compensation" (superseded). This pronouncement encouraged firms to recognize the estimated value of stock options as an expense, but allowed this expense to be disclosed in the footnotes to the financial statements. However, the FASB urged companies to voluntarily disclose the fair value of the compensation expense associated with stock options in their financial statements.

Criticism of the footnote disclosure requirement became more vocal in the early 2000s because of the widespread concern over deceptive accounting practices at companies accused of fraud (e.g., Enron, Tyco, and WorldCom). In several of these situations, corporations used stock options to avoid paying U.S. taxes while overstating earnings, and company executives who held substantial stock options were motivated to artificially inflate stock prices for their own financial gain.

Stock options helped companies avoid paying taxes because when they were exercised, corporations took a tax deduction for the difference between what employees paid for the stock and its current value. But under the accounting rules in force at the time, companies didn't treat stock options transactions as expenses. For example, Microsoft had a tax savings of $2.7 billion in stock option tax benefits during the period from 1996 to 1998. The savings were realized largely because stock option tax benefits are dependent on how much a company's stock has gone up in value. Consequently, the tax savings were especially large in high-tech industries whose market valuations increased substantially during that same three-year period.

The disclosures arising from these cases increased the demand for more transparency in corporate reporting. The FASB responded to these concerns with the release of *SFAS No. 123R* (see FASB ASC 718) in December 2004. This guidance requires companies issuing stock options to estimate the compensation expense arising from the granting of stock options by using a fair value method and to disclose this estimated compensation expense on their income statements.

Under the fair value method, companies measure the expected future value of stock options by using either the model developed by Fisher Black and Myron

Scholes[27] or the binomial lattice model. FASB ASC 718-10-55 does not favor the use of either model; rather, it indicates that "The measurement objective for equity instruments awarded to employees is to estimate the fair value at the grant date of the equity instruments that the entity is obligated to issue when employees have rendered the requisite service and satisfied any other conditions necessary to earn the right to benefit from the instruments" (see FASB ASC 718-10-30-6). Both models satisfy this objective and use the same basic inputs:

1. The underlying stock price
2. The risk-free rate of interest
3. The strike price
4. The dividend yield
5. The volatility of the company's stock price
6. The expected term of the option

The difference between the models is that the binomial lattice method allows companies to change the parameters. It takes into consideration that in any period, a stock price can increase or decrease. Additionally, though the Black-Scholes model assumes that option holders will not exercise until the end of the option period, the binomial lattice model allows for early exercise. The binomial lattice model results in a number of potential outcomes whose present values are summed at the risk-free rate of return. These values are then averaged to arrive at the fair value of the option.

The opposition to the FASB ASC 718 guidance did not end with the issuance of *SFAS No. 123R*. In 2006, twenty-seven noted economists and business leaders, including Nobel Prize–winning economist Milton Friedman and former cabinet officer George Schultz, issued a position paper opposing its provisions. The signatories to this position paper opposed expensing stock options because they believed it to be improper accounting that results in the serious impairment of the financial statements of companies that are users of broad-based stock option plans. Additionally, they believed that the requirements result in damage to companies' bottom lines, compromise their ability to attract talented employees, and make them less competitive against foreign rivals that don't face similar requirements.[28]

Stock Warrants

Stock warrants are certificates that allow holders to acquire shares of stock at certain prices within stated periods. These certificates are generally issued under one of two conditions:

1. As evidence of the *preemptive right* of current shareholders to purchase additional shares of common stock from new stock issues in proportion to their current ownership percentage

27. This model, termed Black-Scholes, was further refined by Scholes and Robert Merton to incorporate other areas of finance. They were rewarded for their work by receiving the Nobel Prize for economics in 1997. Fisher Black, who died in 1995, was ineligible for the Nobel Prize because it is not awarded posthumously.

28. K. Hagopian, "Expensing Employee Stock Options Is Improper Accounting," *California Management Review* 48, no. 4 (2006): 136–56.

2. As an inducement originally attached to debt or preferred shares to increase the marketability of these securities

Under current practice, the accounting for the preemptive right of existing shareholders creates no particular problem. These warrants are recorded only as memoranda in the formal accounting records. In the event warrants of this type are exercised, the value of the shares of stock issued is measured at the amount of cash exchanged.

Detachable warrants attached to other securities require a separate valuation because they may be traded on the open market. The amount to be attributed to these types of warrants depends on their value in the securities market. Their value is measured by determining the percentage relationship of the price of the warrant to the total market price of the security and warrant and then applying this percentage to the proceeds of the security issue. This procedure should be followed whether the warrants are associated with bonds or with preferred stock.

In *APB Opinion No. 14* (see FASB ASC 470), the APB supported this approach when it stated:

> The Board is of the opinion that the portion of the proceeds of debt securities issued with detachable stock purchase warrants which is applicable to the warrants should be accounted for as paid-in capital. The allocation should be based on the relative fair value of the two securities at the time of issuance.[29]

If the warrants are exercised, their value will be added to the cash received to arrive at the carrying value of the common stock. In the event the warrants are not exercised within the designated period, the portion of the cost of the security allocated to the warrants will remain on the books as paid-in capital.

Retained Earnings

Legal restrictions in most states allow corporations to pay dividends only when there are accumulated, undistributed earnings. These restrictions have resulted in the reporting of earned capital as a component of owners' equity separate from paid-in capital. Although some states allow dividends from paid-in capital in the event of deficits, corporate managements generally do not wish to deplete capital, and distributions of this type are rare.

Retained earnings represent the accumulated net profits of a corporation that have not been distributed as dividends. It also should be noted that accumulated retained earnings do not necessarily mean that a corporation has the cash available to pay dividends. Accumulated earnings allow corporations to distribute dividends; the actual cash funds to pay these dividends must be available or acquired from other sources.

In many cases the retained earnings balance disclosed on the financial statements is divided into appropriated and unappropriated sections. Appropriated retained earnings comprise that portion of retained earnings that is not available to distribute as dividends. Appropriations may arise from legal restrictions, contractual restrictions, or internal decisions. However, an appropriation does not

---

29. Accounting Principles Board, *Opinion No. 14*, "Accounting for Convertible Debt and Debt Issued with Stock Purchase Warrants" (New York: AICPA, 1969), para. 16.

provide the funds to accomplish stated objectives, and it can be argued that these disclosures might be just as effective if presented as footnotes.

Stock Dividends

As noted previously, corporations may have accumulated earnings but not have the funds available to distribute these earnings as cash dividends to stockholders. In such cases, the company may elect to distribute some of its own shares of stock as dividends to current stockholders. Distributions of this type are termed *stock dividends*. When stock dividends are minor, relative to the total number of shares outstanding, retained earnings are reduced by the market value of the shares distributed. Capital stock and additional paid-in capital are increased by the par value of the shares and any excess, respectively. In theory, a relatively small stock dividend will not adversely affect the previously established market value of the stock. The rationale behind stock dividend distributions is that the stockholders will receive additional shares with the same value per share as those previously held. Nevertheless, stock dividends are not income to the recipients. They represent no distribution of corporate assets to the owners and are simply a reclassification of ownership interests.

Stock Splits

A procedure somewhat similar to stock dividends, but with a different purpose, is a *stock split*. The most economical method of purchasing and selling stock in the stock market is in blocks of 100 shares, and this practice affects the marketability of the stock. The higher the price of an individual share of stock, the smaller the number of people who can purchase the stock in blocks of 100. For this reason, many corporations seek to maintain the price of their stock within certain ranges. When the price climbs above that range, the firm may decide to issue additional shares to all existing stockholders (or split the stock). In a stock split, each stockholder receives a stated multiple of the number of shares currently held (usually 2 or 3 for 1), which lowers the market price per share. In theory, this lower price should be equivalent to dividing the current price by the multiple of shares in the split; but intervening variables in the marketplace frequently affect prices simultaneously. A stock split does not cause any change in the stockholder's equity section except to increase the number of actual shares outstanding and reduce the par or stated value per share. No additional values are assigned to the shares of stock issued in a stock split, because no distribution of assets or reclassification of ownership interests occurs.

A question sometimes arises as to whether a stock dividend is in actuality a stock split and should be treated accordingly. In a stock dividend, no material change in the market price of the shares is anticipated, whereas stock splits are undertaken specifically to change the market price of the shares. A large stock dividend can cause market prices to decline regardless of the terminology attached to the distribution. A rule of thumb is that if a stock dividend is at least 20 to 25 percent of the outstanding shares, the distribution should be recorded in a manner similar to a stock split. Stock distributions of this magnitude are termed *large stock dividends*. When large stock dividends are declared, standard practice is to capitalize an amount of retained earnings equal to the par value of the shares issued.

Treasury Stock

Capital may be reduced by formally repurchasing and canceling outstanding shares of stock; however, the corporation may informally reduce capital by acquiring shares on the open market without canceling them. These reacquired shares are termed *treasury stock*. Reacquisition of a company's own stock reduces both assets and stockholder equity and results in a legal restriction on retained earnings. The amount of shares repurchased is usually limited by the amount of a company's retained earnings.

In general, finance theory interprets stock repurchase announcements as an indication that management views them as underpriced in the marketplace.[30] In addition, a company may reacquire its own shares in order to offer employee stock options.

Two methods of accounting for treasury stock are found in current practice: the cost method and the par value method. Under the *cost method*, the presumption is that the shares acquired will be resold, and two events are assumed: (1) the corporation purchases the shares, and (2) the shares are reissued to a new stockholder. The reacquired shares are recorded at cost, and this amount is disclosed as negative stockholders' equity by deducting it from total capital until the shares are resold. Because treasury stock transactions are transactions with owners, any difference between the acquisition price and the sales price is generally treated as an adjustment to paid-in capital (unless sufficient additional paid-in capital is not available to offset any "loss"; in such cases, retained earnings are charged).

Under the *par value method*, it is assumed that the corporation's relationship with the original stockholder is ended. The transaction is in substance a retirement; hence, the shares are considered constructively retired. Therefore, legal capital and additional paid-in capital are reduced for the original issue price of the reacquired shares. Any difference between the original issue price and the reacquisition price is treated as an adjustment to additional paid-in capital (unless a sufficient balance is not available to offset a "loss," and retained earnings are charged). The par value of the reacquired shares is disclosed as a deduction from capital stock until the treasury shares are reissued.

The disclosure requirements for treasury stock in financial statements are not clearly defined by generally accepted accounting principles. For example, *APB Opinion No. 6*, since superseded, stated:

> When a corporation's stock is acquired for purposes other than retirement (formal or constructive), or when ultimate disposition has not yet been decided, the cost of acquired stock may be shown separately, as a deduction from the total capital stock, capital surplus, and retained earnings, or may be accorded the accounting treatment appropriate for retired stock, or in some circumstances may be shown as an asset.[31]

This opinion, in effect, allowed for virtually any presentation of treasury stock desired by a corporation and disregarded the reasons for the acquisition of the shares. Treasury stock is clearly not an asset because a company cannot own itself, and dividends are not paid on treasury shares. Similarly, "gains" and "losses" on treasury stock transactions are not to be reported on the income statement because of the possibility of income manipulation and because gains and losses cannot result from investments by owners or distributions to owners. FASB ASC 505-30-45-1 now indicates that the cost of treasury stock should be shown

---

30. Ibid.

31. Accounting Principles Board, *Opinion No. 6*, "Status of Accounting Research Bulletins" (New York: AICPA, 1965), para. 12.

separately as a deduction from the total of capital stock, additional paid-in capital, and retained earnings.

Other Comprehensive Income

Items recorded as other comprehensive income arise from events not connected with the issuance of stock or the normal profit-directed operations of the company. They result from the need to recognize assets or changes in value of other balance sheet items that have been excluded from the components of income by an authoritative body. The recognition issues for these items are discussed elsewhere in the text. The major examples of other comprehensive income are (1) unrealized gains and losses on investments in debt and equity securities classified as available for sale securities (discussed in Chapter 8), and (2) unrealized gains and losses resulting from the translation of certain investments in foreign subsidiaries (discussed in Chapter 16).

Quasi-Reorganizations

A corporation that suffers losses over an extended period of time may find it difficult to attract new capital. That is, debt holders and stockholders wish to receive a return on their investments, but a period of unprofitable operations may restrict the corporation's ability to offer interest and dividend payments. This is particularly true for stockholders who cannot receive dividends unless there is a positive retained earnings balance.

In some cases a corporate reorganization allowed under the provisions of state law may be attempted as an alternative to bankruptcy. These situations are termed *quasi-reorganizations*, and the company is given a fresh start by eliminating the deficit balance in retained earnings and writing down any overvalued assets. If a quasi-reorganization is undertaken, the corporation must clearly disclose its plan to the stockholders and receive their formal approval.

Modigliani and Miller found that the actual payment of dividends did not affect the market value of an enterprise, whereas the ability to pay dividends did affect a firm's market value.[32] A quasi-reorganization gives a firm the ability to pay dividends sooner than it would have been able to without a quasi-reorganization, and a quasi-reorganization can positively affect the market value of a reorganized enterprise. Therefore a firm that is unable to pay dividends because of negative retained earnings will be able to raise new capital more economically if it first engages in a quasi-reorganization.

The steps involved in a quasi-reorganization are as follows:

1. Assets are written down to their fair market value against retained earnings or additional paid-in capital.

2. The retained earnings deficit is eliminated against additional paid-in capital or legal capital.

3. The zero retained earnings balance is dated, and this date is retained until it loses its significance (typically 5 to 10 years).

---

32. Modigliani and Miller, "Cost of Capital, Corporation Finance and the Theory of Investment," 261–97.

Financial Analysis of Stockholders' Equity

The financial analysis of investment returns was introduced in Chapter 7. The return-on-assets (ROA) ratio measures the average return on investment to all investors regardless of their relationship to the company. This ratio is based on the entity theory in that it does not distinguish among investors and reports on overall firm performance. A ratio that reports on a company's performance from the point of view of its common stockholders is the return on common shareholders' equity (ROCSE). This ratio is based on the proprietary theory in that borrowing costs are considered expenses rather than a return on investment and is calculated as:

$$\text{ROCSE} = \frac{\text{Net income available to common shareholders}}{\text{Average common stockholders' equity}}$$

When calculating this ratio, transitory items are eliminated in order to reflect sustainable income available to common stockholders. Table 15.1 contains information to calculate ROCSE for Hershey and Tootsie Roll.

TABLE 15.1   *Selected Data ($000 omitted)*

Hershey	2008	2007	2006
Net income	$ 311,405	$ 214,154	
Business realignment and asset impairment charge net of tax	94,801	276,868	
Stockholder's equity	318,199	592,922	683,423
Total assets	3,634,719	4,247,113	4,157,565

Tootsie Roll	2008	2007	2006
Net income	$ 38,777	$ 51,625	
Stockholder's equity	634,770	638,230	630,681
Total assets	812,092	812,725	791,639

Hershey's fiscal 2008 net income was $311,405,000 and its 2007 net income was $214,154,000. The company reported asset impairment charges in 2008 and 2007.

Tootsie Roll's fiscal 2008 net income was $38,777,000. In 2007, the company's net income was $51,625,000.

The ROCSEs for Hershey and Tootsie Roll for fiscal 2008 and 2007 are calculated as follows ($000 omitted).

Return on Common Stockholders' Equity (ROCSE)

	Hershey	Tootsie Roll
2008	$\dfrac{\$311{,}405 + 94{,}801}{(\$318{,}199 + 592{,}922)/2} = 0.892$	$\dfrac{\$38{,}777}{(\$634{,}770 + 638{,}230)/2} = 0.061$
2007	$\dfrac{\$214{,}154 + 276{,}868}{(\$592{,}922 + 683{,}423)/2} = 0.769$	$\dfrac{\$51{,}625}{(\$638{,}230 + 630{,}681)/2} = 0.081$

The ROCSE is affected by both profitability and the extent to which a company employs financial leverage. As discussed in Chapter 11, financial leverage increases the rate of return to common stockholders when the return on investment projects is greater than the cost of the borrowed funds. Hershey's ROCSE increased from 76.9 percent in 2007 to 89.2 percent in 2008. These returns are much higher than the adjusted ROA measure of 11.91 percent for 2008 that was illustrated in Chapter 7. They are also much higher than the five-year industry average of 7.22 percent. Tootsie Roll's ROCSEs of 6.1 percent and 8.2 percent for fiscal years 2008 and 2007, respectively, are slightly lower and slightly higher than the industry average. The differences between Hershey and Tootsie Roll are attributable to the fact that Hershey is much more highly leveraged than Tootsie Roll.

Since ROCSE measures the return to common stockholders, the numerator should be reduced by dividends to preferred stockholders. Neither Tootsie Roll nor Hershey has any preferred stockholders. However, both companies have Class B common stock. Since these shares are similar to preferred shares, a better picture of the return to common stock would exclude their dividends from the numerator and their claim to equity from the denominator. Removal of the effects of the Class B stock for Hershey has only a minor effect on the company's ROCSE. There is insufficient information available to make similar adjustments for Tootsie Roll.

A company's use of financial leverage can be further evaluated by calculating the financial structure ratio (FSR). This ratio indicates the proportion of the company's assets that are being financed by the stockholders and is calculated as:

$$FSR = \frac{\text{Average assets}}{\text{Average common stockholders' equity}}$$

The FSRs for Hershey and Tootsie Roll for 2008 and 2007 are as follows.

Financial Structure Ratio (FSR)

	Hershey	Tootsie Roll
2008	$\dfrac{(\$3,634,719 + 4,247,113)/2}{(\$318,199 + 592,922)/2} = 8.65$	$\dfrac{(\$812,092 + 812,725)/2}{(\$634,770 + 638,230)/2} = 1.28$
2007	$\dfrac{(\$4,247,113 + 4,157,565)/2}{(\$592,922 + 683,423)/2} = 6.59$	$\dfrac{(\$812,725 + 791,639)/2}{(\$638,230 + 630,681)/2} = 1.26$

These ratios indicate that Hershey's use of financial leverage results in a rate of return to the common stockholders that exceeds what it earns on its assets.

International Accounting Standards

The IASB has addressed the following issues relating to stockholders' equity: (1) the presentation of equity on the financial statements in its framework (see below) and (2) share-based payments in *IFRS No. 2*.

In "Framework for the Preparation and Presentation of Financial Statements," the IASC indicated a preference for the proprietary theory when it stated, "*Equity* is the residual interest in the assets of the enterprise after deducting all its liabilities."[33] The IASC then indicated that equity may be subclassified to disclose amounts contributed by stockholders, retained earnings, reserves, and capital maintenance adjustments. These subclassifications are viewed as relevant to the decision-making needs of the users of financial statements because they indicate any current legal restrictions and may reflect the fact that different ownership interests have different rights.

The objective of *IFRS No. 2*, "Share-Based Payment,"[34] is to specify the financial reporting by an entity for the effects of share-based payment transactions, including expenses associated with transactions in which *share options* are granted to employees. The concept of share-based payments outlined in *IFRS No. 2* is broader than the concept of employee share options. *IFRS No. 2* encompasses the issuance of shares, or rights to shares, in return for services and goods. Examples of items included in the scope of *IFRS No. 2* are share appreciation rights, employee share purchase plans, employee share ownership plans, share option plans, and plans where the issuance of shares (or rights to shares) may depend on market or non-market-related conditions. *IFRS No. 2* requires an entity to recognize share-based payment transactions in its financial statements, including transactions with employees or other parties to be settled in cash, other assets, or equity instruments of the entity as an increase in a component of stockholders' equity and an expense.

IFRS No. 2 sets out measurement principles and specific requirements for three types of share-based payment transactions:

1. Equity-settled share-based payment transactions, in which the entity receives goods or services as consideration for equity instruments of the entity (including shares or share options)

2. Cash-settled share-based payment transactions, in which the entity acquires goods or services by incurring liabilities to the supplier of those goods or services for amounts that are based on the price (or value) of the entity's shares or other equity instruments of the entity

3. Transactions in which the entity receives or acquires goods or services, and the terms of the arrangement provide either the entity or the supplier of those goods or services with a choice of whether the entity settles the transaction in cash or by issuing equity instruments

For equity-settled share-based payment transactions, the IFRS requires an entity to measure the goods or services received, and the corresponding increase in equity—directly—at the fair value of the goods or services received, unless that fair value cannot be estimated reliably.

For cash-settled share-based payment transactions, the IFRS requires an entity to measure the goods or services acquired and the liability incurred at the fair value of the liability. Until the liability is settled, the entity is required to remeasure the fair value of the liability at each reporting date and at the date of settlement, and any changes in value are to be recognized in profit or loss for the period.

33. International Accounting Standards Committee, "Framework for the Preparation and Presentation of Financial Statements," (London, IASB, 1989), para. 49(c).

34. International Financial Reporting Standard No. 2, "Share-Based Payment" (London: IASB, 2004).

For share-based payment transactions in which the terms of the arrangement provide either the entity or the supplier of goods or services with a choice of whether the entity settles the transaction in cash or by issuing equity instruments, the entity is required to account for that transaction, or the components of that transaction, as a cash-settled share-based payment transaction if, and to the extent that, the entity has incurred a liability to settle in cash (or other assets), or as an equity-settled share-based payment transaction if, and to the extent that, no such liability has been incurred.

IFRS No. 2 also prescribes various disclosure requirements to enable users of financial statements to understand:

1. The nature and extent of share-based payment arrangements that existed during the period

2. How the fair value of the goods or services received, or the fair value of the equity instruments granted, during the period was determined

3. The effect of share-based payment transactions on the entity's profit or loss for the period and on its financial position[35]

Cases

• Case 15-1 Accounting for Employee Stock Options: Theoretical Arguments

Arts Corporation offers a generous employee compensation package that includes employee stock options. The exercise price has always been equal to the market price of the stock at the date of grant. The corporate controller, John Jones, believes that employee stock options, like all obligations to issue the corporation's own stock, are equity. The new staff accountant, Marcy Means, disagrees. Marcy argues that when a company issues stock for less than current value, the value of preexisting stockholders' shares is diluted.

Required:

a. Describe how Arts Corporation should account for its employee stock option plan, under existing GAAP.

b. Pretend you are hired to debate the issue of the proper treatment of options written on a company's own stock. Formulate your argument, citing concepts and definitions to buttress your case, assuming

  i. You are siding with John

  ii. You are siding with Marcy

---

35. Although the accounting requirements of FASB ASC and IFRS are similar, there are some differences that are beyond the scope of this text. For a summary of those differences see Andrew Mandel and Fred Whittlesey, "Convergence Towards International Financial Reporting Standards Will Require Comprehensive Review of Executive and Equity Compensation Programs," *Insightout* (2008), http://www.buckconsultants.com/buckconsultants/Portals/0/Documents/PUBLICATIONS/White_Papers/WP_Compensation/wp_insight_Compensation_Convergence_IFRS.pdf.

• Case 15-2 Financial Statements under Various Theories of Equity

Drake Company reported the following for 2011:

Current assets	$87,000
Current liabilities	19,000
Revenues	450,000
Cost of goods sold	220,000
Noncurrent assets	186,000
Bonds payable (10%, issued at par)	100,000
Preferred stock, $5, $100 par	20,000
Common stock, $10 par	50,000
Paid-in capital in excess of par	48,000
Operating expenses	64,000
Retained earnings	36,000

Common stockholders received a $2 dividend during the year. The preferred stock is noncumulative and nonparticipating.

Required

a. Ignoring income taxes, prepare an income statement and balance sheet for Drake Company at December 31, 2011, that is consistent with each of the following theories of equity:

  i. Entity theory

  ii. Proprietary theory

  iii. Residual equity theory

b. For each theory cited above, compute the December 31, 2011, debt-to-equity ratio. If none would be computed, discuss why.

• Case 15-3 Accounting for Treasury Stocks

For numerous reasons, a corporation may reacquire shares of its own capital stock. When a company purchases treasury stock, it has two options as to how to account for the shares: the cost method and the par value method.

Required:

Compare and contrast the cost method and the par value method for each of the following:

a. Purchase of shares at a price less than par value

b. Purchase of shares at a price greater than par value

c. Subsequent resale of treasury shares at a price less than purchase price but more than par value

d. Subsequent resale of treasury shares at a price greater than both purchase price and par value

e. Effect on net income

• Case 15-4 Accounting for a Quasi-Reorganization

Carrol, Inc. accomplished a quasi-reorganization effective December 31, 2011. Immediately before the quasi-reorganization, the stockholders' equity was as follows:

Common stock, par value $10 per share	
authorized issued and outstanding 400,000 shares	$4,000,000
Additional paid-in capital	600,000
Retained earnings (deficit)	(900,000)

Under the terms of the quasi-reorganization, the par value of the common stock was reduced from $10 per share to $5 per share and equipment was written down by $1.2 million.

Required:
Discuss the accounting treatment necessary to accomplish this quasi-reorganization.

• Case 15-5 Stock Options: Various Methods

Stock options are widely used as a form of compensation for corporate executives.

Required:

a. Identify five methods that had been proposed for determining the value of executive stock options before the release of *SFAS No. 123R*.

b. Discuss the conceptual merits of each of these proposed methods.

• Case 15-6 Effects of Stock Options

On January 1, 2010, as an incentive to improved performance of duties, Recycling Corporation adopted a qualified stock option plan to grant corporate executives nontransferable stock options to 500,000 shares of its unissued $1 par value common stock. The options were granted on May 1, 2010, at $25 per share, the market price on that date. All the options were exercisable one year later and for four years thereafter, providing that the grantee was employed by the corporation at the date of exercise.

The market price of this stock was $40 per share on May 1, 2011. All options were exercised before December 31, 2011, at times when the market price varied between $40 and $50 per share.

Required:

a. What information on this option plan should be presented in the financial statements of Recycling Corporation at (1) December 31, 2010, and (2) December 31, 2011? Explain.

b. It has been said that the exercise of such a stock option would dilute the equity of existing stockholders in the corporation.

   i. How could this happen? Discuss.

   ii. What conditions could prevent a dilution of existing equities from taking place in this transaction? Discuss.

• Case 15-7 Theoretical Implications of Various Theories of Equity

The proprietary theory, the entity theory, and the funds theory are three approaches to accounting for equities.

Required:

  a. Describe briefly each of these theories.

  b. State your reasons for emphasizing the application of one of these theories to each of the following.

  i. Single proprietorship

  ii. Partnership

  iii. Financial institutions (banks)

  iv. Consolidated statements

  v. Estate accounting

• Case 15-8 Classification of Stockholders' Equity

The total owners' equity is usually under a number of subcaptions on the corporation's balance sheet.

Required:

  a. List the major subdivisions of the stockholders' equity section of a corporate balance sheet, and describe briefly the nature of the amounts that will appear in each section.

  b. Explain fully the reasons for subdividing the amount of stockholders' equity, including legal, accounting, and other considerations.

  c. Describe three kinds of transactions that will result in paid-in or permanent capital in excess of legal or stated capital.

  d. Various accounting authorities have recommended that the terms *paid-in surplus* and *earned surplus* not be used in published financial statements. Explain briefly the reason for this suggestion, and indicate acceptable substitutes for the terms.

• Case 15-9 Stock Dividends

The directors of Lenox Corporation are considering issuing a stock dividend.

Required:

  a. What is a stock dividend? How is a stock dividend distinguished from a stock split from a legal standpoint? From an accounting standpoint?

  b. For what reasons does a corporation usually declare a stock dividend? A stock split?

  c. Discuss the amount, if any, of retained earnings to be capitalized in connection with a stock dividend.

• Case 15-10 Stock Splits and Stock Dividends

A corporation may use stock splits and stock dividends to change the number of shares of its stock outstanding.

Required:

a. What is meant by a stock split effected in the form of a dividend?

b. From an accounting viewpoint, explain how the stock split effected in the form of a dividend differs from an ordinary stock dividend.

c. How should a stock dividend that has been declared but not yet issued be classified in a statement of financial position? Why?

• Case 15-11 Accounting for Employee Stock Option Plans (ESOPs)

Growth Corporation offered the following stock option plan to its employees: Each employee will receive 1,000 options to purchase shares of stock at an option price equal to the market price of the company's common shares on the grant date, January 1, 20x1. On that date:

The market price per share was	$22
The fair value of an option was	$ 3

Required:

a. Describe how the ESOPs would have been reported under the provisions of *APB Opinion No. 25*.

b. Analyze and explain the consequences of the *APB Opinion No. 25* accounting treatment. Your analysis should consider the following:

   i. The conceptual framework

   ii. Any ethical implications

   iii. The impact on financial statements

   iv. The impact on financial ratios

c. The FASB now requires companies to use the fair value method of accounting for ESOPs as described in *FASB ASC 718*. Describe how the ESOPs will be reported under this method.

d. Analyze and explain the consequences of using fair value to measure and report the ESOPs. Your analysis should consider the following:

   i. The conceptual framework

   ii. Any ethical implications

   iii. The impact on financial statements

   iv. The impact on financial ratios

• Case 15-12 Debt versus Equity

The entity theory of equity implies that there should be no need for financial statements to distinguish between debt and equity. Alternatively, proprietary theory implies that such a distinction is necessary and yields information vital to owners and potential stockholders.

Required:

a. Discuss the entity theory rationale for making no distinction between debt and equity.

b. Is entity theory or proprietary theory consistent with modern theories of finance—that is, does the firm's capital structure make a difference? Explain.

FASB ASC Research

For each of the following research cases, search the FASB ASC database for information to address the issues. Cut and paste the FASB requirements that support your responses. Then summarize briefly what your responses are, citing the pronouncements and paragraphs used to support your responses.

• FASB ASC 15-1 Cost to Issue Equity Securities to Effect a Business Combination

Search the FASB ASC database to determine how a company should account for the cost incurred to issue equity securities when it issues equity securities to purchase another company. Cut and paste your findings (citing the source), and write a brief summary of what your research results mean.

• FASB ASC 15-2 Treasury Stock

Search the FASB ASC database to determine whether under current GAAP, treasury stock can be reported as an asset. If not, was treasury stock allowed to be reported as an asset in the past? Cut and paste your findings (citing the source), and write a brief summary of what your research results mean.

• FASB ASC 15-3 Quasi-Reorganizations

Accounting for quasi-reorganizations is contained in the FASB ASC. Find this topic, cite the source, and copy and paste the relevant requirements for accounting for quasi-reorganizations.

• FASB ASC 15-4 Dividends in Arrears

Find the requirements for disclosing cumulative preferred dividends in arrears in the FASB ASC.

• FASB ASC 15-5 Stock Dividends and Splits

Find the FASB ASC guidance on accounting for stock dividends and stock splits and cite it. Write a brief summary of the FASB ASC guidance on accounting for stock splits and stock dividends.

• FASB ASC 15-6 Treasury Stock

Find the FASB ASC guidance on accounting for treasury stock and cite it. Write a brief summary of the FASB ASC guidance on accounting for treasury stock.

Room for Debate

• Debate 15-1 The Nature of Stock Options

In the 1990 discussion memorandum, "Distinguishing between Liability and Equity Instruments and Accounting for Instruments with Characteristics of Both," the FASB presented arguments relating to the presentation and measurement of a company's stock options and warrants. Under current GAAP, stock options and warrants are measured at the historical fair value of consideration received at issuance. The amount received is reported as an element of stockholders' equity.

Some theorists argue that stock options and warrants represent obligations of the issuing entity and should be reported as liabilities. Moreover, a more appropriate measure would be fair value of the options or warrants at the balance sheet date.

Team Debate:

Team 1:   Argue for the current GAAP treatment for the issuance and subsequent reporting of stock options and warrants.

Team 2:   Argue for reporting stock options and warrants as liabilities measured at current fair value.

• Debate 15-2 The Nature of Cumulative Preferred Dividends

Under GAAP, cumulative preferred dividends are reported as liabilities only after they have been declared by the corporation's board of directors. For the following debate, support your arguments by referring to the *SFAC No. 6* definition of liabilities and the consequent characteristics of liabilities.

Team Debate:

Team 1:   Argue that cumulative preferred dividends are liabilities, even if not declared.

Team 2:   Argue that cumulative preferred dividends are not liabilities unless they are declared.

• Debate 15-3 Distinguishing Between Debt and Equity

In its 1990 discussion memorandum on distinguishing between liabilities and equity, the FASB posed the question, "Should the sharp distinction between liabilities and equity be effectively eliminated?" To do so would be consistent with the entity theory of equity and with the notion that the capital structure (debt versus equity) of a firm is irrelevant to users of financial information.

Team Debate:

Team 1:   Argue for elimination of the distinction between debt and equity. Support your argument by citing the entity theory of equity as well as the finance theory asserting that capital structure is irrelevant.

Team 2:   Argue against elimination of the distinction between debt and equity. Support your argument by citing the proprietary theory of equity as well as the finance theory asserting that capital structure is relevant.

Accounting for

Multiple Entities

Since the inception of the corporate form of organization, business enterprises have found it beneficial to combine operations to achieve economies of scale. These combined operations may vary from corporate joint ventures in which two or more corporations join together as a partnership for a project, such as drilling an offshore oil well, to the acquisition of one company by another. Accounting for the acquisitions of companies is complicated because various terms may be used to describe them. Such terms as *consolidation, combination, merger,* and *purchase* have all been used interchangeably even though they are not all the same, and some are subclassifications of others. In this chapter we focus on three aspects of accounting for multiple entities: (1) the acquisition of one company by another—*business combinations,* (2) the reporting of parent and subsidiary relationships—*consolidations* and *segment reporting,* and (3) foreign currency translation for international subsidiaries.

Business Combinations

Combining two or more previously separate business organizations into a single economic unit has been an observable phenomenon since the late 1800s. Wyatt categorized this phenomenon as follows:

- *The classical era.* The period from 1890 to 1904, following the passage of the Sherman Act. These combinations were generally accomplished through a holding company whose purpose was vertical integration of all operations from the acquisition of raw materials to the sale of the product.

- *Second wave.* The period from the end of World War I to the end of the 1920s. These combinations were generally piecemeal acquisitions whose purpose was to expand the operations of the acquiring company.

- *Third wave.* The period from the end of World War II through the 1960s. Again these were piecemeal acquisitions designed to strengthen competitive position, diversify into new areas, or keep up with technological changes.[1]

In addition to the foregoing reasons, several other factors may cause a business organization to consider combining with another organization:

- *Tax consequences.* The purchasing corporation may accrue the benefits of operating loss carry-forwards from acquired corporations.

- *Growth and diversification.* The purchasing corporation may wish to acquire a new product or enter a new market.

- *Financial considerations.* A larger asset base may make it easier for the corporation to acquire additional funds from capital markets.

- *Competitive pressure.* Economies of scale may alleviate a highly competitive market situation.

- *Profit and retirement.* The seller may be motivated by a high profit or the desire to retire.[2]

Accounting for Business Combinations

As an accounting concept, a business combination is the bringing together of two or more business entities into one accounting entity.[3] A *business combination* occurs when a transaction or event in which one entity (the acquirer) obtains control of one or more businesses (see FASB ASC 805-10-65-1). Under current generally accepted accounting principles (GAAP), *control* typically occurs when one company has a majority of the equity interest in another company. There are two methods of achieving majority ownership in another corporation: (1) the acquiring corporation purchases the voting stock of the acquired corporation for cash, or (2) the acquiring corporation exchanges its voting stock for the voting stock of the acquired corporation.

In accounting for business combinations, it is essential to recall that consistent with the qualitative characteristic of reliability, fair reporting of the results of economic events is the essence of the accounting process. Financial statements that report the results of a business combination should not be biased in favor of any group and must be based on the underlying substance of economic events. After the SEC was established during the 1930s, two methods of accounting for business combinations evolved: purchase and pooling of interests.

A *pooling of interests* was considered to have occurred when the ownership of two or more previously separate entities were combined and continued as the result of the exchange of ownership shares. The acquiring company would obtain control by issuing shares to the owners of the acquired company. Thus the stock of the acquiring company, which was issued to obtain the acquired entity, replaced

1. Arthur R. Wyatt, *A Critical Study of Accounting for Business Combinations* (New York: AICPA, 1963), 1–5.

2. Ibid., 6–8.

3. Accounting Principles Board, *Opinion No. 16*, "Business Combinations" (New York: APB, 1970).

the stock of the acquired entity. Given that a pooling of interests represented a continuation of business ownership in two or more previously separate businesses, the business combination was accounted for as the uniting of ownership interests. As a result, it was not accounted for as an acquisition but rather as a fusion of two or more previously separate entities. For example, the book values of the assets and liabilities of the merging companies were added together and reported on a consolidated balance sheet. No adjustments were made to reflect the fair values of the assets and liabilities, and goodwill was *not* reported. In addition, income for the new reporting unit included the income since the last reporting date for each of the previously separate companies.

Note that when voting stock is exchanged, all the previous owners are still present, and the companies have simply united to carry on their previously separate operations. It follows that the pooling of interests method may be considered appropriate when the ownership of two or more entities is combined. Alternatively, when the acquiring company pays cash to acquire control over another company, only the parent company stockholders remain. In this case, the business combination is really no different from the purchase of an asset, such as a building. The only difference is that the acquiring company has, in effect, acquired all the assets of another business and has also assumed its liabilities. Clearly, a business combination that is effected by a cash purchase of equity shares should be accounted for as though it were a purchase. But is the acquisition of control over another business through an exchange of equity shares really a "pooling" of previously separate interests, or is it really a purchase where the acquiring company has issued shares of its stock, in lieu of cash, as a means of effecting a purchase?

The APB reviewed this question and in 1970 issued *Opinion No. 16*, "Business Combinations"[4] (since superseded). The Board found merit in the use of both the pooling of interests and the purchase methods and did not propose that one method be used to the exclusion of the other. The APB noted that the two methods were not alternatives for accounting for the same transaction and established specific criteria for determining whether a combination should be accounted for as a purchase or as a pooling of interests. Under *APB Opinion No. 16*, all transactions that involved the exchange of cash were accounted for as purchases, whereas exchanges of voting stock were reported as pooling of interests subject to twelve specific pooling criteria. If any of the criteria were violated, the combination was treated as a purchase. The pooling criteria were established to ensure that a combination could not be accounted for as a pooling of interests in those cases where one group of stockholders achieved an advantage over another, or where the combined entity did not plan to carry on the activities of the previously separate companies.

It should be emphasized that pooling of interests was considered appropriate only when there had been an exchange of voting stock and each of the *APB Opinion No. 16* conditions for a pooling was met. Where a combination was effected by a cash transaction or when any of the twelve pooling conditions was violated, the purchase method had to be used.

4. Ibid.

Criticism of the Pooling of Interests Method

Critics argued that business combinations reported under the pooling of interests method were, in substance, similar to those reported under the purchase method; yet pooled financial statements were substantially different from those produced by the purchase method. Unlike the purchase method, pooling ignored the values exchanged in a business combination. As a result, under the pooling method, information regarding how much was invested to acquire an equity interest is not disclosed, and assets that were not previously reported by the combining companies were ignored. The consequent understatement of assets and overstatement of income in subsequent years hampered the investor's ability to assess return on investment. Moreover, because the acquired assets were not measured in a manner similar to other acquisitions, it was difficult to compare the performance of pooled entities to other companies. The end result was perhaps the disruption of the efficient allocation of resources in the capital markets.

Another consideration was that the pooling of interests method is not allowed under international accounting standards. This condition might have further exacerbated intercompany comparisons of financial condition and performance. In early 2000, the FASB voted to eliminate the pooling of interests method for all business combinations occurring after January 1, 2001.

This decision resulted in economic consequences arguments about its potential effect on mergers. Proponents of the pooling method contended that its elimination will have a negative effect on the ability of companies to engage in mergers in the future and that many of the mergers that took place during the 1990s would not have been consummated if the ruling to eliminate pooling of interests had been in place at that time. As a result, on October 3, 2000, two members of Congress, Representatives Christopher Cox (R–CA) and Calvin Dooley (D–CA) introduced a bill in the House of Representatives that would delay completion of the project on business combinations. This action was immediately criticized by the chairman of the FASB, Edmund Jenkins, as legislative interference with the FASB's ability to do its job. Subsequently, five members of Congress (four of whom were CPAs) issued Dear Colleague letters opposing the bill. These events caused the FASB to revisit the issue, but in early 2001 the Board reaffirmed its decision to eliminate pooling of interests accounting. In June 2001, the FASB issued *SFAS No. 141*, "Business Combinations" (see FASB ASC 805), which abolished further use of the pooling of interests method for business combinations.

The Fresh-Start Method

A stumbling block to the FASB's efforts to eliminate the pooling of interests method was the notion that some business combinations are essentially mergers of equals. In these cases none of the combining entities continues. Instead, a new combined entity that is substantially different from its predecessor companies emerges. In a 1998 position paper, the FASB determined that neither the purchase nor the pooling of interests methods may be appropriate for these types of business combinations; it proposed a new method, termed the *fresh-start method*. Under the fresh-start method, all assets of the combined, surviving entity would be revalued. The resulting financial statements would depict net assets and performance as though the enterprise were a newly formed business entity.

Such a revaluation would be similar to that under the purchase method; all the net assets of all combined parties would be revalued rather than just those of the acquired entity.[5]

The Purchase Method

Opponents of the pooling of interests method argue that all two-party business combinations (except perhaps for joint ventures) are essentially acquisitions of one or more acquirees by an acquiring company. The FASB issued *SFAS No. 141* in support of this contention. Its release required all business combinations that were excluded from its scope to be accounted for under the purchase method. This requirement meant that the purchase method would be used when one company acquired the net assets of a business and also obtained control over that business.

The FASB subsequently felt that the scope of *SFAS No. 141* was not broad enough because it was limited to business combinations where control was obtained only by transferring consideration, such as cash or the acquiring company's stock. In 2007, the standard was revised and is now referred to as *SFAS No. 141(R)* (see FASB ASC 805).

The Acquisition Method

The FASB believes that essentially all business combinations are acquisitions. Therefore, in issuing *SFAS No. 141(R)*, the Board not only broadened the scope of business combinations that should be accounted for as though they are purchases but also changed the name of the method of accounting for those acquisitions from the purchase method to the acquisition method.

In addition to making acquisitions in which control is obtained by transferring consideration subject to its provisions, the acquirer is now defined as an entity that obtains control of one or more businesses and establishes the acquisition date that control is achieved. A business is defined as an integrated set of activities or assets whose purpose is to provide a return to its investors, owners, members, or other participants (FASB ASC 805-20). Thus the acquisition method is not required for transactions that form joint ventures, acquisitions of assets that do not constitute a business, combinations of entities or businesses that are already under a common control, or not-for-profit entities.

In order to apply the acquisition method, the acquiring entity must first be identified. Obviously, if the business combination is effected by a cash exchange, the acquiring entity is the one that pays cash to acquire the voting shares of the acquired entity. On the other hand, when the business combination is effected by an exchange of equity shares, the acquiring entity may not be so clearly evident. In this case, FASB ASC 805-10-55-12 requires that the following "pertinent facts and circumstances" be taken into consideration:

1. The *relative voting rights* of the combined entity. All else being equal, the acquiring entity would be the one whose owners retained or received the larger portion of the voting rights of the combined entity.

5. Invitation to Comment, "Methods of Accounting for Business Combinations: Recommendations of the G4 + 1 for Achieving Convergence," FASB, December 15, 1998.

2. The *existence of a large minority voting interest* in the combined entity when no other owner or group of owners has a significant voting interest. All else being equal, the acquiring entity would be the one with the large minority voting interest.

3. The *composition of the governing body* of the combined entity. All else being equal, the acquiring entity's owners or governing body would be the one that has the ability to elect or appoint a majority of the governing body of the combined entity.

4. The *composition of senior management* of the combined entity. All else being equal, the acquiring entity's senior management would dominate that of the combined entity.

5. The *terms of exchange of equity securities*. All else being equal, the acquiring entity would be the one that pays a premium over the market value of the equity securities of the other combining entities.

After the acquiring entity has been identified, the next step in the acquisition method is to determine the cost of the acquisition. According to the historical cost principle, the cost of acquiring an asset is equal to the cost to purchase it and to get it ready for its intended use. This concept was applied to acquisitions before the revision of *SFAS No. 141*. In addition to including the cost incurred to acquire control, such as the cash paid to purchase the shares of the acquired entity, the cost of acquisition also included all direct costs incurred to effect the business combination, such as finder's fees, legal and accounting fees, and fees paid to appraisers and other consultants. The revised requirements are that these direct costs are to be expensed as incurred. One could easily argue that we are no longer applying the historical cost principle fully to business acquisitions. An argument in favor of the FASB's position on this issue is similar to the one made for expensing research and development costs. When research and development costs are incurred, there is uncertainty as to whether a viable result will be forthcoming. Similarly, when finder's fees and other such costs are incurred to effect a business combination, the company does not yet know whether the acquisition will actually take place. The current GAAP rules continue to require that the costs of issuing equity securities to acquire the shares of another entity be treated as a reduction of paid-in capital. Moreover, all indirect costs continue to be expensed as incurred.

Under the revised standard for business combinations, the acquirer must recognize all assets acquired, liabilities assumed, and any noncontrolling interest at fair value, measured as of the acquisition date (the date that control is attained). Fair value is defined by FASB ASC 820-10-20 *as* an exit value. It is the exchange price that would occur in an orderly transaction to sell an asset or transfer a liability in the most advantageous market. Thus fair value is market based and is not entity specific. Fair value excludes transaction costs because they are the incremental direct costs incurred to sell an asset or settle a debt. As such, they are specific to the transaction and have nothing to do with the value of the asset acquired itself or the liability assumed.

Fair value must be applied to assets and liabilities that meet the definition of assets and liabilities under *SFAC No. 6*. This means that the acquirer must recognize all assets and liabilities of the acquiree—even those that are not on the acquiree's books. Thus the acquirer must identify and measure intangibles such as brand names and even in-process research and development as well as advertising jingles. In order to recognize such an intangible asset, it must meet either of the two following criteria: (1) separability or (2) contractual or legal. Separability means that the intangible can be sold, transferred, licensed, rented, or exchanged. The contractual/legal criterion is that the asset arises from some contractual or legal right.

Exceptions to the fair value measurement requirement are deferred taxes, pensions and other postemployment benefits (OPEBs), share-based compensation, and assets held for sale. Long-lived assets, such as buildings and equipment, that are expected to be sold are to be measured at fair value minus the expected cost of disposal. In general, restructuring costs are to be treated as post-acquisition expenses. Restructuring costs are those associated with exit activities such as closing plants and providing severance pay.

Fair value measurement of noncontrolling interest is controversial. FASB ASC 805-20-30-7 indicates that the acquisition date market value of a share of the acquired entity's stock can be used, but that the value can be determined by other valuation techniques. Lack of guidance on this issue should be forthcoming. Some say that it should be based on the value inferred from the purchase price paid by the acquirer. It results from an arm's-length transaction and is thus market based. However, one could argue that it may not measure the true fair value of the acquiree because the price paid could include a control premium paid to effect the acquisition itself.

Once the acquisition cost and the fair values of all assets, liabilities, and noncontrolling interest are known, if the acquisition cost and the fair value of noncontrolling interest exceed the fair values of the identifiable net assets, the difference is deemed to be goodwill. Conversely, if there is an excess of the fair value of identifiable net assets over the cost of the acquisition plus the fair value of noncontrolling interest, the difference is deemed to be a bargain purchase. The amount of the bargain purchase is recognized in the income statement as a gain.

Recognition of a gain from a bargain purchase is a complete reversal from prior practice. Previously, any amount recognized as excess of fair value over cost was deemed to be caused by inefficient use of long-term assets. As a result, the fair value of those assets was reduced and the excess was brought into income over time by reductions in the amount of annual depreciation expense. One could argue that treating such an excess as a gain goes against the principles of economic exchange. The exchange price agreed upon in an arm's-length transaction is equal to fair value; thus, there is no bargain.

The acquisition method will result in financial statement measurements that are quite different from those of its predecessor, the purchase method. Under the purchase method, the assets are measured at the historical cost of the acquiree plus the proportion of the difference between the fair value of the asset and its acquiree's cost multiplied times the acquirer's proportionate interest in the asset. For example, under the purchase method, if the asset is on the books of the acquiree at $90,000, its fair value is $100,000, and the acquirer acquires 90 percent of the acquiree's outstanding shares of common stock, the acquirer would report the asset at $99,000 ($90,000 + ($100,000 − $90,000) × 90 percent. Under the acquisition method, the acquirer will report 100 percent of the fair value of the asset. Noncontrolling interest will be at 100 percent of its fair value, which will include 10 percent of the $100,000.

In those business combinations where the acquired entity is dissolved, the values assigned to the net assets as well as the noncontrolling interest in that entity are added to the books of the acquiring entity. The acquiring entity will then depreciate or amortize the assigned values and report them in the same manner as any other acquired net assets that the company might have. When the acquired entity is not dissolved, the two companies continue to keep separate sets of books. At year-end, their respective financial information must then be consolidated.

Business Combinations II

The FASB has undertaken a two-stage project with the IASB. The first phase resulted in the issuance of pronouncements by both boards on the valuation of intangible assets, *IFRS No. 3* and *SFAS No. 141*. The second phase is aimed at developing a standard that would include a common set of principles intended to improve the completeness, relevance, and comparability of financial information about business combinations.

At its meetings on April 18–19, 2007, the FASB determined that the measurement attribute in a business combination should be fair value and agreed that the FASB ASC 820 definition of fair value—the amount for which an asset could be exchanged, or a liability could be settled, in an arm's-length process—should be used to measure the assets in a business combination. This definition of fair value focuses on the price that would be received to sell an asset or the amount that would be paid to transfer a liability (i.e., exit prices). This definition is now used under the guidelines contained at FASB ASC 805.

Consolidations

Consolidation is presenting one set of financial statements for a reporting entity (the parent company) and its subsidiaries. Consolidation is required when one business entity has a controlling financial interest in one or more other business entities. When control is attained, the stockholders of the acquiring company (the *parent* company) have an interest in the net assets of the combined parent/*subsidiary* entity. It is logical to presume that financial statements combining the results of both parent company and subsidiary operations and financial position would be more meaningful, at least to parent company stockholders, than would separate financial statements of the parent company and each individual subsidiary company.[6] Thus the purpose of consolidated financial statements is to present one set of financial statements, primarily for the benefit of the owners and creditors of the parent company, as if the consolidated group were a single economic entity. For accounting purposes, the entire group is considered a unified whole, and FASB ASC 810-10-25 requires majority-owned subsidiaries to be *consolidated* unless the parent is precluded from exercising control or control is expected to be temporary. The criteria for preparing consolidated financial statements were originally described in *Accounting Research Bulletin No. 51* as follows:

1. A parent-subsidiary relationship must exist. (The parent must own at least 51 percent of the subsidiary.)
2. The parent exercises control over the subsidiary. (Where the courts are exercising control as in a bankruptcy, consolidation is not appropriate.)

6. Committee on Accounting Procedure, *Accounting Research Bulletin No. 51*, "Consolidated Financial Statements" (AICPA, New York, 1959), para. 1.

3. The parent plans to maintain control over the subsidiary during the near future. (Subsidiaries that are to be sold in the near future should not be consolidated.)

4. The parent and subsidiary should operate as an integrated unit, and non-homogeneous operations should be excluded.

5. The fiscal years of the units should approximate each other. (Generally, they should fall within 93 days of each other), or appropriate adjustments should be made to reflect similar closing dates.[7]

The underlying philosophy of both *ARB No. 51* and the guidance contained at FASB ASC 810 is the presentation of a single, though fictional, entity with economic but not legal substance. In the preparation of consolidated financial statements, two overriding principles prevail. The first is balance sheet oriented, and the second is income statement oriented:

1. The entity cannot own or owe itself.

2. The entity cannot make a profit by selling to itself.

The result of the first principle is to eliminate all assets on one company's books that are offset by liabilities on the other, for example, an account receivable on the parent's books relating to a corresponding account payable on the subsidiary's books. In the preparation of consolidated statements, the parent's account receivable is eliminated against the subsidiary's account payable. In applying the second principle, all intercompany sales and profits are eliminated. For example, a sale by one company is offset against a purchase by an affiliated company. (A detailed discussion of the preparation of consolidated financial statements is beyond the scope of this text.)

The Concept of Control

The impetus for consolidations is the control of the parent company over the subsidiary. Control is defined as "the power of one entity to direct or cause the direction of the management and operating and financing policies of another entity."[8] Control is normally presumed when the parent owns, either directly or indirectly, a majority of the voting stock of the subsidiary. The following exceptions indicating an inability to control a majority-owned subsidiary are cited in FASB ASC 810-10-15-10:

1. The subsidiary is in a legal reorganization or bankruptcy.

2. There are severe governmentally imposed uncertainties.

In some cases control may exist with less than a majority ownership, for example, by contract, by lease, as the result of an agreement with stockholders, or by court decree.

The issuance of *SFAS No. 94* was prompted by concerns over off–balance sheet financing. *ARB No. 51* allowed majority-owned subsidiaries to be excluded

7. *Accounting Research Bulletin No. 51*, "Consolidated Financial Statements" (New York: AICPA, 1959).

8. FASB, Discussion Memorandum: "An Analysis of Issues Related to Consolidation Policy and Procedures" (Stamford, CT: FASB, 1991), para. 122.

from consolidation (1) when the subsidiary is a foreign subsidiary, (2) when the minority interest in the subsidiary (subsidiary shares not owned by the parent company) is large relative to the equity interest of parent company stockholders in the consolidated net assets, and (3) when the subsidiary has nonhomogeneous operations.[9] The last exception, the *nonhomogeneity exception*, allowed parent companies to create financing subsidiaries or leasing companies and keep debt or capital lease obligations off the parent company balance sheets. *SFAS No. 94* eliminated these three exceptions.

In a 1991 discussion memorandum on consolidation policy and procedures, the FASB addressed the issue of whether control and the level of ownership are synonymous.[10] In other words, the Board posed the question: Should consolidation be extended to situations where the parent company has control but less than majority ownership? Subsequently, the FASB issued an exposure draft, "Consolidated Financial Statements: Policy and Procedures," in which control over an entity was defined as "power over its assets."[11] As such, control implies that one entity has the power to use or direct the use of the assets of another entity by

1. Establishing the controlled entity's policies and its capital and operating budgets
2. Selecting, determining the compensation of, and terminating personnel responsible for implementing the controlled entity's policies and decisions

Hence, a controlling entity can use or direct the use of the controlled entity's assets to receive future benefit. It follows that the assets of the controlled entity have future service potential to the controlling entity and should be consolidated.

According to the exposure draft, in the absence of evidence to the contrary, effective control is evident when the controlling entity has one or more of the following:

1. Ownership of a large minority voting interest (approximately 40 percent) when no other party or group has a significant interest
2. An ability to dominate the process of nominating candidates to another entity's governing board and to cast a majority of the votes in electing board members
3. A unilateral ability to obtain a majority voting interest through ownership of convertible securities or other rights that may be converted or exercised to obtain voting shares
4. A relationship with an entity that has no voting stock or member voting rights but has legally enforceable provisions that (a) can be changed only by the creator and (b) limit the entity to activities that provide substantially all of the entity's future economic benefits to the creator
5. A unilateral ability to dissolve an entity and assume control of its assets, subject to claims against those assets, without assuming economic costs in excess of benefits expected from the dissolution
6. A sole general partnership interest in a limited partnership

9. Ibid.
10. Ibid.
11. FASB Board, Exposure Draft, "Consolidated Financial Statements: Policy and Procedures" (Stamford, CT: FASB, October 16, 1995), para. 9.

Opponents of consolidation of entities where legal control (majority owner-ship) does not exist contend that the determination of other than legal control is too subjective for practical implementation. Nevertheless, there is widespread use of the control rather than the majority ownership criterion in other countries, for example, Canada, Australia, and the United Kingdom.

In late 2000 the FASB reviewed its proposed control-based consolidation approach and decided to proceed with the modified approach. Under the *modified approach*, a party that has a financial relationship with an entity would assess whether consolidation is required by applying the four following steps:

1. The party having the financial relationship would assess whether the entity is a qualifying special-purpose entity and whether the party is the transferor or its affiliate. If so, the standard would not apply, and *SFAS No. 140* applies (see FASB ASC 860, discussed in Chapter 9).

2. The party assesses whether the permitted activities and powers of the entity are significantly limited. If not, the modified approach would not apply, and the presumption of control remains.

3. If the permitted activities and powers are significantly limited, the party would assess whether it has a current ability to change the entity's purpose or powers. If so, the party would consolidate only if that ability can be exer-cised (a) without further significant cash outlay or investment or (b) with a significant cash outlaw or investment that is expected to result in benefits that exceed further investments.

4. If the party would not be required to consolidate under step 3, the party would assess whether its financial interests in the entity (a) are a significant portion of all such variable interests and (b) are significantly greater than such variable interests held by any other party. If both of these conditions exist, the party would be required to consolidate unless other circumstances prohibit it from having an ongoing ability to affect the nature, timing, or volume of the entity's operating activities.

The Board had intended to issue an exposure draft on this issue by the second quarter of 2001 and had tentatively decided to establish an effective date of imple-mentation of this treatment for financial statements of companies with fiscal years beginning after June 15, 2002. To date, no exposure draft or pronouncement on this topic has come forth.

Theories of Consolidation

There are two prominent theories of consolidation: *entity theory* and *parent com-pany theory*. Each theory implies a unique philosophy regarding the nature and purpose of consolidated financial statements. Current practice conforms strictly to neither theory; rather, it retains elements of both theories. Beams describes this hybrid of concepts underlying current consolidation practices and theories as *contemporary theory*.[12]

---

12. Floyd A. Beams, *Advanced Accounting*, 5th ed. (Englewood Cliffs, NJ: Prentice-Hall, 1991), 437–39.

Entity Theory

According to entity theory (discussed in Chapter 14), the consolidated group (parent company and subsidiaries) is an entity separate from its owners. Thus the emphasis is on control of the group of legal entities operating as a single unit. Consolidated assets belong to the consolidated entity, and the income earned by investing in those assets is income to the consolidated entity rather than to the parent company stockholders. Consequently, the purpose of consolidated statements is to provide information to all shareholders—parent company stockholders and outside noncontrolling stockholders of the subsidiaries.

The revision of *SFAS No. 141*, now contained at FASB ASC 805, and the FASB's requirements for recording consolidations contained at FASB ASC 810 are consistent with entity theory. Companies are now required to report 100 percent of the fair value of both the assets and liabilities of an acquired company even when there is a noncontrolling interest remaining in the acquired company or subsidiary. The noncontrolling interest must be measured initially at its fair value, which means that its initial value is no longer unaffected by the consolidation process.

SFAS No. 160 (see FASB ASC 810-10-65) requires that the net income to the entity be determined and labeled as "net income." Then the entity net income attributable to noncontrolling interest is subtracted, leaving the entity net income attributable to the parent company. In addition, the balance sheet reports the stockholders' equity attributable to the parent company first, followed by the noncontrolling interest in the subsidiary to arrive at total stockholders' equity of the consolidated entity.

Parent Company Theory

Parent company theory evolved from the proprietary theory of equity, which is described in Chapter 15. Under parent company theory, parent company stockholders are viewed as having a proprietary interest in the net assets of the consolidated group. The purpose of consolidated statements is to provide information primarily for parent company stockholders. Thus, before the issuance of *SFAS No. 160*, consolidated financial statements reflected a parent company perspective. The assets reported on a consolidated balance sheet were those of the subsidiary adjusted by the parent company's share of the difference between subsidiary historical cost and the asset's fair value at the date of the acquisition. The net income reported in the consolidated income statement was equal to the net income of the parent company. Noncontrolling interest income was reported as a deduction to arrive at consolidated net income, and noncontrolling interest was not considered an equity interest.

Noncontrolling Interest

When a portion of a subsidiary's stock is owned by investors outside the parent company, this ownership interest is referred to as *noncontrolling interest* (previously termed *minority interest*) in financial statements. From a noncontrolling stockholder's standpoint, the value of his or her investment results from holding shares in an affiliated company, and the determination of equity, the payment of dividends, and the basis for a claim should a liquidation ensue are all based on a claim against a particular subsidiary. Therefore the noncontrolling interest must gauge its financial status from the subsidiary company, not the parent or the consolidated group. Before the issuance of *SFAS No. 160*, noncontrolling interest was calculated as the percentage ownership in the subsidiary's net assets at the date of acquisition, plus the percentage of retained earnings since acquisition. Under current practice, noncontrolling interest is reported at its initial fair value plus its share of the earnings of the subsidiary. This amount is then adjusted for the noncontrolling interest's share of write-offs for differences between historical cost and acquired fair values, which include its share of any goodwill impairments minus its share of subsidiary dividends.

The classification of noncontrolling interest on consolidated balance sheets has been the subject of debate. The previous guidance on consolidations, *ARB No. 51* and *SFAS No. 141(R)*, neither defined what noncontrolling interest is nor described how it should be treated in published financial statements. Moreover, the prevailing consolidation theories imply different interpretations of the very nature of non-controlling interest. In prior practice, noncontrolling interest has been variously (1) disclosed as a liability, (2) separately presented between liabilities and stock-holders' equity, and (3) disclosed as a part of stockholders' equity.

The first two alternative treatments are consistent with parent company theory. Under parent company theory, only parent company stockholders play a proprietary role; hence, minority shares are an outside interest and should not be included in stockholders' equity. It is argued that the consolidation process has no impact on the reporting entity and is of no benefit to minority sharehold-ers. Yet noncontrolling interest does not fit the definition of liabilities found in *SFAC No. 6*; thus, there is no established theoretical basis for reporting minority interest as debt. At the same time, noncontrolling stockholders do not enjoy the ownership privileges of parent company stockholders. Their interest is in only part of the consolidated entity, over which they cannot exercise control, and thus they are unable to act as owners in the usual sense. Some proponents of parent company theory argue that the unique nature of noncontrolling interest is best portrayed by placing it between liabilities and stockholders' equity.

Entity theory implies that noncontrolling interest is an equity interest. The consolidated enterprise is considered one economic unit, and noncontrolling shareholders contribute resources in the same manner as parent company stock-holders. Moreover, like parent company stockholders, their respective interest is enhanced or burdened by changes in net assets from nonowner sources—a prerequisite for equities as described in *SFAC No. 6*, paragraph 62. *SFAC No. 6* iden-tified noncontrolling interest as an example of an equity interest stating that non-controlling stockholders have ownership or residual interests in the consolidated enterprise.[13] Subsequently, in its 2000 exposure draft on "Accounting for Finan-cial Instruments with Characteristics of Liabilities, Equity, or Both," the FASB pro-posed that the noncontrolling interest in a subsidiary be reported as a component of stockholders' equity.[14] However, the Board omitted this proposed requirement from its subsequent pronouncement, *SFAS No. 150*.

---

13. *Statement of Financial Accounting Concepts No. 6*, "Elements of Financial Statements" (Stamford, CT: FASB, 1985), para. 254.

14. "Accounting for Financial Instruments with Characteristics of Liabilities, Equity, or Both," Proposed Statement of Financial Accounting Standards (Stamford, CT: FASB, October 27, 2000).

Because the FASB has proposed that consolidation should be required for controlled entities in which the controlling entity has less than a majority ownership, the outside interest of a given subsidiary would no longer be composed of a minority of common stockholders in the controlled entity. Hence, the previously used term, *minority interest*, would no longer apply. The 1999 exposure draft on consolidation policy and procedures proposed that the outside interest should be labeled *noncontrolling interest in subsidiaries*. Moreover, consistent with their position in *SFAS No. 6* and the 2000 exposure draft on complex financial instruments, the noncontrolling interest would be reported in the consolidated balance sheet as a separate component of equity. The acquisition method, now required under the guidance contained at FASB ASC 805, and the consolidation guidelines contained at FASB ASC 810 no longer refer to these owners as a minority interest. Instead, they must now be referred to as a noncontrolling interest, and noncontrolling interest must now be reported as a separate component of equity.

Proportionate Consolidation

Because of the controversy surrounding the inability to reach a consensus on the nature of minority interest, some accountants advocate an alternative, proportionate consolidation, which would ignore minority interest altogether. Under proportionate consolidation, the parent company would report only its share of the assets and liabilities of the subsidiary entity, and no minority interest would need to be reported. Rosenfield and Rubin contend that when the parent company acquires the voting stock of the subsidiary, it obtains a right to receive its pro rata share of the subsidiary company's dividends, implying that only the corresponding pro rata share of subsidiary net assets is relevant to parent company stockholders.[15] This argument ignores the concept of control that is fundamental to the very nature of consolidations. If the parent company controls the net assets of the subsidiary entity, then it controls 100 percent of those net assets and not just its proportionate share. It follows that if consolidated financial statements are intended to report the results of using the assets controlled, consolidation of 100 percent of subsidiary net assets would be relevant.

A determination of the nature of minority interest is important because it affects the underlying premises of alternative accounting treatments for the recognition and measurement of consolidated assets and earnings. A complete discussion of the issues involved is beyond the scope of this text. In the next section we describe the implications of consolidation theories and minority interest recognition and measurement. Similar implications apply to other consolidated net assets.

Goodwill

Goodwill, described in Chapter 8 as an intangible asset, is recorded when a business combination occurs and is reported by the parent company in consolidated financial statements. Before the revision of *SFAS No. 141*, the measurement of goodwill was consistent with parent company theory. Goodwill was initially computed as the difference between the cost of the investment made to acquire the subsidiary shares and the fair value of the parent company's proportionate

15. Paul Rosenfield and Steven Rubin, "Minority Interest: Opposing Views," *Journal of Accountancy* (March 1986), 78–80, 82, 84, 86, 88–90.

share of the identifiable net assets of the subsidiary. No goodwill was attributed to noncontrolling interest. The result was that the value of noncontrolling interest reported on the consolidated financial statements was not affected by the consolidation process. Thus it reflected only the noncontrolling interest's share of the reported book value of the subsidiary entity.

Under entity theory, because the emphasis is on the entity and not the parent company, goodwill would be valued at its total market value, implied by the purchase price paid for the parent company investment. In this case, the equity interest in goodwill would be allocated between the parent company and noncontrolling interest. The result would be that the noncontrolling interest, like the parent company interest, would be measured at fair value. The balance sheet would then reflect the total fair value of the goodwill under the control of the parent company.

In its 1999 exposure draft on consolidation principles and procedures, the FASB supported the entity theory for the valuation of identifiable net assets and the parent company theory for the valuation of goodwill. Contrary to the then current GAAP, this proposal would require subsidiary assets, such as inventory, land, and buildings, to be valued at 100 percent of fair value at acquisition. The result would be that a portion of the difference between fair value and book value acquired would be attributed to the noncontrolling interest. Current GAAP is virtually consistent with this proposal. The only difference lies in the manner in which the initial valuation of noncontrolling interest may be determined. Consistent with the proposal, the fair value of noncontrolling interest may be equal to the amount implied by the purchase price paid by the parent company to acquire its share of the net assets of the subsidiary. Alternatively, noncontrolling interest may be valued by multiplying the number of noncontrolling interest shares times the market value of the acquiree's shares on the date control is attained or by some other valuation technique. It is unfortunate that the FASB did not provide better guidance on how the acquiring company should value noncontrolling interest.

Drawbacks of Consolidation

The growth of business combinations has created companies with diversified operations, termed *conglomerates*. The result has been the aggregation of financial information from various lines of business into one set of financial reports. Moreover, if the FASB does extend the definition of control below 50 percent ownership, the result will be even higher levels of aggregation and even greater loss of information regarding the performance of the individual combined companies. Each new business combination results in the loss of some information to the investing public because previously reported data is now combined with existing data in consolidating financial reports.

The loss of information may be further exacerbated by the reporting requirements of the guidance contained at FASB ASC 810. Assets and liabilities of heterogeneous companies are now required to be consolidated. Although empirical research indicates that the liabilities of previously unconsolidated subsidiaries may be perceived by market participants as parent company liabilities, one would expect a loss of comparability among the financial information provided across companies comprising varying combinations of different types of business entities.[16] In addition, proponents of proportionate consolidation argue that the consolidation process exaggerates reported amounts for assets and liabilities and hence affects the calculation of performance measures, such as debt-to-equity ratios.

Some accountants would prefer that in addition to consolidated financial statements, companies also report the separate financial statements of the individual companies that constitute the consolidated group. In this way, users would evaluate the individual as well as the combined performance and financial position of the group and might better be able to assess the incremental addition of each unit to the total combined reporting entity.

Special-Purpose Entities

In Chapter 1, we introduced the issue of special-purpose entities (SPEs) in conjunction with the discussion of the collapse of Enron. A special-purpose entity was originally defined as a partnership, corporation, trust, or joint venture that was created for a limited purpose, with a limited life and limited activities, and that was designed to benefit a single company. The primary motive for most SPEs was off–balance sheet financing, often to avoid reporting capital leases under *SFAS No. 13* (see FASB ASC 840). Under previous GAAP, companies were able to avoid consolidation of many SPEs. An SPE was created by an asset transfer in which the assets were sold to the SPE. To achieve off–balance sheet treatment, a minimum investment from an independent third-party investor was required (originally 3 percent, later 10 percent), in exchange for which the third-party investor controlled the SPE and bore the risk of loss. In other words, the transaction was treated like a sale of assets. As a result, consolidation was not required.

The requirements to qualify an SPE for nonconsolidation were refined in *SFAS No. 140*, "Accounting for Transfers and Servicing of Financial Assets and Extinguishments of Liabilities." According to *SFAS No. 140*, the transferor company surrendered control over the transferred assets (and thus had a sale) when all of the following conditions were met:

1. The transferred assets had been put beyond the reach of the transferor and its creditors.

2. Each transferee (SPE) had the right to pledge or exchange the assets, and no conditions constrained the transferee from taking advantage of its right to pledge or exchange.

3. The transferor did not maintain effective control over the transferred assets through either (1) an agreement that entitled and obligated the transferor to repurchase or redeem the transferred assets before maturity or (2) the ability to unilaterally cause the holder to return specific assets, other than through a cleanup call.[17]

---

16. E. E. Comiskey, R. A. McEwen, and C. W. Mulford, "A Test of Pro Forma Consolidation of Finance Subsidiaries," *Financial Management* (Autumn 1987), 45–50.

17. A cleanup call is defined as the early redemption of the entire balance of a debt issue when a relatively small amount of the original issue remains outstanding.

The intent of these provisions was to ensure that following a transfer, an entity recognized the assets it controls and derecognized liabilities when extinguished.

In December 2003, the FASB issued *FIN No. 46*, "Consolidation of Certain Special Purpose Entities" (later amended by *FIN 46R*) to further address this issue by identifying situations in which a company may have a controlling financial interest in an SPE, but no voting interest (*FIN No. 46* referred to entities subject to its requirements as *variable interest entities,* or VIEs, rather than special-purpose entities). The FASB's intent was to require consolidation only if the VIE did not effectively disperse the risks and benefits of ownership among the various parties involved. *FIN No. 46* modified the first of the above three *SFAS No. 140* conditions as follows:

> The transferred assets have been put beyond the reach of the powers of a bankruptcy trustee or other receiver for the transferor or any consolidated affiliate of the transferor that is not a VIE.

FIN No. 46 added that a qualifying VIE may have the power to dispose of the assets to a party other than the transferor, its affiliate, or agent when the VIE terminates and the manner of disposal is not specified at the inception of the VIE.

Later in December 2009, the FASB issued *SFAS No. 167*, "Amendments to FASB Interpretation No. 46(R)," (see FASB ASC 810-10). *SFAS No. 167* amended *FIN No. 46(R)* to require an enterprise to perform an analysis to determine whether the enterprise's variable interest or interests give it a controlling financial interest in a VIE. This analysis identifies the primary beneficiary of a VIE as the enterprise that has both of the following characteristics:

1. The power to direct the activities of a VIE that most significantly affect the entity's economic performance
2. The obligation to absorb losses of the entity that could potentially be significant to the VIE or the right to receive benefits from the entity that could potentially be significant to the VIE

Additionally, the provisions of *SFAS No. 167* require an enterprise to assess whether it has an implicit financial responsibility to ensure that a VIE operates as designed when determining whether it has the power to direct the activities of the VIE that most significantly affect the entity's economic performance. It also requires ongoing reassessments of whether an enterprise is the primary beneficiary of a VIE. Previous GAAP required reconsideration of whether an enterprise is the primary beneficiary of a VIE only when specific events occurred. *SFAS No. 167* also eliminated the quantitative approach previously required for determining the primary beneficiary of a VIE, which was based on determining which enterprise absorbs the majority of the entity's expected losses, receives a majority of the entity's expected residual returns, or both. *SFAS No. 167* noted that it is possible that application of this revised guidance could change an enterprise's assessment regarding which of the entities it is involved with are VIEs.

Segment Reporting

Current GAAP does not require the reporting of separate financial statements of the companies comprising a consolidated group. Nevertheless, *segment reporting,* the reporting of financial information on a less-than-total-enterprise basis, is required under *SFAS No. 131* (see FASB ASC 280).

Previous GAAP required or recommended segment reporting only in limited areas. For example, *ARB No. 43* recommended certain disclosures about foreign operations, *APB Opinion No. 18* required disclosure of certain information about companies accounted for by the equity method (see FASB ASC 323), and *APB Opinion No. 30* (since superseded) mandated the disclosure of information about discontinued segments. However, segmental information became an increasing part of corporate reporting during the 1970s because of two factors:

1. In 1969, the SEC required line-of-business reporting in registration statements, and in 1970 these requirements were extended to the 10-K reports.

2. In 1973, the New York Stock Exchange urged that line-of-business reporting, similar to that provided on the 10-K reports, be included in the annual reports to stockholders.

The proponents of segmental reporting base their arguments on two points:

1. Various types of operations may have differing prospects for growth, rates of profitability, and degrees of risk.

2. Since management responsibility is frequently decentralized, the assessment of management ability requires less-than-total-enterprise information.[18]

Subsequent study of the problem resulted in the issuance of *SFAS No. 14* in 1976[19] (since superseded). This pronouncement required that a corporation issuing a complete set of financial statements disclose:

1. The enterprise's operations in different industries

2. Its foreign operations and export sales

3. Its major customers[20]

In requiring these disclosures, *SFAS No. 14* provided the following definitions:

1. *Industry segment.* Component of an enterprise engaged in providing a product or service or group of related products and services primarily to unaffiliated customers for a profit

2. *Reportable segment.* An industry segment for which information is required to be reported by this segment

3. *Revenue.* Sales to unaffiliated customers and intersegment transactions similar to those with unaffiliated customers

4. *Operating profit or loss.* Revenue minus all operating expenses, including the allocation of corporate overhead

5. *Identifiable assets.* Tangible and intangible enterprise assets that are used by the industry

---

18. Discussion Memorandum, "An Analysis of Issues Related to Financial Reporting for Segments of a Business Enterprise" (Stamford, CT: FASB, 1974), 6–7.

19. *SFAS No. 14*, "Financial Reporting for Segments of a Business Enterprise" (Stamford, CT: FASB, 1976).

20. Ibid.

In response to criticisms of the reporting requirements of *SFAS No. 14, SFAS No. 131* (see FASB ASC 280) restructured segment reporting to include a greater number of segments for some enterprises and segmentation that correspond more closely to internal decision making regarding business segments. It also extended segment reporting to interim reports. The resulting segment reporting practices are intended to provide information to help users make better assessments of enterprise performance and thereby make more informed decisions about the enterprise as a whole.

Under the provisions of *SFAS No. 131* (see FASB ASC 280-10-50-20 to 25), companies are required to report separately income statement and balance sheet information about each operating segment. In addition to a measure of a segment's profit or loss and total assets, companies are to report specific information if it is included in the measure of segment profit or loss by the chief operating decision maker. The list of such segment disclosures is as follows:

1. Revenues from external users
2. Revenues from transactions with other operating segments of the same enterprise
3. Interest revenue
4. Interest expense
5. Depreciation, depletion, and amortization expense
6. Unusual items
7. Equity in the net income of investees under the equity method
8. Income tax expense or benefit
9. Extraordinary items
10. Significant noncash items other than depreciation, depletion, and amortization expense[21]

Additional disclosures include the amount of investment in equity method investees and total expenditures for long-lived assets, productive assets, mortgage and other servicing rights, and deferred tax assets for those items that are included in total segment assets. Companies are also required to report certain geographic information and information regarding the extent of reliance on major (10 percent or more of total revenue) customers.

Operating Segments

A goal of the guidance contained at *FASB ASC 280* is to use the enterprise's internal organization in such a way that reportable operating segments will be readily evident to the financial statement preparer. The resulting "management approach" to identifying operating segments is based on the manner in which management organizes the segments for making operating decisions and assessing performance.

---

21. *SFAS No. 131*, "Disclosures about Segments of an Enterprise and Related Information" (Stamford, CT: FASB, 1997), para. 27.

FASB ASC 280-10-50-1 defines an operating segment as a component of the enterprise

- That engages in business activities from which it may earn revenues and incur expenses
- Whose operating results are regularly reviewed by the chief operating decision maker of the enterprise in making decisions about allocating resources to the segment and in assessing segment performance
- For which discrete financial information is available

In analyzing segmental information, the user should keep in mind that comparison of a segment from one enterprise with a similar segment from another enterprise has limited usefulness unless both companies use similar disaggregation and cost allocation procedures. Because segments are identified by analyzing a company's internal organization structure, comparisons between companies may be difficult for companies with different organizational structures.

The major problems associated with these disclosures are (1) the determination of reportable segments, (2) the allocation of joint costs, and (3) transfer pricing. In determining its reportable segments, an enterprise is required to identify the individual products and services from which it derives its revenue, group these products by industry lines and segments, and select those segments that are significant with respect to the industry as a whole. These procedures require a considerable amount of managerial judgment, and the following guidelines are presented:

1. *Existing profit centers.* The smallest units of activity for which revenue and expense information is accumulated for internal planning and control purposes represent a logical starting point for determining industry segments.

2. *Management organization.* The company's internal organizational structure generally corresponds to management's view of the major segments.

3. *Investor expectations.* The information provided should coincide with the type of information needed by the public.

4. *Competitive factors.* Although the disclosure of all industry segment information might injure a company's competitive position, the required disclosures are not more detailed than those typically provided by an enterprise operating within a single industry.[22]

The problems associated with the allocation of joint costs and transfer pricing also cause some difficulty in reporting segmental information. Joint costs should be allocated to the various segments in the most rational manner possible. However, since the allocation process is frequently quite arbitrary, this process may have a profound effect on reporting segmental income.

The transfer pricing problem arises when products are transferred from division to division, and one division's product becomes another's raw material. In many cases, these interdivisional transfers are recorded at cost plus an amount of profit. Most accountants advocate eliminating the profit from interdivisional transfers before they are reported as segmental information.

---

22. Ibid., para. 13.

Reportable Segments

Reportable segments include those operating segments that meet any of the following quantitative thresholds:

1. Reported revenue is at least 10 percent of combined revenue.
2. Reported profit (loss) is at least 10 percent of combined profit (loss).
3. Assets are 10 percent or more of combined assets.

FASB ASC 280-10-50-11 allows two or more segments that have similar economic characteristics to be aggregated into a single segment if the segments are similar in each of the following areas:

- Nature of products and services
- Nature of production processes
- Type or class of customers
- Method used to distribute products or services
- Nature of the regulatory environment (if applicable)

In addition, it is required that the combined revenue from sales to all unaffiliated customers of all reportable segments constitutes at least 75 percent of the combined revenue from sales to unaffiliated customers of all industry segments.

Disclosed Information

FASB ASC 280-10-50 requires that the following information be presented for each of the reportable segments:

- Revenues from external customers
- Revenues from transactions among the company's operating segments
- Interest revenue and interest expense
- Depreciation, depletion, and amortization expense
- Unusual items required to be reported separately under *APB Opinion No. 30*
- Equity in the net income of investees accounted for under the equity method
- Income tax expense or benefit
- Extraordinary items
- Significant noncash items other than depreciation, depletion, and amortization expense

If the chief operating decision maker includes the following when reviewing segment assets, these items should be disclosed separately for each reportable segment:

1. The amount of the company's investment in equity method investees
2. Total amounts expended for additions to long-lived assets other than financial instruments, long-term customer relationships of a financial institution, mortgage and other servicing rights, deferred policy acquisition costs, and deferred tax assets

In addition, the reporting entity must provide information regarding the extent of its reliance on major customers. If a single customer provides at least 10 percent of total enterprise revenues, this fact must be disclosed along with the amount of the total revenue generated from that customer. In meeting this disclosure requirement, a group of entities known to be operating under common control shall be considered a single customer.

Foreign Currency Translation

Foreign operations by U.S. corporations have increased substantially in recent years. At the same time, devaluation of the dollar, which allowed it to float on world currency markets, accentuated the impact of foreign currency fluctuation on the accounting information and reporting systems of multinational companies. As a result, foreign currency translation has become an important and widely debated accounting and reporting issue. More specifically, the issue is this: How does a U.S.-based corporation measure monetary unit differences and changes in those differences in its foreign branches and subsidiaries?[23]

The problem arises in the following manner: The foreign subsidiary handles its transactions in foreign currency, which may include anything from long-term borrowing agreements for assets acquired to credit sales carried as accounts receivable. When management or outside investors wish to evaluate the company's operations as a whole, it becomes necessary to express all activities, foreign and domestic, in common financial terms. Useful comparisons and calculations can be made only if measures of a company's profitability and financial position are expressed in a common unit of measurement (usually the domestic currency); foreign monetary measures must be converted to domestic units. This process is known as *translation*.

In translating foreign currency, the foreign exchange rate defines the relationship between two monetary scales. The foreign currency is stated as a ratio to the U.S. dollar, and this ratio becomes the multiplying factor to determine the equivalent amount of domestic currency. For example, if the British pound (£) is quoted as $1.90 and an American subsidiary acquires an asset valued at £10,000, the translation into dollars will be $19,000 (10,000 × $1.90). Foreign exchange rates change over time in response to the forces of supply and demand and to the relative degree of inflation between countries. These changes are classified into three types—fluctuation, devaluation, and revaluation. *Fluctuation* denotes a rate change within the narrow margin (a deviation of ¼ percent above or below that country's official exchange rate) allowed by the International Monetary Fund (IMF). If the IMF allows an entirely new support level of the foreign currency and the dollar rate falls, it is called *devaluation. Revaluation* occurs when the dollar rate of the foreign currency rises to a new support level.

The translation process in no way changes the inherent characteristics of the assets or liabilities measured. That is, translation is a single process that merely restates an asset or liability initially valued in foreign currency in terms of a common currency measurement by applying the rate of exchange factor; it does not

---

23. It has been argued that in reality it is impossible to isolate the translation process from general price-level adjustments, since foreign exchange rates do to some extent reflect changes in the price level. But even though inflationary relationships between countries may be indirectly reflected in official exchange rates, translation is still considered to be an independent process.

restate historical cost. Translation is a completely separate process, just as adjusting for general price changes is a separate process. The translation process is analogous to price-level adjustments in that neither changes any accounting principles; they merely change the unit of measurement.

If the exchange rate remained constant between a particular foreign country and the United States, translation would be a relatively simple process involving a constant exchange rate. However, recent history indicates that this is unlikely, and a method of translation must be established that adequately discloses the effect of changes in exchange rates on financial statements. There has been considerable debate among accountants on how to achieve this objective. In the following sections, we review the proposals advocated by several individuals and groups.

Historically, four methods of translation were proposed by various authors before the release of any official pronouncements by the APB or FASB: the current-noncurrent method, the monetary-nonmonetary method, the current rate method, and the temporal method.[24]

Current-Noncurrent Method

The current-noncurrent method is based on the distinction between current and noncurrent assets and liabilities. It was initially recommended by the American Institute of Certified Public Accountants (AICPA) in 1931 and updated in *Accounting Research Bulletin No. 43* in 1953.[25] This method requires all current items (cash, receivables, inventory, and short-term liabilities) to be translated at the foreign exchange rate existing at the balance sheet date. Noncurrent items (plant, equipment, property, and long-term liabilities) are translated using the rate in effect when the items were acquired or incurred (the historical rate). The rationale for the dichotomy between current and noncurrent items is that those items that will not be converted into cash in the upcoming period (noncurrent) are not affected by changes in current rates. Thus, in using this method, it is assumed that items translated at the historical exchange rate are not exposed to gains and losses caused by changes in the relative value of currencies. In 1965, *ARB No. 43* (Chapter 12) was modified by *APB Opinion No. 6* (since superseded) to allow long-term payables and receivables to be translated at the current rather than historical rate if this treatment resulted in a better representation of a company's position.[26] With respect to the income statement, *ARB No. 43* required revenues and expenses to be translated at the average exchange rate applicable to each month, except for depreciation, that was translated at the historical rate.

Monetary-Nonmonetary Method

The monetary-nonmonetary method was first advocated by Samuel Hepworth,[27] and the National Association of Accountants' support of Hepworth's method in

---

24. See Leonard Lorensen, "Reporting Foreign Operations of U.S. Companies in U.S. Dollars," *Accounting Research Study No. 12* (New York: AICPA, 1972).

25. *Accounting Research Bulletin No. 43* (New York: AICPA, 1953), chap. 12.

26. Accounting Principles Board, *Opinion No. 6*, "Status of Accounting Research Bulletins" (New York: AICPA, 1965), para. 18.

27. Samuel Hepworth, "Reporting Foreign Operations," *Michigan Business Studies* (Ann Arbor: University of Michigan, 1956).

1960 resulted in more widespread acceptance of its provisions.[28] The monetary-nonmonetary method requires that a distinction be made between monetary items (accounts representing cash or claims on cash, such as receivables, notes payable, and bonds payable) and nonmonetary items (accounts not representing claims on a specific amount of cash such as land, inventory, plant, equipment, and capital stock). Monetary items are translated at the exchange rate in effect at the balance sheet date, whereas nonmonetary items retain the historical exchange rate.

The only difference between the two methods for the reporting of assets is in the translation of inventories. If the current-noncurrent method is used, inventories are considered to be current assets (sensitive to foreign exchange gains and losses) and are translated at the current rate, whereas the monetary-nonmonetary method classifies inventories as nonmonetary assets that are subsequently translated at the historical or preexisting rate. A difference also arises in translating long-term debt. The current-noncurrent approach uses the historical translation rate, whereas the monetary-nonmonetary method considers long-term debt to be monetary and uses the current rate. This difference between the two methods disappears, however, if the current-noncurrent approach is modified as was required by *APB Opinion No. 6*. Both approaches result in a foreign exchange gain or loss in order to balance the assets with the liabilities and equities, thereby creating a reporting problem. That is, how should a gain or loss on foreign currency translation be reported on the financial statements? (We discuss this issue later in the chapter.)

Although these two translation methods dominated accounting practices for about 40 years, the late 1960s and the early 1970s produced a proliferation of new proposals for dealing with foreign exchange problems. After 1971, when the dollar was devalued and allowed to float on the world monetary market, dissatisfaction with the traditional methods came to the forefront. Most authors advocating new approaches contend that new problems surfaced in 1971 because foreign currencies were appreciating rather than depreciating in relation to the dollar, and these problems could not be resolved by the traditional approaches. Two other methods, the current rate method and the temporal method, have been advocated to alleviate this problem.

Current Rate Method

The current rate method requires the translation of *all* assets and liabilities at the exchange rate in effect on the balance sheet date (current rate). It is, therefore, the only method that translates fixed assets at current rather than historical rates. Proponents of the current rate method claim that it most clearly represents the true economic facts because stating all items currently presents the true earnings of a foreign operation at that time—particularly since from the investor's point of view the only real earnings are those that can actually be distributed.

Although the current rate method has drawn some support, it is not without critics. Proponents argue that it presents true economic facts by stating all items at the current rate and thus keeping operating relationships intact. However, critics attack the use of the current rate for fixed assets, stating that the resulting figure

---

28. National Association of Accountants, "Management Accounting Problems in Foreign Operations," *NAA Research Report No. 36* (New York, 1960).

on the translated consolidated balance sheet does not represent the historical cost. They maintain that until the entire reporting system is changed, the current rate method will not be acceptable.

Temporal Method

In 1972, Lorensen advocated another approach, termed the *temporal principle of translation.*[29] Under this method, monetary measurements depend on the temporal characteristics of assets and liabilities. That is, the time of measurement of the elements depends on certain characteristics. Lorensen summarized this process as follows:

> Money and receivables and payables measured at the amounts promised should be translated at the foreign exchange rate in effect at the balance sheet date. Assets and liabilities measured at money prices should be translated at the foreign exchange rate in effect at the dates to which the money prices pertain.[30]

This principle is simply an application of the fair value principle in the area of foreign translation. By stating foreign money receivables and payables at the balance sheet rate, the foreign currency's command over U.S. dollars is measured. (Lorensen believes that this attribute, command over U.S. dollars, is of paramount importance.) Nevertheless, the results from use of this method are generally identical to those from the monetary-nonmonetary method except when the inventory valuation is based on the lower of cost or market (LCM) rule.

Lorensen's main concern was that the generally accepted accounting principles being followed should not be changed by the translation process. Consequently, he strongly opposed any translation method that ultimately changed the attributes of a balance sheet account (e.g., historical cost being transformed into replacement cost or selling price). Unfortunately, the temporal method offers no solution to the problem of reporting exchange gains and losses that plague the traditional methods. Moreover, using the historical rate to translate fixed assets while translating the long-term debt incurred to finance those assets at the current rate may be inappropriate and may result in large gains and losses that will not be realized in the near future. Furthermore, it is argued that because subsidiary assets are acquired with foreign currency, not the parent's currency, use of the historic exchange rate is simply irrelevant.

It must be stressed that due to the nature of the world's monetary systems, none of these methods of translation provides a perfect representation of value. A country's currency is basically a one-dimensional scale that measures and compares economic values within that one political entity. Thus even the best translation method that attempts to restate a foreign asset or liability in terms of domestic currency will inevitably be limited in its representation of economic reality.

29. Lorensen, "Reporting Foreign Operations of U.S. Companies in U.S. Dollars."
30. Ibid., 19.

The FASB and Foreign Currency Translation

The FASB took this issue under advisement and originally issued *SFAS No. 8* (since superseded), "Accounting for the Translation of Foreign Currency Transactions and Foreign Currency Financial Statements."[31] The Board stated that the overall objective of foreign currency translation is to measure and express, in dollars and in conformity with U.S. GAAP, the assets, liabilities, revenue, and expenses initially measured in foreign currency. The following translation principles applied:

1. Each transaction was recorded at the historical exchange rate (the exchange rate in effect at the transaction date).

2. All cash, receivables, and payables denominated in foreign currencies were adjusted using the current rate at the balance sheet date.

3. All assets carried at market price were adjusted to equivalent dollar prices on the balance sheet date.

4. For all other assets, the particular measurement basis was used to determine the translation rate.

5. Revenues and expenses were translated in a manner that produced approximately the same dollar amount that would have resulted had the underlying transactions been translated into dollars on the dates they occurred. An average rate could be used in most cases.

6. All exchange gains and losses were included in the determination of net income.

7. Gains and losses on forward exchange contracts (agreements to exchange currencies at a predetermined rate) intended to hedge a foreign-currency-exposed net asset or liability position or to speculate were included in net income, while gains and losses on forward exchange contracts intended to hedge an identifiable foreign currency commitment were typically deferred.

This statement did not specifically advocate any one of the translation methods previously discussed, and none was adopted intact. Nevertheless, the general objectives of translation originally advocated by the FASB are most closely satisfied by the temporal method.

FASB ASC 830

The requirements of *SFAS No. 8* produced some perceived distortions in financial reporting that resulted in questions by many accountants and financial statement users as to the relevance, reliability, and predictive value of the information presented. Among these perceived distortions were the following:

1. The results of the application of *SFAS No. 8* were economically incompatible with reality. Since nonmonetary items such as inventory were translated at the historical rate, a loss could be reported during a period in which a foreign currency actually strengthened in relation to the dollar.

2. Matching of costs and revenues was inappropriate. For example, sales were measured and translated at current prices, whereas inventory was measured and translated at historical rates.

31. *SFAS No. 8*, "Accounting for the Translation of Foreign Currency Transactions and Foreign Currency Financial Statements" (Stamford, CT: FASB, 1975).

3. The volatility of earnings. *SFAS No. 8* required all translation gains and losses to be included in income. However, exchange rate changes are unrealized and frequently short term. This produced a so-called yo-yo effect on earnings. Critics contended that this reporting requirement tended to obscure long-term trends.

Notice that these are all economic consequence arguments, since none of the perceived distortions affected cash flows. Nevertheless, the FASB took these criticisms under advisement and later replaced *SFAS No. 8* with *SFAS No. 52*, "Foreign Currency Translation"[32] (see FASB ASC 830). The following translation objectives were adopted in this release:

1. To provide information that is generally compatible with the expected economic effects of a rate change on an enterprise's cash flow and equity.
2. To reflect in consolidated statements the financial results and relationships of the individual consolidated entities in conformity with U.S. generally accepted accounting principles.

FASB ASC 830 adopts the *functional currency* approach to translation. An entity's functional currency is defined as the currency of the *primary economic environment* in which it operates, which will normally be the environment in which it expends cash (see FASB ASC 830-30). Most frequently the functional currency will be the local currency, and four general procedures are involved in the translation process when the local currency is defined as the functional currency:

1. The financial statements of each individual foreign entity are initially recorded in that entity's functional currency. For example, a Japanese subsidiary would initially prepare its financial statements in terms of yen, for that would be the currency it generally uses to carry out cash transactions.
2. The foreign entity's statements must be adjusted (if necessary) to comply with U.S. GAAP.
3. The financial statements of the foreign entity are translated into the reporting currency of the parent company (usually the U.S. dollar). Assets and liabilities are translated at the current exchange rate at the balance sheet date. Revenues, expenses, gains, and losses are translated at the rate in effect at the date they were first recognized, or alternatively, at the average rate for the period.
4. Translation gains and losses are accumulated and reported as a component of other comprehensive income.

SFAS No. 52 defined two situations in which the local currency would not be the functional currency:

1. The foreign country's economic environment is highly inflationary (over 100 percent cumulative inflation over the previous three years, such as experienced by Argentina and Brazil in the recent past).
2. The company's investment is not considered long term.

---

32. *SFAS No. 52*, "Foreign Currency Translation" (Stamford, CT: FASB, 1981).

In these cases the foreign company's functional currency is the U.S. dollar, and the financial statements are translated using the *SFAS No. 8* approach. Thus the resulting exchange gains and losses are reported as a component of net income.

Proponents feel that the situational approach adopted by FASB ASC 830 gives a true picture of economic reality. When the functional currency is the local currency, the translated accounting numbers parallel the local perspective of foreign operations. Moreover, the major criticism leveled against *SFAS No. 8* is eliminated. Because translation gains and losses are included in other comprehensive income, rather than in ordinary income, the bottom line is not adversely affected by the volatility of foreign exchange rates.

Nevertheless, critics maintain that the functional currency approach may afford management too much leeway in the selection of the functional currency. As a result, a given subsidiary's functional currency may be chosen to manipulate reported net income. Furthermore, when the current rate is applied to historical costs, the result is an accounting model that at best is a hybrid of historical cost. Moreover, when these numbers are aggregated with the parent company's historical costs, the resulting consolidated financial statements are a mixed bag and may not provide useful information.

Translation versus Remeasurement   Under the provisions of FASB ASC 830-10-20, *translation* is the process of expressing in the reporting currency of the enterprise those amounts that are denominated or measured in a different currency. The translation process, which is performed in order to prepare financial statements, assumes that the foreign subsidiary is freestanding and that the foreign accounts *will not* be liquidated into U.S. dollars. Therefore translation adjustments are disclosed as a part of other comprehensive income rather than as adjustments to net income.

Remeasurement is the process of measuring transactions originally denominated in a different unit of currency (e.g., purchases of a German subsidiary of a U.S. company payable in French francs). Remeasurement is required when:

1. A foreign entity operates in a highly inflationary economy

2. The accounts of an entity are maintained in a currency other than its functional currency

3. A foreign entity is a party to a transaction that produces a monetary asset or liability denominated in a currency other than its functional currency

Remeasurement is accomplished by the same procedures as described earlier under the temporal method. That is, the financial statement elements are restated according to their original measurement bases. Remeasurement assumes that the foreign accounts will be liquidated into U.S. dollars and that an exchange of currencies will occur at the exchange rate prevailing on the date of remeasurement. This produces a foreign exchange gain or loss if the exchange rate fluctuates between the date of the original transaction and the date of the assumed exchange. Therefore any exchange gain or loss is included in net income in the period in which it occurs.

Foreign Currency Hedges   In issuing *SFAS No. 133* (see FASB ASC 815), the FASB intended to increase the consistency of hedge accounting guidance by broadening the scope of eligible foreign currency hedges from what was previously allowed in *SFAS No. 52*. Under the provisions of FASB ASC 815, an entity may designate the following types of foreign currency exposure:

1. A fair value hedge of an unrecognized firm commitment or an available-for-sale security
2. A cash-flow hedge of a forecasted foreign-currency-denominated transaction or a forecasted intercompany foreign-currency-denominated transaction
3. A hedge of a net investment in a foreign operation

Foreign currency fair value hedge. A derivative instrument that is designated as hedging changes in the fair value of an unrecognized firm commitment qualifies for the accounting treatment of a fair value hedge if all of the specified criteria for hedge accounting under the guidelines contained at FASB ASC 815 are met. A derivative instrument that is designated as hedging the changes in the fair value of an available-for-sale security also qualifies for the accounting treatment of a fair value hedge if all of the same specified criteria are met.

Foreign currency cash-flow hedge. Nonderivative financial instruments are not allowed to be designated as foreign currency cash-flow hedges. Derivative instruments designated as hedging the foreign currency exposure to the variability in the functional-currency-equivalent cash flows associated with either a forecasted foreign-currency-denominated transaction (a forecasted export sale to an unaffiliated entity with the price to be denominated in a foreign currency) or a forecasted intercompany foreign-currency-denominated transaction (a forecasted sale to a foreign subsidiary) qualify for hedge accounting under the following conditions:

1. The company with the foreign currency exposure is a party to the hedging instrument.
2. The hedged transaction is denominated in a currency other than that unit's functional currency.
3. All of the qualifying criteria for hedge accounting contained in FASB ASC 815 are met.

Hedge of a net investment in a foreign operation. This type of exposure occurs when dealing with a foreign currency to offset the effects of changes in exchange rates on the company's total investment in a foreign operation—for example, borrowing reais to hedge against the possible devaluation of that currency on an investment in Brazil. Accounting for foreign currency gains or losses depends on whether the dollar or the foreign currency is the functional currency. Usually the dollar is the functional currency because devaluations usually take place in highly inflationary economies. In such cases, remeasurement is required and the gain or loss is reported on the income statement. In the event the functional currency is the foreign currency, the gain or loss is reported in other comprehensive income. Derivative instruments that have been designated as hedges of foreign currency exposure of a net investment in a foreign subsidiary shall be reported in the same manner as reported in the translation adjustment required by FASB ASC 830.

In analyzing foreign currency translation information, investors should keep in mind that it is a mixture of exceptional complexity. That is, foreign currency exchange reporting is inextricably intertwined with accounting for business combinations. The question of what constitutes the net income of a consolidated corporation with foreign subsidiaries may never be fully answerable.

International Accounting Standards

The IASB has issued the following pronouncements dealing with multiple entities:

1. A second revision of *IAS No. 27*, "Consolidated Financial Statements and Accounting for Investments in Subsidiaries"
2. A revised *IAS No. 21*, "The Effects of Changes in Foreign Exchange Rates"
3. A revised *IFRS No. 3*, "Business Combinations," which replaces *IFRS No. 3* issued in 2004
4. *IFRS No. 8*, "Operating Segments," which replaces *IAS No. 14*

In the 2008 revision of *IAS No. 27*, the IASB moved accounting for business combinations more in line with U.S. GAAP. This pronouncement outlines the following two situations where the standard is to be applied:

1. In the preparation and presentation of consolidated financial statements for a group of entities under the control of a parent; and
2. In accounting for investments in subsidiaries, jointly controlled entities, and associates when an entity elects, or is required by local regulations, to present separate (nonconsolidated) financial statements

Under *IAS No. 27*, subsidiaries are to be consolidated when a parent exercises control. Control is presumed when the parent acquires more than half of the voting rights of the entity. Additionally, even when the parent does not acquire more than half of the voting rights, control may be evidenced in any of the following ways:

1. Ownership of over more than one-half of the voting rights by virtue of an agreement with other investors
2. The ability to govern the financial and operating policies of the entity under a statute or an agreement
3. The ability to appoint or remove the majority of the members of the board of directors
4. The ability to cast the majority of votes at a meeting of the board of directors

Consolidated financial statements are required for subsidiaries; however, a parent is not required to (but may) present consolidated financial statements if and only if all of the following four conditions are met:

1. The parent is itself a wholly owned subsidiary, or is a partially owned subsidiary of another entity and its other owners, including those not otherwise entitled to vote, have been informed about, and do not object to, the parent not presenting consolidated financial statements.;
2. The parent's debt or equity instruments are not traded in a public market.
3. The parent did not file, nor is it in the process of filing, its financial statements with a securities commission or other regulatory organization for the purpose of issuing any class of instruments in a public market.
4. The ultimate or any intermediate parent of the parent produces consolidated financial statements available for public use that comply with International Financial Reporting Standards.

Noncontrolling interests are still defined as minority interests in *IAS No. 27.* Minority interests are to be disclosed in the consolidated balance sheet within equity, but separate from the parent's shareholders' equity. Minority interests in the profit or loss of the group should also be separately disclosed. Where losses applicable to the minority exceed the minority interest in the equity of the relevant subsidiary, the excess as well as any further losses attributable to the minority are charged to the group unless the minority has a binding obligation to, and is able to, make good the losses. Where excess losses have been taken up by the group, if the subsidiary in question subsequently reports profits, all such profits are attributed to the group until the minority's share of losses previously absorbed by the group has been recovered.

In accounting for the parent's individual financial statements, investments in subsidiaries, associates, and jointly controlled entities should be accounted for either at cost, or in accordance with *IAS No. 39.* Additionally, the parent is to apply the same accounting for each category of investments. Investments that are classified as held for sale in accordance with *IFRS No. 5* shall be accounted for in accordance with that IFRS. Investments carried at cost should be measured at the lower of their carrying amount and fair value less costs to sell. The measurement of investments accounted for in accordance with *IAS No. 39* is not changed in such circumstances.

In *IAS No. 21,* the IASB outlined accounting for foreign currency translation. The objective of *IAS No. 21* is to prescribe how to include foreign currency transactions and foreign operations in the financial statements of an entity and how to translate financial statements into a presentation currency. The principal issues in this standard are which exchange rate(s) to use and how to report the effects of changes in exchange rates in the financial statements. The revised statement was issued to provide additional guidance on the translation method and on determining the functional and presentation currencies.

Under the provisions of *IAS No. 21,* foreign currency transactions are to be initially recorded at the historical exchange rate. Subsequently, monetary items are reported at the balance sheet date exchange rate; nonmonetary items are carried at either the historical rate or the current rate, depending on whether the foreign currency denomination was determined by using historical cost or fair value. Exchange differences resulting from investments in foreign entities are to be classified as stockholders' equity until they are disposed of, at which time they are recognized in income. These procedures are similar to U.S. GAAP contained in *SFAS No. 52.* The major changes in the revised standard include the following:

1. The original *IAS No. 21* concept of "reporting currency" is replaced by two concepts: functional currency (the currency in which the entity measures the items in the financial statements) and presentation currency (the currency in which the entity presents its financial statements). The term *functional currency* replaces *measurement currency* to converge with U.S. GAAP and common usage.

2. The functional currency is defined as the currency of the primary economic environment in which the entity operates in a manner similar to the way it was defined in *SFAS No. 52.*

3. The functional currency of each entity within a group is the currency of the country that drives that entity's economics (usually the country it is incorporated in). It is not a free choice.

4. A reporting entity (single company or group) may present its financial statements in any currency (or currencies) that it chooses; that is, a free choice of presentation currency will be allowed. The financial statements of any operation whose functional currency differs from the presentation currency used by the reporting entity are translated as follows (assuming the functional currency is not hyperinflationary): assets, liabilities, and equity items at closing rate; income and expense items at the rate on the transaction date; and all resulting exchange differences recognized as a separate component of equity.

5. The allowed alternative in the original *IAS No. 21* to capitalize certain exchange differences will be eliminated. In most cases in which *IAS No. 21* has allowed capitalization, the asset is also restated in accordance with *IAS No. 29*, "Financial Reporting in Hyperinflationary Economies." In such cases, to also capitalize exchange differences results in double counting.

6. The choice in *IAS No. 21* of methods for translating goodwill and fair value adjustments to assets and liabilities that arise on the acquisition of a foreign entity is eliminated. Goodwill and fair value adjustments are to be translated at the closing rate.

7. Any ineffectiveness that arises on a hedge of a net investment in a foreign entity should be reported in net profit or loss.

The 2008 revised *IFRS No. 3* resulted in a high degree of convergence between IFRSs and U.S. GAAP in accounting for business combinations, although some potentially significant differences remain. A business combination is defined as a transaction or event in which an acquirer obtains control of one or more businesses. A business is defined as an integrated set of activities and assets that is capable of being conducted and managed for the purpose of providing a return directly to investors or other owners, members, or participants. *IFRS No. 3* requires all business combinations to be accounted for using the acquisition method. It identifies the steps in applying the acquisition method as follows:

1. Identification of the "acquirer"—the combining entity that obtains control of the acquiree.

2. Determination of the "acquisition date"—the date on which the acquirer obtains control of the acquiree.

3. Recognition and measurement of the identifiable assets acquired, the liabilities assumed, and any noncontrolling interest (NCI, formerly called minority interest) in the acquiree.

4. Recognition and measurement of goodwill or a gain from a bargain purchase.

The acquirer measures the cost of a business combination at the sum of the fair values, at the date of exchange, of assets given, liabilities incurred or assumed, and equity instruments issued by the acquirer, in exchange for control of the acquiree, plus any costs directly attributable to the combination. If equity instruments are issued as consideration for the acquisition, the market price of those equity instruments at the date of exchange is considered to provide the best evidence of fair value. If a market price does not exist or is not considered reliable, other valuation techniques are used to measure fair value.

The acquirer recognizes separately, at the acquisition date, the acquiree's identifiable assets, liabilities, and contingent liabilities that satisfy the following recognition criteria at that date, regardless of whether they had been previously recognized in the acquiree's financial statements:

1. An asset other than an intangible asset is recognized if it is probable that any associated future economic benefits will flow to the acquirer, and its fair value can be measured reliably.

2. A liability other than a contingent liability is recognized if it is probable that an outflow of resources will be required to settle the obligation, and its fair value can be measured reliably.

3. An intangible asset or a contingent liability is recognized if its fair value can be measured reliably.

Goodwill is to be measured as the difference between:

1. The aggregate of (i) the acquisition-date fair value of the consideration transferred, (ii) the amount of any noncontrolling interest, and (iii) in a business combination achieved in stages, the acquisition-date fair value of the acquirer's previously held equity interest in the acquiree; and

2. The net of the acquisition-date amounts of the identifiable assets acquired and the liabilities assumed (measured in accordance with *IFRS No. 3*)

If the difference above is negative, the resulting gain is recognized as a bargain purchase in profit or loss.

IFRS No. 8 is a result of the IASB's joint short-term convergence project with the FASB to reduce differences between IFRSs and U.S. GAAP. Research carried out by the boards found that the U.S. standard *SFAS No. 131*, "Disclosures about Segments of an Enterprise and Related Information" (see FASB ASC 280), results in more useful information than the equivalent IFRS, *IAS No. 14*. Therefore *IFRS No. 8* adopts the requirements of *SFAS No. 131*, except for some terminology.

IFRS No. 8 requires segment disclosure based on the components of the entity that management monitors in making decisions about operating matters. Such components (operating segments) would be identified on the basis of internal reports that the entity's chief operating decision maker reviews regularly in allocating resources to segments and in assessing their performance. This "management approach" differs from the previous standard, *IAS No. 14*, which required the disclosure of two sets of segments, business and geographical segments, based on a disaggregation of information contained in the financial statements. Under the standard, operating segments become reportable based on threshold tests related to revenues, results, and assets. *IFRS No. 8* requires the disclosure of a "measure" of profit or loss and total assets, which would comprise the amounts reported to the chief operating decision maker. Further profit or loss information, as well as an explanation of how segment profit or loss and segment assets are measured for each reportable segment, are to be disclosed. Reconciliations of the totals of segment information to the entity's financial statements also are required.

The changes from *IAS No. 14* include the following:

- The scope of segment reporting is expanded to include entities that hold assets in a fiduciary capacity for a broad group of outsiders, such as a bank, insurance company, or pension fund.

- A component of an entity could meet the definition of an operating segment even if it sells primarily or exclusively to other operating segments of the entity (vertically integrated). *IAS No. 14* did not require vertically integrated operations to be identified as business segments.

• *IFRS No. 8* specifies more qualitative disclosures than *IAS No. 14* required, including the factors used to identify the entity's operating segments and the types of products and services from which each reportable segment derives its revenues.

• Even if an entity has only a single reportable segment, *IAS No. 14* requires disclosure about the entity's products and services, geographical areas, and major customers. *IAS No. 14* did not include this requirement.

Cases

• Case 16-1 Consolidated Financial Statements: Various Issues

Because of irreconcilable differences of opinion, a dissenting group within the management and board of directors of the Algo Company resigned and formed the Bevo Corporation to purchase a manufacturing division of the Algo Company. After negotiation of the agreement, but just before closing and actual transfer of the property, a minority stockholder of Algo notified Bevo that a prior stockholder's agreement with Algo empowered him to prevent the sale. The minority stockholder's claim was acknowledged by Bevo's board of directors. Bevo's board then organized Casco, Inc. to acquire the minority stockholder's interest in Algo for $75,000, and Bevo advanced the cash to Casco. Bevo exercised control over Casco as a subsidiary corporation with common officers and directors. Casco paid the minority stockholder $75,000 (about twice the market value of the Algo stock) for his interest in Algo. Bevo then purchased the manufacturing division from Algo.

Required:

a. What expenditures are usually included in the cost of property, plant, and equipment acquired in a purchase?

b. i. What are the criteria for determining whether to consolidate the financial statements of Bevo Corporation and Casco, Inc.?

ii. Should the financial statements of Bevo and Casco be consolidated? Discuss.

c. Assume that unconsolidated financial statements are prepared. Discuss the propriety of treating the $75,000 expenditure in the financial statements of the Bevo as

i. an account receivable from Casco

ii. an investment in Casco

iii. part of the cost of the property, plant, and equipment

iv. a loss

• Case 16-2 Business Combinations

The Whit Company, a manufacturer, and the Berry Company, a retailer, entered into a business combination whereby Whit acquired for cash all the outstanding voting common stock of Berry.

Required:

a. The Whit Company is preparing consolidated financial statements immediately after the consummation of the newly formed business combination. How should Whit determine in general the amounts to be reported for the assets and liabilities of Berry Company? Assuming that the business combination resulted in goodwill, indicate how the amount of goodwill is determined.

b. Why and under what circumstances should Berry be included in the entity's consolidated financial statements?

• Case 16-3 Segmental Reporting: Required Information

A central issue in reporting on industry segments of a business enterprise is the determination of which segments are reportable.

Required:

a. What is a reportable segment?

b. Explain how a preparer would determine which operating segments to report segment information for.

c. What types of segment information must be reported?

• Case 16-4 Foreign Currency Translation: Measure versus Denominate

The FASB has discussed certain terminology essential to both the translation of foreign currency transactions and foreign currency financial statements. Included in the discussion is a definition of and distinction between the terms *measure* and *denominate*.

Required:

Define the terms *measure* and *denominate* as discussed by the FASB. Give a brief example that demonstrates the distinction between accounts measured in a particular currency and accounts denominated in a particular currency.

• Case 16-5 Foreign Currency Translation: Various Methods

Several methods of translating foreign currency transactions or accounts are reflected in foreign currency financial statements. Among these methods are the current-noncurrent, monetary-nonmonetary, current rate, and temporal methods.

Required:

Define the temporal method of translating foreign currency financial statements. Specifically include in your answer the treatment of the following four accounts:

a. Long-term accounts receivable
b. Deferred income
c. Inventory valued at cost
d. Long-term debt

• Case 16-6 Forward Exchange Contracts

Reporting forward exchange contracts continues to be a significant issue in accounting for foreign currency translation adjustments.

Required:

a. Describe a fair value hedge and discuss how to account for forward exchange contracts that are entered into for fair value hedges.
b. Describe foreign currency fair value hedges and discuss the accounting for these types of hedges.
c. Describe foreign currency cash flow hedges and discuss the accounting for these types of hedges.

• Case 16-7 Foreign Currency Translation: Functional Currency Approach

In *SFAS No. 52* (see FASB ASC 280), the FASB adopted standards for financial reporting of foreign currency exchanges. This release adopts the functional currency approach to foreign currency translation.

Required:

a. Discuss the functional currency approach to foreign currency translation.
b. Discuss the terms *translation* and *remeasurement* as they relate to foreign currency translation.

• Case 16-8 Entity Theory of Consolidation

Entity theory is one of the two prominent theories of consolidation.

Required:
Under entity theory

a. How would the value of goodwill be determined? Explain why.
b. How would the initial value of noncontrolling interest be determined? Explain why.
c. How would a company report noncontrolling interest income in the consolidated income statement? Explain why.
d. Where would a company report noncontrolling interest in the consolidated balance sheet? Explain why.

• Case 16-9 Parent Company Theory of Consolidation

Parent company theory is one of the two prominent theories of consolidation.

Required:

Under parent company theory

  a. How would the value of goodwill be determined? Explain why.

  b. How would the initial value of noncontrolling interest be determined? Explain why.

  c. How would a company report noncontrolling interest income in the consolidated income statement? Explain why.

  d. Where would a company report noncontrolling interest in the consolidated balance sheet? Explain why.

• Case 16-10 Consolidation: Current Practice and Entity Theory

Explain how current practice for consolidations is consistent with the entity theory of consolidation.

FASB ASC Research

For each of the following research cases, search the FASB ASC database for information to address the issues. Cut and paste the FASB requirements that support your responses. Then summarize briefly what your responses are, citing the pronouncements and paragraphs used to support your responses.

• FASB ASC 16-1 Cost Allocation for a Patent

Assume that Your Company acquires My Company in a business combination. My Company has a patent for its production process. Search the FASB ASC database to enable you to answer the following questions related to the patent. Cut and paste your findings (citing the source), and write a brief summary of your research findings.

  1. My Company incurred significant cost to develop the patent. On the date of the business combination, the patent is 10 years old and has a useful life of 15 years.

   a. According to *SFAS No. 2* (see FASB ASC 730), how should My Company have accounted for the patent? Would you expect My Company to report an asset for the patent in its balance sheet?

   b. If My Company does not report an asset for the patent, will Your Company report one? If so, how will Your Company measure the initial value to record (or report) for the patent?

  2. My Company purchased the patent from another company three years ago. The patent had a remaining useful life of 12 years when it was purchased. Will the valuation of the patent by My Company be the same as it would be under part 1b above? Explain.

• FASB ASC 16-2 Consolidations and the EITF

The EITF has issued numerous interpretations on the topic of consolidations. These interpretations are subdivided by topic. Choose any three interpretations under the topic "New Basis of Accounting," identify the issue number and topic, and write a brief summary of the interpretation.

• FASB ASC 16-3 Definition of a Business

Included in the guidance for accounting for business combinations is the definition of a business. Find and cite the paragraph, and copy this guidance.

• FASB ASC 16-4 Accounting for Noncontrolling Interests

SFAS No. 165 outlined some issues in accounting for noncontrolling interests in consolidated financial statements. This guidance is now contained in the FASB ASC. Find the sections of the FASB ASC that were originally published as *SFAS No. 160*. Cite the paragraphs and copy this guidance.

• FASB ASC 16-5 Proportionate Consolidation

The FASB ASC discusses proportionate consolidation, Find, copy, and cite the general rule and the exception on proportionate consolidation.

• FASB ASC 16-6 Value beyond Proven and Probable Reserves

The FASB ASC provides a definition of value beyond proven and probable reserves for mining assets in the extractive industries. Find, cite, and copy that definition. How should value beyond proven and probable reserves be accounted for in a business combination? Find, cite, and copy that definition.

• FASB ASC 16-7 Demutualization of Life Insurance Companies

The FASB ASC provides a definition of the demutualization of life insurance companies that are consolidated. Find, cite, and copy that definition.

• FASB ASC 16-8 Affiliated Sales in the Consolidation of Regulated Industries

The FASB ASC discusses accounting for the profit on affiliated sales in the consolidation of regulated industries. Find, cite, and copy this guidance.

Room for Debate

• Debate 16-1 Noncontrolling Interest

In its 1995 exposure draft, "Consolidated Financial Statements: Policy and Procedures," the FASB proposed that a company's outside interest ("noncontrolling interest") be reported as an element of stockholders' equity. Current practice now requires that noncontrolling interest be reported in stockholders' equity, but separate from equity belonging to the parent company. This practice differs from *IAS No. 27*, which requires that noncontrolling interest be presented above stockholders' equity, as well as from the majority of current practice that conforms to the international requirement.

In your arguments for the following debate, you should consider the conceptual framework and be grounded on a theory of consolidation (entity theory or parent company theory).

Team Debate:

Team 1: Argue in favor of presenting the noncontrolling interest as an element of stockholders' equity.

Team 2: Argue in favor of presenting the noncontrolling interest outside of stockholders' equity.

• Debate 16-2 Measurement

Current practice requires that the assets acquired in a business combination be measured at fair value as defined by *SFAS No. 157* (see FASB ASC 820-10).

Team Debate:

Team 1: Argue that the acquiring company should measure the acquired company's plant assets that it plans to use in its operations in accordance with the requirements of *SFAS No. 141* before its revision.

Team 2: Argue that the acquiring company should measure the acquired company's plant assets that it plans to use in its operations in accordance with the *SFAS No. 141* revision.

• Debate 16-3 Goodwill of an Acquired Company

SFAS No. 160 (see FASB ASC 810) required that Goodwill be measured at 100 percent of its fair value.

Team Debate:

Team 1: Argue that Goodwill reported in balance sheets should be measured only at the value purchased by the parent company. Your arguments should refer to parent company theory.

Team 2: Argue that goodwill reported in balance sheets should be the amount of goodwill for the total company acquired. Your arguments should refer to entity theory.

Financial Reporting

Disclosure

Requirements and

Ethical Responsibilities

In the preceding chapters of this text, we have attempted to give a concise yet comprehensive explanation of current generally accepted accounting principles (GAAP). We have given primary attention to those principles promulgated by the Financial Accounting Standards Board (FASB) and its predecessors in their roles as the bodies of the accounting profession authorized to issue financial accounting standards. The discussion, therefore, has frequently been directed toward identifying transactions to be treated as accounting information, the appropriate measurement of those transactions, criteria for classifying the data in the financial statements, and the reporting and disclosure requirements of the various Accounting Principles Board (APB) opinions and Statements of Financial Accounting Standards (SFASs).

This chapter seeks to draw additional attention to the special importance of disclosure in financial reporting. Specifically, we review the disclosure requirements issued by (1) the FASB and (2) the Securities and Exchange Commission (SEC). Additionally, we examine accountants' ethical responsibility to society.

Recognition and Measurement Criteria

Statement of Financial Accounting Concepts (SFAC) *No. 5*, discussed in Chapter 2, outlines the various methods of disclosure that corporations should use in published financial statements. These disclosure requirements are summarized in Exhibit 17.1.

As seen in Exhibit 17.1, *SFAC No. 5* summarizes the building blocks to disclosure as follows:

1. The scope of recognition and measurement
2. Basic financial statements

EXHIBIT 17.1 *Relationship of SFAC No. 5 to Other Methods of Financial Reporting*

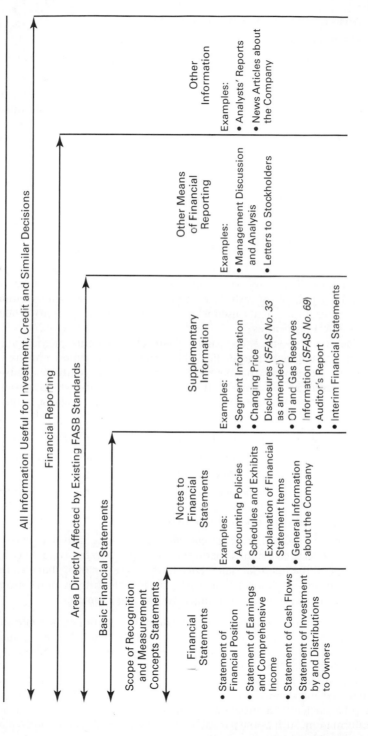

3. Areas directly affected by existing FASB standards

4. Financial reporting

5. All information useful for investment, credit, and similar decisions

The issues addressed under item 1 have been addressed earlier in this text. Therefore, in this chapter, we focus on the issues addressed by items 2 through 5. Note from Exhibit 17.1 that in addition to corporate annual reports, the disclosure vehicles in corporate annual reports include the footnotes to the financial statements; supplementary information, such as segmental information; other methods of financial disclosure, such as management's discussion and analysis; and other company information, such as analysts' reports and news reports. However, the most relevant information should always appear in one of the financial statements, provided that it meets the *SFAC No. 5* criteria for measurement and recognition.

Basic Financial Statements

The financial statements described in *SFAC No. 5* were discussed in Chapters 6 and 7. In addition to the four basic statements (the balance sheet, the income statement, the statement of cash flows, and the statement of owners' equity), a full set of financial statements also includes footnotes, supplementary schedules, and parenthetical disclosures.

The footnotes to a company's financial statements provide a significant amount of additional information about the items on the company's financial statements. In general, the footnotes disclose information that explains, clarifies, or develops items appearing on the financial statements, which cannot easily be incorporated into the financial statements themselves. The most common examples of footnotes are as follows:

1. *Accounting policies* (discussed below)

2. *Schedules and exhibits.* Firms typically report schedules or exhibits concerning long-term debt and income tax, for example.

3. *Explanations of financial statement items.* Some items require additional explanation so that users can make sense of the reported information. Pensions and postretirement benefits are two examples.

4. *General information about the company.* Occasionally, firms face events that may affect their financial performance or position but cannot yet be recognized on the financial statements. In that case, investors have an interest in learning this information as soon as possible. Information concerning subsequent events and contingencies are two examples.

The purpose of supplementary schedules is to improve the understandability of the financial statements. They may be used to highlight trends, such as five-year summaries; or they may be required by FASB pronouncements, such as information on current costs.

Parenthetical disclosures are contained on the face of the financial statements (usually on the balance sheet). They are generally used to describe the valuation basis of a particular financial statement element but also may provide other kinds of information, such as the par value and number of shares authorized and issued for various classes of a company's stock.

Accounting Policies

APB Opinion No. 22, "Disclosure of Accounting Policies" (see FASB ASC 235), required all companies to disclose both the accounting policies the firm follows and the methods it uses in applying those policies. Typically, companies disclose this information in a "Summary of Significant Accounting Policies" preceding the footnotes. Specifically, *APB Opinion No. 22* required that the accounting methods and procedures involving the following be disclosed:

1. A selection from existing acceptable alternatives
2. Principles and methods peculiar to the industry in which the reporting entity operates
3. Unusual or innovative applications of GAAP

The APB's principal objective in issuing *Opinion No. 22* was to provide information that helps investors compare firms across and between industries. Since accounting policies have a significant impact on numbers reported in the financial statements, investors need to know what those policies are so they can draw meaningful comparisons between firms in the same industry, or between firms in different industries. Ultimately, knowing these accounting policies allows investors to make economic decisions with more confidence because they can make legitimate comparisons.

Subsequent Events

Because of the complexities of closing the books, the requirements of the audit, and the length of time it takes to print and distribute the annual report, companies usually issue their financial statements several weeks after the close of their fiscal years. During the period between the end of a company's fiscal year and the issuance of its financial statements, events might occur that aren't reflected in its accounting records. These events are referred to as subsequent events and may be either (1) events that provide further evidence of conditions that existed on the balance sheet date or (2) events that provide evidence of conditions that did not exist at the balance sheet date.

GAAP requires events in the first category to be reported on the company's financial statements. In other words, when a company experiences an event— after the balance sheet date but before it issues its financial statements—that provides further evidence of some condition existing at the balance sheet date, it is required to adjust its records to reflect the financial impact of that condition. If, for example, a company settles litigation for an amount significantly different than the amount it had originally accrued, then it must adjust the amount it originally accrued and report the adjusted accrual on the financial statements. The adjusted disclosure is required because the event that gave rise to the adjustment occurred before the balance sheet date. If such an adjustment were not made, then the financial statements would not fully reflect the true financial condition at the balance sheet date or performance of the company that occurred during the fiscal year.

On the other hand, GAAP does not require adjustments to the financial statements for category 2 events. But we should note that companies frequently disclose these events in the footnotes to their financial statements. These footnote disclosures allow the company to discuss the impact of the new information.

Companies often disclose this type of subsequent event when they issue debt or equity securities, incur casualty losses, sell significant assets, or settle litigation initiated as the result of events that occurred after the balance sheet date. The accompanying text box illustrates a subsequent event disclosure of a category 2 item for Intuit, Inc.

Intuit, Inc.: Disclosure of a Subsequent Event

On September 11, 2009, we entered into a definitive agreement to acquire Mint Software Inc., a provider of online personal finance management services. The cash transaction is valued at approximately $170 million, including the assumption of Mint outstanding stock options. Mint will become part of our Other Businesses segment. The transaction is subject to regulatory approval and customary closing conditions. We expect the transaction to close before the end of calendar year 2009.

Areas Directly Affected by Existing FASB Standards—Supplementary Information

The accounting quality of understandability, defined in *SFAC No. 2*, requires financial statement data to be summarized to enable it to be useful to reasonably informed readers. As a consequence, significant information that does not meet the measurement and reporting requirements for presentation in the financial statements is presented as supplementary information. This information may be included in the footnotes or in a separate section frequently termed *financial highlights*. Supplementary information may also be mandated by the FASB or the SEC. Examples of supplementary information include segment information, information describing the effects of price-level changes, information on oil and gas reserves for companies in the extractive industry, the auditor's report, and interim financial reports. Segment information was discussed in Chapter 15, and the disclosure of information on oil and gas reserves is beyond the scope of this text.

Price-Level Information

The high level of inflation experienced in the United States during the 1970s caused concerns that financial statements were being distorted. As a result, both the SEC (*ASR No. 190*) and the FASB (*SFAS No. 33*, superseded) issued pronouncements requiring the disclosure of supplemental information on the effects of changing prices in the 10-K and annual report to stockholders. These disclosures were generally made in separate schedules. Later, after inflation subsided in the 1980s, these requirements were suspended; consequently, supplemental disclosure of this information is no longer required.

Auditor's Report

The SEC requires every company that sells securities to the general public to obtain an auditor's opinion. The auditor is an independent accountant whose responsibility it is to examine the financial statements prepared by management and determine if they are presented "fairly" and in conformity with GAAP. The auditor's opinion is not a method of disclosure, but an unqualified opinion implies that the company's level of disclosure is, at least, adequate. The following guidelines for preparing the auditor's report were developed by the AICPA:

1. The report shall state whether the financial statements are presented in accordance with generally accepted accounting principles.

2. The report shall identify those circumstances in which such principles have not been consistently observed in the current period in relation to the preceding period.

3. Informative disclosures in the financial statements are to be regarded as reasonably adequate unless otherwise stated in the report.

4. The report shall either contain an expression of opinion regarding the financial statements taken as a whole, or an assertion to the effect that an opinion cannot be expressed. When an overall opinion cannot be expressed, the reasons therefore should be stated. In all cases where an auditor's name is associated with financial statements, the report should contain a clear-cut indication of the character of the auditor's work, if any, and the degree of responsibility the auditor is taking.

In most cases, the audit will result in the issuance of a standard, or unqualified, audit report that contains three sections:

1. An opening paragraph that indicates an audit was performed and includes a statement that the financial statements are the responsibility of management

2. A scope paragraph that indicates the audit was performed in accordance with generally accepted auditing standards

3. An opinion paragraph that states the financial statements are presented fairly in accordance with generally accepted accounting principles

In the event the auditor cannot satisfy the criteria necessary to make the above three assertions, he or she may issue one of the following types of opinions:

1. *Qualified opinion.* This type of audit report indicates that except for the effects to which the qualification relates, the financial statements are presented fairly. A qualified audit opinion is issued when

   a. Circumstances prevent the auditor from performing all audit procedures necessary to comply with generally accepted auditing standards,

   b. The financial statements contain a material departure form GAAP, or

   c. All informative disclosures have not been made in the financial statements.

2. *Disclaimer of opinion.* This type of opinion states that the auditor does not express an opinion on the financial statements because

   a. The auditor cannot gather all of the necessary evidence, or

   b. There is concern about the ability of the company to continue as a going concern.

3. *Adverse opinion.* This type of opinion results when the statements are not prepared in accordance with generally accepted accounting principles.

Exhibit 17.2 illustrates the 2008 fiscal year auditor's report for Hershey Company.

EXHIBIT 17.2   *Hershey Company 2008 Independent Auditor's Report*

REPORT OF INDEPENDENT REGISTERED PUBLIC ACCOUNTING FIRM

The Board of Directors and Stockholders
The Hershey Company:

We have audited the accompanying consolidated balance sheets of The Hershey Company and subsidiaries (the "Company") as of December 31, 2008 and 2007, and the related consolidated statements of income, cash flows and stockholders' equity for each of the years in the three-year period ended December 31, 2008. These consolidated financial statements are the responsibility of the Company's management. Our responsibility is to express an opinion on these consolidated financial statements based on our audits.

We conducted our audits in accordance with the standards of the Public Company Accounting Oversight Board (United States). Those standards require that we plan and perform the audit to obtain reasonable assurance about whether the financial statements are free of material misstatement. An audit includes examining, on a test basis, evidence supporting the amounts and disclosures in the financial statements. An audit also includes assessing the accounting principles used and significant estimates made by management, as well as evaluating the overall financial statement presentation. We believe that our audits provide a reasonable basis for our opinion.

In our opinion, the consolidated financial statements referred to above present fairly, in all material respects, the financial position of The Hershey Company and subsidiaries as of December 31, 2008 and 2007, and the results of their operations and their cash flows for each of the years in the three-year period ended December 31, 2008, in conformity with U.S. generally accepted accounting principles.

As discussed in Note 1, the Company adopted Statement of Financial Accounting Standards No. 158, *Employers' Accounting for Defined Benefit Pensions and Other Postretirement Plans,* at December 31, 2006.

We also have audited, in accordance with the standards of the Public Company Accounting Oversight Board (United States), the effectiveness of the Company's internal control over financial reporting as of December 31, 2008, based on criteria established in Internal Control-Integrated Framework issued by the Committee of Sponsoring Organizations of the Treadway Commission (COSO), and our report dated February 19, 2009 expressed an unqualified opinion on the effectiveness of the Company's internal control over financial reporting.

KPMG LLP
New York, New York
February 19, 2009

Interim Financial Statements

The SEC requires companies to issue quarterly summary financial statements on Form 10-Q. Information on financial performance and operating results for periods of less than a year are termed *interim financial reports*. Most publicly traded companies also release information on their periodic performance through various news media. The major value of interim financial reports and news releases is their timeliness. Stated differently, investors need to be aware of any changes in the financial position of the company as soon as possible. In addition, much of the information disclosed in interim financial statements enters into the analytical data used by the government to develop information on the state of the economy, the need for monetary controls, or the need for modifications in the tax laws. There is also evidence that interim reporting has an impact on stock prices, indicating that investors do use interim financial information. It is therefore important that interim information be as reliable as possible.

A wide variety of practices have existed with regard to the methods of reporting in interim periods. Thus, such things as seasonal fluctuations in revenues and the application of fixed costs to the various periods have a significant impact on the reported results for interim periods.

In 1973 the APB studied this problem and issued its conclusions in *APB Opinion No. 28*, "Interim Financial Reporting" (see FASB ASC 270). In reviewing the general question, the Board noted that two views existed as to the principal objective of interim financial reporting.

1. One view held that each interim period was a separate accounting period and that income should be determined in the same manner as for the annual period, thus revenues and expenses should be reported as they occur (*discrete view*).

2. The other view held that interim periods were an integral part of the annual period, thus revenues and expenses might be allocated to various interim periods even though they occurred only in one period (*integral view*).[1]

In *Opinion No. 28*, the APB stated that interim financial information is essential to provide timely data on the progress of the enterprise and that the usefulness of the data rests on its relationship to annual reports. Accordingly, the Board determined that interim periods should be viewed as integral parts of the annual period and that the principles and practices followed in the annual period should be followed in the interim period. However, certain modifications were deemed necessary to provide a better relationship to the annual period.

Additionally, publicly traded companies that present summary information for financial analysis should provide, at minimum, certain information for the interim period in question and the same interim period for the previous year. These guidelines are intended to offset partially the reduction in detail from interim reports. Among the items to be disclosed are sales, earnings per share, seasonal revenues, disposal of a business segment, contingencies, and changes in accounting principles.

Interim financial information is essential to provide timely data on the progress of the enterprise. Moreover, the usefulness of the data rests on its relationship to annual reports. In short, interim periods should be viewed as integral parts of the annual period, and the principles and practices followed in the annual period should be followed in the interim period.

---

1. Accounting Principles Board, *Opinion No. 28*, "Interim Financial Reporting" (New York: American Institute of Certified Public Accountants, 1973), para. 5.

Other Means of Financial Reporting

The financial statements, footnotes, and supplementary schedules constitute the company's financial report. And all significant information should be included in the financial report. Additionally, other relevant information, which can assist in understanding the financial report, is presented in narrative form. Examples of these types of items are management's discussion and analysis and the letter to stockholders.

Management's Discussion and Analysis (MD&A)

The SEC requires all publicly held companies to include an MD&A section in their annual reports. The reasons for including this information in the annual report are outlined in *SFAC No. 1*, which states:

> Management knows more about the enterprise and its affairs than investors, creditors, or other "outsiders" and can often increase the usefulness of financial information by identifying certain transactions, other events, and circumstances that affect the enterprise and explaining their financial impact on it.[2]

Basically, the MD&A section evaluates the causes and explains the reasons for a company's performance during its preceding annual period. The required disclosures include information about liquidity, capital resources, and the results of operations. The SEC also requires management to highlight favorable or unfavorable trends and to identify significant events or uncertainties that affect those three factors. Since a company must disclose matters that could affect its financial statements in the future, the MD&A allows financial statement users to evaluate a company's past performance and its likely impact on future performance. Of course, in order to discuss the influence of past performance on the future, management must use various estimates or approximations. Although these particular discussions often depend on subjective estimates, the SEC indicated that the information's relevance to users exceeds its potential lack of reliability. In fact, in an effort to encourage these presentations, the SEC has provided "safe harbor" rules that protect the firm against fraud charges as long as the estimates management uses are prepared in a reasonable manner and disclosed in good faith.[3]

In 1997 the SEC issued new disclosure rules in an amendment to Regulation S-X titled "Disclosure of Accounting Policies for Derivative Financial Instruments and Derivative Commodity Instruments and Disclosure of Quantitative and Qualitative Information about Market Risk Inherent in Derivative Financial Instruments, Other Financial Instruments, and Derivative Commodity Instruments." As

2. Financial Accounting Standards Board, *SFAC No. 1*, "Objectives of Financial Reporting by Business Enterprises" (Stamford, CT: FASB, 1974), para. 54.

3. Safe-Harbor Rule for Protection, *Release No. 5993* (Washington, DC: Securities and Exchange Commission, 1979).

indicated by its title, this release requires the disclosure of qualitative and quantitative information about market risk by all companies registered with the SEC. Market risk is defined as the risk of loss arising from adverse changes in market rates and prices from such items as

- Interest rates
- Currency exchange rates
- Commodity prices
- Equity prices

The required disclosures are designed to provide investors with forward-looking information about a company's exposures to market risk, such as the risks associated with changes in interest rates, foreign currency exchange rates, commodity prices, and stock prices. The information should indicate the market risk a company faces as well as how the company's management views and manages its market risk. This amendment was issued in response to the large derivative losses that were incurred by companies in the early 1990s, such as Showa Shell Sekiya's $1.5 billion loss on currency derivatives, Procter and Gamble's $157 million loss on leveraged currency swaps, and Arco's employee earnings loss of $22 million on money market derivatives.

The expanded disclosure requirements mandate the inclusion of quantitative and qualitative information about the market risk inherent in market-risk-sensitive instruments. This information is disclosed both outside the financial statements and in the related notes.

The quantitative information about market-risk-sensitive instruments is to be disclosed by using one or more of the following alternatives:

1. Tabular presentation of fair value information and contract terms relevant to determining future cash flows, categorized by expected maturity dates
2. Sensitivity analysis expressing the potential loss in future earnings, fair values, or cash flows from selected hypothetical changes in market rates and prices
3. Value-at-risk disclosures expressing the potential loss in future earnings, fair values, or cash flows from market movements over a selected period and with a selected likelihood of occurrence.

These three alternative methods were allowed because the SEC wanted to permit disclosure requirements about market risk that were flexible enough to accommodate different types of registrants, different degrees of market risk exposure, and alternative methods of measuring market risk.

A primary objective of the quantitative disclosure requirements is to provide investors with forward-looking information about a registrant's potential exposures to market risk. Consequently, in preparing quantitative information, registrants are required to categorize market-risk-sensitive instruments into instruments entered into for trading purposes, and instruments entered into for purposes other than trading. Specifically, companies must disclose:

1. Their primary market risk exposures at the end of the current reporting period
2. How they manage those exposures (such as a description of the objectives, general strategies, and instruments, if any, used to manage those exposures)

3. Changes in either the primary market risk exposures or how those exposures are managed, when compared to the most recent reporting period and what is known or expected in future periods

An examination of Hershey's and Tootsie Roll's financial statements revealed that both companies use derivative financial instruments to manage risk. The following information about Hershey's use of derivatives was contained in its 2008 10-K report:

> We use certain derivative instruments, from time to time, including interest rate swaps, foreign currency forward exchange contracts and options, and commodities futures and options contracts, to manage interest rate, foreign currency exchange rate and commodity market price risk exposures, respectively. We enter into interest rate swap agreements and foreign exchange forward contracts and options for periods consistent with related underlying exposures. These derivative instruments do not constitute positions independent of those exposures. We enter into commodities futures and options contracts for varying periods. These futures and options contracts are intended to be, and are effective as hedges of market price risks associated with anticipated raw material purchases, energy requirements and transportation costs. We do not hold or issue derivative instruments for trading purposes and are not a party to any instruments with leverage or prepayment features. In entering into these contracts, we have assumed the risk that might arise from the possible inability of counterparties to meet the terms of their contracts. We mitigate this risk by performing financial assessments prior to contract execution, conducting periodic evaluations of counterparty performance and maintaining a diverse portfolio of qualified counterparties. We do not expect any significant losses from counterparty defaults.

In 2003 the SEC published new interpretive guidelines regarding the disclosure of items in the MD&A section of the 10-K report.[4] Specifically, additional guidance was provided for the following areas:

1. *The overall presentation of MD&A.* Within the universe of material information, companies should present their disclosures so that the most important information is most prominent; companies should avoid unnecessary duplicative disclosure that can tend to overwhelm readers and act as an obstacle to identifying and understanding material matters; and many companies would benefit from starting their MD&A with a section that provides an executive-level overview that provides context for the remainder of the discussion.

2. *The focus and content of MD&A (including materiality, analysis, key performance measures, and known material trends and uncertainties).* In deciding on the content of MD&A, companies should focus on material information and eliminate immaterial information that does not promote understanding of companies' financial condition, liquidity and capital resources, changes

4. Interpretation: Commission Guidance Regarding Management's Discussion and Analysis of Financial Condition and Results of Operations. Release No. 33-8350; 34-48960; IC-21399 December 19, 2003.SEC, www.sec.gov/news/press/2003-179.htm.

in financial condition, and results of operations (both in the context of profit and loss and cash flows); companies should identify and discuss key performance indicators, including nonfinancial performance indicators, that their management uses to manage the business and that would be material to investors; companies must identify and disclose known trends, events, demands, commitments, and uncertainties that are reasonably likely to have a material effect on financial condition or operating performance, and companies should provide not only disclosure of information responsive to MD&A's requirements but also an analysis that is responsive to those requirements that explains management's view of the implications and significance of that information and that satisfies the objectives of MD&A.

3. *The disclosure of liquidity and capital resources.* Companies should consider enhanced analysis and explanation of the sources and uses of cash and material changes in particular items underlying the major captions reported in their financial statements, rather than recitation of the items in the cash flow statements; companies using the indirect method in preparing their cash-flow statements should pay particular attention to disclosure and analysis of matters that are not readily apparent from their cash-flow statements; and companies also should consider whether their MD&A should include enhanced disclosure regarding debt instruments, guarantees, and related covenants.

4. *The disclosure of critical accounting estimates.* Companies should consider enhanced discussion and analysis of these critical accounting estimates and assumptions that supplements, but does not duplicate, the description of accounting policies in the notes to the financial statements and that provides greater insight into the quality and variability of information regarding financial condition and operating performance.

Letter to Stockholders

Management's letter to the stockholders has four main purposes. It indicates that management:

1. Is responsible for preparation and integrity of statements
2. Has prepared statements in accordance with GAAP
3. Has used its best estimates and judgment
4. Maintains a system of internal controls

Other Useful Information for Investment, Credit, and Similar Decisions

Information about companies is also available outside the company's annual report and 10-K. Examples of these types of information include analysts' reports and news articles about the company.

Analysts' Reports

Individual investors make essentially three investment decisions:

1. *Buy.* A potential investor decides to purchase a particular security on the basis of all available disclosed information.

2. *Hold.* An investor decides to retain a particular security on the basis of all available disclosed information.

3. *Sell.* An investor decides to dispose of a particular security on the basis of all available disclosed information.

As discussed in Chapter 4, the decision process used by most investors is termed *fundamental analysis.* Fundamental analysis attempts to identify securities that are mispriced by reviewing all available information. The investor then incorporates the associated degree of risk to arrive at an expected share price. The expected share price is then compared to the current price, allowing the investor to make buy–hold–sell decisions.

Professional security analysts also make investment analyses. They frequently specialize in certain industries, using their training and experience to process and disseminate information more accurately and economically than individual investors. There are three categories of financial analysts:

1. *Sell side.* These analysts work for full-service broker dealers and make recommendations on securities they cover. Many work for the most prominent brokerage firms, which also provide investment banking services to companies, including those whose securities the analysts cover.

2. *Buy side.* These analysts work for institutional money managers, such as mutual funds, that purchase securities for their own accounts. They counsel their companies to buy, hold, and sell.

3. *Independent.* These analysts are not associated with firms that underwrite the securities they cover. They often sell their recommendations on a subscription basis.

Many analysts work in a world of built-in conflicts of interest and competing pressures. Sell-side firms want their investor clients to be successful over time because satisfied long-term investors are the key to the firm's reputation and success. On the other hand, several factors can create pressure on an analyst's independence and objectivity. Such pressures don't necessarily mean analysts are biased, but investors should understand these points:

1. An analysts' firm may be underwriting a company's securities offering, and client firms prefer favorable research reports.

2. Positive reports can generate additional clients and revenues.

3. Arrangements frequently tie compensation to continuation of clients.

4. Analysts may own securities individually, or the securities may be owned by the analyst's firm.

Consequently, investors should confirm whether the analyst's firm underwrote a recommended company's stock by looking at the prospectus, which is part of the registration statement for the offering. A list of the lead or managing underwriters can be found on the front cover of both the preliminary and final copies of the prospectus. Additionally, a company's registration statement and its annual report on Form 10-K will disclose the identities of the beneficial owners of more than 5 percent of a class of equity securities and list the private sales of the company's securities during the past three years.

If a financial analyst or the firm acquired ownership interests through venture investing, the shares generally will be subject to a "lock-up" agreement during and after the issuer's initial public offering. Lock-up agreements prohibit company insiders—including employees, their friends and family, and venture capitalists—from selling their shares for a set period of time without the underwriter's permission. While the underwriter can choose to end a lock-up period early, whether because of market conditions, the performance of the offering, or other factors, lock-ups generally last for 180 days after the offering's registration statement becomes effective.

After the lock-up period ends, the firm or the analyst may wish to sell the stock. Anyone considering investing in a company that has recently conducted an initial public offering will want to check whether a lock-up agreement is in effect and when it expires, or whether the underwriter waived any lock-up restrictions. This is important information because a company's stock price may be affected by the prospect of lock-up shares being sold into the market when the lock-up ends. It is also a data point to consider when assessing research reports issued just before a lock-up period expires; those reports are sometimes known as "booster shots."

Above all, it must be remembered that even the soundest recommendation from the most trustworthy analyst may not be a good choice. That's one reason investors should never rely solely on an analyst's recommendation when buying or selling a stock. Before acting, investors should determine whether the decision fits with their goals, time horizon, and tolerance for risk. In other words, they should know what they are buying or selling—and why.

Securities and Exchange Commission

Many of the disclosure techniques and accounting conventions discussed in the preceding section are the result of evolving GAAP and consensus. However, since the mid-1930s, the U.S. government has also been involved in standard-setting and disclosure issues. The SEC is the regulatory agency responsible for administering federal securities laws. The purpose of these laws is to protect investors and to attempt to ensure that investors have all relevant information about companies that issue publicly traded securities. The SEC is also responsible for enforcing all of the laws passed by Congress that affect the public trading of securities. Among these laws are the Securities Act of 1933, the Securities Exchange Act of 1934, the Foreign Corrupt Practices Act of 1977, and the Sarbanes-Oxley Act of 2002. These acts stress the need to provide prospective investors with full and fair disclosure of the activities of a company offering and selling securities to the public.

The Securities Act of 1933

The Securities Act of 1933 regulates the initial public sale and distribution of a corporation's securities (*going public*). The goal of this legislation is to protect the public from fraud when a company is initially issuing securities to the general public. The provisions of the Securities Act of 1933 require a company initially offering securities to file a registration statement and a prospectus with the SEC. The registration statement becomes effective on the 20th day after filing unless the SEC requires amendments. This 20-day period is termed the *waiting period*, and it is unlawful for a company to offer to sell securities during this period. Registration of securities under the provisions of the 1933 act is designed to provide adequate disclosures of material facts to allow investors to assess the degree of potential risk. Nevertheless, registration does not completely protect investors from the possibility of loss, and it is unlawful for any company officials to suggest that registration prevents possible losses.

The Securities Exchange Act of 1934

The Securities Exchange Act of 1934 regulates the trading of securities of publicly held companies (*being public*). This legislation addresses the personal duties of corporate officers and owners (*insiders*) and corporate reporting requirements, and it specifies information that is to be contained in the corporate annual reports and interim reports issued to shareholders. The act established extensive reporting requirements to provide continuous full and fair disclosure. Each corporation that offers securities for sale to the general public must select the appropriate reporting forms. The most common reporting forms, all of which can be obtained from the SEC's website, are as follows:

- *Form 10.* The normal registration statement for securities to be sold to the public
- *Form 10-K.* The annual report
- *Form 10-Q.* The quarterly report of operations[5]
- *Proxy statement.* Used when a company makes a proxy solicitation for its stockholder meetings

A major goal of the 1934 act is to ensure that any *corporate insider* (broadly defined as any corporate officer, director, or shareholder owning 10 percent or more) does not achieve an advantage in the purchase or sale of securities because of a relationship with the corporation. The act also established civil and criminal liabilities for insiders making false or misleading statements when trading corporate securities. The specific SEC reporting requirements for going public and being public are beyond the scope of this text; however, note that the SEC's stipulation that much of the information provided in the 10-K, 10-Q, and proxy reports must be certified by an independent certified public accountant has been a significant factor in the growth and importance of the public accounting profession in the United States.

The Foreign Corrupt Practices Act of 1977

The Foreign Corrupt Practices Act (FCPA) of 1977 contains two main elements. The first makes it a criminal offense to offer bribes to political or governmental officials outside the United States and imposes fines on offending firms. It also provides for fines and imprisonment of officers, directors, or stockholders of offending firms.

The second element of the FCPA is a requirement that all public companies must (1) keep reasonably detailed records that accurately and fairly reflect company financial activity and (2) devise and maintain a system of internal control that provides reasonable assurance that transactions were properly authorized, recorded, and accounted for. This element is an amendment to the Securities Exchange Act of 1934 and therefore applies to all corporations that are subject to the act's provisions.

---

5. The SEC first required quarterly reports to be issued in 1970.

The major goals of this legislation are to prevent the bribery of foreign officials and to ensure the maintenance of adequate corporate financial records.

The Sarbanes-Oxley Act of 2002 (SOX)

During the early 2000s, dozens of major companies either went bankrupt or faced extreme financial difficulties. These included such familiar names as Enron, WorldCom, Xerox, Global Crossing, Arthur Andersen, Merrill Lynch, Tyco International, and Halliburton Oil Services. As a result, Americans lost billions of their investment dollars, jobs vanished, and thousands of people lost their entire retirement savings. Subsequently, "corporate reform" became a watchword; and the feelings of the public can be illustrated by this observation from noted economist and television commentator Larry Kudlow:

> It's not the economy that is driving the stock market down. There's a malaise over Wall Street because people are worried, fearful, aggravated, and downright blown away by the incongruous behavior of our leaders and elected officials. This level of indecision, finger pointing, and suspended animation shouldn't be happening in this great country, but it is happening. What's the solution? Where are the answers? No one knows for sure. But decisive action by our nation's leaders in business, finance, accounting, law, and governance must emerge.[6]

In addition to the scandals, the cavalier attitude of the executives of some of the failed companies further unsettled the nation. For example, in congressional testimony, Jeffrey Skilling, CEO of Enron, maintained that detailed financial reporting and disclosure vigilance was the proper domain not of a CEO but of Enron's accountants and lawyers. Similarly, Bernie Ebbers, the CEO of WorldCom, alleged that he was totally unaware of his CFO's financial reporting wrongdoing. Public unrest resulted in a hearing before Congress, and on April 25, 2002, the House of Representatives passed the Oxley Bill. On July 15, 2002, the Senate passed the Sarbanes Bill. Together these two bills became known as the Sarbanes-Oxley Act of 2002 (SOX), which President George W. Bush signed into law on July 30, 2002.

Here are some major provisions of this legislation:

1. *Creation of the Public Company Accounting Oversight Board (PCAOB)*. The PCAOB oversees audits of public companies that are subject to the Securities Act of 1933 and the Securities Exchange Act of 1934. The PCAOB contains five members appointed from among prominent individuals of integrity and reputation. These individuals must have a demonstrated commitment to the interests of investors and the public and an understanding of the responsibilities for the financial disclosures required in the preparation of financial statements and audit reports. PCAOB duties include

   a. Registering public accounting firms that prepare audit reports

   b. Establishing auditing, quality control, ethics, independence, and other standards relating to the preparation of audit reports

---

6. Larry Kudlow, "Investing America's on Hold Because the World's Turned Upside Down," NRO Online (June 5, 2002), http://66.216.126.164/.

   c. Conducting inspections of registered public accounting firms

   d. Conducting investigations and disciplinary proceedings and, where appropriate, imposing appropriate sanctions where justified upon registered public accounting firms and CPAs within those firms

   e. Performing any other duties or functions necessary or appropriate to promote high professional standards among, and to improve the quality of audit services offered by, CPA firms and CPAs within those firms

   f. Enforcing compliance with the Securities Exchange Act of 1934

   Among the PCAOB's powers are

   a. To sue and be sued, complain and defend, in its corporate name and through its own counsel, with the approval of the SEC, in any federal, state, or other court

   b. To conduct its operations and exercise all rights and powers authorized by the SEC, without regard to any qualification, licensing, or other provision of law in effect in any state or political subdivision

2. *Establishment of auditing, quality control, and independence standards.* The PCAOB is required to cooperate with various professional groups of CPAs related to the standard-setting process. The PCAOB may adopt standards proposed by the profession; however, it has the authority to amend, modify, repeal, and/or reject any standards suggested by the profession. Additionally, CPA firms are required to prepare, and maintain for a period of not less than seven years, audit work papers and other information in sufficient detail to support the conclusions reached in each of its audit reports. CPA firms must also use a second-partner review and approval of its audit reports. The PCAOB developed an audit standard to implement internal control reviews. This standard requires auditors to evaluate whether internal controls include records that accurately and fairly reflect transactions of the reporting entity and provide reasonable assurance that the transactions are recorded in a manner that will permit the preparation of financial statements in accordance with the technical literature; auditors must also disclose any material weaknesses in internal controls they discover during audits.

3. *Inspection of CPA firms.* The PCAOB will conduct annual quality reviews for CPA firms that audit financial statements of more than 100 publicly traded entities. Other firms must undergo this quality review/inspection process every three years. The SEC and/or the PCAOB may order a special inspection of any CPA firm at any time.

4. *Establishment of accounting standards.* The SEC is authorized to recognize as generally accepted accounting principles those that are established by a standard-setting body that meet all of the criteria within the Sarbanes-Oxley Act, which include requirements that the standard-setting body

   a. Be a private entity.

   b. Be governed by a board of trustees or equivalent body, the majority of whom are not or have not been associated with a CPA firm within the two-year period preceding service on this board of trustees.

    c. Be funded in a manner similar to the PCAOB, through fees collected from CPA firms and other parties.

    d. Have adopted procedures to ensure prompt consideration of changes to accounting principles by a majority vote. Consider when adopting standards the need to keep the standards current and the extent to which international convergence of standards is necessary or appropriate.

5. *Delineation of prohibited services.* The legislation makes it unlawful for a CPA firm to provide any nonaudit service to the reporting entity contemporaneously with the financial statement audit. Prohibited services include the following:

    a. Bookkeeping or other services related to the accounting records or financial statements of the reporting entity

    b. Financial information systems design and implementation

    c. Appraisal or valuation services, fairness opinions, or contribution-in-kind reports

    d. Actuarial services

    e. Internal audit outsourcing services

    f. Management functions or human resources

    g. Broker-dealer, investor advisor, or investment banker services

    h. Legal services and expert services unrelated to the audit, or any other service that the board rules is not permissible

The legislations allow the board, on a case by case basis, to provide an exemption to these prohibitions, subject to review by the SEC, and does not make it unlawful to provide other nonaudit services (those not prohibited) if those services are approved in advance by the audit committee. The audit committee must disclose to investors in periodic reports the decision to preapprove those services. The preapproval requirement is waived if the aggregate amount of the fees for all of the services provided constitutes less than 5 percent of the total amount of revenues paid by the issuer to the auditing firm.

6. *Prohibition of acts that influence the conduct of an audit.* The act makes it unlawful for any officer or director of an entity to fraudulently influence, coerce, manipulate, or mislead a CPA performing an audit.

7. *Requirement for specified disclosures.* Each financial report must reflect all material correcting adjustments a CPA determines are necessary. Each annual or quarterly financial report must disclose all material off–balance sheet transactions and other relationships with unconsolidated entities that may have a material current or future effect on the financial condition of the entity. The SEC will issue rules providing that pro forma financial information must be presented in a manner such that it does not contain an "untrue statement" or omit a material fact necessary in order for the information not to be misleading.

8. *Requirement for CEO and CFO certification.* CEOs and CFOs must certify in each annual and quarterly report that the officer has reviewed the report, that based on the officer's knowledge the report contains no untrue statement of a material fact or omit a material fact, and that based on the officer's

knowledge, the financial statements and other financial information included in the report fairly present the financial condition and results of operations of the issuer. They must also attest that they are responsible for establishing and maintaining internal controls, that they have designed such controls to ensure that material information is made known to the officers, that they have presented their conclusions about the effectiveness of those controls in the report, and that they have disclosed both to the outside auditors and to the company's audit committee (1) all significant deficiencies in the design or operation of internal controls that could adversely affect the issuer's ability to record, process, summarize, and report financial data; and (2) any fraud, whether or not material, involving any employee who has a significant role in the issuer's internal controls.

Section 404

Section 404 is one of the more controversial provisions of SOX. It contains two subsections—404(a) and 404(b). Section 404(a) outlines management's responsibility under the act and requires that the annual report include an internal control report by management that (1) acknowledges its responsibility for establishing and maintaining adequate internal control over financial reporting and (2) contains an assessment of the effectiveness of internal control over financial reporting as of the end of the most recent fiscal year. It also requires the principal executive and financial officers to make quarterly and annual certifications as to the effectiveness of the company's internal control over financial reporting. Section 404(b) outlines the independent auditor's responsibility. It requires the auditor (1) to report on the internal control assessment made by management and (2) to make a separate independent assessment of the company's internal controls over financial reporting.

The result of these provisions initially was to require the auditor to issue two separate opinions. The first opinion stated whether management's assessment of internal control was fairly stated, in all material respects. The second opinion indicated whether, in the auditor's opinion, the company maintained, in all material respects, effective internal control over financial reporting as of the specific date, based on the control criteria used by management. In summary, the auditor reported on (1) whether management's assessment of the effectiveness of internal control was appropriate, and (2) whether he or she believed that the company had maintained effective internal control over financial reporting.

The cost of compliance with this legislation was seen by some as excessive. According to one study, the net private cost amounted to approximately $1.4 trillion.[7] This amount was obtained by an econometric estimate of the loss in total market value caused by SOX. It measured the costs minus the benefits as perceived by the stock market as the new rules were enacted. This study's results were later questioned on the grounds that no single factor can be attributed as the cause of stock market behavior. Critics noted that all of the stock market trends around the time SOX was enacted were attributed to the legislation, while the

---

7. I. X. Zhang, "Economic Consequences of the Sarbanes-Oxley Act of 2002" Unpublished working paper (Rochester, NY: William E. Simon Graduate School of Business Administration, University of Rochester, 2005).

subsequent increase in market value was ignored.[8] Nevertheless, a survey by the Financial Executives Institute in 2005[9] estimated that companies' total costs for the first year of compliance with SOX averaged $4.6 million.

The SOX 404 provisions that emphasize the importance of internal control have obvious benefit; however, a standard rule of thumb for internal control measures is that the benefits should outweigh their costs. Some critics of SOX maintain that its effect has been that the costs of regulation exceed its benefits for many corporations.[10] SOX was originally effective for companies meeting the definition of accelerated filers (having an equity market capitalization of over $75 million and filing a report with the SEC) for fiscal years ending on or after December 15, 2004; consequently, December 31, 2004, was the first filing date for most of these companies. Companies that did not meet the definition of accelerated filers were initially required to comply with SOX's provisions for fiscal periods ending on or after July 15, 2006.

A subsequent study of the economic consequences of SOX Section 404 indicated that audit fees for the companies meeting the definition of accelerated filers increased by an average of 65 percent in the first year SOX was effective and by 0.9 percent in the second year.[11] This increased cost was found to cause an average decrease in earnings of 0.5 percent during the first year of compliance. Similar analyses apparently caused the SEC to revisit the issue. In June 2007, the PCAOB released *Auditing Standard No. 5 (AS No. 5)* to supersede the previous guidelines under which auditors were seen as so focused on the detail and the shear breadth of the internal controls that there was little room for judgment and a clear perspective over the overall process goals. *AS No. 5* adopts an integrated top-down, risk-based, and materiality-focused approach to the audit. As such, the auditor's report on internal control over financial reporting will express one opinion—an opinion on whether the company has maintained effective internal control over financial reporting as of its fiscal year-end. For the auditor to render an opinion, *AS No. 5* requires the auditor to evaluate and test both the design and the operating effectiveness of internal control to be satisfied that management's assessment about whether the company maintained effective internal control over financial reporting as of its fiscal year-end is correct and, therefore, is fairly stated.

The cost of complying with the Section 404 provisions was also viewed as especially burdensome for smaller companies. In an attempt to reduce this impact, in May 2006, the SEC announced it intended to take a series of actions to improve the implementation of Section 404 of SOX; and in December 2006, it first extended the date for compliance by non-accelerated filers to fiscal years ending on or after December 15, 2007. Later, The SEC extended the date for compliance for non-accelerated filers to June 15, 2010.

8. See, for example, C. Creelman, "Estimated SOX Year-One Compliance Costs $1.4 Trillion: Increase in Investor Confidence Priceless," Pennsylvania Institute of Certified Public Accountants (2006), www.cpazone.org.

9. "404 Compliance: Is the Gain Worth the Pain?" *Financial Executive* 21 (2005): 30–32.

10. W. J. Carney, "The Costs of Being Public After Sarbanes-Oxley: The Irony of Going Private," *Emory Law Journal* 55 (2006): 141–59.

11. S. Bhamornsiri, R. Guinn, and R. Schroeder, "International Implications of Section 404 of the Cost of Compliance with Section 404 of Sarbanes-Oxley," *International Advances in Economic Research*.15 1 (Feb. 2009) 17–29.

Initially, the SEC did not play an active role in the accounting standard setting process and encouraged the private sector to develop accounting standards. However, in recent years the SEC has taken a more proactive role. For example, in 2008 the SEC issued a study on the impact of mark-to-market accounting (discussed in Chapter 7). Earlier in July 2007, the SEC chartered the Advisory Committee on Improvements to Financial Reporting. This committee's mandate was to examine the U.S. financial reporting system in order to make recommendations intended to increase the usefulness of financial information to investors, while reducing the complexity of the financial reporting system to investors, preparers, and auditors.

In August, 2008 the committee issued its final report.[12] Among its recommendations were the following:

1. *The usefulness of the information in SEC reports should be increased.* One of the committee's primary objectives was to make financial information more useful to investors while minimizing additional burdens on preparers. As part of this effort, the committee recommend including a short executive summary at the beginning of a company's annual report on Form 10-K. This recommendation was in response to the committee's belief that individual investors find a company's periodic reports overly complex and detailed. The summary should describe concisely the most important themes or other significant matters management is primarily concerned with, along with a page index showing where investors could find more detailed information on particular subjects. The committee also encouraged the private sector to develop key performance indicators, on an activity and industry basis, that would capture important aspects of a company's activities that may not be fully reflected in its financial statements or may be nonfinancial.

2. *The accounting standards-setting process should be enhanced.* The committee maintained that the financial reporting system would be best served by recognizing the preeminence of the perspective of investors because they are the primary users of financial reports. To promote this perspective, it supported increased investor representation on the FASB and in the Financial Accounting Foundation. The committee believed that increasing investor direct and indirect representation in the process was the best way to assure that financial reports will be useful to investors.

3. *The substantive design of new accounting standards should be improved.* The committee asserted that some accounting standards do not clearly articulate their underlying objectives and principles and are sometimes obscured by dense language, detailed rules, and numerous exemptions. In an attempt to overcome this shortcoming, the committed supported the objective of the FASB's project on financial statement presentation to divide a company's individual financial statements into cohesive components. Although recognizing that the current mixed-attribute system of historic cost and fair value was likely to continue, it urged a judicious approach to further expansions of fair value. Additionally, the committee advocated portraying the different sources of changes in a

---

12. Final Report of the Advisory Committee on Improvements to Financial Reporting to the United States Securities and Exchange Commission, SEC (August 1, 2008), www.sec.gov/ about/offices/oca/acifr/acifrfinalreport.pdf.

company's income—for example, by clearly distinguishing cash receipts from unrealized changes in fair value. This distinction was seen as helping companies better explain to investors the earnings volatility during each accounting period. The committee also opposed rule-based bright-line tests since such tests might result in very different accounting for transactions with quite similar economics. To decrease complexity and increase comparability, the committee advocated a move away from industry-specific guidance in authoritative literature—unless it was justified by strong conceptual arguments. The committee held that a better approach would be to focus on the nature of the business activity itself. Finally, the committee recommended that the FASB eliminate alternative accounting methods for the same transaction, unless the alternative has a compelling rationale.

4. *Authoritative interpretive guidance should be delineated.* The committee noted that historically, interpretive guidance on implementing accounting standards proliferated from many public and private sources and thus increased the volume of U.S. GAAP. To reduce the avoidable complexity associated with the proliferation of U.S. GAAP, the committee voiced support for the FASB's efforts to complete the codification of all U.S. GAAP in one document, which would clearly delineate authoritative from nonauthoritative literature. To help integrate SEC accounting guidance into this codification, the committee recommended that the SEC should formulate its guidance in a format consistent with the one used by the FASB. The committee also voiced its belief that there should be a single standards setter for all authoritative accounting standards and interpretive implementation guidance of general significance.

5. *Guidance on financial restatements and accounting judgments should be clarified.* The committee noted that in 2006, more than 9 percent of all U.S. public companies restated their financial statements because of accounting errors. This restatement process, which frequently takes longer than 12 months, imposes significant costs on investors as well as preparers. As a result, companies often go into a dark period and issue very little financial information to the public. Consequently, the committee recommend that the determination of whether an accounting error is material be separated from the decision on how to correct the error, and supported a stricter rule than the current practice on accounting errors. That is, a company should promptly correct and prominently disclose any accounting error unless clearly insignificant. In addition, the correction and disclosure of any accounting error should not automatically result in a financial restatement. Also, due to the high probable cost to investors during the dark period, prior period financial statements should be amended only if the error would be material to investors making current investment decisions. The committee also noted that the preparation and audit of financial statements has always required the exercise of judgment and that a recent trend in accounting has been to move away from prescriptive guidance toward greater use of judgment. In recognition of the increasing exercise of accounting and audit judgments, the committees recommend that the SEC and PCAOB adopt policy statements on this subject. These policy statements should provide more transparency into how these regulators evaluate the reasonableness of a judgment, so that investors can have more confidence in the ways that accounting and auditing judgments are being exercised.

The committee went on to make numerous recommendations on how to implement these recommendations. They can be accessed through the web address contained in the reports' citation.

Ethical Responsibilities

From a philosophical perspective, the study of ethics explores and analyzes moral judgments, choices, and standards, and asks the question: How should I act? Consequently, society's moral value judgments and the bases for choices of moral beliefs and standards require more comprehensive analysis than is attainable from the data of other disciplines. For example, consider the distinction between science and philosophy. While acting in a professional capacity, the scientist does not find it necessary to pass value judgments on his or her work. In fact, the scientist may disclaim responsibility for the uses of his or her findings, as in the case of biological and nuclear weapons. However, philosophers do evaluate and pass moral judgments on the work of scientists, since the goal of philosophy is to evaluate all aspects of human character, conduct, and experience. Similarly, the scientist (and the accountant), as a thinking person, is required to make value judgments concerning his or her own work and its consequences.

The terms *ethics* and *morals* are not used interchangeably. In general, ethics (derived from the Greek *elhike*—"the science of character") is the study of moral issues, whereas morals (derived from the Greek *mores*—"customs and manners") are standards that individuals observe in their daily conduct. The professions, including accounting, provide an exception to this general rule. Professional codes of conduct delineate minimum standards for the practice of a profession. Violation of these standards makes a professional unethical. For a layperson, the violation of his or her personal code of ethics makes the individual immoral.

The ethical philosophy of Western civilization is based largely on the concept of *utilitarianism*, the greatest happiness of the greatest number, as defined by John Stuart Mill.[13] Professional ethics by accountants prescribes a duty that goes beyond that of an ordinary citizen. The special responsibility accountants have to society was summarized by Chief Justice Warren Burger, as discussed in Chapter 1 (see page 21). Meeting this responsibility requires accountants to maintain high ethical standards of professional conduct. Society has granted many of the professions autonomy, including self-regulation, as a privilege. In return, these professions must assume the obligation to promote ethical conduct among their members, or public policymakers may react by reducing or removing self-regulation and autonomy. Ethical conduct by accountants, based on the concept of utilitarianism, should include consideration of all possible consequences of professional decisions for all individuals or groups affected by a decision. Among these individuals or groups are actual and potential stockholders, creditors, suppliers, customers, employees, and society as a whole.

The practice of professional accounting is characterized by uncertainties that can create ethical dilemmas. Loeb has identified several major ethical issues or dilemmas that may confront individual accountants and accounting firms.[14]

13. See, for example, J. B. Schneewind, *Mill's Ethical Writings* (New York: Collier, 1965).

14. Stephen E. Loeb, "Ethical Committees and Consultants in Public Accounting," *Accounting Horizons* (December 1989): 1–10.

1. *Independence.* The concept of independence requires the complete separation of the business and financial interests of the public accountant from the client corporation. Consequently, the auditor must serve the role of an impartial observer maintaining the public watchdog function. How do firms develop policies to ensure that this duty is maintained?

2. *Scope of services.* What other services (e.g., consulting, tax return preparation, tax advice) are compatible with financial auditing? At what point does the auditor lose independence by providing nonaudit services to a client?

3. *Confidentiality.* When does the auditor's public watchdog function conflict with his or her duty to keep client activities confidential?

4. *Practice development.* The removal of the rule prohibiting advertising (discussed later in the chapter) allows a great deal of latitude; however, an advertisement cannot be misleading or untrue. How do firms develop policies to delineate the nature and extent of practice development activities?

5. *Differences on accounting issues.* How do public accounting firms develop policies to deal with situations in which a company wishes to account for a transaction in a manner not believed to be acceptable to the firm? (In these situations, the company may threaten to fire the auditor and seek a public accounting firm that will agree with management's position on the accounting issue. This practice is termed *opinion shopping*.)

The resolution of ethical dilemmas can be assisted through a framework of analysis. The purpose of such frameworks is to help identify the ethical issues and to decide on an appropriate course of action. For example, the following six-step approach may be used:

1. Obtain the relevant facts.
2. Identify the ethical issues.
3. Determine the individuals or groups affected by the dilemma.
4. Identify the possible alternative solutions.
5. Determine how the individuals or groups are affected by the alternative solutions.
6. Decide on the appropriate action.

Another aspect of the ethics issue is the legal-ethical question. That is, if a particular action is legal, does that automatically make it ethical? The obvious answer to this question is no, given that slavery was once legal in the United States. In fact, there is a presumption in our society that ethical behavior should be at a higher level than legal behavior. Consequently, acts that are consistent with current ethical standards but inconsistent with current legal standards may point to a need to change unethical legal standards. For example, consider the issues of sexual and racial discrimination. Not long ago, public accounting firms hired neither women nor racial minorities. Various actions throughout society, including some that violated the law, helped eliminate these practices to the point that today over 50 percent of new hires by large public accounting firms are women; and the profession and public accounting firms are currently engaging in a variety of activities to encourage racial minorities to choose accounting as a career.

The Professional Code of Conduct

Accountants, as professionals, are expected to maintain a level of ethical conduct that goes beyond society's laws. The reason for this high level of ethical conduct is the need for public confidence in the quality of services provided by the profession, regardless of the individual providing the service. Public confidence in the quality of professional service is enhanced when the profession encourages high standards of performance and ethical conduct by its members.

Over the years, the AICPA has represented itself as an ethical professional body engaged in practicing an art rather than a science. Accounting was to be viewed by society, in a manner similar to the medical and legal professions, as more influenced by a service motive than by a profit motive. As an art, the judgmental nature of accounting precludes a uniform set of rules to cover all situations; consequently, the foundation of the profession rests not on standardization and regulation but on ethical conduct.

In attempting to solidify this view by society, the accounting profession in the United States has had some form of the Code of Professional Conduct since the early twentieth century. The original code, which was part of the bylaws of the American Association of Professional Accountants (AAPA), a predecessor of the AICPA, was first published in 1905 and contained only two rules. One prohibited members from allowing nonmembers to practice in the member's name, thereby requiring all members of the firm, not just the managing partner, to join the AAPA. The second rule prohibited the payment of referral fees, now commonly known as kickbacks. The limited scope of the earliest version of the code was based on a belief that a written code could not and should not be taken as a complete representation of the moral obligations of accounting's responsibility to society.

Later, in 1917 and through subsequent adopted rules, the renamed organization, the American Institute of Accountants, amended the Code of Professional Conduct to include rules prohibiting various actions such as contingency fees, competitive bidding, advertising, the formation of partnerships, forecasts, and a substantial financial interest in a public corporation client. In addition, in response to the securities acts of 1933 and 1934, a rule on independence was adopted in 1934. Later, in 1941, the rules were recodified to include a section on technical standards.

As discussed in Chapter 1, after the collapse of the stock market in 1929, accountants were viewed very favorably by society. Consequently, it was not necessary for the profession to undertake any drastic measures to attain the public's confidence. Up to 1941, the profession's main concerns were bound up with the concepts of confidentiality, competence, and independence. The main emphasis of the profession's disciplinary actions during this period, and even somewhat later, was directed toward restrictions on unprofessional competitive practices such as competitive bidding, advertising, encroachment on the practice of other CPAs, and the pirating of other firms' employees. The rules prohibiting such actions were based on the belief that they would erode independence and destroy harmony among practitioners.[15]

---

15. W. E. Olson, *The Accounting Profession: Years of Trial: 1969–1980* (New York: AICPA, 1982).

In 1962 the Code of Professional Conduct was again amended. Although the amended code contained essentially the same rules as did the 1941 code, they were classified into five articles. Article 1, "Relations with Clients and Public," contained a more explicit description of independence. Article 2 defined "Technical Standards." Article 3, "Promotional Practices," covered advertising, promotional practices, and competitive bidding. Article 4 discussed the rules of membership and was termed "Operating Practices." Finally, Article 5, "Relations with Fellow Members," defined unacceptable client and employee acquisition practices.

The subsequent social upheaval of the 1960s, and the impact of the Watergate investigation of 1974, affected the accounting profession. For example, it was found that many of the largest corporations had made illegal contributions to the Republican Party, and investigations discovered secret bank accounts that were used to hide bribes and kickbacks. The profession argued that it was difficult, if not impossible, to discover such transactions in a normal audit. In addition, it was maintained that, even if detected, such illegal transactions would not have a material effect on companies' financial statements and therefore did not require disclosure. Nevertheless, the failure to uncover these illegal activities by normal audits served to erode confidence in the ethical conduct of the accounting profession. As a result of these issues, and because public accounting firms had failed to detect the imminent bankruptcies of several large audit clients such as National Student Marketing, Penn Central, and Equity Funding, in 1977 Congress published a study asserting that the largest accounting firms had both an alarming lack of independence and a lack of dedication to public protection.[16]

During this period, the House Subcommittee on Oversight and Investigations (the congressional body that oversees the SEC) was engaging in an inquiry of accounting practices in the oil and gas industry that culminated in a much larger investigation. In a report issued in 1978, the committee's chair, John Moss, summarized Congress's concern over the incidents that had occurred.[17] Especially troubling were events such as bankruptcies with no warnings from auditors to investors that anything was amiss, the demise of more than 100 brokerage firms in the late 1960s because of inconsistent methods of determining capital ratios, lack of uniform accounting procedures in the energy industry, and the incidents discovered in relation to the Watergate incident.

In the mid-1980s congressional interest in the accounting profession emerged again in the form of more hearings before the House Subcommittee on Oversight and Investigations, chaired by Representative John Dingell. The committee's primary concern was the role of auditors in fraud detection. Dingell questioned whether the public's and the profession's perception of accountants' responsibility coincided. He also asked: Were the rules deficient? Were the qualifications to be a CPA sufficient? Was self-policing of the accounting profession adequate?[18] In other words, he was questioning the maintenance of ethical standards by the profession and suggesting that the profession did not have the ability to regulate itself.

16. U.S. Congress, *The Accounting Establishment: 95th Congress*, 1st session (Washington, DC: U.S. Government Printing Office, 1977).

17. U.S. Congress, *Accounting and Auditing Practices and Procedures: 95th Congress*, 1st session (Washington, DC: U.S. Government Printing Office, 1978).

18. J. Dingell, "Accountants Must Clean Up Their Act: Rep. John Dingell Speaks Out," *Management Accounting* (May 1985), 52–55.

Public policymakers were not the only ones voicing concerns. During the 1970s some accountants were joining the critics of the accounting profession. For example, Abraham Briloff (an accounting professor at Baruch College, City University of New York), in a series of books, articles, and testimony before Congress, maintained that many published financial statements were not "prepared fairly" in accordance with GAAP; the FASB had not fulfilled its responsibility to develop accounting standards; and public accounting firms had not adequately resolved their ethical dilemmas (discussed above), thus resulting in several cases of successful opinion shopping.[19]

The events of the 1970s and 1980s served to question the ability of accountants to detect fraud, uncover illegal contributions, and predict bankruptcy; consequently, their competence as professionals was also being questioned. As a result, the profession was facing legislation that threatened to regulate the practice of accounting.

Partially in response to these issues, the AICPA engaged in several activities in an attempt to neutralize criticism of the accounting profession. In 1973 the Code of Professional Conduct was again amended. A major feature of the amended code was the requirement to comply with auditing standards and the prohibition from expressing an opinion that financial statements are prepared in conformity with GAAP if such statements depart from an accounting principle. As discussed earlier in the text, the inclusion of this rule made *ARBs*, *APB Opinions*, *SFASs*, and now the FASB ASC enforceable under the Code of Professional Conduct. The 1973 code also included a discussion of the philosophical fashion by which the rules flow from the concepts and why these concepts were of importance to the profession.

Next, in 1974 the AICPA formed a commission on auditors' responsibilities. The commission's final report, known as the Cohen Report, called upon the Auditing Standards Executive Committee to consider developing an improved auditor's report. It also recommended the development of criteria for the evaluation of internal accounting controls and the establishment of independent audit committees. Later, the AICPA established a new division for CPA firms with two sections, one for firms with clients registered with the SEC and one for firms that had clients in private practice. Membership in the SEC Practice Section requires self-regulation, including external peer review of its practice procedures. In addition, the activities of the SEC Practice Section are monitored by the PCAOB. As noted by Representative Dingell, some of the criticism of the professional practice of accounting can be attributed to an *expectations gap*. That is, there is a difference between what financial statement users and society as a whole perceive as the responsibility of public accountants versus what accountants and the profession perceive as their responsibility. As a result, the AICPA's Auditing Standards Board issued nine new standards in 1988 in an attempt to narrow this expectations gap. Specifically, the effect of these new standards was to (1) broaden auditors' responsibility to consider the reliability of a company's

---

19. See, for example, *Unaccountable Accounting* (New York: Harper & Row, 1972); *More Debits Than Credits* (New York: Harper & Row, 1976); *The Truth about Corporate Accounting* (New York: Harper & Row, 1981); "Standards Without Standards/Principles Without Principles/Fairness Without Fairness," *Advances in Accounting* 3 (1986), 25–50; and "Accounting and Society: A Covenant Desecrated," *Critical Perspectives on Accounting* 11 (March 1990), 5–30.

internal control system when planning an audit; (2) delineate the responsibility of auditors for reporting errors, irregularities, and illegal acts by clients; and (3) require auditors to evaluate a company's ability to continue as a going concern.[20]

At the same time, the Code of Professional Conduct was undergoing a review. In 1983 the AICPA appointed a committee to study the relevance and effectiveness of the code in the contemporary environment. The committee's report, commonly known as the Anderson Report, indicated that effective performance should meet six criteria:

1. Safeguard the public's interest.
2. Recognize the CPA's paramount role in the financial reporting process.
3. Help ensure quality performance and eliminate substandard performance.
4. Help ensure objectivity and integrity in public service.
5. Enhance the CPA's prestige and credibility.
6. Provide guidance as to proper conduct.[21]

The members of the AICPA accepted the recommendations of the Anderson Report and amended the Code of Professional Conduct in 1988. The code now consists of four sections:

1. *Principles.* The standards of ethical conduct stated in philosophical terms
2. *Rules of conduct.* Minimum standards of ethical conduct
3. *Interpretations.* Interpretations of the rules by the AICPA Division of Professional Ethics
4. *Ethical rulings.* Published explanations and answers to questions about the rules submitted to the AICPA by practicing accountants and others interested in ethical requirements

The first two sections of the Code of Professional Conduct consist of general statements emphasizing positive activities that encourage a high level of performance (principles) and minimum levels of performance that must be maintained (rules). Consequently, implicit in the Code of Professional Conduct is the expectation that CPAs will abide by the rules at the minimum and strive to achieve the

---

20. In 2008 the FASB issued an exposure draft on going concern. The proposed statement would require disclosures when either the financial statements are not prepared on a going concern basis or there is substantial doubt as to an entity's ability to continue as a going concern. Later in 2010, the FASB decided that the project should provide guidance that defines a going concern and clarify that the time period for the going concern assessment is not a bright-line 12 months but also is not intended to be an indefinite look-forward period. The Board also decided to broaden the scope of the project to address three additional areas: (1) enhance the disclosures of short-term and long-term risks, specifically risks for which there is more than a remote likelihood of occurrence; (2) define substantial doubt in terms of an entity's ability to continue as a going concern; and (3) develop guidance surrounding the adoption and application of the liquidation basis of accounting. A final statement was expected in the third quarter of 2010, as of the time this text was published.

21. *Recruiting Professional Standards to Achieve Professional Excellence in a Changing Environment* (New York: AICPA, 1986), 11.

principles at the maximum. The following six ethical principles, which are not enforceable, are contained in the Code of Professional Conduct:

1. *Responsibilities.* In carrying out their responsibilities as professionals, members should exercise sensitive professional and moral judgments in all their activities.

2. *The public interest.* Members should accept the obligation to act in a way that will serve the public interest, honor the public trust, and demonstrate commitment to professionalism.

3. *Integrity.* To maintain and broaden public confidence, members should perform all professional responsibilities with the highest level of integrity.

4. *Objectivity and independence.* A member should maintain objectivity and be free of conflict of interest in discharging professional responsibilities. A member in public practice should be independent in fact and appearance when providing auditing and other attestation services.

5. *Due care.* A member should observe the profession's technical and ethical standards, strive continually to improve competence and the quality of services, and discharge professional responsibility to the best of the member's ability.

6. *Scope and nature of services.* A member in public practice should observe the Principles of the Code of Professional Conduct in determining the scope and nature of services to be provided.

The principles, which are goal oriented, also provide the framework for the rules, which represent the enforceable provisions of the code. The rules deal with issues such as independence, integrity, and objectivity; compliance with standards of practice; confidentiality of client information; advertising; and contingent fees and commissions. Later, some of these rules were required to be liberalized because of a consent decree between the AICPA and the Federal Trade Commission arising from a claim of restraint of fair trade. For example, CPA firms may now accept contingent fees from nonattest clients, and advertising by CPA firms is now an acceptable practice.

The issue of ethical principles gained new prominence during the accounting scandals of the early 2000s, which resulted in the demise of Arthur Andersen. Before the passage of SOX, the SEC had established a list of nonaudit functions that a CPA firm could not perform in conjunction with an audit. These prohibited functions are the same as those contained in part 5 of the SOX (discussed above). Additionally, companies were required to disclose the amounts received from auditors from nonaudit services in the notes to the financial statements. Although no substantial legal evidence has been uncovered that indicates Arthur Andersen engaged in any of the forbidden nonaudit functions, in each of the company failures the amounts of AA's nonaudit fees exceeded their audit fees. As a result, it is now unlawful for a CPA firm to provide any nonaudit services to its clients.

The need for interpretations of the Code of Professional Conduct arises when individuals or firms have questions about a particular rule. Ethical rulings are explanations concerning specific factual situations. They have been published in the form of questions and answers. A detailed review of the interpretations and ethical rulings is beyond the scope of this book.

In summary, the past two decades have brought forward questions from some critics concerning the ethical conduct of professional accountants. The profession has responded by further delineating its responsibilities and by attempting to narrow the expectations gap. The accounting scandals at the beginning of the decade resulted in a less favorable view of the profession; however, a Gallup poll in 2008 found the profession's image to be recovering. According to the poll's analysis, the profession whose image has improved the most compared to the previous year's is accounting. Its rating rose from a net rating of 0 percent (i.e., as many people gave it a negative rating as a positive one) to + 30 percent. [22] Yet, the profession has still not recovered to the + 39 percent rating it received in 2001, before the Enron and other scandals cast such negative light on accounting firms' roles in these companies' alleged malfeasance. However, the accounting profession must strive to improve this perception, and the Code of Professional Conduct should be viewed as a starting point in determining the ethical behavior of professional accountants. It may also be necessary to revisit the scope of services issue because this same Gallup poll detected some concerns over the variety of services offered by CPA firms to the same client. This and other issues that trouble the public must be resolved in order for accounting to continue to serve its public watchdog function in a manner that is accepted by society.

International Accounting Standards

The IASB standard that addresses disclosure requirements and ethical responsibilities is *IAS No. 1*, "Presentation of Financial Statements." The objective of *IAS No. 1* is to prescribe the basis for presentation of general-purpose financial statements so as to ensure comparability both with the entity's financial statements of previous periods and with the financial statements of other entities. *IAS No. 1* sets out the overall requirements for the presentation of financial statements, guidelines for their structure, and minimum requirements for their content. Standards for recognizing, measuring, and disclosing specific transactions are addressed in specific standards and interpretations. This statement replaced *IAS No. 1*, originally titled "Disclosure of Accounting Policies" (as well as *IAS Nos. 5* and *13*). It requires companies to present a statement disclosing each item of income, expense, gain, or loss required by other standards to be presented directly in equity and to provide the total of these items. It also requires that the notes to the financial statements present information about the basis on which financial statements were prepared and the specific accounting policies selected, disclose all other information required by IASB standards not presented elsewhere in the financial statements, and provide all other information necessary for a fair presentation.

The IASB also addressed interim financial reporting in *IAS No. 34*, "Interim Financial Reporting." This release defined the minimum content of an interim financial report, provided presentation and measurement guidance, and defined

22. Lydia Saad, "Nurses Shine, Bankers Slump in Ethics Ratings." Gallup (Nov. 24, 2008), www.gallup.com/poll/112264/Nurses-Shine-While-Bankers-Slump-Ethics-Ratings.aspx.

the recognition and measurement principles to be followed in the presentation of interim financial reports. The IASB went on to conclude that the decision to publish and the frequency of reporting are matters best decided by national law.

The minimum content of an interim financial report was defined as a condensed balance sheet, condensed income statement, condensed statement of cash flows, condensed statement of changes in stockholders' equity, and all footnotes necessary to understand the financial statements. *IAS No. 34* requires companies to use the same accounting principles in interim financial reports that are used in the annual report and thus adopts the integral view of interim financial reports.

Cases

• Case 17-1 Two Viewpoints on Accounting Standards

The proponents of neoclassical, marginal economics (see Chapter 4) maintain that mandatory accounting and auditing standards inhibit contracting arrangements and the ability to report on company operations. Opponents of this view argue that market forces alone cannot be relied on to produce the high-quality information required by society.

Required:
Present arguments support both viewpoints. What is your opinion? [*Hint:* You may wish to consult Richard Leftwich, "Market Failure Fallacies and Accounting Information," *Journal of Accounting and Economics* (December 1980): 193–221; and Steven Johnson, "A Perspective on Solomon's Quest for Credibility in Financial Reporting," *Journal of Accounting and Public Policy* 7, no. 2 (1988): 137–54.]

• Case 17-2 Ethical Dilemma

Barbara Montgomery is a first-year auditor for Coppers and Rose, a large public accounting firm. She has been assigned to the audit of Lakes Brothers, a clothing retailer with retail outlets throughout the United States. This audit has proved troublesome in the past, and during a staff meeting preceding the audit, Robert Cooley, the supervisor on the audit, says: "We are going to be required to work several hours 'off-the-clock' each week until this audit is completed." He also observes that the client is putting a great deal of pressure on the firm to maintain an acceptable level of fees.

Barbara has just been to staff training school, where it was emphasized that not charging a client for hours actually worked is a violation of Coppers and Rose's employment policy, a violation that could cause her to be dismissed. She also knows that only staff personnel are paid overtime and that supervisors are evaluated on successfully completing audits within allowable budgets. Barbara discusses the issue with John Reed, a second-year staff accountant. John says, "Don't worry, if you go along nobody will find out and Robert will give you a good evaluation." John also says that Robert is very highly regarded by the senior members of the firm and is likely to be promoted to manager in the near future.

Required:

    a. Is it ethical for Barbara to work hours and not charge them to the client?

    b. Use the six-step approach outlined in this chapter to resolve this ethical dilemma.

• Case 17-3 Types of Disclosure

Lancaster Electronics produces electronic components for sale to manufacturers of radios, television sets, and phonographic systems. In connection with his examination of Lancaster's financial statements for the year ended December 31, 2011, Don Olds, CPA, completed fieldwork two weeks ago. Mr. Olds is now evaluating the significance of the following items before preparing his auditor's report. Except as noted, none of these items has been disclosed in the financial statements or footnotes.

    1. Recently, Lancaster interrupted its policy of paying cash dividends quarterly to its stockholders. Dividends were paid regularly through 2009, discontinued for all of 2010 to finance equipment for the company's new plant, and resumed in the first quarter of 2011. In the annual report, dividend policy is to be discussed in the president's letter to stockholders.

    2. A 10-year loan agreement, which the company entered into 3 years ago, provides that dividend payments may not exceed net income earned after taxes subsequent to the date of the agreement. The balance of retained earnings at the date of the loan agreement was $298,000. From that date through December 31, 2011, net income after taxes has totaled $360,000, and cash dividends have totaled $130,000. Based on these data, the staff auditor assigned to this review concluded that there was no retained earnings restriction at December 31, 2011.

    3. The company's new manufacturing plant building, which cost $600,000 and has an estimated life of 25 years, is leased from the Sixth National Bank at an annual rental of $100,000. The company is obligated to pay property taxes, insurance, and maintenance. At the conclusion of its 10-year noncancelable lease, the company has the option of purchasing the property for $1. In Lancaster's income statement, the rental payment is reported on a separate line.

    4. A major electronics firm has introduced a line of products that will compete directly with Lancaster's primary line, which is now being produced in the specially designed new plant. Because of manufacturing innovations, a competitor's line will be of comparable quality but priced 50 percent below Lancaster's line. The competitor announced its new line during the week following completion of fieldwork. Mr. Olds read the announcement in the newspaper and discussed the situation by telephone with Lancaster executives. Lancaster will meet the lower prices with prices that are high enough to cover variable manufacturing and selling expenses but will permit recovery of only a portion of fixed costs.

Required:

For each of the preceding items, discuss any additional disclosures in the financial statements and footnotes that the auditor should recommend to his client. (The cumulative effect of the four items should not be considered.)

• Case 17-4 Preparation of Footnotes

You have completed your audit of Carter Corporation and its consolidated subsidiaries for the year ended December 31, 2010, and are satisfied with the results of your examination. You have examined the financial statements of Carter for the past three years. The corporation is now preparing its annual report to shareholders. The report will include the consolidated financial statements of Carter and its subsidiaries and your short-form auditor's report. During your audit, the following matters came to your attention:

1. The Internal Revenue Service, which is examining the corporation's 2008 federal income tax return, questions the amount of a deduction claimed by the corporation's domestic subsidiary for a loss sustained in 2008. The examination is still in process, and any additional tax liability is indeterminable at this time. The corporation's tax counsel believes that there will be no substantial additional tax liability.

2. A vice president who is also a stockholder resigned on December 31, 2010, after an argument with the president. The vice president is soliciting proxies from stockholders and expects to obtain sufficient proxies to gain control of the board of directors so that a new president will be appointed. The president plans to have a footnote prepared that would include information about the pending proxy fight, management's accomplishments over the years, and an appeal by management for the support of stockholders.

Required:
   a. Prepare the footnotes, if any, that you would suggest for the foregoing listed items.
   b. State your reasons for not making disclosure by footnote for each of the listed items for which you did not prepare a footnote.

• Case 17-5 Interim Reporting

The unaudited quarterly statements of income issued by many corporations to their stockholders are usually prepared on the same basis as annual statements— the statement for each quarter reflects the transactions of that quarter.

Required:
   a. Why do problems arise in using such quarterly statements to predict the income (before extraordinary items) for the year? Explain.
   b. Discuss the ways in which quarterly income can be affected by the behavior of the costs recorded in an account for *repairs and maintenance of factory machinery.*
   c. Do such quarterly statements give management opportunities to manipulate the results of operations for a quarter? If so, explain or give an example.

• Case 17-6 Methods of Disclosure

The concept of adequate disclosure continues to be one of the most important issues facing accountants, and disclosure may take various forms.

Required:

  a. Discuss the various forms of disclosure available in published financial statements.

  b. Discuss the disclosure issues addressed by each of the following sources:

    i. The AICPA Code of Professional Ethics

    ii. The Securities Act of 1933

    iii. The Securities Exchange Act of 1934

    iv. The Foreign Corrupt Practices Act of 1977

    v. Section 404 of the Sarbanes-Oxley Act of 2002

• Case 17-7 The Securities Acts of 1933 and 1934

The Securities Act of 1933 and the Securities Exchange Act of 1934 established guidelines for the disclosures necessary and the protection from fraud when securities are offered to the public for sale.

Required:

  a. Discuss the terms *going public* and *being public* as they relate to these pieces of legislation.

  b. Regulation S-X requires management to discuss and analyze certain financial conditions and results of operations. What are these items?

• Case 17-8 Code of Professional Conduct

Certified public accountants have imposed on themselves a rigorous code of professional conduct.

Required:

  a. Discuss the reasons that the accounting profession adopted a code of professional conduct.

  b. One rule of professional ethics adopted by CPAs is that a CPA cannot be an officer, director, stockholder, representative, or agent of any corporation engaged in the practice of public accounting, except for the professional corporation form expressly permitted by the AICPA. List the arguments supporting the rule that a CPA's firm cannot be a corporation.

• Case 17-9 Consolidated Reporting

As discussed in Chapter 14, leases that are in-substance purchases of assets should be capitalized—an asset and associated liability should be recorded for the fair value acquired. Mason Enterprises is considering acquiring a machine and has the option to lease or to buy by issuing debt. Mason also has debt covenants that restrict its debt-to-equity ratio to 2:1. The purchase alternative would increase the debt-to-equity ratio precariously close to the restrictive limit and could result in the company's going into default. Also, management bonuses are affected when the debt-to-equity ratio exceeds 1.5:1.

Mason's management is aware that majority-owned subsidiaries must be consolidated. The president, Penny Mason, persuades the board to form a subsidiary that would own 49 percent of the stock. The rest of the stock would be sold to the public. Mason would retain control of the subsidiary by maintaining membership on the board of directors and selling the majority shares in small blocks to a number of investors.

Required:

a. What is the economic substance of the lease transaction from the perspective of Mason Enterprises? Discuss.

b. By forming the subsidiary, is Mason able to lease the equipment and keep the transaction off its balance sheet?

c. According to the efficient market hypothesis, discussed in Chapter 3, would investors be fooled by the Mason financing strategy? Explain.

d. According to agency theory, discussed in Chapter 3, management may act in its own best interest at the expense of owners. In light of this theory, what are the ethical implications of the Mason financing strategy? Discuss.

e. Does the financing strategy provide financial statements that are representationally faithful and unbiased? Discuss.

• Case 17-10 The Ethics of Accounting Choices

The Fillups Company has been in the business of exploring for oil reserves. During 19x1, $10 million was spent drilling wells that were dry holes. Under GAAP, Fillups has the option of accounting for these costs by the successful efforts method or the full cost method. Under successful efforts, the $10 million would be expensed once it was determined that the wells were dry. Under full cost, the $10 million would be capitalized. It would not be expensed until the oil from successful wells is extracted and sold.

Fillups decides to use the full cost method because of its positive effect on the bottom line.

Required:

a. What are the ethical considerations implied in the rationale for Fillups' decision? Explain.

b. Do you believe that an accounting alternative should be selected solely on the basis of financial statement effects? Discuss.

FASB ASC Research

• FASB ASC Research

For each of the following FASB ASC research cases, search the FASB ASC database for information to address the issues. Cut and paste the FASB paragraphs that support your responses. Then summarize briefly what your responses are, citing the pronouncements and paragraphs used to support your responses.

• FASB ASC 17-1 Disclosure of Loss Contingency and Subsequent Event

A company car is in a wreck and the company expects to have to pay a substantial sum to persons who were injured. Search the FASB ASC database to determine what type of disclosure, if any, is required under each of the following two circumstances. For each circumstance, cut and paste your findings (citing the source) and then write a brief summary of what your research results mean. In both cases, assume the company's year-end is December 31.

1. The accident occurred in November.
2. The accident occurred in January of the following year. Financial statements will not be issued until February.

• FASB ASC 17-2 Accounting Policies

APB Opinion No. 22 and the EITF both addressed the disclosure of accounting policies.

1. Search the FASB ASC database to find the paragraphs relating to the disclosure of accounting policies. Cite and summarize these paragraphs.
2. Cite and summarize the FASB ASC paragraphs where supplemental guidance was provided by the EITF.

• FASB ASC 17-3 Accounting for Changing Prices

The FASB ASC indicates that a business entity that prepares its financial statements in U.S. dollars and in accordance with U.S. GAAP is encouraged, but not required, to disclose supplementary information on the effects of changing prices. It also describes the information that should be disclosed if such supplemental information is provided. Find, cite, and copy the FASB ASC paragraphs that discuss this issue.

• FASB ASC 17-4 Interim Financial Reports in the Oil and Gas Industry

The FASB ASC provides guidance on the disclosure of certain events in the oil and gas industry in interim financial reports. Find, cite, and copy the FASB ASC paragraphs that discuss this issue.

• FASB ASC 17-5 Interim Financial Reports in the Construction Industry

The FASB ASC provides guidance on disclosures specific to the construction industry. Find, cite, and copy the FASB ASC paragraphs that discuss this issue.

• FASB ASC 17-6 Disclosure of Foreign Activities

The SEC has issued regulations requiring the disclosure of foreign activities when certain financial statement elements exceed 10 percent of the corresponding financial statement amount. Find, cite, and copy the FASB ASC paragraphs that discuss this issue.

- **FASB ASC 17-7 Common Interest Realty Associations**

The FASB ASC addresses disclosure requirements for common interest realty associations. Find, cite, and copy the FASB ASC paragraphs that define common interest realty associations. Additionally, find, cite, and copy the FASB ASC paragraphs that proscribe the additional disclosures requited for common interest realty associations.

Room for Debate

- **Debate 17-1 Ethical Consideration of Off–balance Sheet Financing**

Snappy Corporation enters into a lease agreement with Long Leasing. Long requires that the lease qualify as a sale. Snappy can fill this requirement by either guaranteeing the residual value itself or having a third party guarantee the residual value. Self-guarantee of the residual value will result in a capital lease to Snappy. The third-party guarantee will allow Snappy to report the lease as an operating lease (off–balance sheet financing).

Team Debate:

Team 1:   Argue for recording the lease as a capital lease. Your arguments should take into consideration the definition of relevant elements of financial statements found in *SFAC No. 6*, representational faithfulness, and the substance and form of the lease transaction. In addition, discuss the ethical implications of selecting this alternative as opposed to the operating lease.

Team 2:   Argue for treating the lease as an operating lease. Your arguments should take into consideration the definitions of relevant elements of financial statements found in *SFAC No. 6*, representational faithfulness, and the substance and form of the lease transaction. In addition, discuss the ethical implications of selecting this alternative as opposed to the capital lease.

Debate 17-2 Booking the Budget

In 2002 the SEC investigated Microsoft's accounting practices that occurred during the late 1990s. The Commission found that Microsoft typically reported budgeted marketing expenses in its interim reports. At year end, Microsoft reported actual marketing expenses in its annual report.

Team Debate:

Team 1:   Argue in favor of Microsoft's interim reporting practices. Use the integral view of interim reporting to support your argument.

Team 2:   Argue against Microsoft's interim reporting practices. Use the discrete view of interim financial reporting to support your argument.

• Debate 17-3 Full Disclosure

Investors, creditors, and other users of financial statements often argue that there should be more transparency in published financial statements. This argument is based, at least to some extent, on concerns that management has too much leeway in the selection of accounting alternatives.

Team Debate:

Team 1: Argue that management should continue to be allowed to choose among different accounting alternatives because full disclosure in the notes to financial statements provides sufficient transparency.

Team 2: Argue that there should be a narrowing of accounting alternatives because full disclosure in the notes is not sufficient to curb potential management abuses.

Index